ASCENT®

CENTER FOR TECHNICAL KNOWLEDGE

Autodesk® Navisworks® 2026 Fundamentals

Learning Guide

Edition 1.0

ASCENT - Center for Technical Knowledge®
Autodesk® Navisworks® 2026
Fundamentals

Edition 1.0

Prepared and produced by:

ASCENT Center for Technical Knowledge
630 Peter Jefferson Parkway, Suite 175
Charlottesville, VA 22911

866-527-2368
www.ASCENTed.com

Lead Contributor: Jeff Morris

ASCENT - Center for Technical Knowledge (a division of Rand Worldwide Inc.) is a leading developer of professional learning materials and knowledge products for engineering software applications. ASCENT specializes in designing targeted content that facilitates application-based learning with hands-on software experience. For over 25 years, ASCENT has helped users become more productive through tailored custom learning solutions.

We welcome any comments you may have regarding this guide, or any of our products. To contact us please email: feedback@ASCENTed.com.

AS-NVW2601-BIM1IM-SG // IS-NVW2601-BIM1IM-SG

Contents

Chapter 7: Quantification 7-1

Chapter 8: Animator 8-1

Preface

Autodesk® Navisworks® 2026: Fundamentals introduces you to the key features of the Autodesk Navisworks Manage software and demonstrates how to use it in a BIM workflow to better predict project outcomes, reduce conflicts, and minimize risks.

The course explores how to integrate civil, architectural, structural, and MEP models into one comprehensive BIM model and check for potential issues. It also explains how to use the **Review** and **Markup** tools to facilitate clear communication among different disciplines, how to leverage the **Quantification** module to generate precise building material estimates, and how to use features such as **TimeLiner**, **Animator**, and **Clash Detective** to simulate construction activities and identify potential clashes or issues on site.

Additionally, you will examine how **Animation**, **Scripting**, and **Rendering** tools can be used to communicate the design intent clearly to your team and project stakeholders. This course is designed for professionals from diverse fields and both new users of the software as well as those with prior experience in Autodesk Navisworks will find this a valuable resource.

Topics Covered

- Understanding the purpose of Building Information Modeling (BIM) and how it is applied in the Autodesk Navisworks software
- Navigating the Autodesk Navisworks workspace and interface
- Consolidating models from different software and properly aligning them to create a single Navisworks model
- Saving and retrieving views and sectioning a model
- Using basic viewing and investigation tools to locate, review, and measure items
- Adding tags and comments to model components
- Reviewing a model for clashes
- Performing quantification calculations and material takeoffs
- Animating and writing scripts to interact with the model
- Creating and animating a construction timeline
- Creating photorealistic images

Prerequisites

- Access to the 2026.0 version of the software, to ensure compatibility with this guide. Future software updates that are released by Autodesk may include changes that are not reflected in this guide. The practices and files included with this guide might not be compatible with prior versions.
- The **2026.1 Civil 3D Object Enabler** must be installed on the computer running Navisworks.The site drawing is created in Civil 3D with terrain and roadways, as well as Civil Alignments. In order to access them, you need to have either Civil 3D or the Civil 3D enabler installed. For more information on the Civil 3D enabler, see Appendix A - Coordination Best Practices.
- A working knowledge of 3D design and task-scheduling software is recommended.

Note on Software Setup

This guide assumes a standard installation of the software using the default preferences during installation.

Note on Learning Guide Content

ASCENT's learning guides are intended to teach the technical aspects of using the software and do not focus on professional design principles and standards. The exercises aim to demonstrate the capabilities and flexibility of the software, rather than following specific design codes or standards, which can vary between regions.

Lead Contributor: Jeff Morris

Specializing in the civil engineering industry, Jeff authors learning guides and provides training and implementation support for all Autodesk infrastructure solutions.

Jeff has over 25 years of experience in the civil engineering industry. His diverse work experience includes multiple roles as a Trainer, Application Specialist, Implementation and Customization Consultant, CAD Coordinator, and CAD/BIM Manager in civil engineering and architectural firms. He has worked in different countries, from small private firms to large multinational corporations and government organizations. Through his extensive experience in Building and Infrastructure design, Jeff has acquired a thorough understanding of CAD Standards and Procedures and an in-depth knowledge of CAD and BIM.

Jeff studied Architecture and holds a diploma in Systems Analysis and Programming. He is an Autodesk Certified Instructor (ACI) and an Autodesk Certified Professional for Civil 3D and Revit.

Jeff Morris has been the Lead Contributor for *Autodesk Navisworks: Fundamentals* since 2019.

In This Guide

The following highlights the key features of this guide.

Feature	Description
Practice Files	The Practice Files page includes a link to the practice files and instructions on how to download and install them. The practice files are required to complete the practices in this guide.
Chapters	A chapter consists of the following: Learning Objectives, Instructional Content, Practices, Chapter Review Questions, and Command Summary. • **Learning Objectives** define the skills you can acquire by learning the content provided in the chapter. • **Instructional Content**, which begins right after Learning Objectives, refers to the descriptive and procedural information related to various topics. Each main topic introduces a product feature, discusses various aspects of that feature, and provides step-by-step procedures on how to use that feature. Where relevant, examples, figures, helpful hints, and notes are provided. • **Practice** for a topic follows the instructional content. Practices enable you to use the software to perform a hands-on review of a topic. It is required that you download the practice files (using the link found on the Practice Files page) prior to starting the first practice. • **Chapter Review Questions**, located close to the end of a chapter, enable you to test your knowledge of the key concepts discussed in the chapter. • **Command Summary** concludes a chapter. It contains a list of the software commands that are used throughout the chapter and provides information on where the command can be found in the software.
Appendices	Appendices provide additional information to the main course content. It could be in the form of instructional content, practices, tables, projects, or skills assessment.

Practice Files

To download the practice files for this guide, use the following steps:

1. Type the URL *exactly as shown below* into the address bar of your Internet browser to access the Course File Download page.

   Note: If you are using the ebook, you do not have to type the URL. Instead, you can access the page by clicking the URL below.

   https://www.ascented.com/getfile/id/potosiaPF

2. On the Course File Download page, click the **DOWNLOAD NOW** button, as shown below, to download the .ZIP file that contains the practice files.

3. Once the download is complete, unzip the file and extract its contents.

   The recommended practice files folder location is:
   C:\Navisworks BIM Practice Files

   Note: It is recommended that you do not change the location of the practice files folder. Doing so may cause errors when completing the practices.

Chapter 1

Introduction to Autodesk Navisworks

The Autodesk® Navisworks® software is used in the Building Information Modeling (BIM) workflow to review 3D designs. The software enables you to review and mark up models from different disciplines. Navigating the model is a crucial part of efficiently reviewing a BIM model.

Explore the user interface and then uncover constructibility issues using the standard viewing tools, orbiting, and camera settings.

Learning Objectives

- Discover how to use Autodesk Navisworks to manage a project.
- Examine the user interface and understand how to use the parts most effectively.
- Identify constructibility issues in a model using the standard viewing tools.
- Improve your ability to walk and orbit around a model.

1.1 What Is Navisworks?

The Autodesk Navisworks software is used in a Building Information Modeling (BIM) workflow for reviewing 3D designs. It enables you to consolidate 3D models from multiple sources and applications, which helps you to check for clashes between disciplines. As models are consolidated, the size of the model is drastically reduced to make it possible to review multiple large models at the same time. Navisworks provides tools for reviewing and markup, construction simulation, and collaboration between multiple stakeholders.

BIM is a strategy for the entire building life cycle. It includes design, construction, and facilities management. The BIM process supports the ability to coordinate, update, and share design data with team members across disciplines. Using Navisworks in a BIM workflow enables design teams to have a more holistic view of multiple, integrated models and data that make up the project, as shown in Figure 1–1. This enables them to:

- Better communicate design intent
- Ensure that everything fits together properly without clashes
- Set the construction time line and sequencing.

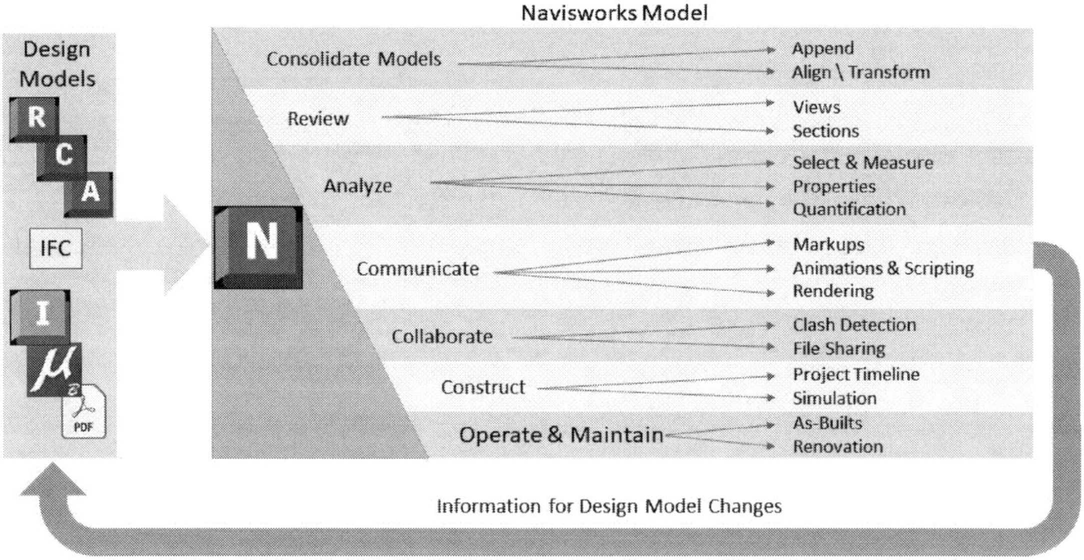

Figure 1–1

There are several components in the Autodesk Navisworks software:

- Autodesk Navisworks Simulate provides review and communication tools for 5D analysis and coordination. It does not include Clash Detection.
- Autodesk Navisworks Manage provides tools for 5D analysis, advanced coordination (Clash Detection), and simulation.

  Note: *5D analysis includes 3D modeling plus time and cost.*

- Autodesk Navisworks Freedom is a 3D viewer that enables stakeholders to review and explore a project model without needing the software that was used by the design team.

In this guide, you will focus on Navisworks Manage, with an emphasis on how to:

- Consolidate models from different disciplines into one complete model.
- Review a model with viewing tools, including the use of walkthroughs, sections, and basic animations.
- Analyze a model by selecting and investigating items.
- Communicate with all members of a project team by marking up views.
- Collaborate with all of the disciplines using clash detection tools that can be useful at all stages from early design development to construction.
- Construct the project virtually by visually reviewing the project schedule using TimeLiner.
- Operate and maintain the finished building by including links to as-builts and other information.

1.2 Overview of the Interface

The Autodesk Navisworks interface (shown in Figure 1–2) includes user interface tools that are common to most Autodesk software, such as the application menu and ribbons. Knowing where to find the tools that you use most and how to maximize screen space by positioning various dockable windows helps you more easily view and review the model.

Figure 1–2

1. Application Menu	6. Scene View
2. Home	7. Dockable Windows
3. Quick Access Toolbar	8. Status Bar
4. Ribbon	9. Plan View
5. InfoCenter	10. Sheet Browser

1. Application Menu

The application menu provides access to file commands, settings, and documents. You can hover the cursor over a command to display a list of additional tools, as shown in Figure 1–3.

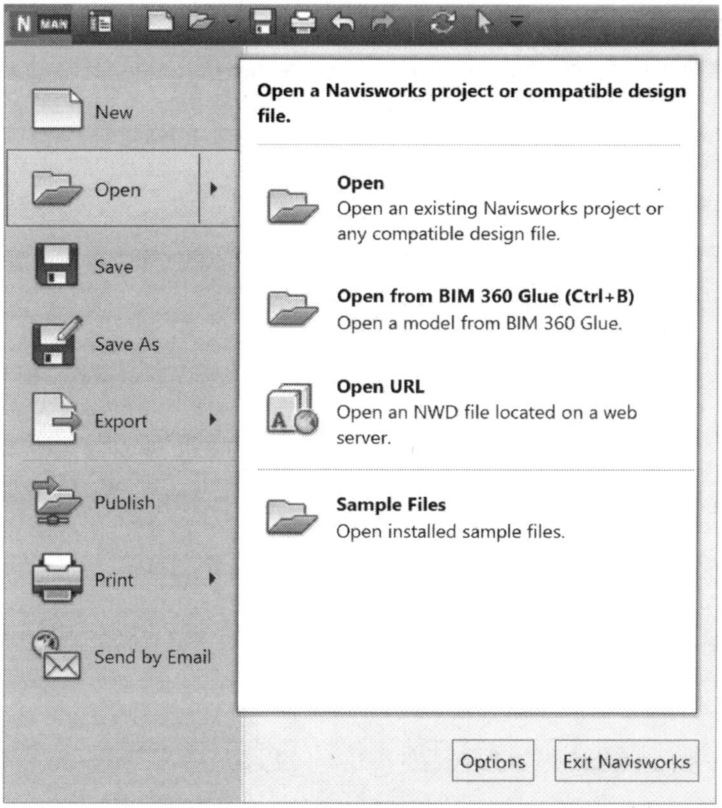

Figure 1–3

__Note:__ Click __Options__ to open the Options Editor where you can setup the user interface and other tools.

- When no command is selected, a list of recently used documents displays. The documents can be reordered if required, as shown in Figure 1–4.
- Click the (Pin) icon next to a document name to keep it available on this list.

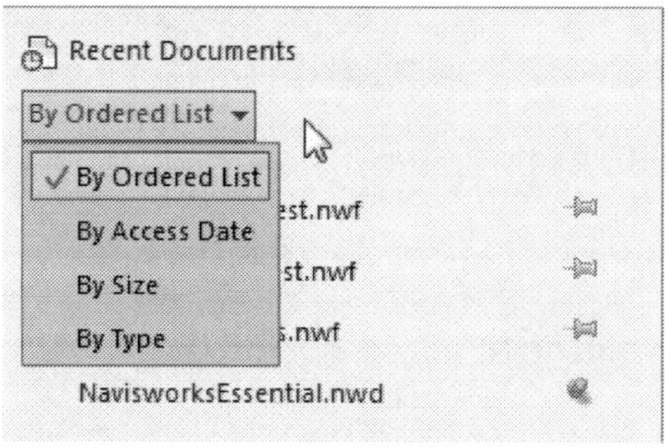

Figure 1–4

2.Homescreen

By default, the *Home screen* is continually available, even when a Navisworks file is open. It enables you to complete several actions, as shown in Figure 1–5:

- Open an existing file or project (1)
- Create new Navisworks project (2)
- Review and open recent documents (3)
- Access Help (online) (4)
- Open various online tools and support (5)
- Browse to Autodesk Docs (6)
- Tiles (or list) of recently opened files or projects (7)
- Search for files / projects (8)

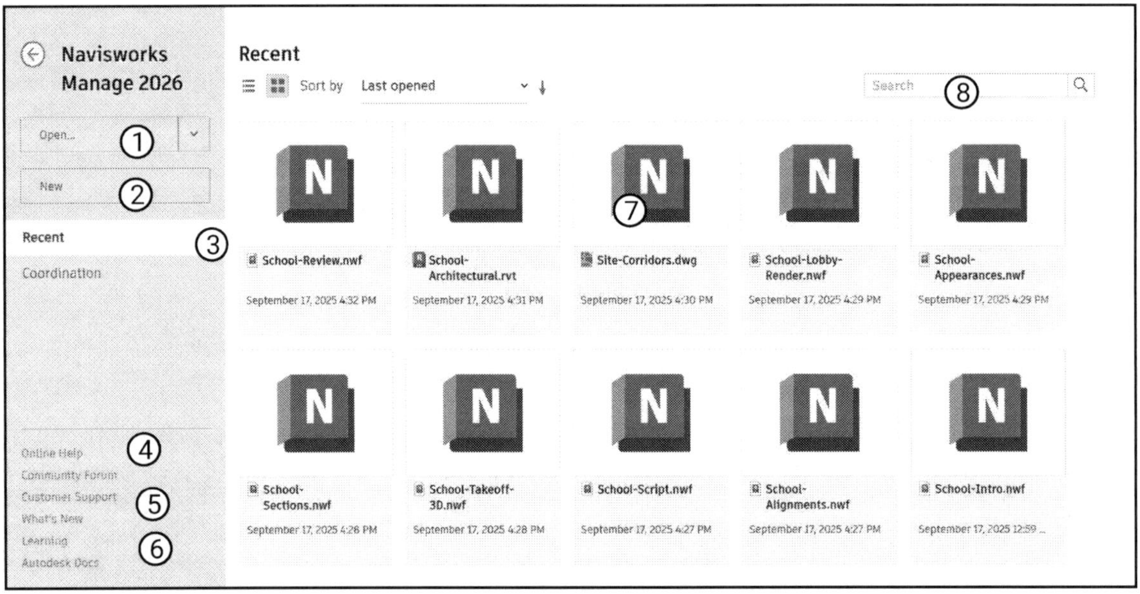

Figure 1–5

On the drop-down menu of the **Open ...** button, you can open files from an URL web address, or explore sample projects that are part of the Navisworks installation, as shown on the left panel in Figure 1–6.

To collapse the *Home* screen and go to the current project, click on , as shown on the left panel in Figure 1–6.

To pin a file to the *Home* screen to be a permanent display on the *Home* screen (until it is unpinned), hover over a file and a pin symbol displays in the upper left corner of the tile, as shown on the right panel in Figure 1–6. When hovering over a file, the full path including the file name is displayed in a tooltip.

Figure 1–6

3. Quick Access Toolbar

The Quick Access Toolbar includes commonly used commands, such as **Home, New**, **Open**, **Save**, **Print**, **Undo**, **Redo**, **Refresh**, and **Select**, as shown in Figure 1–7.

Figure 1–7

Hint: Customizing the Quick Access Toolbar

To change the docked location of the toolbar, or to add, relocate, or remove tools on the toolbar, right-click on the Quick Access Toolbar and use the **Remove from Quick Access Toolbar** or the **Show Quick Access Toolbar below the Ribbon** options, as required. You can also right-click on a tool in the ribbon and select **Add to Quick Access Toolbar**, as shown in Figure 1–8, to add the command to the Quick Access Toolbar.

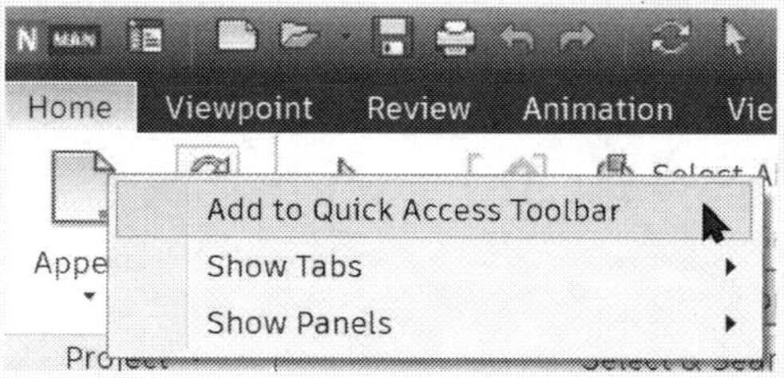

Figure 1–8

4. Ribbon

The ribbon contains tools in a series of tabs and panels, as shown in Figure 1–9. Selecting a tab displays a group of related panels. The panels contain a variety of tools, grouped by task.

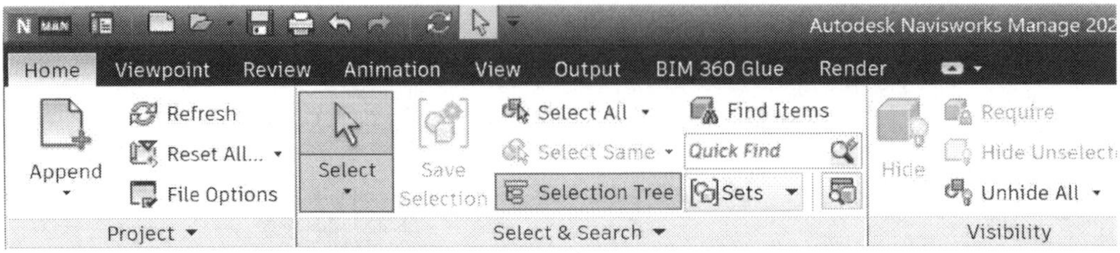

Figure 1–9

When you select an element in the scene view, the ribbon displays the *Item Tools* tab. This contains item specific tools, as shown in Figure 1–10.

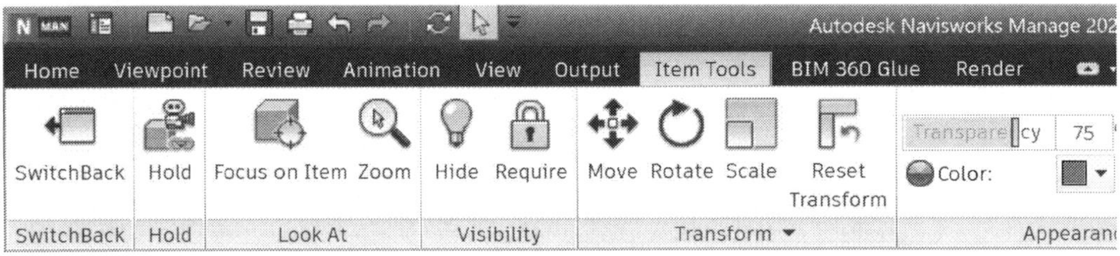

Figure 1–10

- When you hover the cursor over a tool on the ribbon, tooltips display the tool's name and a short description, as shown in Figure 1–11.

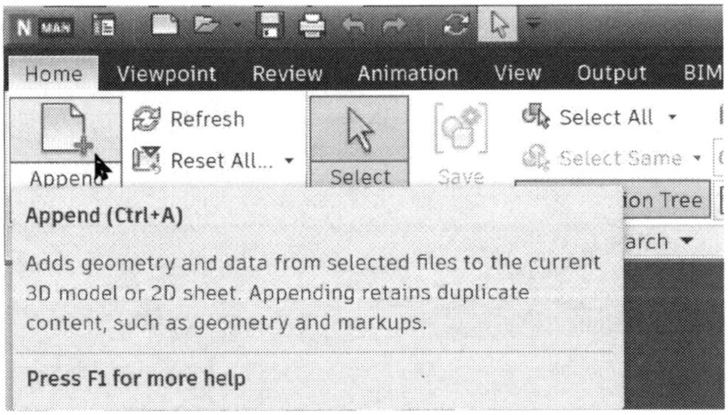

Figure 1–11

- Many commands have keyboard shortcuts. For example, you can press <Ctrl>+<A> for **Append** or <Ctrl>+<1> for **Select**. The keyboard shortcuts are listed next to the name of the command in the tooltips, as shown above in Figure 1–11. Do not press <Enter> when typing shortcuts.

- To rearrange the order in which the ribbon tabs display, select the tab, hold <Ctrl>, and drag the tab to a new location. The location is remembered when you restart the software.
- Any panel can be dragged by its title into the scene view area to become a floating panel. Click **Return Panels to Ribbon** (as shown in Figure 1–12) to return a panel to the ribbon.

Figure 1–12

5. InfoCenter

The InfoCenter (shown in Figure 1–13) includes a search field to find help on the web, and also provides access to the Subscription Center, Communication Center, Autodesk 360 Services sign-in, and other help options.

Click here to collapse the search field to save screen space

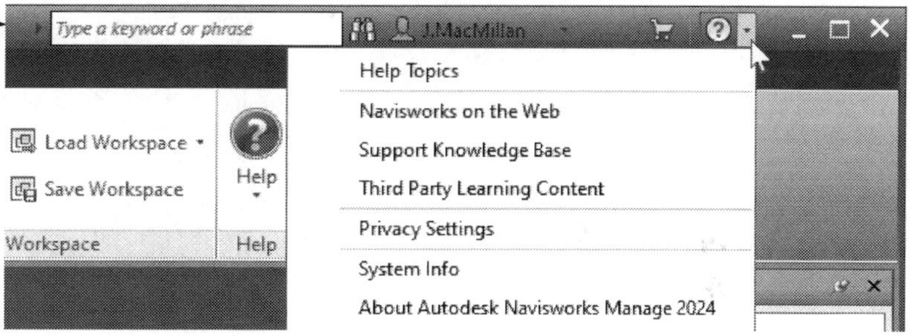

Figure 1–13

6. Scene View

The scene view is where you view the model, as shown in Figure 1–14. You can reorient the view using viewing tools such as the ViewCube and navigation bar. You can also select items in the scene view.

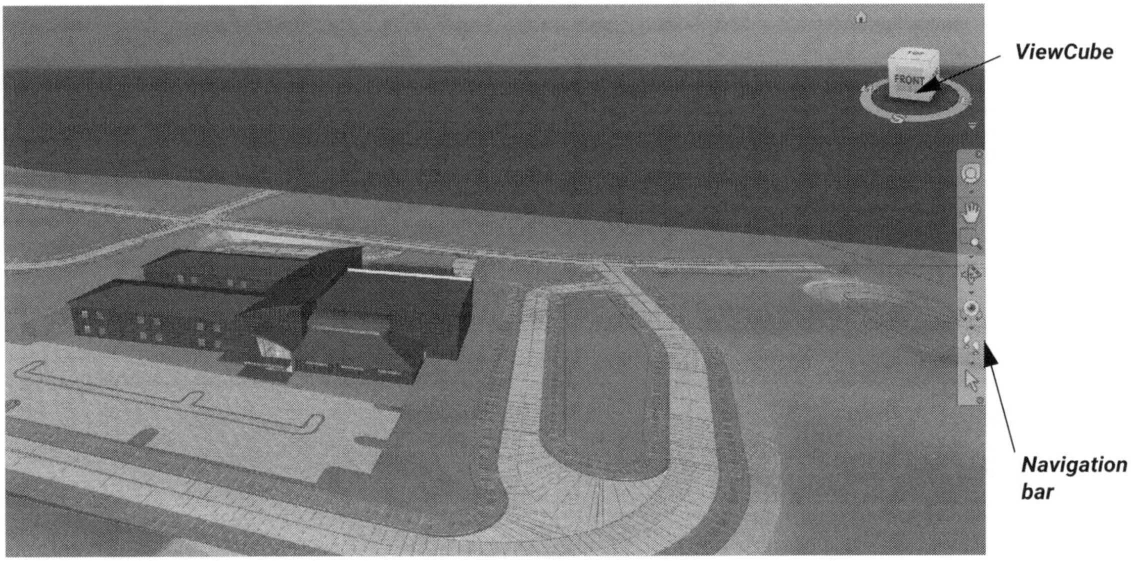

Figure 1–14

Note: *The background of the scene view varies depending on the type of view you are in. Figure 1–14 displays a perspective view with a horizon line with the Render Style set to* ***Full Render.*** *Render styles are discussed in an later topic.*

7. Dockable Windows

Many of the Autodesk Navisworks tools have windows that include information you will use while working. These windows can float in the scene view, or be docked to the top, bottom, or sides of the screen. They can be auto-hidden to display just a tab, as shown in Figure 1–15.

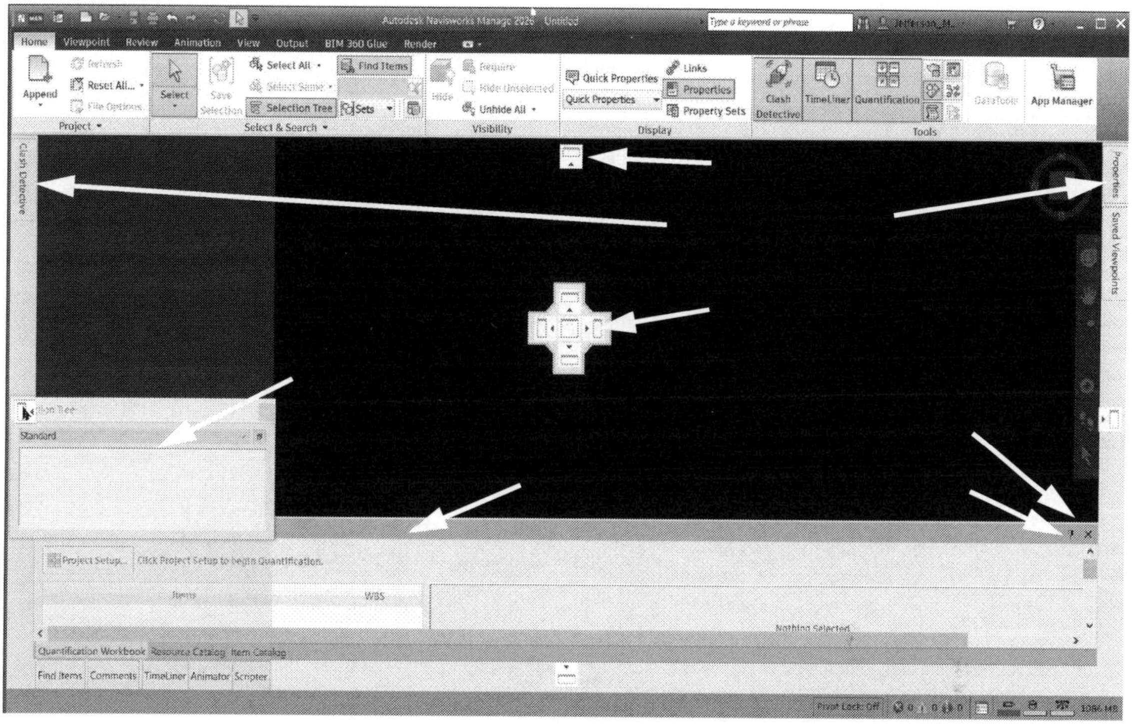

Figure 1–15

- To dock a window, drag it by the title and hover over one of the location icons. A transparent blue box displays where the window can be docked. Release the cursor to place it.
- Only the docking locations on the outer edges of the interface enable you to pin/unpin windows. Inner docking locations cause windows to float.
- Windows can be tiled in the interface.
- To undock a window, drag the title bar into the scene view.
- To hide a docked window, click (Auto Hide).
- To display a hidden window, hover over the tab.
- To close a window, click **X** (Close).

To maximize a floating window (so it fills the entire screen), double-click on the header of the window. To restore a maximized window, use the middle icon in the top right corner, as shown in Figure 1–16.

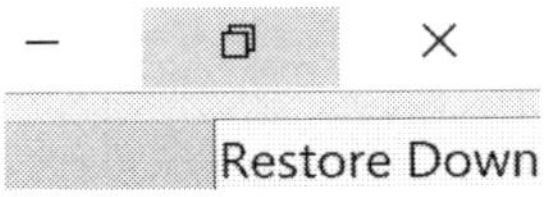

Figure 1–16

- The list of dockable windows are available in *View* tab>*Workspace* panel> (Windows) drop-down list.
- Floating windows can be dragged onto other monitors.

8. Status Bar

The status bar includes the Sheet Browser and File Performance information, as shown in Figure 1–17. The Sheet Browser enables you to access multi-sheet .DWF files (such as shop drawings) that might be attached to a project. The File Performance information displays information about the performance of the project file, such as the amount of memory being used by the software.

Sheet Browser ***File performance***

Figure 1–17

Hint: Right-Click Menus

Right-click menus enable you to quickly access required commands. These menus provide access to basic viewing commands, recently used commands, and all of the major **Viewpoint** commands, as shown in Figure 1–18. Additional options are available if you have an item selected.

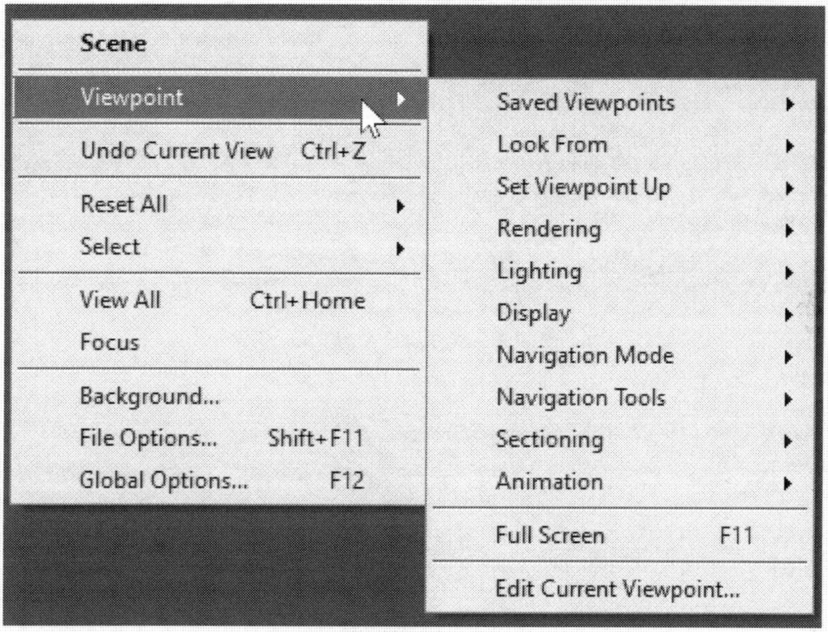

Figure 1–18

9. Plan View

A plan view is a type of reference view to aid in navigation in a 3D workspace. Like a bird's eye view, it gives an overall view of the model and shows where you are. You can quickly navigate to a location through the plan view. The other type of reference view is the section view, which aids in cutting sections through the model. Within the window, there are additional choices through the right-click menu, as shown in Figure 1–19.

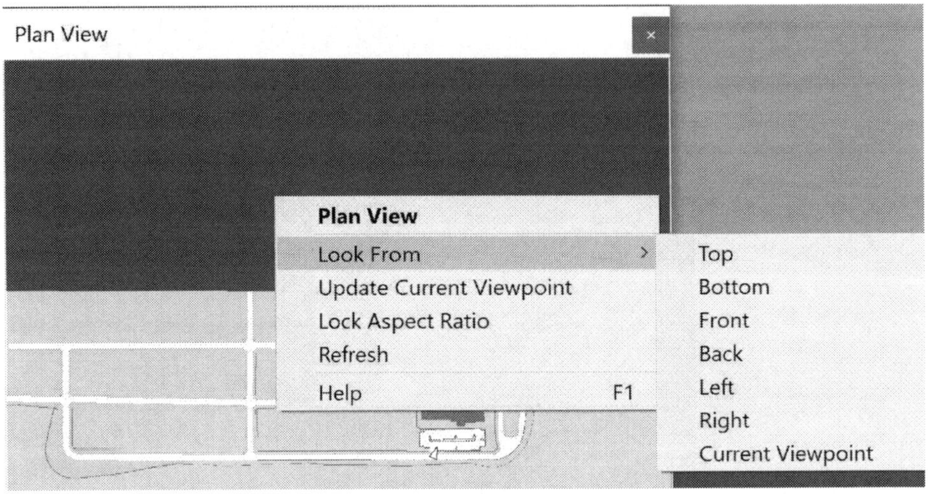

Figure 1–19

10. Sheet Browser

The Sheet Browser lists all the sheets and models in a multi-sheet file. Additional sheets can be contained within a file, such as 2D DWF files. When a particular sheet or model is selected, a preview and the properties of the sheet are displayed, as shown in Figure 1–20.

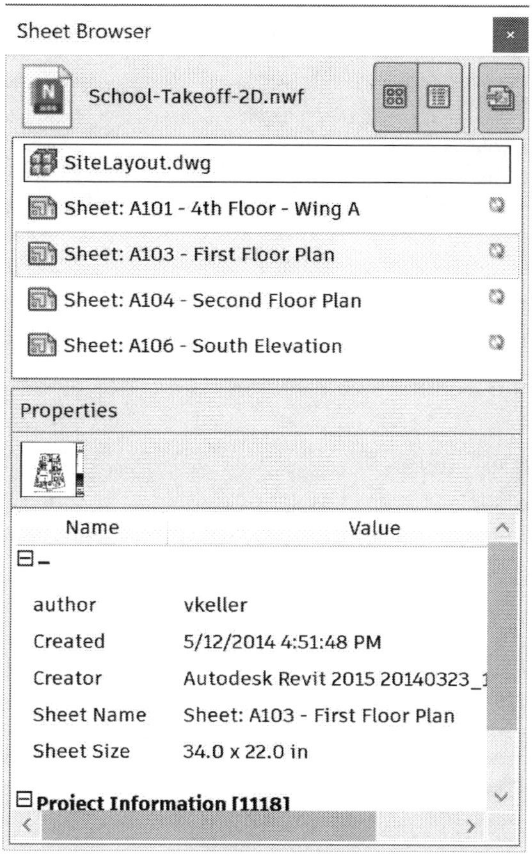

Figure 1–20

Customizing the Interface

You can customize and save the layout of the user interface for easy access to specific commands. This can help you switch between specific toolbars and windows that have the tools you require to perform certain jobs.

- When a workspace is saved, the location and size of each open window is captured.
- Changes to the ribbon or Quick Access Toolbar are not saved in the workspaces.
- Workspaces can then be shared with other users for more efficient access to corporate standards.

When Navisworks is first loaded, four workspaces are available, as shown in Figure 1–21. The default workspace is the **Navisworks Standard** workspace.

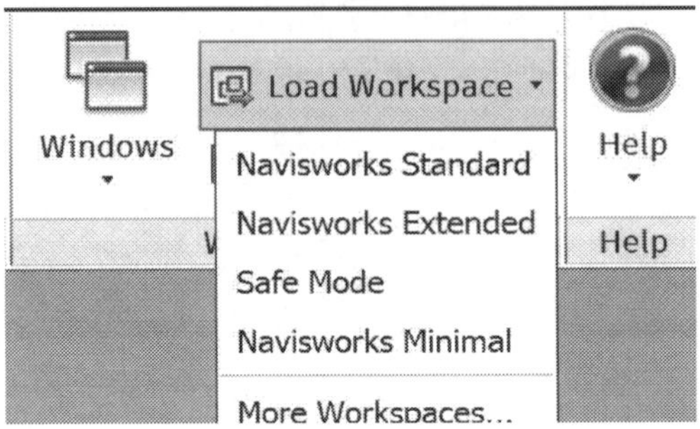

Figure 1–21

How To: Save a Workspace

1. Open, resize, and arrange windows as required.
2. In the *View* tab>*Workspace* panel, click (Save Workspace).
3. In the *Save Current Workspace* dialog box, enter a name for the workspace to create a new workspace or select the name of an existing workspace to overwrite it.
4. Click **Save**.

How To: Load a Workspace

1. In the *View* tab>*Workspace* panel, expand (Load Workspace) to display a drop-down list of all currently saved workspaces.
2. Select a saved workspace to load it.

Practice 1a
Explore the User Interface

Practice Objectives

- Review and configure the user interface layout.
- Save a configured workspace.

In this practice, you will start by loading the Navisworks Standard workspace. Then, you will toggle windows on and off in the workspace to configure it to your needs and save it. You do not need to have a model open for this practice.

1. Launch Navisworks Manage, if not already open.
2. In the *View* tab>*Workspace* panel, expand (Load Workspace) and select **Navisworks Standard**, as shown in Figure 1–22. This is a default workspace that has many of the Navisworks tools open in its default interface.

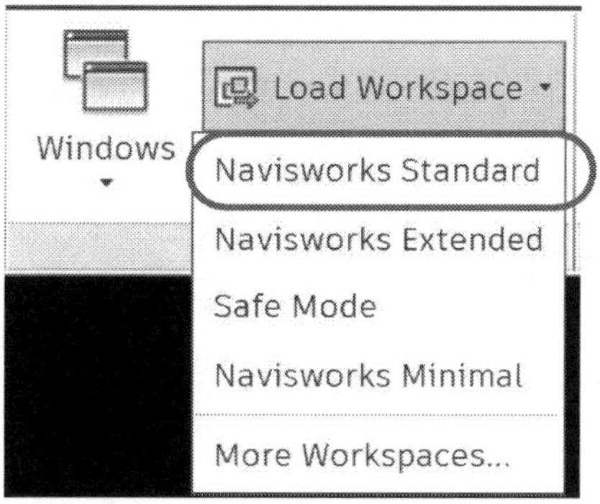

Figure 1–22

3. Review the user interface. Note the hidden, dockable windows to the left, right, and bottom of the scene view.
4. Note that the *Selection Tree* window is currently available on the left side of the scene view.
5. In the *Home* tab>*Select & Search* panel, click (Selection Tree) or press <Ctrl>+<F12> to toggle off the *Selection Tree* window.
6. Click (Selection Tree) again to toggle the *Selection Tree* window back on.
7. Click the *Selection Tree* window title bar, click (Auto Hide) to toggle off auto-hide and force the window to always display (i.e., pin it).
8. Click and drag the *Selection Tree* window title bar and move the window to the middle of the scene view to undock it.

9. Click and drag the *Selection Tree* window title bar to the icon that displays in the scene view.

10. In the *Selection Tree* window title bar, click (Auto Hide) to enable auto-hide. Once enabled, you can select the title bar to display the window and then select in the scene view to hide it.

11. Note that along the bottom of the scene view, the *Quantification Workbook* tab is displayed.

    In the *Home* tab>*Tools* panel, select (Quantification) to clear its selection and note that the tab is no longer displayed along the bottom.

12. Similarly remove the **TimeLiner** tool from the display.

    Note: *The Quantification and TimeLiner tools will be discussed in later topics.*

13. In the *View* tab>*Workspace* panel, click **Save Workspace**. Enter **myworkspace** as the name and click **Save**. Once you learn about all the available tools in Navisworks, you will have a better understanding of which tools will be most valuable to you and you can customize your own workspace accordingly.

14. Before continuing, in the *View* tab>*Workspace* panel, expand (Load Workspace) and select **Navisworks Standard** to return the display to the default standard view.

End of practice

1.3 Using Basic Viewing Tools

One of the most basic and powerful uses of Navisworks is to navigate around and through a model. This enables you to present the model to others and locate any constructibility issues. Because navigating is such a useful tool, there are many different methods to navigate a model, including the mouse wheel, the ViewCube, the navigation bar, and the *Viewpoint* tab>*Navigate* panel, as shown in Figure 1–23.

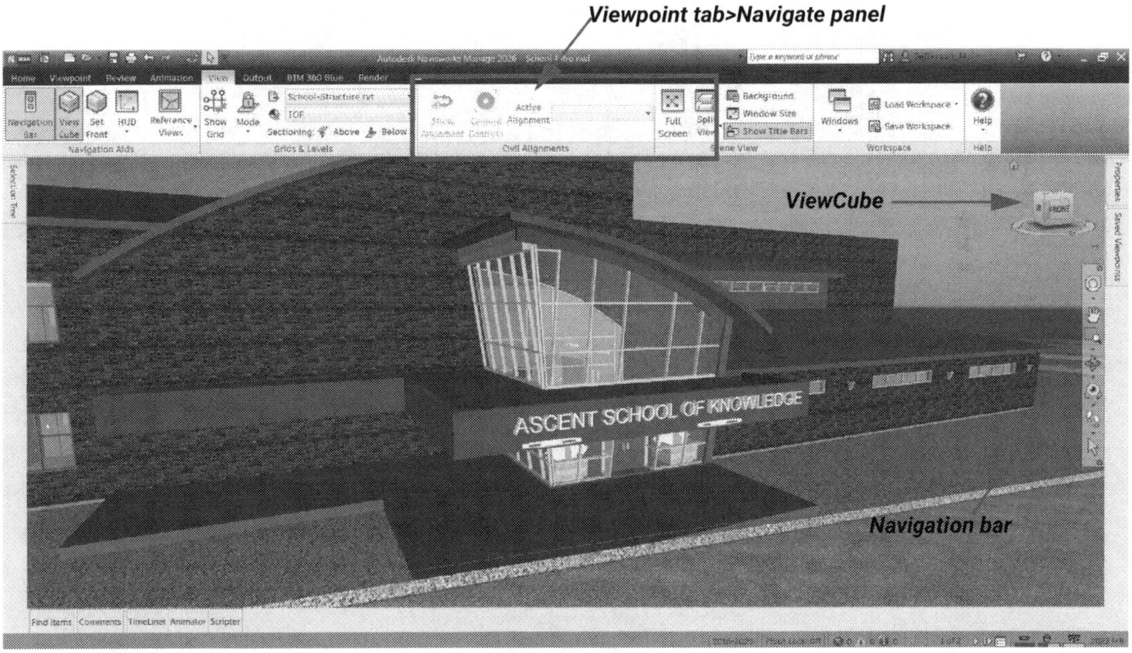

Figure 1–23

- Some of the navigation tools move the model within the view, while others are more like holding a camera.
- In Navisworks, you can walk through walls.
- The camera position (x,y,z) displays at the bottom left of the main view to provide positional feedback, as shown in Figure 1–24.

Figure 1–24

Using the Mouse Wheel

You can use the mouse wheel to move around the scene. The movement is based on the location of the mouse pointer, which becomes the pivot point for the movement, as shown in Figure 1–25.

Figure 1–25

- The mouse wheel functionality changes depending on how you use the mouse wheel. To **Zoom**, **Pan**, or **Orbit** a model, in the Quick Access Toolbar or navigation bar, click  (Select), and then use the mouse wheel as follows:
  - **Zoom:** Scroll the mouse wheel up to zoom in and down to zoom out.
  - **Pan:** Hold the mouse wheel and then move the mouse to pan.
  - **Orbit:** Hold <Shift> and the mouse wheel, and then move the mouse to orbit around the scene.
- When you zoom, the current location of the cursor is the pivot point.
- Pan and Orbit use the pivot point defined by the most recent zoom.

Orbiting Around a Model

Viewing a model from all angles is an important part of using Navisworks. While you can orbit a model using the mouse wheel, there are also several orbiting tools in the navigation bar and the *Viewpoint* tab>*Navigate* panel, as shown in Figure 1–26.

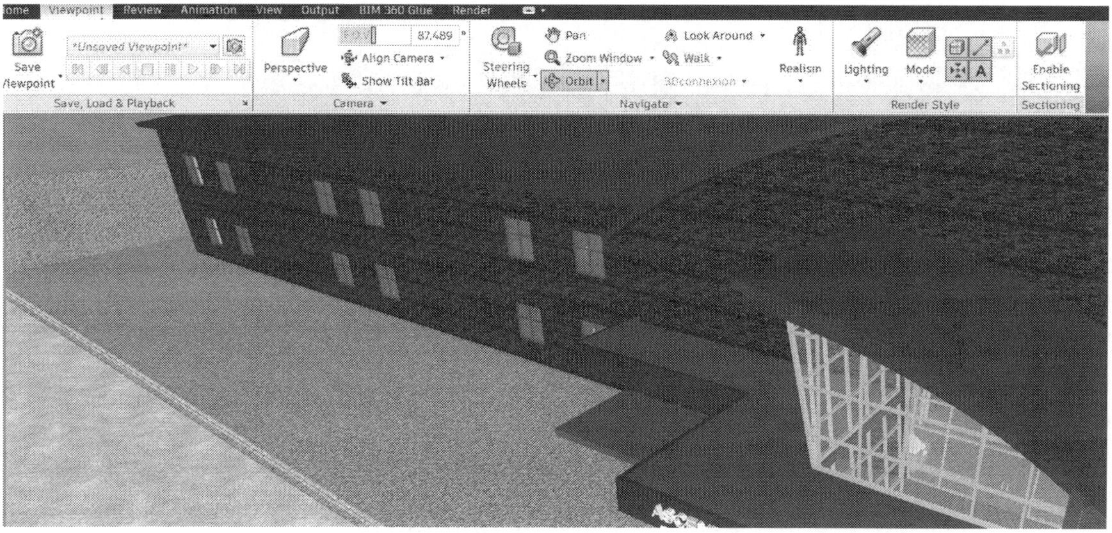

Figure 1–26

- The orbit commands all revolve around a pivot point. To specify the pivot point, reposition your cursor to the required location, press and hold <Ctrl>, and click in the scene before orbiting.
- To use the orbit commands, select the command, click and hold the left mouse button, and then move the mouse:
  - (Orbit): Rotates in all directions while maintaining the "up" orientation.
  - (Constrained Orbit): Rotates with the model remaining on the original plane.
  - (Free Orbit): Rotates freely in any direction.

Using the ViewCube

The ViewCube provides visual clues as to where you are in a 3D view. It helps you move around the model with quick access to specific views (such as **Top**, **Front**, and **Right**), corner views, and directional views, as shown in Figure 1–27.

Figure 1–27

Hover the cursor over any face of the ViewCube to highlight it and then click to reorient the model. You can also click and drag the ViewCube to rotate it and the model.

- (Home) displays when you hover the cursor over the ViewCube. Click to return to the view defined as **Home**. If you get lost in a model, use (Home) to return to a familiar view.
- The drop-down menu connected to the ViewCube includes options to do the following. Alternatively, you can right-click on the ViewCube to access the same options.
  - Switch between **Perspective** and **Orthographic** mode.
  - Set the current view as the **Home** or **Front** view.
  - Open the Options Editor to access the ViewCube Options, including how the ViewCube looks and what happens when you switch views.

Note: *In the View tab>Navigation Aids panel, click (ViewCube) to toggle the ViewCube on or off.*

Hint: Perspective Views and Camera Options

You can switch between (Perspective) and (Orthographic) mode in the *Viewpoint* tab>*Camera* panel. When in a perspective view, you can modify the **F.O.V.** (Field of View) using the slider bar. Alternatively, expand the *Camera* panel and specify the exact position and target of the camera, as shown in Figure 1–28.

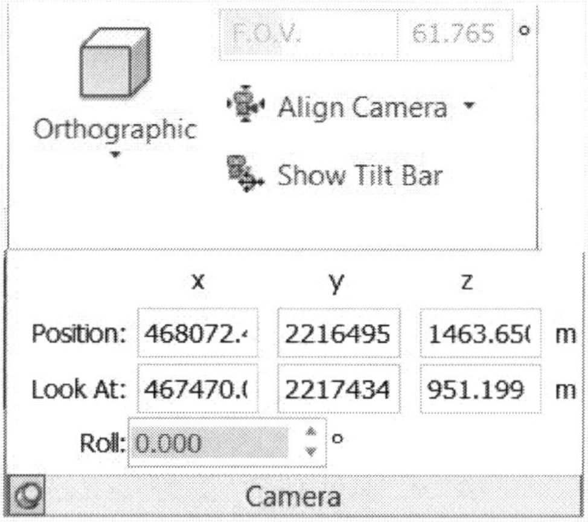

Figure 1–28

- (Align Camera) provides options to straighten the camera or focus on the X-, Y-, or Z-axes. These are similar to the faces of the ViewCube.
- (Show Tilt Bar) toggles a window with a slider bar where you can move the model up and down. This is similar to scrolling the mouse wheel up and down.

Zoom and Pan Commands

The navigation bar includes several standard viewing commands that are similar to those used in other Autodesk software. These options are also available in the *Viewpoint* tab>*Navigate* panel, as shown in Figure 1–29.

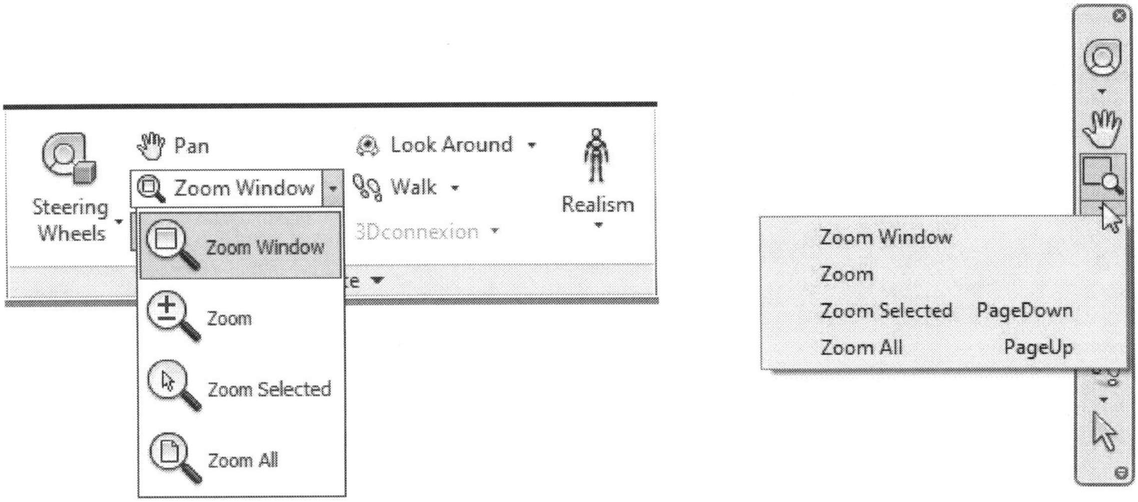

Figure 1–29

The pan and zoom options are as follows:

- (Pan): Move across a scene using the left mouse button.
- (Zoom Window): Zooms in to a region that you define. To define the rectangular area you want to zoom in to, drag the cursor or select two points. This is the default command.
- (Zoom): Zoom in and out of a scene using the left mouse button.
- (Zoom Selected): Zooms in on any selected item in the scene.
- (Zoom All): Zooms in or out to fit the full model on the screen.

  Note: *The zoom icons in the Navigate panel may vary from the zoom icons in the navigation bar. The icons above are those available in the Navigate panel.*

- (Steering Wheel): Provides cursor-specific access to **Zoom** and **Pan**. Additional commands on the Steering Wheel also allow for orbiting and rewinding.

  Note: *In the View tab>Navigation Aids panel, click (Navigation Bar) to toggle it on and off.*

Walk

The (Walk) command works as if you are walking along a camera path. Drag the left mouse button to move forward or back as you walk around and through the model.

- To help you know where you are going, you can toggle on an avatar, such as the construction worker shown in Figure 1–30. In the navigation bar, expand the *Walk* drop-down list and select **Third Person** (or press <Ctrl>+<T>).

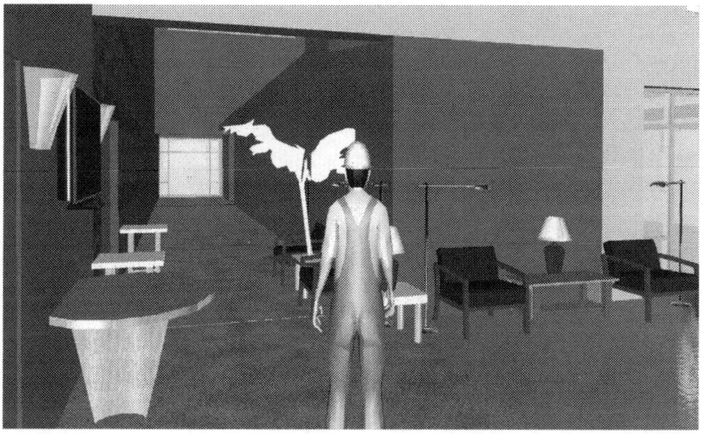

Figure 1–30

> ***Note:*** *To change the avatar, in the Options Editor> Viewpoint Defaults> Collision pane, click* ***Settings****.*

Use the following controls to walk around a model:

- Hold <Shift> as you drag to double the movement speed.
- Scroll the mouse wheel to move up and down, or press the wheel to move side to side. This changes the position of the camera.
- You can set the *F.O.V.* and camera *Position* (including the **Z**, which controls the height of the camera) in the *Viewpoint* tab>*Camera* panel.

Look Around

The (Look Around) command is a stationary camera that enables you to look right and left, up and down by pressing and holding the left mouse button and dragging.

Fly

The (Fly) command is similar to game navigation tools. The camera follows the direction of the mouse. Click the mouse and move it forward to start moving. Ascend or descend by moving the mouse up or down. Move left and right by moving the mouse in that direction.

Realism

The (Realism) options enable you to change how the camera interacts with the model. There are four settings you can turn on or off, as shown in Figure 1–31:

- **Collision:** Causes the camera to stop when it runs into a solid object in the model.
- **Gravity:** Causes the camera to remain a set distance from the top of objects to simulate walking on top of them.
- **Crouch:** Permits the camera to dip below objects in the model to get around them if there is enough room.
- **Third Person:** Toggles on an avatar to simulate a person being in the model.

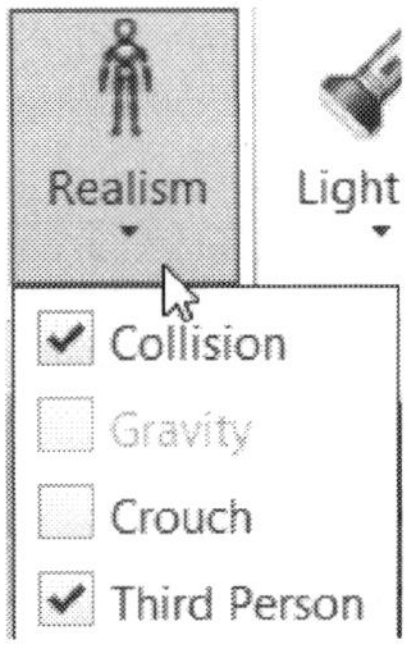

Figure 1–31

> **Hint: Controlling the Speed of Navigation Commands**
>
> In the *Viewpoint* tab, expand the *Navigate* panel to modify the *Linear Speed* and *Angular Speed*, as shown in Figure 1–32.

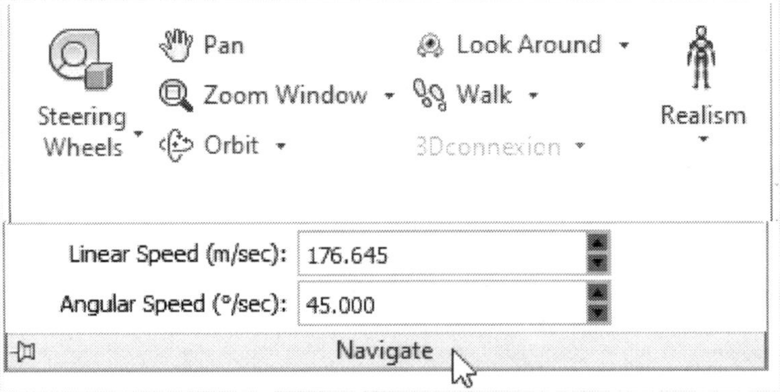

Figure 1–32

Viewpoints

In Navisworks, you can save the position you are in the model and its vantage points. Such saved views are called viewpoints, which can be accessed through the *Saved Viewpoints* window, as shown in Figure 1–33.

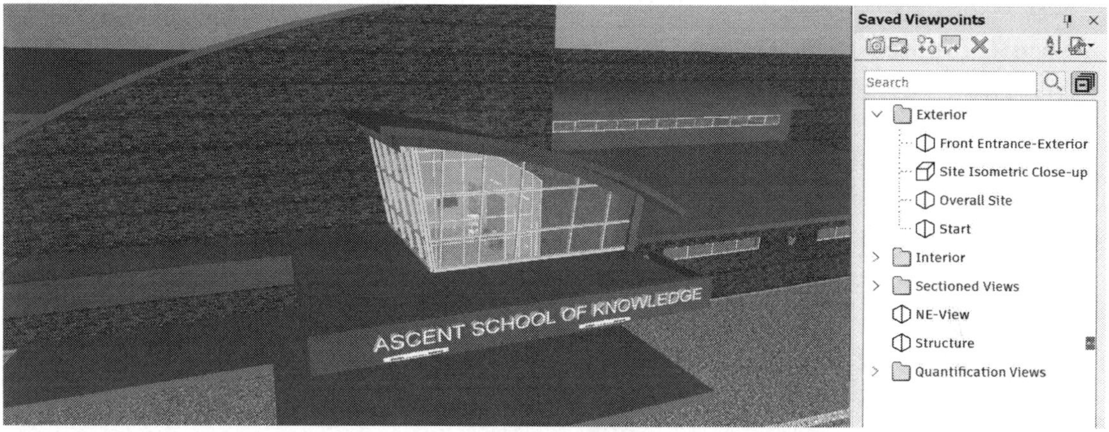

Figure 1–33

These viewpoints also save the conditions of the current scene, such as material variations, overrides, lighting conditions, objects that are hidden, etc. Viewpoints help you focus on specific conditions in a scene so that you can share information quickly with others.

Hint: Quickly Returning to a Previous View

To return to a previous view orientation, you can use the Steering Wheel () option in the navigation bar or in the *Viewpoint* tab>*Navigation* panel. Once selected, move your mouse onto the **Rewind** area of the wheel, as shown on the left in Figure 1–34. Select once to return to the previous view orientation, or press and hold to rewind through your previous movements using a slider bar, as shown on the right.

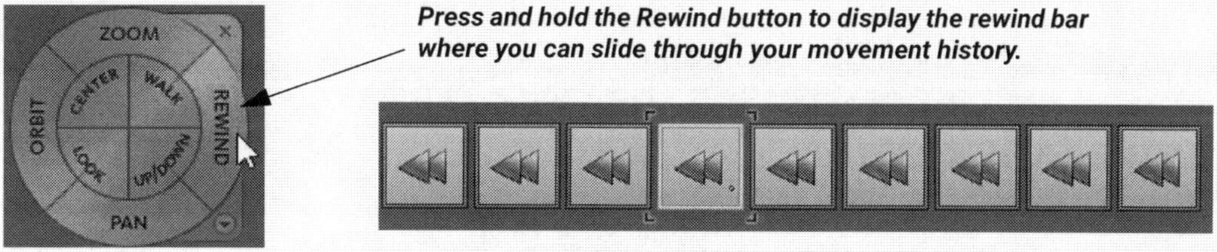

Figure 1–34

Practice 1b
Use Basic Viewing Tools

Practice Objectives

- Navigate the scene using the mouse.
- Navigate the scene using the ViewCube.
- Navigate the scene using the navigation bar.

In this practice, you will open a Navisworks file of a school located on a Civil 3D site. Once opened, you will look around the model outside of the building and inside the building (shown in Figure 1–35) using various navigation tools. Note that the views you see in the software may vary from those shown in the practice images.

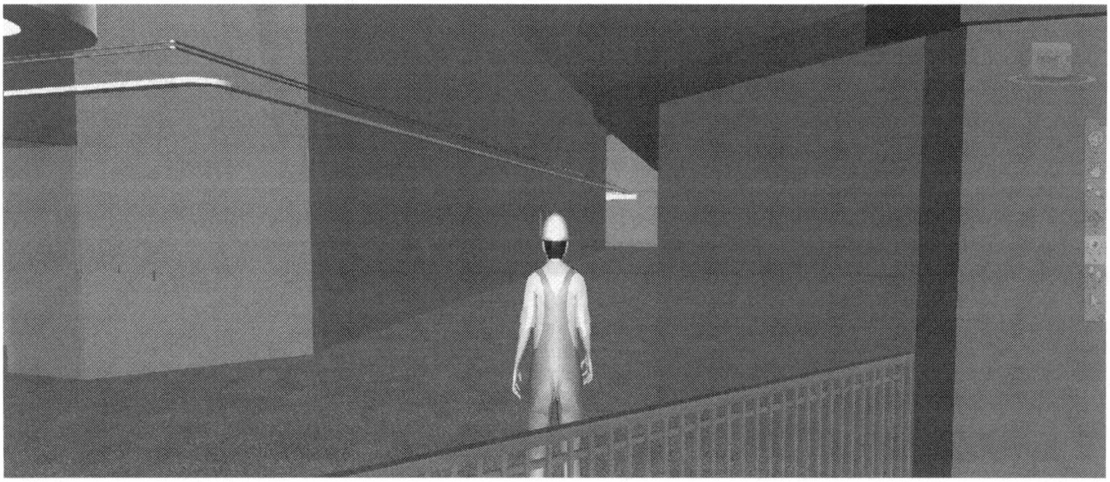

Figure 1–35

Task 1: Navigate the model with the mouse and keyboard.

1. In the Quick Access Toolbar, click  (Open).
2. In the *Open* dialog box, navigate to the *Navisworks BIM Practice Files* folder and review the list of subfolders that will be used in the practices in this learning content.

   Note: *Having project files stored in a common folder structure emulates proper BIM procedures. For training purposes, these folders reside on the local C drive, but in practice, these folders should be on a shared network drive so that the whole project team has access to them.*

3. In the *File type* drop-down list, select **All Files (*.*)**, if not already selected.

4. Double-click on the *Introduction* practice files folder, select **School-Intro.nwf**, and click **Open**.

   Note: *The file may take some time to load as it is retrieving data from Revit and AutoCAD.*

5. In the *View* tab>*Grids & Levels* panel, select  (Show Grid) to display the grids on the Revit school building. When **Show Grid** is enabled, the icon will display with a blue background, as shown in Figure 1–36. Turn off the display of the grids by selecting the option a second time. Ensure that **Show Grid** is off (white background) before continuing.

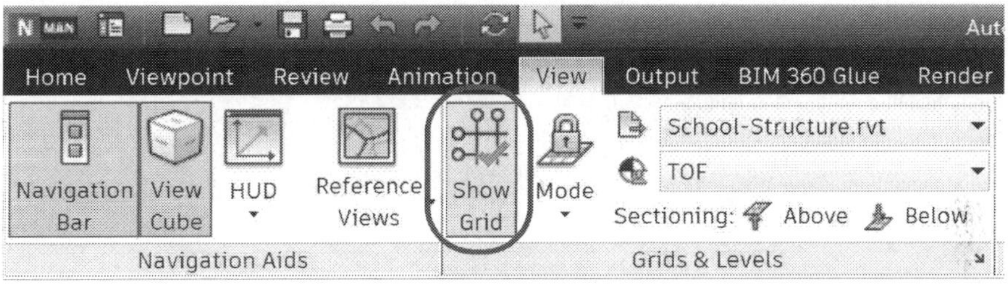

Figure 1–36

   Note: *The Show Grid toggle affects all saved viewpoints in the current model as well as all models to be opened in Navisworks.*

6. Return to the *Home* tab on the ribbon.
7. In the navigation bar, click on the small down arrow to expand the zoom options and select **Zoom**, as shown in Figure 1–37.

   Note: *The zoom icon that displays in your navigation bar may vary. It changes depending on the currently active zoom setting.*

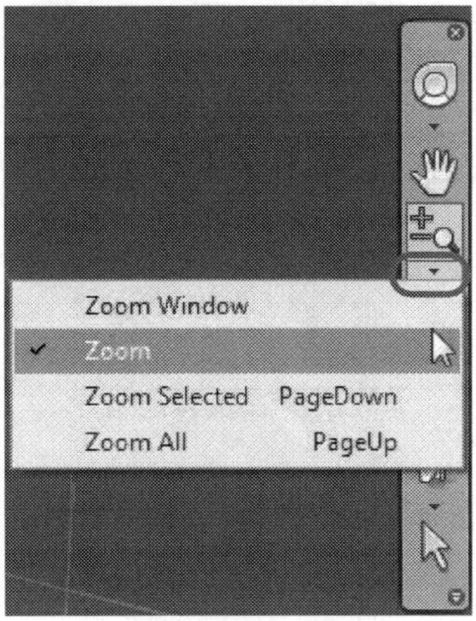

Figure 1–37

8. In the model, center the cursor over the building (as shown in Figure 1–38) and scroll with the mouse wheel to zoom in and out. The cursor location when you begin scrolling defines the pivot point (in this case, it is the center point for scrolling).

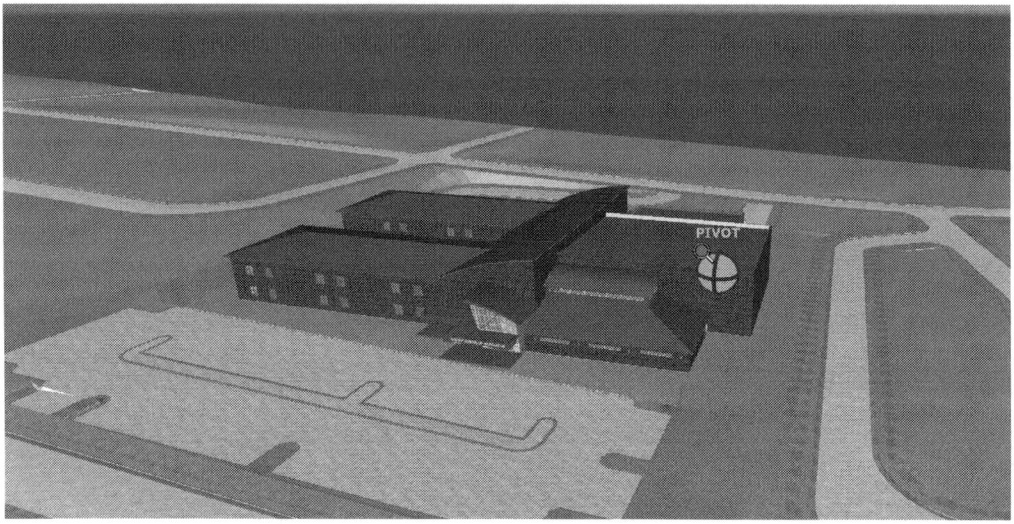

Figure 1–38

9. Hold <Shift> along with pressing and holding the mouse wheel button to orbit around the scene until the view of the model is similar to that shown in Figure 1–39. Release the mouse wheel and <Shift>.

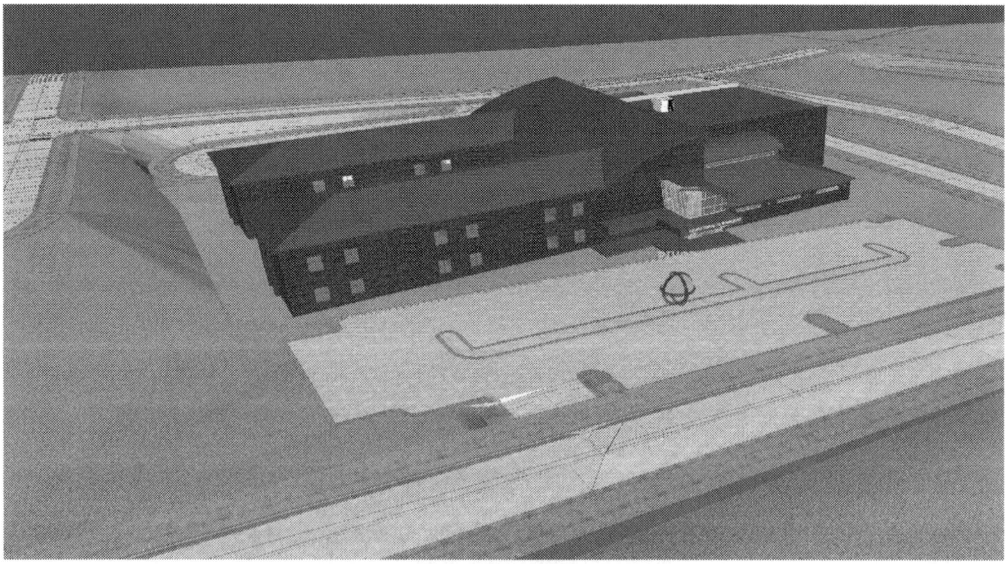

Figure 1–39

10. Press and hold the mouse wheel and move the mouse to the right to pan the scene and display the south side of the building, as shown in Figure 1–40. Release the mouse wheel.

Figure 1–40

11. Hover your mouse near the front entry shown above in Figure 1–40.
12. Use the mouse to zoom and pan the scene until you can see the foyer inside the building, such as the view shown in Figure 1–41. Alternatively, you can double-click the left mouse button to zoom in with small increments.

Figure 1–41

13. To stop zooming, click (Select) in the Quick Access Toolbar or in the *Home* tab>*Select & Search* panel, as shown in Figure 1–42.

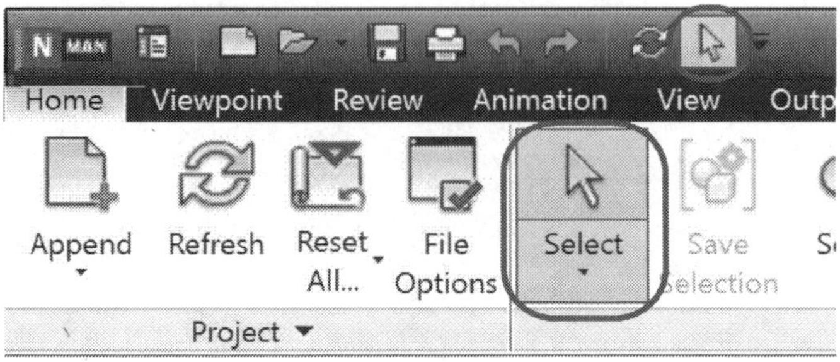

Figure 1–42

14. In the *View* tab>*Workspace* panel, expand (Windows) and verify that **Selection Tree** and **Saved Viewpoints** are selected in the list.

    Note: *All items in the Windows drop-down list that are checked are displayed on the screen. This is an alternate method to enable the tools on the Home tab.*

15. On the right side of the interface, select **Saved Viewpoints** to open its window.
16. In the *Saved Viewpoints* window, expand the **Exterior** folder and select the **Start** saved viewpoint. This will reorient you to a view of the model from the exterior. The **Start** saved viewpoint is not a default view in Navisworks. It has been created in the file for you and was the view that the file was in when it was originally saved.
17. In the *Saved Viewpoints* window, select the **Front Entrance-Exterior** saved viewpoint in the *Exterior* folder. This is another viewpoint that has been saved for you. In a later topic, you will learn how to create your own viewpoints and about the viewpoints that are currently in the folders.
18. Return to the *Home* tab on the ribbon, if not already active.

Task 2: Navigate the model using the navigation bar and Navigation panel.

1. On the left side of the interface, select **Selection Tree** to open its window.
2. In the *Selection Tree*, expand **School-Architectural.rvt>Second Floor>Railings>Railing>Guardrail - Rectangular** and then select the second **Railing**, as shown in Figure 1–43.

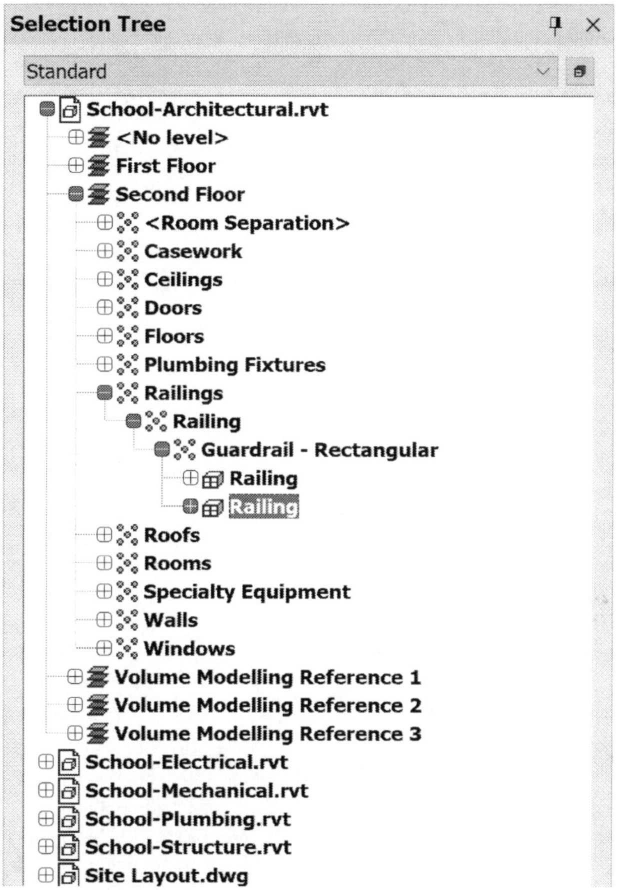

Figure 1–43

3. In the navigation bar, click (Zoom Selected) in the drop-down list, as shown in Figure 1–44. (You can also press the <PageDown> keyboard button.) This zooms into the railing inside the building.

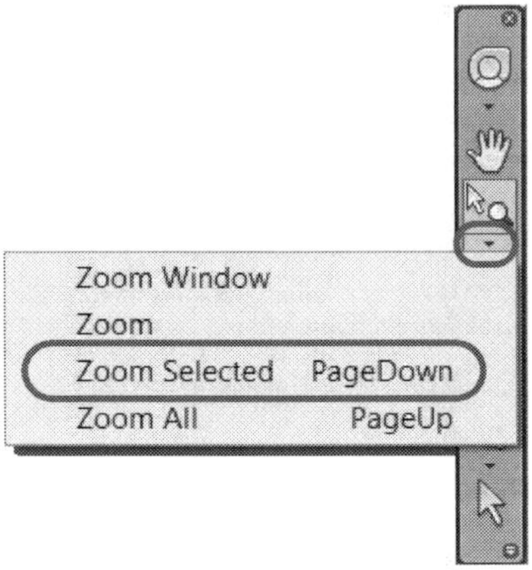

Figure 1–44

4. In the navigation bar, click (Look Around). Hold the left mouse button, move the cursor, and use the mouse wheel to zoom in and pan as required, until you are looking the other way down the hall. Depending on your previous vantage point, you may have to pan (by pressing and holding the mouse wheel) to get to a view similar to the one shown in Figure 1–45.

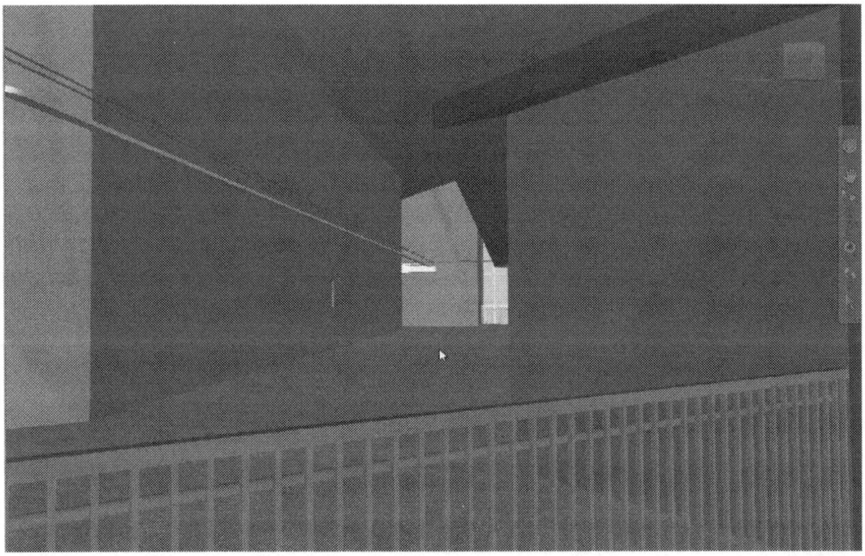

Figure 1–45

5. In the navigation bar, click  (Walk).
6. Hold the left mouse button as you move the mouse slowly forward to simulate walking forward.
7. In the *Viewpoint* tab>*Navigate* panel, expand the *Realism* drop-down list and select **Third Person** to display the construction worker avatar, similar to that shown in Figure 1–46. The distance you move your mouse controls the speed of your walking. If moving too fast, pull your mouse back. If you pull back too much, you reverse your walking.

   Note: *If your avatar displays lower than the floor, pan the view so that you are higher than the floor.*

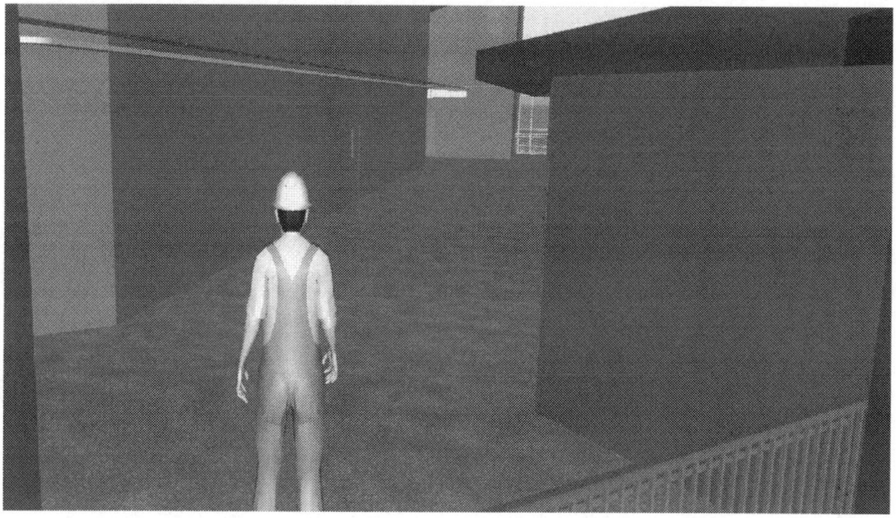

Figure 1–46

8. Continue dragging the mouse forward until you are half way down the hall. Then, pull the mouse backward slightly to simulate walking backward. Finally, move the cursor forward and to the right and watch as you walk through the wall into the bathroom.
9. Once in the bathroom, in the navigation bar, click  (Look Around).
10. Hold the left mouse button as you move the mouse slowly forward to simulate looking up, then pull it back to look down. Next, move the mouse to the right to look around the room. Move it left to return to the original focus.
11. Hover the cursor over the ViewCube and click  (Home) to return the model to its default zoomed out overall model view.
12. The avatar does not scale to fit. Press <Ctrl>+<T> to toggle off the **Third Person** view.

13. Expand the *Selection Tree* window in the interface. The **Railing** remains selected. In the *Home* tab>*Select & Search* panel, expand the *Select All* drop-down list and click (Select None) to clear the selection.
14. Practice zooming, orbiting, and panning to view the back of the building. Consider using the **Start** viewpoint to initially get closer to the model.
15. Hover the cursor over the ViewCube, press and hold your left mouse button on it, and move your mouse to further orbit the model.
16. On the ViewCube, click any of the eight corners (as shown in Figure 1–47) to view the model in an alternate perspective view. Note how this reorients the entire model because nothing is selected.

Figure 1–47

17. In the *Selection Tree*, select **School-Architectural.rvt**.
18. On the ViewCube, click any of the eight corners. Continue to select the next adjacent corner until you are viewing the back of the school.
19. On the ViewCube, select the **BACK** planar face to reorient to a planar view.
20. In the graphics window, select away from the model to deselect the school. The model should display as shown in Figure 1–48.

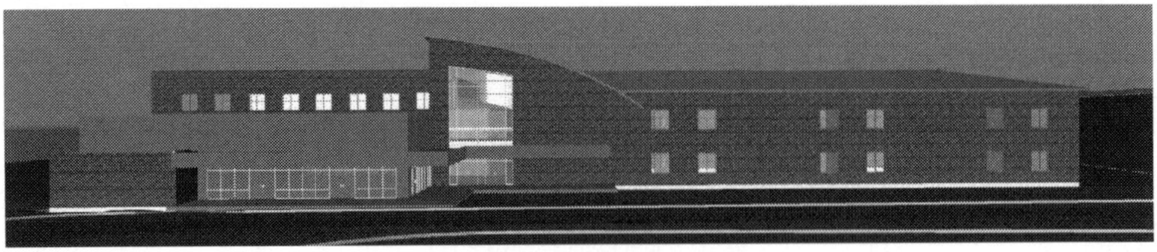

Figure 1–48

21. In the navigation bar, expand the (Walk) option and click (Fly).
22. Click the left mouse button and then move the mouse forward to start moving. Ascend or descend by moving the mouse up or down. Move left and right by moving the mouse in that direction.

23. In the *Viewpoint* tab>*Navigate* panel, expand (Realism) and toggle on **Collision**. Alternatively, you can access this option in the expanded **Fly** menu in the navigation bar. With collision enabled, you are unable to fly through walls.
24. Purposely move directly into the building and note how the camera stops as it collides.
25. Click (Home) on the ViewCube.
26. In the navigation bar, expand **Fly**, toggle off **Collision**, and then select **Walk**.
27. In the Quick Access Toolbar, click (New). This closes the current file and opens a blank file. There is no prompt to save the file as no changes (markups) were made.

End of practice

Chapter Review Questions

1. If you have lost all of your dockable windows and tools, what is the fastest way to get them back?
   a. Use the Undo arrow in the Quick Access Toolbar.
   b. Close and restart the software.
   c. Select the required workspace.

2. In the following areas of the user interface, where are you most likely to find viewing tools?
   a. Quick Access Toolbar
   b. Dockable Window
   c. Scene View
   d. Status Bar

3. What do you do if you want a window available but not taking space from the scene view?
   a. Dock it to the side and pin it.
   b. Dock it to the side and set it to auto-hide.
   c. Move it off the screen.
   d. Open and close it.

4. How do you pan sideways in a model using your mouse?
   a. Hold the mouse wheel and drag the mouse sideways.
   b. Hold the left mouse button and drag the mouse sideways.
   c. Hold the right mouse button and drag the mouse sideways.

5. How do you ensure that the camera cannot go through walls?
   a. Toggle on the **Collision** option.
   b. There is no way to prevent the camera from going through walls.
   c. Toggle on the **Background** option.
   d. Toggle on the **Gravity** option.

6. How do you quickly return to a default preset view of a model?
   a. Use the mouse wheel to zoom out.
   b. Hover the cursor over the ViewCube and click (Home).
   c. In the navigation bar, click (Zoom All).
   d. Click on the top south-east corner of the ViewCube.

Command Summary

Button	Command	Location
	**Constrained Orbit**	• **Navigation Bar** • **Ribbon:** *Viewpoint* tab>*Navigate* panel, expand *Orbit*
	**Fly**	• **Navigation Bar:** expand Walk • **Ribbon:** *Viewpoint* tab>*Navigate* panel, expand *Walk*
	**Free Orbit**	• **Navigation Bar** • **Ribbon:** *Viewpoint* tab>*Navigate* panel, expand *Orbit*
	**Load Workspace**	• **Ribbon:** *View* tab>*Workspace* panel
	**Look Around**	• **Navigation Bar** • **Ribbon:** *Viewpoint* tab>*Navigate* panel
	**Navigation Bar**	• **Ribbon:** *View* tab>*Navigation Aids* panel
	**Open**	• **Application Menu** • **Quick Access Toolbar**
	**Orbit**	• **Navigation Bar** • **Ribbon:** *Viewpoint* tab>*Navigate* panel
	**Orthographic**	• **Navigation Bar** • **Ribbon:** *Viewpoint* tab>*Camera* panel
	**Pan**	• **Navigation Bar** • **Ribbon:** *Viewpoint* tab>*Navigate* panel
	**Perspective**	• **Navigation Bar** • **Ribbon:** *Viewpoint* tab>*Camera* panel
	**Save Workspace**	• **Ribbon:** *View* tab>*Workspace* panel
	**Steering Wheel**	• **Navigation Bar** • **Ribbon:** *Viewpoint* tab>*Navigate* panel
	**ViewCube**	• **Ribbon:** *View* tab>*Navigation Aids* panel

Button	Command	Location
	**Walk**	• **Navigation Bar** • **Ribbon:** *Viewpoint* tab>*Navigate* panel
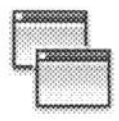	**Windows**	• **Ribbon:** *View* tab>*Workspace* panel
	**Zoom**	• **Navigation Bar:** expand Zoom • **Ribbon:** *Viewpoint* tab>*Navigate* panel, expand *Zoom*
	**Zoom All**	• **Navigation Bar:** expand Zoom • **Ribbon:** *Viewpoint* tab>*Navigate* panel, expand *Zoom*
	**Zoom Selected**	• **Navigation Bar:** expand Zoom • **Ribbon:** *Viewpoint* tab>*Navigate* panel, expand *Zoom*
	**Zoom Window**	• **Navigation Bar:** expand Zoom • **Ribbon:** *Viewpoint* tab>*Navigate* panel, expand *Zoom*

Chapter 2

Consolidate Trade Models

The Autodesk® Navisworks® software is an advanced Building Information Modeling (BIM) tool that allows design teams to view project information, regardless of which software was used to create the original designs. With Navisworks, you can open multiple models and combine them within the application to ensure all project components are coordinated and compatible. The process involves opening a model and then appending additional models, making it easier to consolidate all project data in a BIM workflow.

Learning Objectives

- Open and save Navisworks-specific files.
- Consolidate a model using files from different types of software.
- Set the units for an appended model.
- Align models from different design team members.

BIM Workflow: Consolidate Models

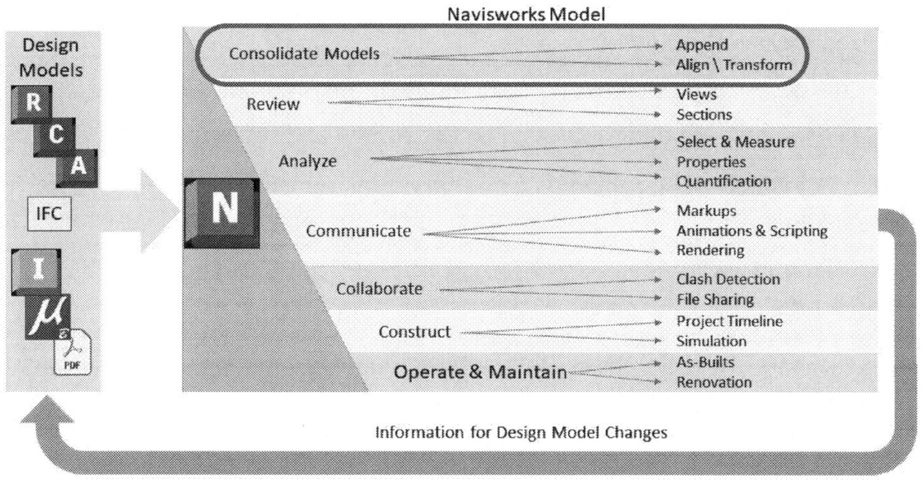

2.1 Consolidating the Model

Autodesk Navisworks is primarily used to combine CAD and BIM files from different disciplines into one composite model. These files can be 2D or 3D, and can be created in Autodesk software (e.g., AutoCAD®, Autodesk® Civil 3D®, Autodesk® Revit®, etc.) or in software provided by other vendors. The advantage of using Navisworks to combine models is the reduction in file sizes. For instance, if you have a 30 MB Revit file, when you bring it into Navisworks, it is reduced to 4 MB. The software simplifies the model to speed up visualization without losing details.

Many different file formats can be opened directly in Navisworks or can be appended together into a single consolidated model. Figure 2–1 shows five appended models representing the architectural, electrical, mechanical, plumbing, and structural designs for a school.

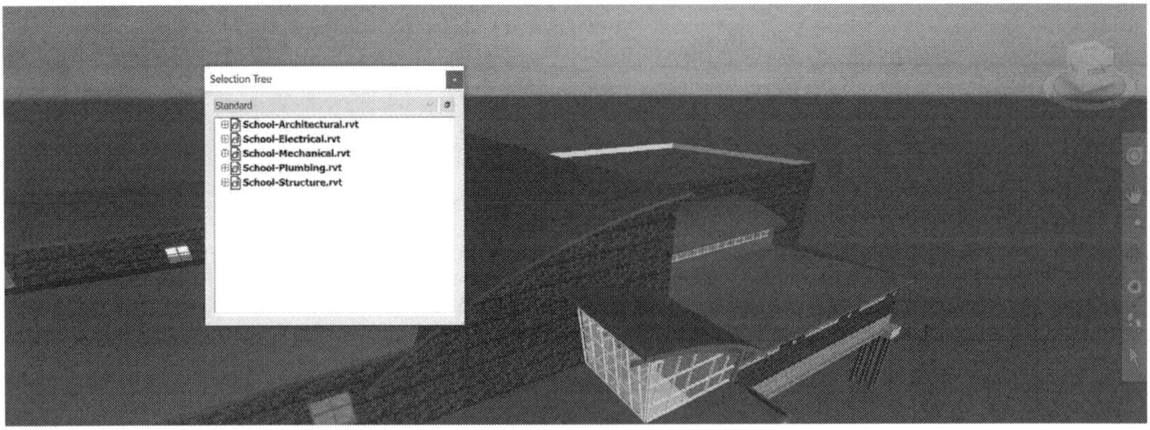

Figure 2–1

There are three main file types created by Navisworks:

- **Navisworks (.NWD):** The current state (or "snapshot") of a project, with all of the model geometry and markups included.
  - These files do not update if a change is made to the original linked files.
  - A .NWD file is typically sent out for others to review at set stages of the project.
- **Navisworks File Set (.NWF):** Includes links to the original files that form a Navisworks model and markups.
  - The model updates in these files when changes are made to the linked files.
  - The .NWF file is typically the file that you work in the most.
- **Navisworks Cache (.NWC):** Snapshots of each original file that are created automatically when you open or append files from other software.

- As long as the original file is not updated, Navisworks uses these cache files as the data source when a file set is opened.
- You typically do not work in cache files.

Note: *To refresh an updated model in the .NWF file, you might need to delete the .NWC file.*

How To: Start a Navisworks Project

1. In the Quick Access Toolbar or (Application Menu), click (New). You can also start a new project from the *Home* screen. Alternatively, you can open a compatible file type.
2. In the *Home* tab>*Project* panel, click (Append). Alternatively, in the Quick Access Toolbar, expand (Open) and click **Append**, or press <Ctrl>+<A>.
3. In the *Append* dialog box, expand the *Files of type* drop-down list and select the file format you want to use, as shown in Figure 2–2. You can open or append many types of files, including Navisworks, Revit, AutoCAD, .DWG, and .DWF formats, as shown in Figure 2–2.

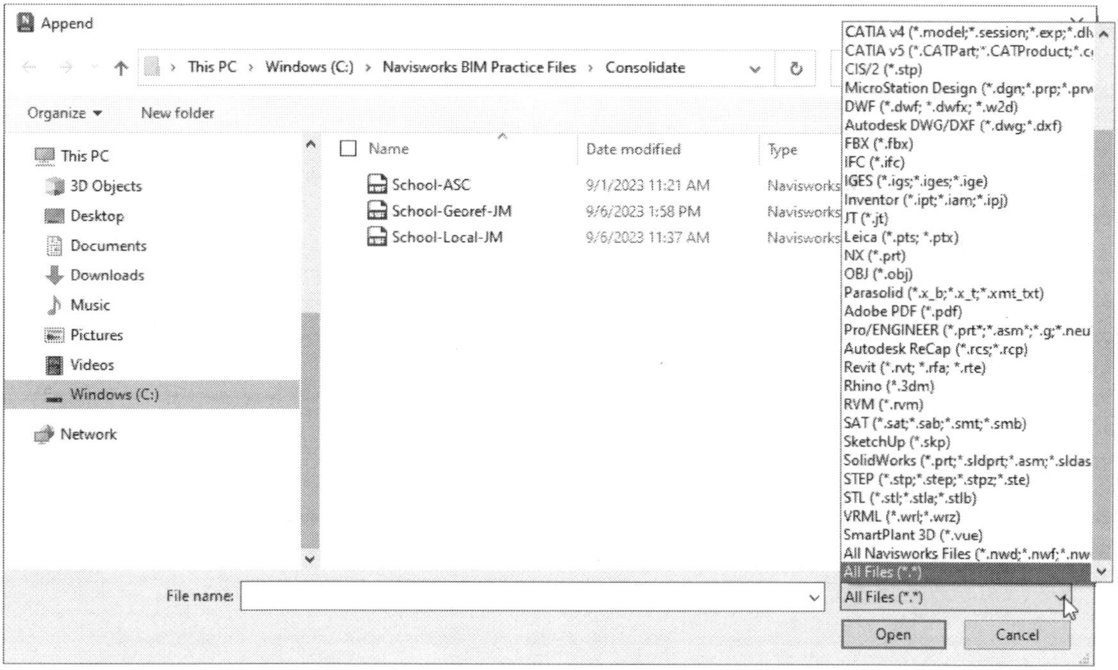

Figure 2–2

4. Navigate to the appropriate folder and select a file.

   Note: *You can select multiple files to open or append by holding either <Shift> or <Ctrl>.*

5. Click **Open**.
6. Continue appending other models as required.
7. In the Quick Access Toolbar or  (Application Menu), click  (Save). The first time you save a file, the *Save As* dialog box opens. Select the type of Navisworks file you want to save.
    - Files can be saved as Navisworks File Set (.NWF) or Navisworks (.NWD). You can also save files so that they are compatible with previous versions of Navisworks, as shown in Figure 2–3.

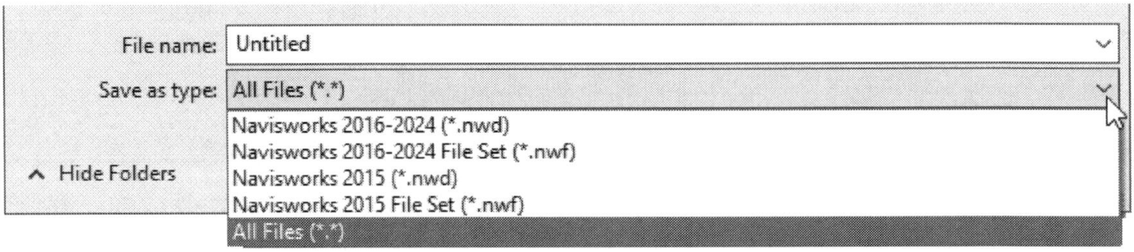

Figure 2–3

2.2 Aligning Models

When appending multiple models together, it is important to ensure that they are scaled properly and line up with each other correctly. By doing this, you can ensure that you get the correct measurements when you measure the model, and that clash detections are as accurate as possible. You are not asked for an insertion point or a scale factor when appending files. These are set after the model is added using the *Units and Transform* dialog box.

Display Units

Each file has its own units. When you append files, they inherit the units of the base file and are scaled to match. The base file's units are determined by the Display Units settings. This determines the scale of the model in Navisworks, and is the unit of measure for scene geometry. If the units do not match as expected, you can modify each model's units.

How To: Set the Display Units

1. Expand (Application Menu) and select **Options**.
2. In the *Options Editor* dialog box, set the units for the base Navisworks model as follows, as shown in Figure 2–4:
   - In the left panel, expand the **Interface** node and select **Display Units**.
   - In the right panel, select the required units for *Linear Units* and *Angular Units*. Select the units you want to use for your measurements in the Navisworks model.
   - Set the *Decimal Places* precision for the units.

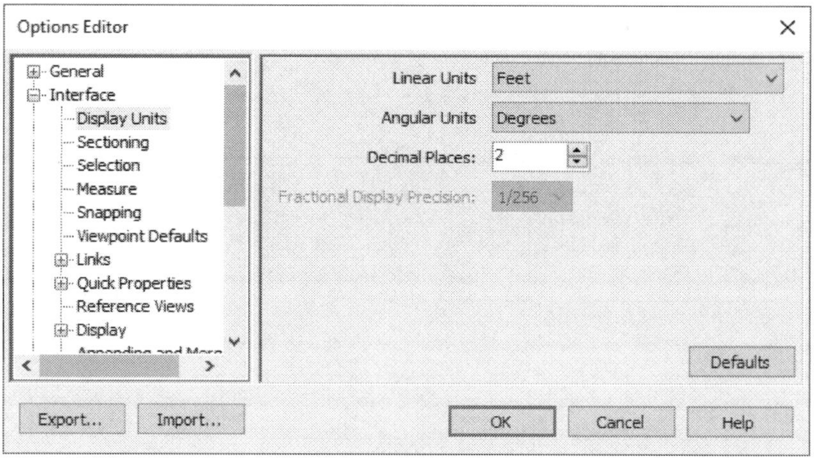

Figure 2–4

3. Click **OK**.

File Transformation

Civil engineers typically work in real world coordinates. Each of their models often have a different base point according to where their projects are located. On the other hand, architects often have a model base point of 0,0,0, unless they input the project base point manually inside Autodesk Revit. You must perform a file transformation when the models from different design team members do not line up correctly. There are two ways to transform a file:

- **Using real world coordinates:** This setting uses the real world coordinates located at the centroid of the appended model. Note that each model must be transformed individually when using this method.
- **Using a difference in coordinates:** This enables you to enter the distance you need the models to move in the X-, Y-, and Z-directions. This method can be used on multiple models simultaneously if they all need to move the same distance.

How To: Transform a File Using Real-World Coordinates

1. Confirm which coordinate system was used to create the model.
2. In the *Selection Tree*, select an appended model, right-click on it, and select **Units and Transform** to set the model's units.
3. In the *Units and Transform* dialog box, enter coordinates, as shown in Figure 2–5.

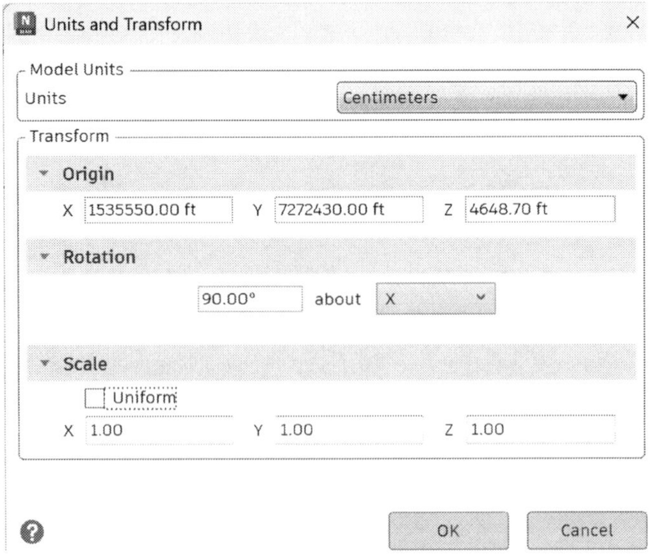

Figure 2–5

4. Click **OK**.

   ***Note:** Only one model can be transformed at a time using the Units and Transform dialog box. Additionally, you can use the Rotation and Scale options to reorient and scale the file.*

How To: Transform Models Using Relative Values

1. In the *Selection Tree*, select all of the files that need to be transformed.
2. Right-click on any one of the selected files and select **Override Item>Override Transform**.
3. In the *Override Transform* dialog box, enter the required X-, Y-, and Z-distances to move the models (as shown in Figure 2–6) relative to their current locations.

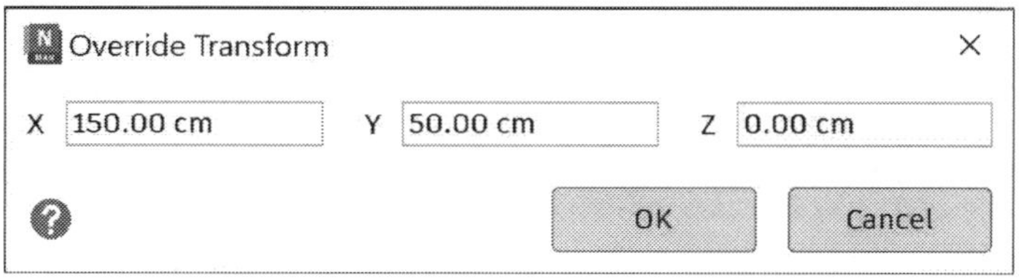

Figure 2–6

4. Click **OK**.

Hint: Heads Up Display (HUD)

You might need to determine where you are in a model before you can calculate the transformation coordinates to use. The Heads Up Display (HUD) information displays in the lower-left corner of the scene view, as shown in Figure 2–7.

- The location information that displays is the current camera location.
- Panning and zooming in the scene causes the coordinates in the HUD to change without moving the cursor.
- To toggle the display the various HUD elements, in the *View* tab>*Navigation Aids* panel, expand (HUD) and select **XYZ Axes**, **Position Readout**, or **Grid Location**.

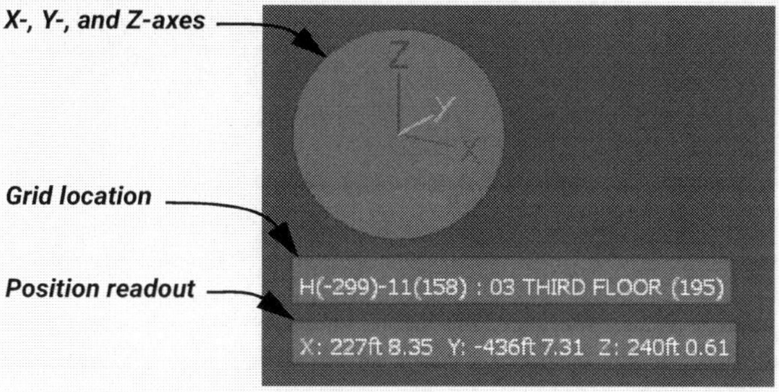

Figure 2–7

How To: Transform Models Using the Measure Tool

1. In the *Review* tab>*Measure* panel, expand (Measure) and ensure that **Point to Point** is selected, as shown in Figure 2–8.

   ***Note:** You will use the Point to Point measure tool to measure between the one model and the location it should be positioned. The measurement value will define the distance the model will be transformed.*

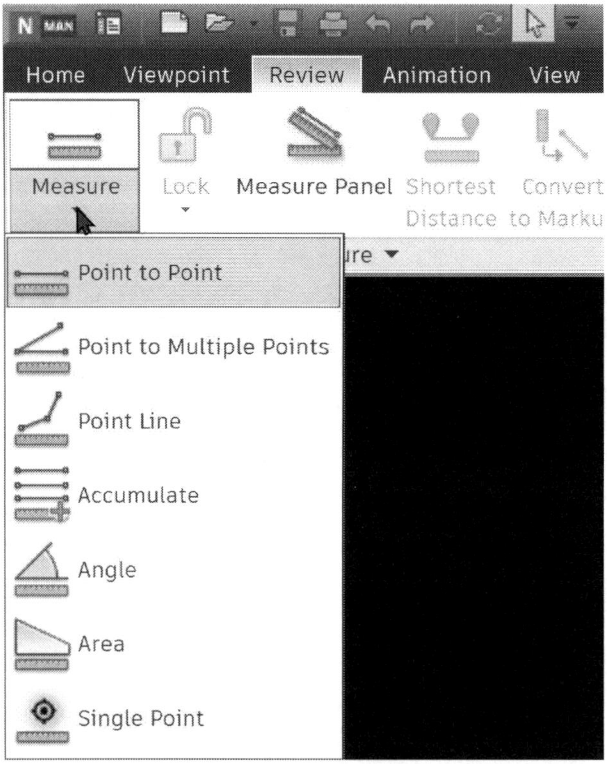

Figure 2–8

2. Select a point on the model that is to be transformed (moved). Once the point is selected, you can drag and see a measurement value.
3. Select the second point to define where the model will be transformed to. A value displays on the screen identifying the distance between the two points.
4. In the *Selection Tree*, select the model(s) that is to be transformed.

5. In the *Review* tab, expand the *Measure* panel and select **Transform Selected Items**, as shown in Figure 2–9.

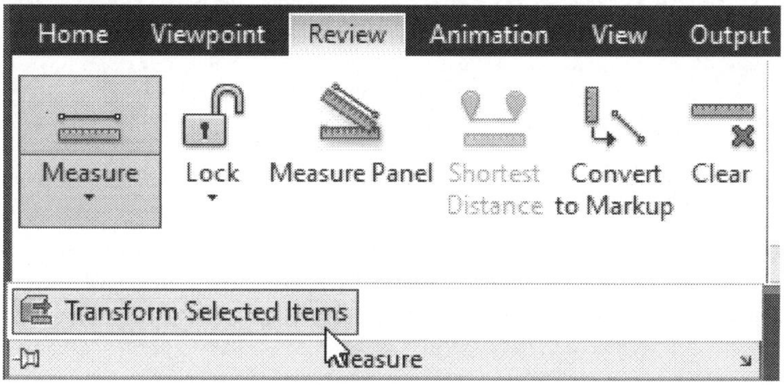

Figure 2–9

Civil 3D/Revit Coordination

Autodesk Civil 3D and Autodesk Revit are the two Autodesk "flagships" for civil engineering and building design respectively. There are many workflows to coordinate between these two applications, some of which involve the Autodesk Construction Cloud. These workflows may involve adding a site to the Revit model, where the Revit project basepoint is geo-referenced to coincide with the Civil 3D coordinate system.

If the authors of the Revit models that are being incorporated into a Navisworks model have access to these coordination tools, they should be encouraged to set a site in the Revit models that is geo-referenced and make it current prior to issuing the models.

Practice 2a
Consolidate Models

Practice Objectives

- Consolidate models from multiple software sources.
- Align models with each other.

In this practice, you will open the preliminary planning phase to review the initial project layout, as shown in Figure 2–10. This file was designed in the Autodesk InfraWorks program and exported as an .FBX file for review purposes only. To complete the practice, you will consolidate design models from Revit and AutoCAD into one Autodesk Navisworks file to highlight the first step in the BIM workflow when working with Navisworks.

Figure 2–10

Task 1: Open the preliminary design and review the project.

In this task, you will open an .FBX file that was created from an Autodesk InfraWorks model during the preliminary planning phase of the project. This enables you to review the early design of the project.

1. In the Quick Access Toolbar, click  (Open).
2. In the *Open* dialog box, set the *Files of type* to **FBX (*.fbx)**.
3. Navigate to the *Navisworks BIM Practice Files\Project Files\InfraWorks Files* folder and select **SiteLayout.fbx**.

4. Click **Open**.
5. On the ViewCube, click the SW corner to view the model in a south-west isometric view.
6. Zoom and pan the model to become familiar with it. Finish orienting the model so that it is oriented as shown in Figure 2–11.
7. In the *Selection Tree*, expand **SiteLayout.fbx>ID 0>ID -1** and select the first seven **Mesh 1** items one at a time to view the items that are highlighted in the scene. Some will be difficult to see, but the sixth and seventh are noticeable as they are the school's roofs and walls, as shown in Figure 2–11 for the seventh mesh item.
   - If the *Selection Tree* window is not displayed, go to the *View* tab>*Workspace* panel, expand **Windows**, and select **Selection Tree**.

Figure 2–11

8. Press <Esc> to release the selection.

This file was the initial project layout, as designed in the Autodesk InfraWorks program. It was provided in an .FBX file format so that it could be reviewed. No further work is required in this file.

Task 2: Consolidate multiple models into one Navisworks file.

In this task, you will open an AutoCAD drawing that represents the site design to create a new Navisworks .NWF file. You will then append multiple Autodesk Revit models into the Navisworks file to represent the building on the site.

1. In the Quick Access Toolbar, click  (Open).

2. Navigate to the *Navisworks BIM Practice Files\Project Files\Civil Files* folder, set the file format to **All Files (*.*)**, and open **Site Console .dwg**. Opening a file automatically closes any other open file.

   ***Note:** This drawing file is a Civil 3D file. Navisworks supports the use of Civil 3D drawings and, to view files created in Autodesk Civil 3D, you must have the Civil 3D Object Enabler installed on your system if you do not have Civil 3D installed.*

3. In the *View* tab>*Navigation Aids* panel, expand (HUD) and in the drop-down list, select **XYZ Axes** and **Position Readout**, as shown in Figure 2–12. This is for the Heads Up Display, which displays the coordinates in the lower-left corner of the scene view.

   ***Note:** The **Grid Location** option is grayed out since no grids are displayed.*

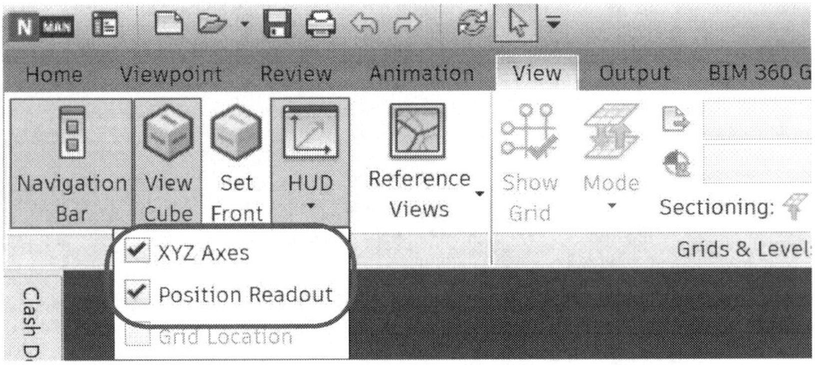

Figure 2–12

4. Review the coordinates in the lower-left corner of the scene view. This file was created in Civil 3D and has real-world coordinates and was properly geo-referenced for the site. Note that the values are quite large for X, Y, and Z.
5. In the *Home* tab>*Project* panel, click (Append).
6. In the *Append* dialog box, expand the drop-down list associated with the file types and set the file format to **Revit (*.rvt; *.rfa; *.rte)**.
7. Navigate to the *Navisworks BIM Practice Files\Project Files\Revit Files* folder. Select **School-Architectural.rvt**, press and hold <Ctrl>, and select the following Revit files,:
   - **School-Electrical.rvt**
   - **School-Mechanical.rvt**
   - **School-Plumbing.rvt**
   - **School-Structure.rvt**

   ***Note:** Do NOT select **School-Architectural_Revised.rvt**.*

8. There should be five files selected in the *Append* dialog box. Click **Open** to load these files into the project.
9. Note that the Revit models are appended.Use the Viewcube to display the South East view and zoom into the model, similar to that shown in Figure 2–13.

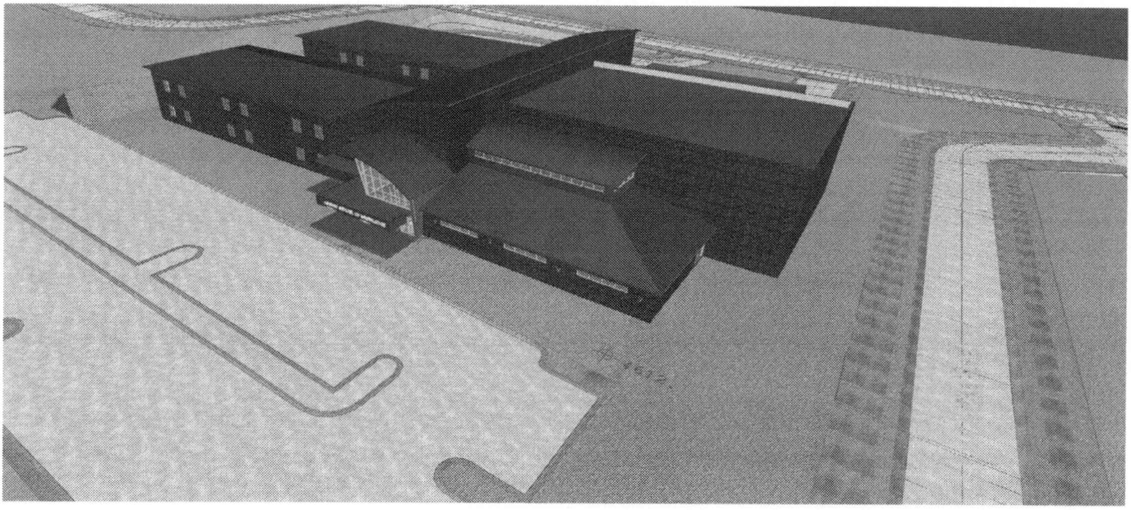

Figure 2–13

10. In the *Home* tab, expand the *Select & Search* panel and set the *Selection Resolution* to **File** by selecting it from the drop-down list, as shown in Figure 2–14. You will learn more about the *Selection Resolution* in later topics. In general, by setting it to **File**, it allows you to easily select entire models in the scene view.

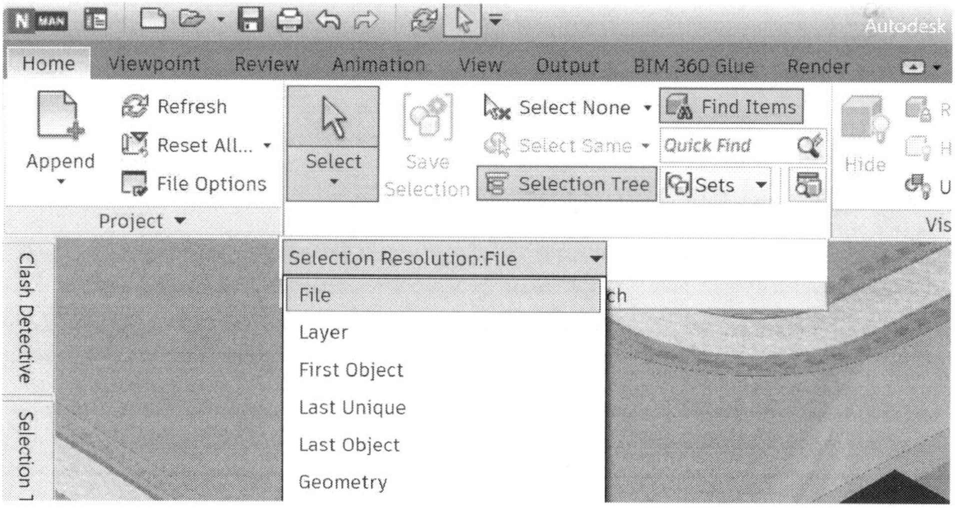

Figure 2–14

11. You can hide the architectural model to be able to see the other models. Select any part of the architectural model, for example a wall or roof, then press <Ctrl>+<H> to hide the architectural model. The entire model is hidden because you had just set the *Selection Resolution* to **File**.
12. Note that all the electrical, mechanical, plumbing, and structural models have also aligned on the site design.
13. Press <Ctrl>+<H> again to unhide the architectural model.
14. Press <Esc> to clear the selection of the school building.
15. In the Quick Access Toolbar or (Application Menu), click (Save).
16. Save the file in the *Navisworks BIM Practice Files\Consolidate* folder as **School-<your initials>.nwf**.

Task 3: Append and transform models.

In the previous task, all of the models aligned correctly because the Revit files were saved using the required coordinates of the site design. This is the ideal scenario; however, this is not always the case. In many cases, you will be required to transform models to their required locations in Navisworks.

In this task, you will once again create a new file with the site design and then append five different Revit models. In this case, you will see that these Revit files were not saved with the required coordinates and you will learn to transform them.

1. In the Quick Access Toolbar, click (Open).
2. Navigate to the *Navisworks BIM Practice Files\Project Files\Civil Files* folder, set the file format to **All Files (*.*)**, and open **Site Console.dwg**.

   Note: *The previous file will be automatically closed when you open the new file. Because the file was saved in the previous task, you will not be prompted; however, if a file were not saved, you would be prompted to save it before a new file is opened.*

3. In the *Home* tab>*Project* panel, click (Append).
4. In the *Append* dialog box, expand the drop-down list associated with the file types and set the file format to **Revit (*.rvt; *.rfa; *.rte)**.
5. Navigate to the *Navisworks BIM Practice Files\Project Files\Revit Files\Local Files* folder. Select **School-Architectural-Local.rvt**, press and hold <Ctrl>, and select the remaining Revit files, as follows:
   - **School-Electrical-Local.rvt**
   - **School-Mechanical-Local.rvt**
   - **School-Plumbing-Local.rvt**
   - **School-Structure-Local.rvt**

6. There should be five files selected in the *Append* dialog box. Click **Open** to load these files into the project.
7. Once the appending process is complete, note that the files do not display on the site. However, they are listed in the *Selection Tree*.
8. The **Site Console.dwg** model is still displayed. In the lower left-hand corner of the scene view, note the coordinates of this model.
9. In the *Selection Tree*, select **School-Architectural-Local.rvt**.
10. Press <Page Down> on your keyboard to reposition the view to the selected school model.

    Note: *<Page Down> can be used as an alternative to using the* **Zoom Selected** *option in the Navigation panel or navigation bar.*

11. With the **School-Architectural-Local.rvt** model still selected, press <Ctrl>+<H> to hide the architectural model. Note that all the electrical, mechanical, plumbing, and structural models have also aligned to the same location.
12. Press <Ctrl>+<H> again to unhide the architectural model.
13. In the lower left-hand corner of the scene view, note the coordinates of the Revit models. Their coordinates are significantly different.

It is assumed that the model designed in Civil 3D was created with the required geo-referenced coordinates and the Revit models must be transformed (moved) to the site design model.

14. Expand  (Application Menu) and select **Options**.

15. In the *Options Editor* dialog box, complete the following (as shown in Figure 2–15) to set the units for the base Navisworks model:
    - In the left pane, select **Interface>Display Units**.
    - In the right pane, set *Linear Units to* **Feet**.
    - Set *Angular Units* to **Degrees**.
    - Set *Decimal Places* to **2**.
    - Click **OK**.

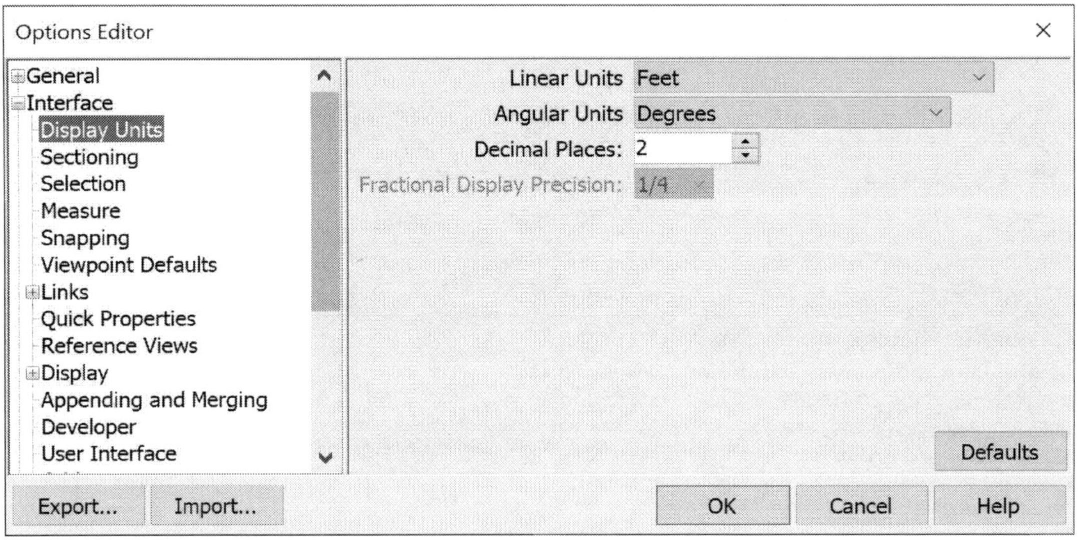

Figure 2–15

16. With the **School-Architectural-Local.rvt** model still selected, use the Viewcube to change the view to **South East** view of the model. Use the Navigation tools to zoom in to the front entrance of the school.
17. Press <Esc> to ensure that nothing is currently selected in the model.

18. In the *Review* tab>*Measure* panel, expand (Measure) and ensure that **Point to Point** is selected, as shown in Figure 2–16. Also ensure that the (None) lock option is active.

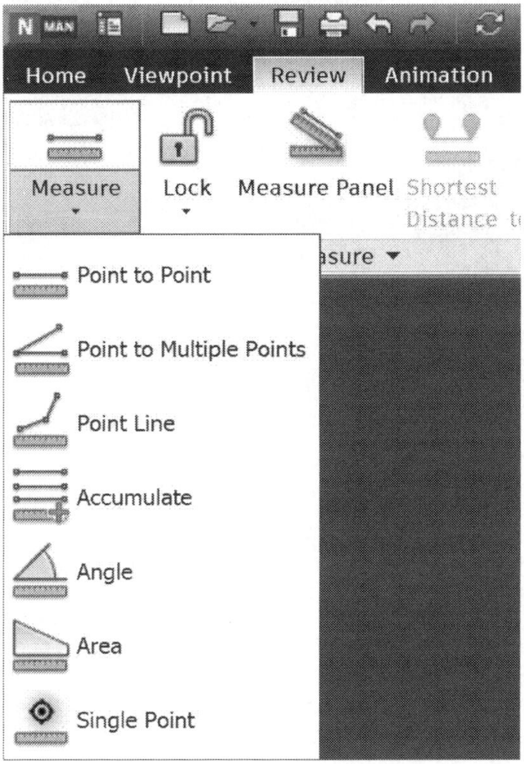

Figure 2–16

Note: *You will use a* ***Point to Point*** *measurement between the current architectural model and the location it should be positioned on the site model to transform and reposition the Revit models.*

19. Select the point at the bottom of the front entrance slab of the school as shown in Figure 2–17.

Figure 2–17

20. Once the point is selected, you can move the mouse and see a measurement value. Do not select a second point yet.
21. In the *Selection Tree*, select the **Site Console.dwg** file and press <Page Down> to zoom to this file in the scene view. Note that the measure tool is still active.
22. Press <Esc> to deselect the site model.
23. Zoom in to the site in the approximate location shown in Figure 2–18. Do not select the second point yet.

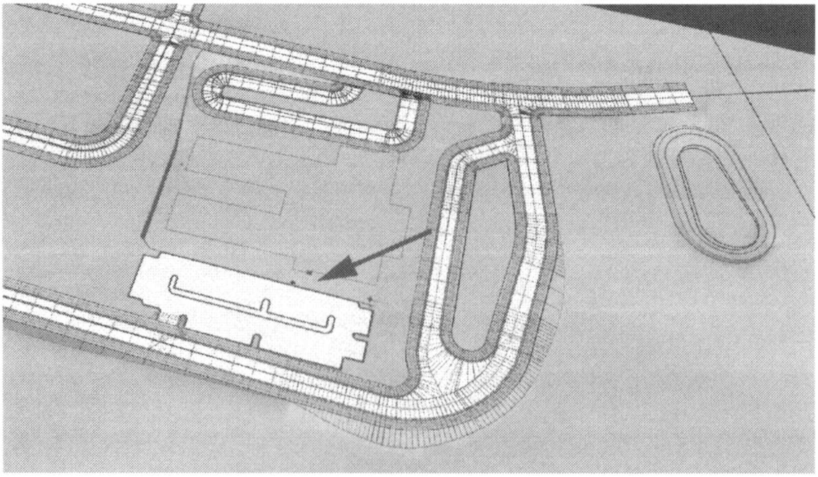

Figure 2–18

24. Continue to zoom to the building pad on the site and select the point shown in Figure 2–19 as the second point in the measurement.

Figure 2–19

25. In the *Selection Tree*, press and hold <Ctrl> and select the five Revit models.
26. In the *Review* tab, expand the *Measure* panel and select **Transform Selected Items**, as shown in Figure 2–20.

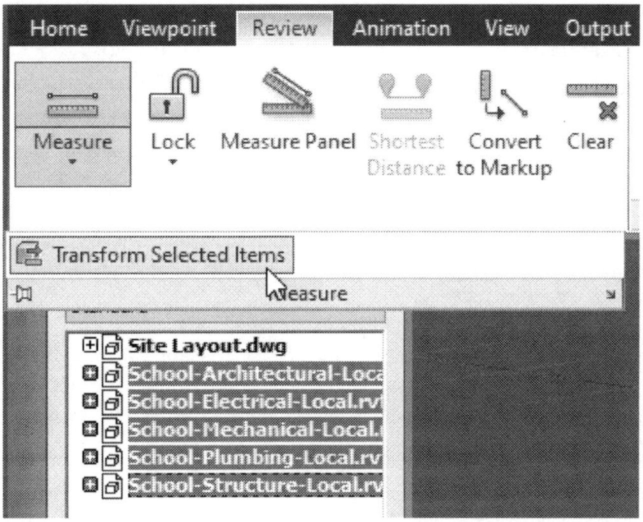

Figure 2–20

27. Press <Page Down> with the Revit models still selected and note that they are now positioned correctly on the site design model (at its coordinate system).
28. Press <Esc> to ensure that nothing is currently selected in the model.

29. Orbit the model to review its placement, as shown in Figure 2–21. There might be some discrepancies between the building and the ground.

Figure 2–21

Note: *In general, Navisworks can help you identify such discrepancies. In such cases, you should coordinate with the Civil engineering firm to update the site model with the required corrections.*

30. In the Quick Access Toolbar or (Application Menu), click (Save).

31. Save the file in the *Navisworks BIM Practice Files\Consolidate* folder as **School-Transformed-<your initials>.nwf**.

Task 4: Append and transform an Inventor model.

In this task, you will append an air conditioning model that was designed with Autodesk Inventor to learn an alternative method that you can use to transform models in a Navisworks file.

1. On the ViewCube, select the **Home** icon, as shown in Figure 2–22, to return to the default view orientation.

Figure 2–22

2. Zoom in to view the school from the front.
3. In the *Home* tab>*Project* panel, click (Append).
4. In the *Append* dialog box, expand the *Files of type* drop-down list and set the file type to **Inventor (*.ipt, *.iam, *.ipj)**.
5. Navigate to the *Navisworks BIM Practice Files\Project Files\HVAC Files* folder and select **1Unit_CommercialAC.iam**. Click **Open**.

   Note: *The AC unit will not display in this view because Inventor also does not use geo-referenced coordinates. You can verify this using the same approach that was previously discussed. Select the unit in the Selection Tree and press <Page Down> to zoom to it and review its coordinates.*

6. If not already displayed, ensure the school is displayed in the scene view.
7. In the *Selection Tree*, right-click on the newly appended Autodesk Inventor file and select **Units and Transform**.

8. In the *Units and Transform* dialog box, set the following, as shown in Figure 2–23:
   - *Units:* **Centimeters**
   - *Origin (ft):* (X) **1535550** (Y) **7272430** (Z) **4648.70**
   - *Rotation:* **90.00**
   - *about:* Select **X** to rotate the AC unit about only the X-axis.
   - Click **OK**.

   Note: *These values have been provided for you, but in general you would have to determine them yourself; therefore, using the measure technique and transforming to a selected location avoids having to find and enter X, Y, and Z coordinates.*

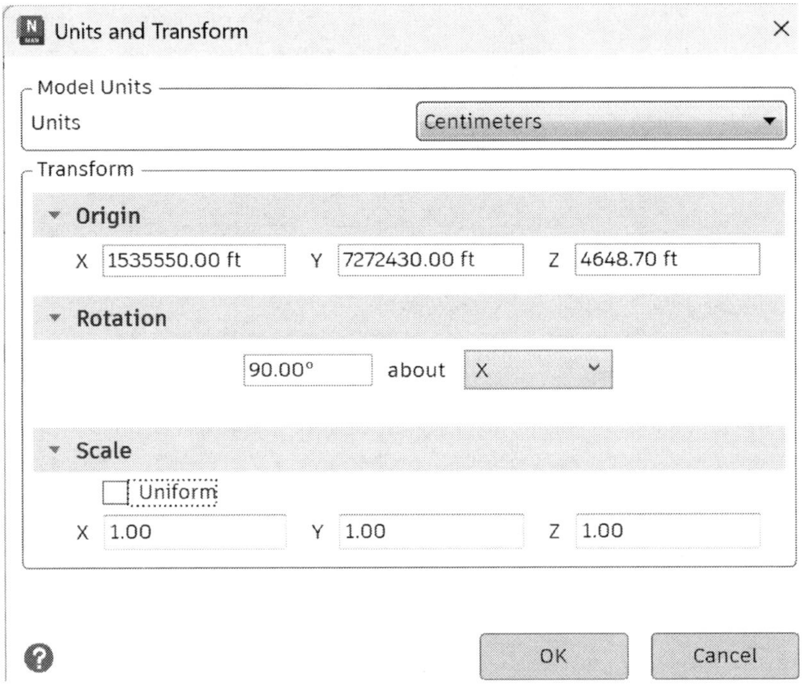

Figure 2–23

Note: *To make further changes to the AC unit's coordinates, you can also right-click on the file and select* ***Override Item>Override Transform*** *and use the Override Transform dialog box. This dialog box only allows for translation from the current location, not from the location that the file was appended to.*

9. The AC unit should display on the flat roof, as shown in Figure 2–24.

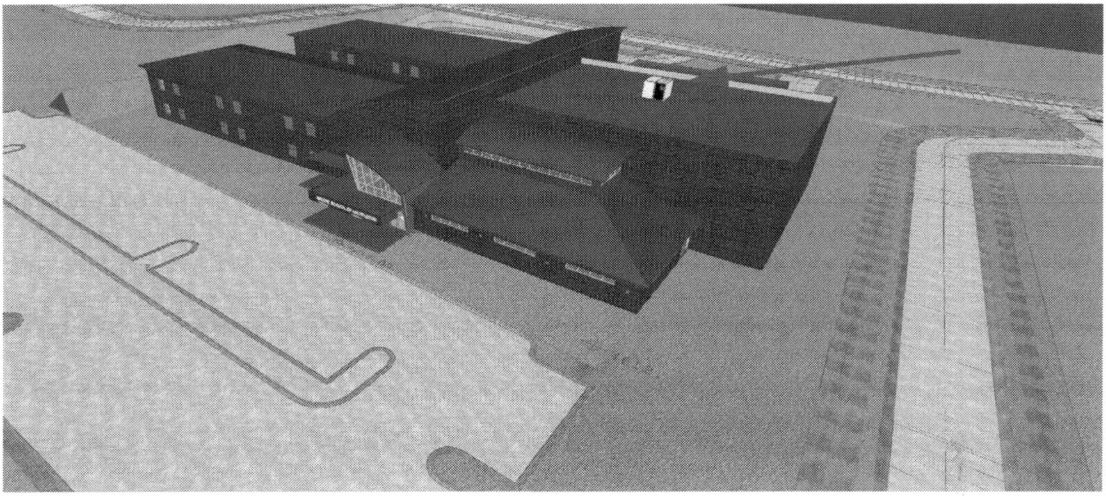

Figure 2–24

10. In the Quick Access Toolbar or (Application Menu), click (Save) to save the file.

    Note: *The models that will be used for the remainder of the practices will be provided for you to ensure that the files have been consolidated properly.*

End of practice

Chapter Review Questions

1. In Autodesk Navisworks, if you open a file that was created in a different software program, can you append other types of files to it?
    a. Yes
    b. No
    c. It depends on the file type

2. Which file format is automatically created when you open or append a file into an Autodesk Navisworks project?
    a. .NWD
    b. .NWF
    c. .NWC

3. Which file format should you use if you want an Autodesk Navisworks project to stay linked to the original models and update as the original models update?
    a. .NWD
    b. .NWF
    c. .NWC

4. How do you change the measurement units for an Autodesk Navisworks model?
    a. You cannot change the units.
    b. In the *Options* dialog box, change the *Display Units*.
    c. You must start the project using the correct template at the beginning.
    d. The units must be changed in the original model.

5. How would you change the units for just one appended model?
    a. In the *Options* dialog box, change the *Display Units*.
    b. You cannot change one appended model independently, you must change them all at the same time.
    c. In the *Selection Tree*, right-click on the model name and select **Override Item>Override Transform**.
    d. In the *Selection Tree*, right-click on the model name and select **Units & Transform...**.

Command Summary

Button	Command	Location
	**Append**	• **Ribbon:** *Home* tab>*Project* panel • **Quick Access Toolbar:** Expand *Open*
N/A	**File Units**	• **Right-click:** (with an item selected) **Units and Transform...**
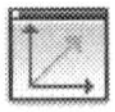	**HUD**	• **Ribbon:** *Views* tab>*Navigation Aids* panel
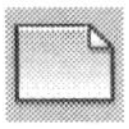	**New**	• **Application Menu** • **Quick Access Toolbar**
	**Open**	• **Application Menu** • **Quick Access Toolbar**
N/A	**Options**	• **Application Menu**
	**Save**	• **Application Menu** • **Quick Access Toolbar**
	**Save As**	• **Application Menu** • **Quick Access Toolbar**

Chapter

3

Review Models

In a BIM workflow, once you have consolidated the models, you need to review them. Model review enables stakeholders to preview the project with all of the components included. In doing so, sight lines, lighting, security, and many other criteria can be reviewed and verified. Learn how to section the model and save views for easy reuse. Also, set up appearances and view options.

Learning Objectives

- Save scenes for later reuse.
- Section a model.
- Set up view options.

BIM Workflow: Review

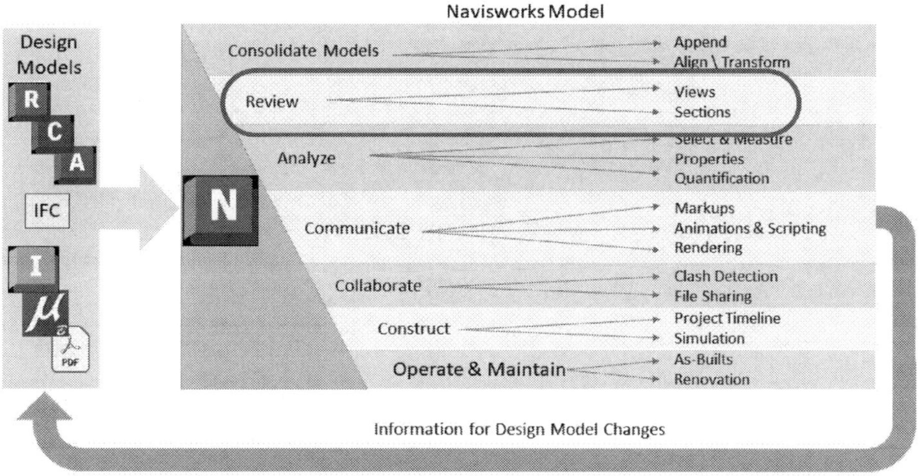

3.1 Saving and Retrieving Views

In Autodesk® Navisworks®, saved views are called viewpoints, which can be accessed through the *Saved Viewpoints* window, as shown in Figure 3–1. Viewpoints help you focus on specific conditions in a scene so that you can share information quickly with others. Viewpoints save the scene conditions, such as varying materials, lighting, or what is displayed or hidden. They can also include comments and markup tags. To open the *Saved Viewpoints* window, in the *View* tab>*Workspace* panel, expand (Windows) and select *Saved Viewpoints*. In the *Saved Viewpoints* window, select any view to make it current.

How To: Retrieve a Viewpoint

1. In the *Saved Viewpoints* window, select the name of the view.
2. To switch to another view, select an alternate view.

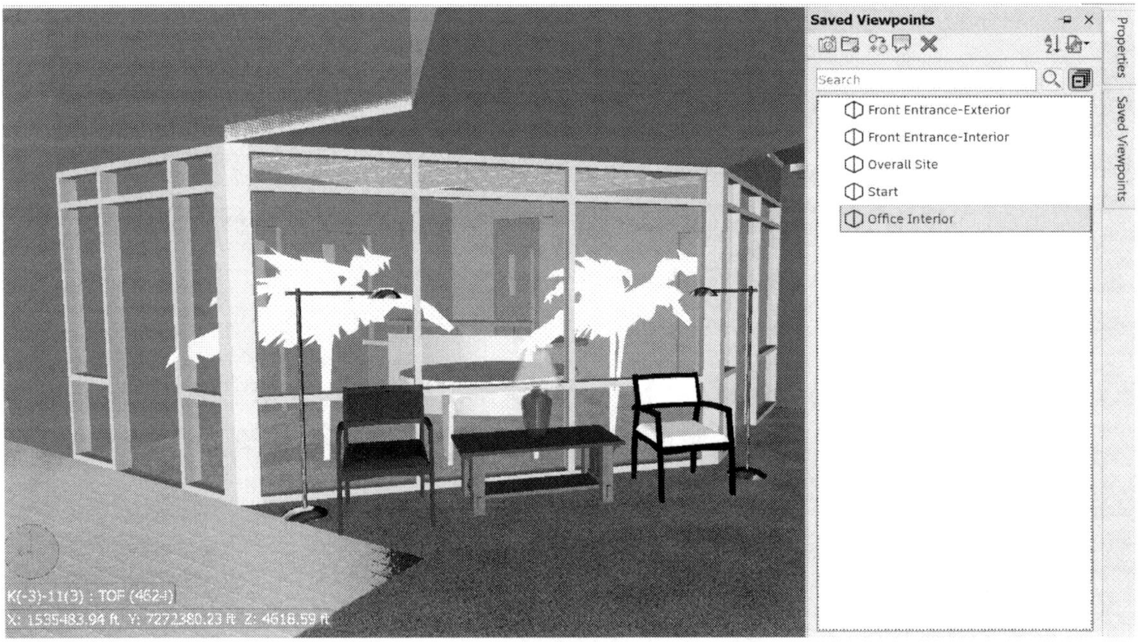

Figure 3–1

> ***Note:*** *Once a viewpoint is active and the model is saved, this viewpoint becomes the default view when the model is next opened.*

How To: Save a Viewpoint

1. Set up the view as required.
2. In the *Saved Viewpoints* window, right-click on a blank space under the list and select **Save Viewpoint**, as shown in Figure 3–2. Alternatively on the *Viewpoint* tab>*Save, Load & Playback* panel, click  (Save Viewpoint).

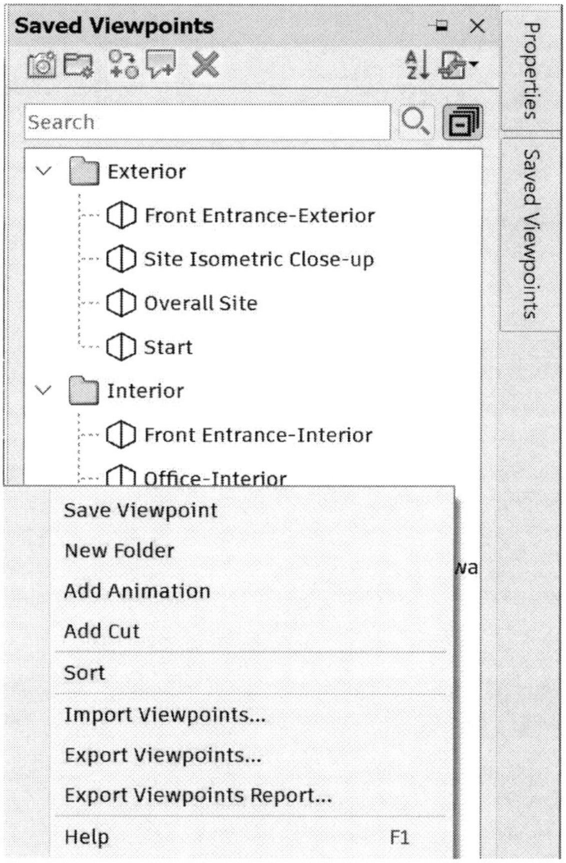

Figure 3–2

3. Enter a name for the viewpoint and press <Enter>.

Editing Viewpoints

Once viewpoints have been created and saved, you can edit and update them. In the *Saved Viewpoints* window, right-click on a viewpoint name to display the menu shown in Figure 3–3.

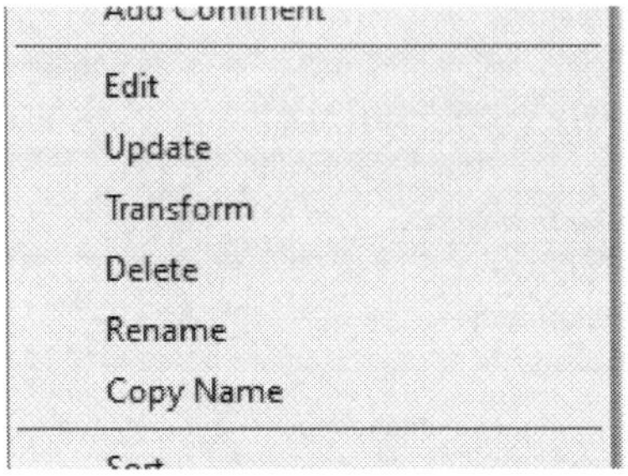

Figure 3–3

> ***Note:*** *You might want to make a copy of a viewpoint before you start editing it. To do this, select* ***Add Copy*** *in the same right-click menu.*

The viewpoint editing options are as follows:

- **Edit:** Opens the *Edit Viewpoint* dialog box shown in Figure 3–4. The available options include changes to the camera, animation, saved attributes, and collision settings for the view.

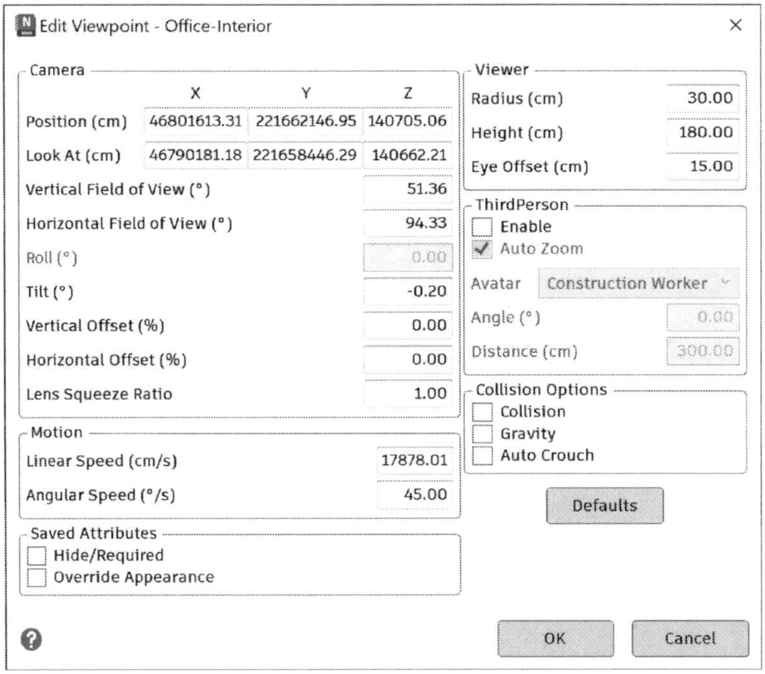

Figure 3–4

- **Update:** If you have made changes of any kind to the view, this option updates the saved viewpoint with those changes.

  ***Note:** Once you have reoriented the scene, ensure that you simply right-click on the viewpoint name to access the menu. Selecting first and then right-clicking will reset the view to that of the selected viewpoint.*

- **Transform:** Opens the *Transform* dialog box (shown in Figure 3–5), which enables you to specify X, Y, and Z values to move the entire view these distances.

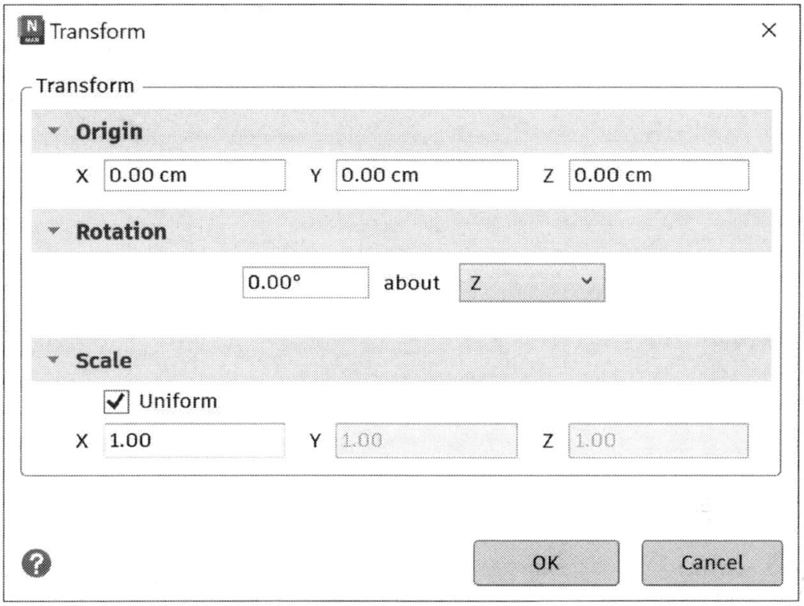

Figure 3–5

- **Delete:** Removes the view from the project.
- **Rename:** Enables you to assign a new name. You can also slowly click twice on the name to do this.

Viewpoint Defaults

The viewpoint defaults impact all new viewpoints.

How To: Change the Viewpoint Defaults

1. Expand (Application Menu) and select **Options**.
2. In the *Options Editor* dialog box, set the following, as shown in Figure 3–6:
   - In the left pane, select **Interface>Viewpoint Defaults**.
   - In the right pane, select the viewpoint settings required.

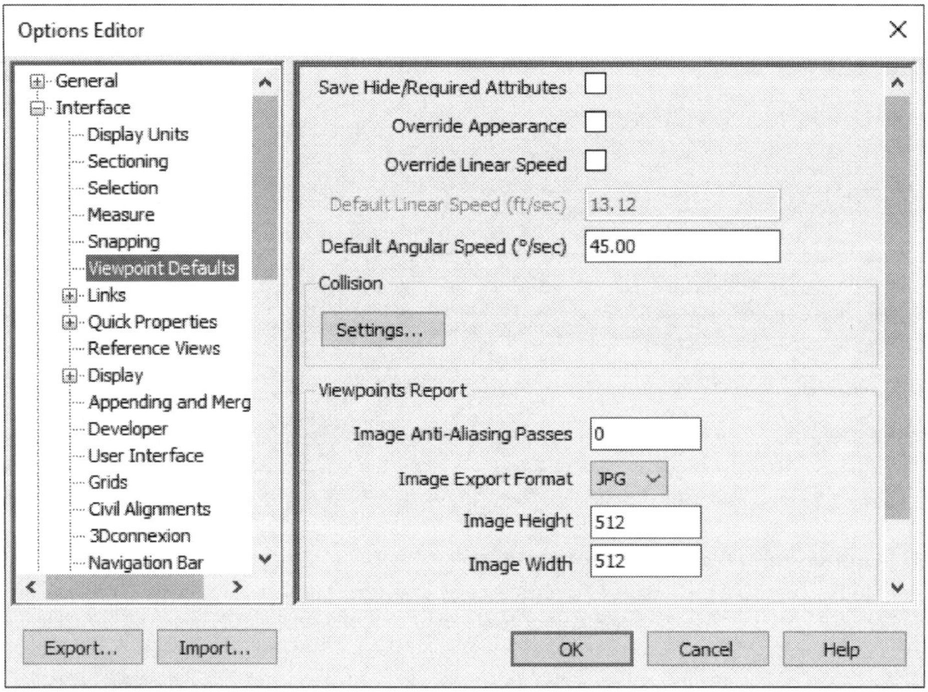

Figure 3–6

3. Click **OK**.

   Note: *The* ***Viewpoint Defaults*** *options also enable you to set the defaults for how the images are saved for viewpoint reports.*

Organizing Viewpoints

You can sort viewpoints in the following ways:

- Alphanumerically
- Manually sorted into custom order
- Moved into folders which can also be sorted alphanumerically

How To: Organize Viewpoints into Folders

1. In the *Saved Viewpoints* window, right-click and select **New Folder**.
2. Enter a name for the new folder and press <Enter>.
3. Drag and drop any saved views into the new folder.
4. In the *Saved Viewpoints* window, right-click and select **Sort** to sort the folders and views alphanumerically.

Hint: Importing Autodesk Revit Views

If a 3D view exists inside Autodesk Revit, it will be imported with the model. To ensure the view is recognized, you must ensure that you set the options shown in Figure 3–7 before appending the Revit model.

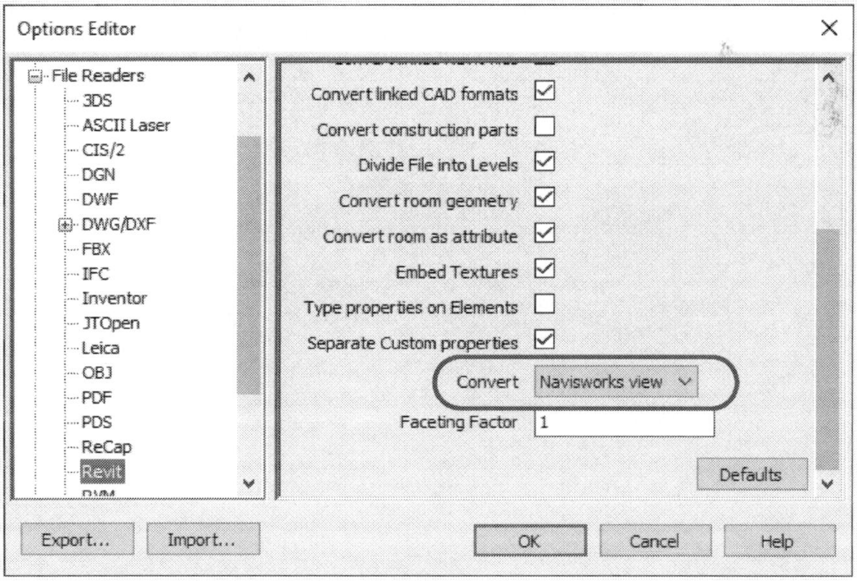

Figure 3–7

Practice 3a
Save and Retrieve Viewpoints

Practice Objectives

- Restore existing saved viewpoints.
- Create new viewpoints.
- Modify a saved viewpoint.
- Organize saved viewpoints into folders.

In this practice, you will review several existing viewpoints, create interior and exterior viewpoints, and separate them into folders. Once the practice is complete, your *Saved Viewpoints* window will display similar to that shown in Figure 3–8.

Figure 3–8

Task 1: Restore viewpoints.

1. In the Quick Access Toolbar, click (Open).
2. In the *Open* dialog box, navigate to the *Navisworks BIM Practice Files\Review* folder, select **School-Viewpoints.nwf**, and click **Open**.

   Note: *If the file is not displayed in the Review folder, ensure that the file type list is set to* ***All Files (*.*)****.*

3. Expand the *Saved Viewpoints* window, if not already visible.
   - By default, the *Saved Viewpoints* window is usually in a hidden state in the top-right corner of your software. If this window is not enabled, in the *View* tab>*Workspace* panel, expand (Windows) and select **Saved Viewpoints** to open the window.
4. In the *Saved Viewpoints* window, review the four existing saved viewpoints listed outside of the folders (**Front Entrance-Exterior**, **Front Entrance-Interior**, **Overall Site**, and **Start**).
5. The other viewpoints that are showing in folders were originally imported with and are associated to the Autodesk Revit files. These views may or may not be useful in Navisworks. In this case, you will remove them. Press and hold <Shift> and select all of the folders, then right-click and select **Delete**.
6. Select the saved viewpoint **Front Entrance-Interior**. You are automatically zoomed in to the front entry area of the school, as this was the saved location of this viewpoint.
7. Save the file. Once saved, this will be the view that opens the next time the file is opened.

Task 2: Save new viewpoints.

1. From the front entrance area, use the viewing tools to look around the interior of the building.
2. Reorient the view as shown in Figure 3–9 to look at the angled front office.
3. In the *Viewpoint* tab>*Save, Load & Playback* panel, click  (Save Viewpoint).
4. In the *Saved Viewpoints* window, enter the name **Office-Interior** and press <Enter>. The new viewpoint is listed, as shown in Figure 3–9.

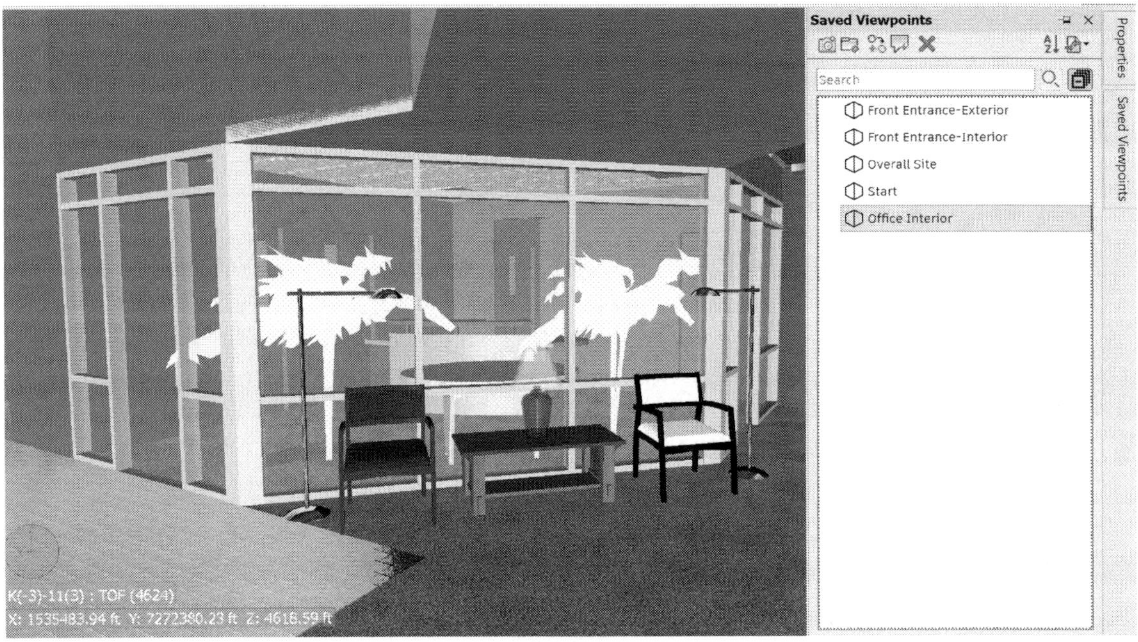

Figure 3–9

5. Continue viewing the interior of the building and make several additional viewpoints.
6. Save the file.

Task 3: Edit a viewpoint.

1. In the *Saved Viewpoints* window, right-click on **Overall Site** and select **Add Copy**.
2. Select the copy, right-click, and select **Rename**. Rename the viewpoint as **Site Isometric Close-up**. Alternatively, you can slowly double-click to rename the saved viewpoint.
3. Zoom in on the building.
4. In the *Viewpoint* tab>*Camera* panel, expand  (Perspective) and select  (Orthographic), as shown in Figure 3–10.

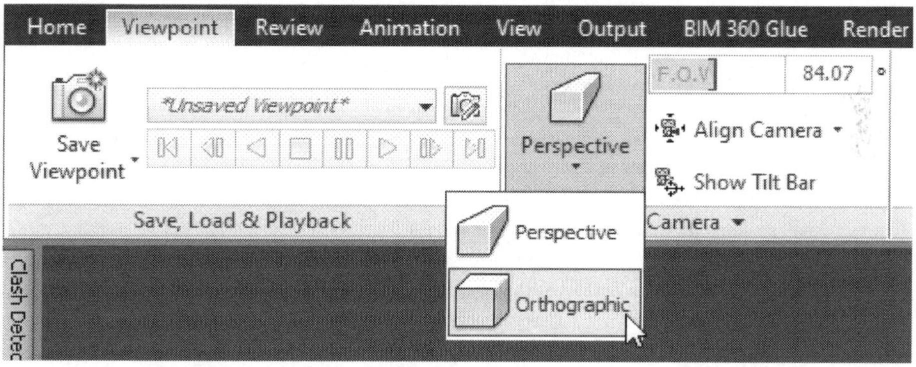

Figure 3–10

5. In the *Saved Viewpoints* window, right-click on **Site Isometric Close-up** and select **Update**.
6. Switch between the two viewpoints and note the differences.
7. Save the file.

Task 4: Organize the new viewpoints.

1. To prevent the *Saved Viewpoints* window from auto-hiding, open and pin the *Saved Viewpoints* window by selecting the  icon at the top of its title bar.
2. In the *Saved Viewpoints* window toolbar, select  (New Folder) or right-click in the window and select **New Folder**. Do this again to add a second new folder.
3. Rename the new folders **Interior** and **Exterior**.

4. Drag and drop the viewpoints into the appropriate folder, as shown in Figure 3–11. The exact names in your model may vary depending on the views that you created.

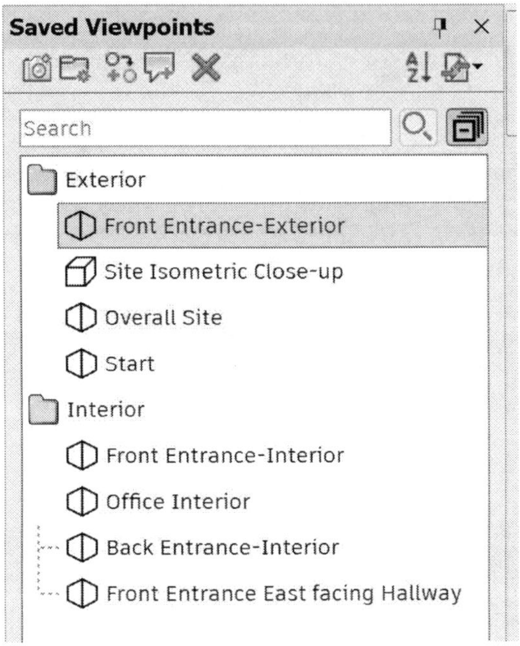

Figure 3–11

5. Select **Front Entrance-Exterior**, if not already active.
6. Save the file.

   Note: *When a file is saved, the active viewpoint is also saved. The next time you open the file, that viewpoint will be displayed.*

End of practice

3.2 Sectioning the Model

A powerful way to view the model in Navisworks is to create sections. When you enable sectioning, you can create and modify cut planes or a cut box to customize the views you need. There are two modes used in sectioning:

- (Planes): Enables you to toggle and modify any of six preset planes.
- (Box): Automatically cuts all six planes of the box.

  ***Note:** You can also cut the model along building levels and grid lines. This option is covered later in this chapter.*

How To: Create Sections in Planes Mode

1. In the *Viewpoint* tab>*Sectioning* panel, click (Enable Sectioning).
2. In the *Sectioning Tools* tab>*Mode* panel, select (Planes) from the drop-down list, if not already enabled.
3. In the *Sectioning Tools* tab>*Transform* panel, click (Move), if not already active. If the gizmo does not display, toggle **Move** off and then on again.

   ***Note:** If the scene view displays as gray only (i.e., no model geometry is shown), it indicates that the default location of the planes is below the model. With the default Plane1 active, select the blue gizmo arrow and slowly drag it upwards in the Z direction. Note how the model is sectioned as you move the plane through the model. Reposition the plane above the model to begin sectioning.*

4. Plane 1 and the section gizmo display in the scene view. Note that **Plane 1** is set as the default active plane, as shown in Figure 3–12. This plane is aligned with the **Top** of the ViewCube.

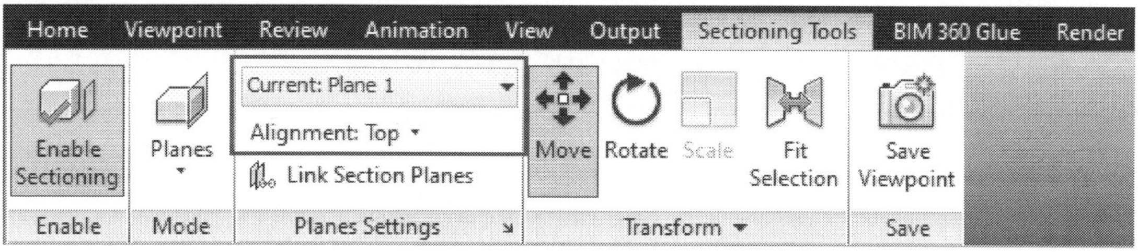

Figure 3–12

5. Review the ViewCube and determine which plane defines the cutting plane that is required.

6. In the *Planes Settings* panel, click ↘ (Section Plane Settings) to open the *Section Plane Settings* dialog box, as shown in Figure 3–13. This dialog box provides you with the Plane # as associated with the assigned ViewCube sides. As you become more familiar with Navisworks, you may not need to review this. You can also use this to reset the orientation of the section planes relative to the ViewCube.

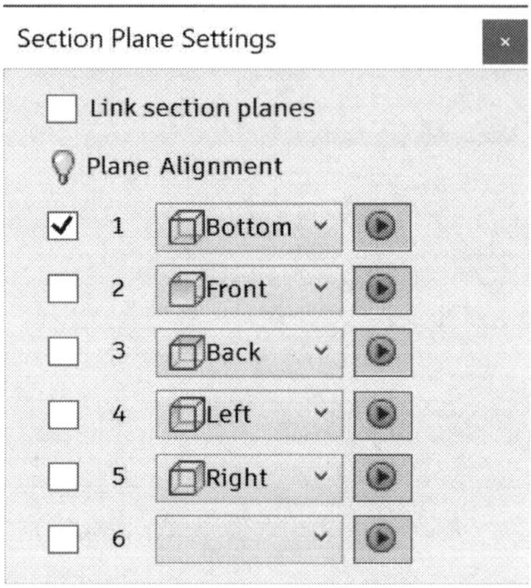

Figure 3–13

7. To change the active plane (i.e., to section from a different plane, in this case the front of the model (Plane 3)), in the *Planes Settings* panel, expand the *Current Plane* drop-down list and select **Plane 3** to make it the active plane for editing. The *Plane Settings* panel updates as shown in Figure 3–14.

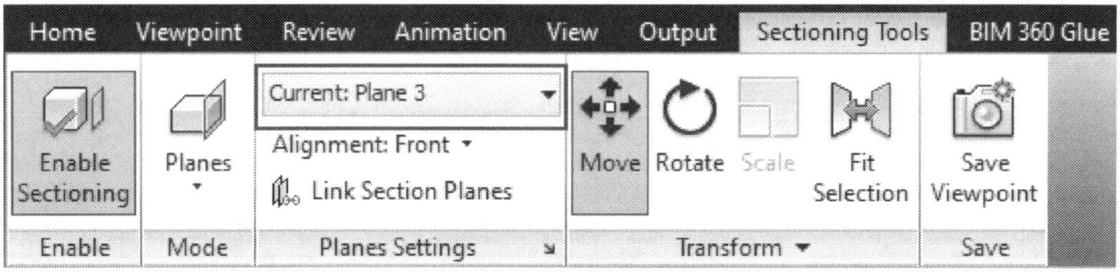

Figure 3–14

8. Drag the blue gizmo arrow (perpendicular to the plane) and position it as required to section the model (in this case, parallel to the front of the model), as shown in Figure 3–15.

Figure 3–15

9. Continue to activate planes in the *Planes Settings* panel and further section the model in other directions, as needed.

How To: Create Sections in Box Mode

1. In the *Viewpoint* tab>*Sectioning* panel, click  (Enable Sectioning).
2. In the *Sectioning Tools* tab>*Mode* panel, select  (Box) from the drop-down list, if not already enabled.
3. The default section box and gizmo display in the scene view, similar to that shown in Figure 3–16. Note that the *Planes Settings* section of the ribbon is disabled because the box mode is being used. When using Box mode, all of the planes are transformed at the same time.

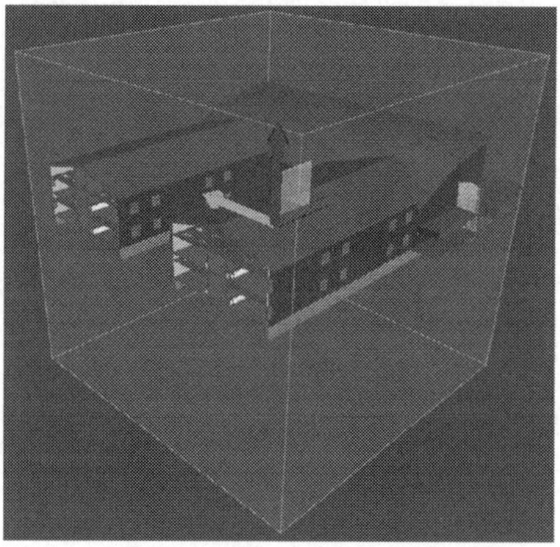

Figure 3–16

4. In the *Sectioning Tools* tab>*Transform* panel, use the (Move), (Rotate) and (Scale) transform options as needed to transform the location of the box to define the required section view. These transform options are discussed further in the next section.

Consider the following tips when working with the Planes and Box sectioning modes:

- Multiple planes can be incorporated at the same time to section the model in multiple directions all at once. Whether the section is included or not is controlled with the light bulb icon that is listed adjacent to the plane name in the *Current Plane* drop-down list, as shown in Figure 3–17. A yellow light bulb icon ( ) indicates the plane is included in the view and the gray icon ( ) indicates it is not included (turned off). To control the display, simply toggle the icon on/off as needed.

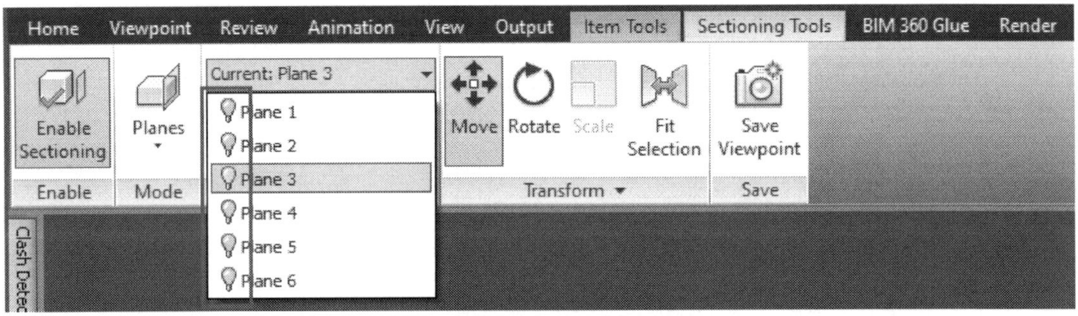

Figure 3–17

- To set the box to a selection set, select the item in the model and click (Fit Selection).
- Once the section view is created, you can reorient the model as needed using the standard navigation tools and use the (Save Viewpoint) command to save the view, as shown in Figure 3–18.

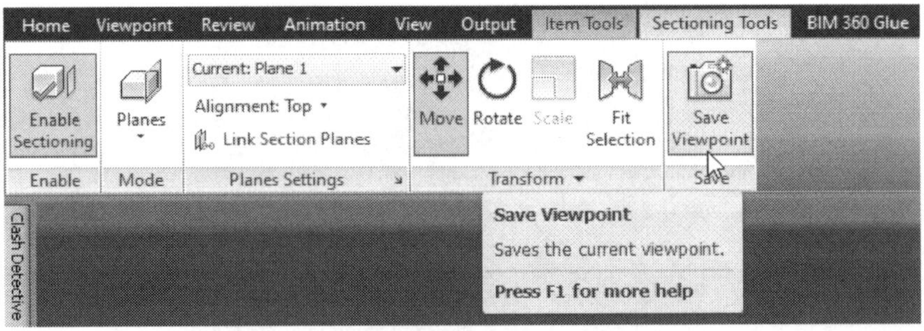

Figure 3–18

- Additional transformation tools can be used to position/rotate the planes. These options are discussed further in the next section.

Transforming Sections

The transform tools enable you to modify the location of the plane or box to create the exact section you need, such as the rotated plane shown in Figure 3–19. Each of the primary transform tools use the gizmo to modify the locations of the planes or box.

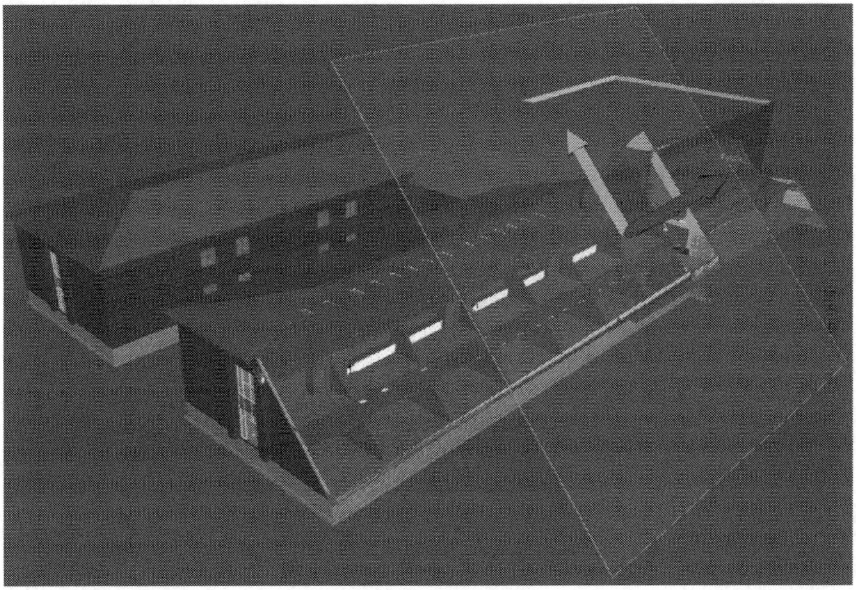

Figure 3–19

Each gizmo is based on the Cartesian coordinate system and has three directional arrows and three planes, as shown in Figure 3–20. These are used to transform the plane or box.

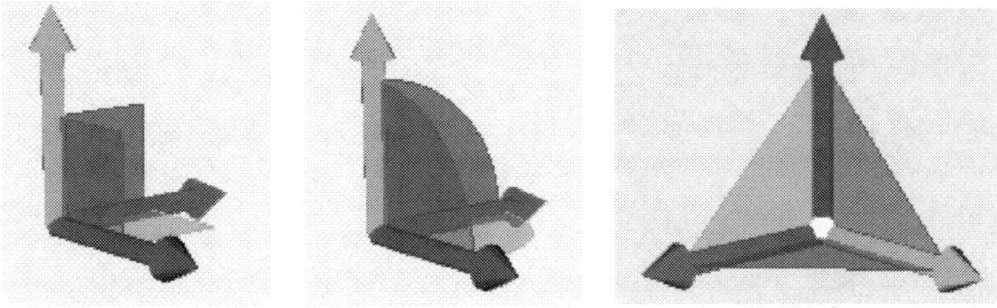

Move ***Rotate*** ***Scale***

Figure 3–20

- In Planes mode, the gizmo is fixed on the current plane. You can move and rotate in this mode.
- In Box mode, the gizmo is fixed at the center of the box. You can move, rotate, and scale in this mode.

Transform Tools

- (Move): Moves the current plane or the entire box based on the arrow or plane you select on the gizmo.
- (Rotate): In Planes mode, the tool enables you to rotate the current plane. In Box mode, the tool rotates the entire box. For this transfom option, you can only use the planes of the gizmo, not the arrows.
- (Scale): Available only in Box mode, the tool enables you to drag the arrows on the gizmo to scale the opposing sides of the box equally to create a rectangle. Alternatively, you can select the triangular planes between arrows to scale in all directions.
- (Fit Selection): In Planes mode, the tool moves the current plane so that the selected items are in the displayed area of the section. In Box mode, the tool fits the box tightly around the selected items. This tool does not use a gizmo.

In general, when using Box mode, you will use a combination of move and scale actions to obtain the required section. In the example shown in Figure 3–21, the Y-axis arrow was used to create a cut on both the front and back of the building.

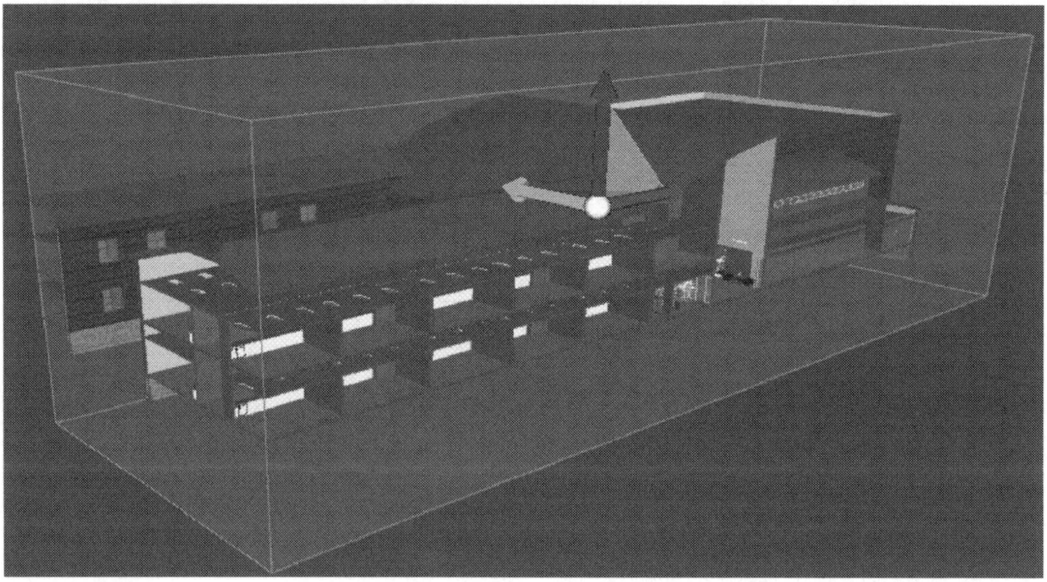

Figure 3–21

Plane Alignment

When using Planes mode to create a section, you have access to the *Planes Settings* panel to customize the plane alignment.

> ***Note:*** *By default, planes 1 through 6 are aligned to the sides of the ViewCube. The default alignments are Plane 1 = Top, Plane 2 = Bottom, Plane 3 = Front, Plane 4 = Back, Plane 5 = Left, and Plane 6 = Right.*

To customize the plane alignment, use the drop-down list shown in Figure 3–22 to reassign the alignment of the current plane (i.e., the plane listed in the *Current:* field) to an alternate side.

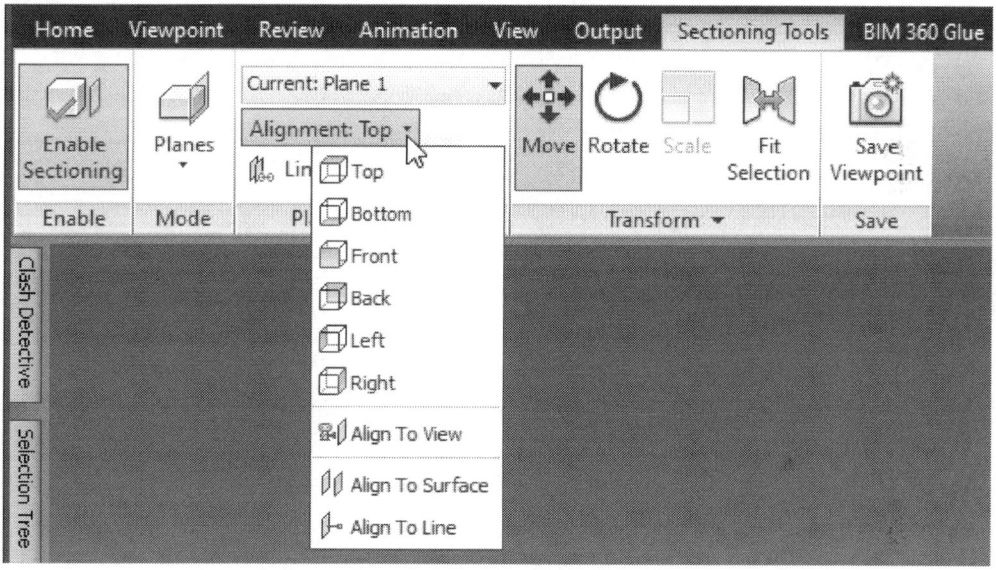

Figure 3–22

Note that if you change a plane alignment, you can end up with two planes aligned to the same side. It is recommended that you review the *Section Plane Settings* dialog box (shown in Figure 3–23) after making a change to ensure that each plane is set as required. To access the *Section Plane Settings* dialog box, click ↘ in the bottom-right corner of the *Planes Settings* panel title.

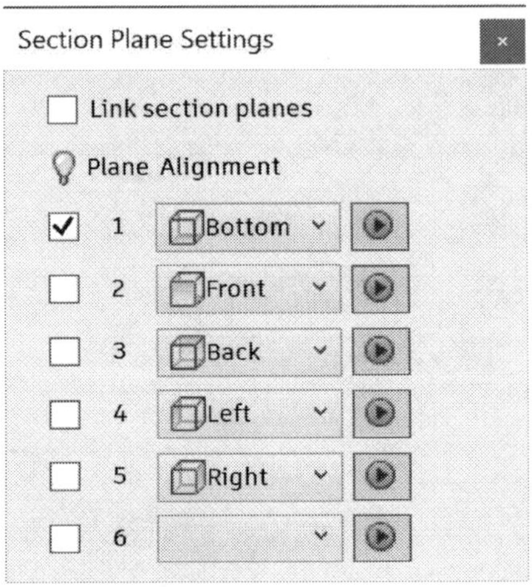

Figure 3–23

Planes 1 through 6 are listed from top to bottom and their initially assigned ViewCube sides are listed adjacent to each number. To reassign a side to a plane, select the drop-down list (as shown in Figure 3–24) and select an alternate side name. Reassigning sides in this dialog box enables you to ensure all planes are set as required.

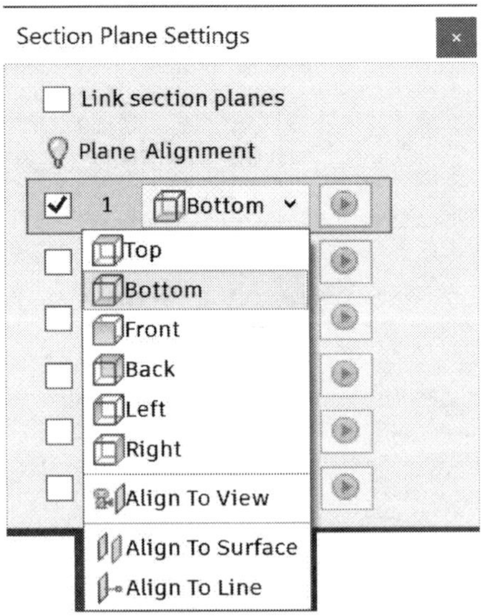

Figure 3–24

The following additional alignment options are available for each plane to further help customize the section view. These options are available at the bottom of each plane's drop-down list, as shown above in Figure 3–24.

- The **Align To View** option orients the plane so that it is parallel to the plane of the current scene view orientation, as shown in Figure 3–25.

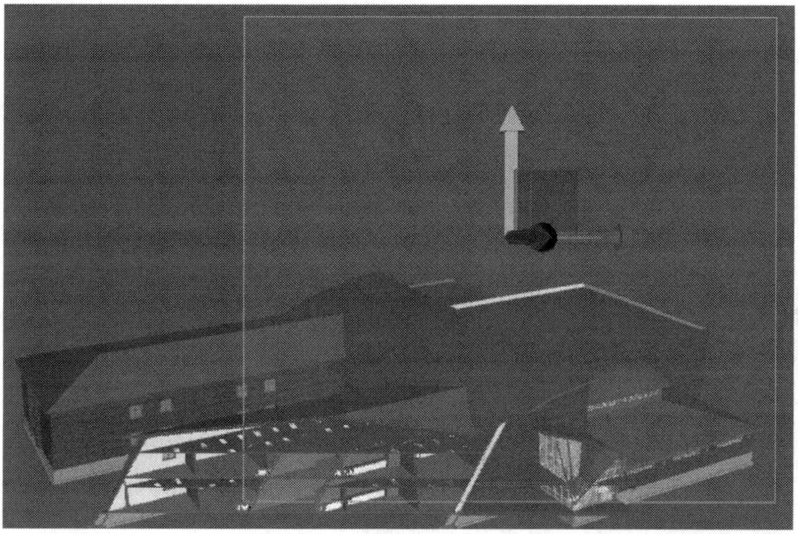

Figure 3–25

- The **Align To Surface** option orients the plane to a selected surface in the 3D model.
- The **Align To Line** option orients the plane to a selected line entity in the model.

When using any of these options you can reorient or select a new surface or line and click 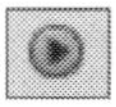 (Re-select) to update the view.

Linking Section Planes

The **Link section planes** option enables you to select two parallel planes to move them together. In the *Section Plane Settings* dialog box, enable the two planes by selecting their associated checkboxes and then selecting **Link section planes**, as shown in Figure 3–26. Once enabled, you can select which plane to use for moving and drag the gizmo as needed to move the planes at the same time.

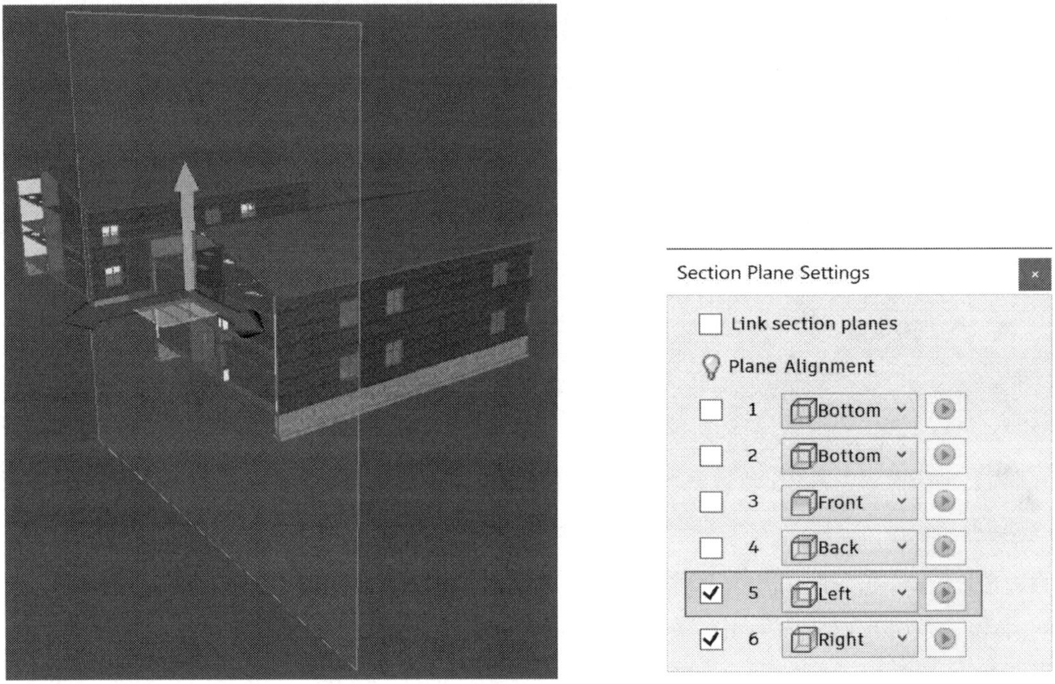

Figure 3–26

Note: *Two linked planes cannot be rotated at the same time.*

Hint: Reference Views

Plan and section reference views can be displayed in a window to help identify where you are in the model. A marker in the reference view enables you to navigate the scene by holding the left mouse button over it and dragging the triangle to a new location. Reference views are regular Navisworks windows that can be docked or floating. In the *View* tab>*Navigation Aids* panel, expand (Reference Views) and select **Plan View** or **Section View**. Alternatively, you can enable their windows on the *View* tab using the *Windows* drop-down list.

- **Plan View** displays the entire model from the top by default, as shown in Figure 3–27.
- **Section View** displays the entire model from the front.

Within either reference view window, there are additional options in the right-click menu to reorient the view, as shown in Figure 3–27.

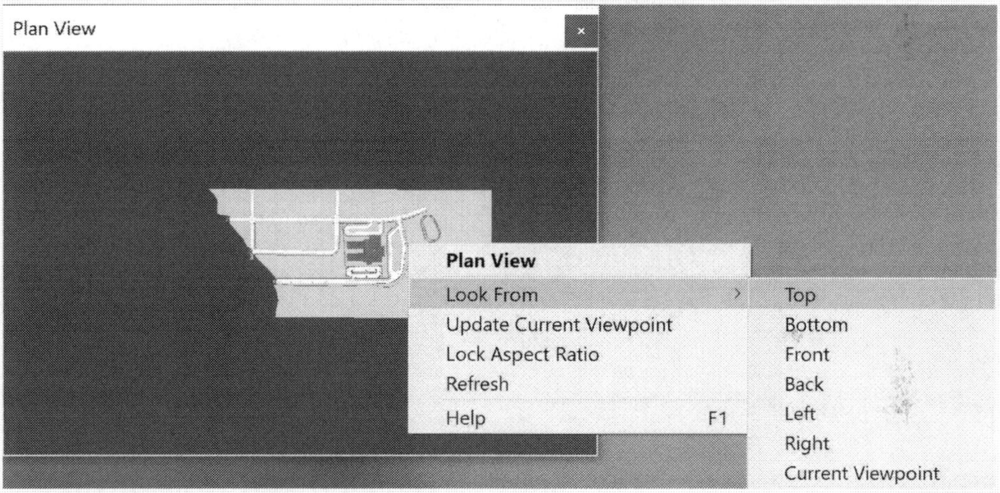

Figure 3–27

Practice 3b
Section the Model

Practice Objective

- Create sections of a model.

In this practice, you will cut sections using individual planes and a box section, as shown in Figure 3–28. You will then modify the sections using the Transform tools.

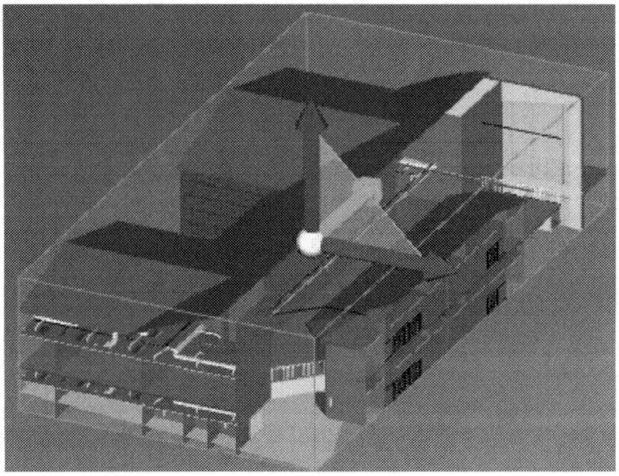

Figure 3–28

Task 1: Create plane sections.

1. Open **School-Sections.nwf** from the *Navisworks BIM Practice Files\Review* folder.
2. Open the saved viewpoint **Exterior for Sectioning** that has been created for you.
3. In the *Viewpoint* tab>*Sectioning* panel, click  (Enable Sectioning). Note that the default section may not show the model.
4. In the *Sectioning Tools* tab>*Mode* panel, select  (Planes) from the drop-down list, if not already enabled.
5. In the *Sectioning Tools* tab>*Transform* panel, click  (Move), if not already active. If the gizmo does not display, toggle **Move** off and then on again.

6. The scene view may not currently display the full model because the default location of the planes is not in an appropriate location. If the full model is not currently displayed, select the blue gizmo arrow and slowly drag it upwards in the Z direction. Note how the model is sectioned as you move the plane through the model. Ensure that Plane 1 is above the model and does not section any geometry, as shown in Figure 3–29.

Figure 3–29

7. In the *Planes Settings* panel, expand the *Current Plane* drop-down list and click the light bulb icon next to **Plane 3** to toggle its section display on. Select **Plane 3** to make it the active plane for editing, as shown in Figure 3–30.

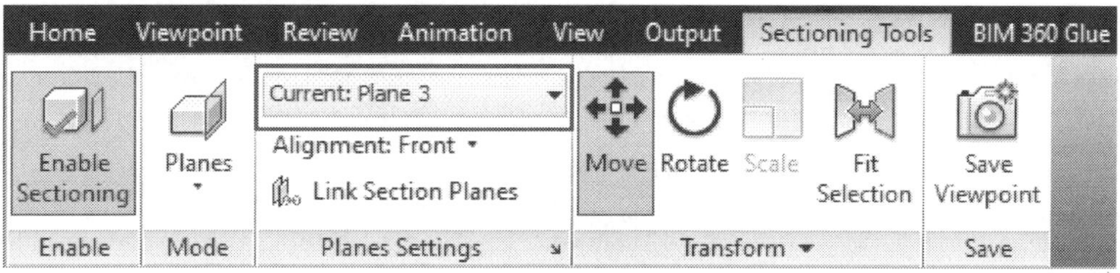

Figure 3–30

Note: *Switching to Plane 3 does not toggle off the display (light bulb icon) of Plane 1. If Plane 1 was cutting the model, its section would also be included.*

8. Click and drag the blue gizmo arrow forward to position the section as shown in Figure 3–31. The section should cut through the AC unit on the roof.

Figure 3–31

9. If the gizmo needs to be relocated to get it closer to the model, hover over it until a hand displays, then you can move the gizmo, as shown in Figure 3–32.

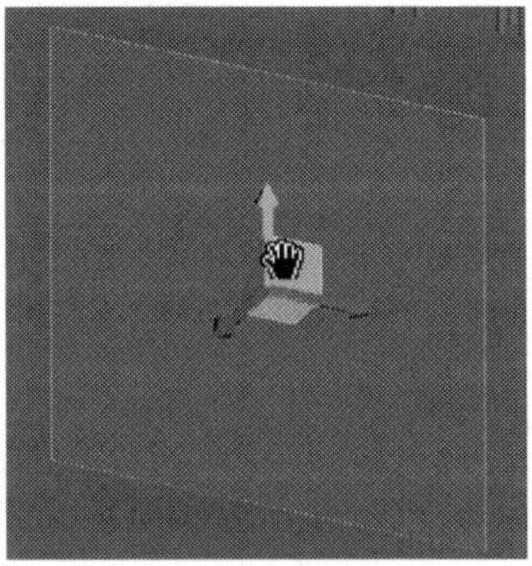

Figure 3–32

10. In the *Sectioning Tools* tab>*Save* panel, click (Save Viewpoint) to save the section position. Enter **Section-North Wing** for the viewpoint name and press <Enter>.

11. In the *Current Plane* drop-down list, click the **Plane 4** light bulb icon to toggle the plane on, then click the **Plane 3** light bulb icon to toggle that plane off.

12. In the *Planes Settings* panel, make **Plane 4** current and set the *Alignment* to **Right**, as shown in Figure 3–33.

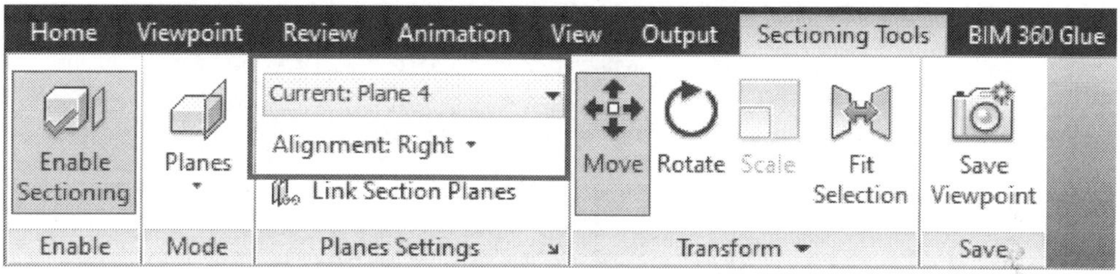

Figure 3–33

13. In the *Sectioning Tools* tab>*Transform* panel, click (Move), if not already active and to display the gizmo. Click and drag the blue gizmo arrow to position the section so that it cuts through the building entrance, as shown in Figure 3–34.

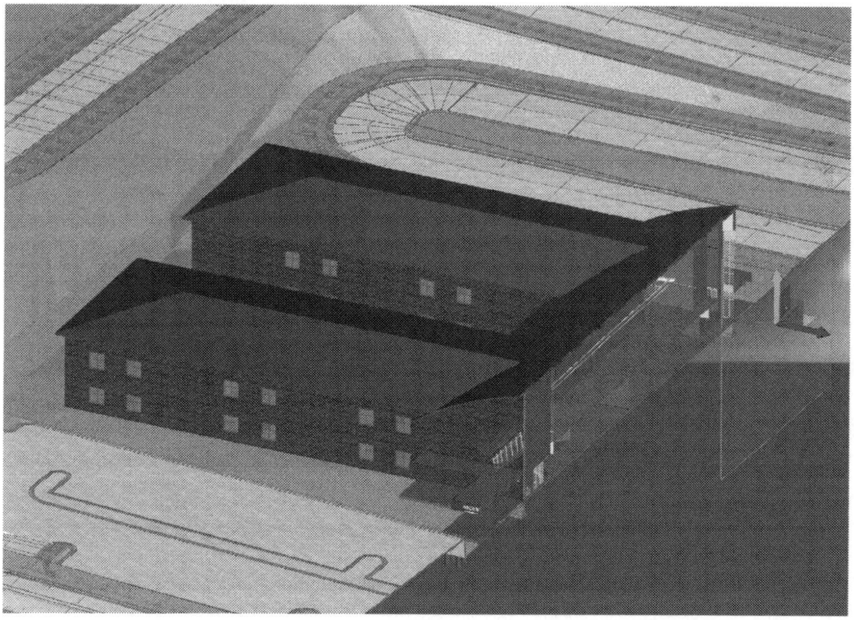

Figure 3–34

14. Click (Move) to toggle off the move gizmo.

15. Further reorient the view similar to that shown in Figure 3–35, then in the *Sectioning Tools* tab>*Save* panel, click (Save Viewpoint) to save the section view. For the viewpoint name, enter **Section-Entrance** and press <Enter>.

Figure 3–35

16. In the *Sectioning Tools* tab>*Enable* panel, click (Enable Sectioning) to disable sectioning.

Task 2: Edit and save a viewpoint.

1. In the *Saved Viewpoints* window, select **Section-North Wing**.
2. Pan, zoom, and orbit to adjust the view for a closer look at the rooftop AC unit, as shown in Figure 3–36. Note that your section may vary slightly from that shown, based on where you sectioned the model.

Figure 3–36

3. In the *Saved Viewpoints* window, right-click on a blank space and select **Save Viewpoint**.
4. Enter **Section-AC Unit** for the name and press <Enter>.

Task 3: Create a box section.

1. Select the saved viewpoint **Exterior for Sectioning**.
2. In the *Selection Tree*, select **School-Architectural.rvt**. The school highlights in blue in the scene view.
3. In the *Viewpoint* tab>*Sectioning* panel, click (Enable Sectioning).
4. In the *Sectioning Tools* tab>*Mode* panel, select (Box) in the expanded **Planes** menu.
5. In the *Sectioning Tools* tab>*Transform* panel, click (Fit Selection). The section box is resized to exactly fit the selected model (the school building), as shown in Figure 3–37.

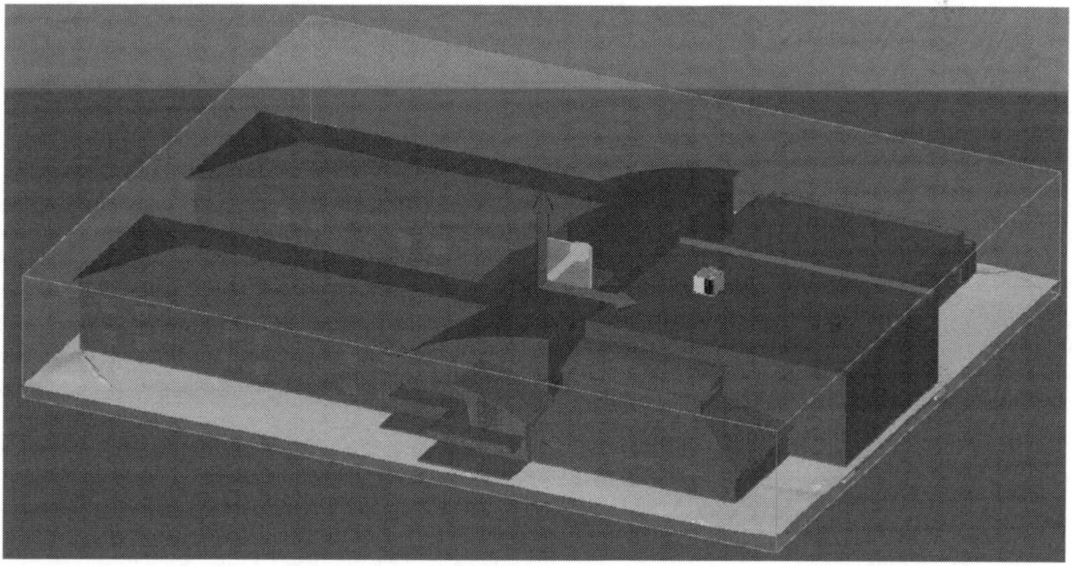

Figure 3–37

6. Press <Esc> to release the selection.
7. In the *Sectioning Tools* tab>*Transform* panel, click (Scale).

8. Click and drag the Z-axis (blue arrow) on the gizmo to scale the box and position the section so that the building roof and its slab are cut off, as shown in Figure 3–38.

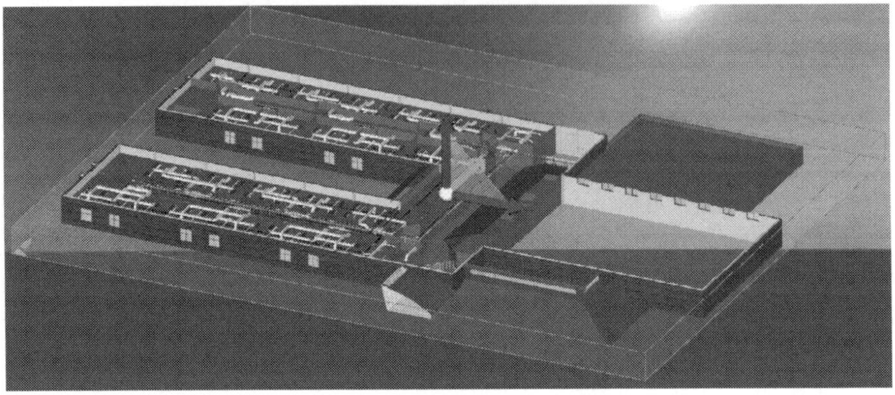

Figure 3–38

9. Save the viewpoint as **Section-Ductwork**.

10. In the *Sectioning Tools* tab>*Enable* panel, click  (Enable Sectioning) to disable sectioning.

11. In the *Saved Viewpoints* window, select the **Start** viewpoint in the *Exterior* folder, then save the file.

End of practice

3.3 Setting View Options

Controlling how a scene displays can help you visualize how the coordinated models work together. You can change the way the view is rendered and toggle the display of structural grids.

Render Style Modes

One of four render styles can be set to view the overall scene. They enable you to display the scene as rendered (as shown in Figure 3–39), shaded, wireframe, and hidden line.

Figure 3–39

The **Render Style** options are found in the *Viewpoint* tab>*Render* Style panel. The list below describes each type of render style mode available.

- (Full Render): Displays the materials and textures of items, including lights, reflections, and shadows. This is the default view type.
- (Hidden Line): Displays the lines, edges, and surfaces of the elements, but it does not display any colors.
- (Wireframe): Displays the lines and edges of elements, but hides the surfaces. This can be useful when you are dealing with complex intersections.

- (Shaded): Displays the surface color but not the textures of materials, as shown for the same school lobby scene in Figure 3–40.

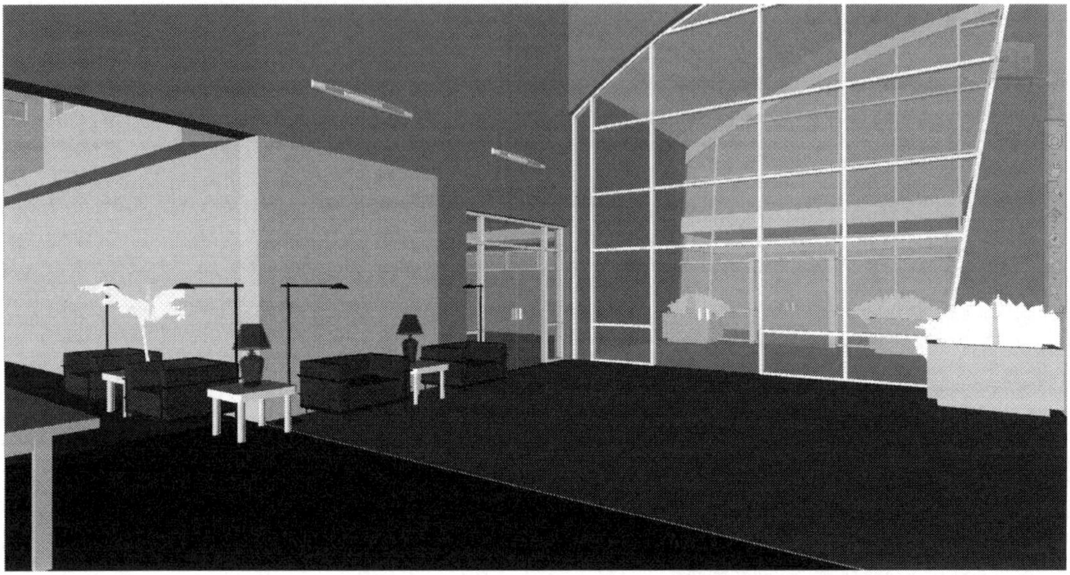

Figure 3–40

Photorealistic scenes can also be created using the Autodesk Rendering system, as shown in Figure 3–41, which is included in Navisworks. This functionality is discussed in a later topic.

Figure 3–41

Hint: Lighting Modes

You can control how a 3D scene is lit using one of the following lighting modes:

- **Full Lights:** Lights defined by the Autodesk Rendering tool.
- **Scene Lights:** Lights defined by the native CAD file. If the original file did not include lights, the light is defined by two default opposing lights.
- **Head Light:** Single directional light positioned at the same location as the camera and pointing in the same direction as the camera.
- **No Lights:** All lights are switched off, leaving the scene shaded with flat rendering.

3.4 Displaying Grids

Autodesk Revit model often include grids, which can be displayed in the Autodesk Navisworks model, as shown in Figure 3–42. When working in a large project or when identifying a specific area, toggling on grids can help you describe feature locations in the model.

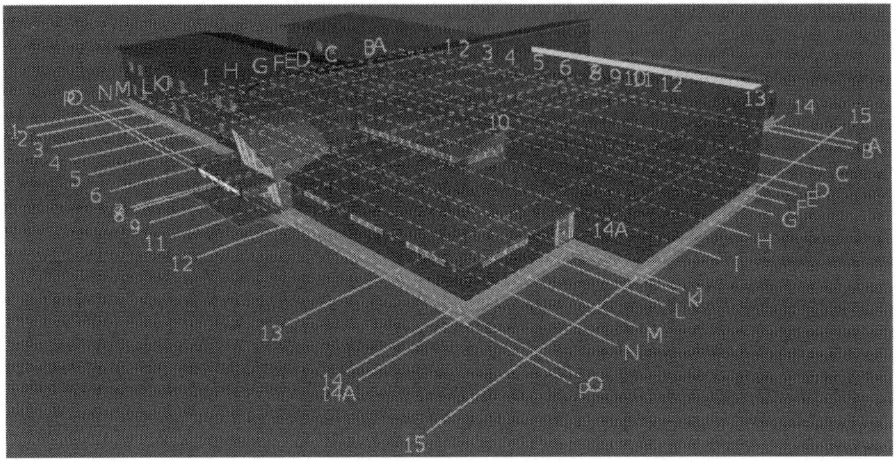

Figure 3–42

It is usually the structural model that contains the building grids. If grids are contained in multiple models, you can select the model in the *View* tab>*Grids & Levels* panel, as shown in Figure 3–43. You can also select which grid level to be displayed.

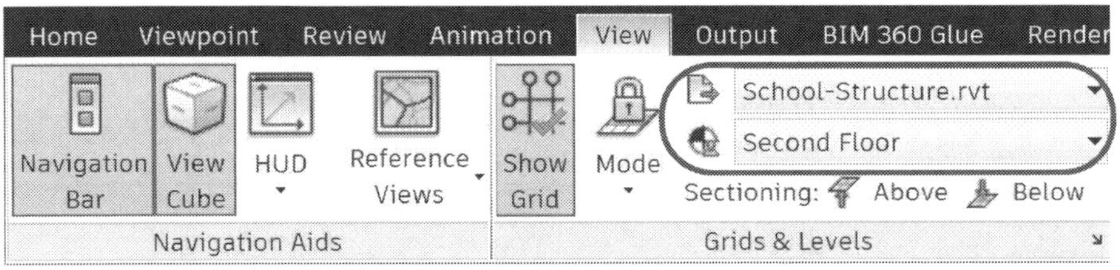

Figure 3–43

If grids are not included in any of the appended Autodesk Revit models, the **Show Grid** tool is grayed out.

- To toggle the display of the grid, in the *View* tab>*Grids & Levels* panel, click (Show Grid).
- If you have multiple files, the (Active Grid) drop-down list enables you to specify which model grid to use.

- Grid modes control the display of the grids in relation to the current camera position. The following options are available in the *View* tab>*Grids & Levels* panel, in the *Mode* drop-down list:
  - (Above and Below): Displays red grids above and green grids below.
  - (Above): Displays only red grids.
  - (Below): Displays only green grids.
  - (All): Displays red and green grids, as well as halftone images of all of the other grid locations.
  - (Fixed): Displays grids at the level specified in the drop-down list for the (Display Level). It does not change the location of the grid as you orbit around the model.

If the *Mode* is set to **Fixed**, then you have the option of slicing the model at the grid lines by clicking the *Sectioning* options in the *View* tab>*Grids & Levels* panel (as shown in Figure 3–44.

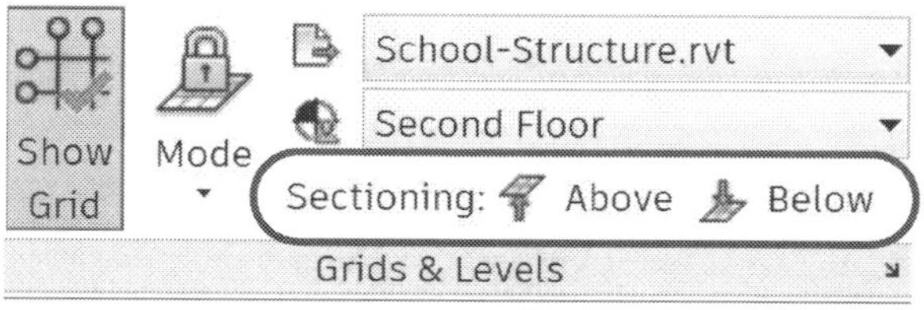

Figure 3–44

The *Sectioning* options are as follows:

- (Above): Clips the model at the ceiling of the chosen grid level to hide the upper levels.
- (Below): Clips the model at the floor of the chosen grid level to hide the lower levels.
- (Above) AND (Below): Clips the model at the floor and the ceiling of the chosen grid level to only display the selected level.

3.5 Setting Up Appearances

From time to time, an object might display in its wireframe color. This is because the material or texture for the object that was imported from the original model is unsupported. When this happens, you might have to override an object's appearance.

How To: Override Appearances on Selected Items

1. In the model, click on the objects that need to be changed to select them.
2. In the *Item Tools* contextual tab>*Appearance* panel, expand (Color) and select a color square, as shown in Figure 3–45.

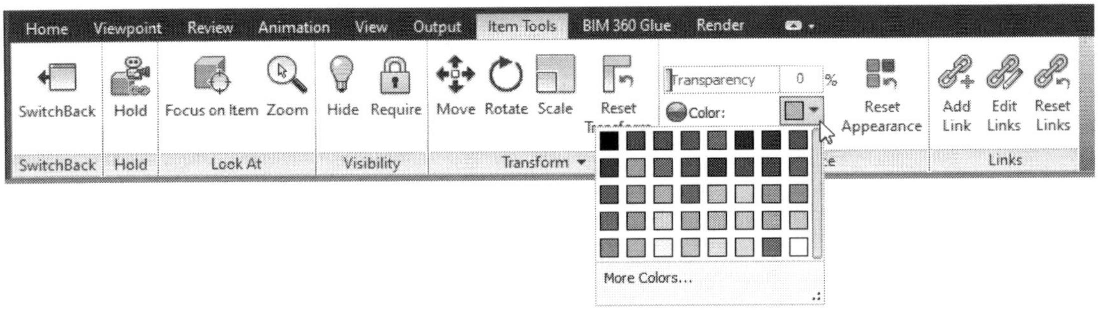

Figure 3–45

3. In the *Item Tools* contextual tab>*Appearance* panel, click and drag the *Transparency slider* to make the object more or less opaque, as required.
4. If the changes did not have the required results, or if you need to revert back to the original color or transparency, in the *Item Tools* contextual tab>*Appearance* panel, click (Reset Appearance).
5. Press <Esc> to clear the selection and view the changes.

   Note: *Changes to the appearance of a model will display in all viewpoints.*

Materials can be edited in all viewpoints globally using the *Options Editor* dialog box.

How To: Override Appearances on Assigned Materials

1. Expand (Application Menu) and select **Options**.
2. In the *Options Editor* dialog box, do the following, as shown in Figure 3–46:
   - In the left pane, expand Interface and select **Viewpoint Defaults**.
   - In the right pane, select **Override Appearance**.

   Note: *Defaults affect all new Viewpoints.*

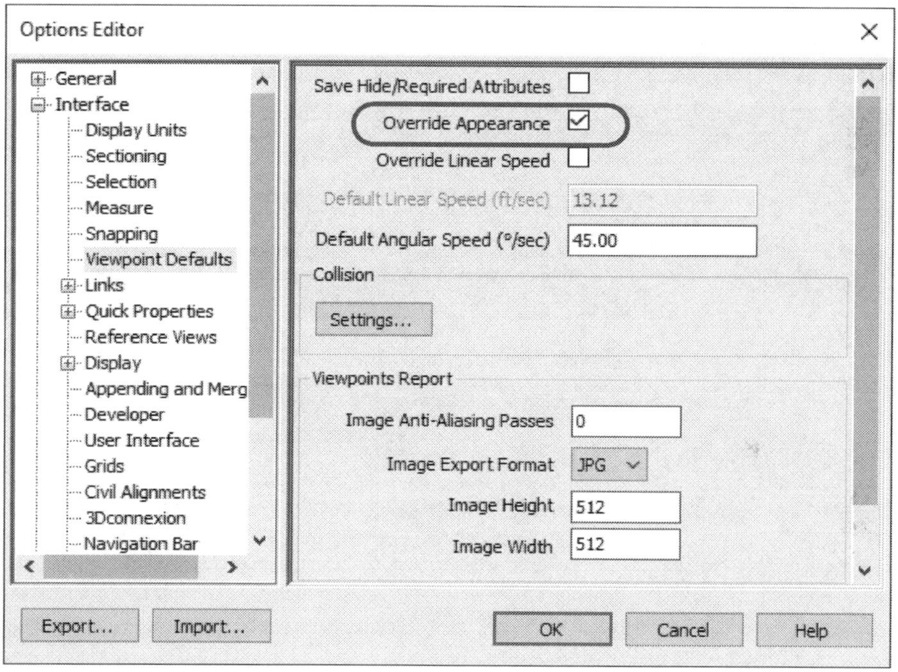

Figure 3–46

3. Click **OK**.
4. In the scene view, select the objects that need a material override.
5. In the *Item Tools* contextual tab>*Appearance* panel, expand (Color) and select a color square.
6. In the *Item Tools* contextual tab>*Appearance* panel, click and drag the *Transparency* slider to make the object more or less opaque.
7. Press <Esc> to clear the selection and view the changes.
8. In the *Saved Viewpoints* window, right-click on the viewpoint that you want to set to appearance override and select **Update**.

Practice 3c
Set Up the Display

Practice Objectives

- Display a grid to help communicate where something is in the model.
- Set up appearances.

In this practice, you will turn on the grid that was imported with the Autodesk Revit model and change the display appearances for the site and the AC unit, as shown in Figure 3–47.

Figure 3–47

Task 1: Display a grid.

1. Open **School-Appearances.nwf** from the *Navisworks BIM Practice Files\Review* folder.
2. In the *Saved Viewpoints* window, expand the *Exterior* folder and select **Site Isometric Close-up**.
3. In the *View* tab>*Grids & Levels* panel, click (Show Grid) to toggle the grid on. Toggle the grid off and on a couple times. Note how the grid displays in the model. With the grid toggled on, continue to the next step.
4. Open another exterior viewpoint. Note that the grid displays in this view as well. The grid display affects all saved viewpoints.

5. In the *Selection Tree*, select the **Site Layout.dwg** model. Note that the grids are easier to see against the dark blue of the selection color, as shown in Figure 3–48.

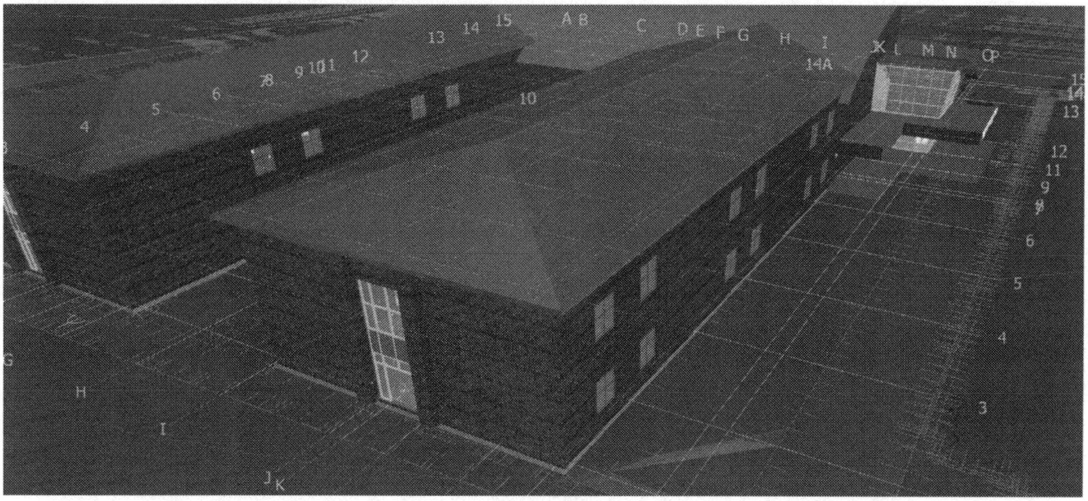

Figure 3–48

6. In the *View* tab>*Grids & Levels* panel, *Mode* drop-down list, pick (Display Level) to set the level to **Second Floor**. In the *Mode* expanded menu, select (Below), as shown in Figure 3–49. You only see the green lower grid lines.

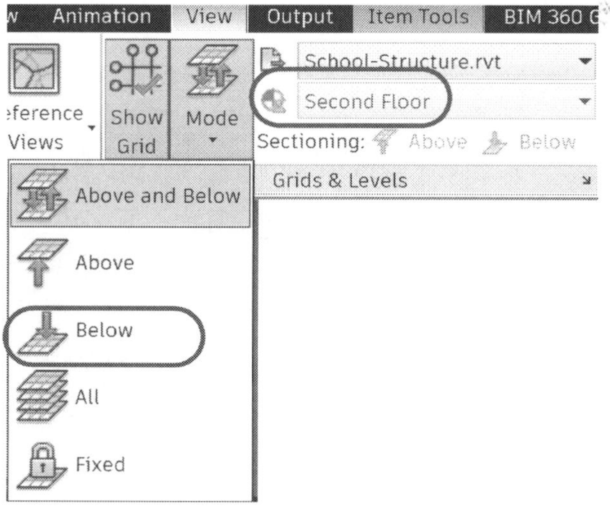

Figure 3–49

7. Experiment with the other *Mode* options and note the change in the grids in the model. End up with the (Fixed) mode.

8. Click on (Above) in the *Sectioning* options in the *View* tab>*Grids & Levels* panel. This clips the model at the ceiling of the current grid level to hide the upper levels, as shown in Figure 3–50.

Figure 3–50

9. Click on (Below) in the *Sectioning* options in the *View* tab>*Grids & Levels* panel so that both **Above** and **Below** are selected. This clips the model at the ceiling of the current grid level as well as the floor below to isolate only the selected level, as shown in Figure 3–51.

Figure 3–51

10. Click on (Above) in the *Sectioning* options in the *View* tab>*Grids & Levels* panel to deselect it. Verify that only **Below** is selected. This clips the model at the floor of the current grid level to hide the lower levels, as shown in Figure 3–52.

Figure 3–52

11. Click on (Below) to deselect it so the entire model is displayed.

Task 2: Change appearances.

1. In the *View* tab>*Grids & Levels* panel, toggle off (Show Grid).
2. Note the curb lines of the roadways and parking lots are magenta, as shown in Figure 3–53.

Figure 3–53

3. With the site model still selected, in the *Item Tools* contextual tab>*Appearance* panel, expand 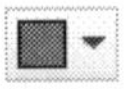 (Color) and select the dark green color shown in Figure 3–54.

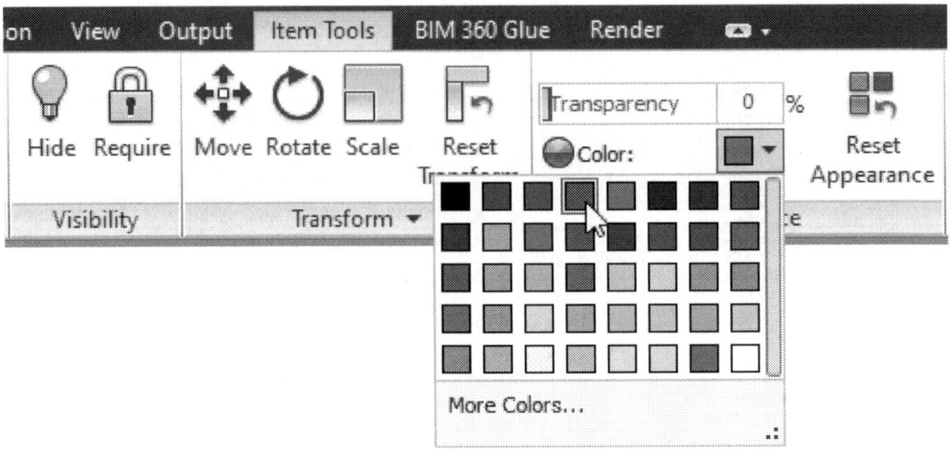

Figure 3–54

4. Press <Esc> to clear the selection and view the changes. Note that the curblines are now dark green. The rendering material of the grass however remains unaffected.
5. In the *Viewpoint* tab>*Render Style* panel>*Mode* drop-down list, select **Shaded** as the Rendering Style mode, as shown in Figure 3–55.

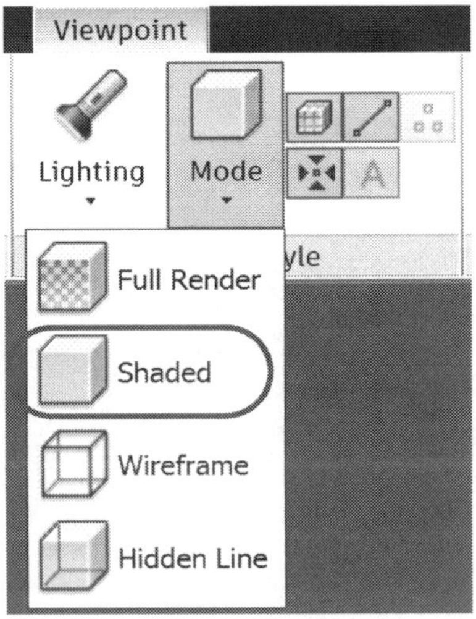

Figure 3–55

6. Now you see the model as solid colors rather than the rendering material assigned. All of the Site-Layout is now a solid green, as shown in Figure 3–56.

Figure 3–56

7. Select the **Site Layout.dwg** again.
8. In the *Item Tools* contextual tab>*Appearance* panel, click and drag the *Transparency slider* near **80%** to make the surface more transparent.
9. Press <Esc> to clear the selection and view the changes.
10. Change to another exterior view and note that the change to the **Site Layout.dwg** file is reflected in all the viewpoints although the rendering style reverts back to the one originally assigned to the viewpoint.
11. Open the **Section-AC Unit** saved viewpoint.
12. In the *Home* tab>*Select & Search* panel, expand (Select) and click (Select) from the drop-down list, if not already active, as shown in Figure 3–57.

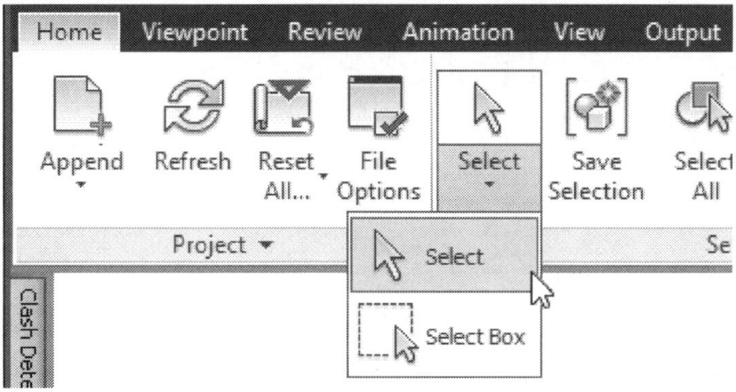

Figure 3–57

13. Expand the *Select & Search* panel and set the *Selection Resolution* to **First Object**, as shown in Figure 3–58.

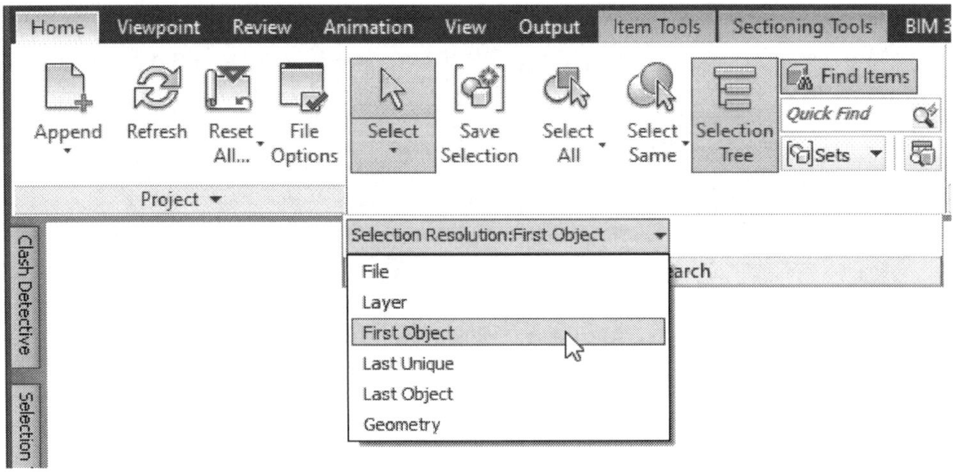

Figure 3–58

14. The AC unit consists of two parts, so you need to select both sides. Select the first part of the AC unit on top of the roof, hold <Ctrl>, and select the second part, then release <Ctrl>. Once selected, both sides should display blue, as shown in Figure 3–59. Because the **First Object** selection resolution was set, this ensures that only the first objects in the selection are selected.

15. Open the *Selection Tree* and verify that only the two objects are selected, as shown in Figure 3–59. The frame at the bottom of the unit remains unselected.

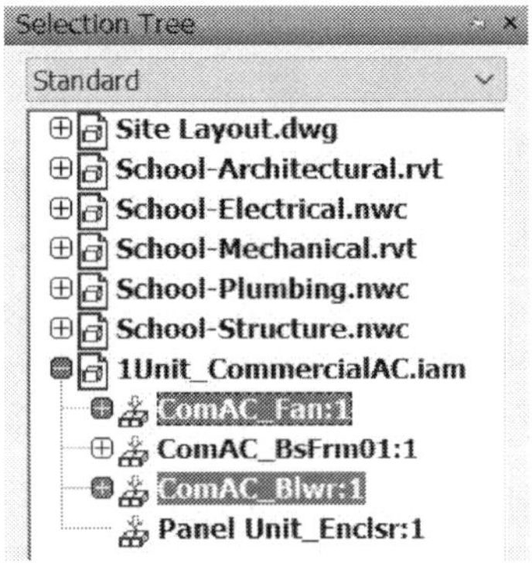

Figure 3–59

***Note:** Alternatively, you can use the Box select mode and draw a bounding box around the AC unit. Keep in mind that it is a good practice to verify what is selected in the Selection Tree.*

16. In the *Item Tools* contextual tab>*Appearance* panel, expand 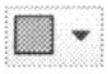 (Color) and select the cyan square shown in Figure 3–60.

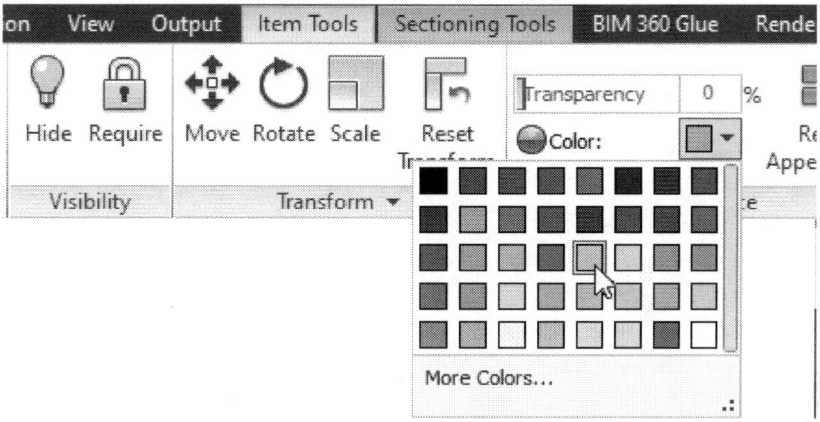

Figure 3–60

17. Press <Esc> to clear the selection of the AC unit. Note that the two components now display in the cyan color.
18. Save the file.

End of practice

Chapter Review Questions

1. Which of the following can be edited for a saved viewpoint? (Select all that apply.)
   a. Position of the camera
   b. Focus point of the camera
   c. Sun settings
   d. Section planes

2. Viewpoints can be sorted alphanumerically on demand.
   a. True
   b. False

3. When creating a section with the Box option, how many section planes are cut at one time?
   a. 1
   b. 2
   c. 4
   d. 6

4. Which render style mode includes the materials and textures of items, including lights, reflections, and shadows?
   a. Full Render
   b. Hidden Line
   c. Wireframe
   d. Shaded

5. How do you create a grid in a scene to help you describe where something is in the model?
   a. In the *Home* tab>*Visibility* panel.
   b. In the *Viewpoint* tab>*Navigate* panel.
   c. You cannot create a grid in the Autodesk Navisworks software. It must be included in the original Autodesk Revit model.
   d. In the *View* tab>*Grids & Levels* panel.

6. Why would an object display in its wireframe color?
   a. The Render Style Mode is set wrong for the scene.
   b. The material or texture for the object that was imported from the original model is unsupported.
   c. The lighting mode is set wrong for the scene.
   d. Objects do not display in wireframe in the Autodesk Navisworks software.

Command Summary

Button	Command	Location
Viewpoints		
N/A	**Add Animation**	• **Right-Click:** in the Saved Viewpoints Window>**Save Viewpoint**
	**Animation Tools**	• **Ribbon:** *Viewpoint* tab>*Save, Load & Playback* panel
	**Edit Current Viewpoint**	• **Ribbon:** *Viewpoint* tab>*Save, Load & Playback* panel
	**Save Viewpoint**	• **Ribbon:** *Viewpoint* tab>*Save, Load & Playback* panel • **Right-Click:** in the Saved Viewpoints Window>**Save Viewpoint**
	**Saved Viewpoints Dialog Launcher**	• **Ribbon:** *Viewpoint* tab>*Save, Load & Playback* panel title
Sectioning		
	**Box**	• **Ribbon:** *Sectioning Tools* tab>*Mode* panel
	**Enable Sectioning**	• **Ribbon:** *Viewpoint* tab>*Sectioning* panel
	**Fit Selection**	• **Ribbon:** *Sectioning Tools* tab>*Transform* panel
	**Move**	• **Ribbon:** *Sectioning Tools* tab>*Transform* panel
	**Planes**	• **Ribbon:** *Sectioning Tools* tab>*Mode* panel
	**Rotate**	• **Ribbon:** *Sectioning Tools* tab>*Transform* panel
	**Scale**	• **Ribbon:** *Sectioning Tools* tab>*Transform* panel
	**Clip Above**	• **Ribbon:** *Views* tab>*Grids & Levels* panel
	**Clip Below**	• **Ribbon:** *Views* tab>*Grids & Levels* panel

Button	Command	Location
Other Viewing Tools		
	**Full Render**	• **Ribbon:** *Views* tab>*Render Style* panel, expand *Mode*
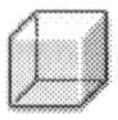	**Hidden Line**	• **Ribbon:** *Views* tab>*Render Style* panel, expand *Mode*
	**Reference View**	• **Ribbon:** *Views* tab>*Navigation Aids* panel
	**Shaded**	• **Ribbon:** *Views* tab>*Render Style* panel, expand *Mode*
	**Show Grid**	• **Ribbon:** *Views* tab>*Grids & Levels* panel
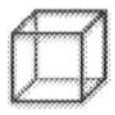	**Wireframe**	• **Ribbon:** *Views* tab>*Render Style* panel, expand *Mode*

Chapter 4

Analyze Models

When you review a BIM model, you should also analyze the model at the same time. Performing a model analysis helps stakeholders predict the project outcome and reduce the number of requests for information (RFIs) and changes that are required during construction. Learn how to select features to investigate their properties and save selection sets. You will also learn how to hide features to gain a clearer view of specific parts of the model.

Learning Objectives

- Select items in a model to evaluate their properties.
- Drill down into the content of a model using the *Selection Tree*.
- Save selections so that they can be retrieved later.
- Find items by using the selection filtering options.
- Hide and unhide items.

BIM Workflow: Analyze

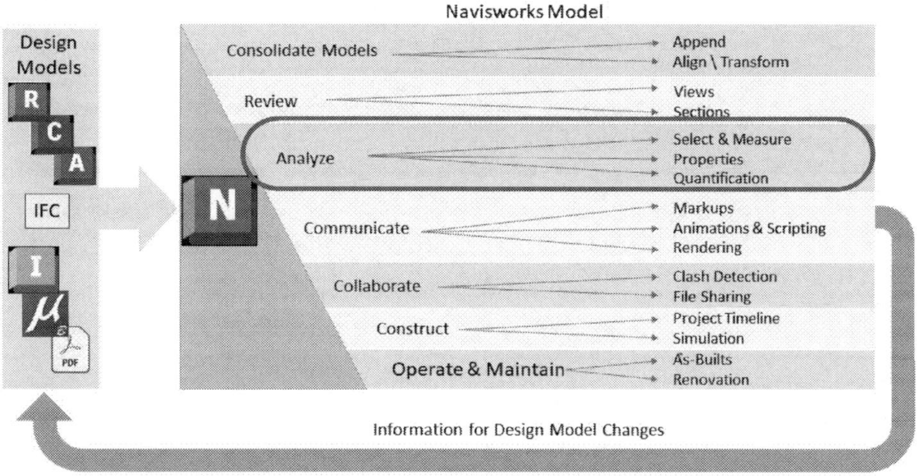

4.1 Selecting Items

A powerful part of using Autodesk® Navisworks® is the variety of selection tools that are available. The majority of the selection tools are available on the ribbon in the *Home* tab>*Select & Search* panel, as shown in Figure 4–1.

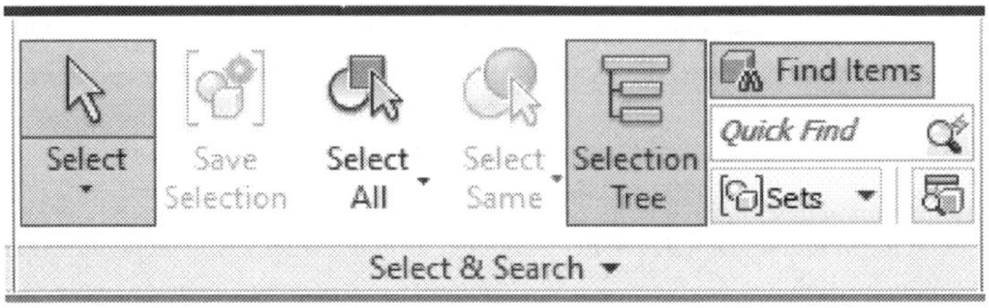

Figure 4–1

The options include the following:

- Press <Ctrl>+<1> to toggle on the (Select) tool. Alternatively, this (Select) tool is available in the Quick Access Toolbar and in the navigation bar. This option must be enabled to select individual items. With the (Select) tool active, press and hold <Ctrl> while selecting to add items to a selection set. Items can be selected in the scene view or in the *Selection Tree*.
- The (Select Box) selection mode enables you to draw a window around groups of items. Only items that are totally inside the box are selected. Expand the **Select** tool to locate this option.
- The (Select All) option selects everything in a project.
- The (Select None) option clears the selection. You can also press <Esc> to do this. Expand the **Select All** tool to locate this option.
- The (Invert Selection) option switches the selection to everything that was not previously selected. Expand the **Select All** tool to locate this option.
- With at least one item selected, use the (Select Same) tool to add other similar items to the selection set. You can choose from a list of categories that match the selected item, as shown in Figure 4–2.

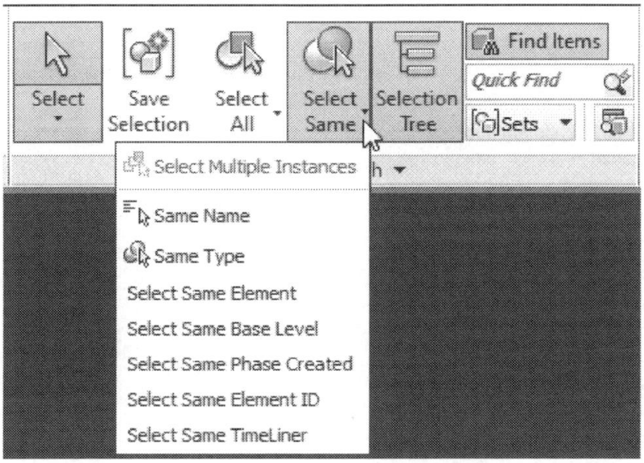

Figure 4–2

*Note: If multiple items are selected, the Select Same list displays only the overlapping properties, such as **Same Name** and **Same Type**.*

Selection Sets

If you select the same group of features frequently, it is recommended that you save them as a selection set. Once created, the selection set can be reselected in the future to avoid having to individually make the selections again.

How To: Create a Selection Set

1. Select the items you want to save in a selection set.
2. In the *Home* tab>*Select & Search* panel, click (Save Selection).
3. The *Sets* window displays with the new selection set, as shown in Figure 4–3.

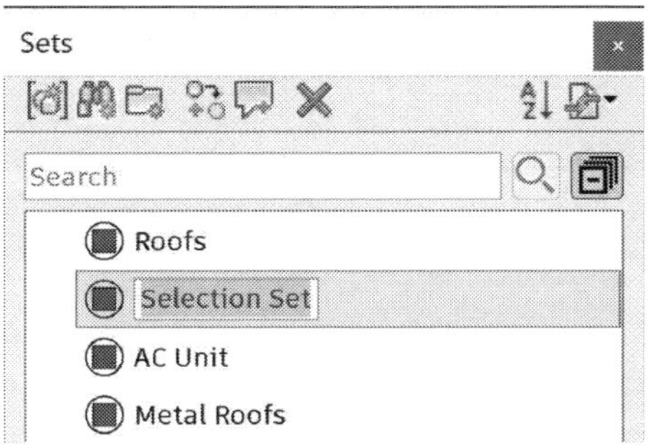

Figure 4–3

4. Enter a descriptive name for the selection set and press <Enter>.

Using Saved Selections

To display the *Sets* window (shown in Figure 4–4), expand the *Sets* drop-down list and select **Manage Sets** or in the *View* tab>*Workspace* panel, select **Sets** from the *Windows* drop-down list to enable the window. To activate a selection set, simply select its name in the Sets window, or in the *Home* tab>*Select & Search* panel, expand the *Sets* drop-down list and select a set name.

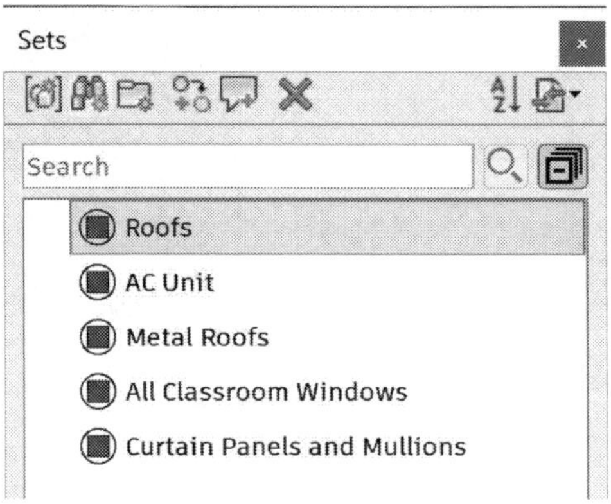

Figure 4–4

Note: *The Sets window can be docked and set to auto-hide, similar to other windows.*

The following options are available in the *Sets* window:

- (Save Selection): Saves the current selection. This option is also available in the *Select & Search* panel.
- (Save Search): Saves a search selection.

  Note: *Search selections are created using the Find Items window. They enable to you focus on a specific file and define criteria to search for.*

- (New Folder): Adds a folder that you can name and use to organize sets.
- (Duplicate): Duplicates an existing set
- (Add Comment): Opens the *Add Comment* dialog box, where you can enter in information about the set.
- (Delete): Deletes the selected selection set from the list.
- (Sort): Organizes the sets into alphabetical order.
- (Import/Export): Enables you to import and export selection sets.

4.2 Investigating Properties

Once items are selected, you can review item properties. These properties include basic information, such as the *Item Name* and *Item Type*, as shown using the Quick Properties (by default) in Figure 4–5, or the full list of properties that are displayed in the *Properties* window (shown on the following page in Figure 4–6).

Figure 4–5

Viewing Properties

To quickly display the *Item Name* and *Item Type* properties directly in the scene view (as shown above in Figure 4–5), in the *Home* tab>*Display* panel, click (Quick Properties) to enable it. Once enabled, you can hover over any item in the scene view to display the properties in a tooltip.

To display the additional properties associated with a selected item, enable the (Properties) window in the *Home* tab>*Display* panel. The *Properties* panel allows you to investigate the full range of properties for a selected item. They are divided by categories accessed through a series of tabs, as shown across the top of the window in Figure 4–6.

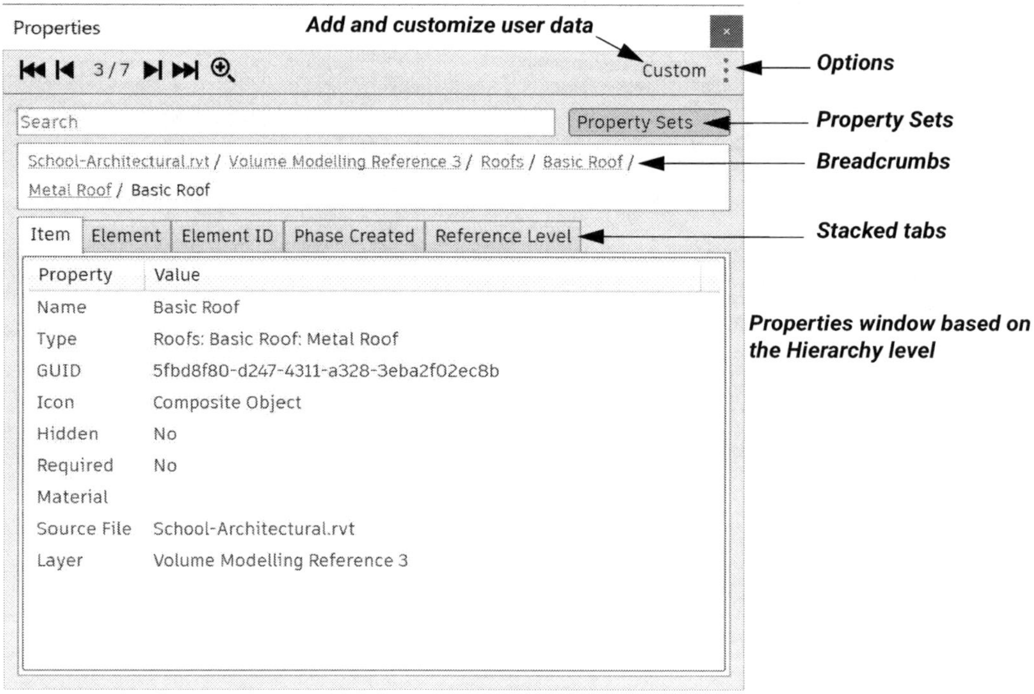

Figure 4–6

Depending on the authoring software of the original file, there could potentially be many properties. For example, an item from Autodesk® Civil 3D® might only have a few categories, while an Autodesk® Revit® model might have more. Revit items, such as walls, might have many more tabs, especially if rooms or spaces are assigned to the model.

The *Properties* panel has multiple sections and displays the following information, based on your settings:

- **Breadcrumbs**: A view of the hierarchical nodes for the object and its parent nodes. (**Nodes** are covered in more detail later in this chapter when discussing *Selection Trees.)*
- Stacked tabs for the different property categories.
- The *Properties* window with a *Property* column and corresponding value column.

- A **Custom** section for adding and managing user data, as shown in Figure 4–7.

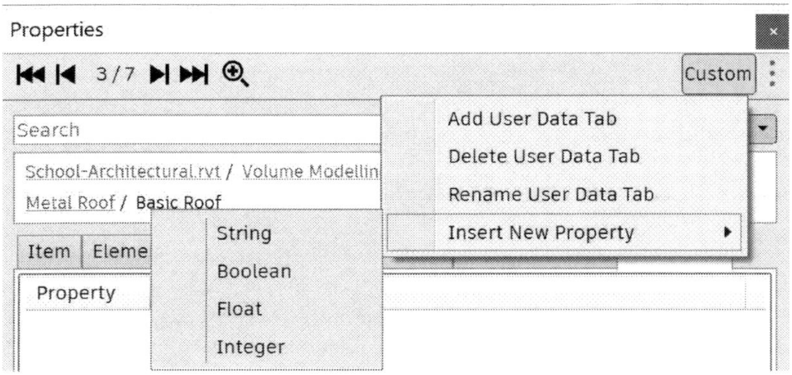

Figure 4–7

- An **Option** section for adding and managing user data, as shown in Figure 4–8.

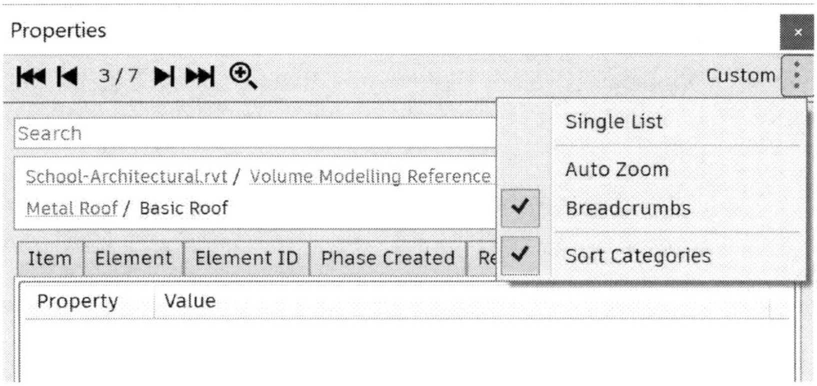

Figure 4–8

- The **Property Sets** drop-down menu for selecting which property set you want to make current, as shown in Figure 4–9.

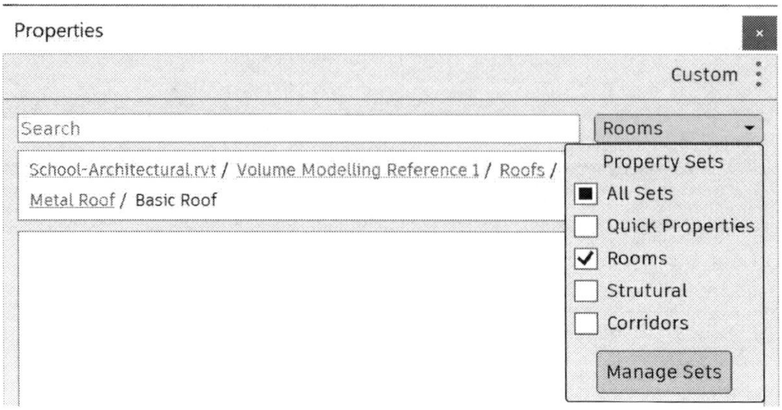

Figure 4–9

Multiple objects

When multiple objects are selected, a navigation bar is displayed in the top left corner showing how many objects are in the selection set and which object is the current one, as shown in Figure 4–10.

Figure 4–10

You can navigate through the selection set as follows:

-  Go to the first object of the selection set.
-  Go to the previous object of the selection set.
-  Go to the next object of the selection set.
-  Go to the last object of the selection set.
-  Zoom to current object of the selection set. (Suitable only if **Auto Zoom** is not enabled).

The numbers in the middle refer to the total number of objects in the selection set and the position of the current object in the set.

Options section

In the upper right corner, when clicking on (Options), a drop-down list opens. An additional list for *Favourites* is also available, as shown in Figure 4–11.

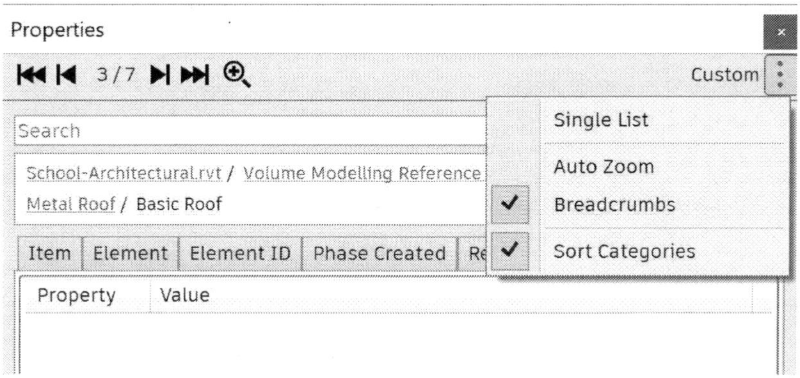

Figure 4–11

- **Single List** combines all the category tabs into one list. When enabled, the tabs vanish and the current window is populated with all the properties of the object.
- **Auto Zoom** automatically zooms to current object of the selection set.
- **Breadcrumbs** displays the breadcrumb section.
- **Sort Categories** sorts the category names alphabetically.

Using the right-click menu of the *Properties* panel, you can copy either the contents of the entire panel or only specific properties to the clip board. The copied contents can be pasted later into other applications as text. For spreadsheets, you can copy the contents to a Comma-Separated Values (CSV) file, which then will be pasted to separate rows in the spreadsheet.

Right-click menu options

The right-click menu of the *Properties* panel can be used to create a search condition for the current row and to add that condition to an existing search. When doing this, it is best to keep the *Find* panel open to ensure that the search condition is added properly, as shown in Figure 4–12. This tool is covered in more detail later in this chapter.

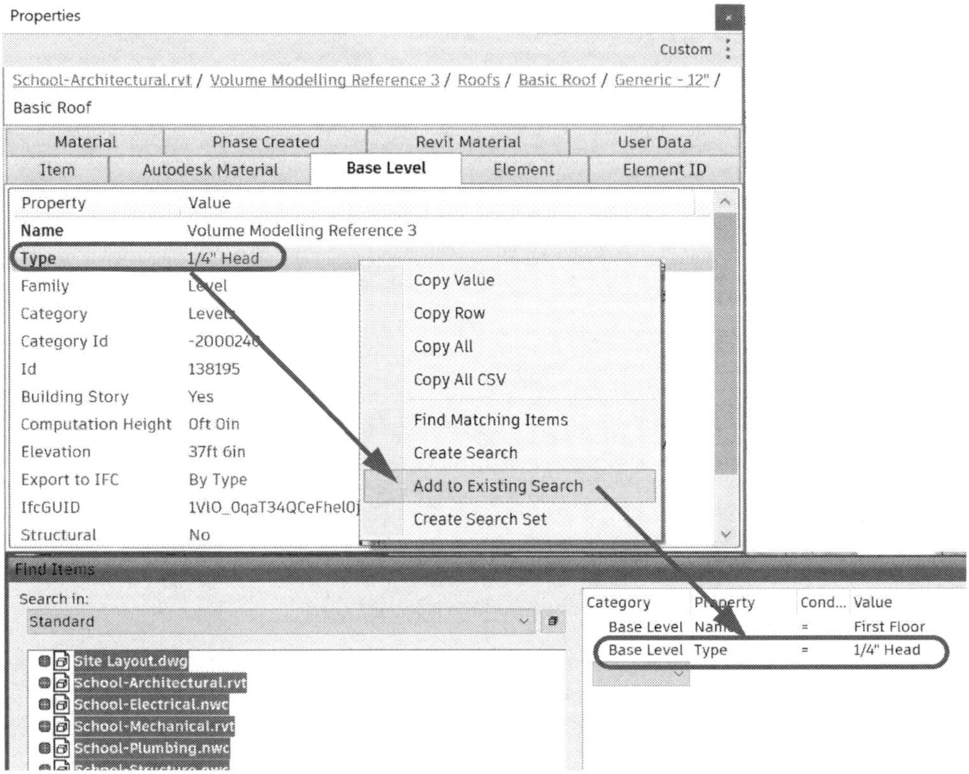

Figure 4–12

Using the right-click menu of the *Properties* panel, you can **Find Matching Items** based on the selected row. The results are listed in the *Selection Tree* and the tally in the navigation bar at the top left corner of either panel (as shown on the left in Figure 4–13). You can also create a **Search Set**, and the result will display in the *Sets* window, (as shown on the right in Figure 4–13). These tools will be covered in more detail later in this chapter.

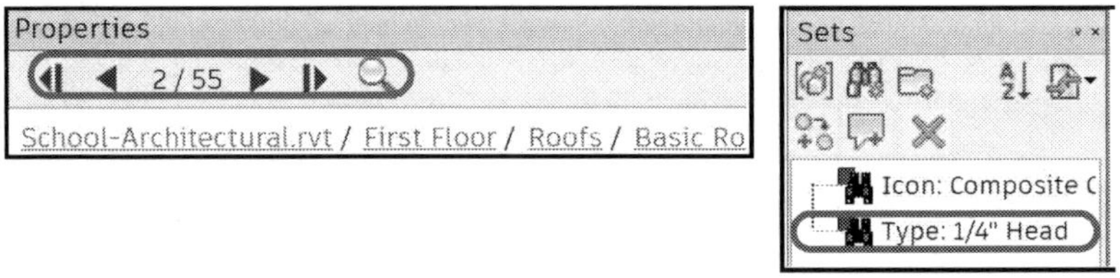

Figure 4–13

Finally, in the *Properties* panel, using the *Options* drop-down menu, you can add the current condition to the *Quick Properties* and / or the *Current Search Properties*.

Hint: How to Create User Data

You can add custom tabs to the *Properties* window to display specific user data.

1. On the header of the *Properties* window, select **Custom** and select **Add User Data Tab**, as shown in Figure 4–14.

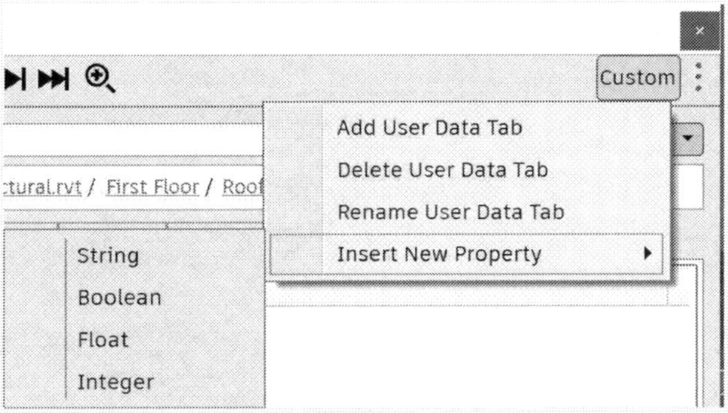

Figure 4–14

2. Select the new tab, select **Custom** and select **Rename User Data Tab** to enter a custom tab name.
3. Select **Custom** again, expand **Insert New Property**, select the type of data you want to add, and enter a name. The available data types are:
   - **String:** Alphanumeric characters
   - **Boolean:** Either **Yes** or **No**
   - **Float:** Decimal-based numbers
   - **Integer:** Numbers without any decimal
4. Once you have the new property in place, right-click and select **Rename** from the right-click menu.
5. In the *User Data* tab>*Value* field, select **Edit Values** from the right-click menu. Click the green checkmark, as shown in Figure 4–15. You can also press <Enter>.

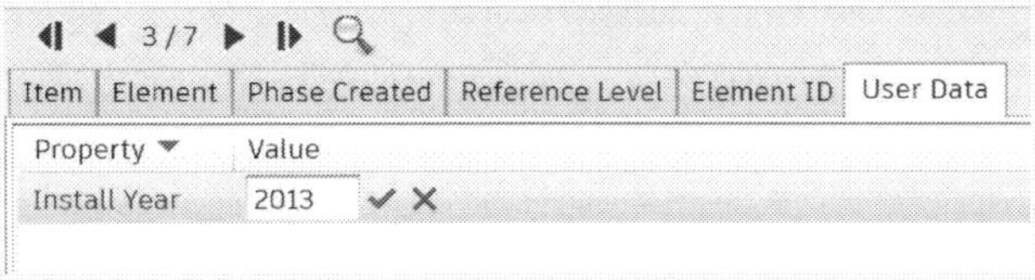

Figure 4–15

6. If you set up a Boolean option, you are prompted to select either **Yes** or **No**.

Selection Inspector

To view the Quick Properties of more than one item, you can select a selection set and use the Selection Inspector to view its items' properties, as shown in Figure 4–16. To open the Selection Inspector, in the *Home* tab>*Select & Search* panel, click  (Selection Inspector).

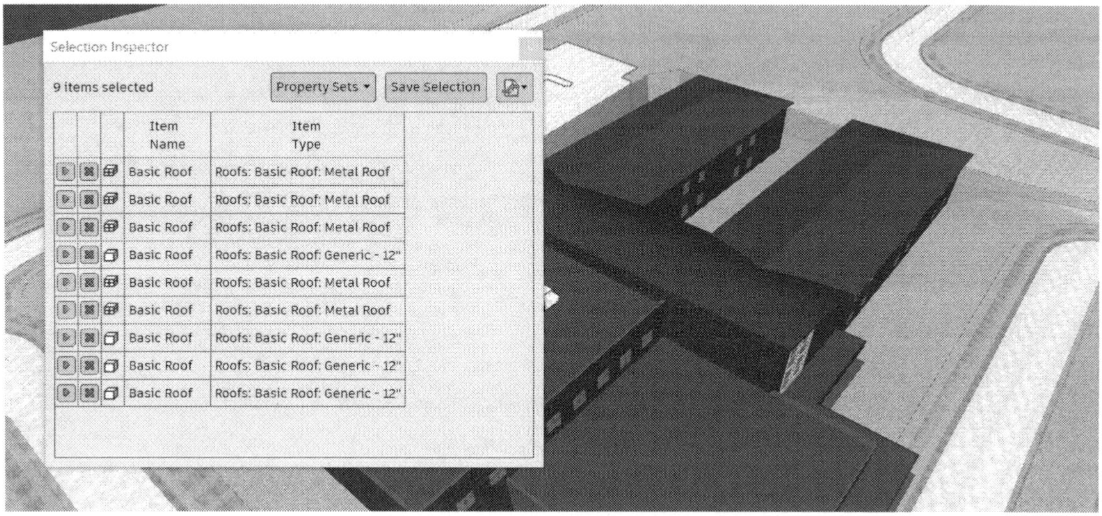

Figure 4–16

The options in the Selection Inspector are as follows:

-  (Show Item): Zooms in on the selected item in the view.
-  (Deselect): Removes the item from the selection set.
- 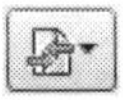 (Export): Sends the information from the window to a .CSV file.
- **Quick Property Definitions:** Enables you to customize the Selection Inspector to add other properties to the window.
- **Property Sets**: Provides a drop-down menu for you to select which property set you want to use.
- **Save Selection:** Adds a new set to the Sets list.

Property Sets

Property sets are a collection of predefined properties you can define to use for filtering and reviewing aspects of objects for review and study. to quickly filter, review and export object properties.

The *Property Sets* panel can be opened from the *Home* tab, *Display* panel or from the *Property Sets* panel or the *Selection Inspector* panel drop-down and selecting the **Manage Sets** option, as shown in Figure 4–17.

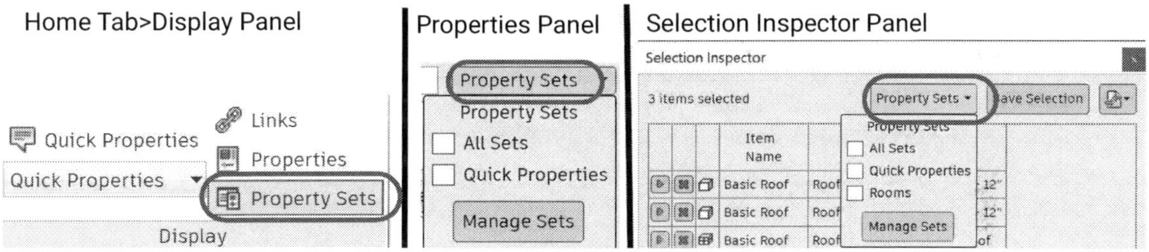

Figure 4–17

The *Property Sets* panel lists all the Property Sets that reside in the file. By default, a *Quick Properties* set exists and can be edited, as shown in Figure 4–18.

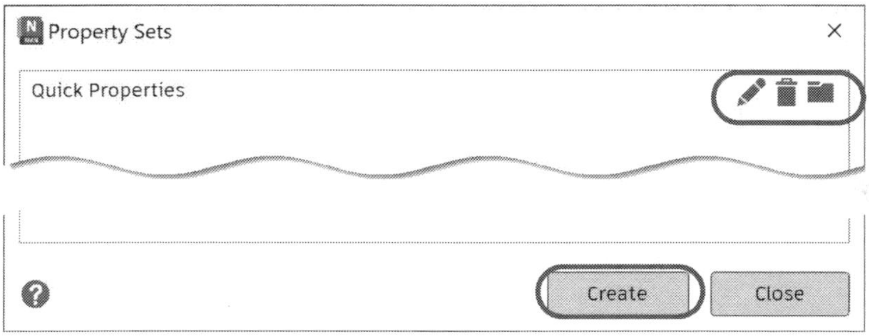

Figure 4–18

You can create new Property Sets by clicking on the **Create** button. You can also edit ( ) or delete ( ) existing property sets. Additionally, you can browse to the folder ( ) which stores the XML files of the property set definition. These icons are to the right of the corresponding property set.

When you create a new property set or edit an existing one, you are launched to the *Create Property Set* or *Edit Property Set* dialog box, as shown in Figure 4–19. Here you can name the Property Set, and build the set by selecting the properties you want to include by expanding the appropriate branch and clicking on the box next to the property to place a checkmark. You can also use the search box to find a particular property.

Figure 4–19

On the *Display* panel of the *Home* tab is a drop down menu to select which property set you want to make current, as shown in Figure 4–20.

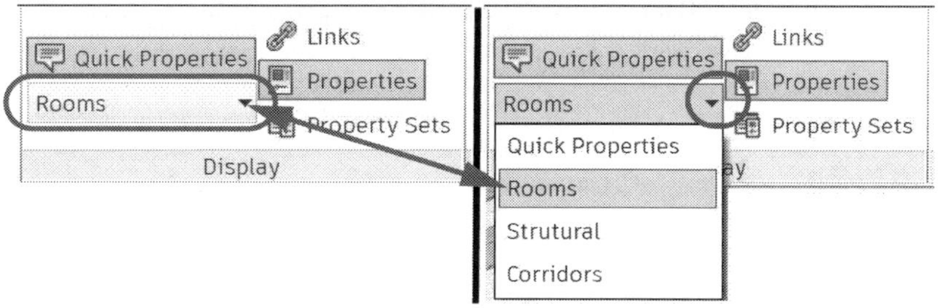

Figure 4–20

If Quick Properties is enabled, then this property set will be displayed in the tooltip when hovering over objects, as shown in Figure 4–21.

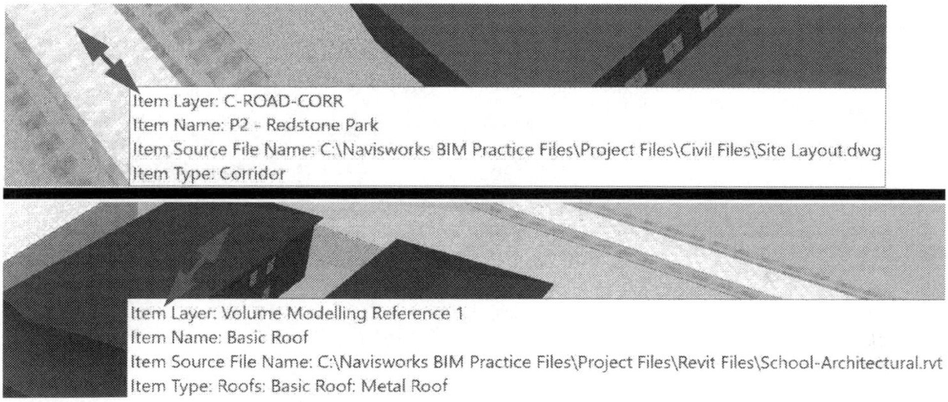

Figure 4–21

Practice 4a
Select and Investigate Items

Practice Objectives

- Select objects in the model.
- Save selection sets.
- Review object properties.

In this practice, you will select objects in the model and create selection sets, as shown in Figure 4–22. You will then review the properties of selected items.

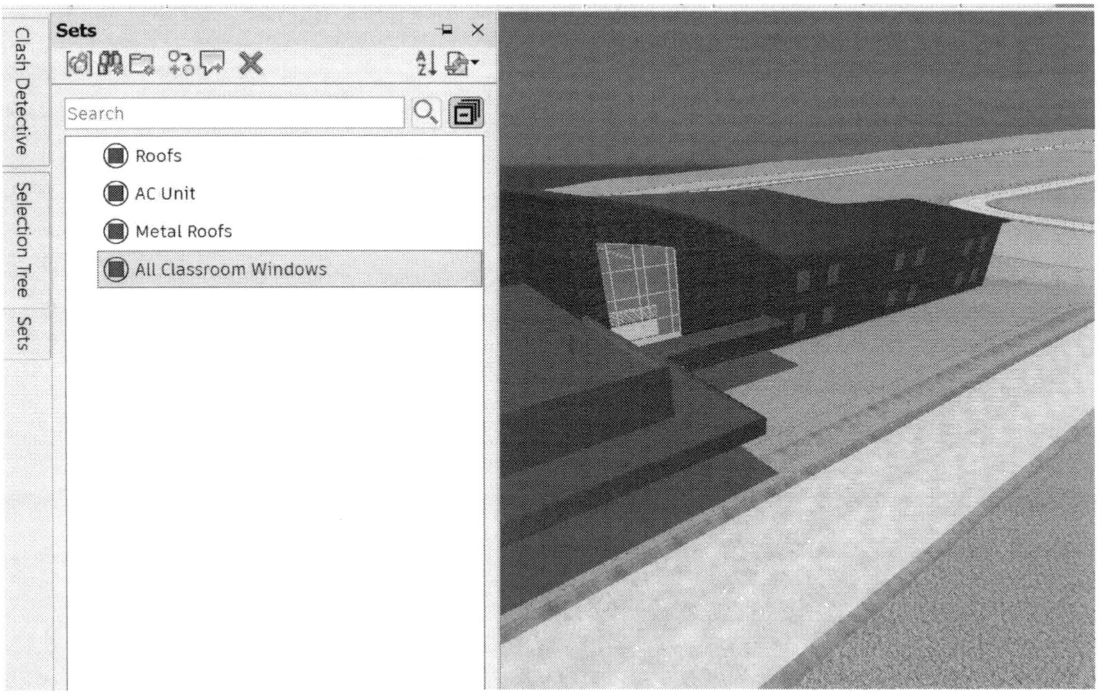

Figure 4–22

Task 1: Use selection tools to select model features.

1. Open **School-Select.nwf** from the *Navisworks BIM Practice Files\Analyze* folder.
2. In the *Saved Viewpoints* window, select **NE-View**. Note that the sections viewpoints have all been reorganized into a folder for you. The NE-View provides an orientation where you can easily see the roofs.

3. In the *Home* tab, expand the *Select & Search* panel and ensure that *Selection Resolution* is set to **First Object**, as shown in Figure 4–23.

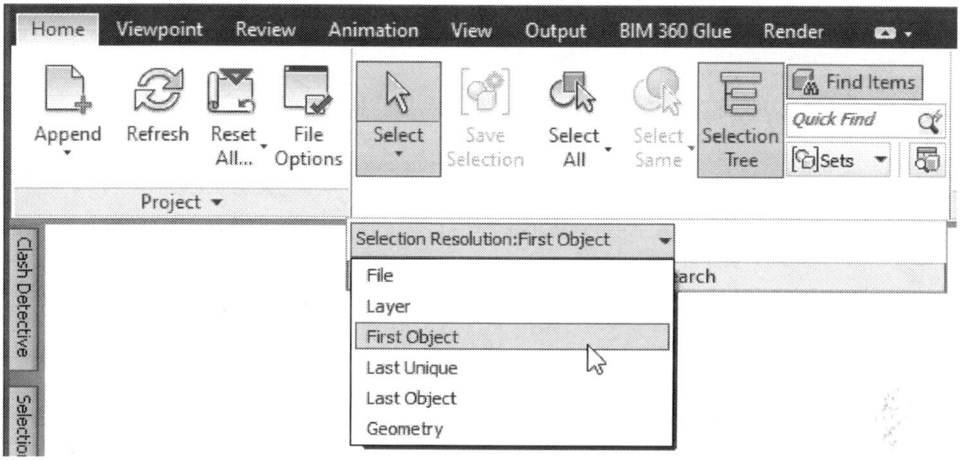

Figure 4–23

4. In the *Home* tab>*Select & Search* panel, click (Select), if not already selected.
5. In the scene view, press and hold <Ctrl> and select the seven rooftops as per their numbers, as shown in Figure 4–24.

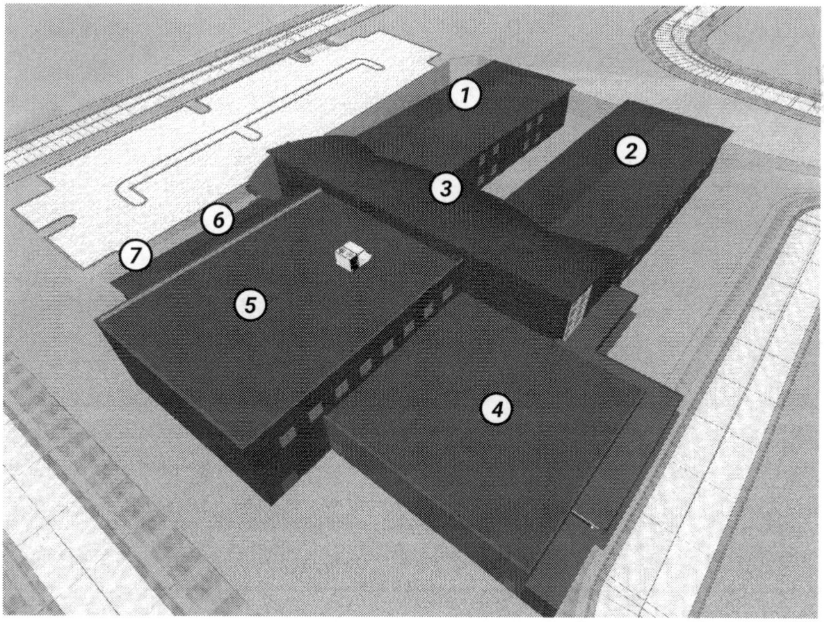

Figure 4–24

6. In the *Home* tab>*Select & Search* panel, click (Save Selection). Enter **Roofs** for the name and press <Enter>.

7. In the *Home* tab>*Select & Search* panel, expand (Select All) and click (Select None) to clear the selection of the roof tops. You can also press <Esc> to clear the current selection.

8. In the *Home* tab>*Select & Search* panel, expand (Select) and click (Select Box). Draw a selection box around the AC unit that is sitting on top of the central flat roof.

9. Save the selection as **AC Unit**.

Task 2: Investigate the model's Quick Properties.

1. In the *Home* tab>*Select & Search* panel, expand the *Sets* drop-down list and select **Roofs**.

2. In the *Home* tab>*Display* panel, click (Quick Properties) to toggle the tool on, if required.

3. Hover the cursor over one of the roofs to display the default *Quick Properties* for that particular roof type within the selection set, as shown in Figure 4–25.

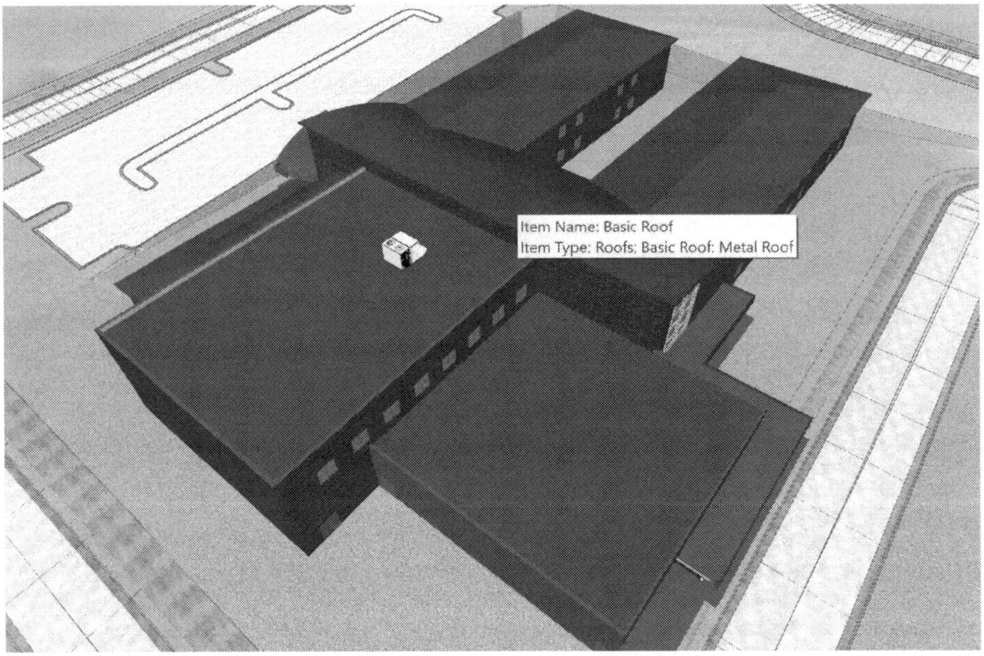

Figure 4–25

4. Open the *Property Sets* panel from the *Home* tab, *Display* panel, as shown in Figure 4–26.

Figure 4–26

5. In the *Property Sets* panel, a *Quick Properties* set exists by default. It was those properties you had seen of the roof just now. To create a new property set, click on **Create**, as shown in Figure 4–27.

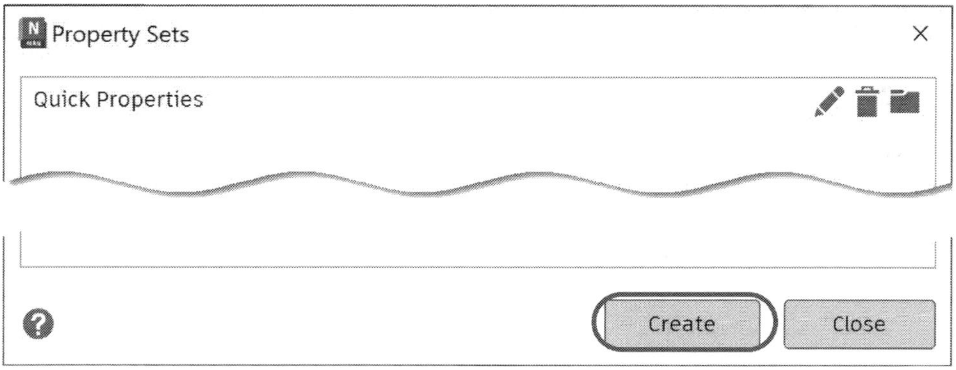

Figure 4–27

6. In the *Create Property Set* dialog box, do the following as shown in Figure 4–28:
   - For *Name* type **Source ID**
   - For *Select properties to include in this set* type **Item** and press <Enter>. This narrows the list of property branches to a single branch matching the search criteria.
   - Expand the *Item* branch by clicking on the ▷ icon to the left.
   - In the *Item* expanded branch, select the following:
     - **Layer**
     - **Name**
     - **Source File Name**
     - **Type**
   - Click **Create** to create the property set.

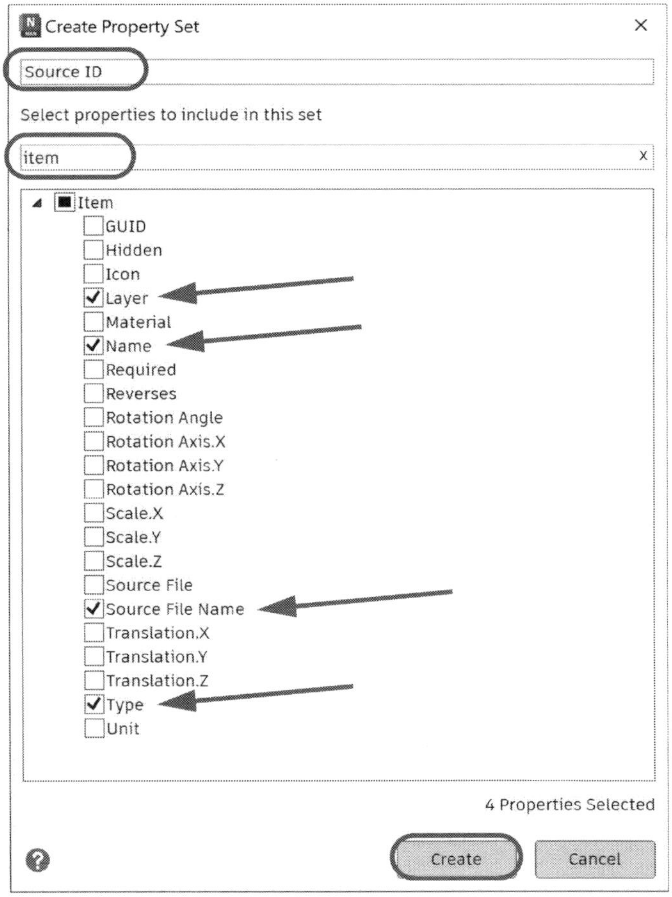

Figure 4–28

7. In the *Property Sets* panel, click **Close**.
8. On the *Display* panel of the *Home* tab, use the drop down menu to select the **Source ID** property to make it current, as shown in Figure 4–29. Ensure that the **Quick Properties** is still enabled.

Figure 4–29

9. Now when you hover over items in the model, the tooltip will display information about its source, as shown in Figure 4–30.

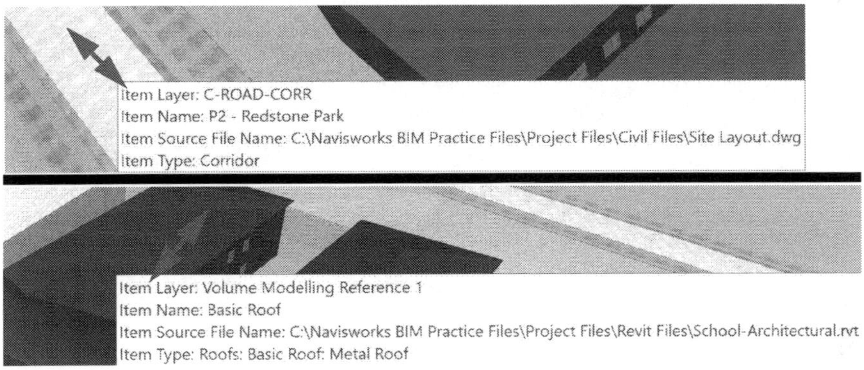

Figure 4–30

Task 3: Investigate the model's feature properties.

1. In the *Home* tab>*Display* panel, click  (Properties) to toggle the tool on, if required.

2. Expand the *Properties* window (which might be docked on the right-side of the window). In the upper right corner, click on ⋮ (Options) and select only **Auto Zoom** and **Breadcrumbs**, leaving the other options unchecked, as shown in Figure 4–31.

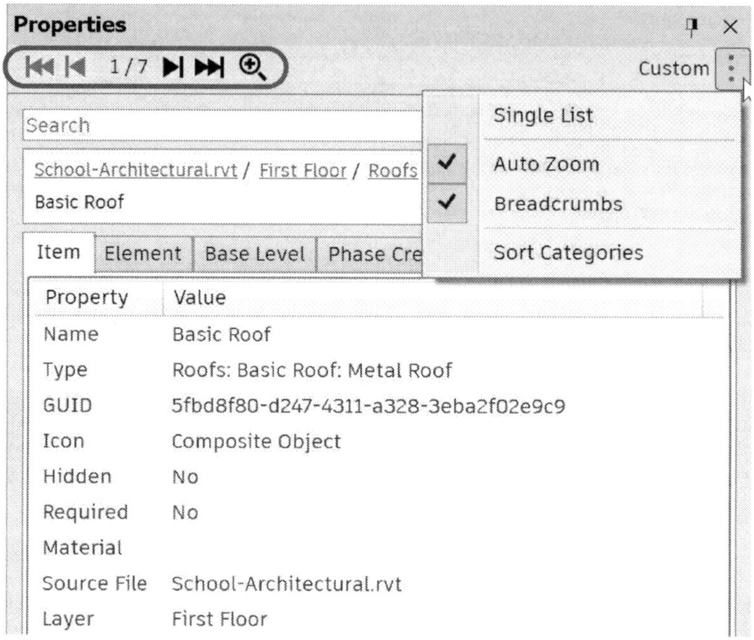

Figure 4–31

3. In the left corner, click on the arrows to view the properties of the different roofs, as shown in Figure 4–31. Each time you click on an arrow, the viewpoint changes to the best view of the selected roof.
4. Select Roof **3/7** with the arrows.
5. Review each of the available tabs in the *Properties* window to review the properties of this roof.

6. Click on (Options) in the upper right corner of the *Properties* window, clear the checkboxes for **Auto Zoom** and **Breadcrumbs**, and select **Single List**. Now the *Properties* window no longer displays the breadcrumbs in the header, the **Custom** button, or the various property tabs, as shown in Figure 4–32. Everything is displayed in a single list, which has grown considerably in length. Scroll down to see the entire list.

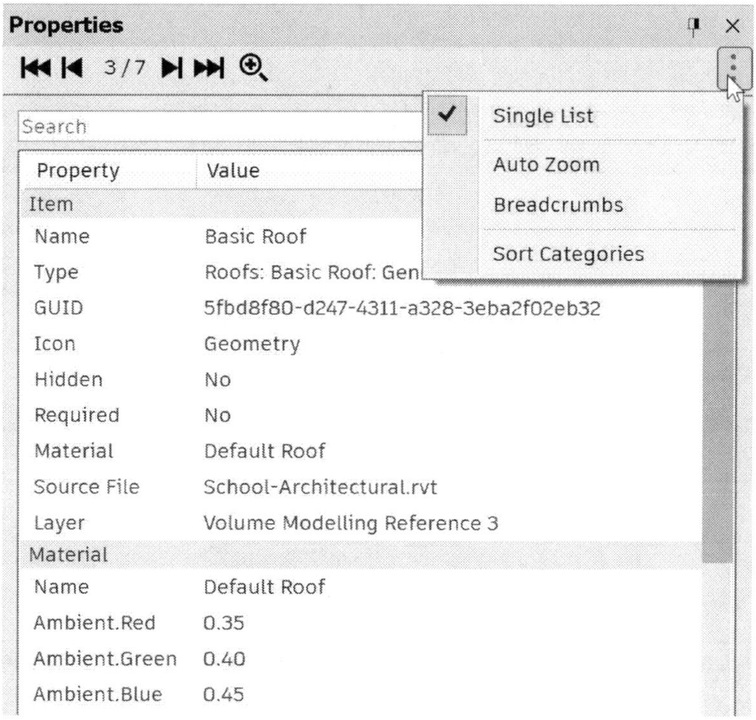

Figure 4–32

7. Now with **Auto Zoom** disabled, when you select a different roof with the arrows, the viewpoint does not change but remains fixed in its current location. Select Roof **4/7** with the arrows.

8. To zoom to the selected item, click on . The 4th selected roof now fills the screen, along with all the information in the *Properties* window.

9. Click on (Options) in the upper right corner of the *Properties* window and clear the **Single List** checkbox. Now the *Properties* window displays the **Custom** button and the various property tabs, but not the breadcrumbs.

10. Click the **Custom** button in the header, and in the drop-down list, click **Add User Data Tab,** as shown in Figure 4–33.

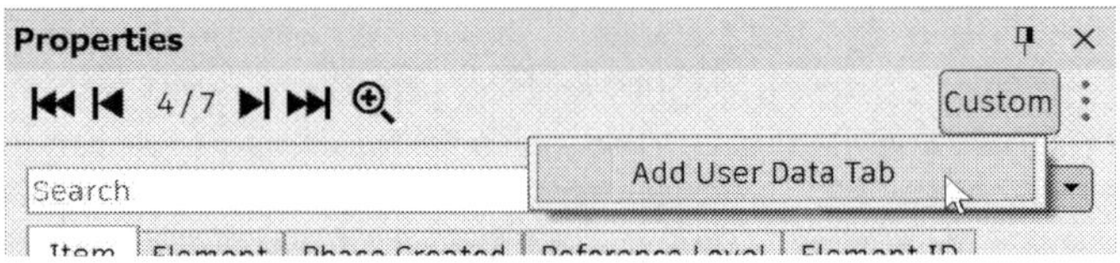

Figure 4–33

11. Click on the new *User Data* tab (if it isn't already selected), and then click the **Custom** button in the header. In the drop-down list, select **Insert New Property>Integer,** as shown in Figure 4–34.

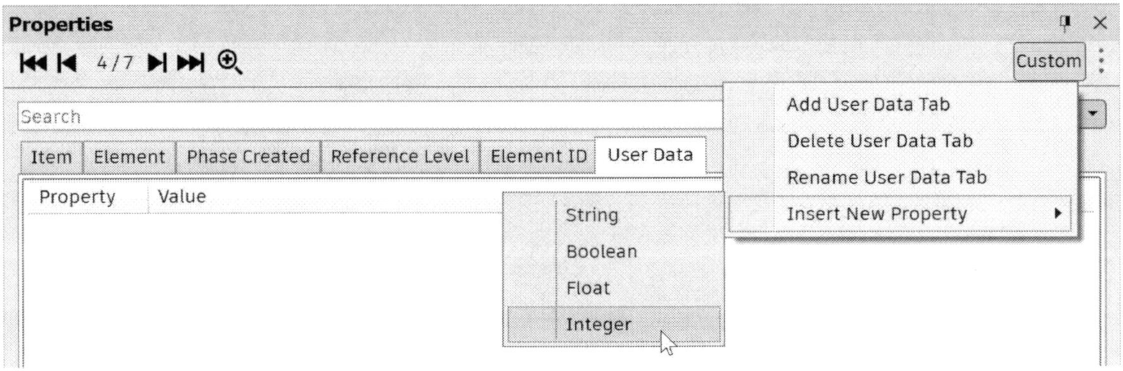

Figure 4–34

12. In the *User Data* tab, right-click in the new row on the *Property* column, and select **Rename**. Name the property **Install Year.**
13. In the *User Data* tab>*Value* field, select **Edit Values** from the right-click menu.
14. Type **2013** and click the green checkmark, as shown in Figure 4–35. You can also press <Enter>.

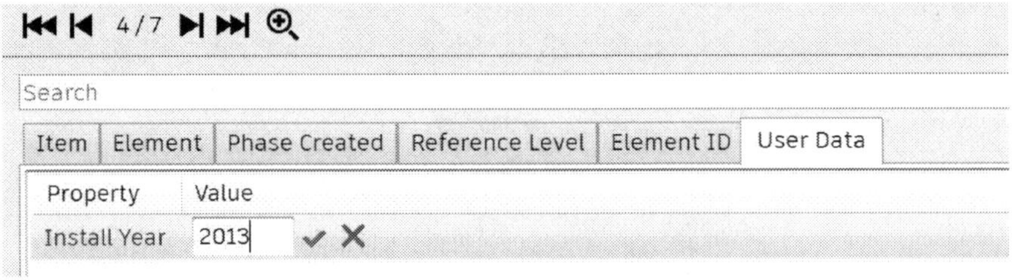

Figure 4–35

15. Add three more properties as follows (Use **Custom>Insert New Property** and select the *Type* from the list):

Type	Property	Value
String	Coverage	**Material and Labor**
Float	Warranty Period	**5.5**
Boolean	Depreciation	No (clear the checkbox)

16. Click the **Custom** button in the header, and from the drop-down list, select **Rename User Data Tab.**
17. In the *Rename User Data Tab* dialog box, type **Warranty** and click **OK**.
18. The completed *Warranty* tab is shown in Figure 4–36.

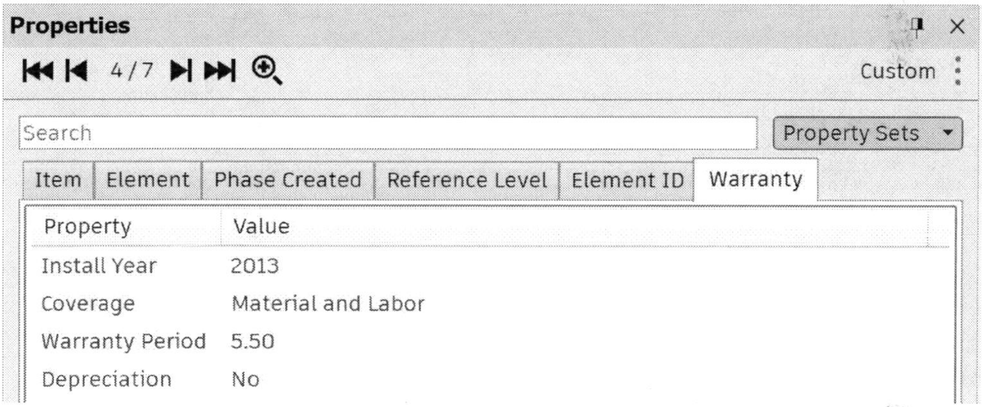

Figure 4–36

19. Click on  (Options) and select **Auto Zoom** and **Breadcrumbs**, and leave **Single List** as unchecked.

20. Select the *Item* tab. As you select different breadcrumbs (the blue text in the element heading), the *Item* tab displays the properties of only the selected hierarchy level, as shown in Figure 4–37. If you notice that any of the tabs have disappeared, it is because these tabs are no longer relevant for the level of breadcrumbs you are currently at.

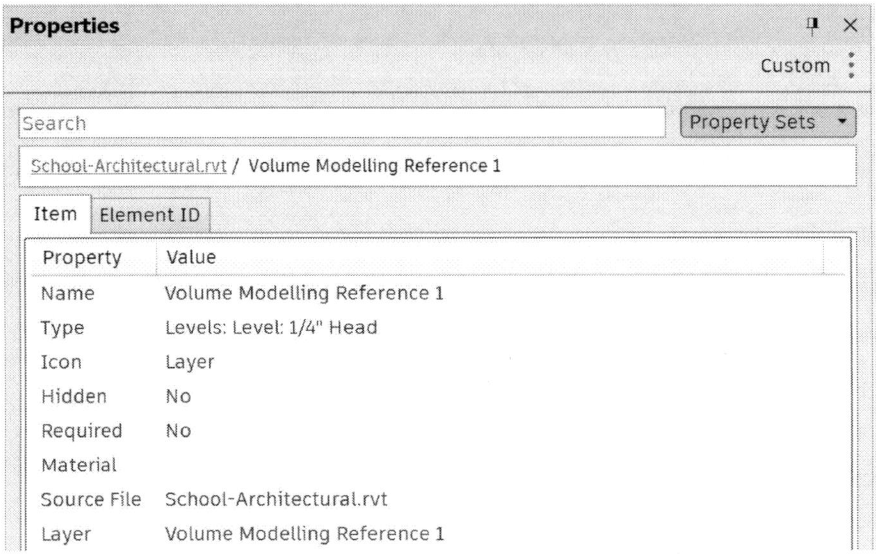

Figure 4–37

21. You can click (Undo) in the Quick Access Toolbar to restore the breadcrumbs after you have collapsed the hierarchy.

22. When you go to another roof element with the arrow keys, note that the *Warranty* tab is not available. It is only present for the roof you created it in.

23. In the *Home* tab>*Select & Search* panel, click (Find Items) to open the *Find Items* window. If the *Find Items* window does not display, select the *Find Items* tab located in the left side tabs near the bottom of the screen and pin it. Arrange the *Properties* window so that it is not overlapping it.

24. In the *Properties* window, in the *Item* category, select the **Type** row, and then from the right-click menu, select **Create Search**. Notice that this criteria has been used to create a new search, as shown in Figure 4–38.

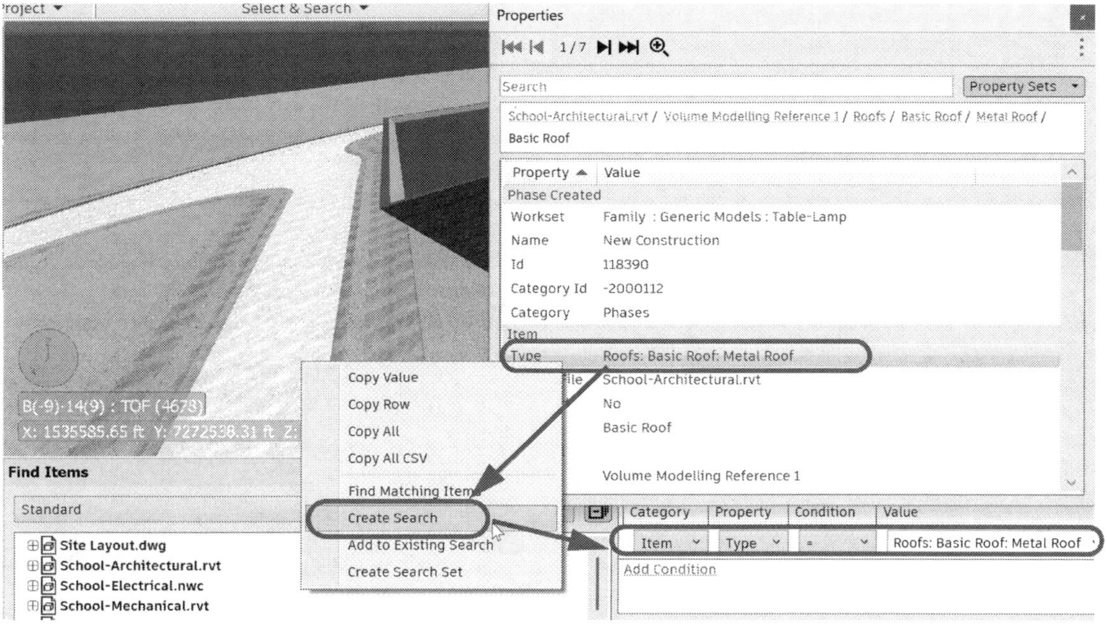

Figure 4–38

25. Select the **Base Level> Name** row and, from the right-click menu, select **Add to Existing Search**. Notice that this criteria has been added as another condition in the existing search.

26. Save the file.

Note: *The Find tool is covered in more detail later in this chapter.*

Task 4: Use the System Inspector.

1. Continue to work in the **School-Select.nwf file**. In the *Home* tab>*Select & Search* panel, click (Selection Inspector).

2. In the *Selection Inspector* window, beside the two **Generic - 12"** roofs, click (Deselect) to remove the items from the selection set. The view updates as shown in Figure 4–39, and the two flat roofs are removed from the selection.

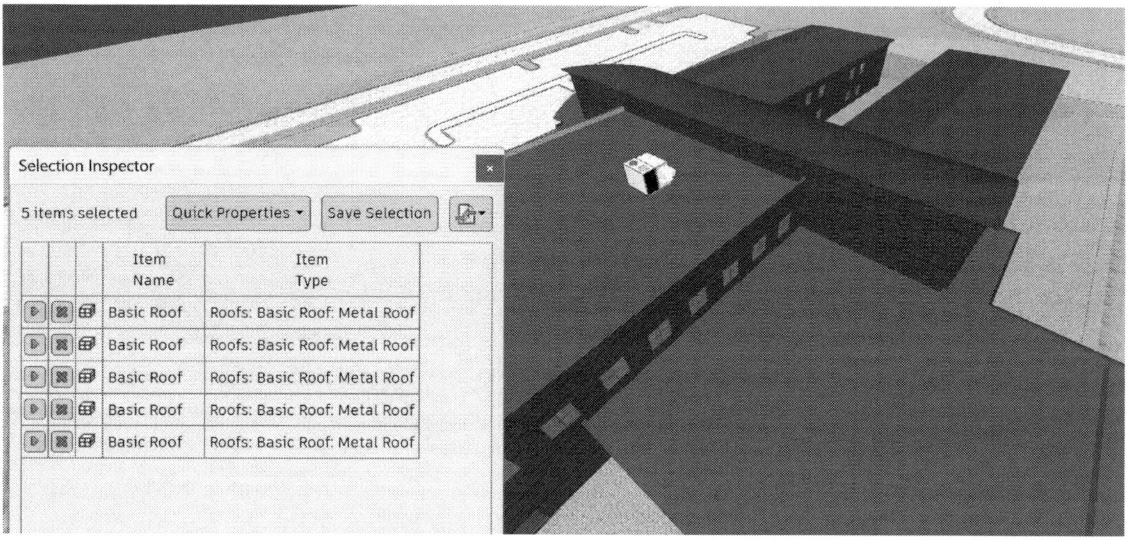

Figure 4–39

3. In the *Selection Inspector* window, click (Show Item) next to the first **Basic Roof** item in the list, as shown in Figure 4–40. The scene view zooms in to the item.

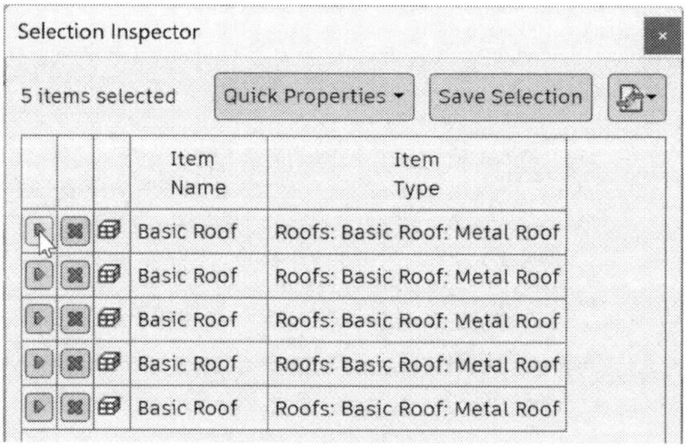

Figure 4–40

4. In the Quick Access Toolbar, click (Undo) to return to viewing the entire building.
5. In the *Selection Inspector* window, click **Save Selection** and name the set **Metal Roofs**.
6. Close the *Selection Inspector* window.
7. Press <Esc> or, in the *Home* tab>*Select & Search* panel, click (Select None) to clear the selection of the roofs.
8. In the *Home* tab>*Select & Search* panel, expand (Select Box) and click (Select), if not already active.
9. In the scene view, click on the terrain surface surrounding the building.
10. Expand the *Properties* window to review the surface properties, as shown in Figure 4–41. Review each of the available tabs in the *Properties* window to review all of the surface properties.

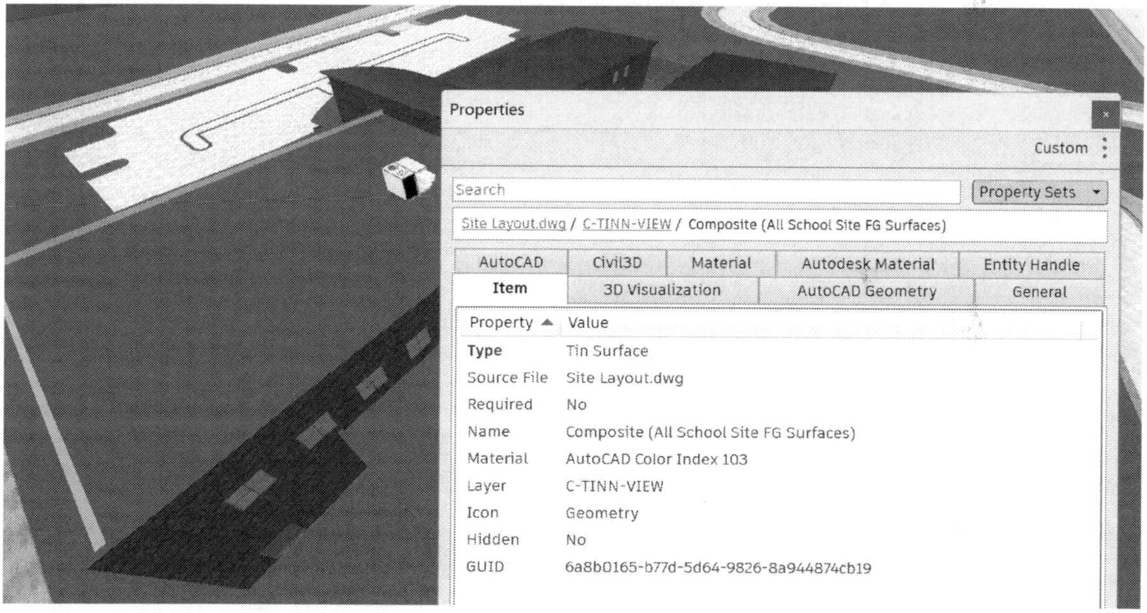

Figure 4–41

11. Press <Esc> to clear the surface selection.
12. Close the *Properties* window.

13. Reorient the model similar to that shown in Figure 4–42.

14. In the *Home* tab>*Select & Search* panel, click (Select), if not already active. In the model, select any one of the visible windows in the classroom wings, as shown in Figure 4–42.

Figure 4–42

15. In the *Home* tab>*Select & Search* panel, expand (Select Same) and select **Same Type** from the list. All classroom windows are selected.
16. Save the selection as **All Classroom Windows**.
17. In the *Home* tab>*Select & Search* panel, expand **Sets** and select **Manage Sets**. The Sets window displays with the created sets listed.
18. Save the file.

End of practice

4.3 Using the Selection Tree

The *Selection Tree* includes all of the models in the project and all of the geometry in every model. It can be used to select very specific information in the model, including materials, as shown in Figure 4–43.

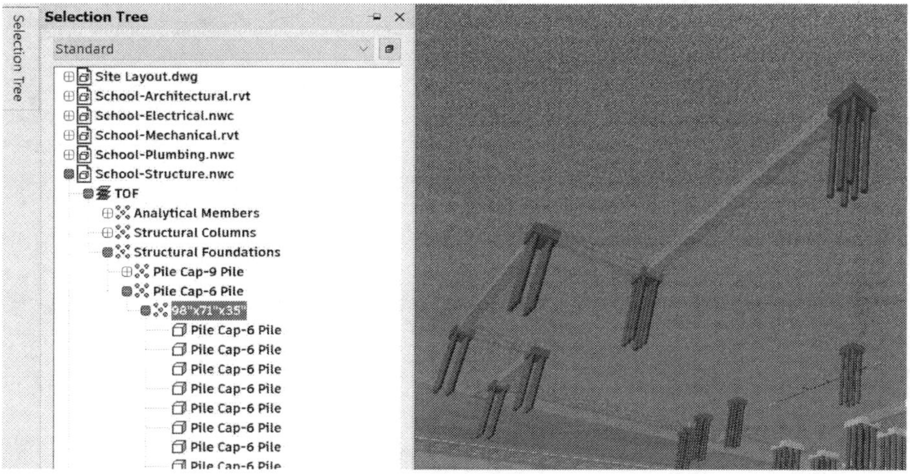

Figure 4–43

When you select items in the model, the *Selection Tree* expands so that you can view the item that is shown highlighted in blue. Similarly, if you select items in the *Selection Tree*, they highlight in the model.

Consider the following:

- To open the *Selection Tree*, in the *Home* tab>*Select & Search* panel, click (Selection Tree) or press <Ctrl>+<F12>. Alternatively, you can enable the window in the *View* tab> expanded **Windows** option.
- The *Selection Tree* is a window and can be docked and set to auto-hide.
- To select multiple items in the *Selection Tree*, hold <Ctrl> or <Shift> while selecting the items.
- To zoom in on a selected item, right-click on it in the *Selection Tree* and select **Focus on Item**.
- To save sets of selections, in the *Home* tab>*Select & Search* panel, click (Save Selection).
- To clear the current selection, press <Esc> or select away from any items in the scene view.

Selection Resolution

You can refine the selection of items to the various levels of the hierarchy in the *Selection Tree* by setting the *Selection Resolution*. In the *Home* tab, expand the *Select & Search* drop-down list, as shown in Figure 4–44, or right-click on an item in the *Selection Tree* to select from the menu.

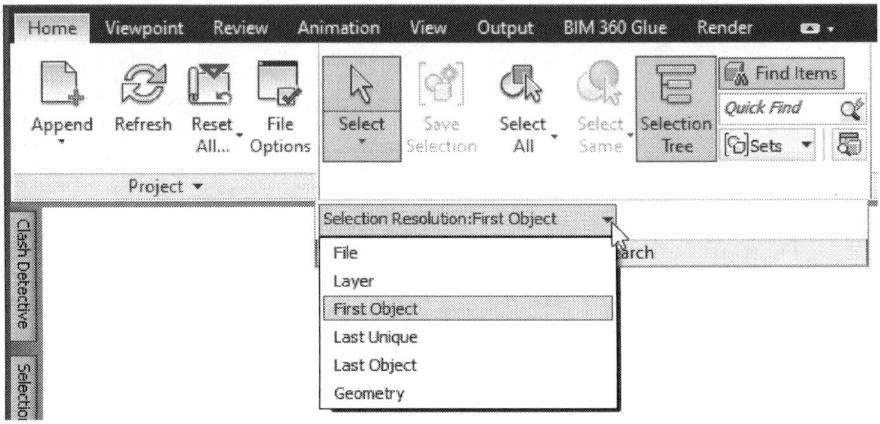

Figure 4–44

Note: *To cycle through selection resolution options, hold <Shift> and click on an item in the scene view to cycle through the resolutions. It helps to have the Selection Tree open to see how this works.*

The **Selection Resolution** options (shown in Figure 4–45) are as follows:

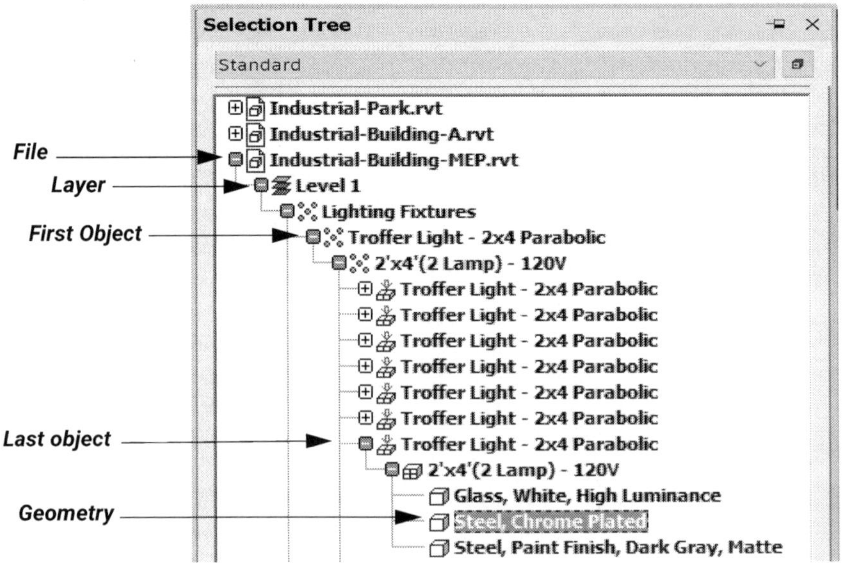

Figure 4–45

- **File:** Selects all of the elements in a file.
- **Layer:** Selects all of the elements on a specific layer. For the example shown in Figure 4–46, selecting the door on the first floor selects all of the other elements on that layer, in this case the windows and visible items such as the first floor interior walls.

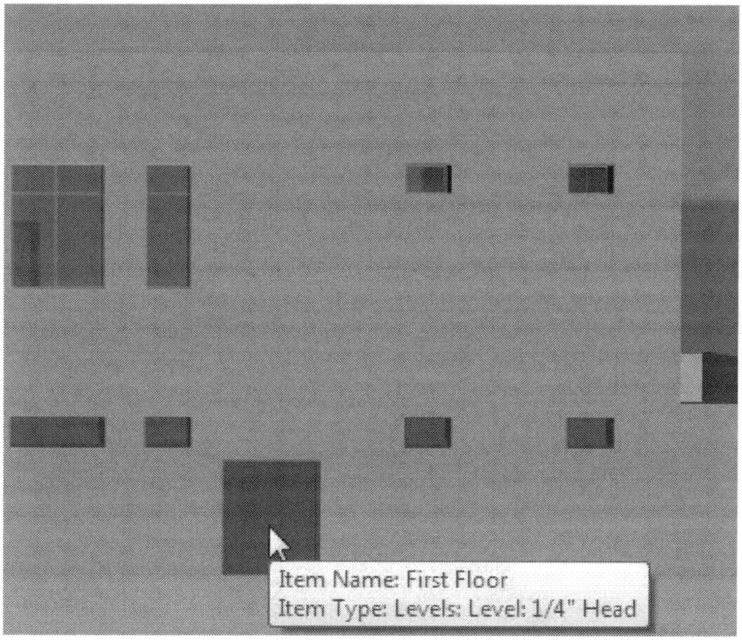

Figure 4–46

- **First Object, Last Object**, and **Last Unique** are based on their location below the level, but typically each option selects the exact item you pick, such as a specific wall, column, or lighting fixture in an Autodesk Revit model. AutoCAD-based models might be different because of the underlying geometry.
- **Geometry:** Selects the base geometry of the item, such as the material of a lighting fixture, or a line, polyline, or arc element in an AutoCAD project.

Hint: Selection Options

There are several options that can help you be more precise in selecting and viewing items. These options are found in the *Options Editor* in the **Interface>Selection** pane, as shown in Figure 4–47.

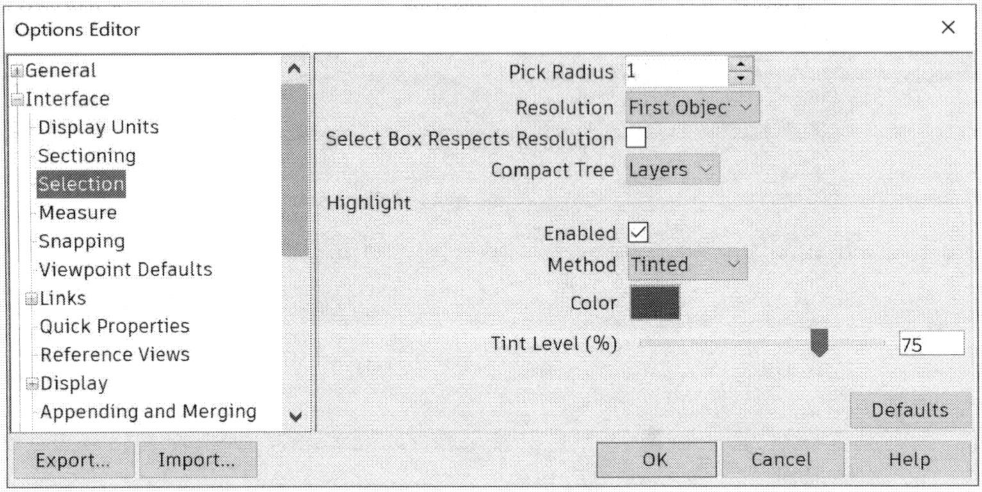

Figure 4–47

- **Pick Radius:** Sets the size (in pixels) of the point where you click the cursor to select an element.
- **Resolution:** Establishes the default pick order.
- **Select Box Respects Resolution:** Sets the Box select mode to respect the selection resolution that is set.
- **Compact Tree:** Establishes the default presentation of the *Selection Tree*.
- **Highlight:** Sets the method (**Tinted**, **Shaded**, or **Wireframe**), color, and tint level of selected items.

Setting the Viewing Order

The *Selection Tree* can be very complex, depending on the number of models included in the project and the number of items within each model. There are at least three ways to view the information, as shown in Figure 4–48.

Figure 4–48

- **Standard:** Displays all of the nodes from *File* to *Geometry*.
- **Compact:** Displays only the nodes for *File* and *Layers*.
- **Properties:** Displays all of the properties of every item in the model by category. For example, in an Autodesk Revit model, each room is considered a category, and you can find properties such as the Area of the room. When you select the room, all of the related items (such as the exterior wall and windows) are selected, as shown in Figure 4–49.

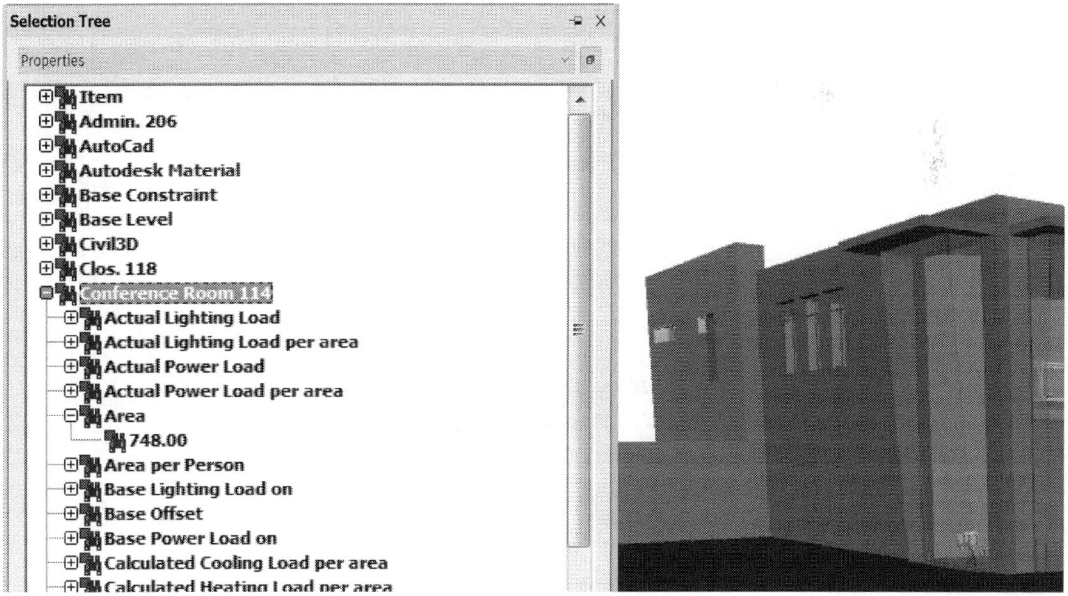

Figure 4–49

- **Sets:** Only available when you have saved selections in the project, and displays those sets.

Practice 4b
Use the Selection Tree

Practice Objectives

- Change the selection resolution.
- Use the *Selection Tree* to familiarize yourself with the model.

In this practice, you will become more familiar with the school model shown in Figure 4–50 by using the *Selection Tree* to select items and focus on them. You will also change the selection resolution to make selecting individual items much easier.

Figure 4–50

Task 1: Change the selection resolution.

1. Open **School-Tree.nwf** from the *Navisworks BIM Practice Files\Analyze* folder.
2. In the *Saved Viewpoints* window, select **NE-View**.
3. In the *Home* tab>*Select & Search* panel, ensure that the (Select) selection method is set.
4. In the *Home* tab, expand the *Select & Search* panel and ensure that the *Selection Resolution* is set to **First Object**, as shown in Figure 4–51. This selection option ensures that the object directly below the cursor is selected.

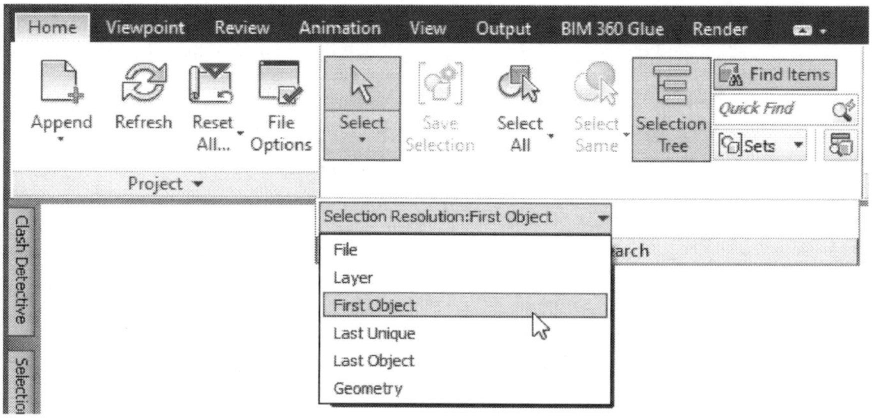

Figure 4–51

5. Open the *Selection Tree* window and pin it open.
6. In the scene view, click on the lower flat roof, as shown in Figure 4–52. Only that one roof should be selected. The *Selection Tree* expands to display the selected item. If it does not expand, ensure the **Standard** view setting is set at the top of the window.

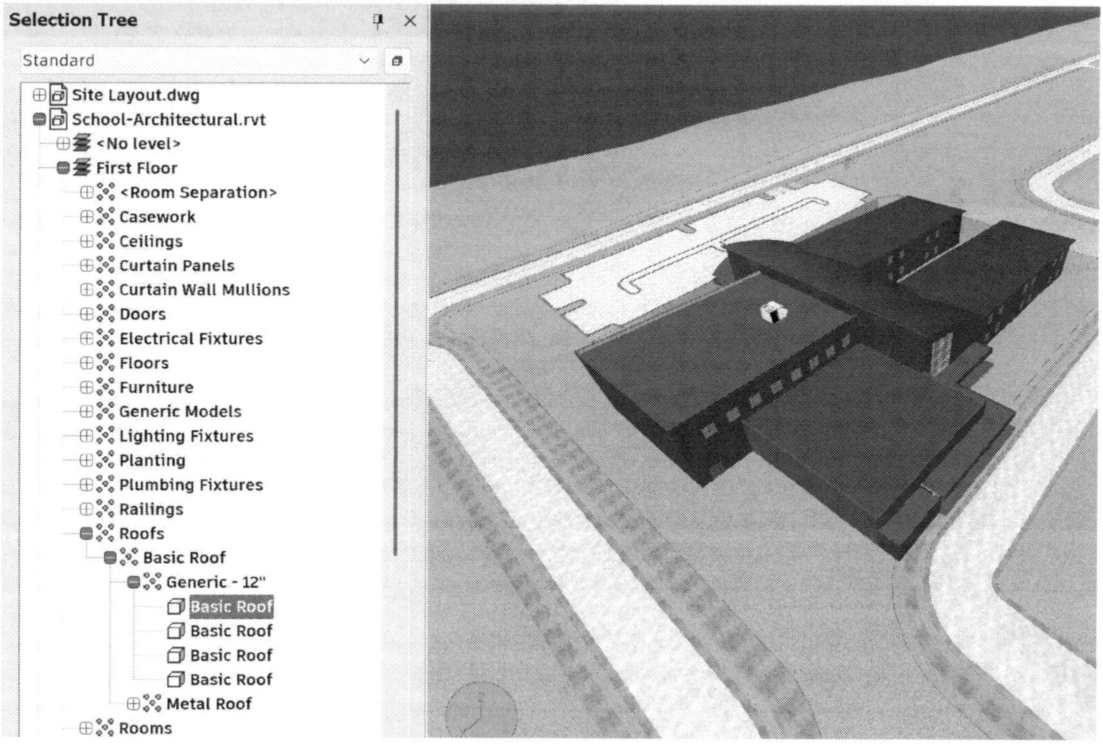

Figure 4–52

7. Click away from all elements or press <Esc> to clear the selection.
8. In the *Home* tab, expand the *Select & Search* panel title and in the *Selection Resolution* drop-down list, select **File**.
9. Select the same roof again and note how the entire **School-Archtectural.rvt** building model is now selected, both in the scene view and in the *Selection Tree*.
10. Clear the selection, change the *Selection Resolution* to **Layer**, and reselect the same roof. Note that only the First Floor elements are selected, as shown in Figure 4–53.

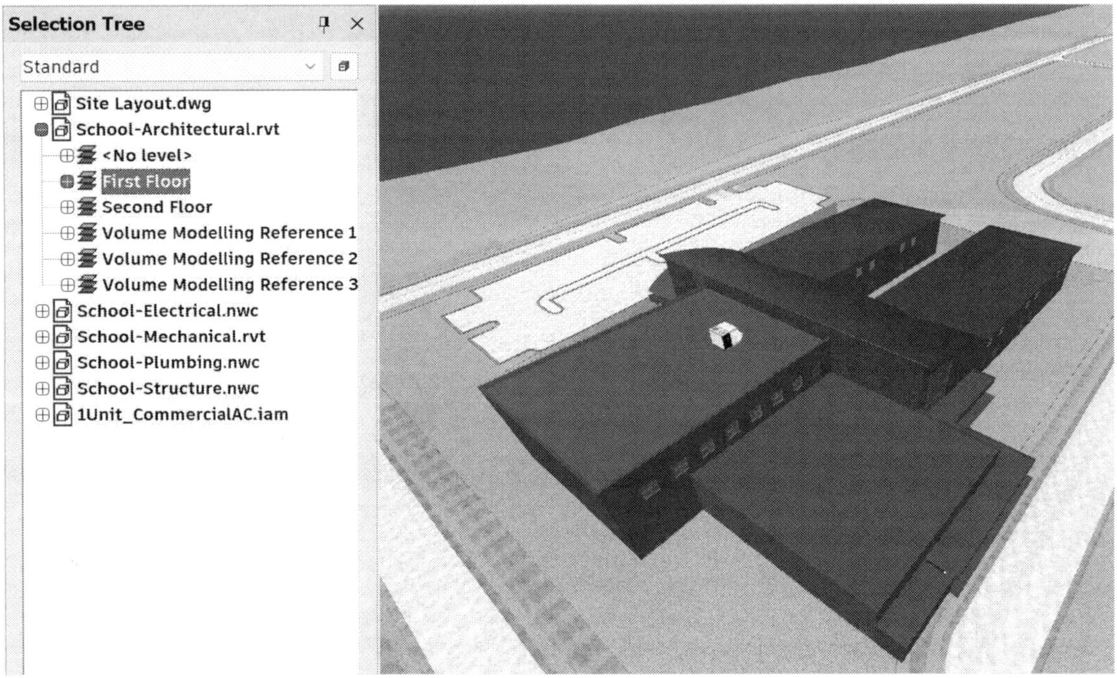

Figure 4–53

11. Reset the resolution to **First Object**. This is generally the most commonly used setting.
12. Auto-hide the *Selection Tree* and clear the First Floor selection.

Task 2: Modify a selection set.

1. In the *Home* tab>*Select & Search* panel, expand the *Sets* drop-down list and select **AC Unit**, as shown in Figure 4–54. If the selection set does not immediately display in the scene view, select **AC Unit** in the *Sets* window that opens.

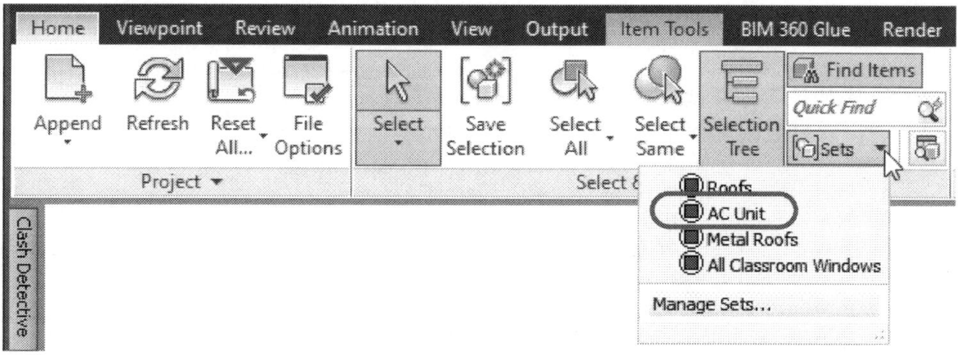

Figure 4–54

2. Scroll through and review the *Selection Tree*. Note that other elements that are not in the AC Unit file were also selected. This occurs because the set was created using the *Select Box* tool and the selection set was not created correctly.
3. Press <Esc> to clear all selections.
4. In the *Selection Tree*, select **1Unit_Commercial AC.iam** (the top level node).
5. In the *Sets* window, right-click on **AC Unit** and then select **Update**.
6. Clear the selection and test the AC Unit selection set to be sure that it has been corrected by reviewing what is selected in the *Selection Tree*.
7. Clear any selection in the model before continuing.

Task 3: Use the Selection Tree to select objects.

1. In the *Saved Viewpoints* window, select **NE-View**, if you are no longer displaying this viewpoint.
2. In the *Selection Tree*, expand *School-Architectural.rvt>First Floor* and select **Doors**.
3. Orbit around the model and note that there are multiple door types selected in the scene view (e.g., double, single, glass and they are on both the exterior and interior of the building).
4. Expand the **Doors** node and select **Double Door**. Note that fewer doors are now selected.
5. Continue to select the remaining door types (**SINGLE**, **DOUBLE**, **Curtain Wall Sgl Glass**, and **Curtain Wall Dbl Glass**) and review them in the model.
6. In the *Saved Viewpoints* window, select the **Section-Ductwork** viewpoint in the *Sectioned Views* folder.
7. In the *Selection Tree*, select **School-Mechanical.rvt**. The mechanical ducting components display.
8. Continue selecting different items in the *Selection Tree* to become more familiar with the model.
9. Press <Esc> to clear the selection.

10. In the *Saved Viewpoints* window, select the **Front Entrance-Exterior** viewpoint in the *Exterior* folder.
11. In the *Selection Tree*, expand *School-Architectural.rvt><No Level>* and select **Curtain Panels**. All of the glass panels at the front entrance highlight in the model.
12. Press and hold <Ctrl> and also select **Curtain Wall Mullions**. The *Selection Tree* and scene view display as shown in Figure 4–55.

Figure 4–55

13. In the *Home* tab>*Select & Search* panel, expand (Select Same) and select **Same Name**.
14. Orbit around the model and note that all of the curtain panels and curtain wall mullions are now selected in the model.
15. In the *Home* tab>*Select & Search* panel, click (Save Selection). Enter **Curtain Panels and Mullions** for the name and press <Enter>.
16. Clear the selection and test that the new **Curtain Panels and Mullions** selection set works.
17. Save the file.

End of practice

4.4 Finding Items and Saving Search Sets

Due to the large amount of information that can be stored in an Autodesk Navisworks project, the tools that help you find objects become very important. For example, you can use **Quick Find** for simple searches or **Find Items** for more complex searches. Additionally, the items that you find can be saved to a convenient search set that can be easily accessed in the future.

Using Quick Find

You can use **Quick Find** (located in the *Home* tab>*Search & Select* panel) to search based on a text string. For example, in a Civil 3D model, enter **road** (as shown in Figure 4–56) and press <Enter>, or click the (Quick Find) button. The first related item in the *Selection Tree* is highlighted, as shown in Figure 4–57.

Figure 4–56

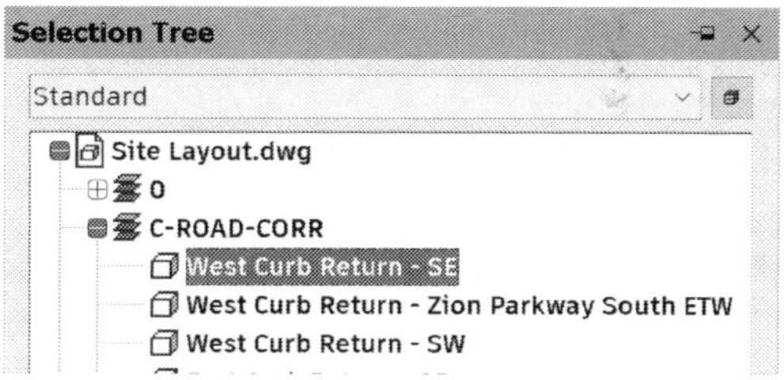

Figure 4–57

Repeatedly pressing <Enter> or clicking (Quick Find) will continue to the next item in the *Selection Tree*. Quick Find drills down to the geometry level with each click before moving to the top level of the next related item.

Using Find Items

The *Find Items* window enables you to specify models to be searched and define criteria to search on.

How To: Use the Find Item Dialog Box

1. In the *Home* tab>*Select & Search* panel, click (Find Items) to open the *Find Items* window.
2. In the *Find Items* dialog box, use the left pane to select the level where you want to start searching. You can select model names or expand the list and select specific items. To select multiple items, press and hold <Ctrl> while selecting.
3. In the right pane, define the criteria to search on. Expand each drop-down list and select the *Category*, *Property*, *Condition*, and *Value* settings to fully define the criteria that should be searched on. Multiple criteria can be set, as needed.

The options in each drop-down list depend on the item. The available criteria are as follows:

- **Category:** A list that corresponds to the tabs in *Properties*
- **Property:** A list of properties within the selected category
- **Condition:** How you want to search
- **Value:** What you want to search for based on the condition

Figure 4–58 shows the *Find Items* window set up to search the **School-Architectural.rvt** model for all items that have the **Birch** material name assigned.

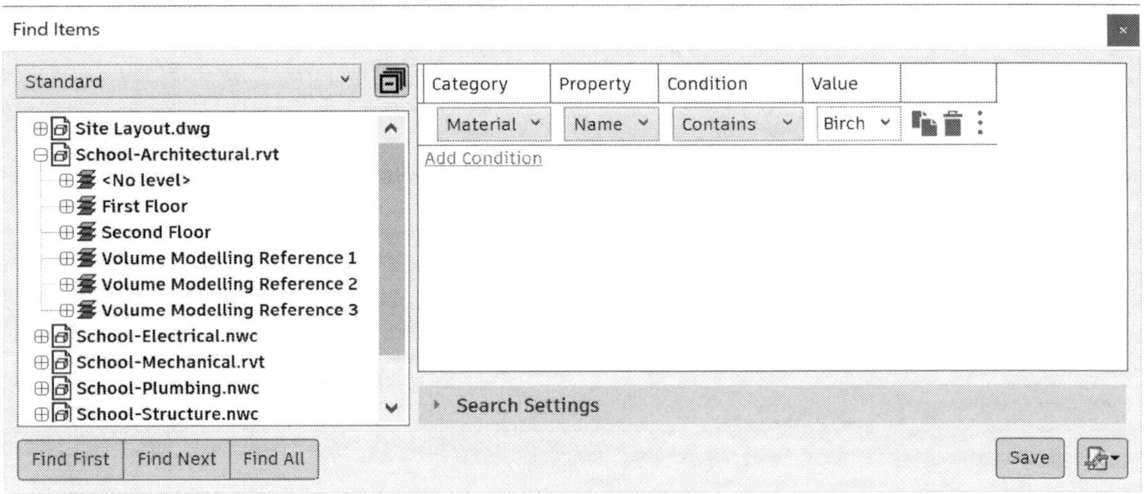

Figure 4–58

4. You can copy ( ) or delete ( ) the current search condition. Copying the condition will create a new criteria which can easily be edited. You can also manually add a condition by clicking the **Add Condition** button, as shown in Figure 4–59.
5. For an added condition, the default is the *AND* condition. You can change that to *OR* by clicking the ( ) icon which opens a fly-out menu.This menu offers other options as well, as can be seen in Figure 4–59.

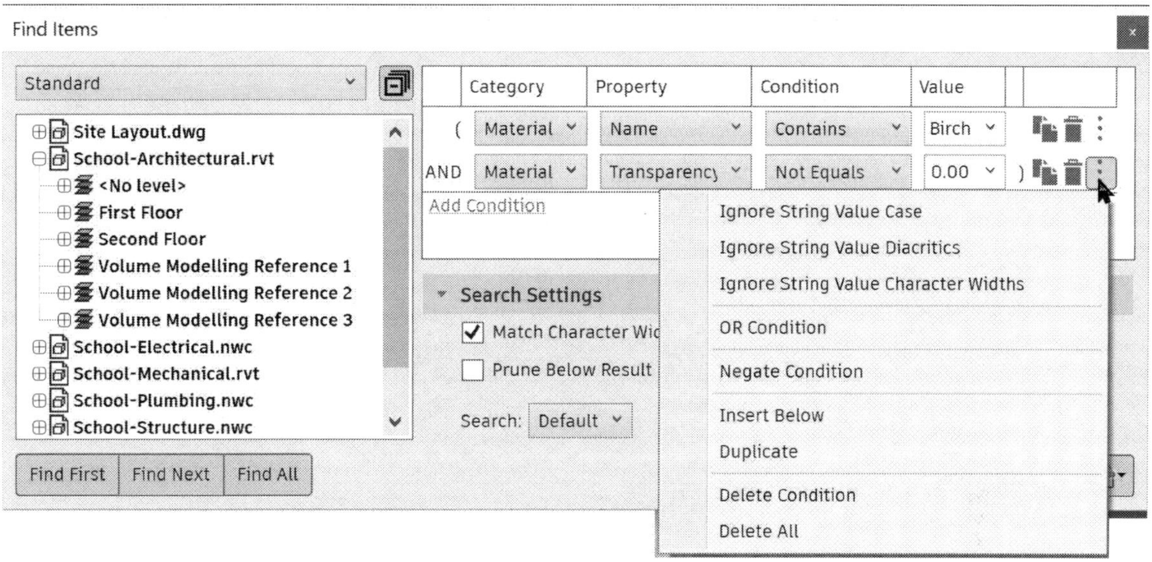

Figure 4–59

When there are multiple rows of criteria included, an *ADD* statement is automatically assigned. This means that both conditions must be matched to find any items. Consider the following:

- If you want to change a row to an *OR* statement, click the (⋮) icon which opens a fly-out menu and select **Or Condition**. The row is distinguished by a **+** sign, as shown in Figure 4–60.

Category	Property	Condition	Value
Item	Name	Contains	Column
Level	Name	=	Level 1
+ Base Level	Elevation	=	10'-0"

Figure 4–60

- To search for the opposite of a condition, select **Negate Condition**.
- To remove a row from the list, select **Delete Condition**.
- You can also select **Delete All Conditions** to start over.

6. When you expand the *Search Settings* section, you can further define the search. Select the Match options as required, as shown in Figure 4–61. You can:

   - **Match Character Widths**, which is also available through the ⋮ fly-out menu.
   - **Match Diacritics**, which is also available through the ⋮ fly-out menu.
   - **Match Case**, which is also available through the ⋮ fly-out menu.
   - **Prune Below Result**
   - **Search Selected Parts only**
   - **Search Below Selected Parts**

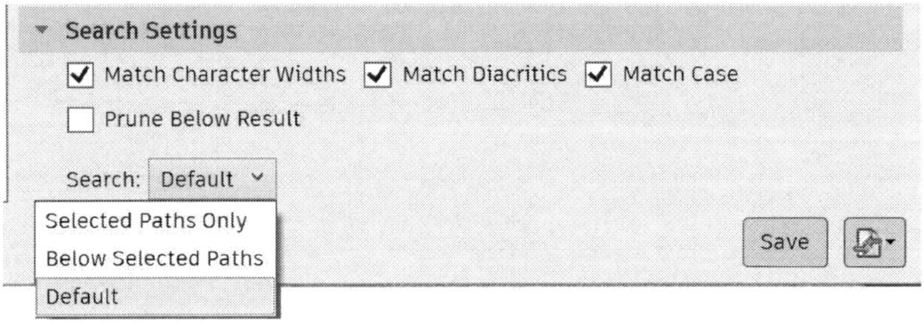

Figure 4–61

The conditions that are available when defining the Find Item criteria depend on whether the property is text based (as shown in Figure 4–62) or number based (as shown in Figure 4–63).

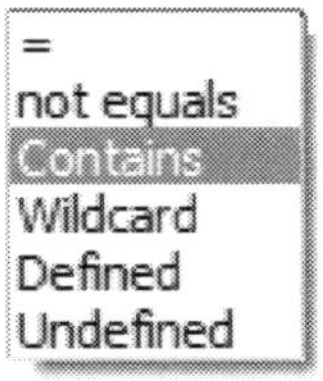

Figure 4–62

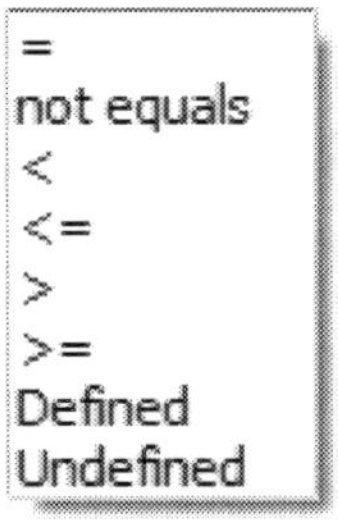

Figure 4–63

7. Click **Find First**, **Find Next**, or **Find All**, as required.

Saving Search Sets

Once you have used the *Find Item* window to locate items in the model, you can save the search as a search set. The advantage of a search set over a saved selection set is that as new models are appended, the search set updates automatically to include new objects, while saved selection sets do not update automatically. Searches are based on information stored in item properties.

How To: Save a Search Set

1. In the *Find Items* window, create a search condition and use **Find All** to select all items in the model that match the defined criteria.
2. In the *Sets* window, click (Save Search) or right-click and select **Save Search**.
3. Enter a descriptive name for the search. Note that the icon for a saved search varies from that of a saved selection set, as shown in Figure 4–64.

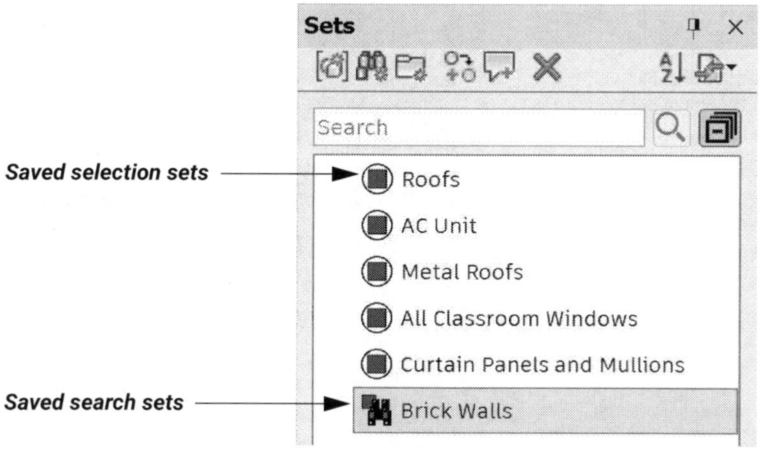

Figure 4–64

- Search sets update when new geometry is added to the model if it matches the search criteria.
- Click (Duplicate) to make a copy of a search set to use as the base for another search set. You can then return to the *Find Items* window and edit the criteria, as needed.

Practice 4c
Find Items and Save Search Sets

Practice Objectives

- Create a search criteria.
- Save a search set for later use.

In this practice, you will run a quick search to find all of the HVAC ducts. Then, you will create a saved set based on the type of walls (interior vs. exterior) for use later, as shown in Figure 4–65.

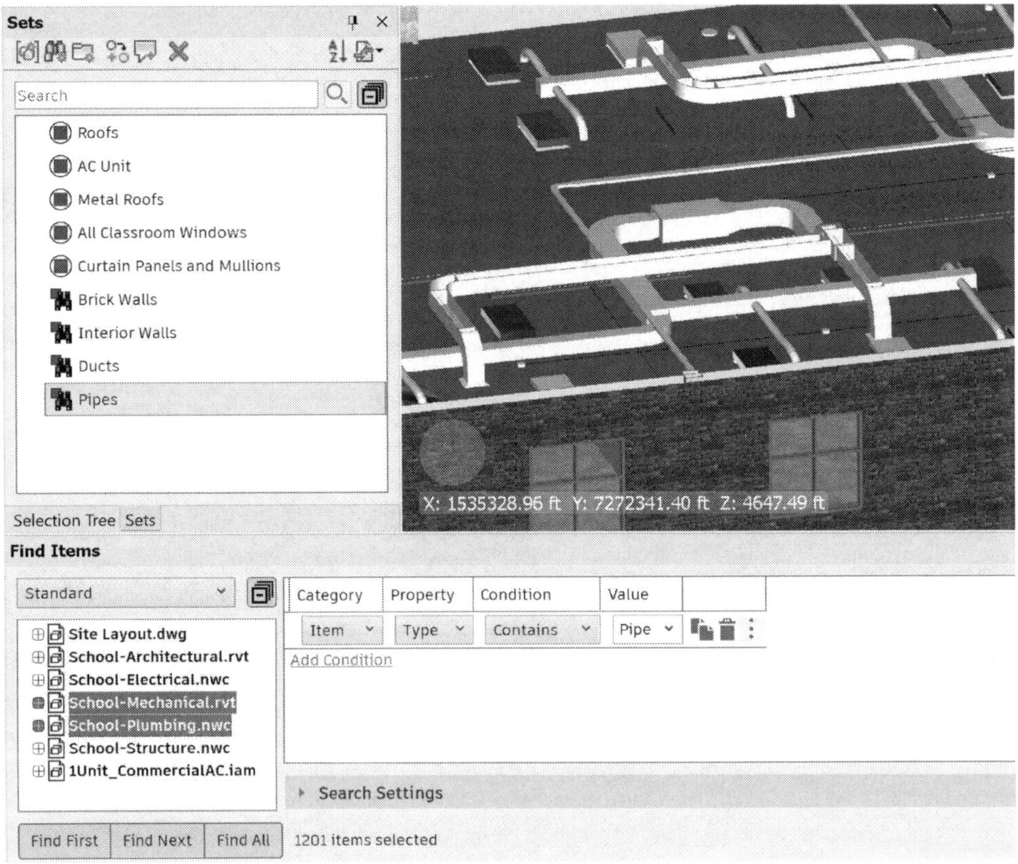

Figure 4–65

Task 1: Do a quick search.

1. Open **School-Sets.nwf** from the *Navisworks BIM Practice Files\Analyze* folder.
2. In the *Saved Viewpoints* window, select **Section-1stFloorUtilities** in the *Sectioned Views* folder.
3. Open the *Properties* window and pin it. Note that the *Properties* window shows **0 Items Selected**.
4. In the *Home* tab>*Select & Search* panel, next to the (Quick Find) button, enter **Ducts** and press <Enter>. Note that Ducts are selected in the *Selection Tree* and all of the ducts in the project and are highlighted in blue in the scene view.
5. Review the ducts' properties in the *Properties* window, as shown in Figure 4–66.

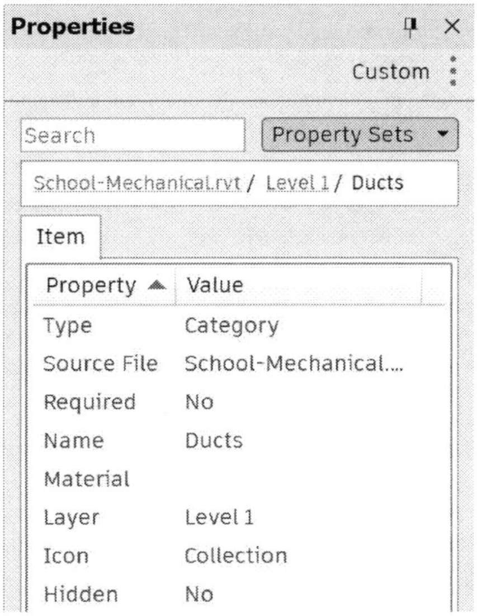

Figure 4–66

6. Click the (Quick Find) button or press <Enter>. Navisworks moves down one level in the *Selection Tree* and highlights **Radius Elbows/Taps**.

7. Click the (Quick Find) button or press <Enter> again. Now only one duct is selected. Note that there are more properties for individual ducts than for the group of ducts, as shown in Figure 4–67.

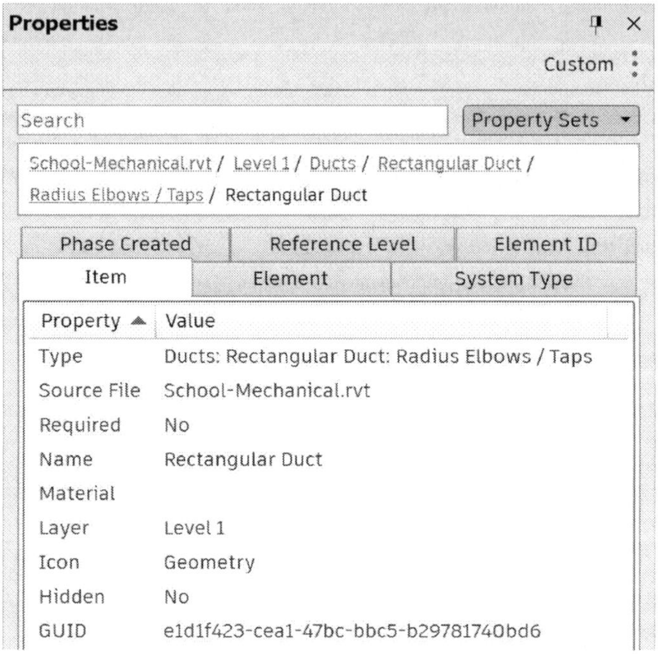

Figure 4–67

8. Continue clicking **Quick Find** to cycle through the ducts in the model, reviewing each duct's properties.
9. Unpin the *Properties* window.

Task 2: Use the Find Items window for an advanced search.

1. Open and pin the *Find Items* window so that it is docked on the bottom of the screen. If the *Find Items* window is not open as a tab along the bottom of the window, in the *Home* tab> *Select & Search* panel, click (Find Items), as shown in Figure 4–68.

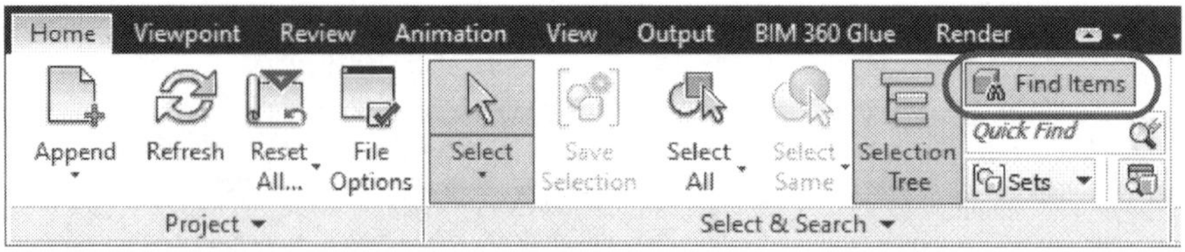

Figure 4–68

2. In the *Find Items* window, in the left pane, select **School-Architectural.rvt**.
3. In the right pane, do the following, as shown in Figure 4–69 (expand the width of the columns to see the information, if needed):
   - Click on **Add Condition** to display the table.
   - Under *Category*, select **Material**.
   - Under *Property*, select **Name**.
   - Under *Condition*, select **Contains**.
   - Under *Value*, enter **Brick**. (Note: Clear the checkmark from **Match Case**.)

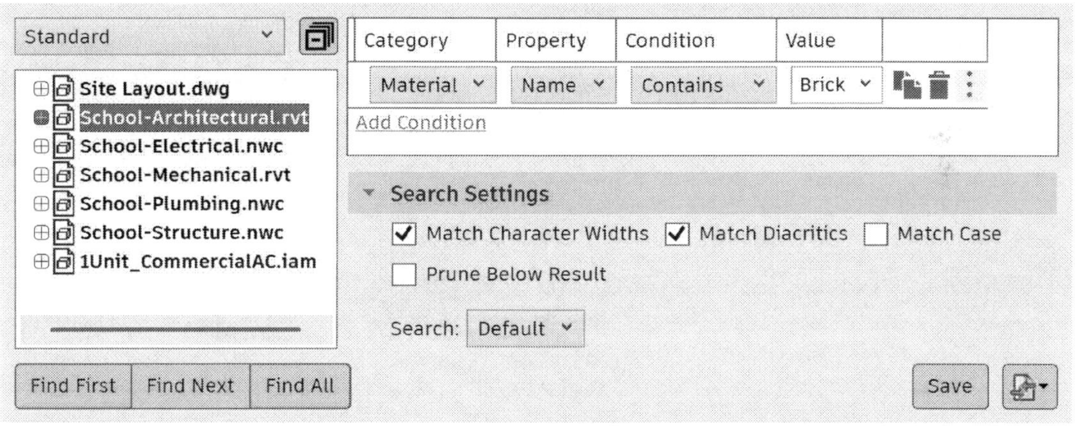

Figure 4–69

4. In the *Search Settings*, maintain the default Match options that are set.
5. Click **Find First**, **Find Next**, and then **Find All** and note what is selected in the model as you select each option.

Task 3: Save search sets.

1. In the *Sets* window, click  (Save Search), as shown in Figure 4–70. If the *Sets* window is not visible, in the *View* tab>*Workspace* panel, expand the *Windows* drop-down list and check the **Sets** checkbox to open the *Sets* window.
2. Enter **Brick Walls** for the search name and press <Enter>. Note that the icon indicates that it is a search set, as shown in Figure 4–70.

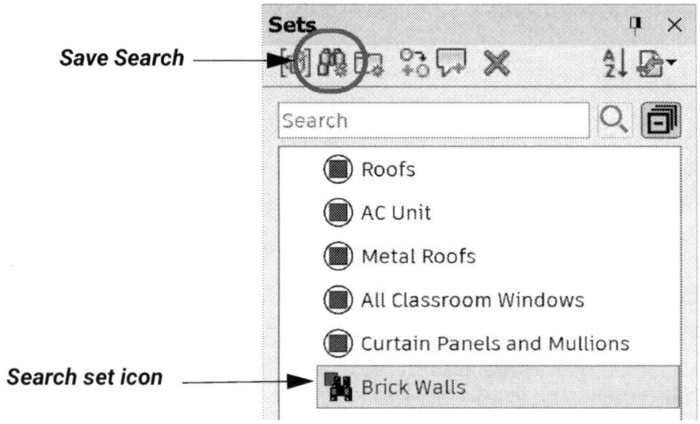

Figure 4–70

3. Clear the selection set.
4. In the *Find Items* window, create another search set that searches **School-Architectural.rvt** with the criteria shown in Figure 4–71. To create a new search, overwrite the existing cell's value by selecting it from the list or by entering a new value.

Category	Property	Condition	Value
Item	Type	Contains	Interior

Figure 4–71

5. Find all items with this criteria and in the *Sets* window, save the search and name it **Interior Walls**.

6. In the *Find Items* window, create another search in the **School-Architectural.rvt** model using the criteria shown in Figure 4–72.

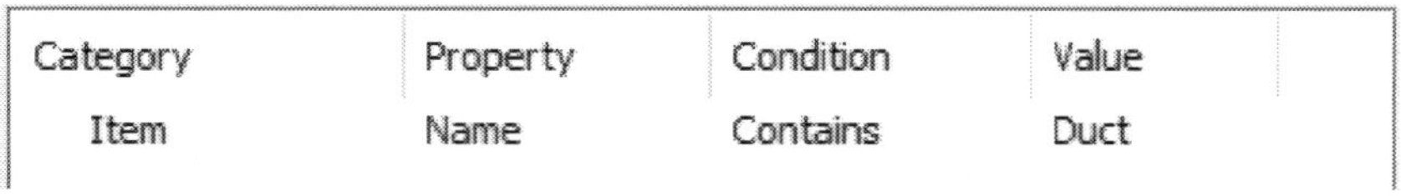

Figure 4–72

7. Click **Find First**. Note that **No Items Found** is displayed, as shown in Figure 4–73. This indicates that there are no objects that match this criteria in the selected architectural model. Click **OK**.

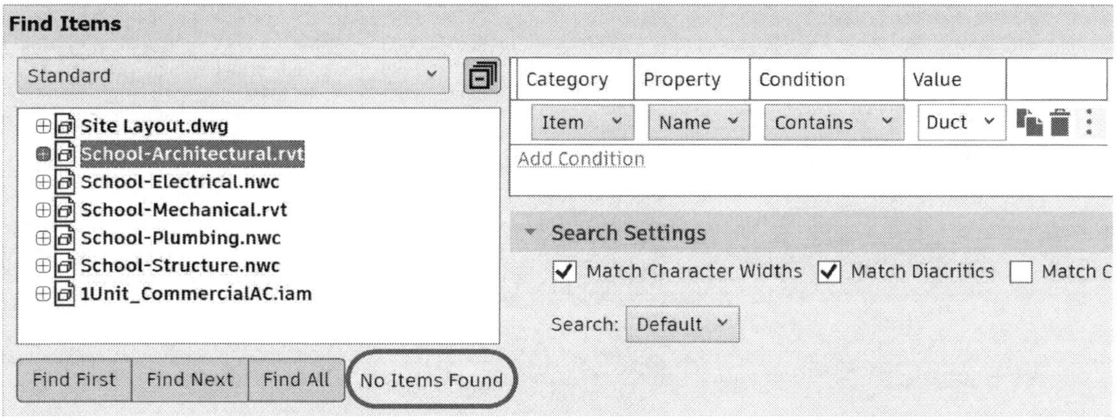

Figure 4–73

8. In the *Find Items* window, in the left pane, select **School-Mechanical.rvt** and then click **Find All**. The ducts are now selected.

9. In the *Saved Viewpoints* window, select **Section - 2ndFloorUtilities**. The ducts are also selected in this view. This is because the Find Items option is not affected by the viewpoint that is selected; it selects all items with the defined criteria. Open the *Selection Tree* and note that all items in the mechanical model that have "Duct" in their name are selected, as shown in Figure 4–74.

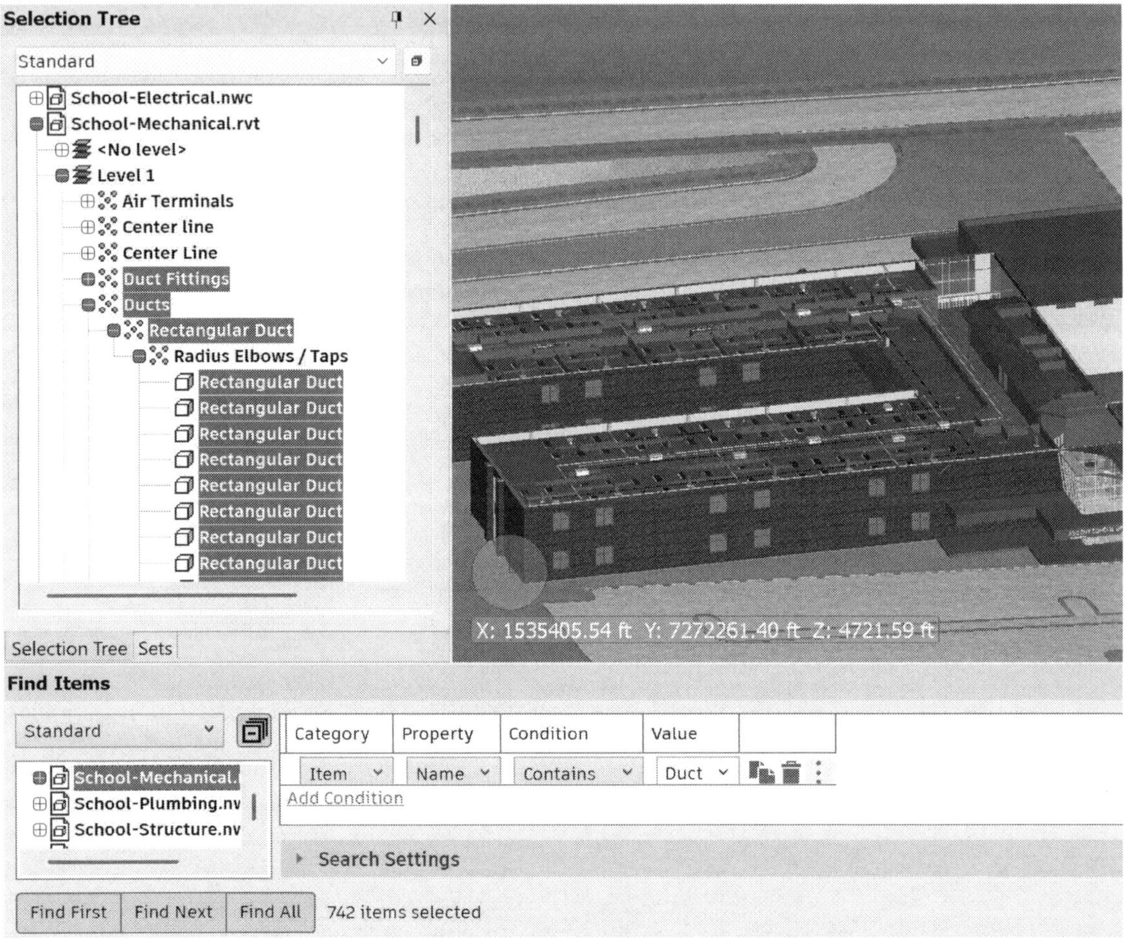

Figure 4–74

10. In the *Sets* window, click (Save Search), enter **Ducts** as the search name, and press <Enter>.

11. Clear the selection set. Zoom in on the lower-left corner of the building so that the pipes display as shown in Figure 4–75.

Figure 4–75

12. In the *Find Items* window, in the left pane, select **School-Mechanical.rvt** and then press <Ctrl> and select **School-Plumbing.nwc**.
13. In the right pane, set the criteria as shown in Figure 4–76. Ensure that you clear the **Match Case** option.

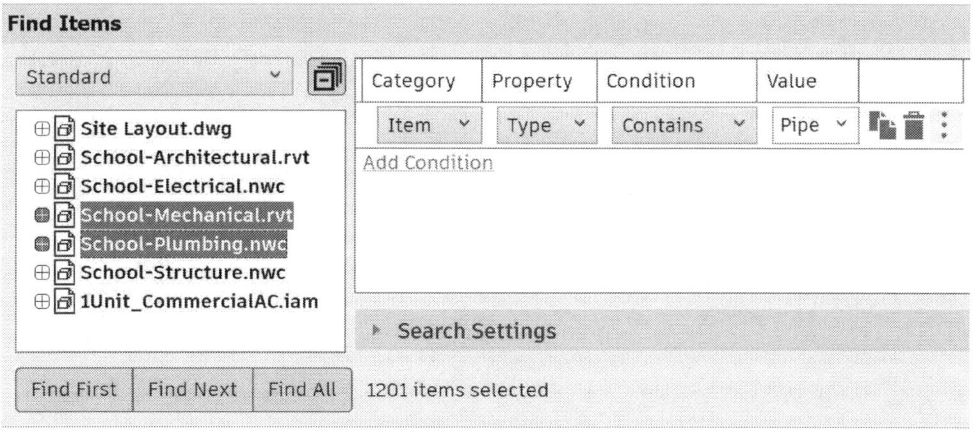

Figure 4–76

14. Click **Find All**. Pipes in both the mechanical and plumbing should highlight.

15. In the *Sets* window, click (Save Search), enter **Pipes** as the search name, and press <Enter>.
16. (Optional) As you have time, create separate saved searches for piping in the mechanical and plumbing files.
17. Save the file.

End of practice

4.5 Hiding and Unhiding Items

As you work in a model, it can help to hide items that are in the way or to isolate them so that you can investigate them more thoroughly. In the example shown in Figure 4–77, the brick walls, windows, AC unit, and structural model have been hidden to make viewing interior features easier.

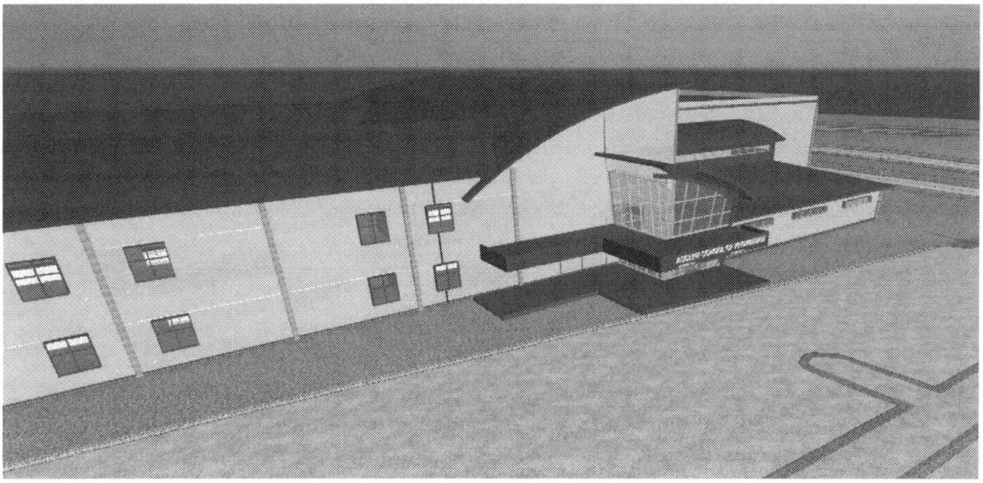

Figure 4–77

> ***Note:*** *Incorporating the use of saved sets and search sets can be helpful when you want to hide and unhide elements.*

How To: Hide Items

1. Select individual items in a scene view, in the *Selection Tree*, or using the *Sets* window. In the *Sets* window, you can select either a saved set or a search set.

2. In the *Home* tab>*Visibility* panel, click (Hide). The selected items are removed from the scene view and their names are displayed in gray in the *Selection Tree*, as shown in Figure 4–78.

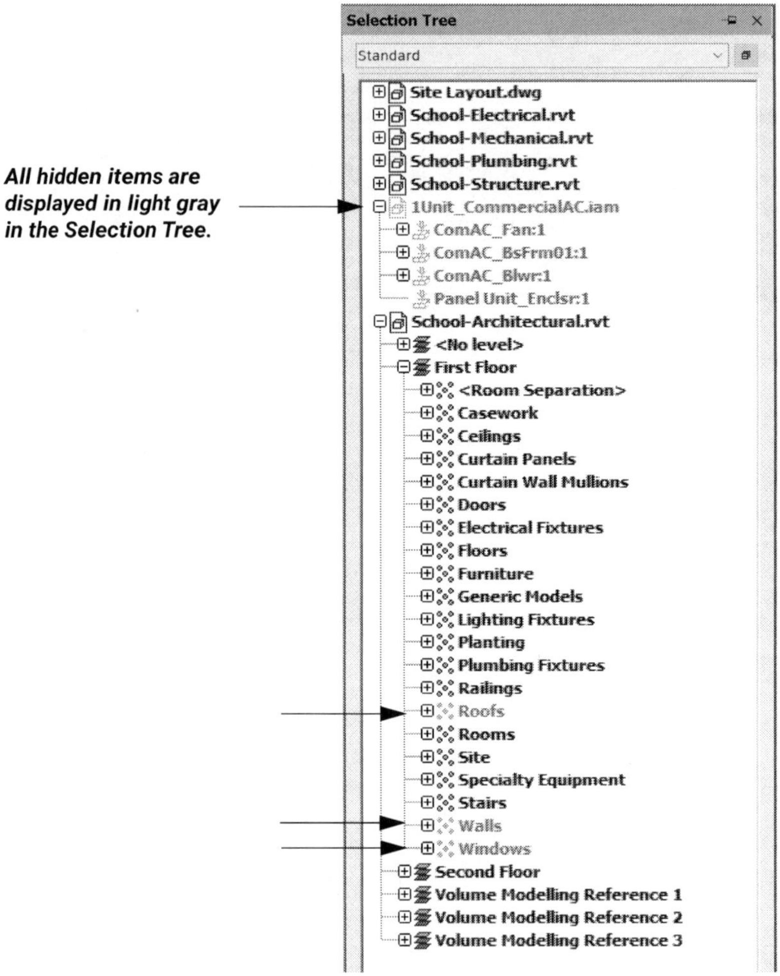

Figure 4–78

How To: Isolate Items

1. Select individual items in a scene view, in the *Selection Tree*, or using the *Sets* window. In the *Sets* window, you can select either a saved set or a search set.

2. In the *Home* tab>*Visibility* panel, click (Hide Unselected). Any items that are not in the selection are hidden.

Unhiding Items

- To unhide all hidden items, in the *Home* tab>*Visibility* panel, click (Unhide All).
- To unhide only specific hidden items, select them in the *Selection Tree*, right-click, and select **Hide**, as shown in Figure 4–79, to clear the selection. This toggles off the checkmark and unhides the items.

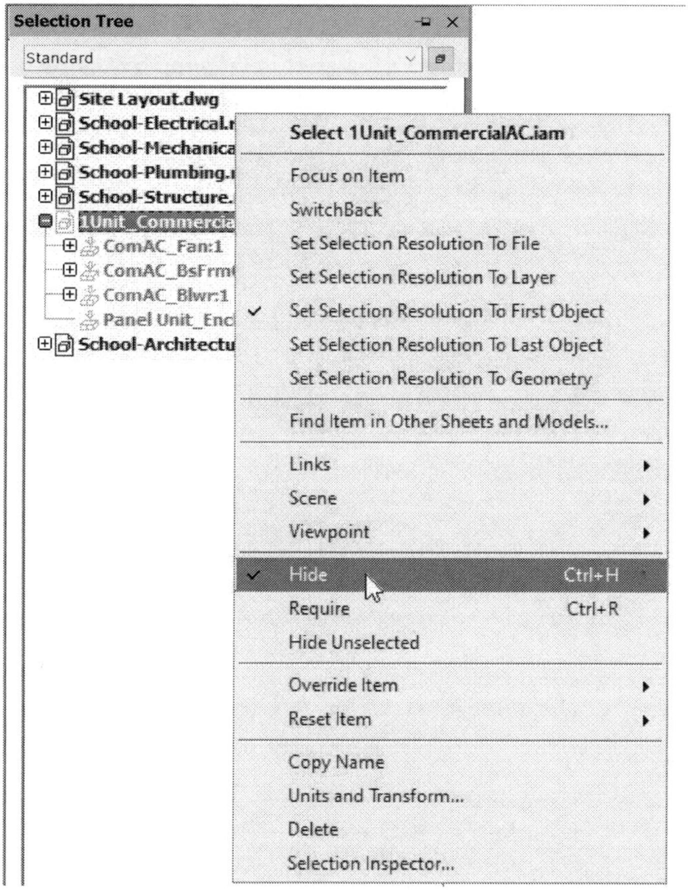

Figure 4–79

Hint: Required Items

To keep selected items displayed as you navigate through a model, you can select items and, in the *Home* tab>*Visibility* panel, click (Require). This can be helpful when you are using complex models so you do not lose the items when the scene regenerates. To toggle this option off, expand (Unhide All) and select (Unrequire All).

Practice 4d
Hide and Unhide Objects in a Model

Practice Objectives

- Hide objects in the scene.
- Unhide hidden objects.

In this practice, you will test out hiding sets of elements and use the *Selection Tree* to hide other elements as shown in Figure 4–80.

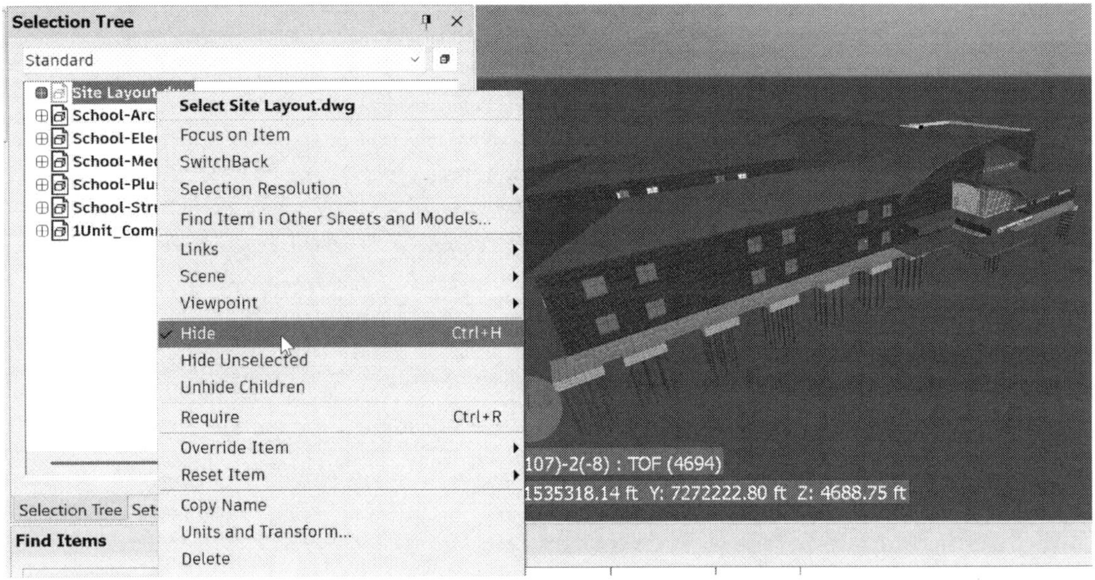

Figure 4–80

Task 1: Hide walls.

1. Open **School-Hide.nwf** from the *Navisworks BIM Practice Files\Analyze* folder.
2. Open the **Section-Entrance** saved viewpoint in the *Sectioned Views* folder.
3. In the *Sets* window, select **Interior Walls**.
4. Zoom in and reorient the view so that you have a clear view of all the walls that are selected, as shown in Figure 4–81.

Figure 4–81

5. In the *Home* tab>*Visibility* panel, click (Hide).
6. Clear the selection set.
7. Note that the selected items are hidden from display in the scene view and are grayed out in the *Selection Tree* (***School-Arcitectural.rvt*** *>First Floor >Walls*), as shown in Figure 4–82.

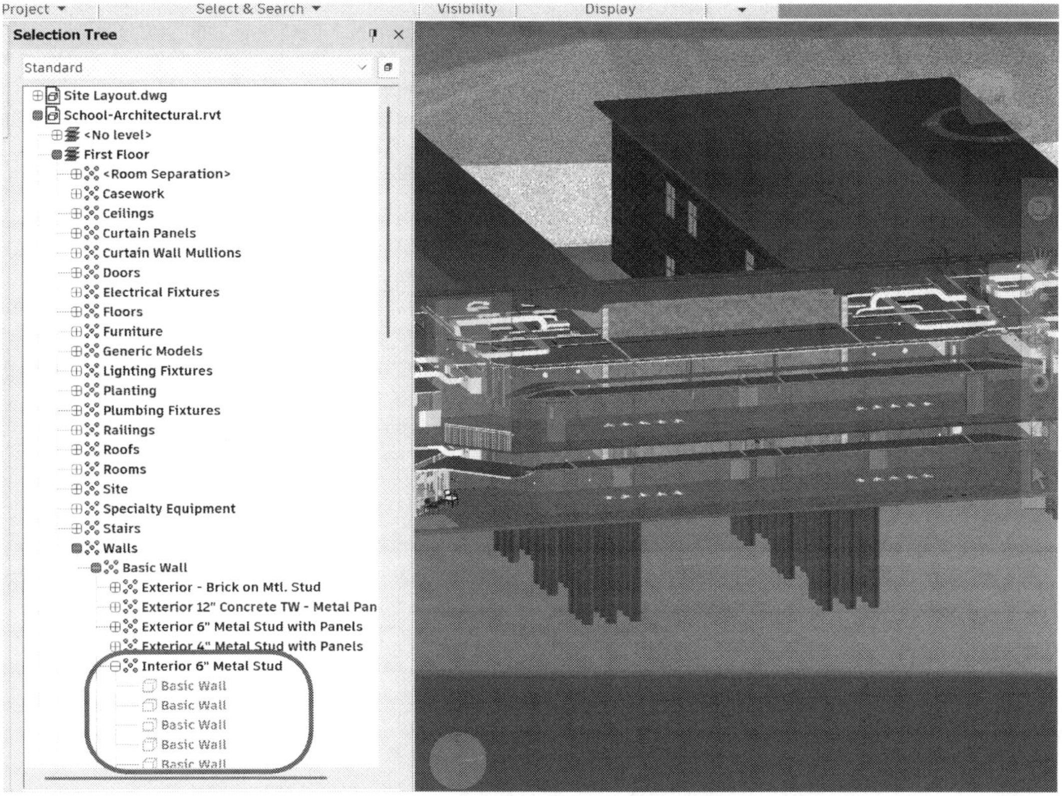

Figure 4–82

Task 2: Hide site elements.

1. In the *Selection Tree*, in the expanded **School-Arcitectural.rvt** file, expand **Second Floor** and select the **Rooms** site element.
2. In the *Home* tab>*Visibility* panel, click (Hide Unselected). All but the **Rooms** site elements on the second floor are hidden.
3. In the *Home* tab>*Visibility* panel, click (Unhide All). All items are returned to the display. You will remain in the sectioned viewpoint. Unhiding does not affect the active viewpoint.
4. With the second floor **Rooms** site element still selected, in the *Home* tab>*Visibility* panel, click (Hide). This hides only the selected **Rooms** site element.
5. Unhide all to return all items to the display.
6. In the *Selection Tree*, select **Site Layout.dwg**. Right-click and select **Hide**.
7. Select the **Start** saved viewpoint (*Exterior* folder) and note that all of the site elements are now hidden.
8. Save the file.

End of practice

Chapter Review Questions

1. Which selection tool would you use to clear the current selection while simultaneously selecting everything that is not in the current selection?

   a. (Select All)

   b. (Select None)

   c. (Invert Selection)

   d. (Select Same)

2. Once a selection set is saved, you cannot make any changes to it.

   a. True

   b. False

3. To view the properties of more than one element, which tool do you need to use?

   a. (Selection Inspector)

   b. (Quick Properties)

   c. (Properties)

4. Which Selection Resolution would you use to select the base geometry of an item, such as the material of a lighting fixture?

   a. File

   b. Layer

   c. First Object, Last Object, and Last Unique

   d. Geometry

5. How would you ensure that objects in the model that absolutely need to be visible do not disappear?
    a. Create a saved set.
    b. Create a search set.
    c. In the *Home* tab>*Visibility* panel, click (Require).
    d. You cannot make items remain visible.

Command Summary

Button	Command	Location
Selection Tools		
	Invert Selection	• **Ribbon:** *Home* tab>*Select & Search* panel, expand *Select All*
	Manage Sets	• **Ribbon:** *Home* tab>*Select & Search* panel
	Save Selection	• **Ribbon:** *Home* tab>*Select & Search* panel
	Select	• **Ribbon:** *Home* tab>*Select & Search* panel • **Quick Access Toolbar** • **Navigation Bar** • **Shortcut:** <Ctrl>+<1>
	Select All	• **Ribbon:** *Home* tab>*Select & Search* panel
	Select Box	• **Ribbon:** *Home* tab>*Select & Search* panel, expand *Select*
	Select None	• **Ribbon:** *Home* tab>*Select & Search* panel, expand *Select All*
	Select Same	• **Ribbon:** *Home* tab>*Select & Search* panel
	Selection Inspector	• **Ribbon:** *Home* tab>*Select & Search* panel
	Selection Tree	• **Ribbon:** *Home* tab>*Select & Search* panel • **Shortcut:** <Ctrl>+<F12>
Properties and Options		
Options	**Options**	• **Application Menu**
	Properties	• **Ribbon:** *Home* tab>*Display* panel
	Quick Properties	• **Ribbon:** *Home* tab>*Display* panel

Button	Command	Location
Find Tools		
	**Find Items**	• **Ribbon:** *Home* tab>*Select & Search* panel
	**Quick Find**	• **Ribbon:** *Home* tab>*Select & Search* panel
	**Save Search**	• **Window:** Sets
Visibility Tools		
	**Hide**	• **Ribbon:** *Home* tab>*Visibility* panel
	**Hide Unselected**	• **Ribbon:** *Home* tab>*Visibility* panel
	**Require**	• **Ribbon:** *Home* tab>*Visibility* panel
	**Select**	• **Quick Access Toolbar** • **Navigation Bar** • **Ribbon:** *Home* tab>*Select & Search* panel
	**Select Box**	• **Quick Access Toolbar** • **Ribbon:** *Home* tab>*Select & Search* panel, expand *Select*
	**Unhide All**	• **Ribbon:** *Home* tab>*Visibility* panel
	**Unrequire All**	• **Ribbon:** *Home* tab>*Visibility* panel, expand *Unhide All*

Chapter 5

Review and Mark Up a Model

The next step in the BIM workflow is communication. BIM was originally created as a way to increase communication and reduce RFIs. Learn how to measure the model and convert those measurements into markups to communicate to other team members what corrections need to be made. You will also explore how to mark up a scene using text, tags, and other drawing tools.

Learning Objectives

- Use measure tools to review model information and convert measurements to markups.
- Mark up scenes for review using text and drawing tools.
- Add tags and comments to elements in a model.

BIM Workflow: Communicate

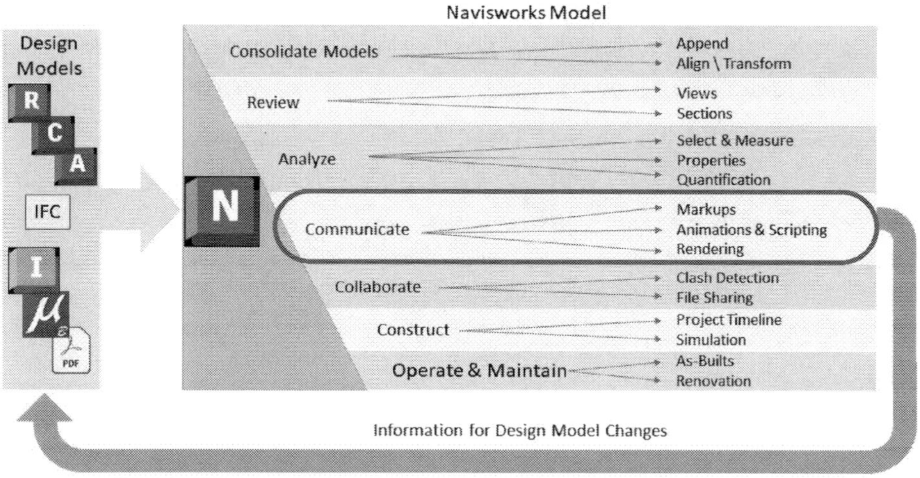

5.1 Using Measuring Tools

Measuring distances, angles, and areas in a model is a critical part of using Autodesk® Navisworks®. This information can be included in markup views sent to the architect or engineer as a request for information (known as an RFI) or to the construction superintendent to clarify a situation.

All measurements are based on coordinate geometry. The actual distance and the X-, Y-, and Z-axis distances can be seen near the item measured, as shown on the left in Figure 5–1. Additionally, you can open the *Measure Tools* window (shown on the right). To open the *Measure Tools* window, in the *Review* tab>*Measure* panel, click (Measure Panel).

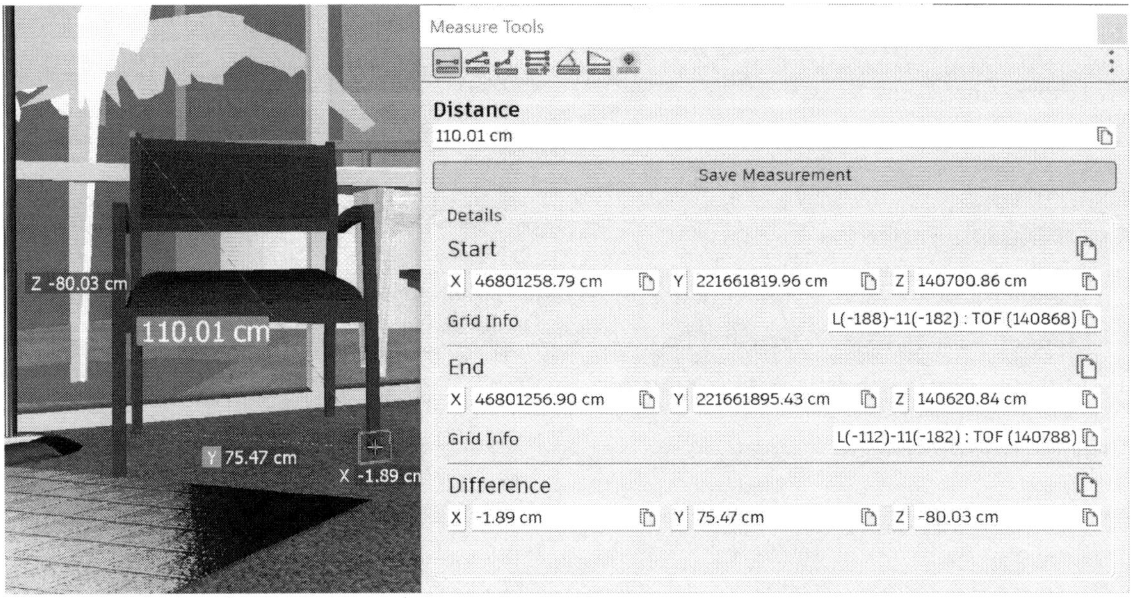

Figure 5–1

Note: *In the past, markups were referred to as "redlines"; however, markups can be of any color, so the term "redlines" is not used anymore.*

How To: Measure Distances

1. In the *Review* tab>*Measure* panel, expand (Measure) and click one of the measurement options (which are listed below).
2. Select the points to define the measurement. The following describes the point selections required for each measurement type:

   - (Point to Point): Select two points to display the distance between them.
   - (Point to Multiple Points): Select the first point and then a second point, then select additional points. The measured distance of each point is based on the original first point.
   - (Point Line): Select the first point and then additional points. The measured distance includes all selections along the path.
   - (Accumulate): Select two points and then two more points, continuing as required. The measured distance of all of the sets of points are added together.

   Note: *Prior to selecting a point on the model, you can hover your cursor over the model to display a tooltip to help identify the item name associated with the item, as shown in the examples in Figure 5–2.*

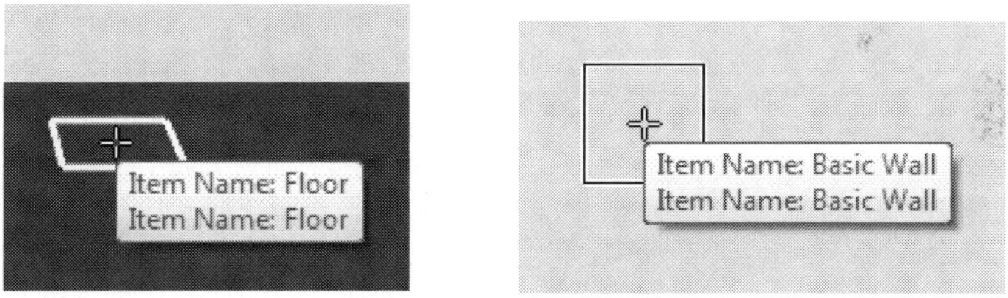

Figure 5–2

To clear a view of measurements, in the *Review* tab>*Measure* panel, click (Clear).

How To: Measure Angles

1. In the *Review* tab>*Measure* panel, expand (Measure) and click (Angle).
2. Select three points to define the angle. The second point defines the vertex of the angle. The dimension displays similar to that shown in Figure 5–3 as soon as the third point is selected.

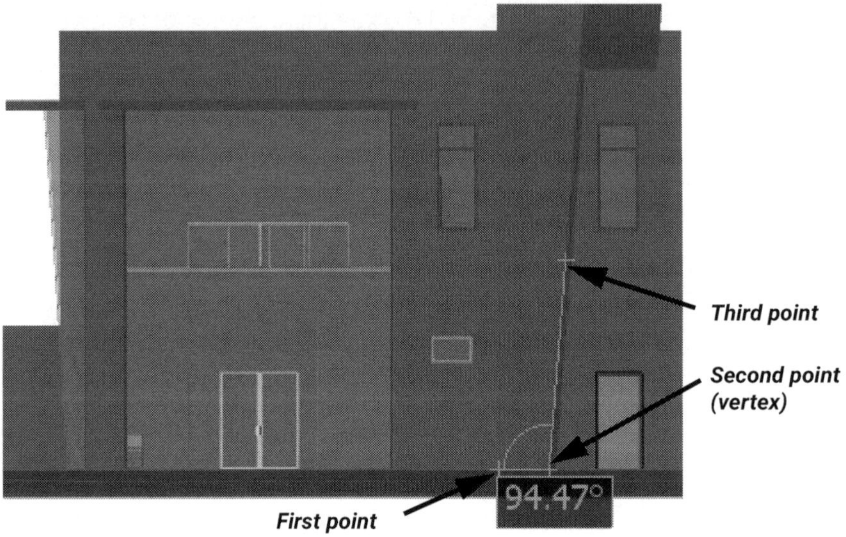

Figure 5–3

How To: Measure Areas

1. In the *Review* tab>*Measure* panel, expand (Measure) and click (Area)
2. Select at least three points to display the area.

3. Continue selecting points as required. The area updates as each additional point is added, as shown in Figure 5–4 with four points selected.

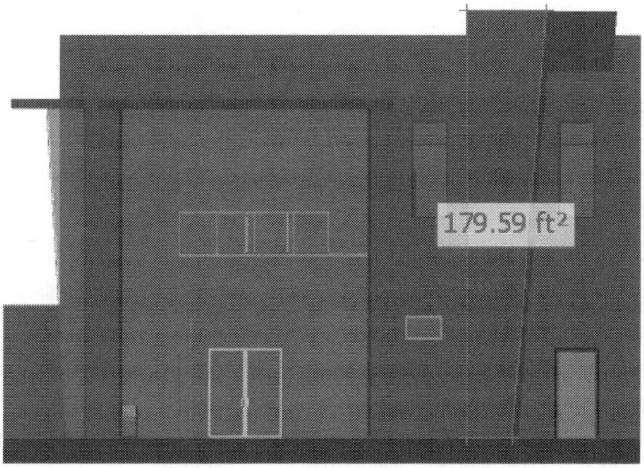

Figure 5–4

How To: Measure the Shortest Distance Between Two Items

1. Select an item, press and hold <Ctrl>, and select a second item.
2. In the *Review* tab>*Measure* panel, expand (Measure) and click (Shortest Distance).
3. The distance displays similar to the example shown in Figure 5–5 that is identifying the shortest distance between a rooftop AC unit and the edge of the roof.

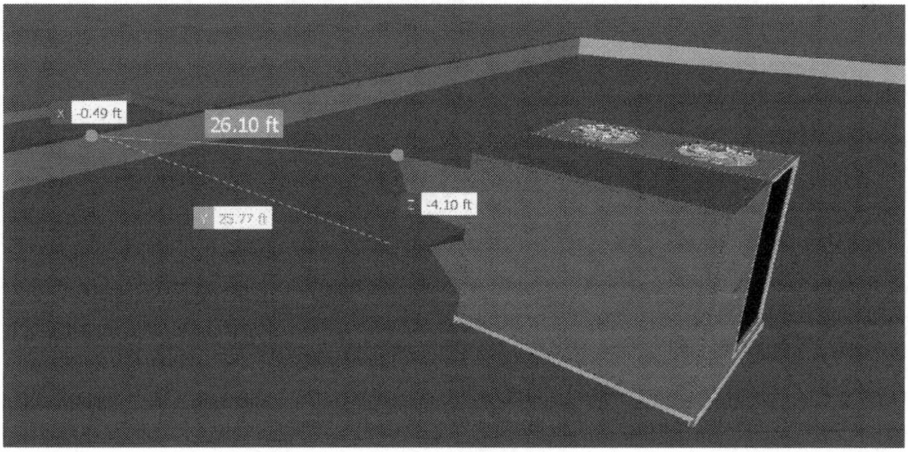

Figure 5–5

Working with the Locking Options

Many times you need to ensure that you are measuring exactly what you are expecting. The Lock options that are available in the *Measure* panel can help you focus the measuring tools to a specific plane. For example, in Figure 5–6, when measuring from the lower-left corner to the top corner, the Z-axis lock was set so that the other axes are not included in the measurement. In the left-hand image, the two points were selected as shown and the Z measurement was assigned. In the right-hand image, the second point was selected further along the X-axis; however, only the Z measurement was shown. The dashed line shows the offset from the Z-axis.

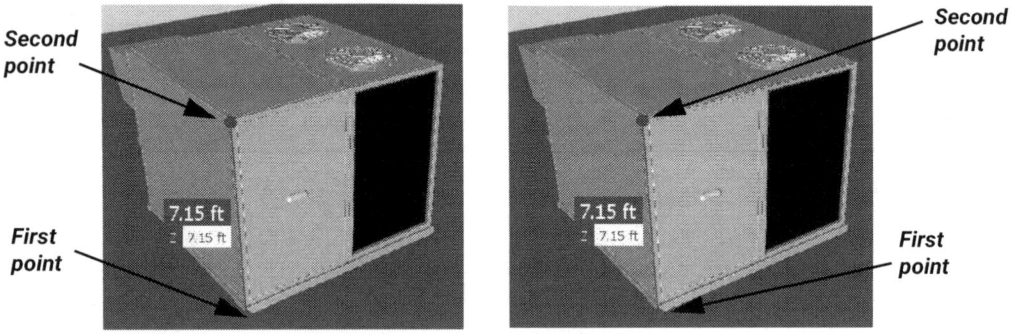

Figure 5–6

Locking Options

When you use any of the lock options, the measurement matches the specific axis direction color (X is red, Y is green, and Z is blue). To set a lock, in the *Review* tab>*Measure* panel, expand the *Lock* drop-down list and select an option from the list. The options are as follows:

- (None): No lock is applied. Measurements are included for all three directions.
- (X Axis), (Y Axis), (Z Axis): The measurement is locked to the specified axis. The color of each lock line matches the axis color shown in the gizmo, HUD icon, and other locations.
- (Perpendicular): The measurement is locked to the plane of the first selected point, and moves perpendicular to that plane.
- (Parallel): The measurement is locked to the plane of the first selected point and moves parallel to it. This is most useful when using the *Area* tool.

  Note: *Measurements of 3D models are based on selecting points on surfaces/planes. Sometimes, it can help to see these exact planes in Hidden Line display as you select the points for measuring. To view the model in Hidden Line display, in the Viewpoint tab>Render Style panel, expand* ***Mode*** *and click (Hidden Line).*

Hint: Measuring and Snapping Options

Many of the default options can be modified to fit your company standards or to help you get more precise measurements. These include setting up the color and thickness of the visual measurement, as well as customizing the tools to clarify what you are measuring.

To open the *Options Editor* to customize measurements, in the *Review* tab>*Measure* panel, click ↘. Alternatively, in the (Application Menu), click **Options**. In the *Options Editor*, expand **Interface** and select **Measure**, as shown in Figure 5–7.

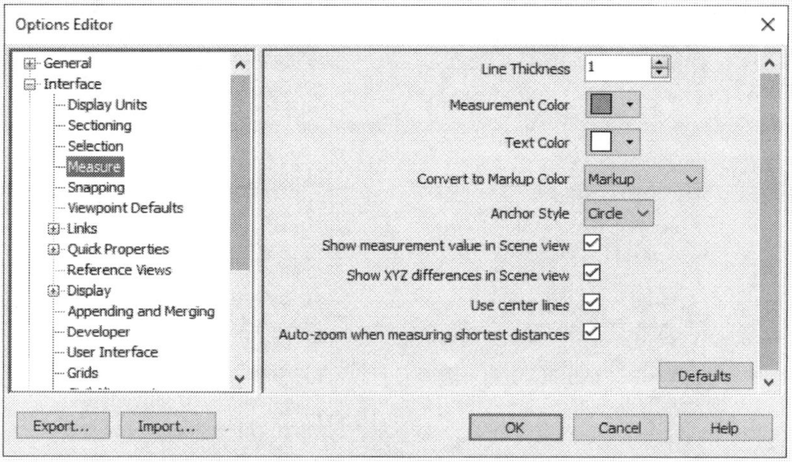

Figure 5–7

Snapping options are also important, especially the **Snap to Vertex** or **Snap to Edge** settings, as shown in Figure 5–8.

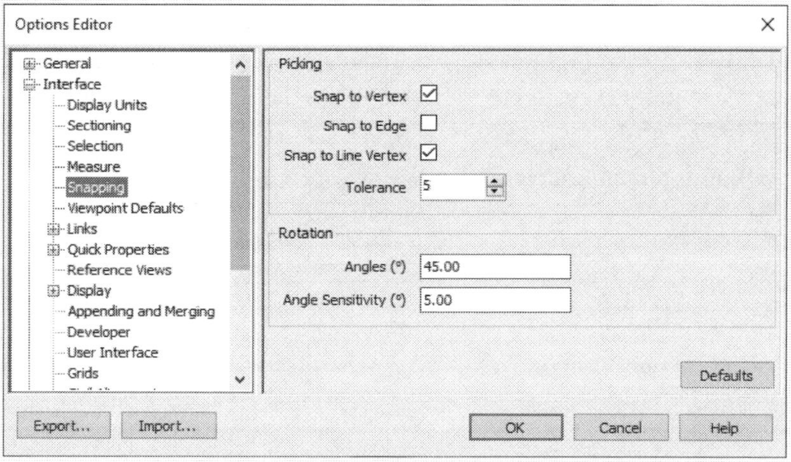

Figure 5–8

Converting Measurements to Markups

As you are measuring items, you might want to use the measured value as a markup dimension, as shown in Figure 5–9. To do this, in the *Review* tab>*Measure* panel, click (Convert to Markup).

Figure 5–9

- Each measurement must be converted separately, after it is created.
- When the first markup is added, a viewpoint is also automatically created in the *Saved Viewpoints* dialog box. Rename the view to help you retrieve it later. Any additional measurements that are converted to markups while the model remains in this viewpoint will also be added to the view.
- Additional markup tools are discussed in the next topic.

Practice 5a
Use Measuring Tools

Practice Objectives

- Measure the model.
- Convert measurements into markups.

In this practice, you will check the building model for accuracy. Then, you will turn those measurements into markups to communicate any issues to the design team, as shown in Figure 5–10.

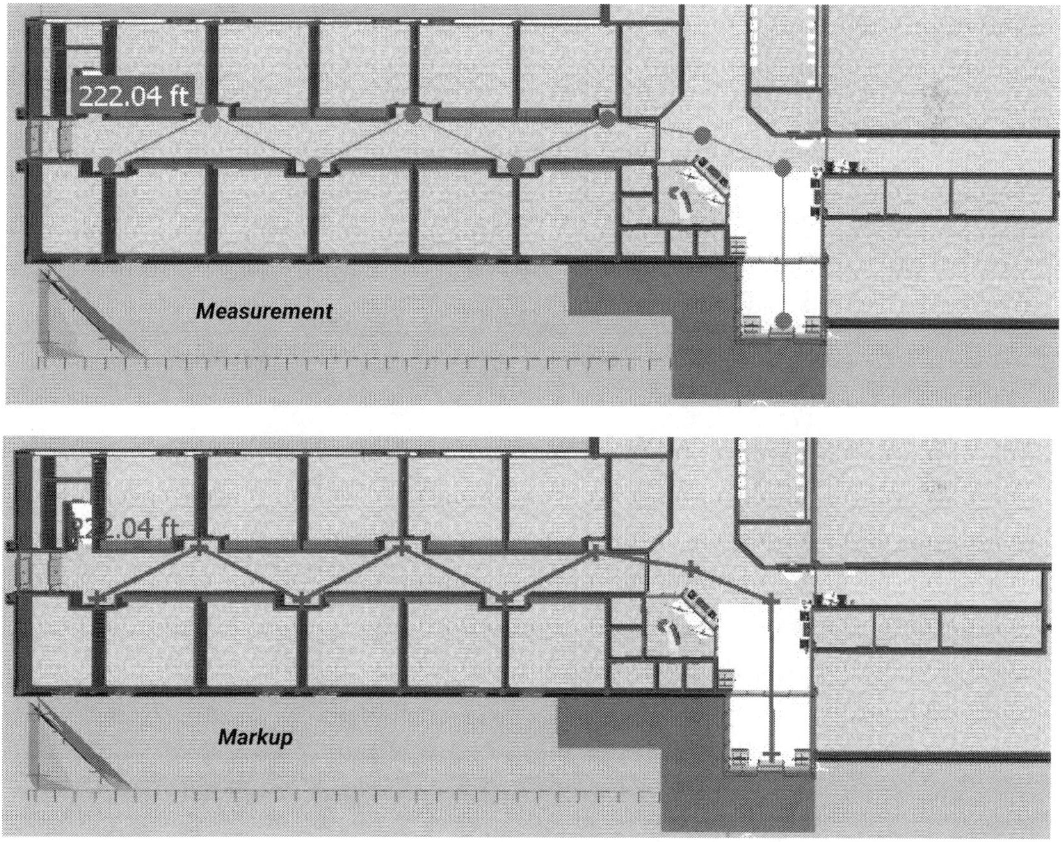

Figure 5–10

Task 1: Measure linear distances.

1. Open **School-Measure.nwf** from the *Navisworks BIM Practice Files\Markup* folder.
2. In the *Saved Viewpoints* window, select **AC Unit** in the *Exterior* folder.
3. Orient the AC unit as shown in Figure 5–11.
4. In the *Review* tab>*Measure* panel, expand (Measure) and click (Point to Point).
5. In the scene view, select the two points shown in Figure 5–11. This measurement displays the approximate size of the AC unit. Four distance values display: actual distance between points (orange), X (red), Y (green), and Z (blue). The dimensions will vary depending on the location of the points you pick.

   Note: *If the values display in units that you are not expecting, in the Options Editor> Interface section, verify the Display Units option is set as required. The dimensions will vary depending on the location of the points you pick.*

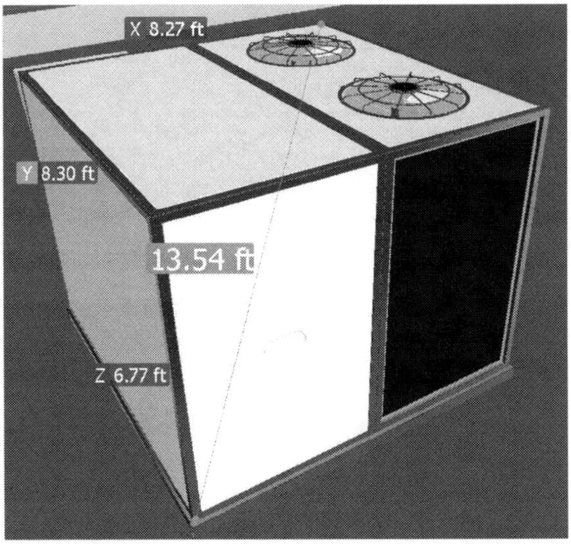

Figure 5–11

6. In the *Review* tab>*Measure* panel, expand (Lock) and click (X Axis).
7. In the scene view, select the same two points that you used in Step 4. Note that only the X (red) value displays this time, as shown in Figure 5–12.

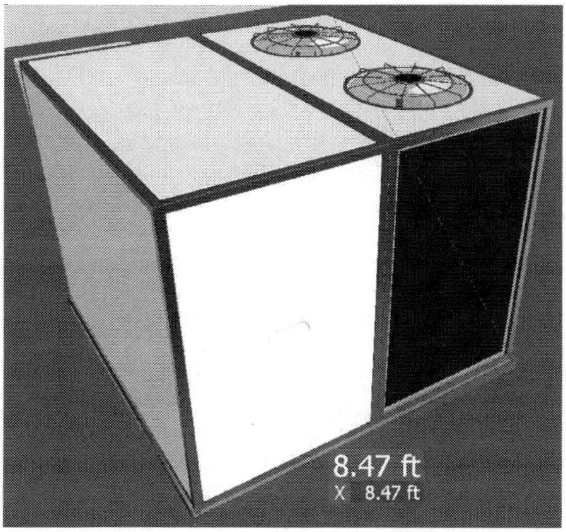

Figure 5–12

8. In the *Review* tab>*Measure* panel, click (Clear).
9. Return to the *Select* mode either by pressing <Ctrl>+<1> or by clicking (Select) in the Quick Access Toolbar.
10. In the *Saved Viewpoints* window, select **Section-1stFloor Layout** in the *Sectioned Views* folder. This viewpoint has been sectioned and oriented to the Top view on the ViewCube to display a plan-like view, as shown in Figure 5–13.
11. In the *Review* tab>*Measure* panel, expand (Measure) and click (Point to Multiple Points).
12. In the *Review* tab>*Measure* panel, expand the *Lock* drop-down list and select (Parallel).
13. Hover your cursor over the floor at the front entry. Once the tooltip displays indicating that you are selecting the **Floor** (as shown in Figure 5–13), click to select the floor as the plane that you will be measuring parallel to.

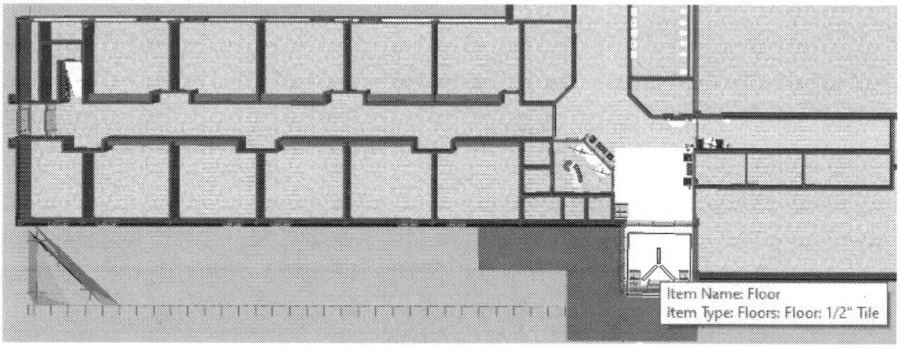

Figure 5–13

14. Clicka point near the front entry doors, and then another point near one of the doors down the hall, as shown in Figure 5–14.

    Note: *The dimensions will vary depending on the location of the points you pick.*

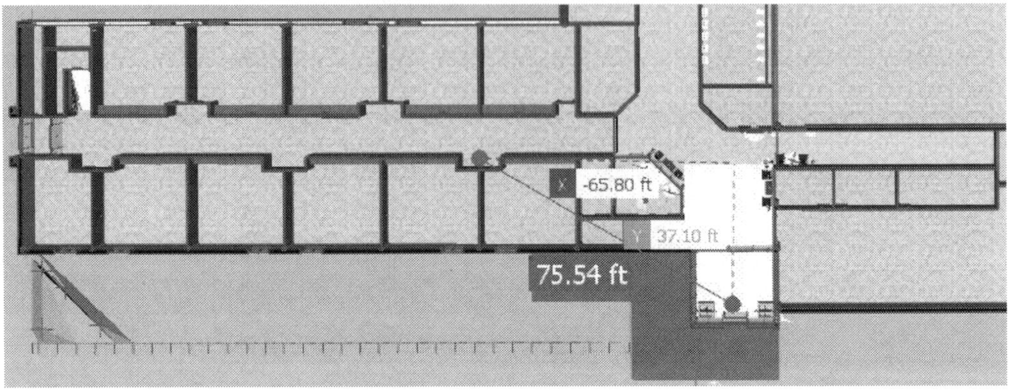

Figure 5–14

15. Select another point on the next door, as shown in Figure 5–15. Note that the first point is remembered. Test the distances for the other door setbacks to check them against egress requirements.

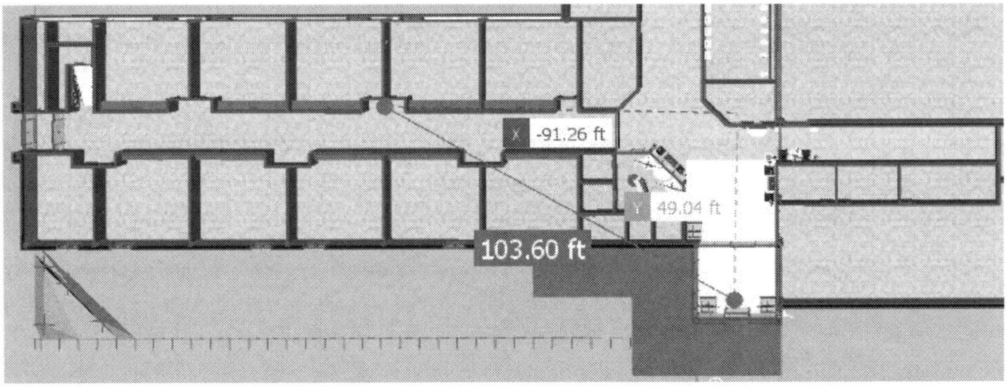

Figure 5–15

16. In the *Review* tab>*Measure* panel, click (Clear) to clean up the view measurements.

17. In the *Review* tab>*Measure* panel, expand (Measure) and select (Point Line).

18. Starting at the front entry, select the points shown in Figure 5–16. Note that the Parallel lock is still set.

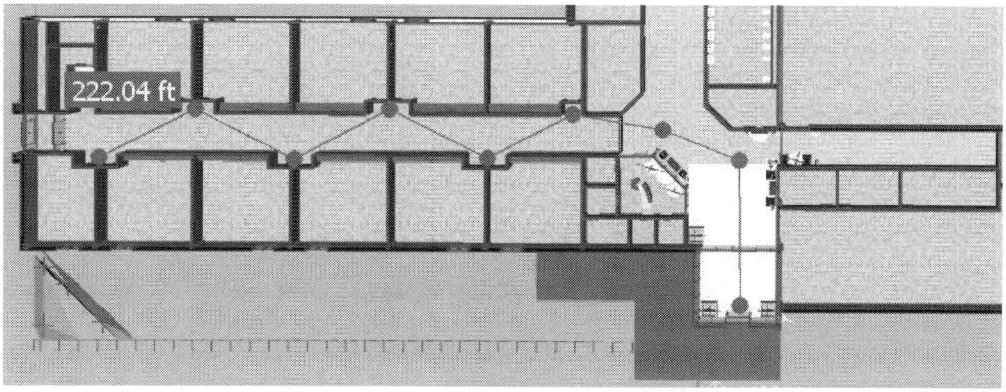

Figure 5–16

19. In the *Review* tab>*Measure* panel, click (Convert to Markup).
20. The viewpoint is saved with the markups included. Verify this by switching to a different viewpoint, then returning to the **Section-1stFloor Layout** viewpoint.

    Note: *If you even slightly change the view (e.g., zoomed or panned), a new viewpoint is automatically created and saved when you convert the measurement to a markup. Select the newly saved viewpoint and note the markups saved.*

21. Return to the *Select* mode either by pressing <Ctrl>+<1> or by clicking (Select) in the Quick Access Toolbar.

Task 2: Create additional linear measurements and convert them to markups.

1. In the *Saved Viewpoints* window, select **Office-Interior** in the *Interior* folder.
2. In the *Review* tab>*Measure* panel, expand (Measure) and click (Point to Point).
3. In the *Review* tab>*Measure* panel, expand (Lock) and click (Z Axis).

4. Hover your cursor over the floor under the chair until the tooltip displays (as shown in Figure 5–17), confirming that you have selected **Floor** as the *Item Name*. Click to set the first measurement point.

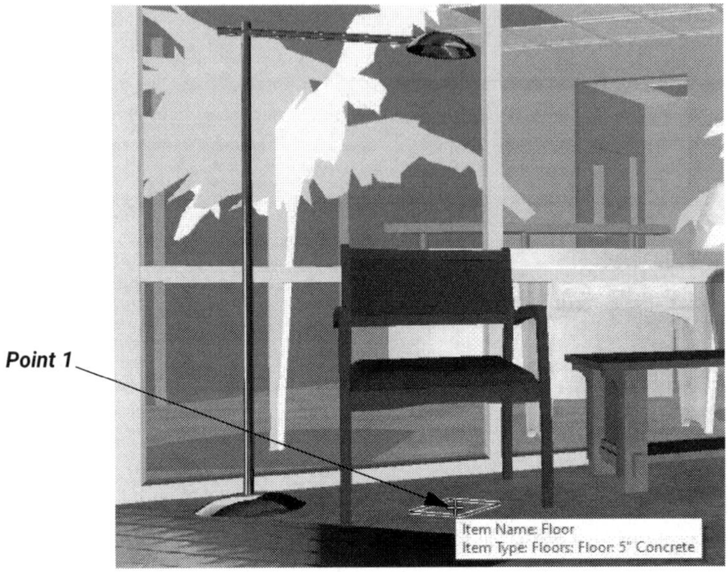

Figure 5–17

5. Select a point on the floor lamp. Ensure that the tooltip indicating that the *Item Name* is **Floor-Lamp** displays before selecting the second point. The Z measurement should display similar to that shown in Figure 5–18.

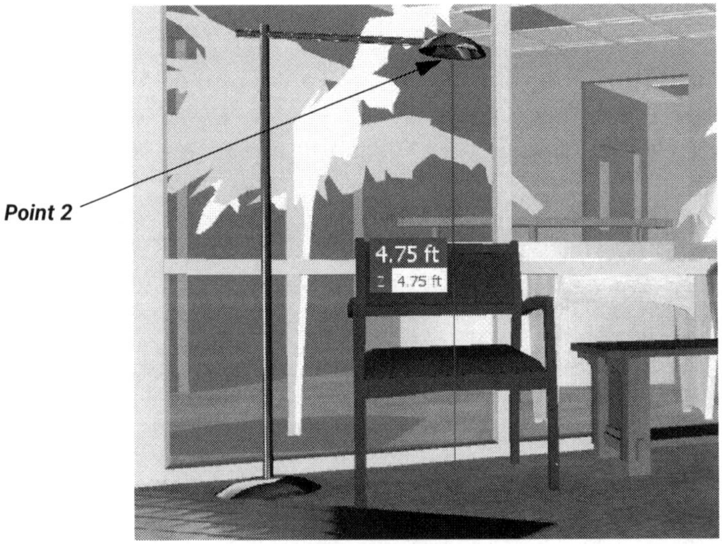

Figure 5–18

Note: *The dimensions will vary depending on the location of the points you pick.*

6. In the *Review* tab>*Measure* panel, click (Convert to Markup).

   Note: *When converting a measurement to a markup, it is added and saved with the current viewpoint. If the exact viewpoint is maintained, then the markup is saved with that viewpoint; however, if you reoriented the viewpoint in any way, a new viewpoint with the saved markup is created.*

   Note: *When you convert a measurement into a markup, it gets added to your current viewpoint. If you keep that exact viewpoint, the markup will be saved with it; but if you reorient or adjust the viewpoint at all, a new viewpoint is created along with the saved markup.*

7. Practice adding a few more linear measurements to the scene view and converting them to markups.

Task 3: Measure areas and angles.

1. In the *Saved Viewpoints* window, select the **Section-1stFloor Layout** viewpoint in the *Sectioned Views* folder or select the new viewpoint that was created with the saved markups in Task 1. This viewpoint contains the markup for the overall distance from the front entry to all the doors in the hall.
2. In the *Saved Viewpoints* window, right-click on **Section-1stFloor Layout** (or the new viewpoint) and select **Add Copy**. A copy of the viewpoint is created.
3. Right-click on the copied viewpoint and select **Rename**. Enter **Hallway** and press <Enter>. Note that this copied viewpoint still has the markup included.
4. In the *Review* tab>*Markup* panel, click (Erase). Draw a selection box around the entire markup by selecting the start point shown in Figure 5–19, pressing and holding the left mouse button, and releasing the mouse button at the end point.

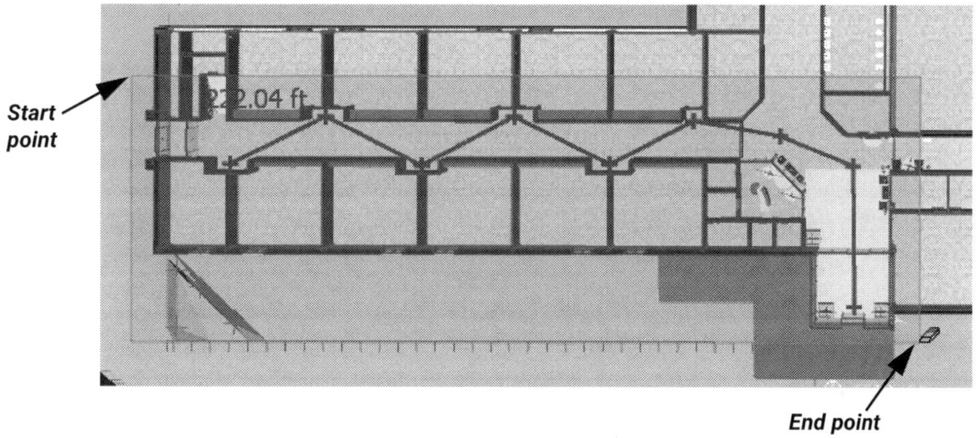

Figure 5–19

5. In the *Saved Viewpoints* window, right-click on **Hallway** and select **Update**. This saves the viewpoint.

6. In the *Review* tab>*Measure* panel, expand (Measure) and click (Area).
7. Set the measurement lock to **Parallel**.
8. Hover your cursor near the center of the hall and when the tooltip indicates that the *Item Name* is **Floor** (as shown in Figure 5–20), click to select the floor for the points to be parallel to.

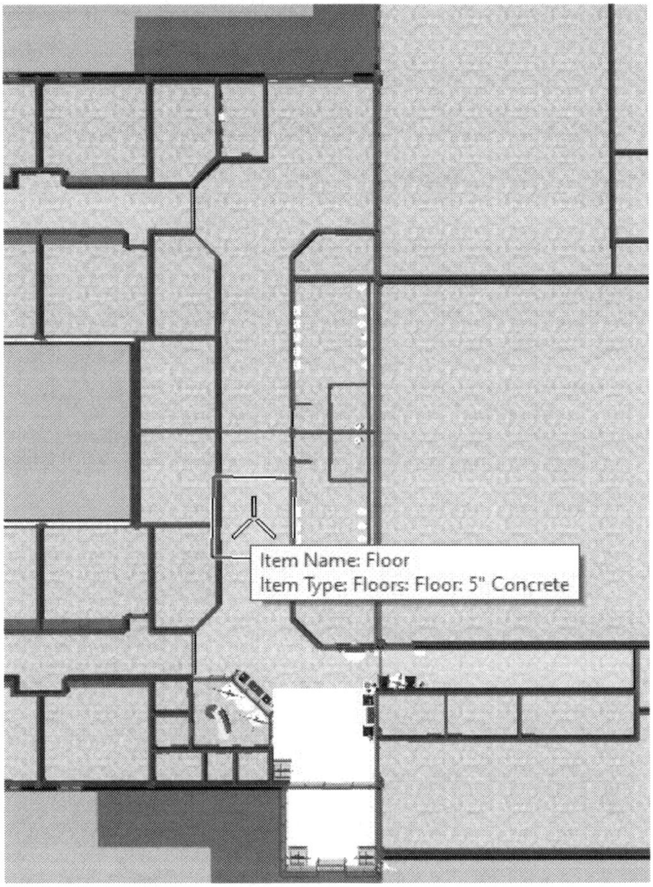

Figure 5–20

9. Begin selecting points that define the area of the hall, similar to that shown in Figure 5–21. It does not matter where you start, and you do not need to select the start point to close the area; this will be done automatically in the next step. This will measure the area of the floor in the hallway.

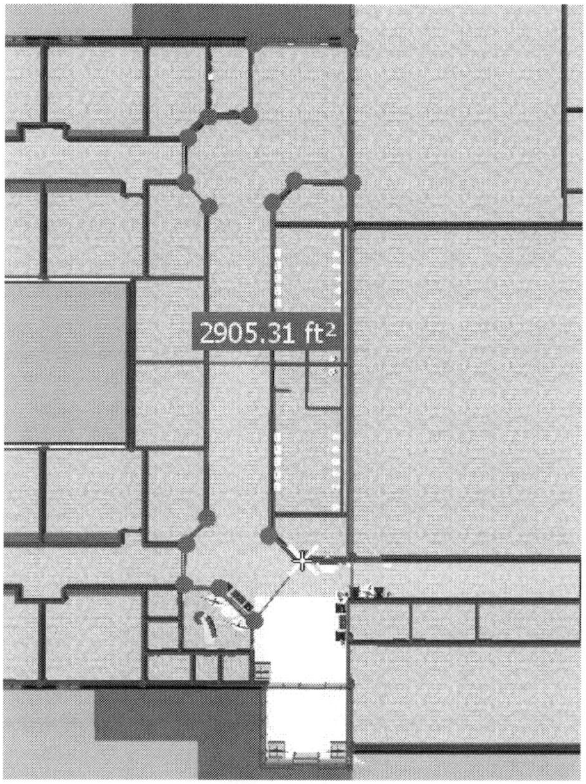

Figure 5–21

10. Convert the measurement to a markup.

    Note: *If you zoomed in to help select the points in the area, a new viewpoint will be created.*

11. In the *Review* tab>*Measure* panel, expand (Measure) and click (Angle).

12. In the scene view, select the points indicated in Figure 5–22.

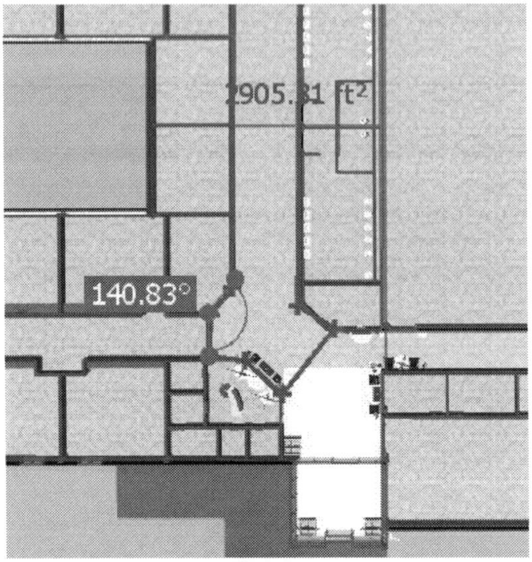

Figure 5–22

13. Click (Clear). This measurement does not need to be converted to a markup. Clearing removes the temporary measurement.

Task 4: Measure shortest distances between two selections.

1. In the *Home* tab, set the *Selection Resolution* i to **File** so that you can select files in the scene view.
2. Hide the **Site Layout.dwg** by selecting it in the scene view and pressing <Ctrl>+<H> or by right-clicking on its name in the *Selection Tree* and selecting **Hide**.
3. Reorient the model similar to that shown in Figure 5–23. Consider using the saved viewpoint called **Start** in the *Exterior* folder to begin.
4. In the Quick Access Toolbar, click (Select).
5. In the *Home* tab, set the *Selection Resolution* to **First Object** so that you can select objects in the scene view.

6. In order to find the shortest distance between the two exterior doors, you first need to select the two items and then start the command. In the scene view, select one of the doors (*Item Name* = **Curtain Wall Dbl Glass**). Press and hold <Ctrl> and select the second door, as shown in Figure 5–23.

7. In the *Review* tab>*Measure* panel, click (Shortest Distance). The shortest distance is **94 ft**, as shown in Figure 5–23.

Figure 5–23

8. In the *Review* tab>*Measure* panel, click (Clear) to clean up the view measurements.
9. Return the view to the **Front-Entrance Exterior** viewpoint in the *Exterior* folder.
10. In the *Selection Tree*, right-click on **Site Layout.dwg** and select **Hide** to clear it. The model is returned to the scene.
11. Save the file.

End of practice

5.2 Marking Up Scenes for Review

Annotating Markup Views

Sometimes it is important to add comments or other geometry in addition to measurements to fully communicate any questions you have regarding the design. In that case, you can mark up scenes for review using text, tags, and drawing tools, as shown in Figure 5–24.

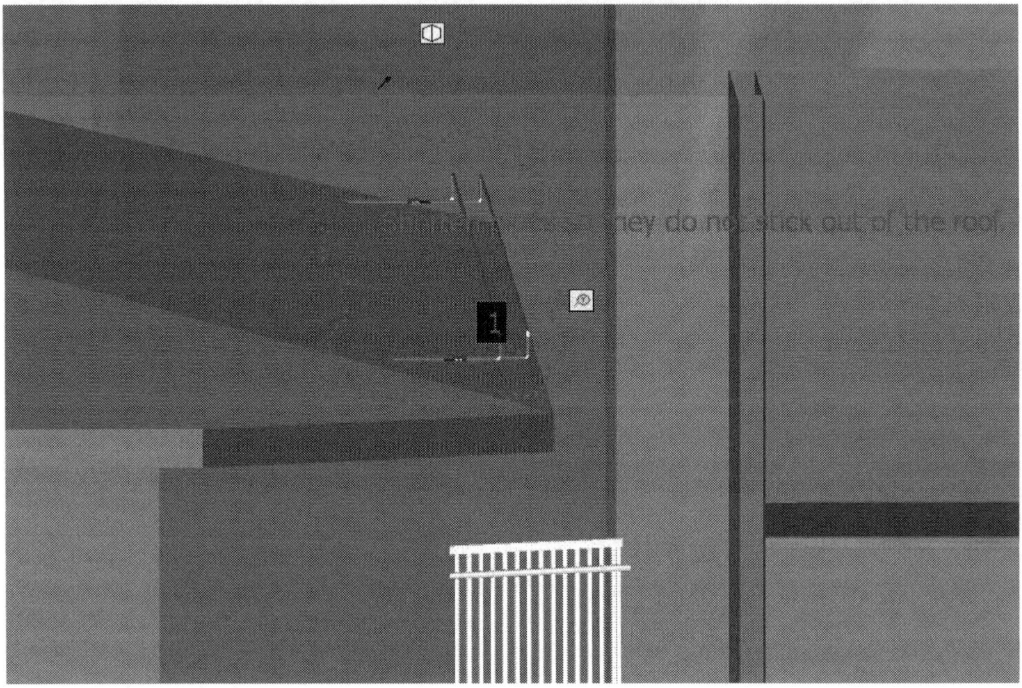

Figure 5–24

Consider the following when working with markups:

- Markups are saved in a viewpoint.
- When you navigate away from the viewpoint, the markups disappear.
- If a viewpoint is not already saved, a viewpoint is automatically added to the *Saved Viewpoints* window upon adding text or other markup geometry to the current view.
- If a viewpoint that contains a markup is deleted, the markup is lost with it.

How To: Add Text to a Viewpoint

1. Open the saved viewpoint where you want to add the text. If the view is not already saved, save a new viewpoint.
2. In the *Review* tab>*Markup* panel, click (Text).
3. Select a location in the model to place the text.
4. In the dialog box, enter the text you want to add (as shown in Figure 5–25) and click **OK**.

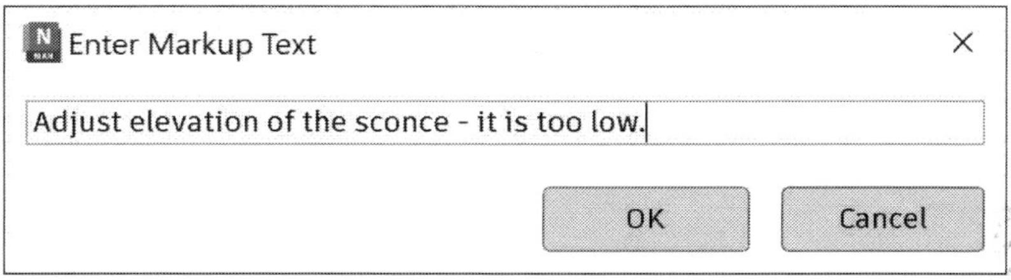

Figure 5–25

- Markup measurements, text, and drawings cannot be moved, but they can be erased. To erase markups, click (Erase) and draw a window around the entire markup item, as shown in Figure 5–26. If you select only part of the markup (as shown in Figure 5–27), the markup is not included in the deletion.

Figure 5–26

Figure 5–27

How To: Use the Draw Tools

1. Open the saved viewpoint where you want to add markups. If the view is not already saved, save a new viewpoint.
2. In the *Review* tab>*Markup* panel, expand **Draw** and select the required markup tool.
3. Draw the markup item by selecting points on the view to fully locate it. The following describes the selections required for each tool:

    - (Cloud): Click two points to create each arc of the cloud. The distance between the clicks determines the size of the arc.
    - (Ellipse): Click and drag to create a bounding box. When you release the mouse button, the ellipse is created inside the bounding box you selected.
    - (Freehand): Click and drag the cursor around to create lines. Release the mouse button to stop drawing.
    - (Line): Click two points to place lines between them. The lines are individual, not connected.
    - (Line String): Click to place the first point and then as many other points as required. The lines are connected.
    - (Arrow): Click to place the end point for the arrow line, and then click again to place where you want the arrow pointing.

    Note: *The most recently used markup tool remains on the top of the drop-down list.*

Hint: Set the Markup Tools' Color and Thickness

You can customize the Markup tools by changing the color and thickness in the *Review* tab>*Markup* panel, as shown in Figure 5–28.

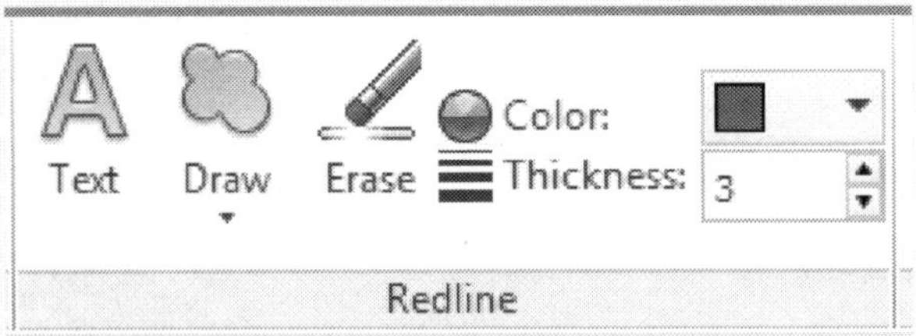

Figure 5–28

Adding Tags and Comments

The difference between adding text and a tag is that a tag places a marker in the scene view, rather than text. Once the tags are placed, you can review the comments added to tags in the order that they were added. In addition, tags enable you to see who added or edited a comment and the date that it was added.

How To: Add Tags

1. Open the saved viewpoint where you want to add a tag. If the view is not already saved, save a new viewpoint.
2. In the *Review* tab>*Tags* panel, click (Add Tag).
3. Click a point to define the placement location for the line.
4. Click a second point to place the tag.
5. In the *Add Comment* dialog box, enter a comment and click **OK**.

How To: Review Tags

1. In the *Review* tab>*Comments* panel, click (View Comments) to toggle the *Comments* window on. It can be resized or docked to make it convenient to review the comments.
2. Use any of the following tools to review the comments:
   - In the *Review* tab>*Tags* panel, step through the tags by selecting the arrow buttons or using their keyboard shortcuts. The comments are highlighted in the *Comments* window as you toggle through the list.
     - (First Tag): <Ctrl>+<Shift>+<Up Arrow>
     - (Previous Tag): <Ctrl>+<Shift>+<Left Arrow>
     - (Next Tag): <Ctrl>+<Shift>+<Right Arrow>
     - (Last Tag): <Ctrl>+<Shift>+<Down Arrow>
   - In the *Review* tab>*Tags* panel, enter a *Tag ID* number and select (Go To Tag) to highlight it in the *Comments* window.
   - If there are a lot of comments, you can use the search options in the *Review* tab>*Comments* panel. You can enter a search string in the Quick Find Comments area or select (Find Comments) and enter search criteria to locate a comment.

Hint: Merging Project Files

Since there might be multiple people reviewing and marking up the model, it might be necessary to merge markups. When project files are merged, markups from other users are copied into one file without creating duplicates.

You can use either of the following methods to merge markups:

- In the *Home* tab>*Project* panel, expand (Append) and click (Merge).
- In the Quick Access Toolbar, expand (Open) and click **Merge**.

Practice 5b
Mark Up Scenes for Review

Practice Objectives

- Add text to communicate a question regarding the design.
- Create markup geometry to draw attention to specific parts of the design.
- Merge project files.

In this practice, you will markup the model to communicate questions and issues to the appropriate teams, as shown in Figure 5–29. You will then merge in another Autodesk Navisworks file and review additional markups.

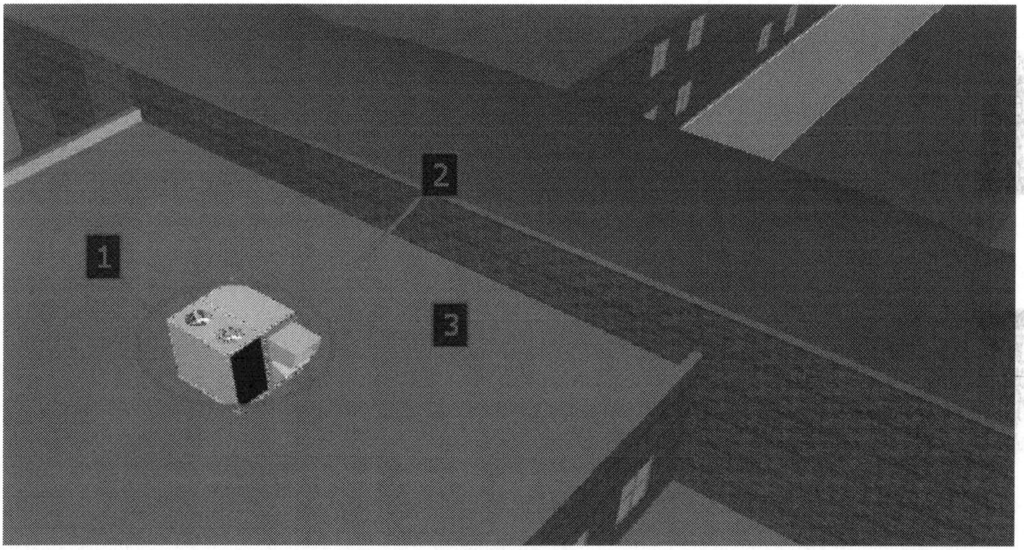

Figure 5–29

Task 1: Add markup dimensions and text to the entrance section.

1. Open **School-Markup.nwf** from the *Navisworks BIM Practice Files\Markup* folder.
2. In the *Saved Viewpoints* window, select **Section-EntrancePlatform** from the *Sectioned Views* folder. This is a view of the front entrance's concrete platform.

3. Hide all but the **Site Layout.dwg** and the **School-Architectural.rvt** files. This will help simplify the display, as shown in Figure 5–30.

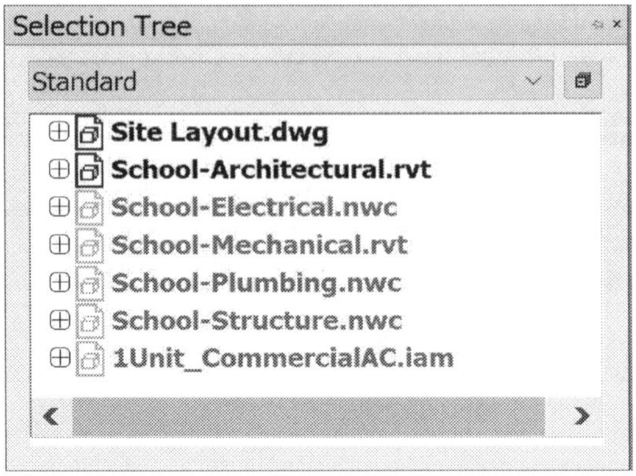

Figure 5–30

4. Zoom and reorient the view similar to that shown in Figure 5–31 to clearly see the ground surface and the concrete platform. Note that the **Site Layout.dwg** file is not exactly positioned under the entrance's concrete platform.
5. Add a **Point to Point** measurement from the base of the entrance concrete platform to the green surface that is representing the topography, as shown in Figure 5–31. Your dimensions might be different depending on the exact points you snap to.

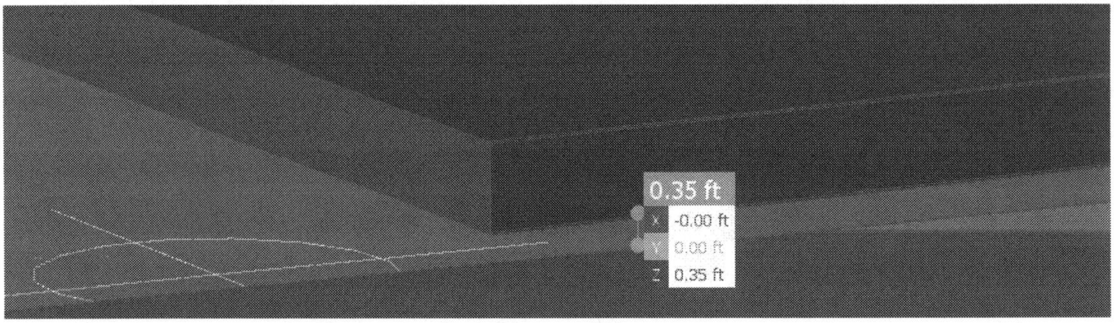

Figure 5–31

6. Once created, convert the measurement to a markup.
7. Because you changed the zoom level, a new view will be created. Click on the new view name in the *Saved Viewpoints* window, enter **Entrance Elevation Change Comments** as its name, and press <Enter>. Select it in the *Saved Viewpoints* window to make it active.

8. In the *Review* tab>*Markup* panel, click (Text).
9. Select below the markup dimension to position the text.
10. In the *Enter Markup Text* dialog box, enter the comment **Adjust elevation of the surface**, as shown in Figure 5–32, and click **OK**.

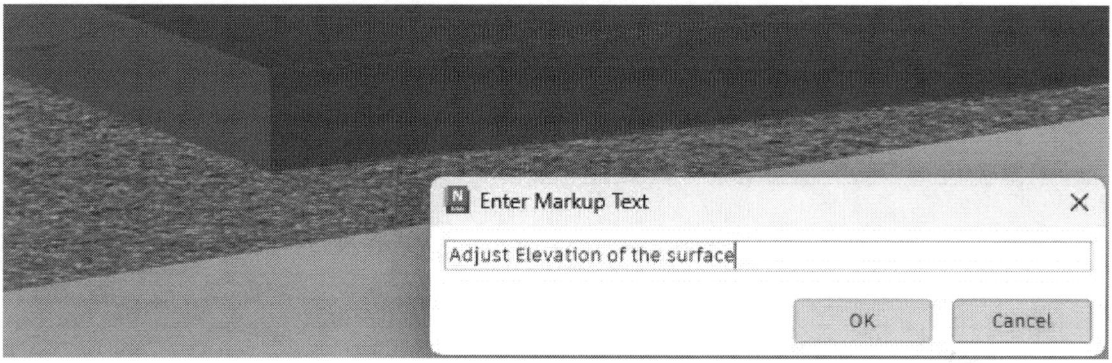

Figure 5–32

11. Without changing the viewpoint, in the *Review* tab>*Markup* panel, expand **Draw** and click (Cloud).
12. In the scene view, click points in a clockwise direction to create each arc of the cloud, as shown in Figure 5–33. The markup information is automatically saved with the viewpoint.

    Note: *The distance between the clicks determines the size of the arc.*

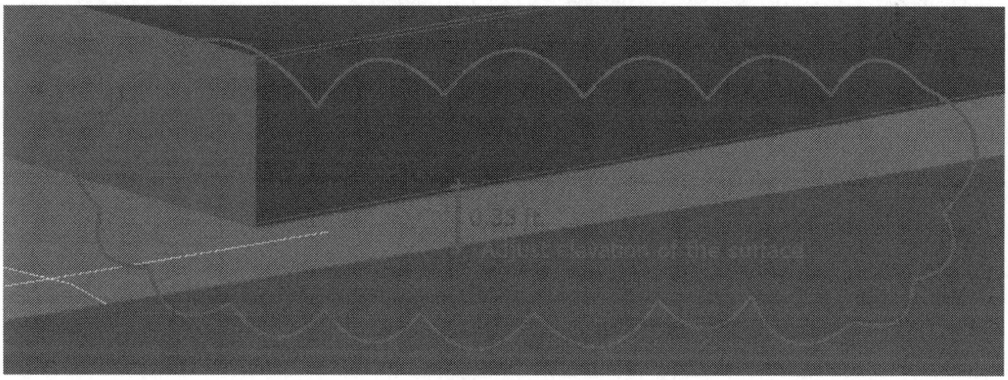

Figure 5–33

13. Save the file.

Task 2: Use markup graphics and tags.

1. In the *Saved Viewpoints* window, select **NE-View**.
2. Right-click on the viewpoint name and click **Save Viewpoint**. Enter **AC Relocation Comments** as the name for the new viewpoint and press <Enter>.
3. Unhide all of the models that were previously hidden. The AC unit is now visible on the roof of the gym.
4. With the **AC Relocation Comments** viewpoint still active, zoom in on the AC unit.
5. In the *Saved Viewpoints* window, right-click on the **AC Relocation Comments** viewpoint and select **Update** to save the changes to the view's zoom level.
6. In the *Review* tab>*Markup* panel, expand **Draw** and click (Ellipse).
7. In the scene view, click and drag to draw the bounding box around the AC unit, as shown on the left in Figure 5–34. When you release the mouse button, the ellipse is created inside the bounding box you selected, as shown on the right in Figure 5–35.

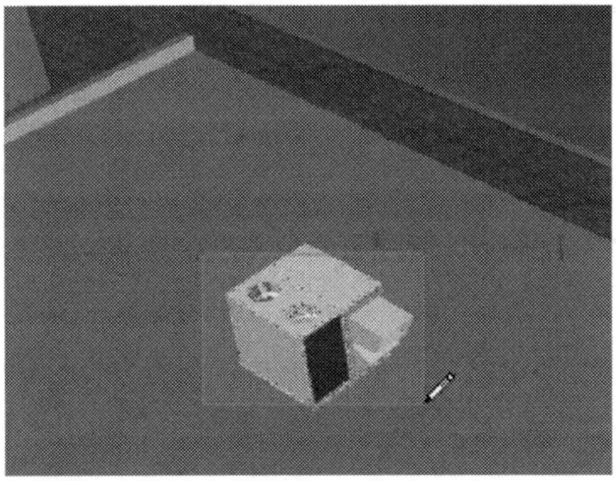

Figure 5–34

Figure 5–35

8. In the *Review* tab>*Tags* panel, click (Add Tag).
9. Click on the ellipse to define the tag's leader start point, similar to that shown in Figure 5–36.
10. Click a second location to place the tag, similar to that shown in Figure 5–36.
11. In the *Add Comment* dialog box, enter the comment **Move AC Unit 10ft towards wall** (as shown in Figure 5–36) and click **OK**.

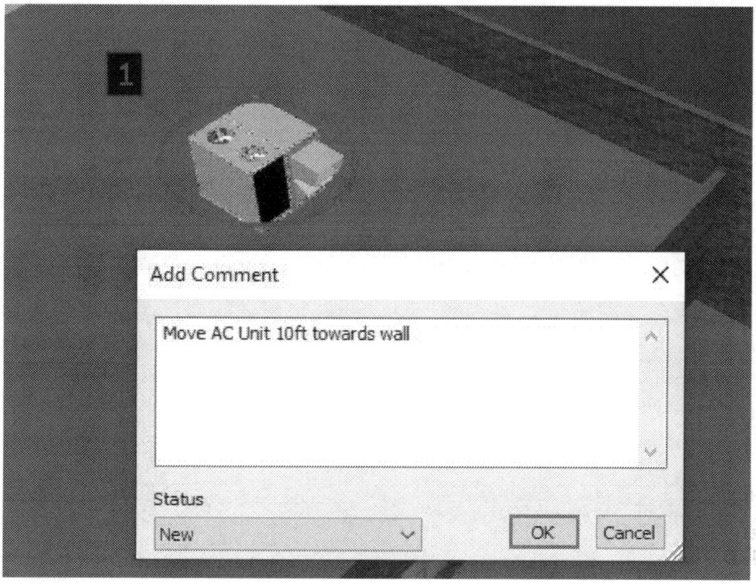

Figure 5–36

12. In the *Review* tab>*Tags* panel, click (Add Tag).
13. Click on the roof (similar to Figure 5–37) to define the tag's leader start point.
14. Click a second location to place the tag, similar to that shown in Figure 5–37.
15. In the *Add Comment* dialog box, enter the comment **New location of the AC Unit** (as shown in Figure 5–37) and click **OK**.

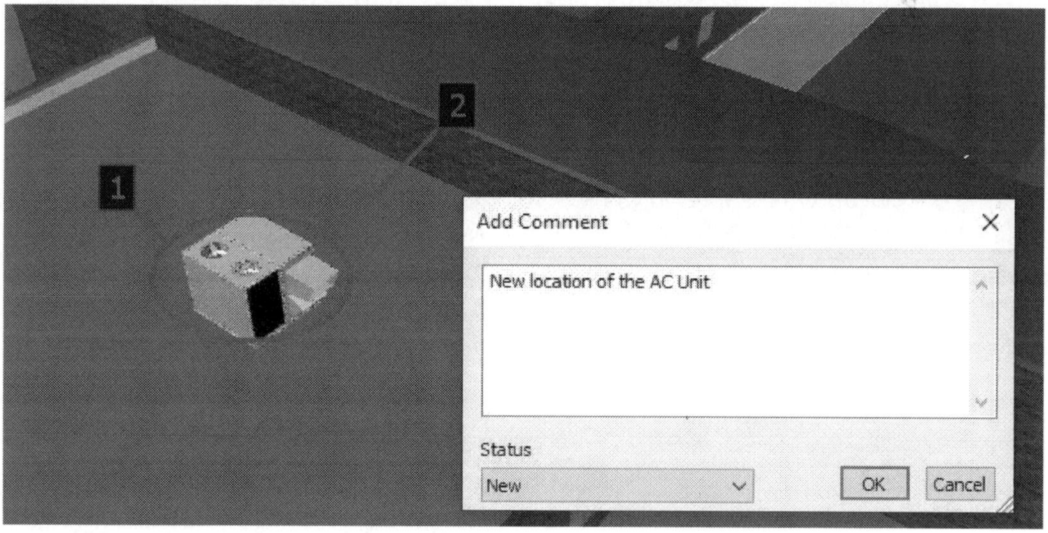

Figure 5–37

16. Add an additional tag to the AC unit with the following comment: **AC Unit is too small for building. Replace with larger unit.** To place the tag without a leader, double-click on the placement location.
17. Open the *Comments* window. By default, it is compressed along the bottom of the interface.
    - The *Comments* window should display at the bottom of the screen. If it does not display, in the *Comments* tab>*Tags* panel, click (View Comments).
18. Pin the *Comments* window.
19. Step through the tags in the *Review* tab>*Tags* panel by selecting the arrow buttons:
    - (First Tag)
    - (Previous Tag)
    - (Next Tag)
    - (Last Tag)
20. Save the file.

Task 3: Merge files and review comments.

1. Pin the *Saved Viewpoints* window open, if not already open. Note the number of viewpoints that are currently listed at the same level as the folders.
2. In the *Home* tab>*Project* panel, expand (Append) and click (Merge).
3. In the *Merge* dialog box, select **School-Markup-Mechanical.nwf** and click **Open**.
4. Review the *Saved Viewpoints* window again. After the merge, two views have been added (**Front** and **Mechanical Redline**). These are viewpoints that existed in the **School-Markup-Mechanical.nwf** file and were merged into the current file.
5. Note in the *Selection Tree* that only one Architectural model exists. This is because merging does not duplicate new geometry. It will only merge new items.
6. In the *Saved Viewpoints* window, select **Mechanical Redline**.

7. Open the *Comments* window and review the comments in this viewpoint, as shown in Figure 5–38.

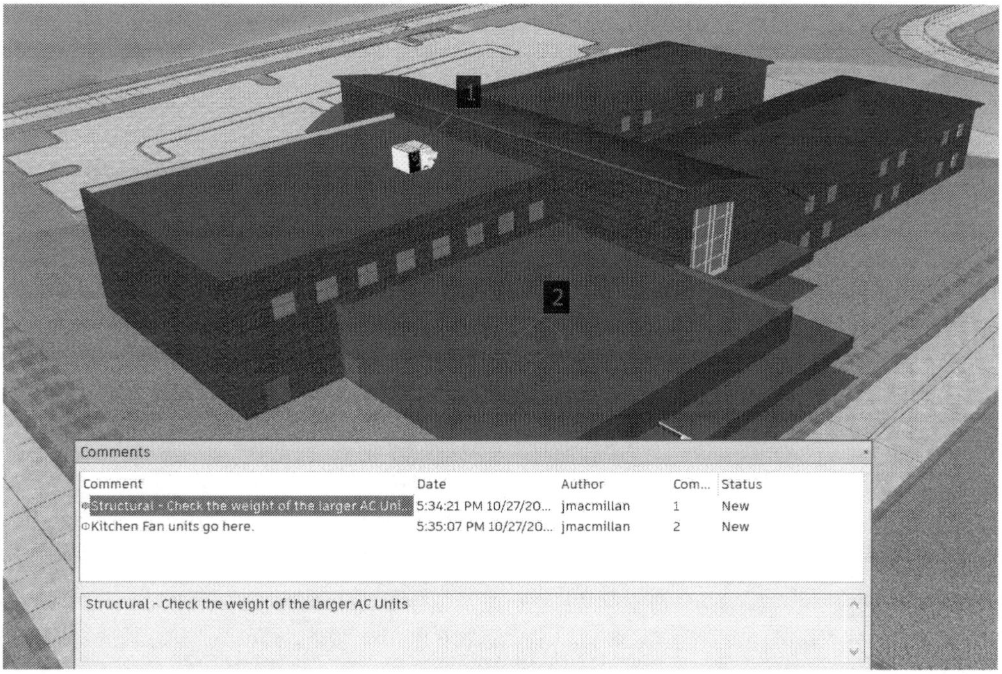

Figure 5–38

8. Save the file.

End of practice

Chapter Review Questions

1. How do you ensure that a measurement remains visible as a markup?

   a. In the *Review* tab>*Measure* panel, click (Convert to Markup).

   b. Take a screen shot and add the image to the file.

   c. Put the dimension in a tag.

   d. Manually draw the dimension with the Draw and Text tools.

2. You can convert more than one measurement to a markup at a time.

   a. True

   b. False

3. What happens when you place a dimension, text, or some other markup geometry in the scene view, and then zoom in/out?

   a. The markups change size with the view.

   b. Nothing. The markup remains the same size (percentage of the screen) no matter how much you zoom in/out.

   c. The markup disappears if the view was not saved.

4. How do you move a markup?

   a. Select the markup and use the gizmo to move it.

   b. Select the markup and click **Move** on the *Markup* contextual tab.

   c. In the *Review* tab>*Measure* panel, click **Clear**.

   d. Markups cannot be moved. They must be erased and redrawn in the new location.

Command Summary

Button	Command	Location
Measuring Tools		
	**Accumulate**	• **Ribbon:** *Review* tab>*Measure* panel, expand *Measure*
	**Angle**	• **Ribbon:** *Review* tab>*Measure* panel, expand *Measure*
	**Area**	• **Ribbon:** *Review* tab>*Measure* panel, expand *Measure*
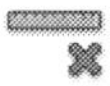	**Clear**	• **Ribbon:** *Review* tab>*Measure* panel
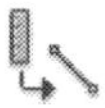	**Convert to Markup**	• **Ribbon:** *Review* tab>*Measure* panel
	**Measure Panel (Measure Tool dialog box)**	• **Ribbon:** *Review* tab>*Measure* panel
	**None**	• **Ribbon:** *Review* tab>*Measure* panel, expand *Lock*
	**Parallel**	• **Ribbon:** *Review* tab>*Measure* panel, expand *Lock*
	**Perpendicular**	• **Ribbon:** *Review* tab>*Measure* panel, expand *Lock*
	**Point Line**	• **Ribbon:** *Review* tab>*Measure* panel, expand *Measure*
	**Point to Multiple Points**	• **Ribbon:** *Review* tab>*Measure* panel, expand *Measure*
	**Point to Point**	• **Ribbon:** *Review* tab>*Measure* panel, expand *Measure*
	**Shortest Distance**	• **Ribbon:** *Review* tab>*Measure* panel
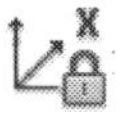	**X Axis**	• **Ribbon:** *Review* tab>*Measure* panel, expand *Lock*

Button	Command	Location
	**Y Axis**	• **Ribbon:** *Review* tab>*Measure* panel, expand *Lock*
	**Z Axis**	• **Ribbon:** *Review* tab>*Measure* panel, expand *Lock*
Markup Tools		
	**Add Tag**	• **Ribbon:** *Review* tab>*Markup* panel
	**Arrow**	• **Ribbon:** *Review* tab>*Markup* panel, expand *Draw*
	**Cloud**	• **Ribbon:** *Review* tab>*Markup* panel, expand *Draw*
	**Color**	• **Ribbon:** *Review* tab>*Markup* panel
	**Ellipse**	• **Ribbon:** *Review* tab>*Markup* panel, expand *Draw*
	**Erase**	• **Ribbon:** *Review* tab>*Markup* panel
	**Find Comments**	• **Ribbon:** *Review* tab>Comments panel
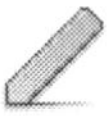	**Freehand**	• **Ribbon:** *Review* tab>*Markup* panel, expand *Draw*
	**Line**	• **Ribbon:** *Review* tab>*Markup* panel, expand *Draw*
	**Line String**	• **Ribbon:** *Review* tab>*Markup* panel, expand *Draw*
	**Text**	• **Ribbon:** *Review* tab>*Markup* panel
	**Thickness**	• **Ribbon:** *Review* tab>*Markup* panel
	**View Comments**	• **Ribbon:** *Review* tab>*Comments* panel

Chapter 6

Clash Detection

The collaboration stage of the BIM workflow is meant to ensure that all of the disciplines are on the same page. For example, it is important that HVAC ductwork does not interfere with the electrical or structural parts of the building, while at the same time, civil engineers need to be sure that they are bringing utilities into a building at the right location for interior connections to be made. Learn how to run clash tests to ensure that everything is properly aligned.

> ***Note:*** *Clash Detection is not available in Navisworks Simulate or Navisworks Freedom. It is only available in Navisworks Manage.*

Learning Objectives

- Run a clash test and review clash test results.
- Fix clashes in the model.
- Communicate clash results using reports.

BIM Workflow: Collaborate

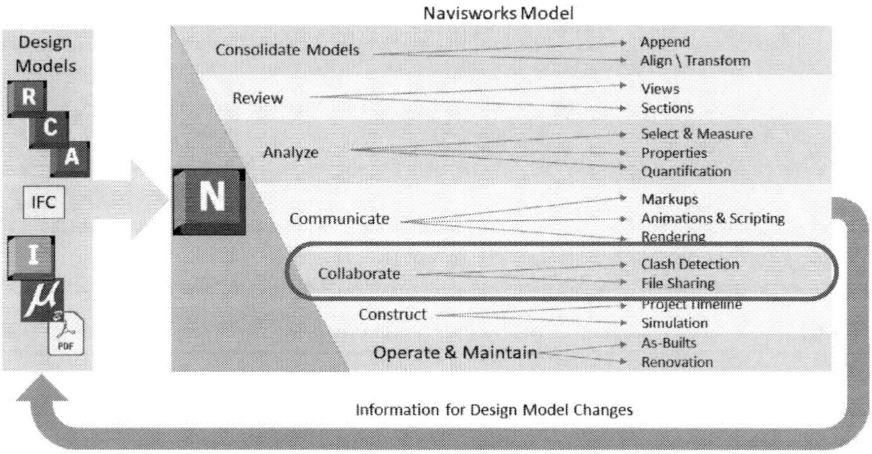

6.1 Overview of the Clash Detective

The Clash Detective eliminates the tedious manual process of inspecting and identifying interference clashes in a 3D project model. This process helps to keep construction costs down by reducing the number of change orders that are caused by objects occupying the same space. You can run clash tests using traditional 3D geometry, or using point clouds generated from laser scans. In addition, you can check stationary objects (buildings) against moving objects (cranes) to ensure that construction equipment does not collide with anything on the project site. When you are doing a clash test, consider the following:

- Always run a clash test on the most up-to-date 3D models.
- Rerun existing clash tests before creating a new test.
- Rules can be created to ignore certain clashes.
- You can minimize the number of clashes that must reviewed at a time by working with groups.
- Clash test parameters can be saved and used on other projects.

The *Clash Detective* window is shown in Figure 6–1. The top pane is where you can manage all of the clash tests and displays a list of previously-created clash tests. The bottom pane contains the following four tabs:

- **Rules:** Configure the rules or list of items to be ignored when a clash test is run. You can create new rules, edit existing rules, or delete rules, as required.
- **Select:** Defines what items the test includes. The items selected in the *Selection A* list are compared against the items selected in the *Selection B* list. You can also set the clash type and tolerance here.
- **Results:** Shows a list of the clashes that were found, as shown in Figure 6–1. You can manage how clashes are handled in this tab.
- **Report:** Manage reports and what they include here.

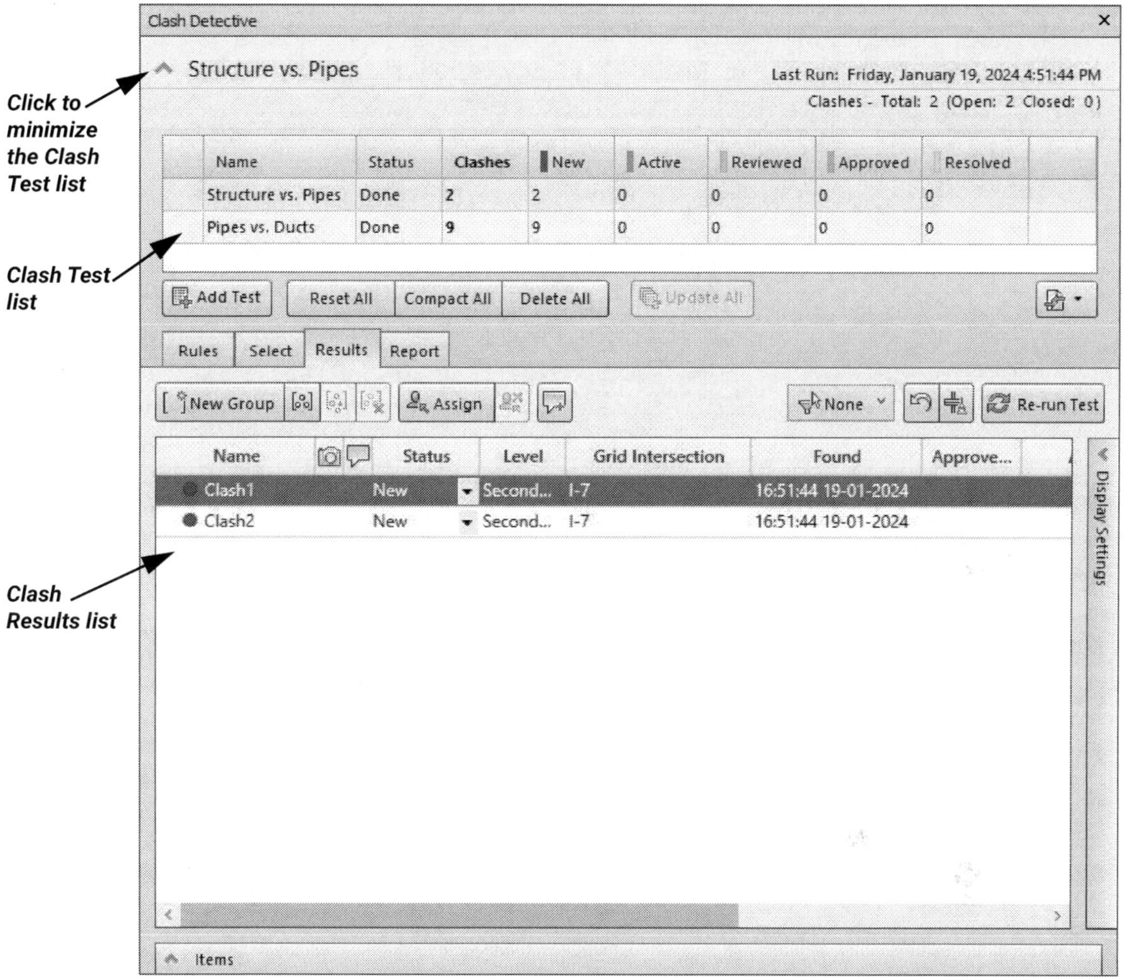

Figure 6–1

How To: Set Up and Run a Clash Test

1. In the *Home* tab>*Tools* panel, click (Clash Detective), or press <Ctrl>+<F2>.

2. In the *Clash Detective* window, click (Add Test). A new test is loaded in the top pane with tabs where you can set up the test in the lower panes, as shown in Figure 6–2.

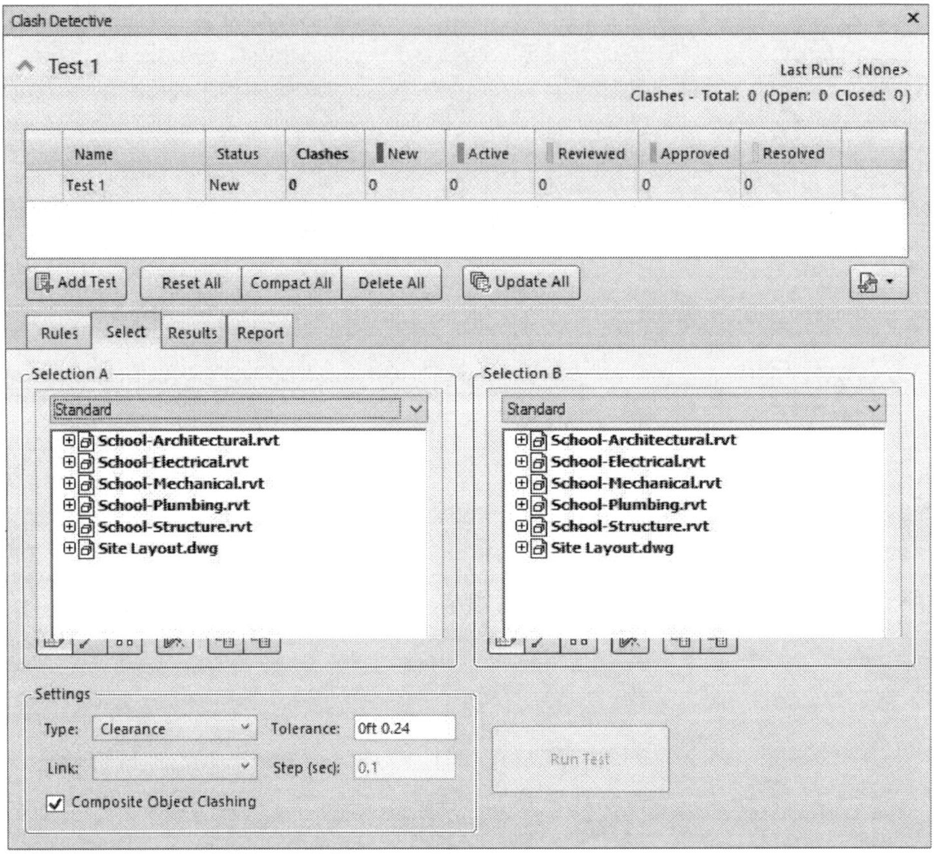

Figure 6–2

3. Double-click in the test *Name* column and enter a descriptive name for the new test.

   Note: *You can rename the clash test later, if required.*

4. In the *Rules* tab, select any of the *Ignore Clashes Between* options, as shown in Figure 6–3.

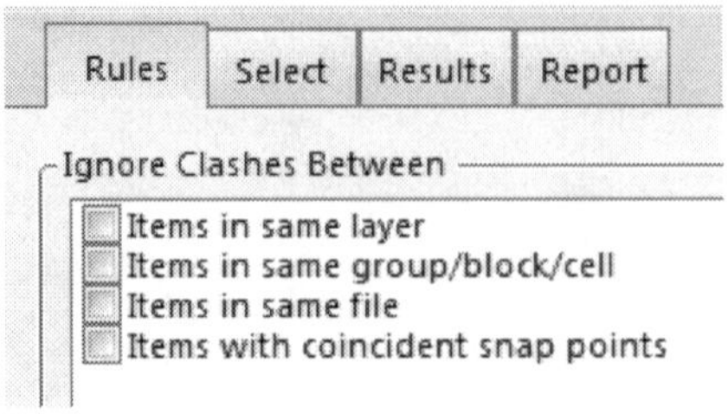

Figure 6–3

5. In the *Select* tab, select the items that will be compared. Selections must be made in the *Selection A* and *Selection B* areas. Their drop-down lists can be used to determine the selection criteria. Use **Standard** to select the models and use **Sets** to select a previously created selection set, as shown in Figure 6–4. This is discussed further in the next topic.

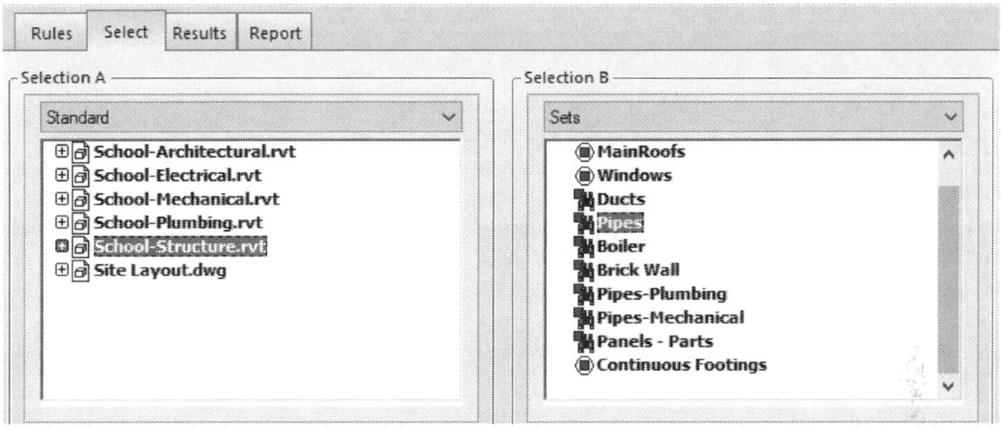

Figure 6–4

6. Define the options in the *Settings* area to set the type of clash and its tolerance value.
7. Click **Run Test**.
8. The *Results* tab opens, displaying a list of clashes, and the scene view zooms in on the first clash, as shown in Figure 6–5. Review the results.

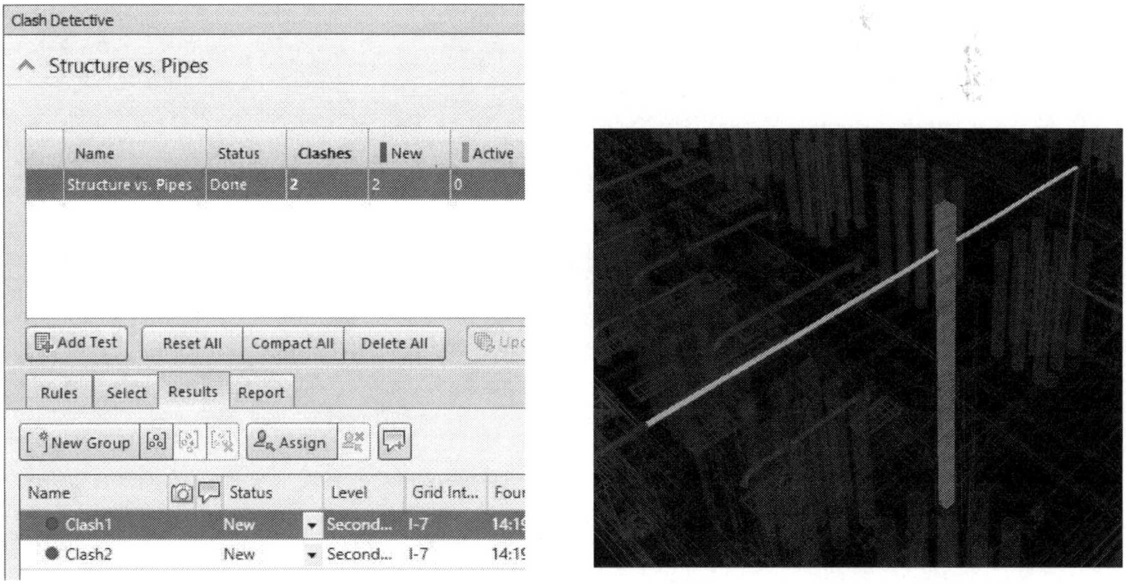

Figure 6–5

9. In the *Report* tab, create a report that can be viewed by others, as required.

After reloading files that have been modified, in the *Clash Detective* window, click **Update All** to re-run the clash test to ensure that everything has been corrected.

Importing and Exporting Clash Tests

Clash tests can be shared between project files. If you set up a clash test to check all of the objects on a specific layer against all of the objects on another layer, you can reuse that test on every project that uses the same standard layer names and definitions.

Clash tests are saved as .XML files.

How To: Export Clash Tests

1. In the *Clash Detective* window, in the *Test* pane, expand (Import/Export Clash Tests) and select **Export Clash Tests**.
2. In the *Export* dialog box, navigate to the location where you want to save the file.
3. Name the file and click **Save**.

   Note: *By default, the clash test is named the same as the Autodesk Navisworks file that you are working in. Rename it to fit a standard so that it can be used in other projects.*

How To: Import Clash Tests

1. In the *Clash Detective* window, in the *Test* pane, expand (Import/Export Clash Tests) and select **Import Clash Tests**.
2. In the *Import* dialog box, navigate to the location of the saved file.
3. Select the file you want to import and click **Open**.

Hint: Customizing Clash Tests

You can edit the .XML file to suit other projects. When you do this, using standard naming conventions for the clash test you are importing are the key to making them work.

6.2 Setting Up Clash Tests

Rules Tab

Use the *Rules* tab to filter out things that you do not want checked, as shown in Figure 6–6. This helps to eliminate false positives and makes the results more meaningful. For example, you might not want to check things that were originally created in the same file, as they are tested separately. For this example, in the *Ignore Clashes Between* area, you would select the **Items in the same file** option.

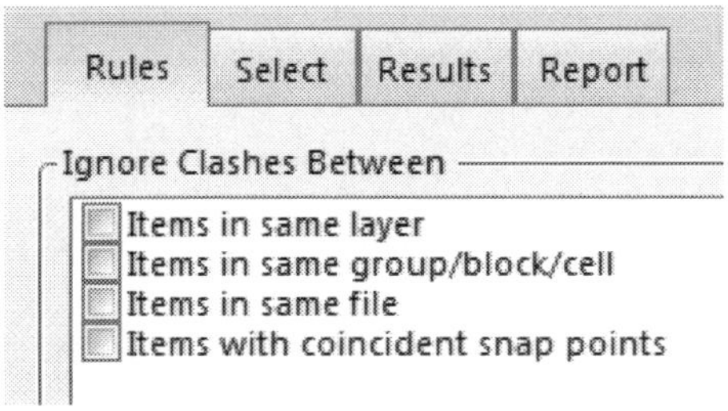

Figure 6–6

- Click **New** to add other options from the Rule Editor.
- Click **Edit** to modify an existing rule.
- Click **Delete** to remove the rule from the list.

Select Tab

The *Selection A* and *Selection B* areas enable you to select which items are compared against each other. The *format* drop-down list in each pane enables you to select the format in which the items are listed, as shown in Figure 6–7.

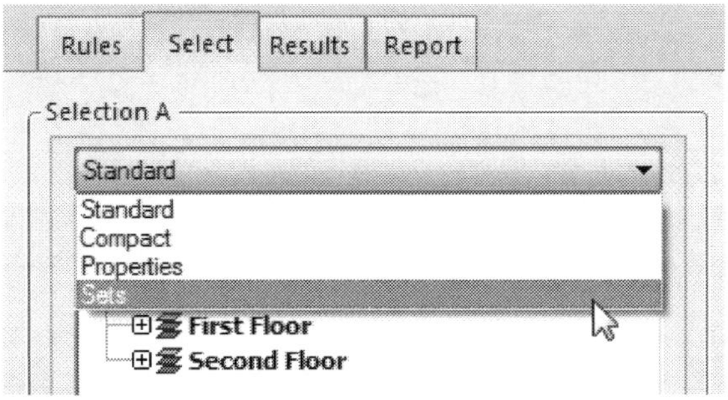

Figure 6–7

The formats are as follows:

- **Standard:** Provides the same list groups according to the appended files found in the *Selection Tree*.
- **Compact:** A simplified version of the Standard list.
- **Properties:** Lists objects according to their properties, such as the same name, material, area name, etc.
- **Sets:** These are the sets that are listed in the *Sets* window, and can be either saved sets or search sets. Using a search set ensures that all of the objects in newly appended files are selected for the clash test.

  Note: *Using the Sets option makes clash tests easier to share and reuse.*

Next, you can select the types of geometry to compare. Select from the following geometry types, which are located below the *Selection* areas, as shown in Figure 6–8:

- (Surfaces): These are the 3D triangles most 3D objects are made out of. This is the default setting.

  Note: *Surfaces refer to 3D planar objects,* **NOT** *to topo surfaces from Civil applications (such as Civil 3D).*

- (Lines): These represent linear objects that have centerlines, such as pipes.
- (Points): These are point clouds that are created using laser scan data.
- (Self-Intersect): Clash tests a selection against itself.
- (Use Current Selection): Selects anything in the selection list that is already selected in the scene view.
- (Select in Scene): Enables you to select items in the scene view to populate the selection list.

  Note: *Hold <Ctrl> to select multiple items.*

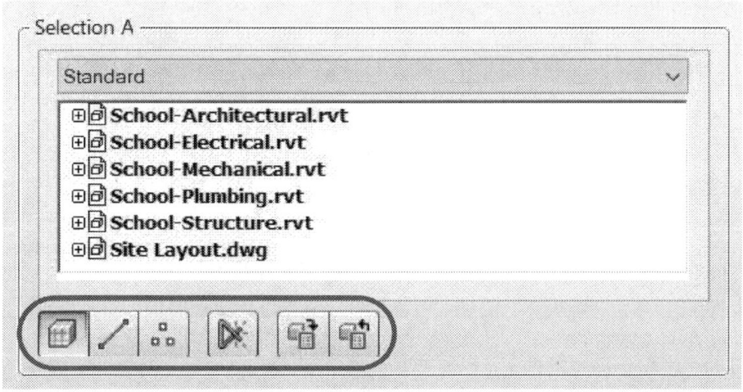

Figure 6–8

Clash Settings

The *Settings* area is used to set the type of clash to run and the tolerance factor for the clash, as shown in Figure 6–9. There are four clash types, as follows:

- **Hard:** Two objects reside in the same space or intersect each other.
- **Hard (Conservative):** A more thorough method than Hard that returns two objects that might clash. You might receive false positives using this method, but it is a more thorough test.
- **Clearance:** Two objects are within the tolerance distance of each other. When using this method, hard clashes are also detected.
- **Duplicates:** Two objects are the same type and reside in the same position.

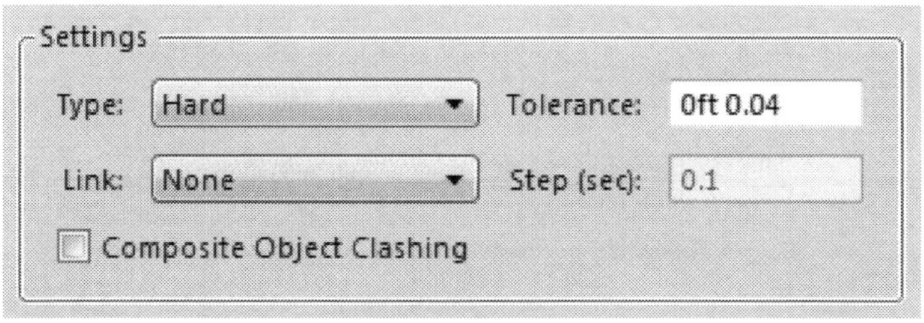

Figure 6–9

It is possible to run a clash test against construction equipment or other items that might move on site. To do this, link the clash test to a TimeLiner schedule or an object animation scene using the *Link* drop-down list in the *Settings* area.

Then, set the period of time between clash tests in the *Step (sec)* field. Since multiple clash tests are run at set intervals throughout the simulation sequence, it does take more time to complete a clash test with a link.

If a clash test is taking too much time to finish, you can stop the test by clicking **Cancel** in the *Working* dialog box, as shown in Figure 6–10. The progress bar displays how much of the model was tested. All of the clashes that were found before the test was canceled are reported, and the test displays a **Partial** status in the Clash list, as shown in Figure 6–11.

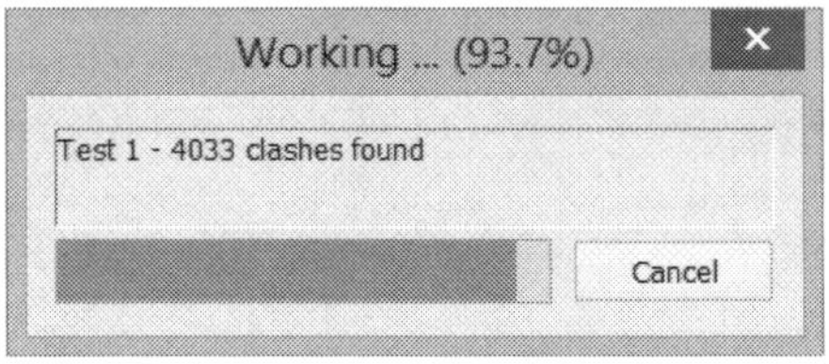

Figure 6–10

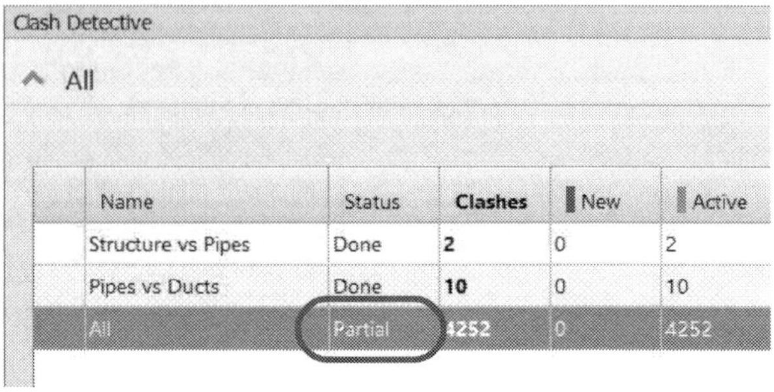

Figure 6–11

How To: Select Items to Test

1. In the *Selection A* area, expand the *Search in:* drop-down list and select the format of how you want to view the potential items, as shown in Figure 6–12.
   - Create and use sets if you expect to recheck the same clashes when models are updated.

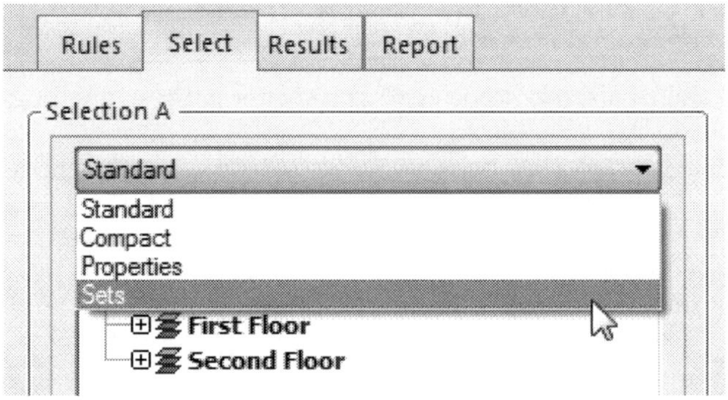

Figure 6–12

2. Select the items or sets you want to compare.
   - Hold <Ctrl> or <Shift> to select multiple options.
3. Repeat the process in the *Selection B* area.
4. Specify the geometry types and settings you want to use.

Practice 6a
Create Clash Tests

Practice Objective

- Check for clashes between objects.

In this practice, you will check the model for clashes against the structural columns and pipes, as shown in Figure 6–13.

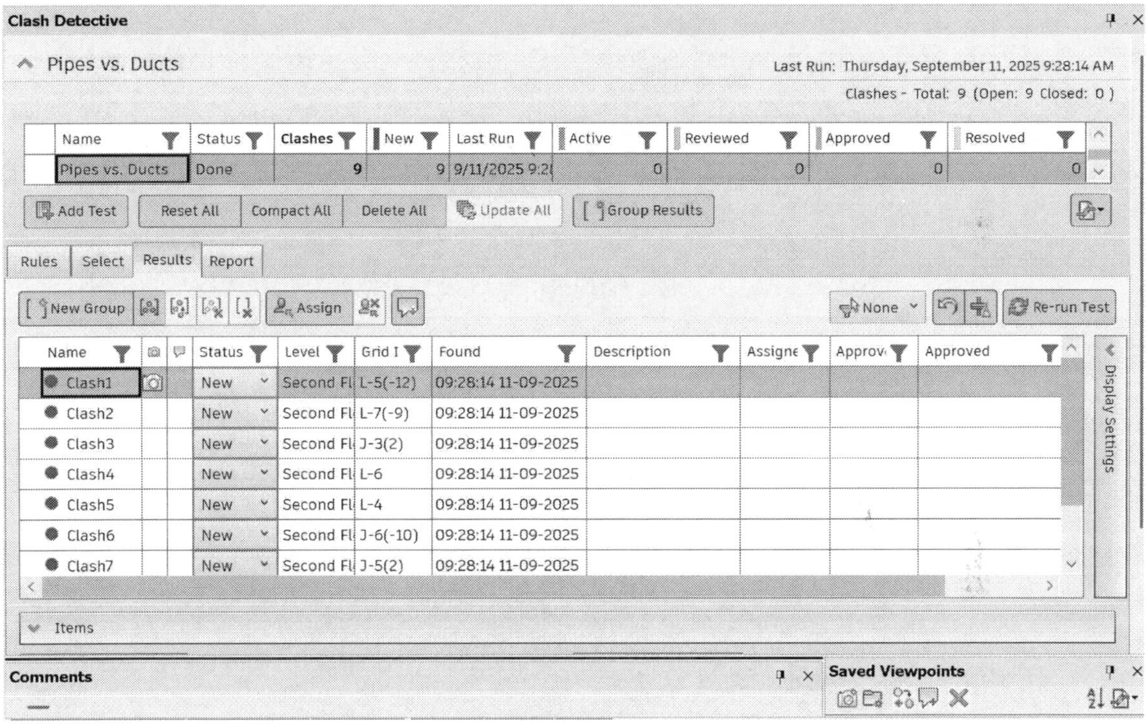

Figure 6–13

Note: *Clash Detection is only available in Navisworks Manage. It is not available in Navisworks Simulate or Navisworks Freedom.*

Task 1: Create a simple clash test.

1. Open **School-Simple.nwf** from the *Navisworks BIM Practice Files\Clash Detection* folder.
2. Open the *Clash Detective* window. If this window is not currently docked on the left side of the software interface, in the *Home* tab>*Tools* panel, click (Clash Detective).
3. In the *Clash Detective* window, click the down arrow icon in the top-left corner, as shown in Figure 6–14, to reveal the *Test* pane. Because no tests have yet been defined, this area is compressed by default.

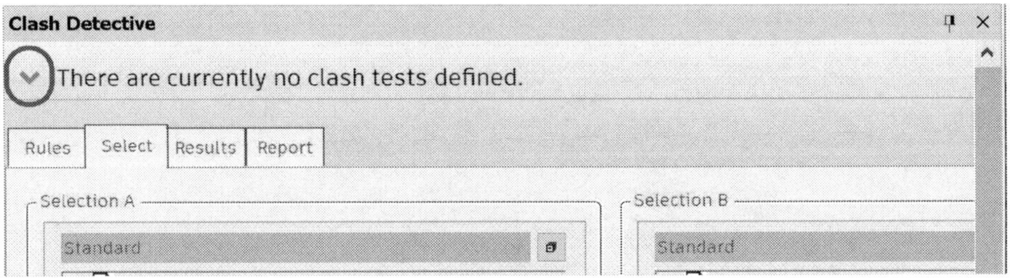

Figure 6–14

Note: *If the window does not display properly, dock it to the top edge of the screen.*

4. In the *Test* pane, click Add Test (Add Test).
5. In the *Test* pane, in the *Name* column, double-click on the name to rename it. Enter **Structure vs. Pipes** for the name, as shown in Figure 6–15, and press <Enter>.

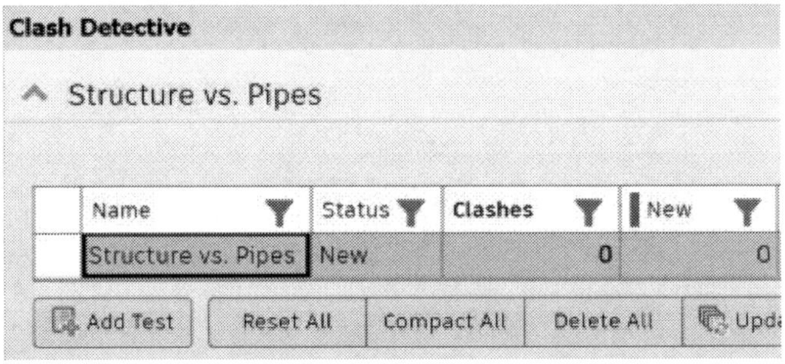

Figure 6–15

6. In the *Rules* tab, ensure that all of the *Ignore Clashes Between* options are unchecked, as shown in Figure 6–16.

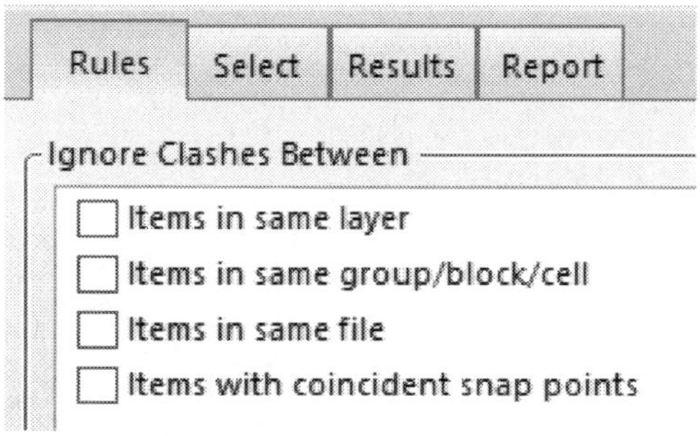

Figure 6–16

7. In the *Select* tab, set up the clash criteria, as follows:
   a. In the *Selection A* area, select **Standard** from the drop-down list, then select **School-Structure.rvt**.
   b. In the *Selection B* area, select **Sets** from the drop-down list and select the **Pipes** search set, as shown in Figure 6–17.

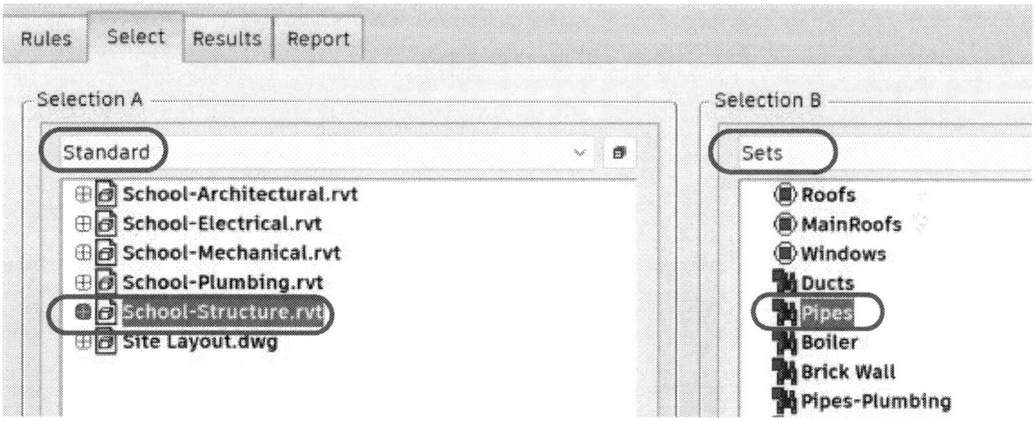

Figure 6–17

   c. In the *Settings* area, ensure the clash *Type* is set to **Hard** and the *Tolerance* value is **0.00 ft**.
   d. Click **Run Test**.

8. The *Results* tab displays a list of clashes and the scene view zooms in on the first clash, as shown in Figure 6–18.

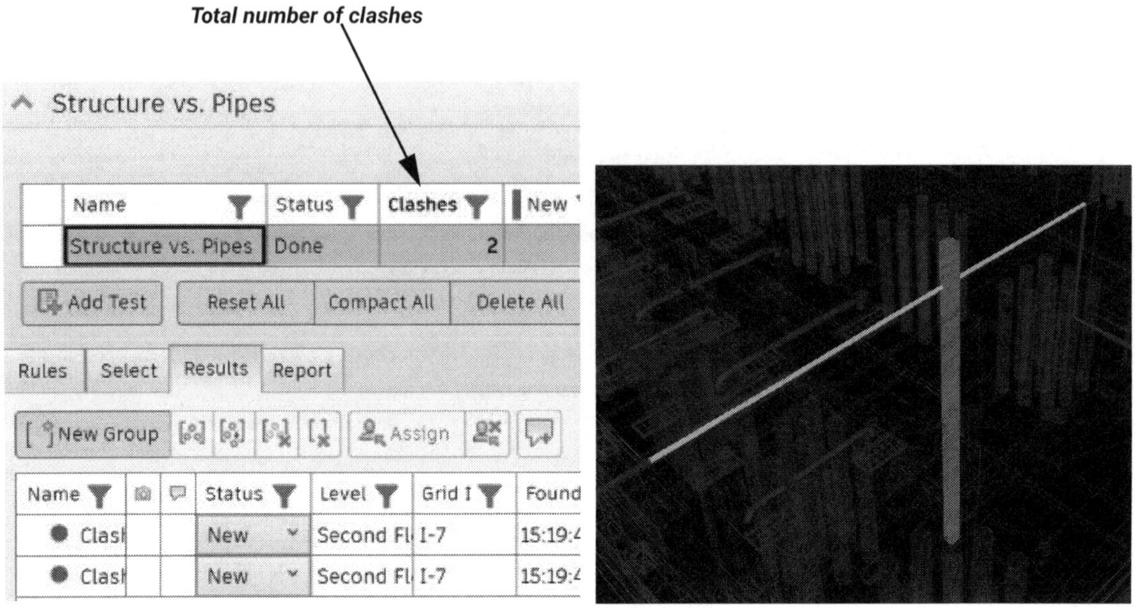

Figure 6–18

9. Select **Clash2** in the lower portion of the window to review it. The scene view updates to show the clash.
10. Save the file.

Task 2: Run a clash test on pipes and ducts.

1. In the *Clash Detective* window, click (Add Test).
2. Select the test name, and rename it to **Pipes vs. Ducts**.
3. In the *Rules* tab, ensure that all of the *Ignore Clashes Between* options remain unchecked.
4. In the *Select* tab, set up the clash criteria as follows (as shown in Figure 6–19):
   - In the *Selection A* area, select **Sets** from the drop-down list, then select the **Pipes** search set.
   - In the *Selection B* area, select **Sets** from the drop-down list, then select the **Ducts** search set.
   - In the *Settings* area, change the *Type* to **Clearance** and set the *Tolerance* to **0.02 ft** so that you check for things that are less than a quarter of an inch apart.

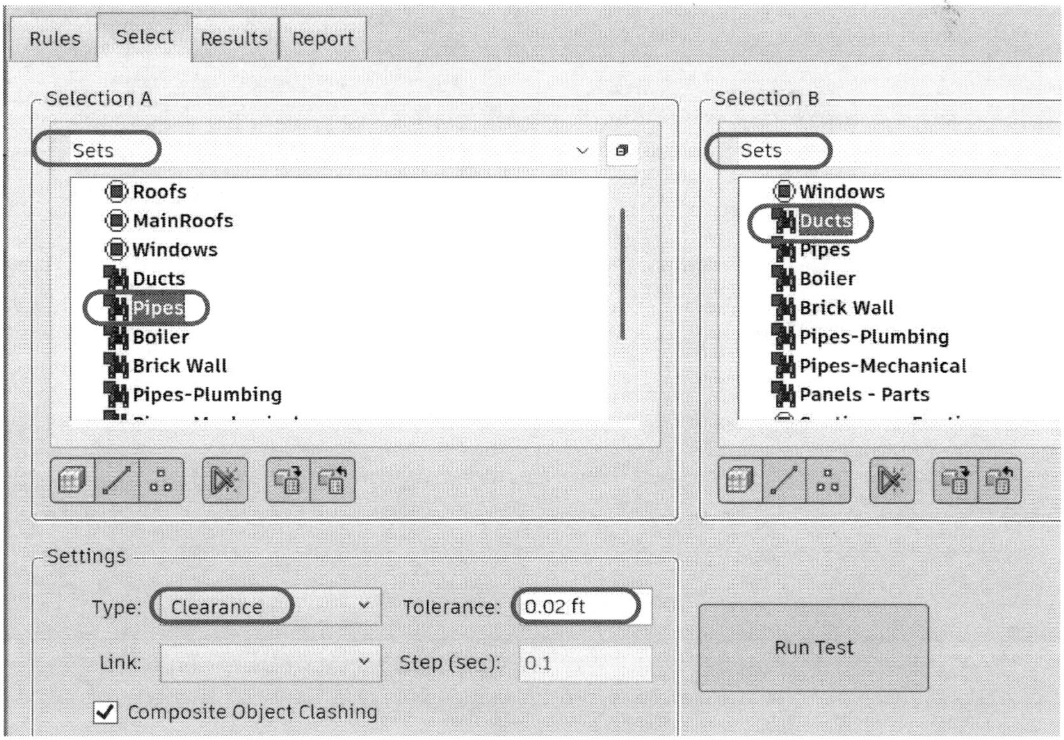

Figure 6–19

5. Click **Run Test**.

6. The *Results* tab displays a list of clashes and the scene view zooms in on the first clash, as shown in Figure 6–20. Review the results.

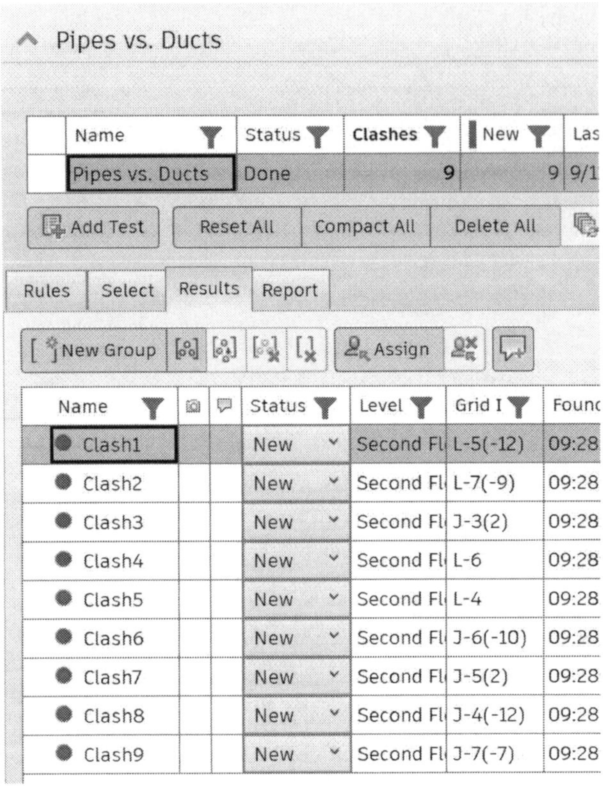

Figure 6–20

7. Save the file.

End of practice

6.3 Reviewing Clash Results

The *Results* tab of the *Clash Detective* window enables you to review the clashes that were found during each clash test. Selecting a clash test in the top pane displays a list of clashes in the bottom pane, as shown in Figure 6–21. Use this pane to:

- View clash results and change how they display.
- Set the status of a clash.
- Add comments to each clash.

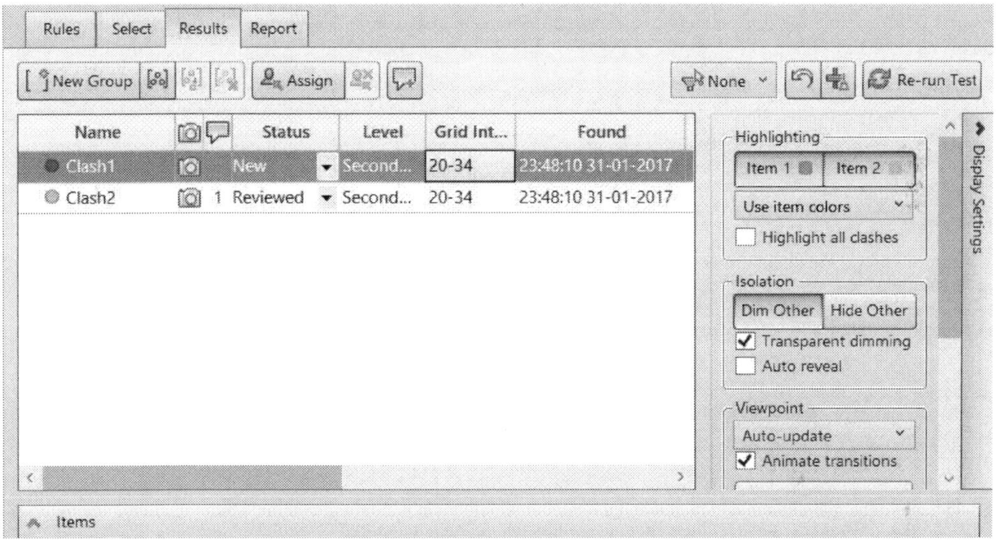

Figure 6–21

- Click the arrow next to the *Items* title to display or hide the tests at the top or the selected items at the bottom, as shown in Figure 6–22.

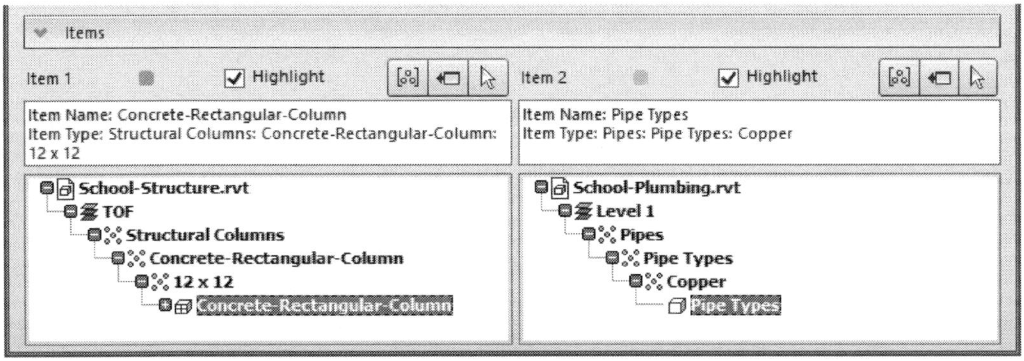

Figure 6–22

Viewing Clashes

Click on a clash to zoom to it in the scene view. If you Pan or Zoom the scene view while a clash is selected, the view is saved and the Camera icon displays (as shown in Figure 6–23) to indicate that there is a saved viewpoint available.

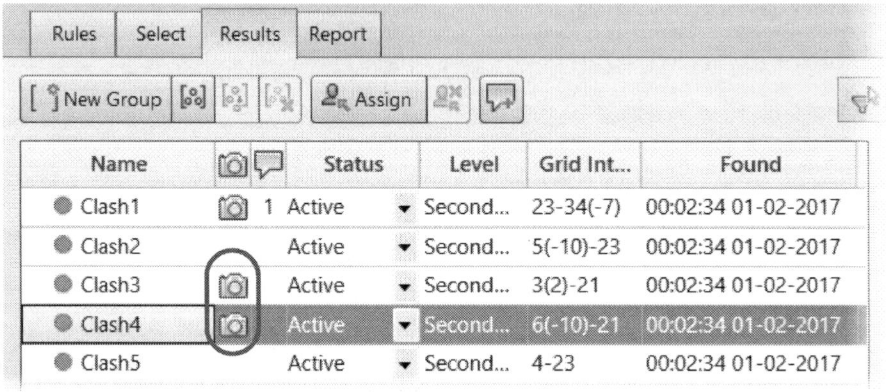

Figure 6–23

Display Settings

The *Display Settings* panel (shown in Figure 6–24) enables you to set how clashed items and other items display in the scene view. Each of the clash items can be set to its own color, and you can fade or completely hide everything else in the scene view. By isolating clashed items, you can get a cleaner picture of the corrections that need to be made.

Click on the *Display Settings* title to open the panel.

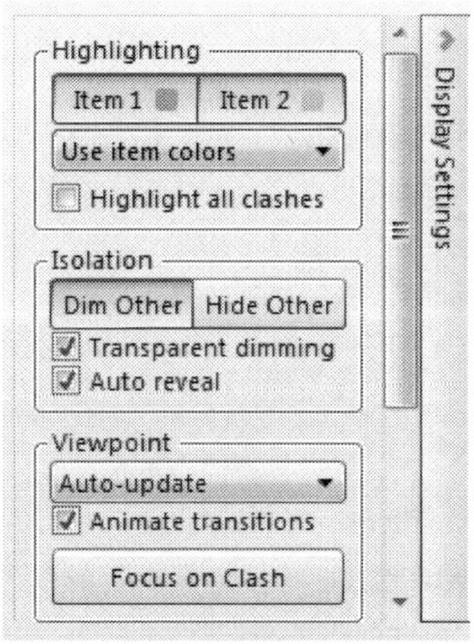

Figure 6–24

Highlighting

Highlighting can help you see which items are clashing, as shown in Figure 6–25.

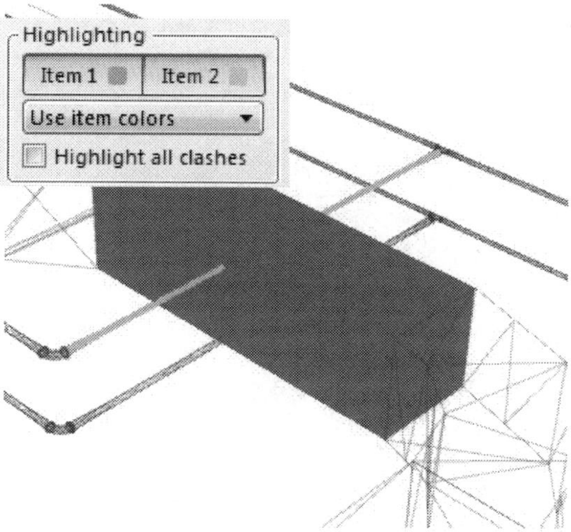

Figure 6–25

- Select the **Item 1** and **Item 2** buttons to toggle the highlighting on and off.
- In the drop-down list, use the **Use item colors** option to display the highlight colors, or use the **Use status color option** to display both items using the color defined for the status options.
- Select **Highlight all clashes** to display all clashes. This can be especially helpful if you have more than one item clashing with the same item (as shown in Figure 6–26), or if you want to see an overview of all of the clashed areas.

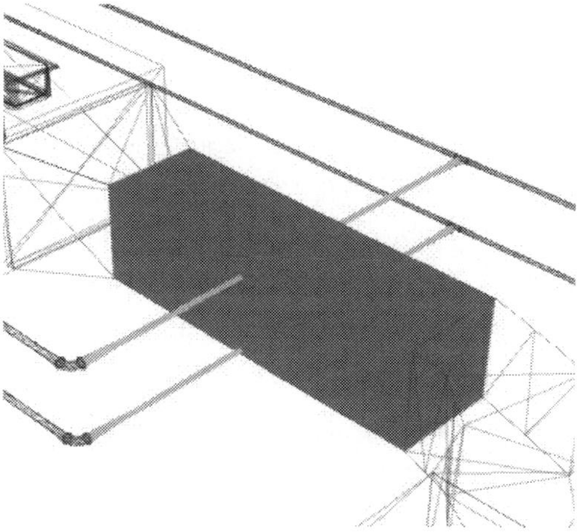

Figure 6–26

Isolation

By default, all of the other elements around the clashing elements are dimmed and display in wireframe (as shown previously in Figure 6–26). You can change this behavior in the Isolation area, shown in Figure 6–27. In the *Isolation* area, click **Hide Other** to display only the items in the current clash. This automatically toggles off the **Transparent dimming** option.

Figure 6–27

- If neither option is selected, the clash items are highlighted but the other elements display in the current Render Style Mode.
- **Auto reveal** temporarily hides any elements that might be obscuring the clash. It is a good idea to have this selected.

Viewpoint

In the *Viewpoint* area, you can specify how the viewpoint displays when you select clashes, as shown in Figure 6–28.

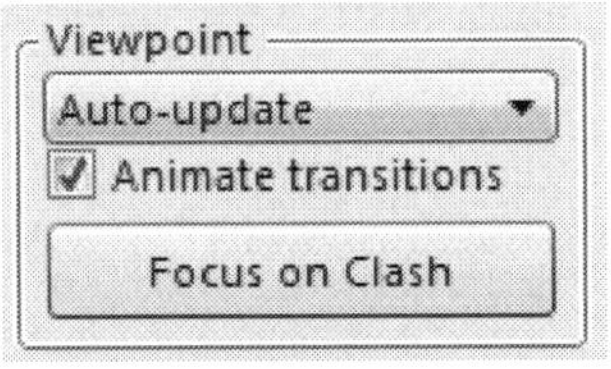

Figure 6–28

The *Viewpoint* area options are as follows:

- **Auto-update:** Automatically zooms in on an appropriate viewpoint and saves any changes you make to the viewpoint.
- **Auto-load:** Automatically zooms in on the default viewpoint, but does not save it as a new viewpoint if you navigate away.
- **Manual:** Does not change the viewpoint when you select clashes. You might want to use this option to display each clash in the context of the overall view.
- **Animate transitions:** Zooms out from the existing clash to the full model and then back in on the selected clash. This can help you locate a specific clash in the model.
- **Focus on Clash:** Zooms in on the clash again if you have moved away from it. This also turns on the **3rd Person** avatar by default.

You can right-click on a camera icon in the *Results* tab to load or save a viewpoint other than the automatic viewpoint. You can also specify **Focus on Clash** or delete the selected viewpoint or all viewpoints.

Hint: Clash Detective Options

You can specify how viewpoints display and animate when you select clashes, how clash tests are imported and exported, and set the default custom highlight colors.

To access these options, in the (Application Menu), click **Options**. In the *Options Editor*, expand **Tools>Clash Detective**, as shown in Figure 6–29.

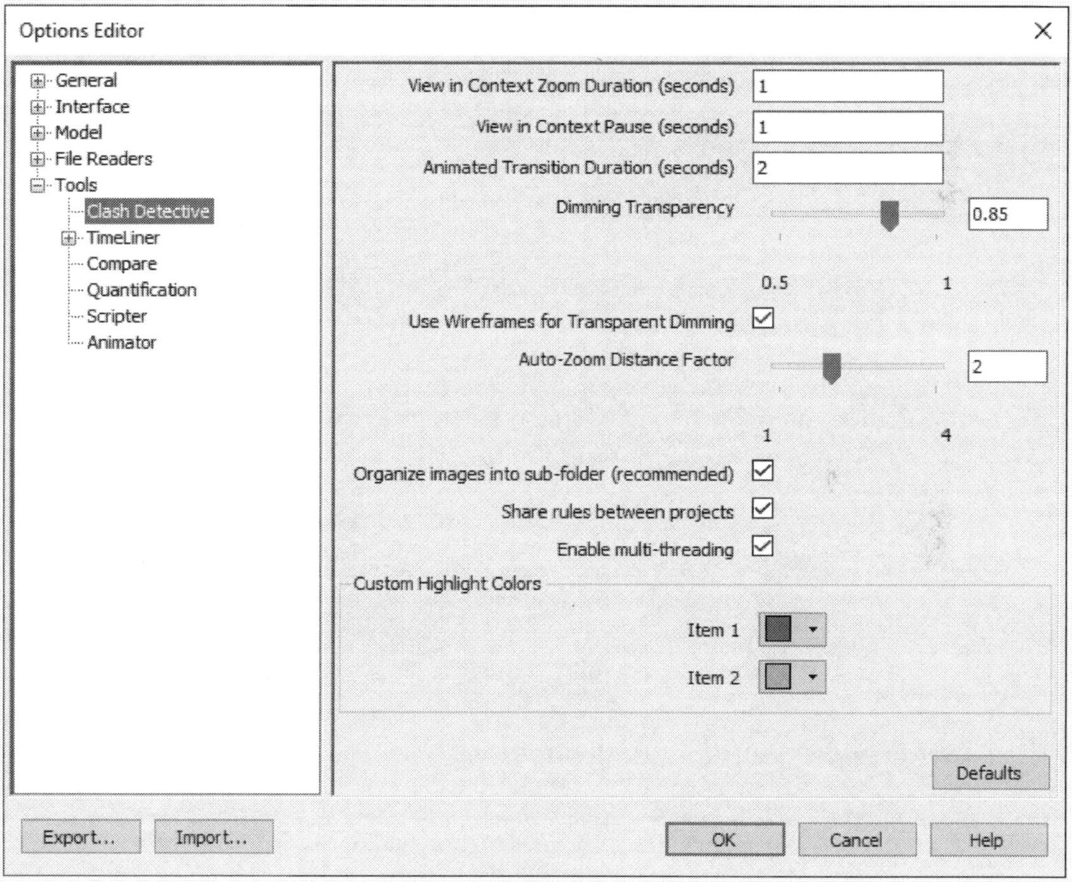

Figure 6–29

6.4 Assigning Clash Fixes

Assigning and Commenting

Clashes are most often found between different disciplines that do not work together. For example, electrical cable trays, plumbing pipes, and ducts are usually modeled by separate firms trying to occupy the same space in a plenum. You can assign responsibility for a clash (as shown in Figure 6–30) and add comments.

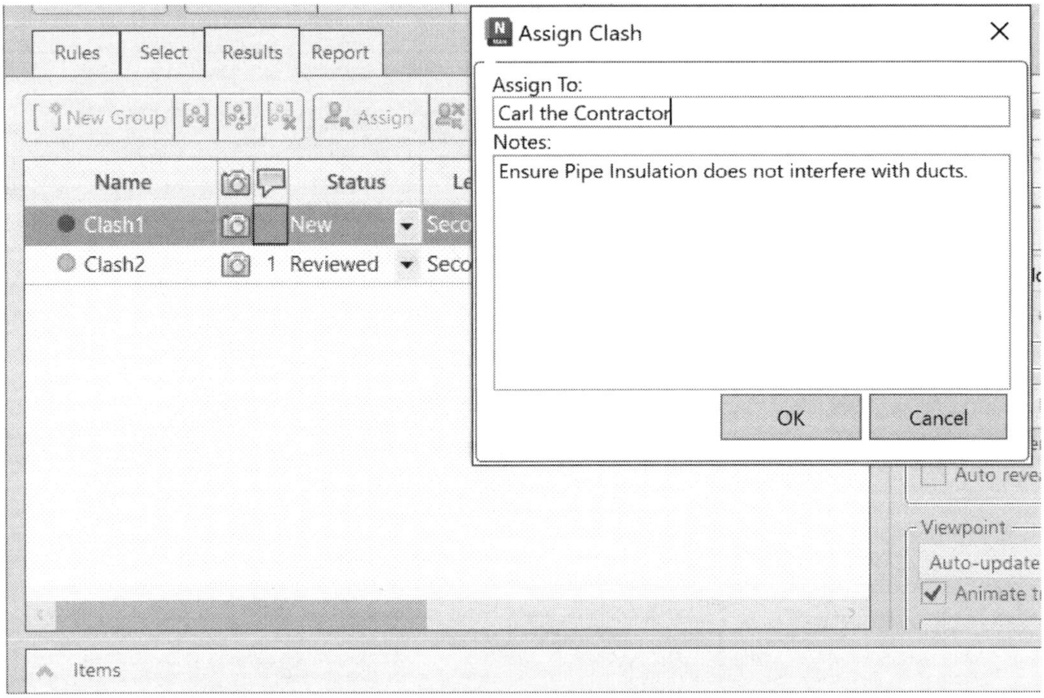

Figure 6–30

How To: Assign and Comment on Clashes

1. In the *Clash Detective>Results* tab, select a clash or clash group.

2. Click  (Assign) or  (Add Comment).

3. In the *Assign Clash* dialog box, enter a name in the *Assign To* field and add any notes (as shown previously in Figure 6–30). If adding a comment, you enter a comment in the dialog box and can assign a status, as shown in Figure 6–31.

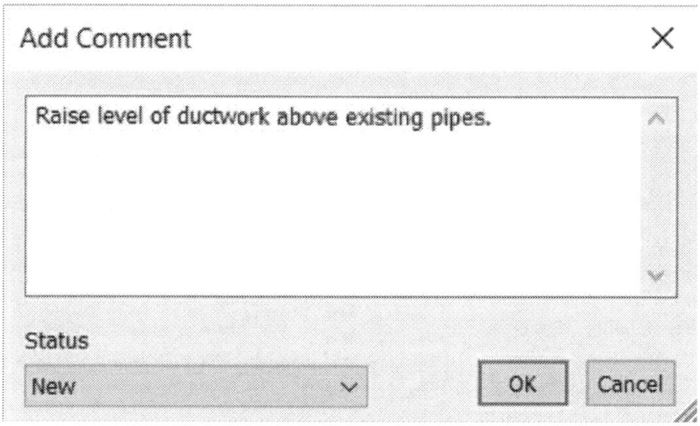

Figure 6–31

4. Click **OK**.

- To remove an assignment, select the clash and click (Unassign).
- Comments and assignments are typically included in any clash test reports.
- To view the comments in Navisworks, in the *Review* tab>*Comments* panel, click (View Comments) to open the *Comments* window (shown in Figure 6–32).

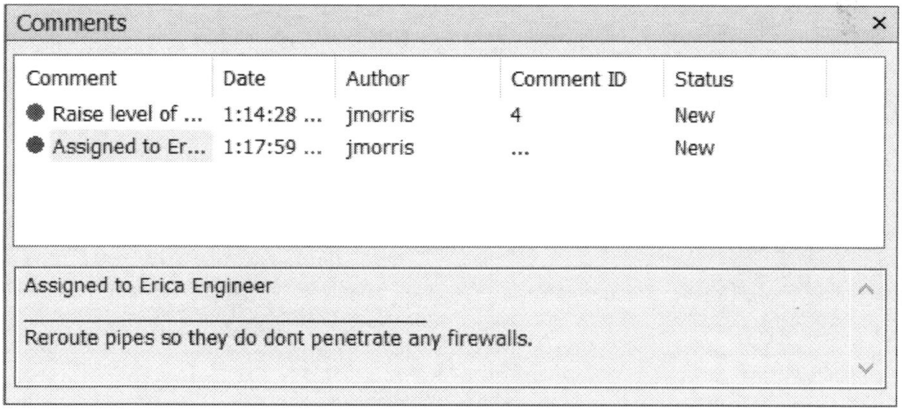

Figure 6–32

Setting the Clash Status

The Clash Status changes automatically as you work through the project. You can also manually apply a clash status, as shown in Figure 6–33.

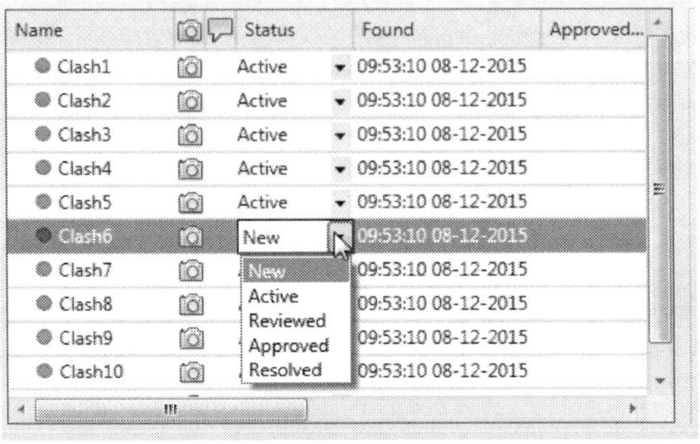

Figure 6–33

Each status displays a different color dot beside the name. The number of clashes for each status also displays in the *Test* pane, as shown in Figure 6–34.

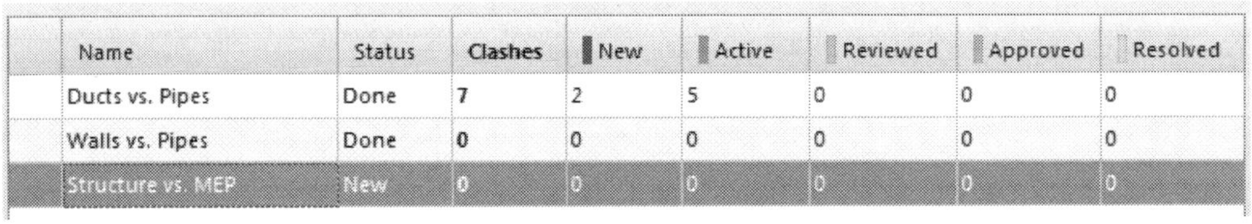

Figure 6–34

The clash statuses are as follows:

- **New:** The first time a clash has been detected.
- **Active:** A Clash test has been run again, and the clash is still unresolved.
- **Reviewed:** The clash has been reviewed, but not modified.
- **Approved:** The clash is approved to remain as is. The user who approved and the time of approval are logged.
- **Resolved:** The clash was in a previous run of the test, but is no longer found and is assumed to be resolved.
    - If a clash is manually changed to Resolved, when the test is run again and the clash still exists, the clash is assigned a New status.
- **Old:** When a model is updated since the test was run, this is a reminder that the current test does not reflect the information in the updated model. Clash tests show this status.

6.5 Clash Grouping

Grouping related clashes together can save everyone time. For example, a series of pipes might be going through a fire-rated wall. Each intersection of pipe and wall is considered one clash. You can group these clashes together (as shown in Figure 6–35) so that they can all be addressed at the same time.

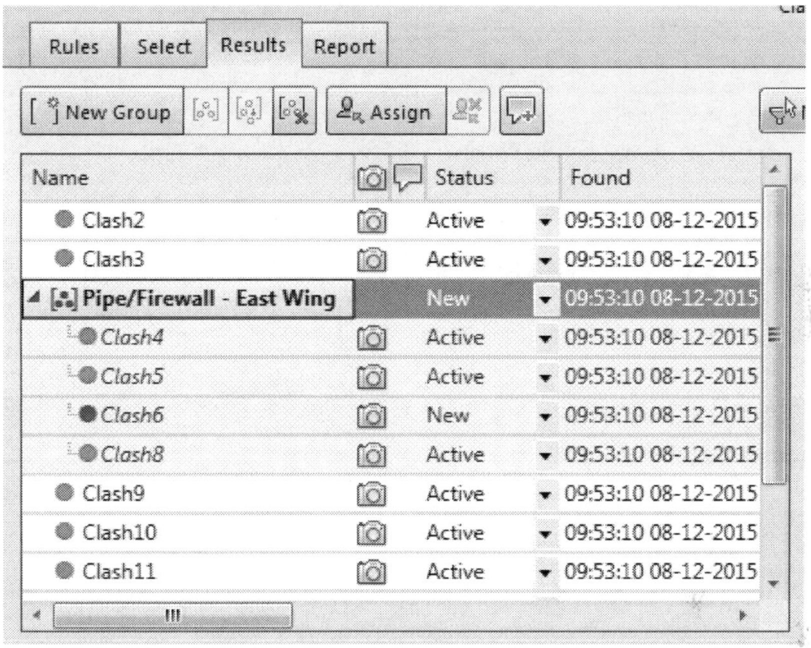

Figure 6–35

You can create groups in any of the following three ways:

- Click  (New Group) and then drag and drop clashes into the group.
- Select several clashes and click  (Group Selected Clashes).
- In the *Results* tab, select the clashes, right-click on them, and then select **Group,** as shown in Figure 6–36.

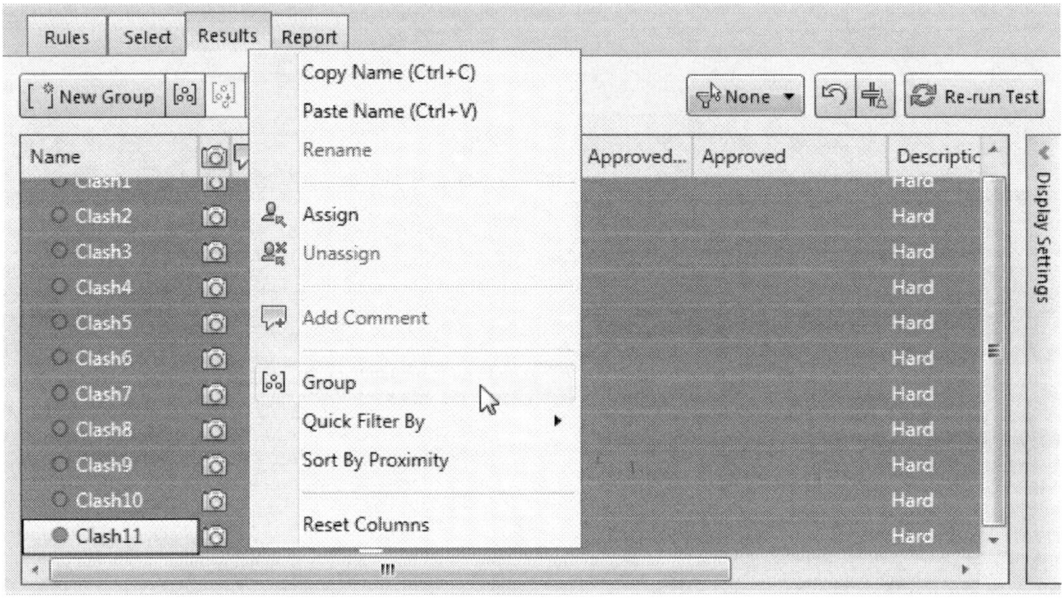

Figure 6–36

- Use <Ctrl> or <Shift> to select multiple names.
- You can rename the groups to make them easily recognizable. Click twice on the name or right-click and select **Rename**.
- To remove a clash from a group, select it and click  (Remove from Group).
- To ungroup, select the group title and click  (Explode Group).

6.6 Sharing Clash Test Results

The *Report* tab of the *Clash Detective* window enables you to create a text file, HTML report, or XML report to communicate the details of the clash tests. You can also save a list of viewpoints for later review. It is good practice to keep reports as short and as easy to read as possible, so only include succinct and necessary information in the report.

The *Reports* tab is broken into the following three areas, as shown in Figure 6–37:

- **Contents:** Provides a list of selectable attributes that can be included in the report.
- **Include Clashes:** The clash status is used to select which clashes are included in the report. Groups can also be used to control the report contents.
- **Output Settings:** Sets the type and format of the report.

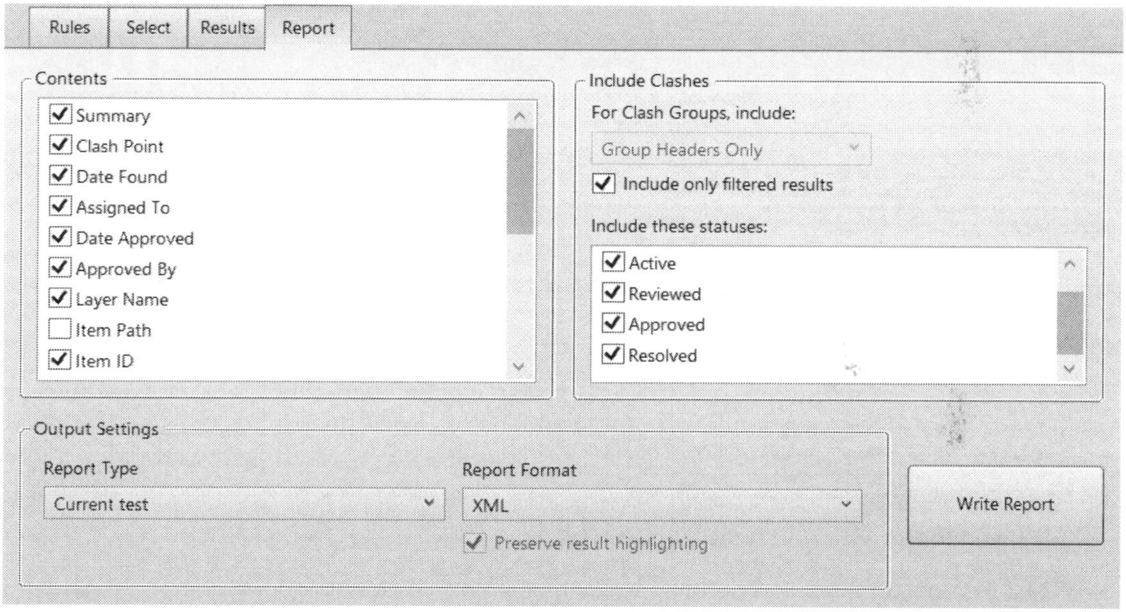

Figure 6–37

Output Settings

There are several types of reports and formats to chose from, as listed below:

Report Type

There are three report types, as shown in Figure 6–38:

- **Current test:** Run a report on the currently-selected clash test.
- **All tests (combined):** Combine all of the clash tests into a single report.
- **All tests (separate):** Create reports for all of the clash tests, with a separate report for each clash test.

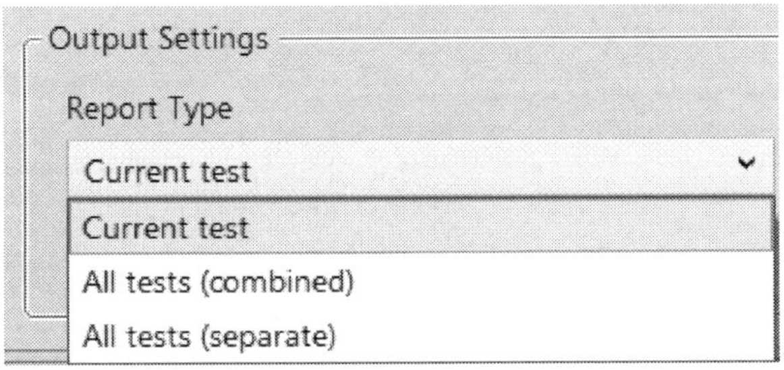

Figure 6–38

Report Format

There are several report formats available for the clash test results. When a report is written, an image file is created for each scene view that contains a clash. These image files are automatically saved to a folder located in the same directory as the report. The following report formats are available:

- **XML:** Includes images and details for clashes in an .XML file.
- **HTML:** Includes images and details for clashes in an .HTML file.
- **HTML (Tabular):** Includes details for clashes in a table which can be opened and edited in Microsoft Excel 2007 or later.
- **Text:** Includes the details for clashes in a text file with references to the image filenames.

  Note: *This format option is helpful for sharing the clash results with anyone using Navisworks Freedom.*

- **As Viewpoint:** Creates a saved viewpoint for each clash and places all of the clash viewpoints within one folder in the *Saved Viewpoints* window. Comments containing the details of each clash are added to the viewpoint automatically.

How To: Write a Clash Test Report

1. Open the *Clash Detective* window.
2. Select the clash test you want to create a report for.
3. In the *Report* tab, do the following, as shown in Figure 6–39:
   - In the *Contents* area, select any information that you want to include in the report.
   - In the *Include Clashes area,* select the grouping level and statuses that you want to include in the report.
   - In the *Output Settings* area, select the type and format of the report that you need.

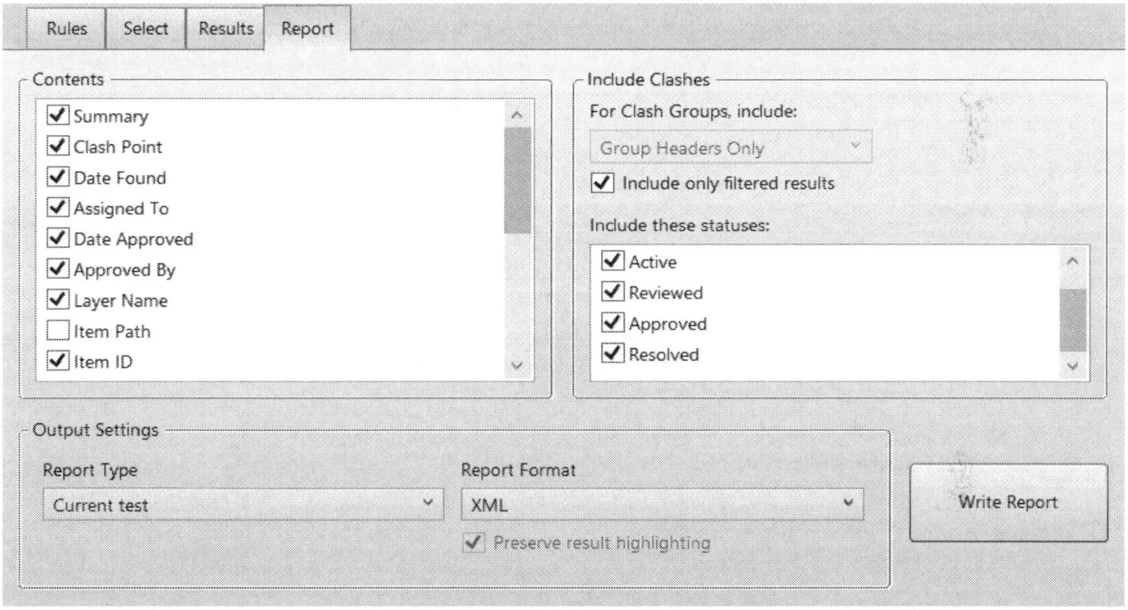

Figure 6–39

4. Click **Write Report**.

6.7 Incorporating Model Updates

Incorporating changes to the source models in Navisworks can easily be done, depending on the file format you are using. Remember, the following file formats are used in Navisworks:

- **Navisworks (.NWD):** The current state (or "snapshot") of a project, with all of the model geometry and markups included.
- **Navisworks File Set (.NWF):** Includes links to the original files that form a Navisworks model and markups.
- **Navisworks Cache (.NWC):** Snapshots of each original file that are created automatically when you open or append files from other software.

The .NWF format are the files you should work with most often as updating this model is the easiest.

- Since the .NWF files include links to the source files, you can simply overwrite the original source file with the latest version of the source file.
- If the source files are on your server, you can chose to keep the .NWF file updated at all times.
- If you are sharing files with team members outside of your office, you can also copy files from an external server or send as an attachment via email.

How To: Incorporate Updated Models in Clash Tests

1. In Windows Explorer, navigate to the Project Files. Paste the updated models into the directory, overwriting the original source files.
2. In Navisworks, on the *Home* tab>*Project* panel, click (Refresh) to force a refresh of the model to the latest file version.
3. If the files do not update in the Navisworks model, close the file, delete the corresponding (.NWC) file, and then re-open the Navisworks model.
4. In the *Clash Detective* window, click Update All (Update All) to re-run all of the clash tests.

Practice 6b
Review Clash Tests

Practice Objectives

- Review clash tests for clashes between objects.
- Assign clashes to individuals for correcting.
- Customize and create a clash report.
- Update the appended plumbing model to resolve the clashes.

> **Note:** *Clash Detection is only available in Navisworks Manage. It is not available in Navisworks Simulate or Navisworks Freedom.*

In this practice, you will review the clash tests ran in the previous practice. Then, you will assign clashes to specific team members for corrections, as shown in Figure 6–40. Finally, you will create reports to share the results with others.

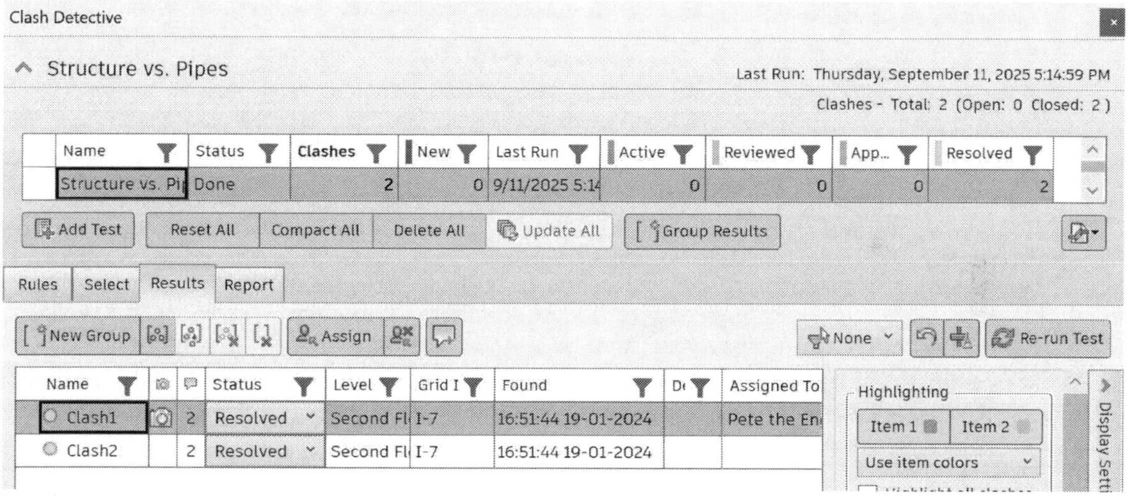

Figure 6–40

Task 1: Review and group the results.

1. Open **School-Review.nwf** from the *Navisworks BIM Practice Files\Clash Detection* folder.
2. In the *Clash Detective* window, select the **Structure vs. Pipes** clash test.
3. In the *Clash Detective* window, note the yellow alert triangles on the clashes.
4. Hover the mouse over a yellow alert triangle. As the tooltip explains, there have been changes to the models or the *Clash Detective* settings since the tests were run, as shown in Figure 6–41. This is because the file was previously saved and now reopened, and there are changes to the model.

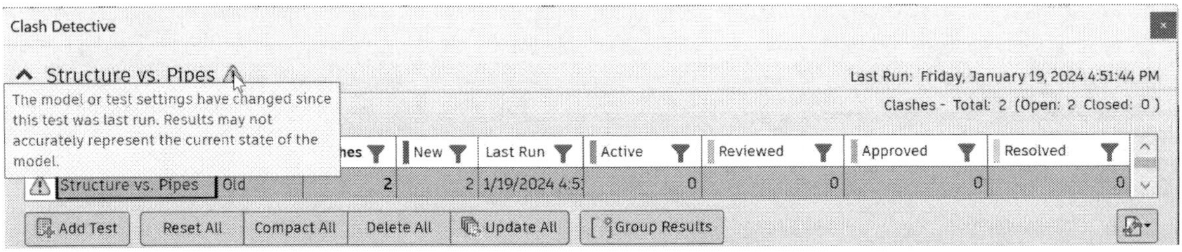

Figure 6–41

5. In the *Clash Detective* window, select  (Update All) to rerun the two clash tests.
6. Select the **Structures vs. Pipes** clash test.
7. Select the *Results* tab, if not already active. The two clashes are listed in the lower section of the window.
8. In the *Results* tab, note that **Clash1** is selected and it is displayed in the scene view. Select **Clash2** and review it.
9. Select the **Pipes vs. Ducts** clash test. (If it is not visible in the list, use the scroll bar arrow to display it.) Review several of the clashes by clicking on them one at a time.

10. In the *Results* tab, select **Clash1**. Press and hold <Ctrl> and select **Clash2**, **Clash4**, and **Clash5** to select them all at once, as shown in Figure 6–42.

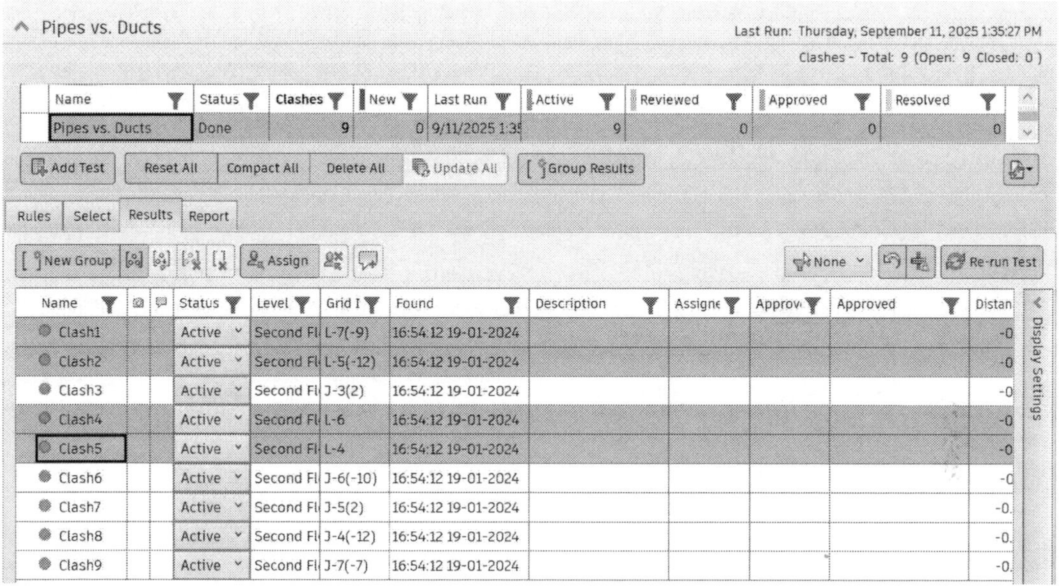

Figure 6–42

11. In the *Results* tab, click  (Group Selected Clashes). Note how the selected four are grouped under the new group as they involve the same pipe.

12. Select and right-click on the new group and select **Rename**. Rename the new group to **South Pipe** and press <Enter>. The new group should display as shown in Figure 6–43.

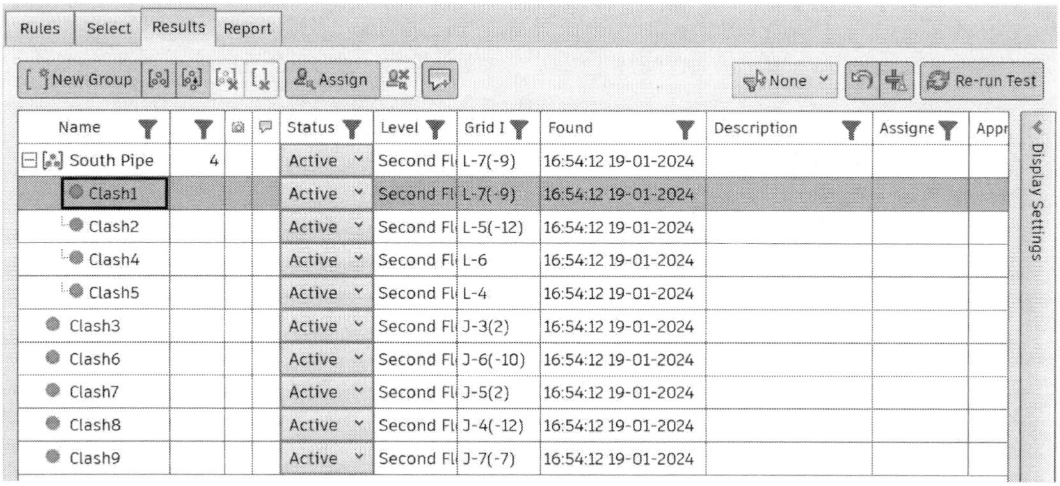

Figure 6–43

13. Select Clashes 3, 6, 7, and 8 and click (Group Selected Clashes).
14. Rename this group as **North Pipe**.

Only three clashes remain in this test, two groups and Clash9 which involves a different pipe.

Task 2: Assign clashes and add comments.

1. Select the **South Pipe** group.
2. Click (Assign).
3. In the *Assign Clash* dialog box, in the *Assign To:* field, enter **Erika the Engineer**, and then in the *Notes:* field, enter **Reroute pipe above the ductwork and ensure a quarter inch clearance.**, as shown in Figure 6–44.

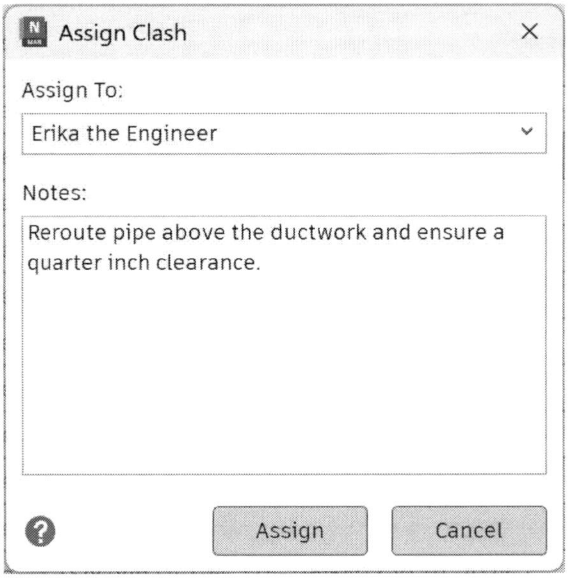

Figure 6–44

4. Click **Assign**.
5. To the right of the **South Pipe** group, expand the *Status* drop-down list and select **Reviewed**. Note the change in color of the group icon and the dot proceeding the clash name and all clashes in the group.
6. In the *Results* tab, select the **North Pipe** group.
7. Click (Assign).
8. In the *Assign Clash* dialog box, set the same assignment as for the **South Pipe** group, as shown in Figure 6–44 above.

9. Click **Assign**.
10. To the right of the **North Pipe** group, expand the *Status* drop-down list and select **Reviewed**.
11. In the *Results* tab, select **Clash9**. Upon review, this should be part of the *North Pipe* clash group as it is in the same area.
12. Click and drag it into the group and release it.
13. As was previously done, assign Clash9 to Erika the Engineer (using the same note) and also update its status to **Reviewed**. The *Clash Detective* window should display as shown in Figure 6–45.

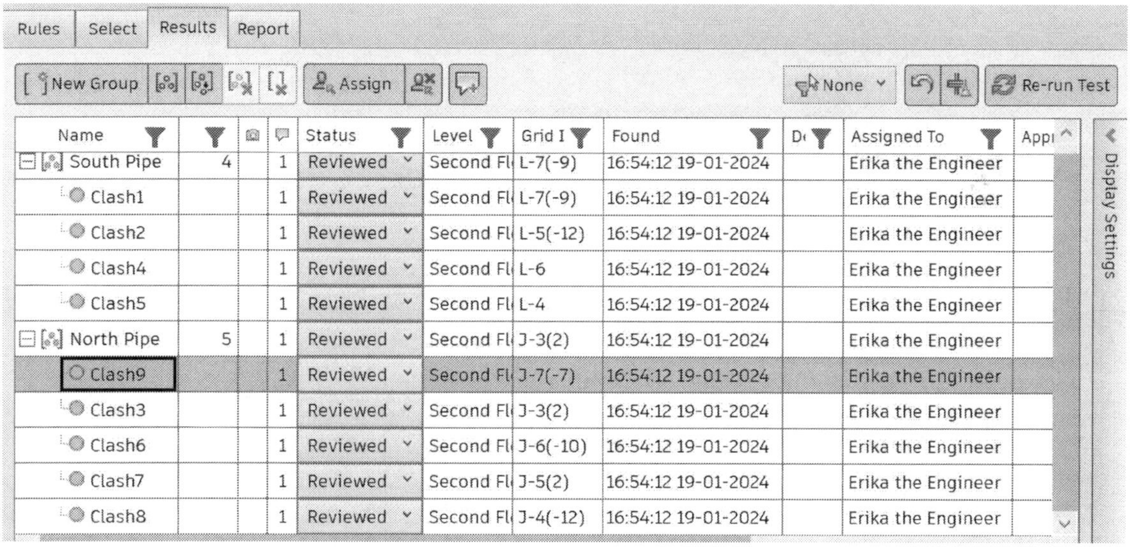

Figure 6–45

14. In the *Clash Detective* window, select the **Structure vs. Pipes** clash test.
15. In the *Results* tab, select **Clash1**, if not already selected.
16. Click 

(Assign).
17. In the *Assign Clash* dialog box, in the *Assign To:* field, enter **Pete the Engineer**, and then in the *Notes:* field, enter **Reroute pipe to the left of the column and ensure a quarter inch clearance.**
18. Click **Assign**.
19. To the right of **Clash1**, expand the *Status* drop-down list and select **Reviewed**.
20. In the *Results* tab, select **Clash2**.
21. Click  (Add Comment).
22. In the *Add Comment* dialog box, enter **Is there enough room to bend this pipe or does it need elbows?**.

23. In the *Status* drop-down list, select **Active**, as shown in Figure 6–46.

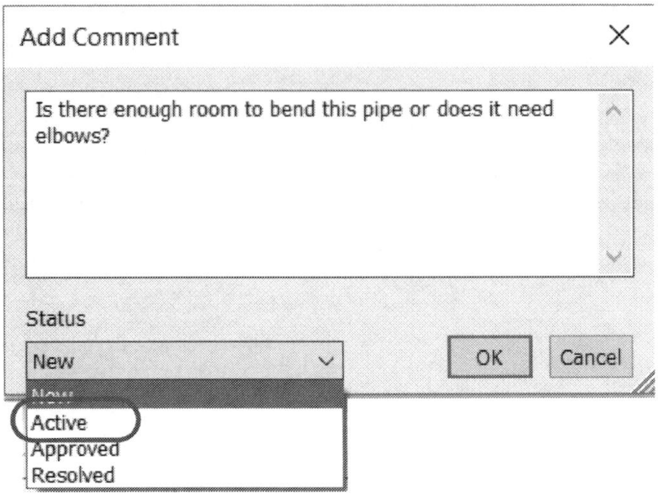

Figure 6–46

24. Click **OK**.

25. To see the comments in Navisworks, in the *Review* tab>*Comments* panel, click (View Comments). The *Comments* window displays, as shown in Figure 6–47. This window might be displayed along the bottom of the screen.

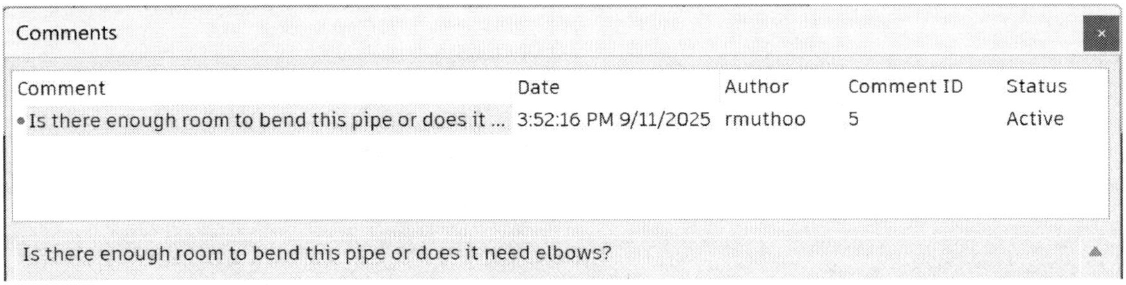

Figure 6–47

Task 3: Create a clash report.

1. In the *Clash Detective* window, select the *Report* tab.
2. In the *Contents* area, select the following options (as shown in Figure 6–48):
   - Summary
   - Clash Point
   - Date Found
   - Assigned To
   - Date Approved
   - Status
   - Description
   - Comments
   - Image
   - Clash Group
   - Grid Location
3. In the *Include Clashes* area, clear the **Include only filtered results** checkbox. Ensure that all of the statuses are selected, as shown in Figure 6–48.
4. In the *Output Settings* area, for *Report Type,* select **All Tests (combined)**, and for *Report Format* select **HTML,** as shown in Figure 6–48.

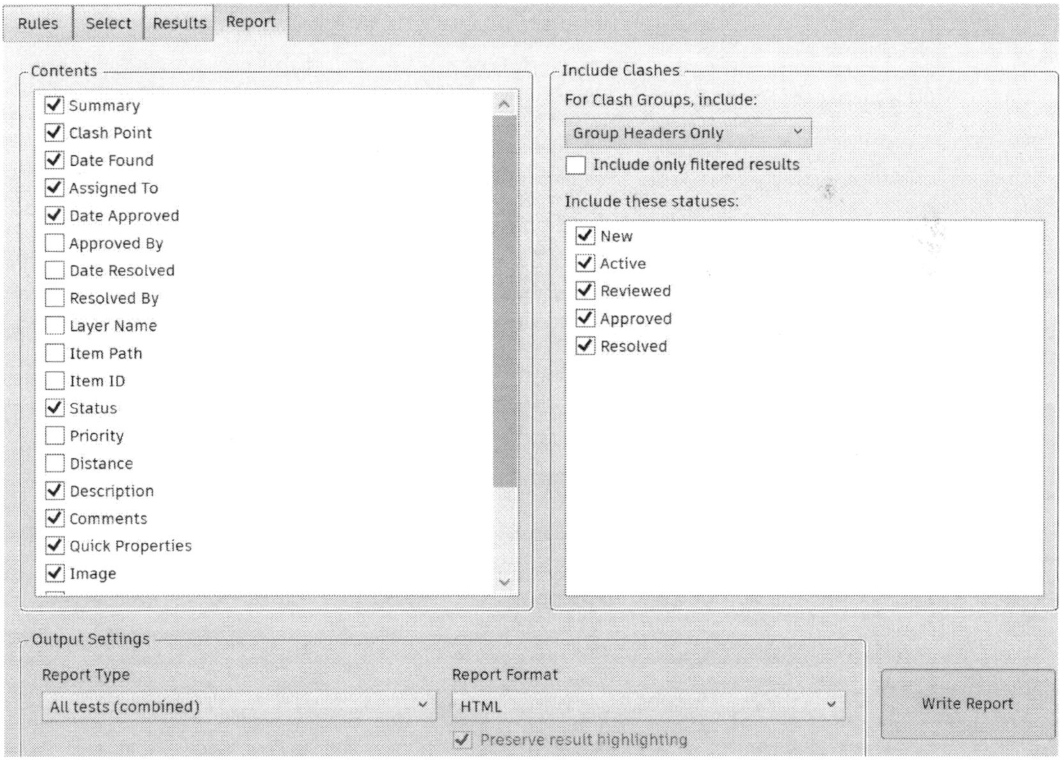

Figure 6–48

5. Click **Write Report**.
6. In the *Save As* dialog box, navigate to the *Navisworks BIM Practice Files\Clash Detection* folder and click **Save** to accept the default filename.
7. In Windows File Explorer, open the HTML file to review the report.
8. Close the HTML file when done reviewing.
9. In Navisworks, save **School-Review.nwf**.

Task 4: Update the plumbing model and re-run the clash tests.

1. In Windows File Explorer, under the *Navisworks BIM Practice Files\Clash Detection* folder, right-click on the **School-Plumbing-Modify.rvt** file and select **Copy**.
2. In Windows File Explorer, navigate to the *Navisworks BIM Practice Files\Project Files\Revit Files* folder. Right-click in the folder window and select **Paste**.
3. Rename the *School-Plumbing.rvt* file to **School-Plumbing-Original.rvt**.
4. Rename the *School-Plumbing-Modify.rvt* file to **School-Plumbing.rvt**.
5. In Navisworks, in the *Home* tab>*Project* panel or in the Quick Access Toolbar, click (Refresh). Navisworks updates to incorporate the change to the Revit file.
6. Note in the *Clash Detective* window that both clash tests show the yellow alert triangle indicating they are **Old** (out of date), as shown in Figure 6–49.

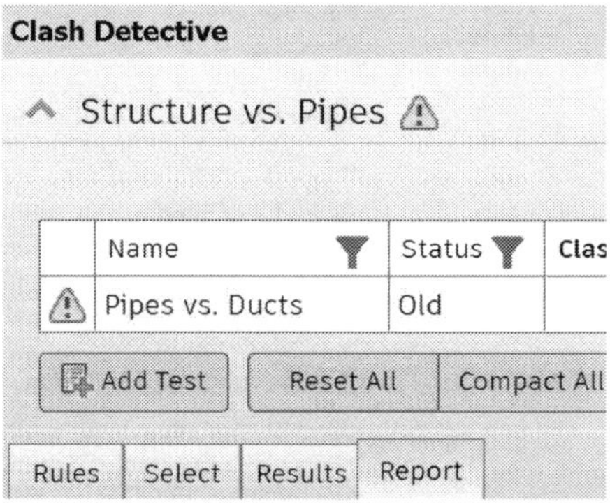

Figure 6–49

7. In the *Clash Detective* window, click Update All (Update All) to re-run the clash tests.

8. Review the clashes individually. All of the clashes in both clash tests should display a status of **Resolved**, as shown in Figure 6–50.

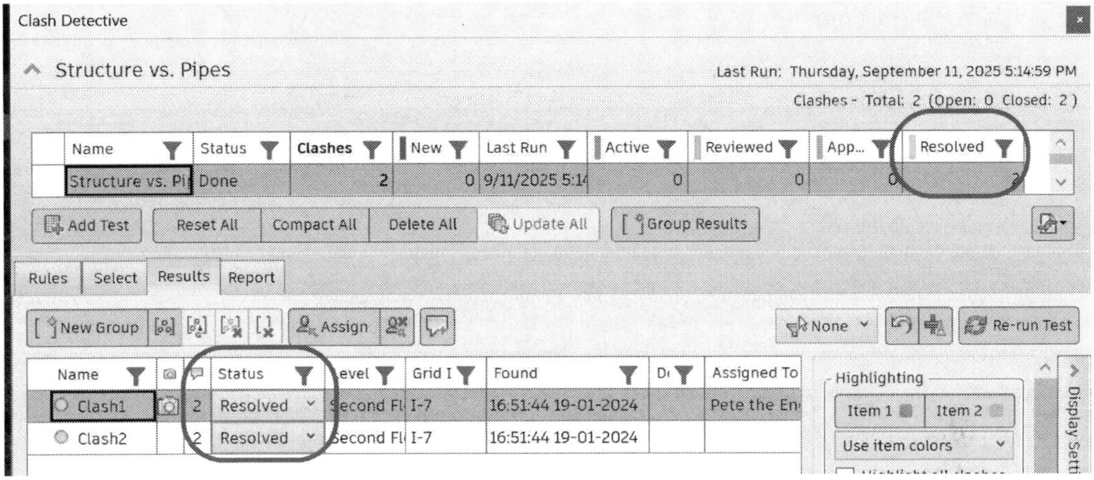

Figure 6–50

9. Save the **School-Review.nwf** file.

End of practice

Chapter Review Questions

1. What are the different types of clashes that you can run? (Select all that apply.)
   a. Hard
   b. Soft
   c. Partial
   d. Clearance

2. Clash test parameters can be saved and used on other projects.
   a. True
   b. False

3. In the *Clash Detective* window, what would you use the *Rules* tab for?
   a. Use Rules to include the things you want to check.
   b. Use Rules to set the clearance tolerance.
   c. Use Rules to filter out things you do not want checked.
   d. Use Rules to change the colors of clashing items.

4. What is the purpose of Groups in the Clash Detective?
   a. To hide non-clashing items easily.
   b. To bring related clashes together.
   c. To run multiple clash tests at the same time.
   d. To view similar comments at the same time.

5. Where can you change the color of items that clash?
   a. In the *Options* dialog box.
   b. In the *Clash Detective* window, under *Display Settings*, in the *Isolation* Area.
   c. In the *Clash Detective* window, under *Display Settings*, in the *Highlighting* Area.
   d. In the *Clash Detective* window, in the *Items* pane.

Command Summary

Button	Command	Location
	**Add Comment**	• **Window:** Clash Detective>*Review* tab
	**Add Test**	• **Window:** Clash Detective
	**Assign**	• **Window:** Clash Detective>*Review* tab
	**Clash Detective**	• **Ribbon:** *Home* tab>*Project* panel • **Hot Key:** <Ctrl>+<F2>
	**Explode Group**	• **Window:** Clash Detective>*Review* tab
	**Group Selected Clashes**	• **Window:** Clash Detective>*Review* tab
	**Import/Export Clash Tests**	• **Window:** Clash Detective
	**New Group**	• **Window:** Clash Detective>*Review* tab
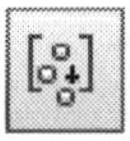	**Remove from Group**	• **Window:** Clash Detective>*Review* tab
	**Unassign**	• **Window:** Clash Detective>*Review* tab
	**View Comment**	• **Ribbon:** *Review* tab>*Comments* panel

Chapter 7

Quantification

An important part of any construction project is estimating how much material is required. This quantification can occur in the authoring applications (such as Civil 3D® and Revit®), at later stages of design development, or at the tendering, pre-construction phase using Autodesk® Navisworks®. Learn how to create material estimates, measure areas, count components, and perform various types of takeoffs on 2D plans.

Note: *Quantification is available for Navisworks Manage and Navisworks Simulate users.*

Learning Objectives

- Set up a *Quantification Workbook*.
- Assign an *Item Catalog* to a project and create resources in the *Resource Catalog*.
- Conduct a model takeoff (3D) and a takeoff from a DWF sheet (2D).
- Export takeoff data from a *Quantification Workbook*.

BIM Workflow: Analyze

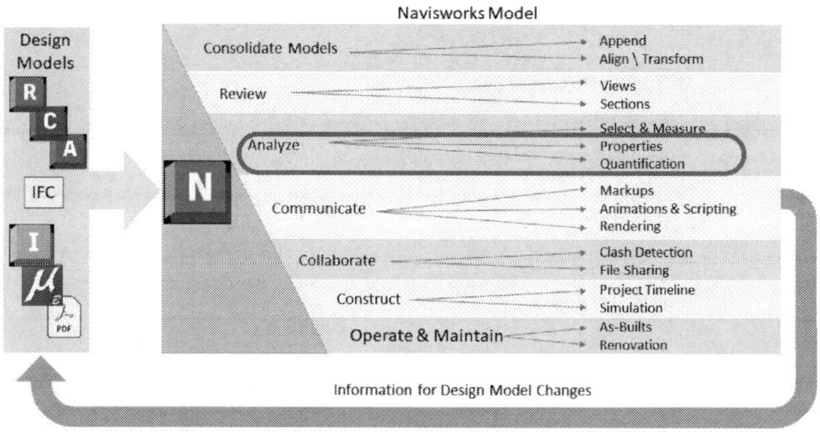

7.1 Quantification Overview

Navisworks Quantification is a feature that is available for both Navisworks Manage and Navisworks Simulate users. It enables you to measure material quantities, measure areas, and count components using data from your 3D models or your 2D drawing sheets. This process of measurement is called takeoff and it is an important part of providing accurate estimates for your construction and renovation projects.

Supported File Formats

Navisworks Quantification supports the following multi-discipline Autodesk file types:

Publishing Application	File Format
AutoCAD Architecture	.DWF, .DWFX
AutoCAD MEP	.DWF, .DWFX
AutoCAD Plant 3D	.DWF, .DWFX
Autodesk Civil 3D	.DWF, .DWFX
Autodesk Inventor	.DWF, .DWFX
Autodesk Revit	.RVT, .NWC, .DWF, .DWFX
Adobe	.PDF

> **Note:** *For 2D takeoff, only .DWF and .DWFX file formats are supported. Consider converting 2D image files (e.g., PDFs) to .DWF using print driver software.*

Quantification Workflow

The Quantification workflow begins with a design file (such as one of those listed above) that is brought into Navisworks. A typical workflow includes the following:

1. Open the file for which a Quantification project is to be created in Navisworks.
2. Set up a project in the Quantification tool.
3. Manage the *Item Catalog* and *Resource Catalog*.
4. Create 3D model and virtual takeoffs, as required.
5. Create 2D takeoffs, as required.
6. Manage takeoff data, as required.
7. Review the takeoff data as changes are made to the source files.
8. Output the takeoff data, as required.

7.2 Setting Up a Quantification Project

The *Quantification Workbook* is your main workspace in a Quantification project. The first time the workbook is accessed in a Navisworks file, you must set up the project, which will consist of your model and any takeoff items that will be used to calculate material quantities. Once a project is created, you will import a catalog and specify project settings, then save it with the Navisworks file. It is accessed each time the Quantification feature is accessed.

How To: Set Up a Quantification Project

1. To access the *Quantification Workbook*, use one of the following methods:

    - On the ribbon, in the *Home* tab>*Tools* panel, click 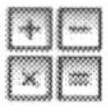 (Quantification), as shown in Figure 7–1.

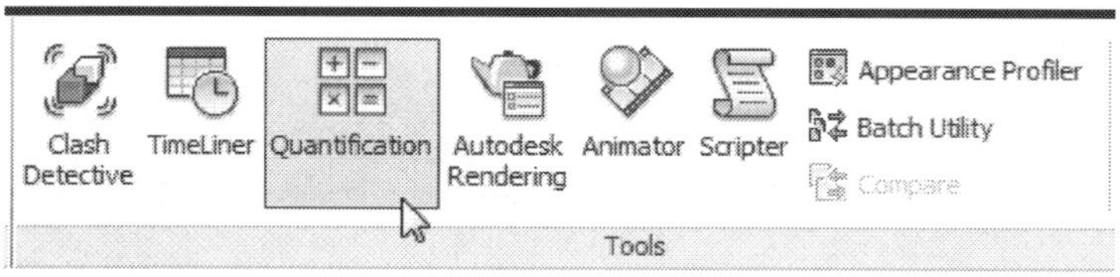

Figure 7–1

    - On the ribbon, in the *View* tab>*Workspace* panel, click the Windows drop-down list and select **Quantification Workbook**, as shown in Figure 7–2.

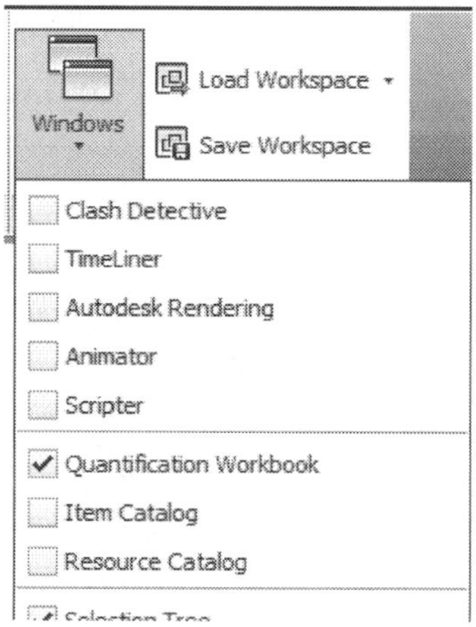

Figure 7–2

2. In the *Quantification Workbook* window, click 

to access the *Quantification Setup Wizard*. If a project already exists in the Navisworks file, setup is not required.

3. Select an option in the *Quantification Getting Started* dialog box, as shown in Figure 7–3. This dialog box provides you with the opportunity to review help on Quantification.

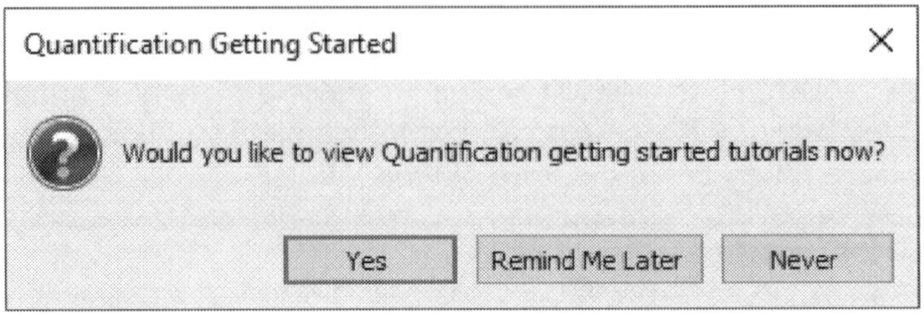

Figure 7–3

4. Select the item catalog that is to be used for the project. Navisworks provides a few default item catalogs or you can load any additional item catalog files (.XML). Browse to or select an existing catalog, as shown in Figure 7–4, and click **Next**.

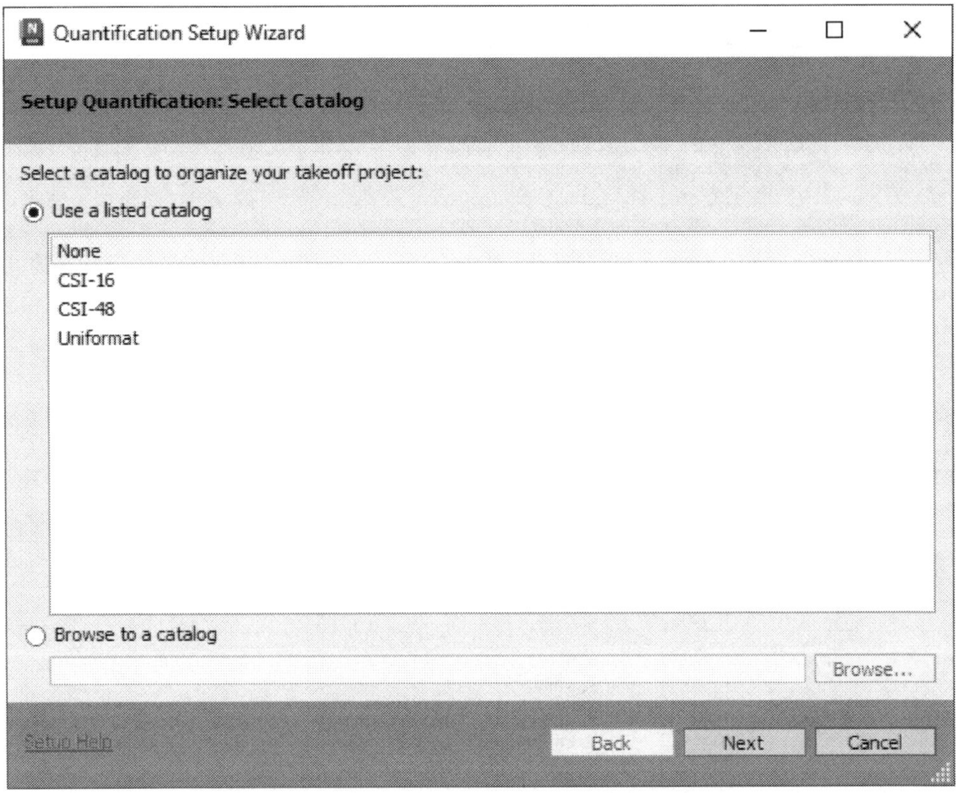

Figure 7–4

Note: *The listed catalogs can also include company-specific catalogs that have been created. If you want to use a custom catalog for your project, it has to have the same units and properties.*

5. If you use a listed catalog option, you can select the overall unit type to be used in the project, as shown in Figure 7–5, and click **Next**. The options include:
   - **Imperial:** Units in the model are converted to imperial (e.g., feet, pounds, or gallons).
   - **Metric:** Units in the model are converted to metric (e.g., meters, kilograms, or liters).
   - **Variable:** Keeps the existing values for the model. The next wizard page will enable you to change each individual takeoff property's unit.

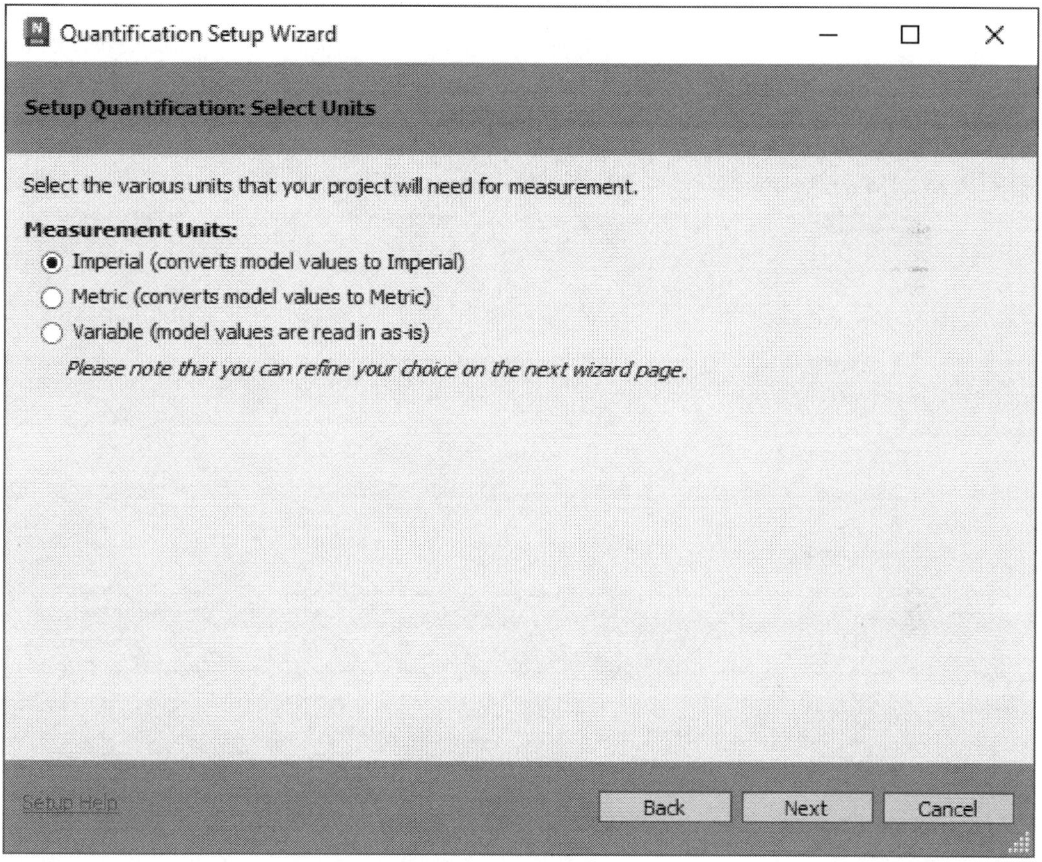

Figure 7–5

6. Refine the units for specific properties by selecting units in the drop-down lists adjacent to each property, as shown in Figure 7–6. Additionally, you can select the **Show Metric and Imperial units for each takeoff property** option, if required, to display both units. Click **Next**.

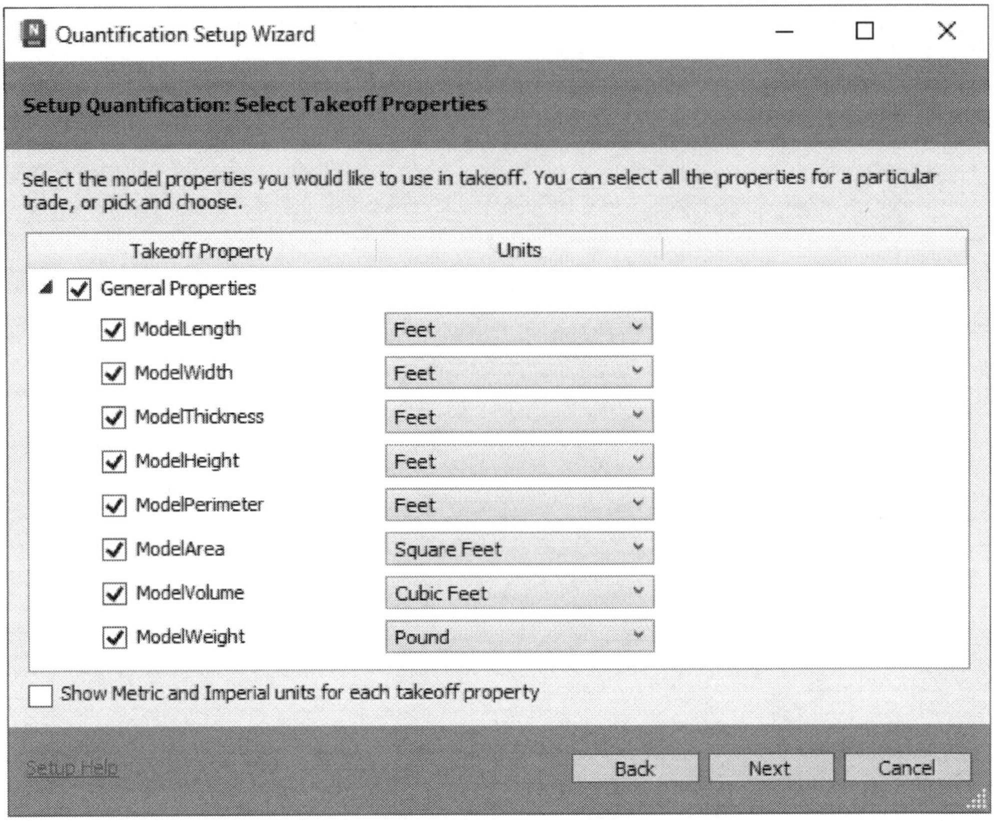

Figure 7–6

7. Click **Finish** to complete the project setup. Once the project has been created, the *Quantification Workbook* updates to display the *Item Catalog* that was selected or imported, as shown in Figure 7–7.

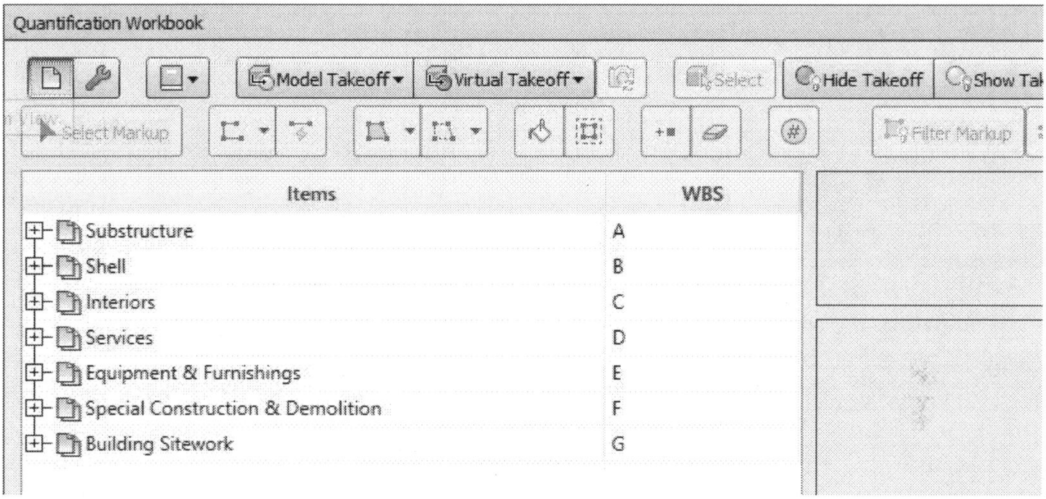

Figure 7–7

Hint: Quantification Catalogs

Quantification catalogs can be imported after the workbook has been created. To import a catalog, click (Import/Export) in the *Quantification Workbook*, select **Import Catalog**, and browse to and open a new catalog. You are prompted if duplicate items are encountered.

Quantification Workbook

The *Quantification Workbook* consists of the following panes and a toolbar, as shown in Figure 7–8:

- **Navigation pane (1):** Contains a list of items or resources and their respective Work Breakdown Structure (WBS) codes. Click  in the toolbar to switch between the list of items (Item View) or resources (Resource View). If the Resource View is displayed, the Resource Breakdown Structure (RBS) codes are displayed.
- **Toolbar (2):** Contains the 2D and 3D Quantification commands.
- **Takeoff pane (3):** Contains a list of all takeoff items. Right-click a column header to change what is displayed in the pane.
- **Rollup pane (4):** Provides a takeoff summary. Right-click on the column headers in this pane to define what is displayed.

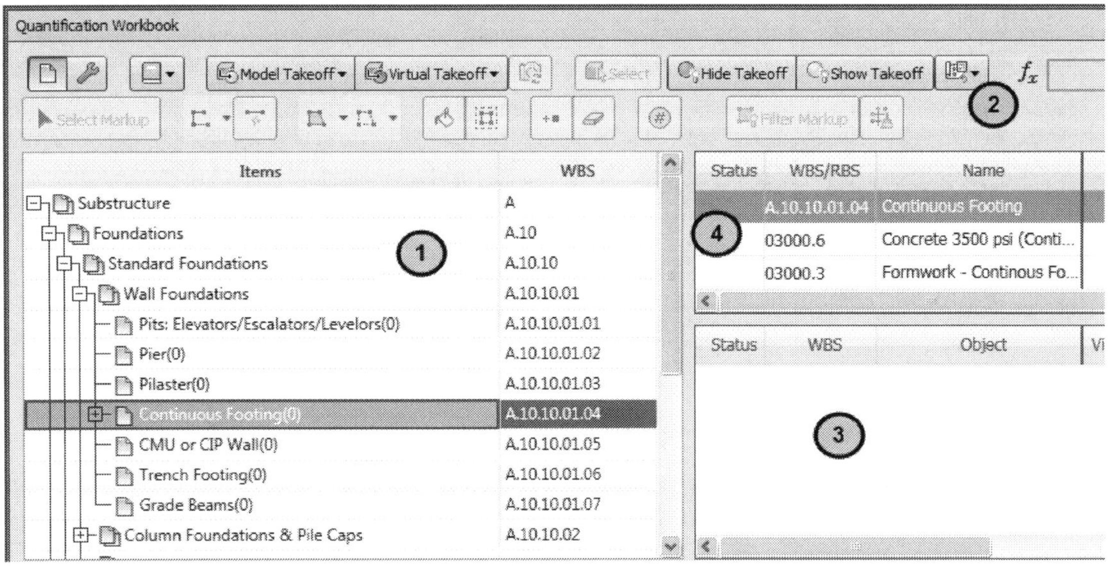

Figure 7–8

7.3 Item and Resource Management

The *Item Catalog* and *Resource Catalog* information is used to classify the elements. These catalogs enhance the model information to generate a more complete quantification/takeoff of the project, not just counts of objects. Basing a project on a catalog enables you to populate the workbook with the takeoff groups in these catalogs. If needed, you can also create additional groups and items by importing specific data from other catalogs or spreadsheets. Once catalogs are created in a project, consider exporting and reusing them in other projects.

Item and Resource Catalog Windows

By default, the *Item* and *Resource* catalogs are nested together in the *Quantification Workbook* window. Each can be displayed by selecting their tab name along the bottom of the window. They can also be displayed as separate windows by double-clicking on their title bar and double-clicking again on the title bar to nest them. To toggle these windows on or off:

- In the *View* tab>*Workspace* panel, expand the *Windows* drop-down list and select **Item Catalog** or **Resource Catalog**, as required.
- On the toolbar in the *Quantification Workbook*, click  and select **Item Catalog** or **Resource Catalog**, as required.
- With either the *Item Catalog or Resource Catalog* window active, you can click either **Resource Catalog** or **Item Catalog** to open the other window.

The *Item Catalog* consists of the following, as shown in Figure 7–9:

- **Items (1)**
- **Resources (2)**
- **Formulas (3):** This area enables you to link variables with a formula to get takeoff values.

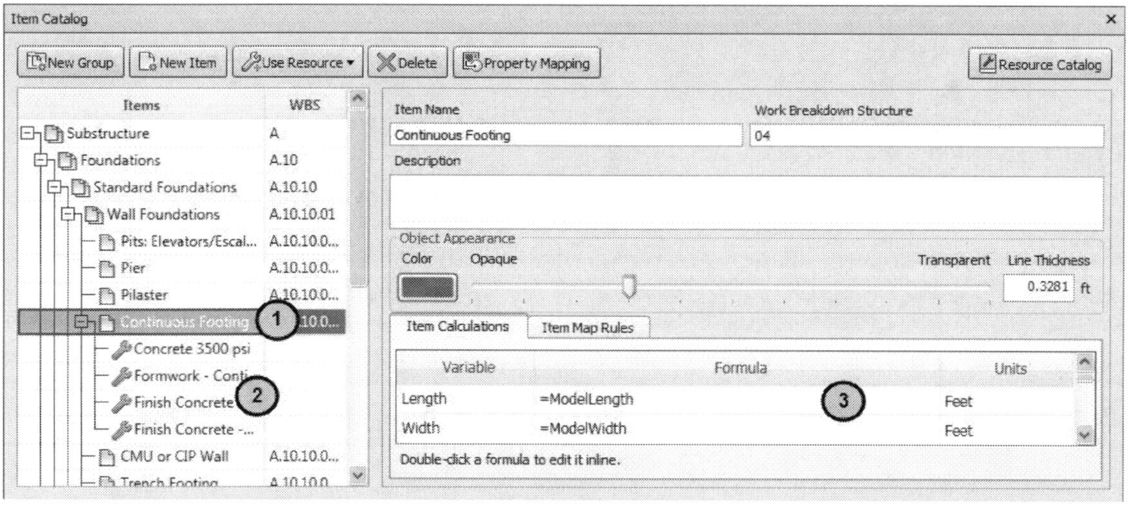

Figure 7–9

The *Resource Catalog* consists of the following, as shown in Figure 7–10:

- **Resource Groups (1)**
- **Resources (2)**
- **Formulas (3):** The *Formula* area enables you to link variables with a formula to measure takeoff values.

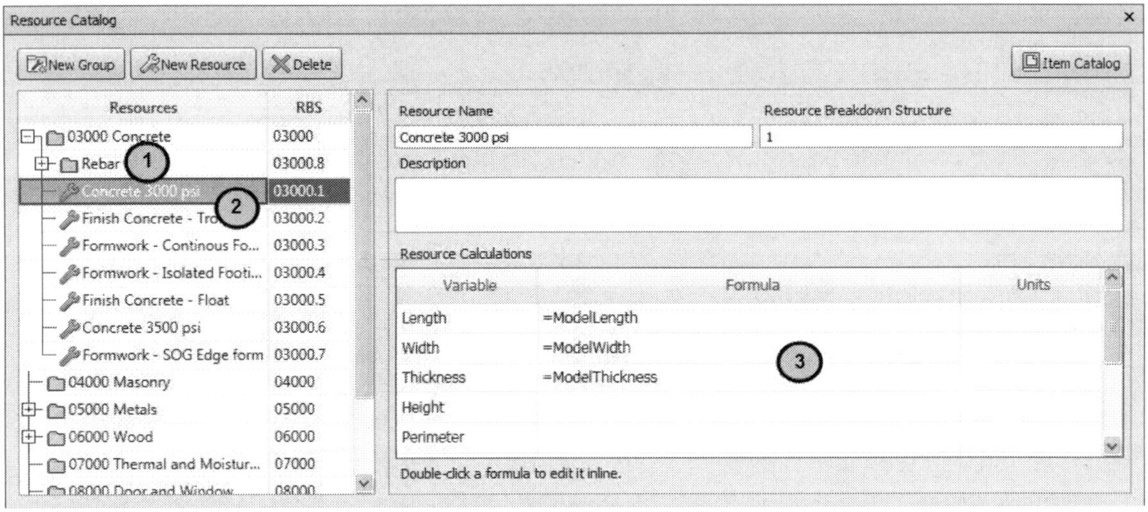

Figure 7–10

Items in the *Item Catalog* can be associated with an object in the model, such as a door or a wall, and can stand alone or contain resources. If resources exist, they are listed in the *Resource Catalog*, which is a database of your project resources.

Creating Groups and Items in the Item Catalog

In Quantification, takeoff data is organized in the following hierarchy in the *Item Catalog*. The icons associated with each help identify them.

- Work Breakdown Structure (WBS) groups ()
- Items ()
- Resources ()

This hierarchy is shown in Figure 7–11 as a navigation tree. There are multiple levels of WBS groups () that contain items (), and the items contain resources (). This structure enables you to create the organizational structure required for your projects.

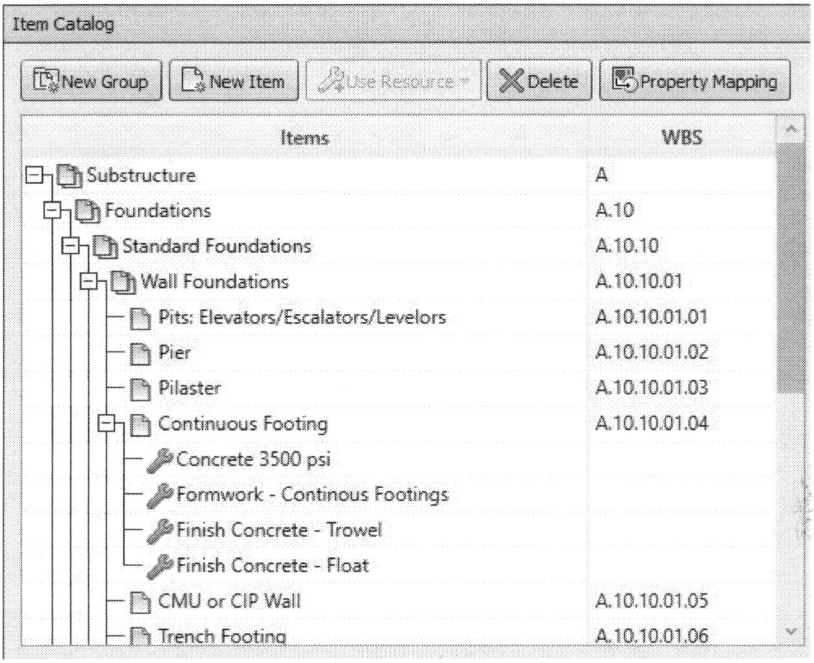

Figure 7–11

How To: Create a New Group

1. In the *Item Catalog* window, click **New Group**. Alternatively, you can right-click in the white space (nothing selected) and select **New Group** to create a new group at the top of the hierarchy, or right-click on an existing group and select **New Group** to create a new group within the selected group.

   Note: *If an existing group is selected, the new group is created in that group. To create a new group at the top of the hierarchy, ensure that no groups are currently selected.*

2. Enter a name for the group and press <Enter>.

How To: Create a New Item

1. In the *Item Catalog* window, expand and select the group in which you want to create the item.

   Note: *The new item is created within the selected group. Items can also be created outside of groups by clearing all of the group selections in the item hierarchy.*

2. Once selected, click **New Item**. Alternatively, you can right-click in the white space (nothing selected) and select **New Item** to create a new item at the top of the hierarchy, or right-click on an existing group and select **New Item** to create a new item in the selected group.
3. Enter a name for the item and press <Enter>.

Hint: Copying Items and Groups

Items and groups can be copied to quickly add items in the *Item Catalog*. To copy, right-click the required item or group and select **Copy**. To paste, right-click the group in which you want the copied item or group to sit and select **Paste**.

Creating Resources in the Resource Catalog

In Quantification, takeoff data is organized in the following hierarchy in the *Resource Catalog*:

- Resource Breakdown Structure (RBS) groups ( )
- Resources ( )

This hierarchy is a navigation tree that supports multiple levels of RBS groups, enabling you to create the organizational structure required for your takeoff project, as shown in Figure 7–12.

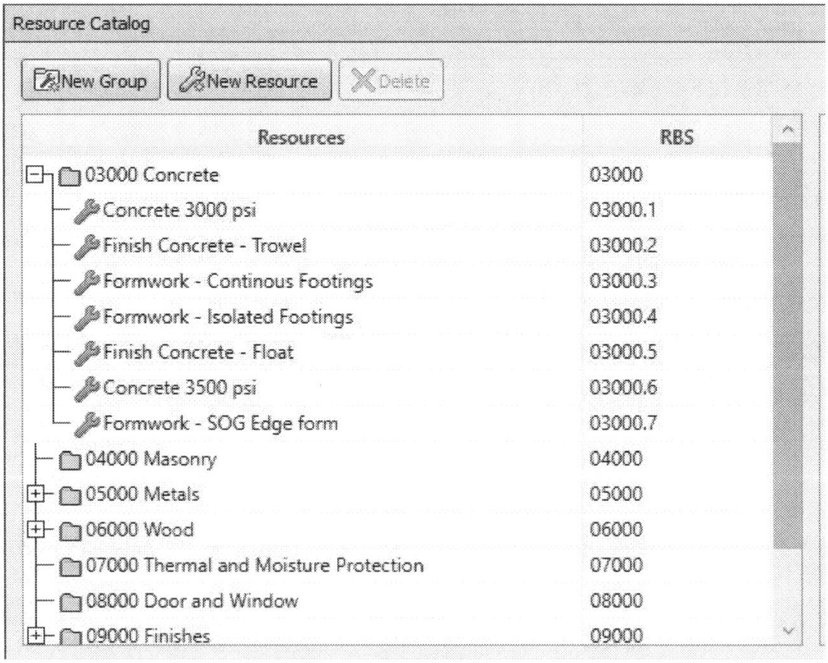

Figure 7–12

How To: Create a New Resource

1. In the *Resource Catalog* window, expand the resource grouping in which you want to create the resource.
2. To create a new group in the *Resource Catalog*, click **New Group**. Sub-groups can also be created to help further manage the resources required for a Quantification project.

   Note: *Groups are only created and used in the Resource Catalog for resource management. The group headings are not used in the Quantification Workbook.*

3. Once the required resource group has been selected, click **New Resource**. The resource is created within the group. Alternatively, you can right-click in the white space (with nothing selected) and select **New Resource** to create a new resource at the top of the hierarchy, or right-click on an existing group and select **New Resource** to create a new resource in a selected group.

   Note: *Resources can also be created outside of groups by clearing all of the group selections in the Resource Catalog hierarchy before creating the resource.*

Adding Resources to the Item Catalog

Resources that are created in the *Resource Catalog* are not automatically added to the Item Catalog. To be used in the project's *Quantification Workbook*, they must be copied into the *Item Catalog*.

How To: Copy a Resource to the Item Catalog

1. In the *Item Catalog* window, expand the item grouping in which to place the new resource.
2. In the *Resource Catalog* window, expand the resource grouping in which the required resource is located.

3. Select the resource to be copied, right-click, and select **Add To Selected Catalog Item**, as shown in Figure 7–13.

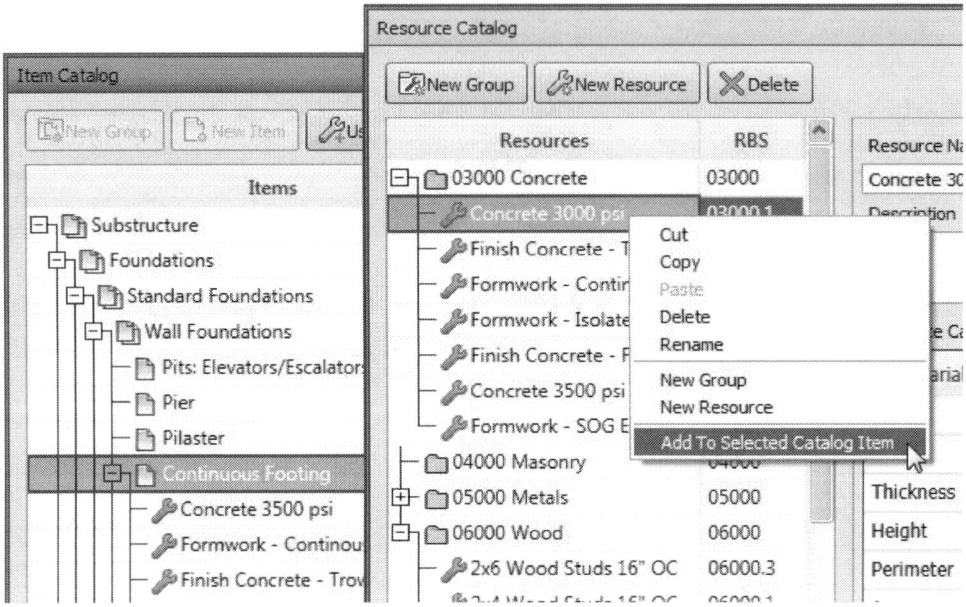

Figure 7–13

Copying Groups and Items in the Item Catalog

An existing group and item structure that is created in the *Item Catalog* can be duplicated as required to create another structure. When copied, all of the groups, items, and resources are also duplicated.

How To: Copy Groups in the Item Catalog

1. In the *Item Catalog* window, select the top level that you want to copy. It can contain groups, items, and resources.
2. Right-click and select **Copy**.
3. Select the level to which you want to paste.
4. Right-click and select **Paste**.
5. Right-click groups or items in the copied structure and select **Rename** to rename them.

Practice 7a
Set Up a Quantification Workbook

Practice Objectives

- Initialize the *Quantification Workbook*.
- Set up and review the *Resource Catalog* and *Item Catalog*.

In this practice, you will begin the Quantification process by setting up the project, the *Resource Catalog*, and the *Item Catalog*. You will then review selected items.

Task 1: Set up the Quantification project.

1. Open **School-Takeoff-Setup.nwf** from the *Navisworks BIM Practice Files\Quantification* folder.
2. Open the *Quantification Workbook* window. If this window is not docked along the bottom of the software interface, in the *Home* tab>*Tools* panel, click (Quantification).
   - Alternatively, in the *View* tab>*Workspace* panel, you can select **Quantification Workbook** in the *Windows* drop-down list.
3. Dock the *Quantification Workbook* at the bottom of the Navisworks screen or on a second monitor, if available.
4. In the *Quantification Workbook* window, click **Project Setup**.
5. Select **Remind Me Later** from the *Quantification Getting Started* dialog box to continue to the Quantification Setup Wizard.
6. Select **Browse to a catalog** and click **Browse**. Navigate to the *Navisworks BIM Practice Files\Quantification* folder and select **School-Quantification Catalog.xml**. This .XML file is the *Item Catalog* that will be used for this project.
7. Click **Open**.

8. In the *Quantification Setup Wizard*, click **Next**, then click **Finish** to complete the project setup. The *Item Catalog* has now been assigned to the file, as shown in Figure 7–14.

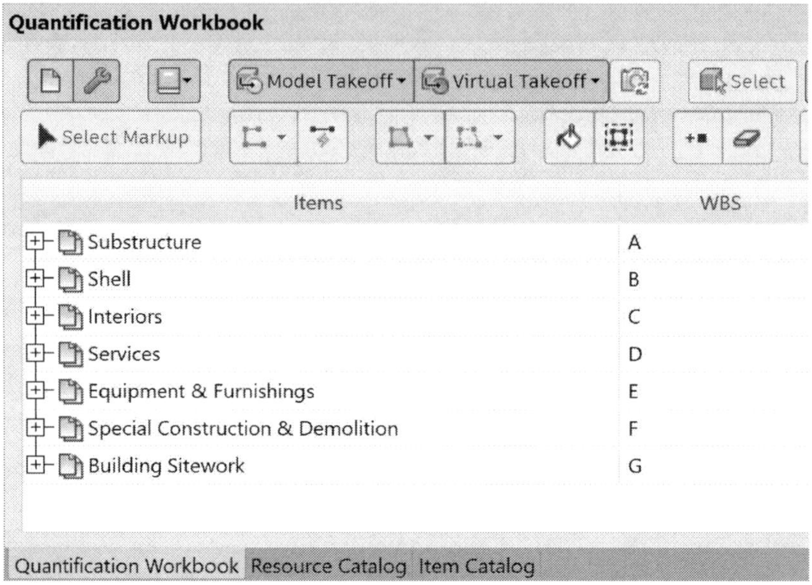

Figure 7–14

Note: *If one of the default project types was selected, the wizard would prompt for additional unit measurement selections. Because an .XML file was selected, the unit definition has already been assigned.*

Task 2: Review the Item and Resource Catalogs and add items.

1. In the *Quantification Workbook* toolbar, click 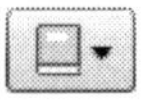 (Show and hide the item and Resource Catalogs) to expand the menu and ensure that the **Item Catalog** and **Resource Catalog** items are selected for display.
   - Alternatively, in the *View* tab>*Workspace* panel, you can select **Item Catalog** in the *Windows* drop-down list.
2. By default, the *Quantification Workbook*, *Item Catalog*, and *Resource Catalog* are all included in the window and are accessed by selecting the appropriate tab at the bottom of the window, when displayed. You can individually drag out any of the windows, as required, to display them separately.

   Note: *Double-clicking on a title bar undocks a docked window.*

3. Select the *Item Catalog* tab at the bottom of the *Quantification Workbook* window, to open the *Item Catalog* window.

4. In the *Item Catalog* window, browse the item collections showing the items in the list, the folder structure, and the WBS numbering, as shown in Figure 7–15.

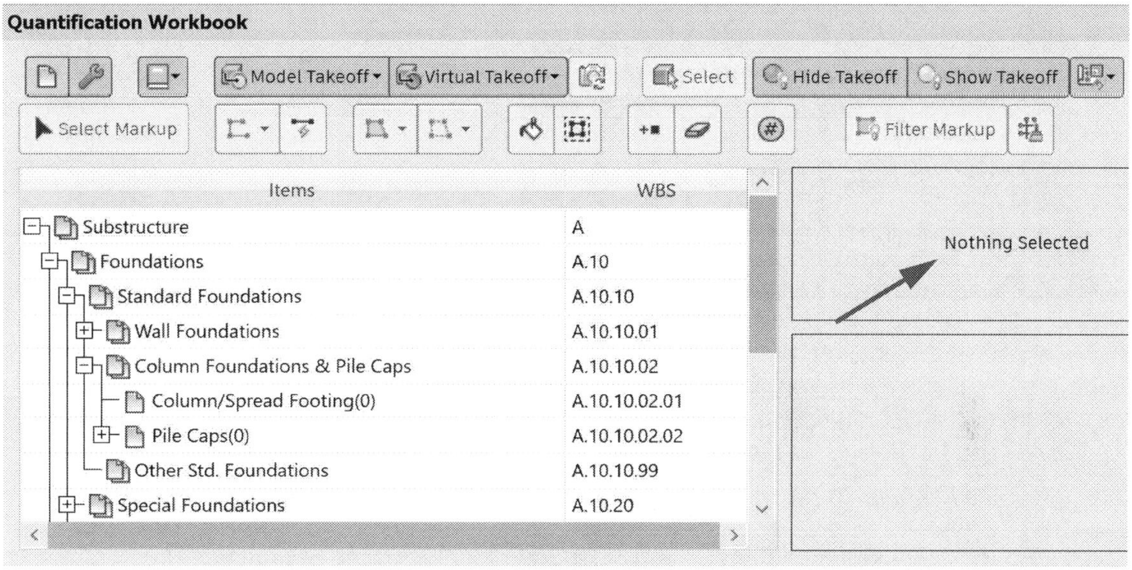

Figure 7–15

5. In the *Item Catalog* window, ensure that no groups are currently selected, and **Nothing Selected** is displayed in the right side pane. This ensures that any new groups are added to the first level of the *Item Catalog* and not to a sub-group. Click **New Group**. Enter **Materials** as the name for the group and press <Enter>.
6. Ensure that the **Materials** group is selected. In the pane on the right, enter **H** as the *Work Breakdown Structure*.
7. With the *Materials* group still selected, click **New Group** again. Enter **Paint** as the name for the group and press <Enter>.
8. In the *Item Catalog* window, select the **Paint** group and click **New Item**. Enter **Blue Paint** as the name for the item and press <Enter>.
9. Select the **Paint** group and click **New Item**. Enter **Beige Paint** as the name for the item and press <Enter>.

10. Add **White Paint** and **Red Paint** as two additional items in the **Paint** group, as shown in Figure 7–16.

Figure 7–16

11. Return to the *Quantification Workbook* and note that the new group named **Materials** containing the items is now available.
12. Select the *Resource Catalog* tab. If it is not a listed tab with the *Quantification Workbook* and *Item Catalog*, you must display it by clicking 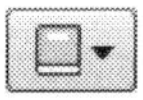 in the *Quantification Workbook* and selecting **Resource Catalog**.
13. Browse the resource collections displaying the resources in the list, folder structure, and RBS numbering, as shown in Figure 7–17.

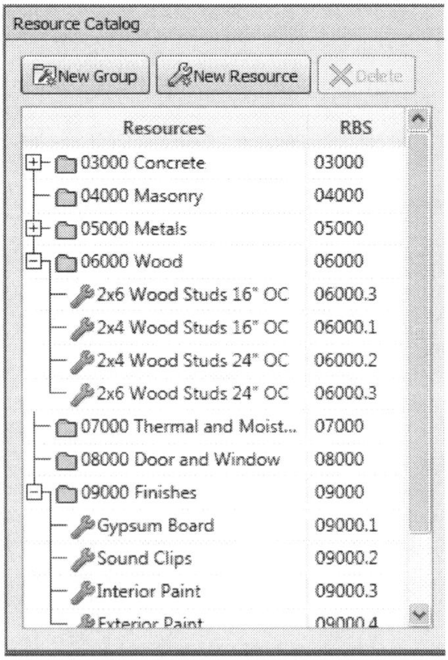

Figure 7–17

14. In the *Resource Catalog* window, expand the **03000 Concrete** resource grouping and select it. Click **New Group** to make a new group within the 03000 Concrete resource. Enter **Rebar** as the name for the resource group and press <Enter>.
15. Ensure that the **Rebar** resource group is selected and click **New Resource**. Enter **Rebar #3** as the name for the resource and press <Enter>.
16. Ensure that the new resource is selected in the catalog. Note the default formulas in the *Resource Calculations* pane, as shown in Figure 7–18. These formulas are used to calculate a takeoff value for this resource once it has been added to the workbook.

Resource Calculations

Variable	Formula	Units
Length	=ModelLength	Feet
Width	=ModelWidth	Feet
Thickness	=ModelThickness	Feet
Height	=ModelHeight	Feet
Perimeter	=ModelPerimeter	Feet
Area	=ModelArea	Square Feet

Figure 7–18

17. Return to the *Item Catalog* window. Expand the *Substructure>Foundations>Standard Foundations>Column Foundations & Pile Caps* group. Select the **Pile Caps** item as the location in which to place the new resource.
18. Return to the *Resource Catalog* window. Verify that the *03000 Concrete>Rebar* resource group is already selected.

19. Select the **Rebar #3** resource, right-click, and select **Add To Selected Catalog Item**, as shown in Figure 7–19.

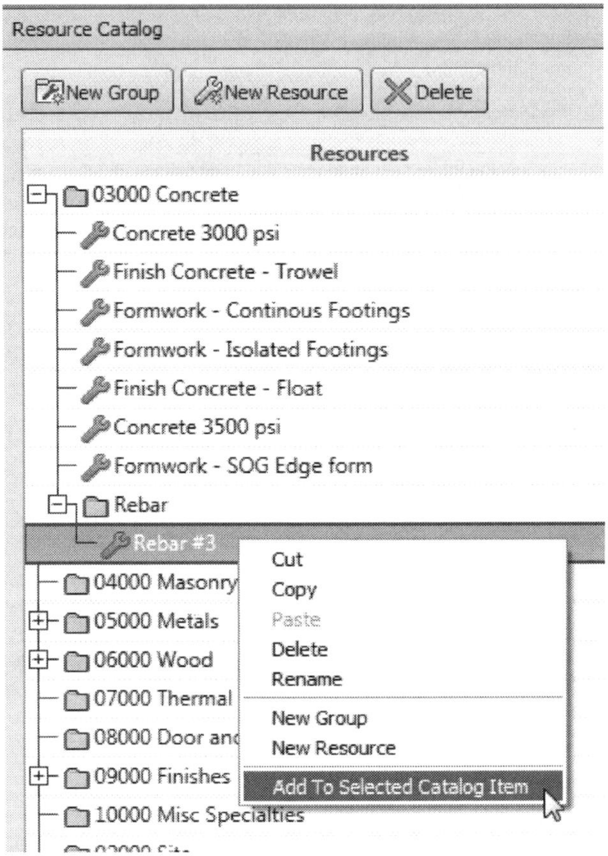

Figure 7–19

20. Return to the *Quantification Workbook*. Note that the **Rebar #3** resource is now included in the *Item Catalog* for the **Pile Caps** item.

Task 3: Duplicate items in the Item Catalog.

1. In the *Item Catalog*, select the **Pile Caps** item. Right-click and select **Copy**, as shown in Figure 7–20.

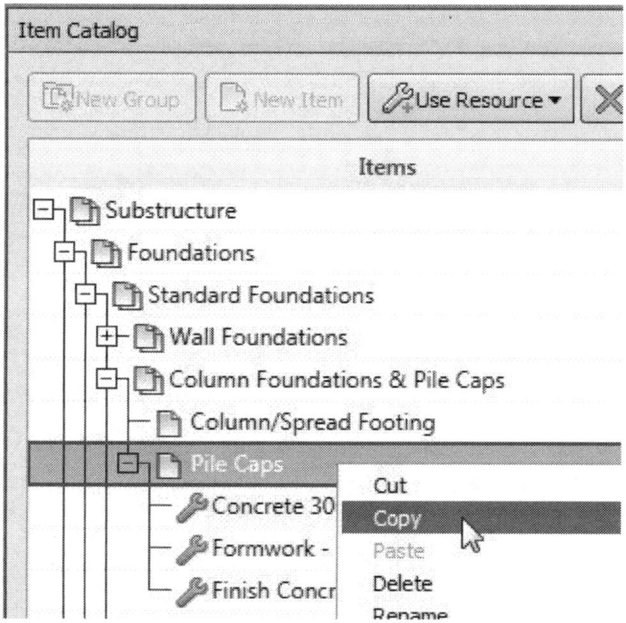

Figure 7–20

2. Select the parent **Column Foundations & Pile Caps** group. Right-click and select **Paste**.
3. Expand the copied *Pile Caps* item and note that all of the resources were copied with it.
4. Right-click on the first (original) *Pile Caps* item and select **Rename**. Enter **Pile Caps-9 Pile** as the new name and press <Enter>.
5. Rename the copied *Pile Caps* item as **Pile Caps-6 Pile**.

6. In the pane on the right, enter **03** as the *Work Breakdown Structure*, as shown in Figure 7–21, and press <Enter>.

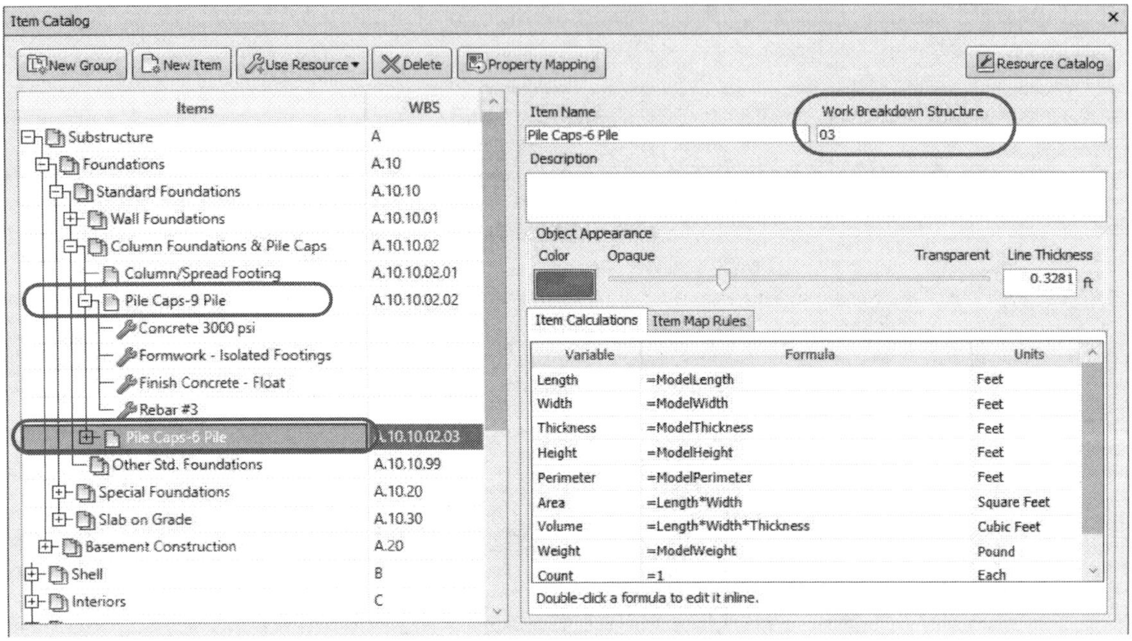

Figure 7–21

7. Return to the *Quantification Workbook* and note that the changes to the *Pile Caps* items are reflected in the *Navigation* pane.
8. Hide the **Site Layout.dwg** drawing for clarity for the next practice.
9. Save the Navisworks file and leave it open. You will continue working on this file in the next practice.

End of practice

7.4 3D Model and Virtual Takeoffs

Using the *Quantification Workbook*, you can perform a 3D model (automatic) takeoff or a virtual (manual) takeoff. The source model data determines if automatic model takeoff is possible. If your files retain their unique properties, including the globally unique identifier (GUID), from the original source software, you can perform model takeoff. A virtual takeoff can be used for items with no associated model geometry or properties.

- **Model takeoff** uses the data that has been exported from the design model (i.e., its properties) to derive the takeoff data for the report. Extracted objects are displayed as items in the *Quantification Workbook*.
- **Virtual takeoff** enables you to manually add takeoff items to the *Quantification Workbook*.

Object Selection for Takeoff

To conduct a model takeoff, you must select items in the scene. Selection can be accomplished using any of the following techniques:

- Select an object (group or above) directly in the scene view using your mouse.
- Expand items in the *Selection Tree* and click an object (group or above). Press and hold <Ctrl> to select multiple objects in the *Selection Tree* or <Shift> to select a range of objects.

  Note: *If using the Selection Tree, ensure that the display is set to* ***Standard Tree****.*

- Use the **Find Items** tool to find objects with the searched criteria. Once found, the objects are automatically selected.

  Note: *Previously found items that were stored as sets can also be used to select objects.*

- To select all of the objects that have the same name or type as an already selected object, you can use the **Select Same** tool. In the *Home* tab>*Select & Search* panel, expand the *Select Same* drop-down list and select **Same Name** or **Same Type**, as shown in Figure 7–22.

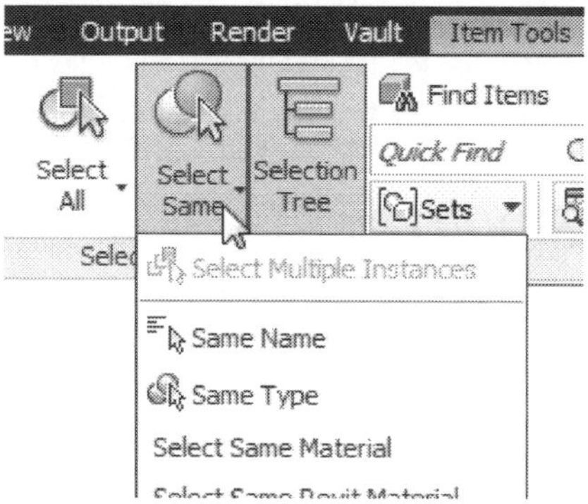

Figure 7–22

Model Takeoff

To conduct model takeoff, objects must be a group () or instance (or). If you try to use an object that is a model (), layer (), collection (), or item (), or if it does not contain a GUID or properties, an error message displays (as shown in Figure 7–23). This indicates the object cannot be taken off.

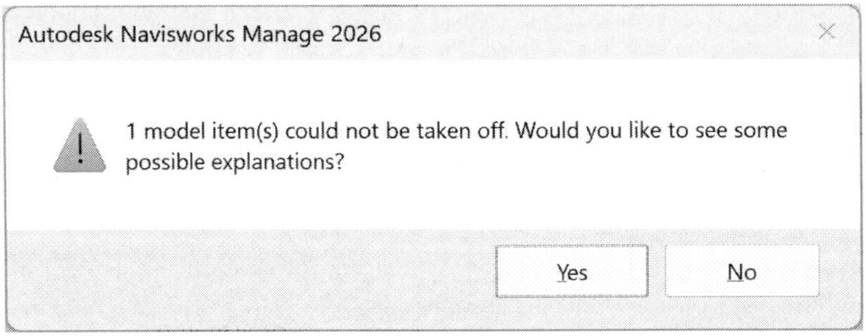

Figure 7–23

Note: *Ensure that your workbook is in Item View before performing takeoff.*

Hint: Globally Unique Identifier (GUID)

A globally unique identifier (GUID) is a unique value that is assigned to each object in a model. It is divided into several fields and written in groups of 8-4-4-4-12 hexadecimal characters (e.g., 71B923D4-ABCD-4BE4-861A-3A26146EF3F0). When exporting files for use in Quantification, ensure that the export settings include object and GUID data.

Conducting a Model Takeoff

Once objects have been selected in the scene view, they can be taken off.

How To: Assign a Selected Scene Object to an Existing Workbook Item

1. In the *Quantification Workbook*, select the item to which you want to assign the scene object.
2. Add the selected object to the *Quantification Workbook* using one of the following:
   - Right-click in the *Selection Tree* and select **Quantification>Take off to: *<Name of Existing Item>*** (where *<Name of Existing Item>* represents the name of the item selected in the *Quantification Workbook*).

- Right-click on a selected object in the *Selection Tree* and select **Quantification>Select Corresponding Takeoff Objects**, as shown in Figure 7–24. The corresponding workbook item must be selected to assign the object(s).

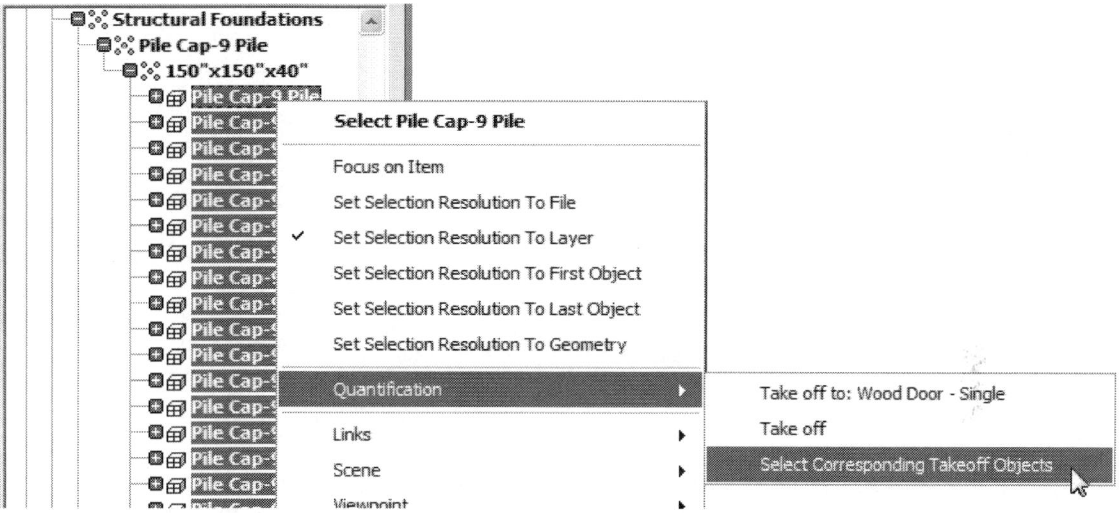

Figure 7–24

- With the object(s) selected in the *Selection Tree*, in the *Quantification Workbook*, right-click on the item to add the selected objects to and select **Take off Selected Model Items**, as shown in Figure 7–25.

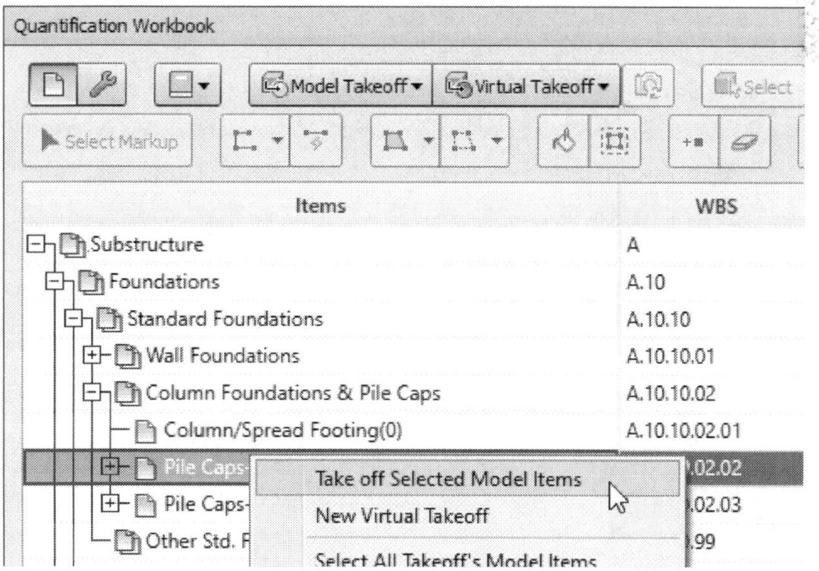

Figure 7–25

- With the object(s) selected in the *Selection Tree*, in the toolbar of the *Quantification Workbook*, click **Model Takeoff** and select **Take off to: <*Selected Item Name*>**, as shown in Figure 7–26.

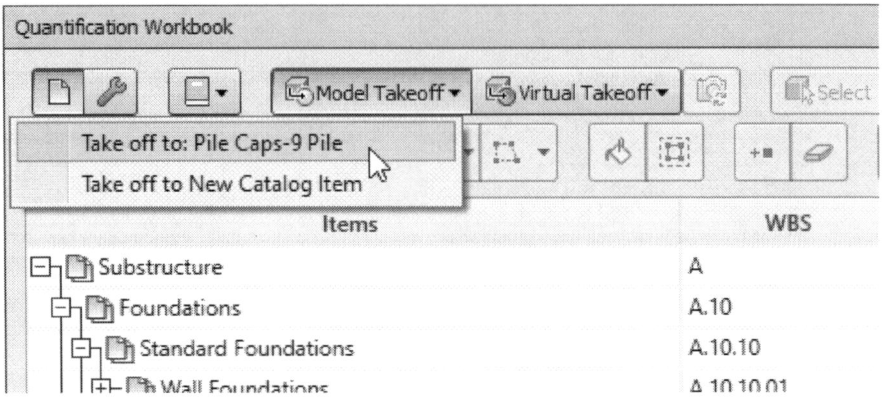

Figure 7–26

- Drag the selected object(s) into the *Quantification Workbook's Navigation* pane, as shown in Figure 7–27. When dragging to the *Navigation* pane, drop the object(s) by releasing the left mouse button on the item type. The item type does not need to be selected for this takeoff creation method.

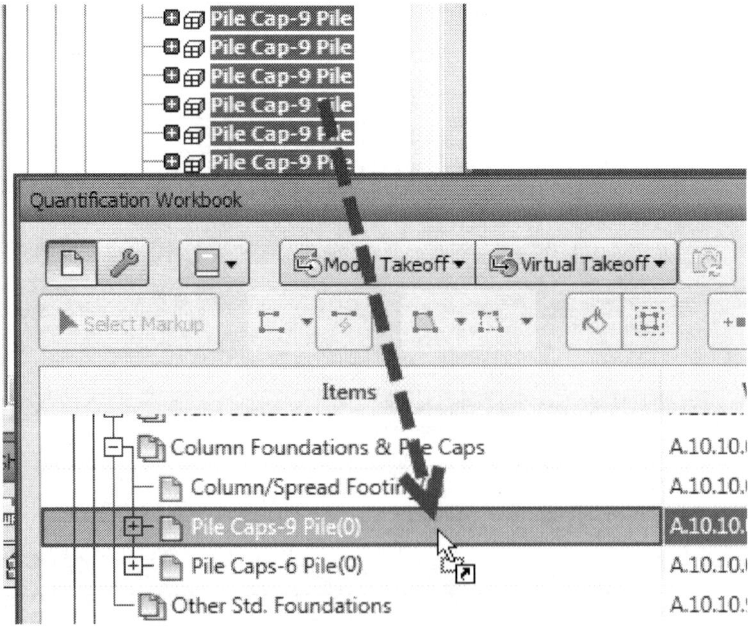

Figure 7–27

- Drag the selected object(s) into the *Quantification Workbook's Takeoff* pane, as shown in Figure 7–28.

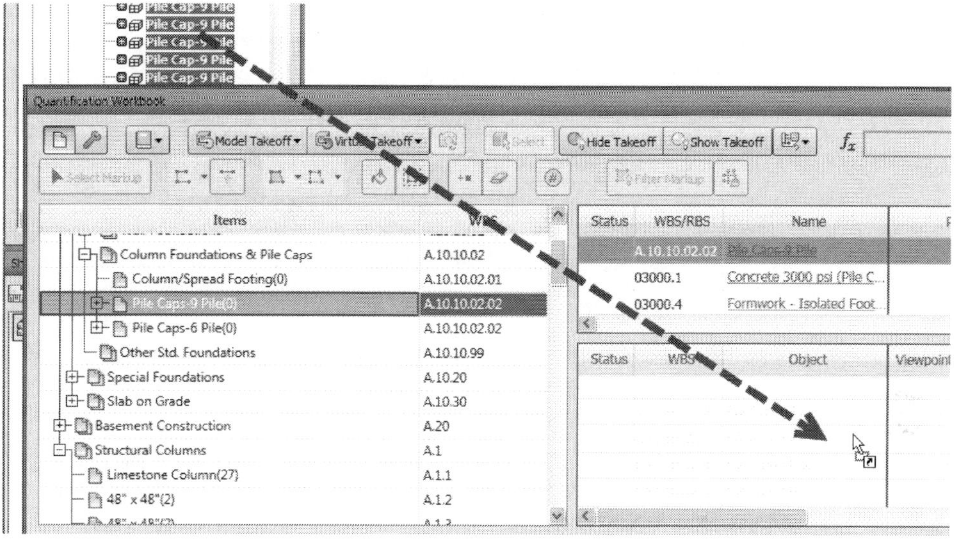

Figure 7–28

Workbook items might have been imported from an existing catalog as a starting point, or you might need to create items as you are generating the takeoff.

How To: Assign a Selected Scene Object to a New Workbook Item

1. Use one of the techniques that were previously discussed to select objects in the scene.
2. Add the selected object to a new item using one of the following:
   - Right-click in the *Selection Tree* and select **Quantification>Take off to new catalog item**, as shown in Figure 7–29.

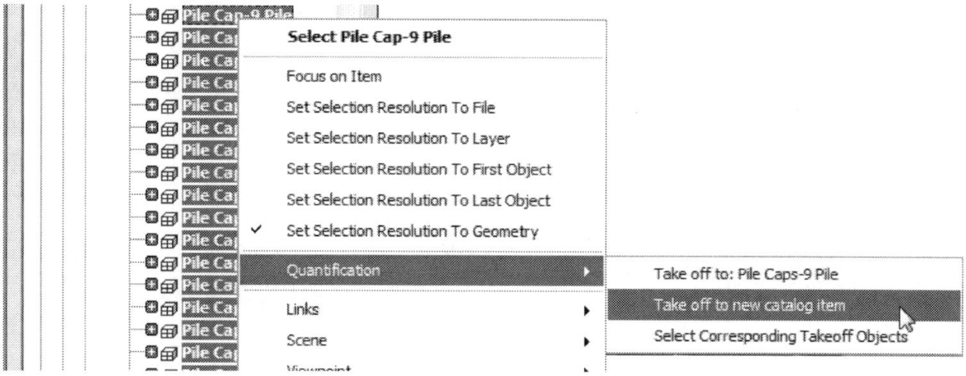

Figure 7–29

- With the object(s) selected in the *Selection Tree*, in the toolbar of the *Quantification Workbook*, click **Model Takeoff** and select **Take off to New Catalog Item**, as shown in Figure 7–30.

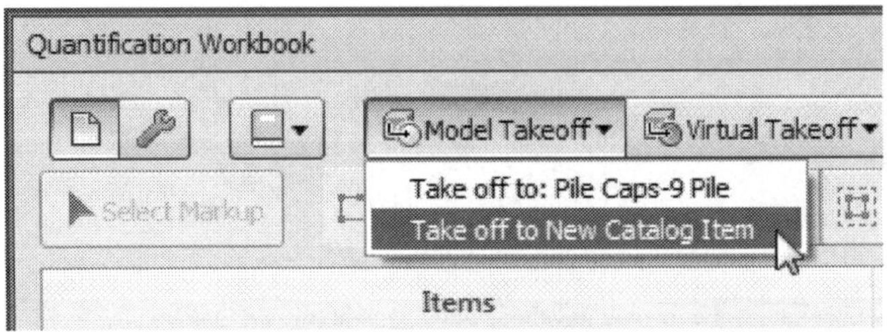

Figure 7–30

3. To rename the new item, double-click on its name in the *Item Catalog*, enter a new name, and press <Enter>.

How To: Use an Object Category to Create Items in a Workbook Group

1. In the *Quantification Workbook*, select the group you want to create new items in. Create a group, if required, using the *Item Catalog*.
2. At the top of the *Selection Tree*, expand the *View Type* drop-down list and select **Properties**. Expand *Category>Name Properties* to obtain a list of all the item types in the model.
3. Add the selected object to a new item using one of the following:
   - Right-click the property type to take off and select **Quantification>Take off to: *<Group to be added to>***, as shown in Figure 7–31.

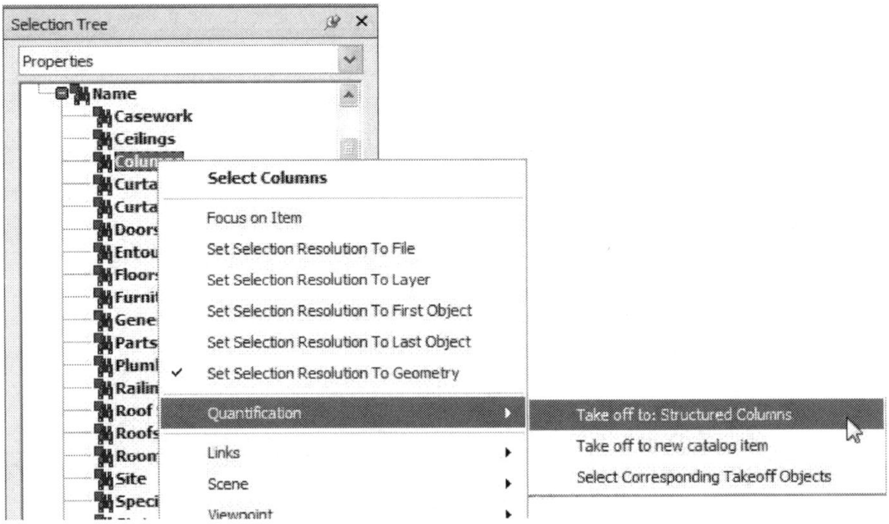

Figure 7–31

- Without any items selected in the *Quantification Workbook*, drag the selected property into the *Quantification Workbook's Navigation* pane, as shown in Figure 7–32. When dragging, drop the object(s) by releasing the left mouse button on the item type.

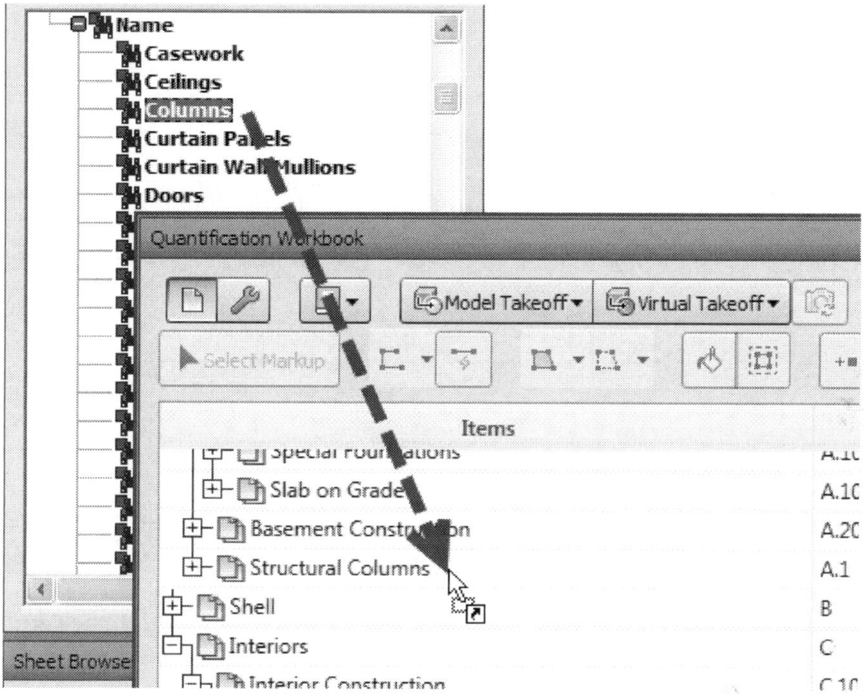

Figure 7–32

4. New item types are automatically added to the assigned group, and the takeoff data for each item is automatically populated, as shown in Figure 7–33.

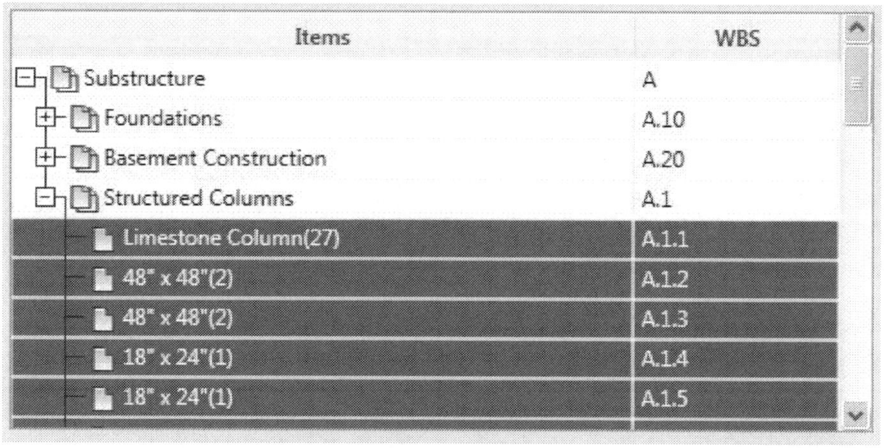

Figure 7–33

Virtual Takeoff

Virtual takeoffs are required when the object properties, whether the source includes geometry or not, cannot be used. Items added to the takeoff virtually are added one at a time.

How To: Create a Virtual Takeoff

1. In the *Quantification Workbook*, click the item ( ) that you want to contain the new virtual takeoff (e.g., Wood Door - Single).
2. To add a new virtual takeoff to the *Quantification Workbook*, use one of the following:
   - In the toolbar, click **Virtual Takeoff** and select **Create in: *<Selected Catalog Item>***, as shown in Figure 7–34.

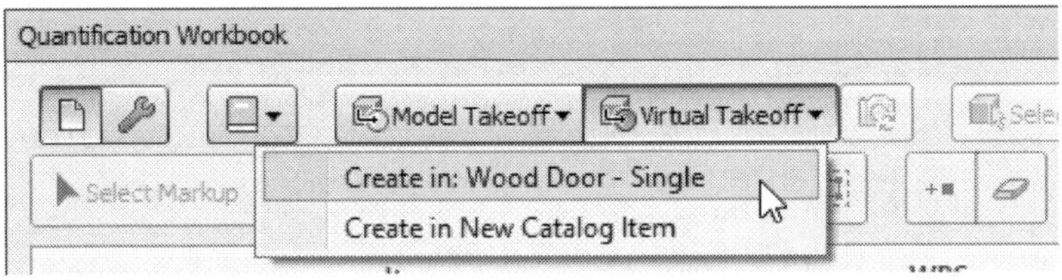

Figure 7–34

   - With the catalog item selected in the *Quantification Workbook*, right-click and select **New Virtual Takeoff**.
3. A new takeoff item is added to the *Takeoff* pane that includes the following:
   - The takeoff item with a default name.
   - A viewpoint based on the current model orientation.
4. To rename the new takeoff, select its default name cell in the *Object* column and enter a new name in the f_x field in the *Quantification Workbook* toolbar.
5. Use the Navisworks measurement tools as well as formulas to add property details, or enter values for those objects that might not be physically modeled in the scene. The takeoff fields may include *Length*, *Width*, *Thickness*, *Height*, *Perimeter*, *Area*, *Volume*, *Weight*, and *Count*.
6. In the *Takeoff* pane in the *Quantification Workbook*, navigate to the takeoff item you want to associate with the measurement. Double-click the takeoff formula cell that you want to change (e.g., *Height* or *Perimeter*) and enter the new measurement. Items that contain explicitly measured and entered values are identified with in the *Status* column of the *Takeoff* pane.

   Note: *Items that are added to the Quantification Workbook using model takeoff can also have overwritten values and are identified with in the Status column of the Takeoff pane.*

Working with Takeoff Viewpoints

A takeoff viewpoint is stored for a takeoff item that is created using Virtual Takeoff. The current orientation of the scene is the viewpoint that is stored when the Virtual Takeoff option is selected. This viewpoint is also stored in the *Saved Viewpoints* window.

- To access the viewpoint for a takeoff item, click in the *Takeoff* pane in the *Quantification Workbook* or select the viewpoint in the *Saved Viewpoints* window.
- To update the viewpoint associated with the virtual takeoff, right-click and select **Takeoff's Viewpoint>Add/Update**, or click (Add Viewpoint) in the *Quantification Workbook* toolbar.
- To remove the viewpoint associated with the virtual takeoff, right-click and select **Takeoff's Viewpoint>Remove**.

Although viewpoints are not automatically created using Model Takeoff, they can be added to the takeoff item.

- To create a viewpoint for a model takeoff item, select the item in the item list or in the *Takeoff* pane and click (Add Viewpoint) in the *Quantification Workbook* toolbar. If the item is selected in the item list, a viewpoint is created for all of its items, while selecting an item in the *Takeoff* pane enables you to select a single item. The icon is added to the *Viewpoint* column in the *Takeoff* pane and also to the *Saved Viewpoints* window.

Hint: Markups in a Takeoff Viewpoint

Markups can also be incorporated with the viewpoints that are stored with model and virtual takeoff data. To add the markup, ensure that the viewpoint is active by clicking in the *Viewpoint* column associated with the takeoff. Then, in the *Review* tab, use the tools on the *Markup* panel to draw and add text as required and highlight areas in the viewpoint. The markup is only saved with the takeoff viewpoint.

Managing Takeoff Data

In the *Quantification Workbook*, there are a number of tools that you can use to manage and more efficiently create a takeoff report. You are able to:

- Change the columns that are displayed in the *Quantification Workbook*.
- Sort the column contents in the *Quantification Workbook*.
- Add comments to takeoff data.
- Change the appearance of the takeoff data.
- Control the display of items in the scene view based on whether they have been taken off or not.
- Delete the takeoff data.
- Remove overrides from the takeoff data.

Changing and Sorting Columns

The columns that are shown in the Takeoff or Rollup panes are assigned by default, but they can be customized for a project. Additionally, you can sort columns in ascending or descending order.

How To: Change the Columns Displayed in the Takeoff and Rollup Panes

1. In the *Takeoff* or *Rollup* pane of the *Quantification Workbook*, right-click a column header and select **Choose Columns**, as shown in Figure 7–35.

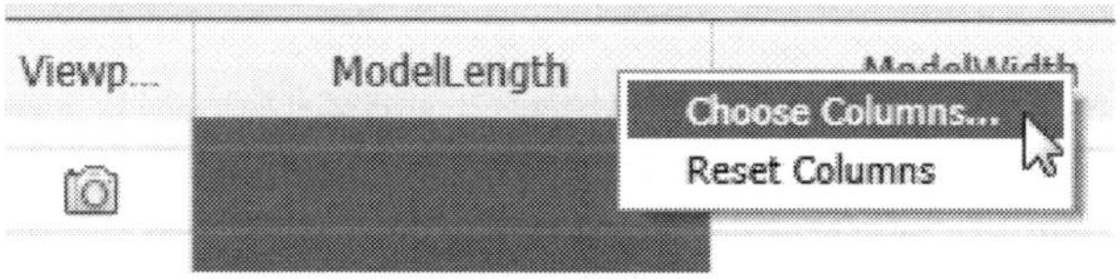

Figure 7–35

2. In the *Choose Details Columns* dialog box, select or clear the columns to be displayed and click **OK**.

Additionally, columns can sorted by clicking on the column header. The ▲ icon indicates the column is sorted alphanumerically in ascending order, and the ▼ icon shows it is in descending order.

Adding Comments

Comments can be added to takeoff data to provide further annotation on takeoff information. A comment is given a number and is added to the *Comments* window with other comments. You can use the *Find Comments* tool to review any comments associated with the takeoff data.

How To: Add a Comment to Takeoff Data

1. In the *Rollup* pane in the *Quantification Workbook*, select a takeoff to display its information.
2. Right-click in the *Comments* field and click **Add Comment**, as shown in Figure 7–36. Alternatively, you can right-click a name in the *Takeoff* or *Rollup* pane and click **Add Comment**.

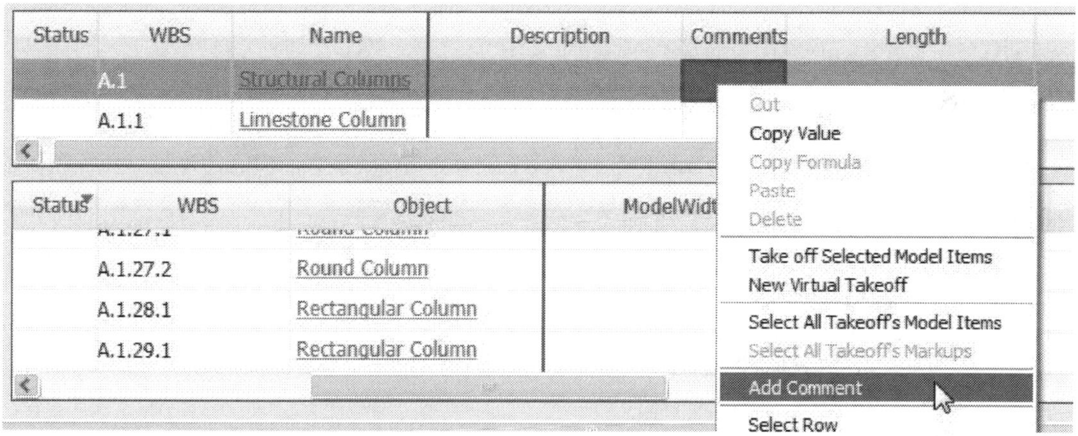

Figure 7–36

3. Enter your comment in the *Add Comment* dialog box and click **OK**.

The comment number displays in the *Comments* cell in the *Rollup* pane and the comment is added to the *Comments* window.

Controlling Takeoff Data Appearance

Once a scene item has been added to the *Quantification Workbook*, you can control its display appearance (color) in the scene based on the original model appearance or the takeoff appearance.

How To: Change the Takeoff Data Appearance

1. In the *Quantification Workbook*, click  and select one of the following:
   - **Reapply Quantification Appearance** sets the scene view to display the specific *Item Catalog* color for those items that have been taken off. All of the items that have been taken off are displayed with their assigned color and those not taken off remain with their original appearance.
   - **Reapply Original Model Appearance** sets the scene view back to its original appearance (color).

   Note: *Controlling the appearance using the*  *options is only available when the model is set to Shaded mode (not Full Render mode).*

Controlling Item Display

When you add model items to the workbook, you can use tools in the *Quantification Workbook* toolbar to clear the display of items from the scene view as they are added, which enables you to ensure that all of the required items are added to the workbook and nothing is missed.

How To: Control the Scene Display Based on Taken Off Items

1. In the *Quantification Workbook*, use one of the following toolbar options:
   - Click 

 to hide all taken off model items and display all other model items.
   - Click 

 to display only the taken off model items and hide the other model items.

   Note: *Click these icons a second time to clear the hide or show display option.*

Deleting Takeoff Data

Model and virtual takeoff data can be deleted from the *Quantification Workbook*, if required.

How To: Delete a Takeoff Item

1. In the *Takeoff* pane for the *Quantification Workbook*, select the takeoff that you want to delete.

2. In the toolbar, expand **Update** and select **Delete Selected Takeoff**, as shown in Figure 7–37.

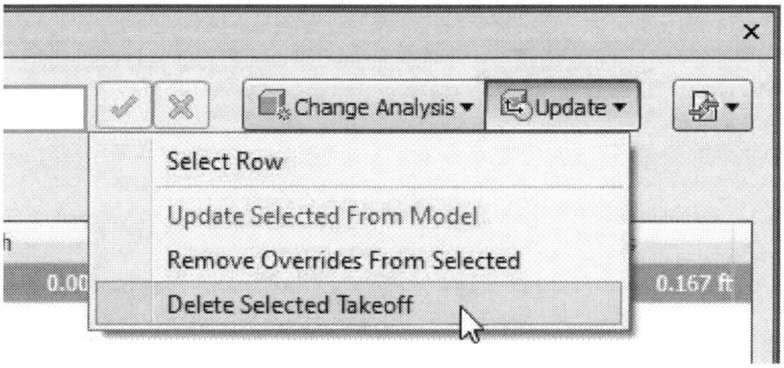

Figure 7–37

Resetting Takeoff Data

Overwritten model and virtual takeoff data can be reset from the *Quantification Workbook*, if required.

How To: Remove Overrides from a Takeoff Item

1. In the *Takeoff* pane for the *Quantification Workbook*, select the takeoff that you want to reset. You can select individual cells in the *Takeoff* pane or you can select an entire row to clear all of the overrides in the row. To select an entire row, click **Update** and select **Select Row**.
2. In the toolbar, expand **Update** and select **Remove Overrides From Selected**, as shown in Figure 7–38.

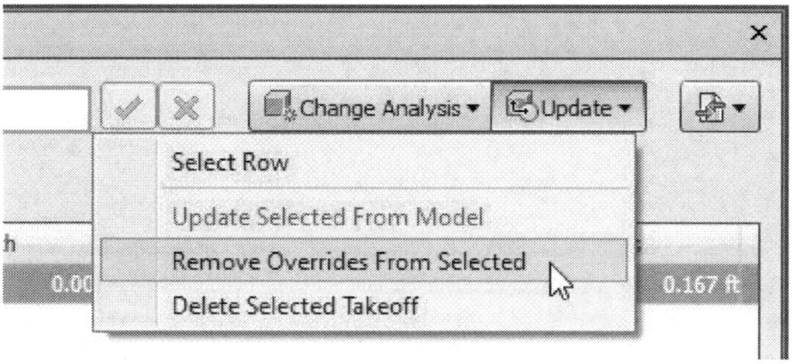

Figure 7–38

Note: *This option is only available if there is an overwritten value for the item. Alternatively, you can right-click a cell and select* ***Remove Override****.*

Practice 7b
Create and Work with 3D Model Takeoff Data

Practice Objectives

- Extract quantities from a model.
- Explore tools for managing the takeoff data.
- Perform a virtual takeoff.

In this practice, you will use the *Quantification Workbook* to extract quantities from the 3D Navisworks model. You will use tools to view the objects in your takeoffs, then conduct a virtual takeoff for objects not yet present in the model.

Task 1: Conduct a model takeoff.

1. Continue to work on the file from the previous practice. If you did not complete that practice, open **School-Takeoff-3D.nwf** from the *Navisworks BIM Practice Files\ Quantification* folder.The **Site Layout.dwg** drawing has been hidden for clarity.
2. Expand  (Application Menu) and select **Options**. In the *Options Editor* dialog box, in the left pane, expand *File Readers* and select **Revit**. In the right pane, enable the **Type properties on Elements** option, if not already enabled. Click **OK** to close the dialog box.
3. Reorient the model similar to that shown in Figure 7–39. In the *Saved Viewpoints* window, save the viewpoint as **Structure**.

Figure 7–39

4. In the *Quantification Workbook*, expand the *Substructure>Foundations>Standard Foundations>Wall Foundations* group. Select the **Continuous Footing** item. This identifies the item to which the quantifications are going to be assigned.

5. Open the *Sets* window and select the **Continuous Footings** set at the bottom of the list. The *Wall Foundation* objects are selected in the *Selection Tree* and are also highlighted in the model.

6. In the *Scene View* area, ensure your mouse is hovering over the sky and not over the school model. Right-click and select **Quantification>Take off to Continuous Footing**, as shown in Figure 7–40. Twenty Wall Foundation items are added.

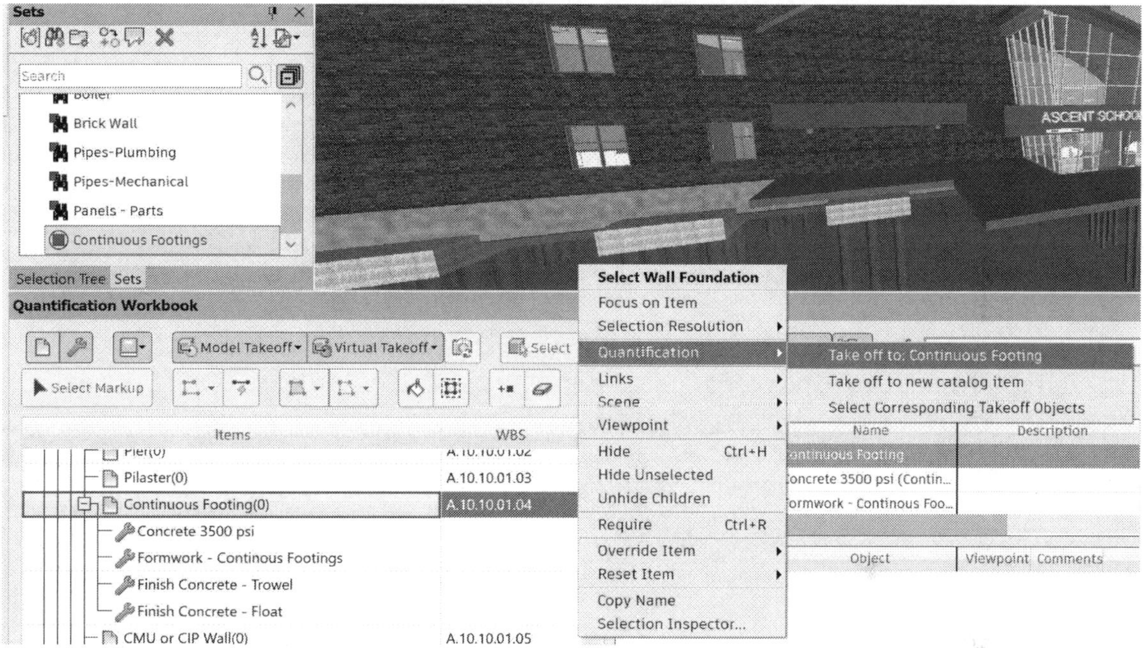

Figure 7–40

7. In the *Rollup* pane of the *Quantification Workbook*, scroll to the right to review the total volume of the *Continuous Footing*, as shown in Figure 7–41. Note how the resources were automatically filled out for the *Continuous Footing* based on the element properties.

Status	WBS/RBS	Name	Perimeter	Area	Volume
	A.10.10.01.04	Continuous Footing	0.000 ft	0.000 ft²	3,993.649 ft³
	03000.6	Concrete 3500 psi (Continu...	0.000	0.000	147.925 yd³
	03000.3	Formwork - Continous Footi...	0.000	0.000 ft²	0.000 ft³
	03000.2	Finish Concrete - Trowel (C...	0.000	3,993.649 ft²	0.000
	03000.5	Finish Concrete - Float (Con...	0.000	3,993.649 ft²	0.000

Figure 7–41

8. Close the *Sets* window.

9. In the *Quantification Workbook*, expand the *Substructure>Foundations>Standard Foundations>Column Foundations & Pile Caps* group. Select the **Pile Caps-9 Pile** item. This identifies the item to which the next quantification is going to be assigned.
10. In the *Home* tab, click **Find Items**. Conduct a search to locate all of the objects with the name *Pile Cap-9*, as shown in Figure 7–42, and click **Find All**.

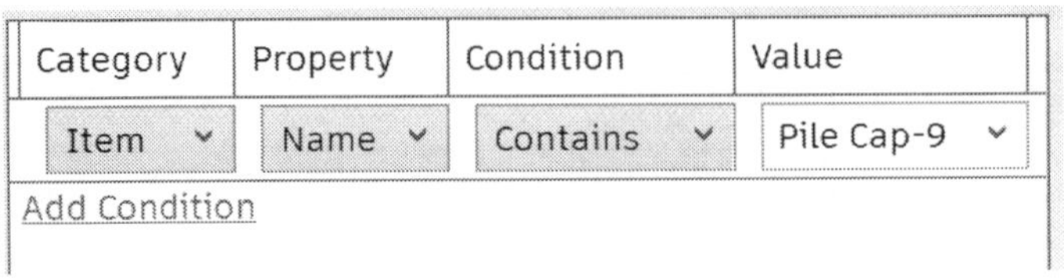

Figure 7–42

11. Once the items have been found, the *Selection Tree* highlights the selected items.
12. Return to the *Quantification Workbook*. Ensure that the **Pile Caps-9 Pile** item is still selected in the *Navigation* pane.
13. Right-click on any one of the selected Pile Cap-9 Pile objects in the *Selection Tree* and select **Quantification>Take off to: Pile Caps-9 Pile**, as shown in Figure 7–43.

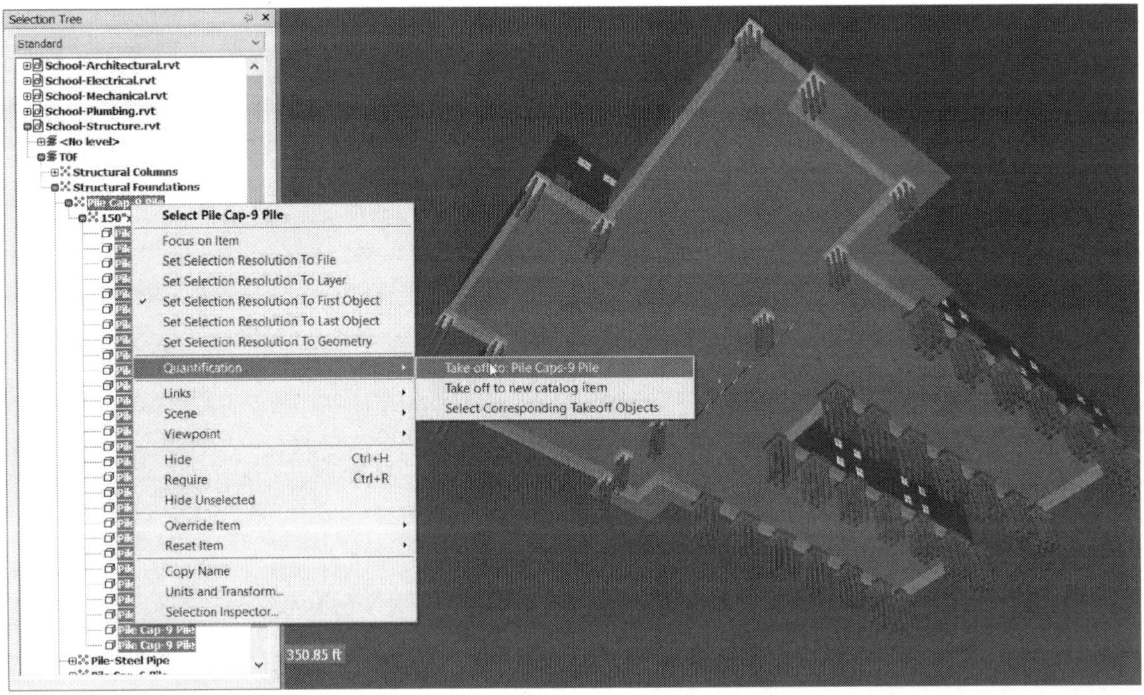

Figure 7–43

14. When prompted that one model item could not be taken off, click **No**. This prompt displays if any item is selected that cannot be taken off (e.g., Collections ⁘). This occurs if the *Find Items* tool is used and locates collection items that have the name that was being searched for but that cannot be taken off.
15. In the *Selection Tree*, press and hold <Ctrl> and click the **Pile Cap-9 Pile** collection item that is listed under *Structural Foundations* to clear it from the selection group.
16. In the *Selection Tree*, right-click on any one of the selected Pile Cap-9 Pile objects and select **Quantification>Take off to: Pile Caps-9 Pile**. In the *Quantification Workbook*, note that twenty-eight Pile Caps are taken off, as shown in Figure 7–44.

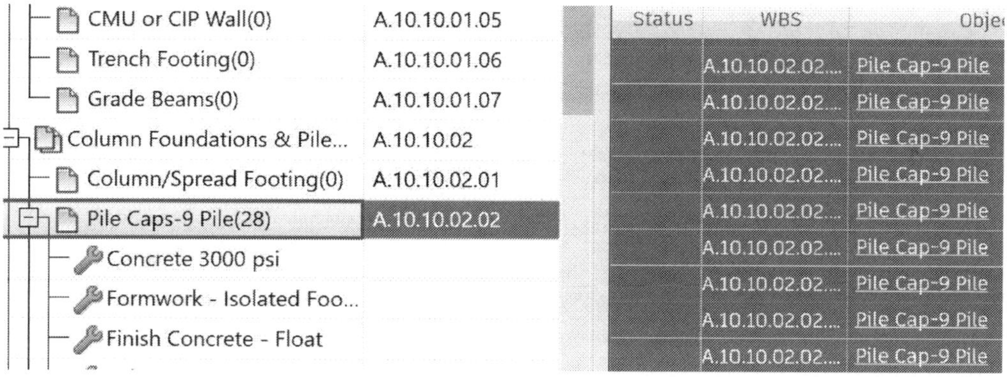

Figure 7–44

17. Select all of the **Pile Cap-6 Pile** objects using any of the selection techniques.
18. Add the Pile Cap-6 Pile objects to their associated item in the *Quantification Workbook*. Thirteen Pile Caps are taken off.
19. In the *Quantification Workbook*, expand the *Interiors>Interior Construction>Interior Doors>Standard Interior Doors* group. Select the **Wood Door - Single** item. This identifies the item to which the quantification is going to be assigned.
20. In the *Home* tab>*Select & Search* panel, enter **SINGLE** in the *Quick Find* field, as shown in Figure 7–45, and press <Enter> to search for a single-flush door.

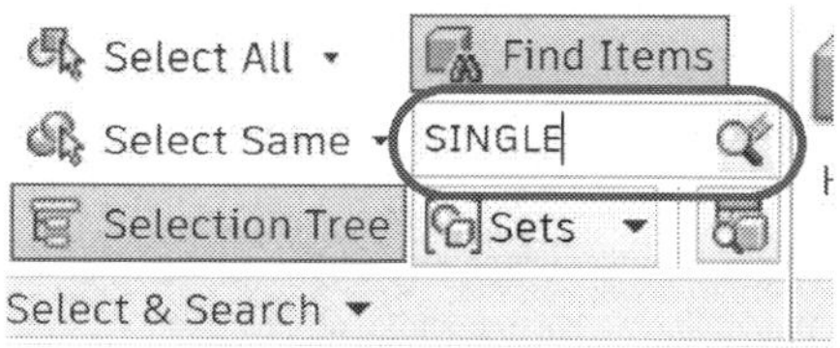

Figure 7–45

21. Once one of the Single-Flush doors has been selected, in the *Home* tab>*Select & Search* panel, click the *Select Same* drop-down list and select **Same Name**. All of the Single-Flush objects are selected in the *Selection Tree*.

22. With the objects selected in the *Selection Tree*, in the toolbar of the *Quantification Workbook*, click **Model Takeoff** and select **Take off to: Wood Door - Single**, as shown in Figure 7–46.

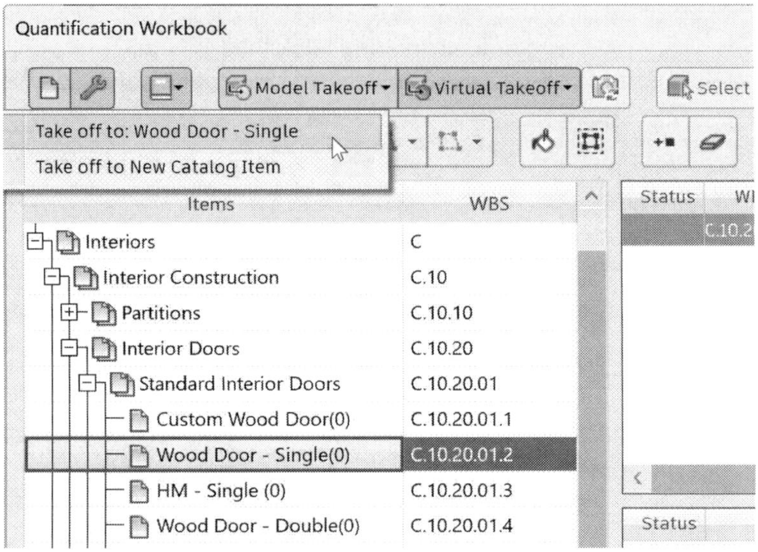

Figure 7–46

23. Click **No** when prompted that model items could not be taken off. As an alternative to clearing collections in the *Selection Tree* manually, you can run another search that only finds the required type. Clear all of the items from selection.

24. Open the *Find Items* window and add the criteria shown in Figure 7–47. Verify that **Match Case** is checked.

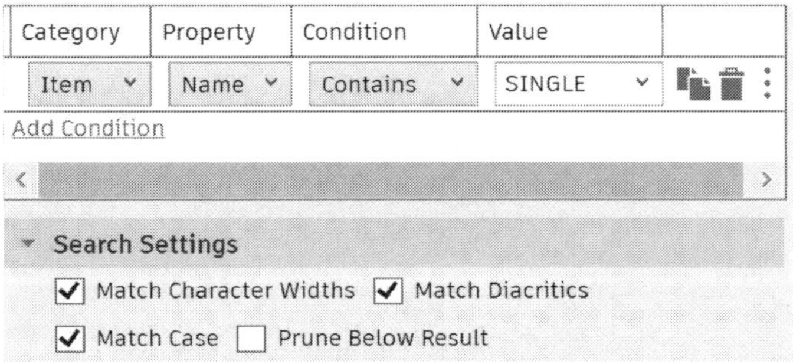

Figure 7–47

25. Conduct the search. As you did previously, in the *Selection Tree*, press and hold <Ctrl> and select the SINGLE collection to clear it from the selection group. There are two such collections, one for the first floor and one for the second floor.

26. Right-click one of the selected items in the *Selection Tree* and select **Quantification>Take off to: Wood Door - Single**. A total of 80 doors have now been added to the workbook, as shown in Figure 7–48.

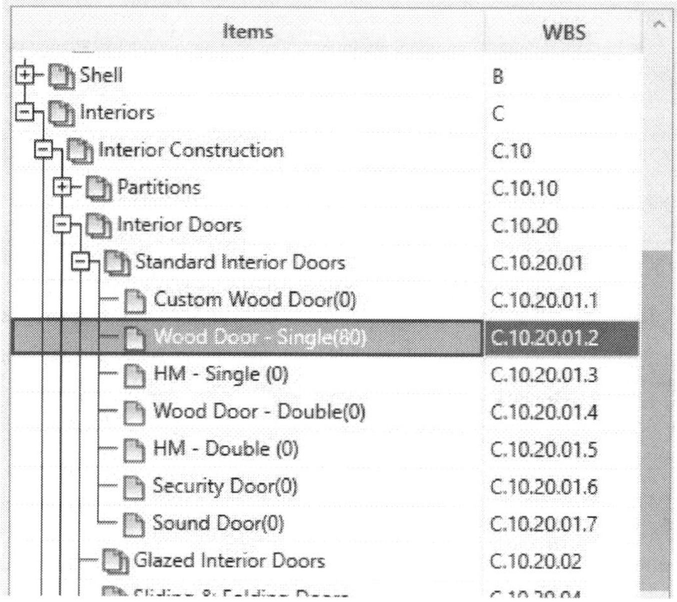

Figure 7–48

27. Close the *Find Items* window and save the file.

Task 2: Add catalog items directly from the model.

1. In the *Item Catalog*, select the **Substructure** group and click **New Group**. Enter **Structural Columns** as the name for the group.
2. With the **Structural Columns** group selected, enter **30** as the *Work Breakdown Structure* in the pane on the right.
3. In the *Selection Tree*, expand *School-Structure.rvt>TOF*. TOF is the Top of Footing Revit level.
4. Select **Structural Columns**. Note that the structural columns in the model are now selected. You will have to navigate around the model to visually see them as they are not easily visible.
5. Right-click the **Structural Columns** property and select **Quantification>Take off to: Structural Columns**.
6. A total of 41 new item types are automatically added to the item list and the takeoff data for each is populated. This approach eliminates having to create the items individually.

Task 3: Manage the quantification data.

1. Ensure that no objects are selected in the scene view.
2. In the *Quantification Workbook*, click 

(Hide Takeoff). All of the Pile Cap, Continuous Footing, Single-Flush Door, and Structural Column items are cleared from display in the scene view. The items are also grayed out in the *Selection Tree*. This helps you to identify which scene objects are still left to take off.

   Note: *This might be difficult to see without zooming into the model.*

3. Click 

(Hide Takeoff) a second time to disable it and display all of the objects in the scene view.
4. Click 

(Show Takeoff) to display only the Pile Cap, Continuous Footing, Single-Flush Door, and Structural Column items in the scene view. This helps identify which items have already been taken off.
5. In the *Viewpoint* tab>*Render Style* panel, set the Mode to **Shaded**.
6. In the *Quantification Workbook*, expand  (Control the appearance of model items) and select **Reapply Original Model Appearance** to set the scene view back to its original appearance (color).

   Note: *Controlling the appearance using the*  *options is only available when the model is set to Shaded mode (not Full Render mode).*

7. Click  and select **Reapply Quantification Appearance** to set the scene view to display the specific *Item Catalog* color for those items that have been taken off. All of the items that have been taken off are displayed with their assigned color (e.g., purple for Pile Caps) and those not taken off retain their original appearance.
8. Click 

(Show Takeoff) a second time to disable it. Note that you will have to hide the **Site Layout.dwg** again if you want it removed from the display. It was returned to the display because it has not been taken off yet.
9. In the *Quantification Workbook*, navigate to and select the **Pile Cap** items (*Substructure>Foundations>Standard Foundations>Column Foundations & Pile Caps*) in the *Navigation* pane. Select the **Pile Caps-9 Pile** item.
10. In the *Takeoff* pane, select the first **Pile Cap** item. Ensure that you select the first object name cell in the *Object* column.
11. In the navigation bar, in the Zoom tools, click **Zoom Selected** to navigate to this item. Zoom out and reorient as required to obtain a good view of this first Pile Cap.

    Note: *<Page Down> is the keyboard shortcut for* ***Zoom Selected****.*

12. In the *Quantification Workbook* toolbar, click (Add Viewpoint) to save a viewpoint for this item. Note that a *Quantification Views* folder has been created in the *Saved Viewpoints* window and the new viewpoint is contained within it.

13. Return to the **Structure** viewpoint. In the *Quantification Workbook*'s *Takeoff* pane, click adjacent to the first **Pile Cap-9 Pile** item, as shown in Figure 7–49, to change to the saved view. As an alternative, you can select the viewpoint in the *Saved Viewpoints* window in the *Quantification Views* folder.

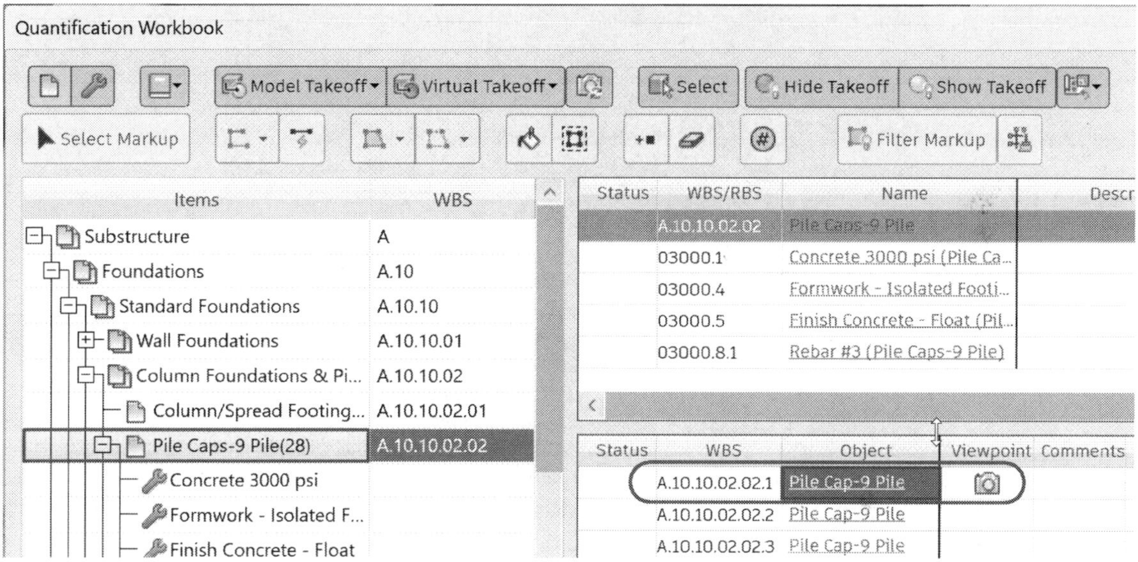

Figure 7–49

Note: *You can select multiple items and create the viewpoints at the same time.*

Task 4: Conduct a virtual takeoff.

1. In the *Saved Viewpoints* window, select **Office-Interior** from the *Interior* folder to change the viewpoint.

2. In the *Quantification Workbook*, expand the *Interiors>Interior Construction>Interior Doors>Standard Interior Doors* group. Select the **Wood Door - Single** item.

Eighty doors have already been added using **Model Takeoff**. However, an office along this hallway is missing a door, as shown in Figure 7–50. Because the door is not included in the source model, a virtual takeoff can be done to communicate this information.

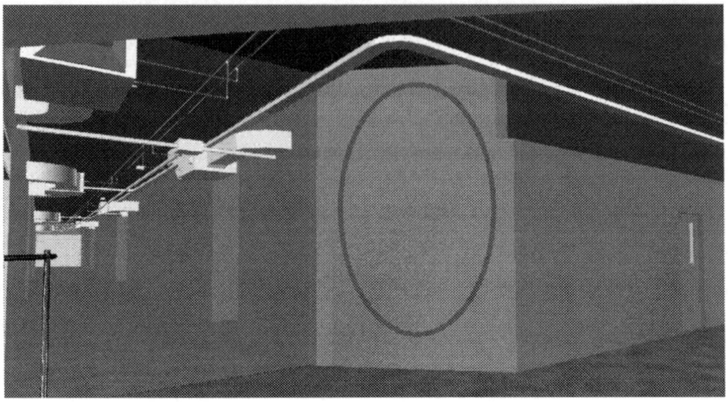

Figure 7–50

3. In the *Quantification Workbook* toolbar, click **Virtual Takeoff** and select **Create in: Wood Door - Single**, as shown in Figure 7–51.

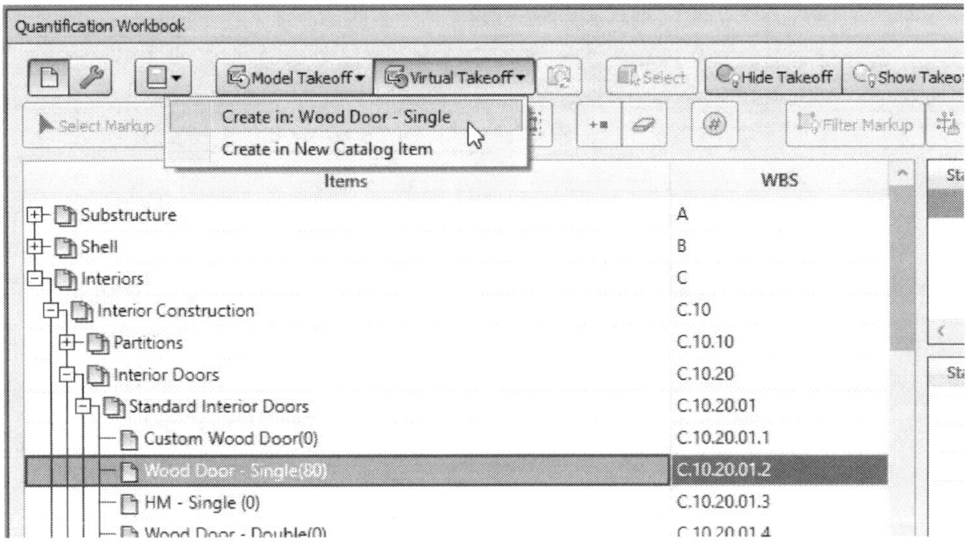

Figure 7–51

4. A new takeoff item is added to the *Takeoff* pane that includes the following:
   - The takeoff item with a default name (No Name).
   - A viewpoint based on the current model orientation.

   Note: *Items added to the takeoff virtually are added one at a time.*

5. Select the *Name* cell in the *Object* column for the virtual takeoff. Enter **Missing Door** in the f_x field in the *Quantification Workbook* toolbar (as shown in Figure 7–52) and press <Enter>.

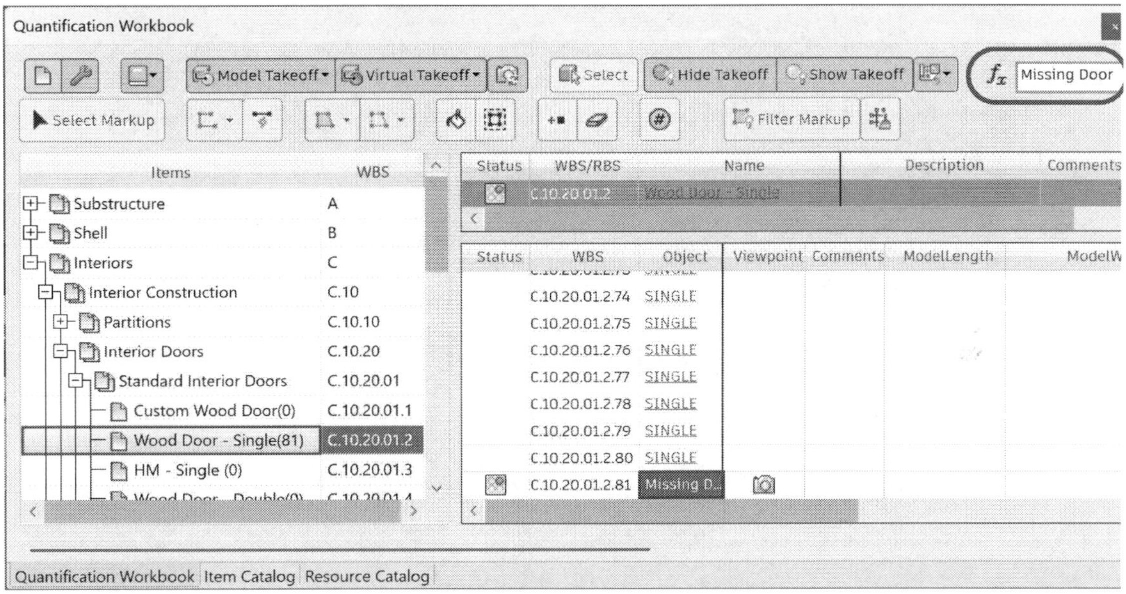

Figure 7–52

6. In the *Rollup* pane, scroll and review the properties for the 81 doors. The quantity includes the virtual door. However, the model properties do not include the virtual property values as these fields are 0 by default.

7. In the columns for the **Missing Door** takeoff, enter the following property values:
   - *ModelWidth* = **3.000 (ft** is added automatically)
   - *ModelThickness* = **0.167 (ft** is added automatically)
   - *ModelHeight* = **7.000 (ft** is added automatically)

   Note: *Additional doors might be missing in this model, but you do not need to add any additional virtual takeoffs at this time.*

8. In the *Rollup* pane, review the properties and note that the property values have been included in the totals for all doors.

9. Note that the status icon displays in the *Status* column for the **Missing Door**. This indicates that fields in this item have been overwritten.

10. Click the camera icon adjacent to the virtual takeoff item to activate it.

11. In the *Review* tab, expand **Draw** and select **Ellipse**.

12. Draw an ellipse on the office wall similar to the one shown in Figure 7–53. Select **Text** and pick a point inside the ellipse. Enter **Add Door** as a note in the viewpoint, as shown in Figure 7–53.

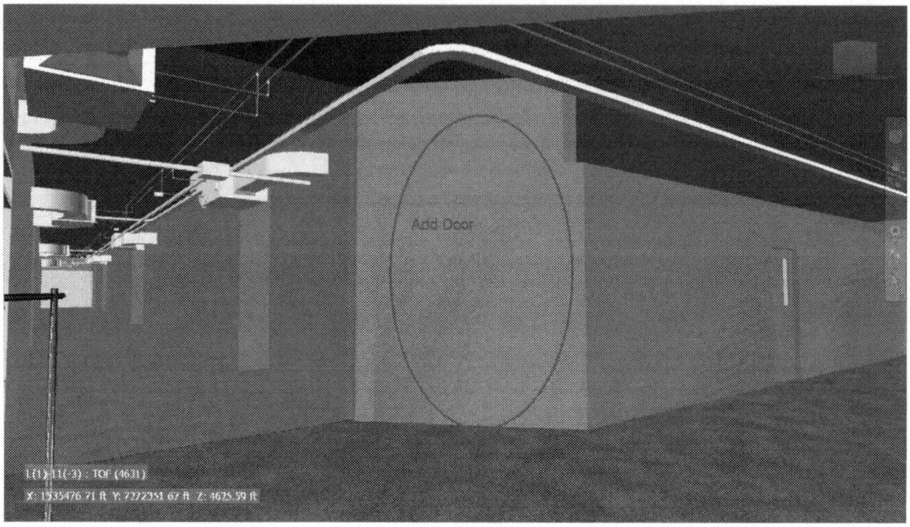

Figure 7–53

13. In the *Saved Viewpoints* window, select the **Office-Interior** viewpoint. Note that the markup is not included in this view.

14. Click [camera icon] adjacent to the virtual takeoff item and note that the markup is included in this view. Alternatively, it is included in the new view that was created in the *Quantification Views* folder in the *Saved Viewpoints* window

15. Save the Navisworks file and leave the file open. You will continue working on this file in the next practice.

End of practice

7.5 2D Takeoffs

By using the 2D data in the project, you can measure and mark up geometry and perform accurate calculations for use in the *Quantification Workbook*. Both 2D and 3D quantification takeoffs can exist in the same workbook.

2D takeoff can be done using both native and scanned .DWF files. Non-native .DWF files (such as PDFs) can easily be converted to .DWF using print driver software for use in 2D takeoff or Autodesk TrueView. (See supported file formats in the Navisworks Help documentation.)

To conduct a 2D takeoff:

- 2D sheets must exist in the Navisworks project. Click (Import Sheets & Models) in the Project Browser.
- The 2D sheets must be prepared/converted for use in the Navisworks project. Right-click a sheet name in the Project Browser and select **Prepare Sheet/Model** or **Prepare All Sheets/ Models**.
- Ensure the scale of the 2D sheets are the same as the 3D model.

Hint: Customizing Sheet Scale

When using 2D .DWFX data, it is important that the measurements taken are at the same scale as the data that is in the 3D model. To customize the sheet scale and display it in the *Set Scale by Measurement* window, complete the following:

1. Activate a 2D sheet.
2. In the *View* tab>*Workspace* panel, expand the *Windows* drop-down list and select **Set Scale by Measure**.
3. Click **New Measure**.
4. On the 2D sheet, trace a line that defines a length of geometry that has a length you already know.
5. In the *Enter Value* dialog box, enter the known length and its unit and click **OK**. Once complete, the average scale displays.

To delete a measurement record, select a row, right-click, and select **Delete**. To delete a scale record, press <Delete> or right-click a row and select **Delete**.

2D Takeoff Tools

Similar to the *3D Takeoff* tool, a Quantification project must be set up and the *Item Catalog* assigned in order to use 2D Takeoff. A 2D sheet must be activated in the Navisworks project using the Project Browser. By activating the 2D sheet, the 2D Takeoff tools are enabled. The tools are located in the second row of the *Quantification Workbook* toolbar, as shown in Figure 7–54.

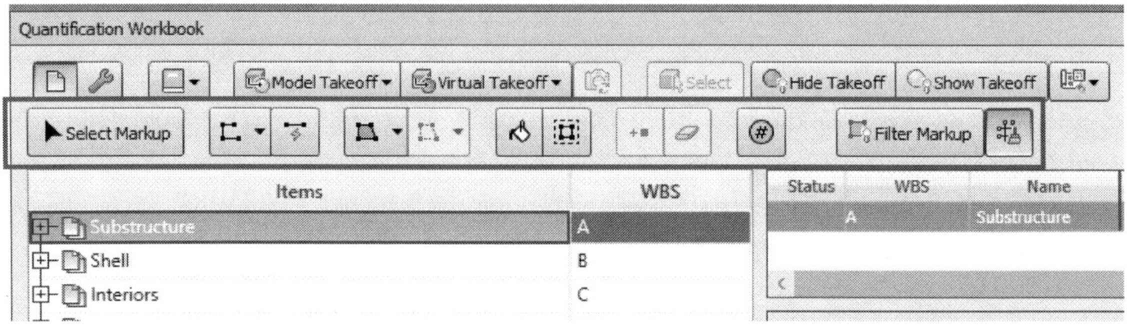

Figure 7–54

The following 2D takeoff types are discussed:

- Linear takeoffs
- Area takeoffs
- Count takeoffs

Linear Takeoffs

There are a number of commands in the *2D Takeoff* toolbar that enable you to measure the length or perimeter of individual or multi-line geometry. The values obtained are added to the *Quantification Workbook*. The commands that can be used (shown in Figure 7–55) include:

- Polyline
- Rectangle Polyline
- Quick Line

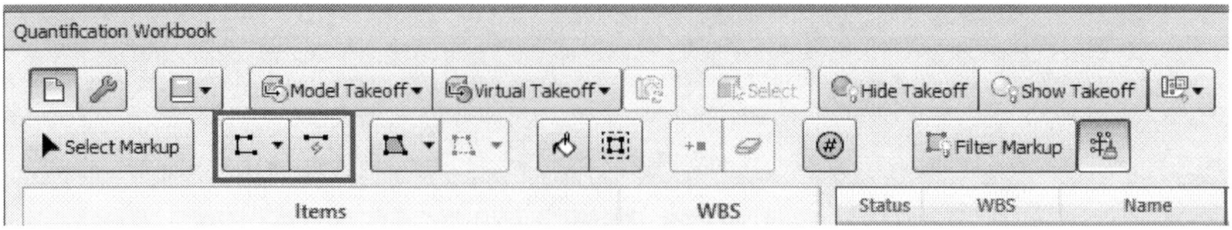

Figure 7–55

How To: Conduct a Linear Takeoff

1. Activate the 2D sheet from which measurements will be taken to populate the takeoff data.
2. In the *Item Catalog*, select the item to which the 2D takeoff will be added.
3. Select a Linear measurement tool in the *2D Takeoff* toolbar.
   - Click (Polyline) to measure single or multi-line segments when the length or perimeter is required and where the geometry is a non-standard shape.
   - Click (Rectangle Polyline) to measure perimeters. The tool creates a square or rectangular shape. Once drawn, you can move the vertices to create a different quadrilateral shape.
4. Conduct the measurement on the 2D sheet.
   - For a **Polyline** measurement, click on the sheet to position the start point for the measurement. As you move over existing geometry, the cursor changes to a snap (green vertex). Continue to select entities on the sheet to define the length or perimeter to be measured. To complete the polyline, select the start point a second time.
   - For a **Rectangle Polyline** measurement, click on the sheet to position the start point for the measurement. Select an entity in the opposite corner to define the rectangle.
5. The measurement is completed when:
   - the start point is selected a second time,
   - the second point in the Rectangular Polyline is selected, or
   - you press <Enter>.

   The takeoff item is added to the active item in the *Item Catalog*.

Hint: Draw Horizontal or Vertical Lines

When drawing a line using the (Polyline) tool, you can press and hold <Shift> to draw one that is perfectly horizontal or vertical.

The *Quick Line* tool in the *2D Takeoff* toolbar is another measurement tool that can be used to obtain a linear takeoff on single or multi-line segments. To use this tool, click (Quick Line) and click an entity on the sheet. Depending on the shape of the line, alternative Quick Line options may be available to more accurately define the measurement of the selected entity (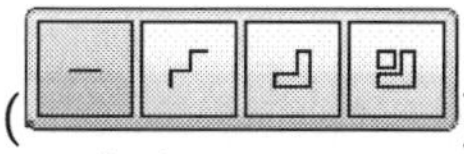). These options enable you to toggle between the selection of the selected single line segment, a polyline of lines connected to the selected line, a curve, or all connected curves.

Hint: Bucket Fill and Quick Box Tools

The Bucket Fill and Quick Box tools enable you to measure both linear and area takeoffs. These tools are discussed later in this section.

Area Takeoffs

Use the Area tools (shown in Figure 7–56) to build up multiple line segments of a polygon or trace a rectangle straight onto the sheet to obtain the area of the traced entities. Once the entities are traced, the area is automatically measured and a new takeoff item is added to the *Quantification Workbook*.

Figure 7–56

How To: Conduct an Area Takeoff

1. Activate the 2D sheet from which the measurements will be taken to populate the takeoff data.
2. In the *Item Catalog*, select the item to which the 2D takeoff will be added.
3. Select an *Area measurement* tool in the *2D Takeoff* toolbar:
   - Click (Area) to measure the size (area) of a non-rectangular area.
   - Click (Rectangle Area) to measure the size (area) of a rectangular area.
4. Conduct the measurement on the 2D sheet.
   - Click on the sheet to position the start point for the **Area** measurement. Continue to select entities on the sheet to define the area to be measured. To complete the area, either select the start point a second time or right-click. As you select entities, a blue highlight displays, defining the area. Once drawn, you can move the vertices to create a different quadrilateral shape.
   - Click on the sheet to position the start point for the **Rectangle Area** measurement. Select an entity in the opposite corner to define the rectangle.

5. The measurement is completed when:
    - the start point is selected a second time,
    - you right-click to automatically close the area,
    - the second point in the Rectangle Area is selected, or
    - you press <Enter>.

The takeoff item is added to the active item in the *Item Catalog*.

Backout Tools

When an area takeoff is conducted, there might be an area within the overall area that is not required in the takeoff value. For example, if an office has a column inside it, the column must be omitted to provide an accurate value for the available floor space, as shown in Figure 7–57. To remove a portion of an overall area, use the **Backout** commands.

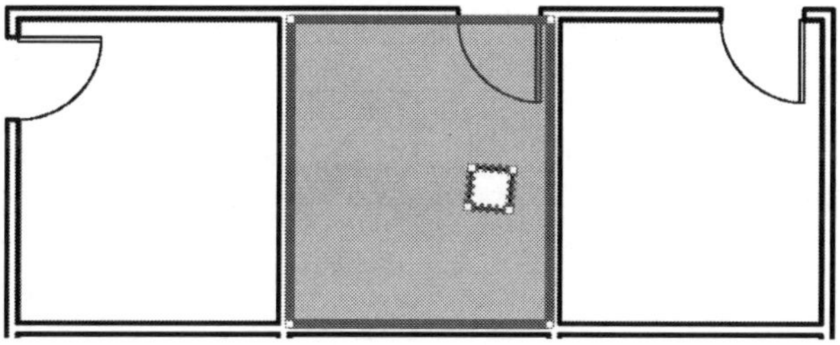

Figure 7–57

How To: Use Backout to Modify an Area Takeoff

1. Ensure that the area takeoff from which an area will be removed is selected in the *Takeoff* pane.
2. Select a *Backout* tool in the *2D Takeoff* toolbar.
    - Click (Backout) to remove a non-rectangular area from a larger takeoff.
    - Click (Rectangle Backout) to remove a rectangular area from a larger takeoff.
3. Trace the area on the 2D sheet.
    - Click on the sheet to position the start point for the **Backout**. As you move over existing geometry, the cursor changes to a snap (green vertex). Continue to select entities on the sheet to define the length or perimeter to be measured. To complete the backout, either select the start point a second time or right-click. Once drawn, you can move the vertices to create a different quadrilateral shape.
    - Click on the sheet to position the start point for the **Rectangle Backout**. Select an entity in the opposite corner to define the rectangle.

4. The backout is completed when:
    - the start point is selected a second time,
    - you right-click to automatically close the area,
    - the second point in the Rectangle Backout is selected, or
    - you press <Enter>.

The original takeoff item is updated to reflect the removal of the backout area.

Bucket Fill and Quick Box Tools

With the *Bucket Fill and Quick Box* tools in the *2D Takeoff* toolbar, you can create either linear or area takeoff entries in the *Quantification Workbook*.

- The **Bucket Fill** tool selects within a geometry boundary to define the linear measurement or area for a takeoff item. Click  (Bucket Fill) and click in an area to select all entities that define a closed area. A linear measurement is identified (as shown on the left in Figure 7–58) with the first selection. Select again in the same area to obtain an area measurement (as shown on the right). While in the command, the last measurement type (linear or area) is used to define each successive selection. Press <Enter> to accept the measurement and add it to the selected item in the *Quantification Workbook*.

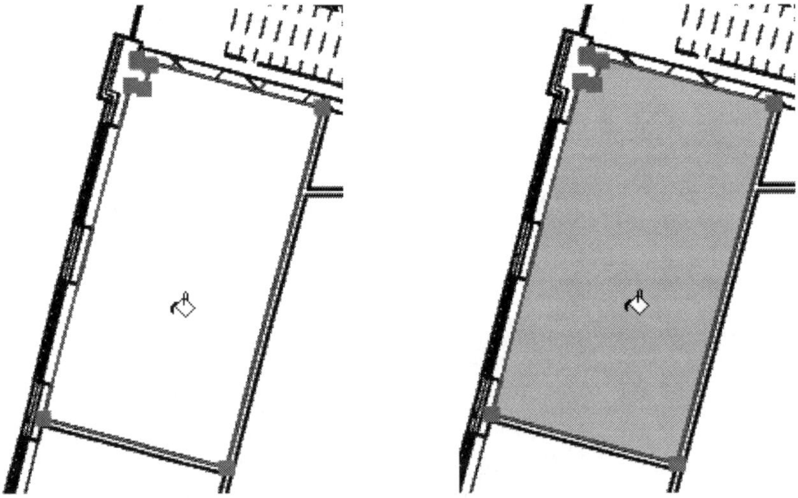

Click once for linear ***Click twice for area***

Figure 7–58

- The **Quick Box** tool enables you to efficiently drag a bounding box over existing geometry to select the length of multiple entities or an area for takeoff measurement. Click (Quick Box) and drag a bounding box over existing entities. Depending on the shape of the entities in the bounding box, Quick Box options display to more accurately define the measurement (). These options enable you to toggle between multiple options. Hover over each item to preview its selection. Select the option to add the takeoff to the selected item in the *Quantification Workbook*. Similar to Bucket Fill, if you select within the enclosed area in the scene view (prior to finalizing the takeoff), it toggles the selection from a linear to an area measurement.

Count Takeoffs

A count takeoff is used to record the number of items. For example, it can be used to count the number of desks in an office. The process involves adding count pins to your 2D sheet. Each pin then becomes a takeoff value in the *Quantification Workbook*.

How To: Conduct a Count Takeoff

1. Activate the 2D sheet from which measurements will be taken to populate the count takeoff data.
2. In the *Item Catalog*, select the item to which the count takeoff will be added.
3. On the *2D Takeoff* toolbar, click (Count) to position a count pin.
4. On the 2D sheet, click to position count pin(s). The *Rollup* pane displays the total count.

   Note: *To delete a count pin, select it and press <Delete>. As an alternative, you can use the Erase tool. Select the count pin so that it displays as blue, click (Erase), and select the pin again on the sheet to remove it. The takeoff value automatically updates.*

Hint: Counting Items Using the Selection Tree

Similar to 3D quantification (in which you can select and use items directly from the 3D model's *Selection Tree*), when doing 2D quantification using a .DWFX file with properties, you can drag items into the *Quantification Workbook* to add a count takeoff. Linear and/or area measurements are not added to the object. This type of count takeoff can only be done on .DWFX files that were created with a source 3D CAD model, where the model's properties were maintained in the .DWFX file.

Additional 2D Takeoff Tools

The following additional 2D Takeoff tools can be used to efficiently work with 2D takeoffs.

- The **Select Markup** option enables you to activate the selection tool for selecting 2D takeoffs on a sheet. Once enabled, you can select single or multiple takeoffs. Multiple takeoffs can be selected by pressing and holding <Ctrl> and clicking the individual takeoffs on the sheet, or by dragging a box around the takeoffs.
- To edit the shape of a linear or area takeoff, you can select and drag any of the vertices that define the shape, or use the  (Add Vertex) tool on the *2D Takeoff* toolbar and select on an active entity to add additional vertices for dragging. Press <Enter> to update the takeoff values.
- The **Filter Markup** option enables you to clear unselected takeoffs from the display on the sheet. Select a takeoff in the *Takeoff* pane (not in the scene view) or select a category or item in the *Quantification Workbook* and use the command. To clear the filter, select the button again.
  - When an item is selected and the **Filter Markup** option is selected, all but the selected markup is removed from the sheet.
  - When a category is selected and the **Filter Markup** option is selected, all items in the selected category remain displayed, while any others outside of the category are removed from the sheet.
- The  (Hide background and annotations) option can be used to help with visibility by toggling off the display of background images and annotations from a 2D worksheet. Once enabled, click  a second time to toggle the background images and annotations on again. This tool will only clear backgrounds and annotations in files that were created with a source 3D CAD model where the backgrounds and annotations are identified as such.
- To quickly review a takeoff item in the *Takeoff* pane (when the item is not easily located), you can select the takeoff in the scene view, right-click, and select **Select Corresponding Takeoff Objects**.
- To temporarily zoom to a selected takeoff, select it in the scene view and press and hold the <Space Bar>. Once you release the <Space Bar>, the viewpoint returns to the previous zoom level and location.

Practice 7c
Create and Work with 2D Takeoff Data

Practice Objectives

- Take off linear 2D elements.
- Take off areas for quantification.
- Perform counting for individual takeoff elements.

In this practice, you will use the *Quantification Workbook* to add quantities by tracing over 2D geometry and counting individual objects.

A new wing planned for the school is in its preliminary state and only 2D sketches are available. Initial quantities are required.

Task 1: Conduct linear and area 2D takeoffs.

1. Continue to work on the file from the previous practice. If you did not complete that practice, open **School-Takeoff-2D.nwf** from the *Navisworks BIM Practice Files\Quantification* folder.
2. In the *View* tab>*Workspace* panel, expand the (Windows) drop-down list and select **Sheet Browser** to display it, if not already displayed. In the Sheet Browser, click (Import Sheets & Models). Open **Proposed-School-Wing.dwfx** from your *Navisworks BIM Practice Files\Quantification* folder. Four 2D sheets are added to the project.
3. If the four new sheets have the icon adjacent to them, they need to be prepared for use in Navisworks. Click on one of the sheets in the Sheet Browser, right-click, and select **Prepare All Sheets/Models**.
4. Double-click on the **Sheet: A103 - First Floor Plan** sheet in the Sheet Browser to activate it.

5. Navigate to the area shown in Figure 7–59.

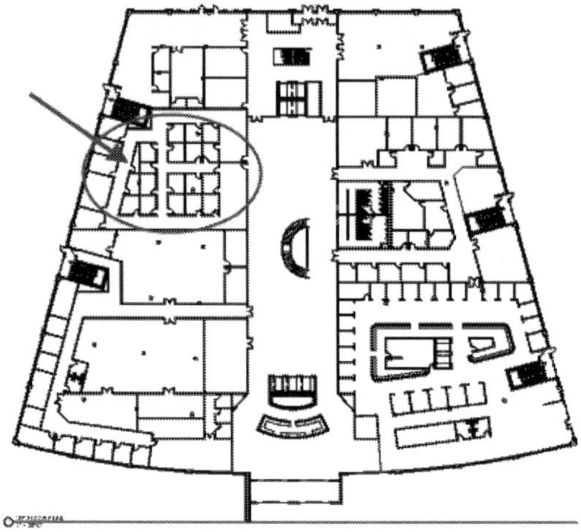

Figure 7–59

6. In the *Item Catalog*, expand *Interiors>Interior Finishes* and select the **Floor Finishes** group. Click **New Item**. Enter **Sheet Vinyl** as the name for the item and press <Enter>. Add **Office Carpet** and **Ceramic Floor** as additional items, as shown in Figure 7–60.

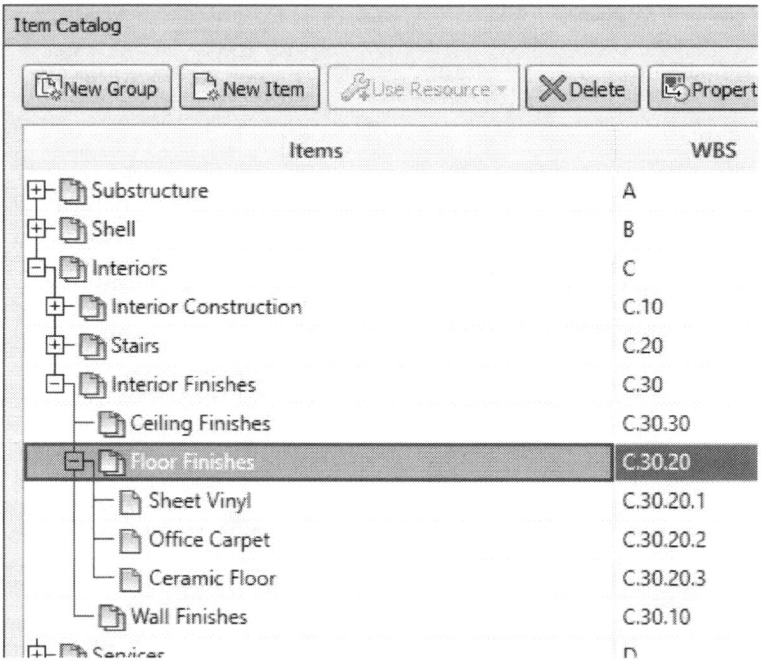

Figure 7–60

7. Open the *Quantification Workbook* and select the **Office Carpet** item, if not already selected.

8. In the *2D Takeoff* toolbar, click (Polyline) to measure the perimeter of a non-rectangular shape.

9. Zoom in to the lower-left corner in the area of focus (shown in Figure 7–59). Select on the sheet at point 1 (inner corners) in Figure 7–61 to position the start point for the Polyline measurement. Continue to select the points (2, 3, 4) that define the shape of this office. To complete the polyline, select the start point (1) a second time. The takeoff is added to the workbook.

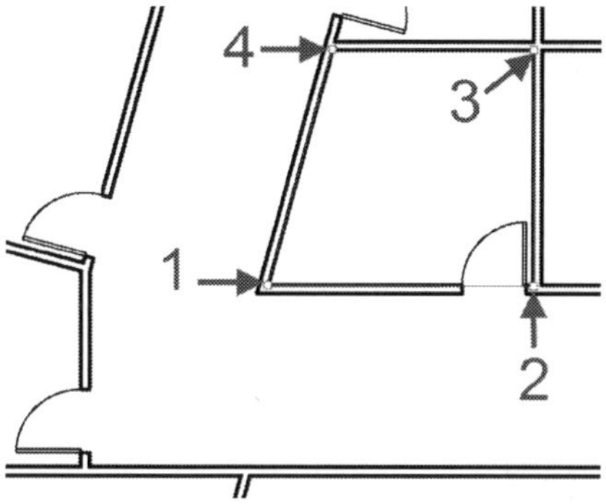

Figure 7–61

10. In the *Quantification Workbook*, review the *Rollup* and *Takeoff* panes for the newly added quantification data for the office, as shown in Figure 7–62. This quantification value measured the perimeter of the office and not the area that is required for a carpet measurement. The values you get may vary slightly depending on your selection locations.

Status	WBS/RBS	Name	Length	Width	Thickness	Height	Perimeter	Area
	C.30.20.2	Office Carpet	44.539 ft	0.000 ft	0.000 ft	0.000 ft	44.539 ft	0.000 ft²

Status	WBS	Object	ModelLength	ModelWidth	ModelThickness	ModelHeight	ModelPerimeter
	C.30.20.2.1	Office Carpet 1	44.539 ft				44.539 ft

Figure 7–62

Note: *It is always important to review the takeoff data to ensure that it is reporting the required information.*

11. In the *Takeoff* pane, right-click **Office Carpet 1** and select **Delete Takeoff** to remove it from the workbook.

12. In the *2D Takeoff* toolbar, click (Area) to measure the area of a non-rectangular shape.

13. Click on the sheet to position the start point for the Area measurement, as shown at point 1 in Figure 7–63. Continue to select the points (2, 3, 4) that define the shape of this office. To complete the area measurement, either select the start point (1) a second time or right-click after making the fourth selection.

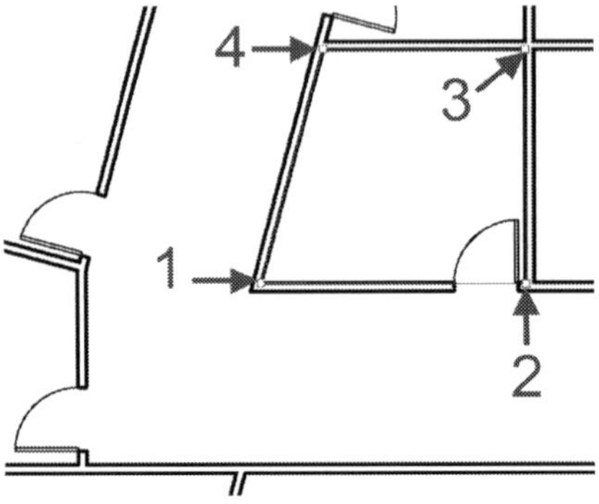

Figure 7–63

14. In the *Quantification Workbook*, review the *Rollup* and *Takeoff* panes for the required quantification data that measures the area of the office, as shown in Figure 7–64. The values you get may vary slightly depending on your selection locations.

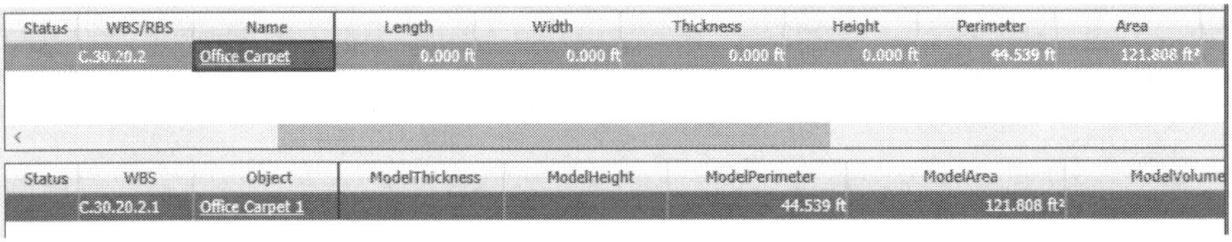

Figure 7–64

Note: *The (Polyline) and (Area) tools are measured in the same way; however, they provide different results. Polyline is for linear measurements and Area measures surface area. Ensure that you select the correct command for the required measurement.*

In a similar way, the (Rectangle Polyline) and (Rectangle Area) tools produce linear and area measurements, respectively.

15. In the *2D Takeoff* toolbar, expand (Area) and click (Rectangle Area) to measure the area of the rectangular office to the right of the previously measured office. Ensure that the **Office Carpet** item is still selected in the *Quantification Workbook*.

16. Click on the sheet to position the start point for the *Rectangle Area* measurement. Click the opposite corner to define the rectangle. Review the *Rollup* and *Takeoff* panes. Notice that two takeoffs now exist, as shown in Figure 7–65.

Status	WBS/RBS	Name	Length	Width	Thickness	Height	Perimeter	Area
	C.30.20.2	Office Carpet	0.000 ft	0.000 ft	0.000 ft	0.000 ft	85.773 ft	227.313 ft²

Status	WBS	Object	ModelThickness	ModelHeight	ModelPerimeter	ModelArea	ModelVolume
	C.30.20.2.1	Office Carpet 1			44.539 ft	121.808 ft²	
	C.30.20.2.2	Office Carpet 2			41.234 ft	105.505 ft²	

Figure 7–65

17. Pan upwards to one of the rectangular offices that have a column, as shown in Figure 7–66.

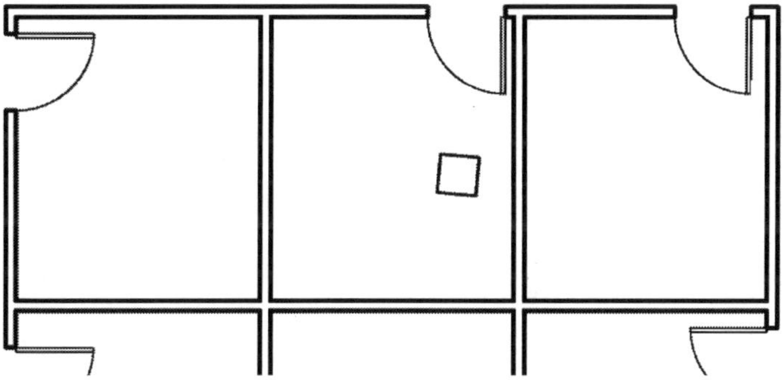

Figure 7–66

18. In the *2D Takeoff* toolbar, click (Rectangle Area) and measure the area of the office. Review the area value in the *Takeoff* pane.

19. In the *2D Takeoff* toolbar, click (Backout) and select the four vertices that define the outline of the column, as shown in Figure 7–67. Right-click to clear the selection once the fourth vertex is selected and press <Esc> to end the command. Review the area in the *Takeoff* pane. The column's area has been removed.

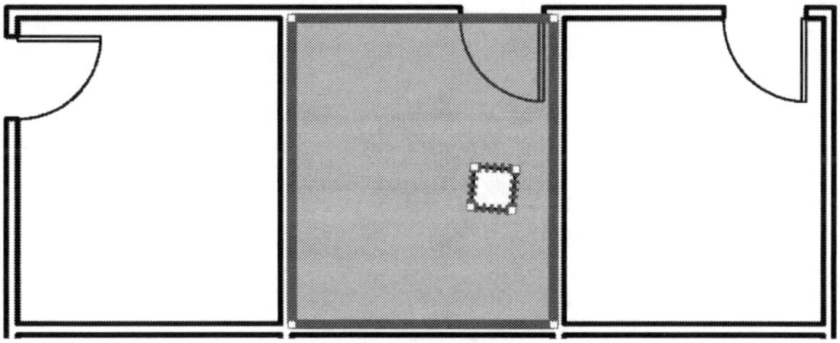

Figure 7–67

20. In the *Quantification Workbook*, select the **Ceramic Floor** item.

21. Zoom into the area of the hallway, as shown in Figure 7–68.

22. In the *2D Takeoff* toolbar, expand (Rectangle Area) and click (Area) and measure the ceramic hallway flooring in the area shown in Figure 7–68. Zoom in and pan as you are selecting vertices for the takeoff to accurately make selections. Once complete, press <Esc> to end the command.

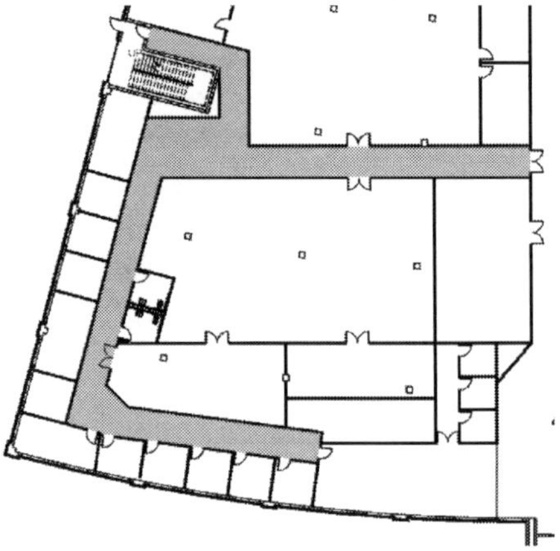

Figure 7–68

23. In the *Quantification Workbook*, return to one of the Office Carpet items and select it in the *Takeoff* pane. The sheet automatically reorients to show these takeoffs. This is a good way to quickly change the view to review the takeoffs.

24. In the scene view, select the takeoff that was done in the hallway (Ceramic), right-click, and select **Select Corresponding Takeoff Objects**. Note that the *Quantification Workbook* now displays the information on this takeoff. This is a good way to locate a takeoff when you do not know its category.

25. In the *Quantification workbook*, select the **Sheet Vinyl** item in the *Floor Finishes* group.

26. Zoom and pan to the location shown in Figure 7–69. Note that this is the office above the original area that was placed. Use the (Area) command to measure the overall area of the room by defining the four corners. This room will be a kitchen with vinyl flooring.

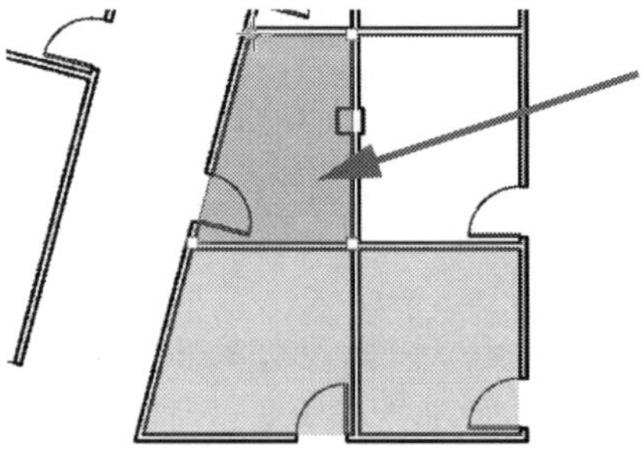

Figure 7–69

27. An area where the column comes into the room must be removed. This is not an enclosed area in the room so the *Backout* tool is not appropriate. With the takeoff still selected, in the *2D Takeoff* toolbar, click (Add Vertex) and make the four selections shown in Figure 7–70 to add four vertices near the column.

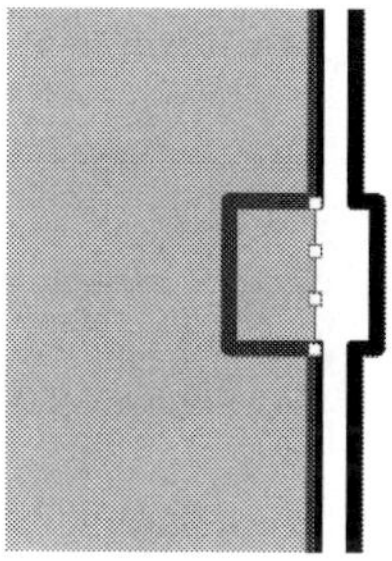

Figure 7–70

28. Press <Esc> to clear the **Add Vertex** command. Drag the two middle vertices to trace the shape of the column, as shown in Figure 7–71. Press <Enter> to complete the edit. The takeoff value updates to reflect the change.

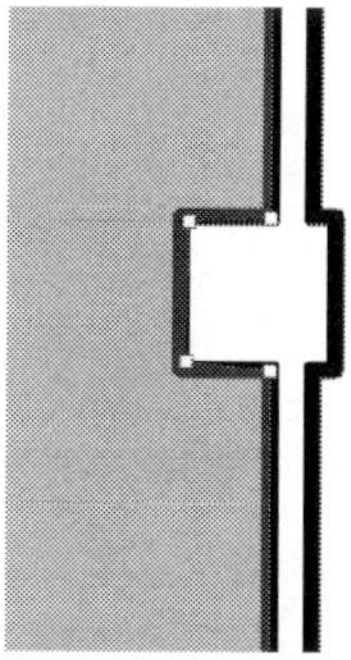

Figure 7–71

29. Zoom out on the drawing to see all five takeoffs. Note that the Carpet, Ceramic, and Vinyl flooring types have different colors. This is because of the color that was defined as the default when the item was created. This can be changed in the *Item Catalog*, if required.
30. In the *Item Catalog*, expand the *Interiors>Interior Construction* group. Click **New Item**. Enter **Column Closures** as the name for the item and press <Enter>.
31. Select the **Column Closures** item in the *Quantification Workbook*, if not already selected.
32. In the *2D Takeoff* toolbar, click (Quick Box) to quickly measure the perimeter of one of the columns in an office. Zoom to an office with a column.

33. Drag a selection box around the column, as shown in Figure 7–72.

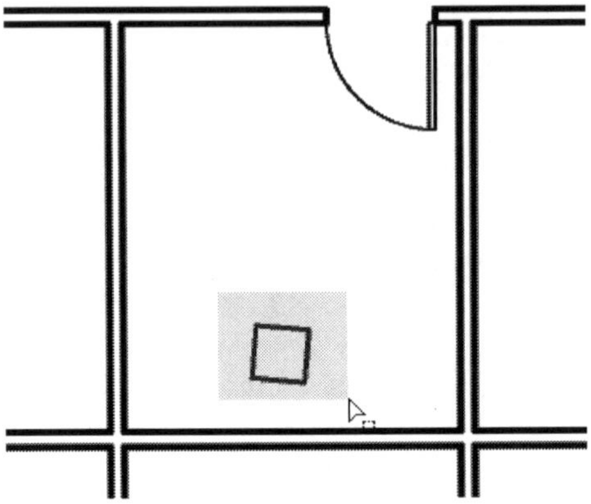

Figure 7–72

34. Once you complete the selection, the Quick Box tools display. Note how the linear perimeter measurement is highlighting. Select again inside the selected area to convert to an Area measurement. The selection highlights in red indicating it is measuring area.

35. Select 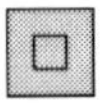 to select the area. It selects the largest boundary area with the least line segments, as shown in Figure 7–73. The area takeoff value is added to the workbook.

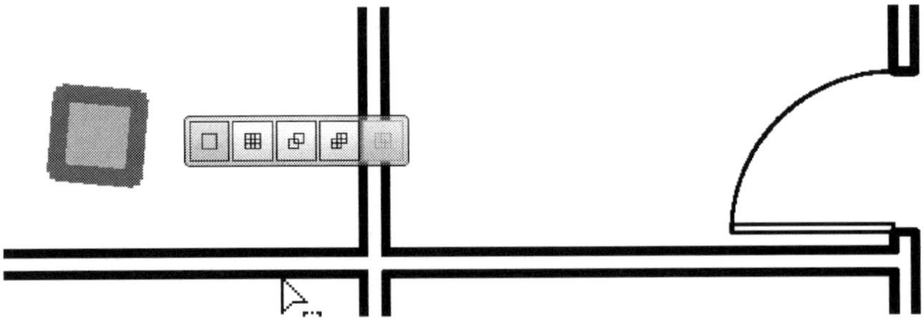

Figure 7–73

36. Zoom out and use the (Quick Box) command and the other options in the Quick Box set to select different entities in the selection box. Note the takeoff values that are added with each selection. Undo this action to clear the addition of these test takeoffs from the workbook.

- As an alternative, you can use the (Bucket) tool to quickly select enclosed areas to take off their perimeters and areas.

***Note:** Review the takeoffs that are created to ensure that they are reporting for the entities that are required. If a takeoff is added that is not required, select it in the Takeoff pane, click **Update**, and select **Delete Selected Takeoff**.*

37. In the *Item Catalog*, expand *Interiors>Interior Finishes* and select the **Wall Finishes** group. Click **New Item**. Enter **Beige Paint** as the name for the item and press <Enter>.
38. Zoom to the kitchen that was taken off using the Sheet Vinyl item, as shown in Figure 7–74. Ensure that the **Beige Paint** item is selected in the *Quantification Workbook*.

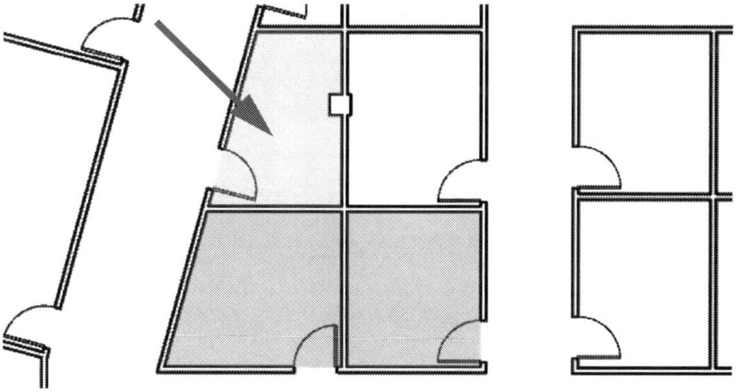

Figure 7–74

39. In the *2D Takeoff* toolbar, click (Polyline). Trace the perimeter of the room to take off its perimeter. Ensure that you trace around the column.
40. In the *Takeoff* pane, scroll through the list of parameters for the new takeoff until you reach the *Height* parameter. Select it, enter **9.000 ft** (as shown in Figure 7–75), and press <Enter>. The icon in the *Status* cell indicates that this is an overwritten field.

Status	WBS	Object	Thickness	Height	Perimeter	Area
	C.30.10.1.1	Beige Paint 1	0.000 ft	9.000 ft	42.673 ft	0.000 ft²

Figure 7–75

41. Select the *Area* parameter field. In the equation field, enter **=Height*ModelPerimeter** and press <Enter> to obtain the *Area* value for the paint takeoff, as shown in Figure 7–76. Note that your area value may differ depending on the point selections you made when tracing the perimeter.

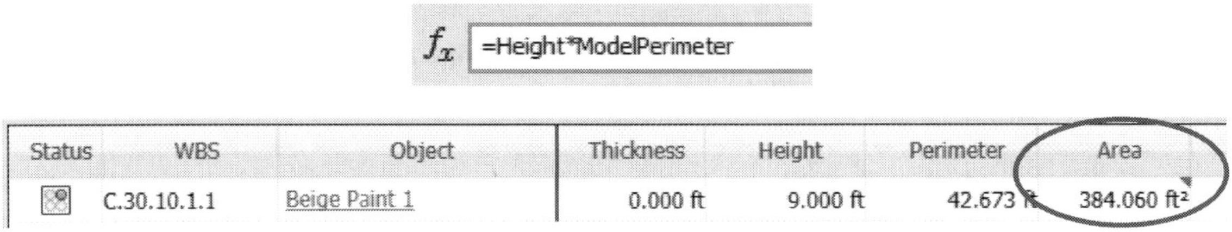

Figure 7–76

Task 2: Conduct a count takeoff.

1. In the Sheet Browser, double-click on the **Sheet: A104 - Second Floor Plan** sheet to activate it. On this sheet there are a number of tables that need to be counted. Zoom in to the tables, as shown in Figure 7–77.

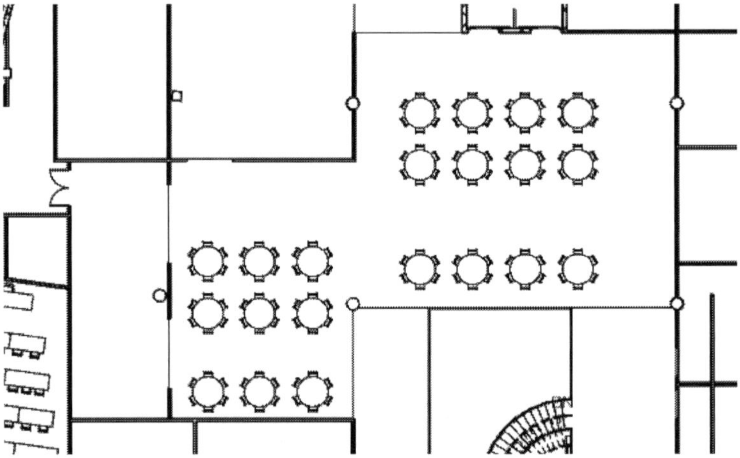

Figure 7–77

2. Add two new items to the *Equipment & Furnishings>Furnishings>Moveable Furnishings* group, one called **Round Table - Med** and the other called **Chair-Breuer**.
3. Select the **Round Table - Med** item in the *Quantification Workbook*.
4. In the *2D Takeoff* toolbar, click  (Count). Select one of the tables on the sheet to position a count pin. Add a total of 21 pins, one on each table, as shown in Figure 7–78. Press <Esc> to end the command.

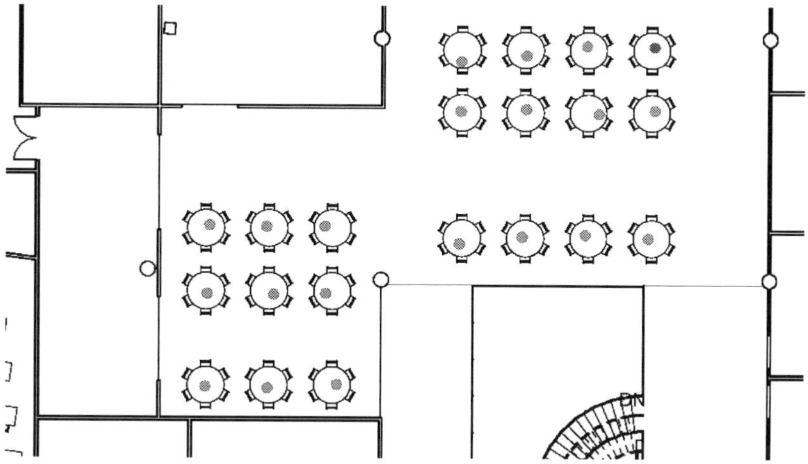

Figure 7–78

5. Review the *Takeoff* and *Rollup* panes to see the total count, as shown in Figure 7–79. There are 21 medium-sized round tables.

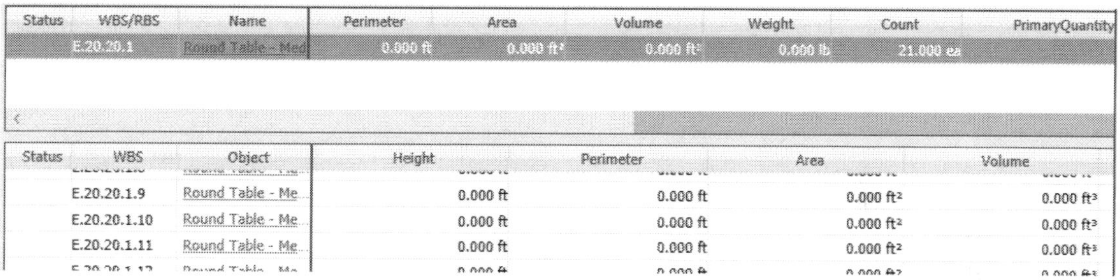

Figure 7–79

Note: *To delete a count pin, select it in the Take Off pane so that the pin displays as blue, right-click on its name, and select* ***Delete****. The takeoff value automatically updates.*

6. Ensure that the *Selection Tree* is displaying the Standard view.
7. Open the *Find Items* window and conduct a search using the criteria shown in Figure 7–80. This represents the types of chairs used at the tables that were just counted. Find all instances of this chair: there should be 126 instances located.

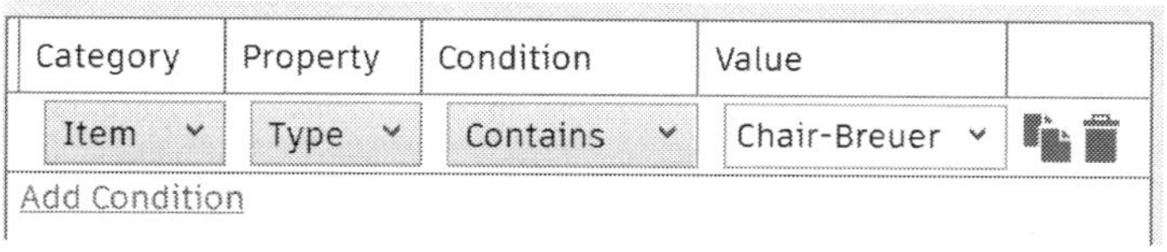

Figure 7–80

8. Ensure that the **Chair-Breuer** item is selected in the *Quantification Workbook*.

9. Right-click on any of the selected items in the *Selection Tree* and select **Quantification>Take off to: Chair-Breuer**. Review the *Rollup* pane and note that all of these 2D items have been counted. Note that you may have to scroll in the *Rollup* pane to see the *Count* column. If properties exist for items in the .DWFX file, this type of count takeoff can be done as an alternative to manually dropping pins.

Task 3: Clear annotations from a sheet.

1. Double-click on the **Sheet: A101 - 4th Floor Wing A** sheet in the Sheet Browser to activate it. On this sheet, note that there are grid lines shown.
2. In the *2D Takeoff* toolbar, click  (Hide background and annotations) to toggle off the display of the grid lines to clear the clutter from the sheet.
3. Save the file.

End of practice

7.6 Working with Takeoff Data

Analyzing Takeoff Data

With Change Analysis, you can compare changes to properties between different versions of a model. If differences are identified or there are changes to the takeoff data, status notifications in the *Quantification Workbook* will indicate what was changed.

The following are the types of notifications that can be presented:

- Warning flags ( ) display adjacent to a changed item or resource in the *Navigation* pane.
- Green triangles display in the corners of cells ( ) to indicate an overwritten value. Hover over the triangle to view a tooltip that shows the original and overridden value, as shown in Figure 7–81.

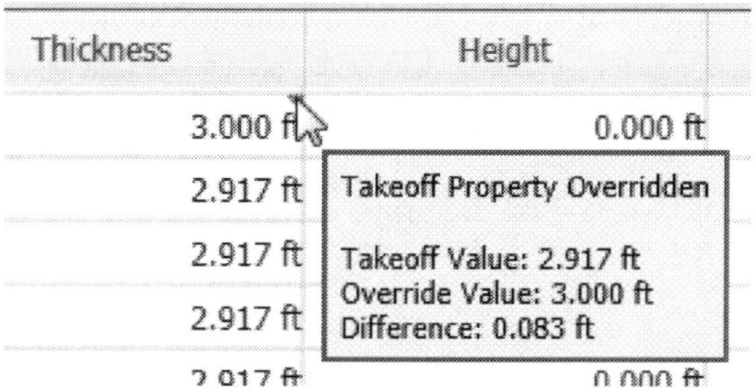

Figure 7–81

- Blue triangles display in the corners of cells ( ) to indicate that a model property has changed. Hover over the triangle to display a tooltip showing the old and new values, as shown in Figure 7–82.

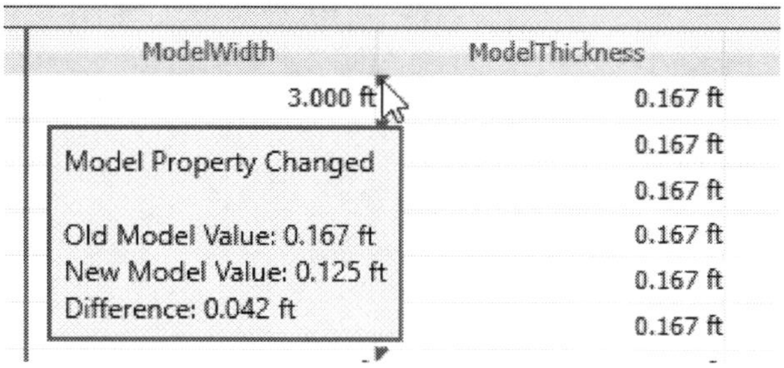

Figure 7–82

Note: *Multiple status notification "lights" might display for one takeoff item.*

- Icons in the *Status* column of the *Takeoff* pane for the *Quantification Workbook* are described as follows. Hover over the icon to display the status in a tooltip.

Icon	Action	Description
	Override (Green)	This icon indicates that a formula has been overridden and Change Analysis is still required.
	Change (Blue)	This icon indicates that an object has changed and is different from the takeoff item in the workbook.
	Error (Red)	This icon indicates that there are errors with either the formula or the item.
	Delete (Black)	This icon indicates that a takeoff's item has been deleted.

- The formula bar displays with a red outline (vs. gray) in the *Quantification Workbook* if an invalid formula was entered. You are prevented from applying the formula.

How To: Analyze and Update Changes in the Quantification Workbook

1. In the *Quantification Workbook*, click **Change Analysis** and select **Analyze Changes**. Virtual takeoffs cannot be analyzed because they are not linked to the model.

2. Review the changes that are identified ( ) in the *Quantification* window.

   - To update the *Quantification Workbook* with the new changes, select a cell in the row, click **Update**, and select **Update Selected from Model**. Items can be updated individually by selecting them in the *Takeoff* pane or you can select all of the items in a catalog item and update them at the same time.

   - For any takeoff item that indicates that the model item has been deleted ( ), select a cell in the row, click **Update**, and select **Delete Selected Takeoff**
   - Click **Change Analysis** and select **Clear Analyze Results** if you want to ignore the changes that have been identified.

Exporting Takeoff Data

Takeoff data can be exported from the *Quantification Workbook* for use in other applications using the .XML or Excel format.

How To: Export Takeoff Data

1. In the *Quantification Workbook*, click .
2. In the drop-down list, select an export option. The available options include:
   - **Export Catalog to XML**
   - **Export Quantities to Excel**
   - **Export Selected Quantities to Excel**

   Note: *The*  *drop-down list can also be used to import a catalog into the Quantification Workbook.*

3. In the dialog box, navigate to the preferred save location. Enter a filename and save the data.

Practice 7d
Analyze and Update Takeoff Data

Practice Objectives

- Update the current Navisworks model with revised models.
- Export the *Quantification Workbook*.

In this practice, you will simulate a project's workflow. The Revit model has been updated to include the missing door that was noted in the previous practice. You will inspect the *Quantification Workbook* with the new changes, then you will export the workbook to a spreadsheet file.

Task 1: Refresh the Navisworks files to reflect changes in the source model.

1. If you have a Navisworks file open, close it by clicking in the Quick Access Toolbar.
2. Open *Windows File Explorer* and navigate to the *Navisworks BIM Practice Files\Project Files\Revit Files* folder.
3. Delete the Navisworks cache file of the architectural model, which is **School-Architectural.nwc.** By deleting this file, Navisworks will open the **School-Architectural.rvt** file rather than the cache file.
4. Rename *School-Architectural.rvt* to **School-Architectural_OLD.rvt**.
5. Rename *School-Architectural_Revised.rvt* to **School-Architectural.rvt**.
6. Return to the Navisworks software and open **School-Takeoff-Export.nwf** from the *Navisworks BIM Practice Files\Quantification* folder.

   Note: *It now takes longer to load the School-Architectural file since you deleted the cache file and the Navisworks* software *has to import and process the Revit file.*

7. In the *Saved Viewpoints* window, select the **Office Interior** viewpoint in the *Interior* folder. Note that a door has been added to the model.

   Note: *The purpose of renaming the files was to simulate a design change in the Revit model, as many training environments do not have access to this software. The* ***School-Architectural_Revised.rvt*** *file has had a design change. In a normal design environment, when a change is made to the Revit model, you can use the* ***Refresh*** *command to incorporate the changes from the source file into Navisworks.*

8. In the upper-right corner of the *Quantification Workbook*, expand **Change Analysis** and select **Analyze Changes**, as shown in Figure 7–83.

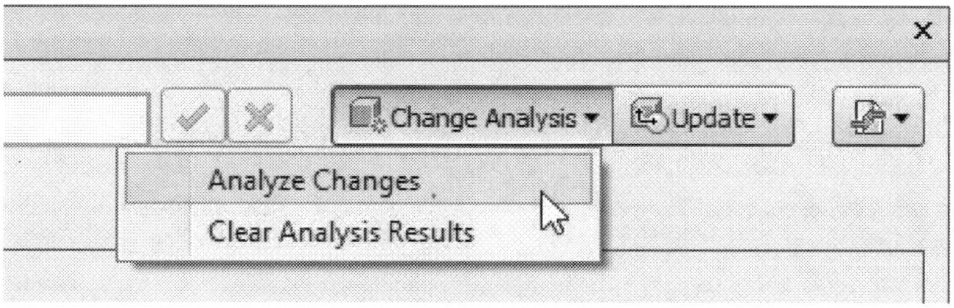

Figure 7–83

9. In the *Quantification Workbook*, note that the icon displays adjacent to the *Interiors* group, helping you to determine where the differences have been found.
10. Expand the *Interiors>Interior Construction>Interior Doors>Standard Interior Doors* group.

    Note that displays in the list for the **Wood Door - Single** item, identifying the change was found here, and that the quantity of Single-Flush doors is 81.
11. Select the **Wood Door - Single** item.
12. In the **School-Architectural_Revised.rvt** file, a door was added where it was initially missing. The virtual takeoff is no longer required. In the *Takeoff* pane of the *Quantification Workbook*, scroll to the bottom of the list and select the **Missing Door** cell in the virtual takeoff row.
13. In the upper right corner of the toolbar, expand **Update** and select **Delete Selected Takeoff,** as shown in Figure 7–84. Note that the quantity of Single-Flush doors is once again 80.

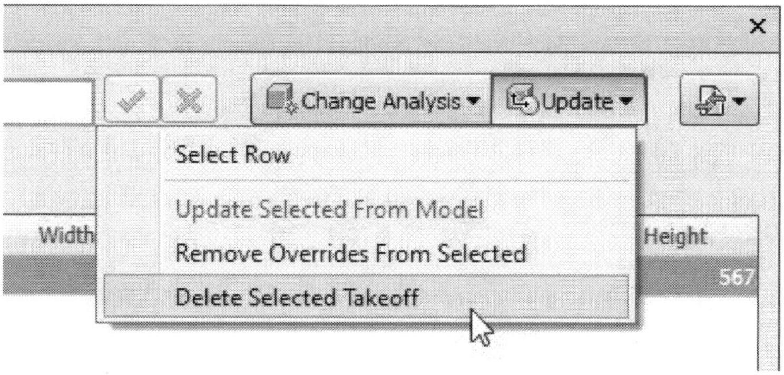

Figure 7–84

14. Select the *Status* column header in the *Takeoff* pane to sort the list. This can be helpful if you only have certain items in the list that change. In this case, all door thicknesses have changed, as shown in Figure 7–85.

Figure 7–85

15. Hover the cursor over the blue triangular icon ( ) for the first item and note that the thickness of the door has been changed, as shown in Figure 7–86. This is the same for all of the doors.

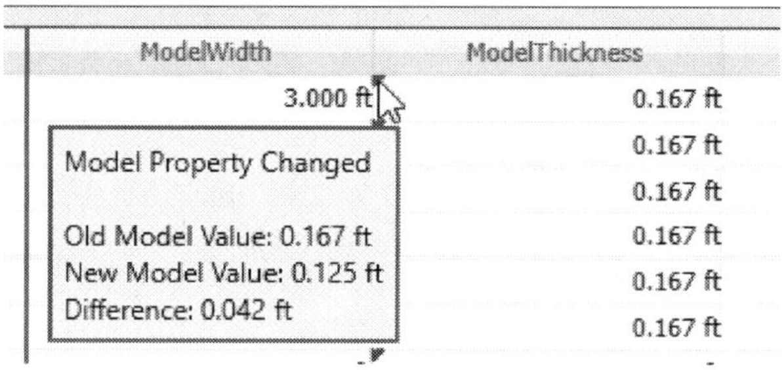

Figure 7–86

16. Select the *ModelThickness* cell for the **C.10.20.01.2.1** object. In the upper right corner of the toolbar, expand **Update** and select **Select Row**.
17. In the toolbar, expand **Update** again and select **Update Selected From Model**. The C.10.20.01.2.1 object's data updates and is no longer marked as changed.
18. Select the **SINGLE** name for the second object. Press and hold <Shift> and scroll to the bottom of the list and select the last object. All of the remaining objects are now selected.
19. Expand **Update** and select **Select Row**. The rows for all remaining objects are now selected.
20. In the toolbar, expand **Update** and select **Update Selected From Model**. Note that no longer displays in the item list because all of the changes have been updated.
21. The new door that was added to the revision of the model must be added to the takeoff. In the *Saved Viewpoints* window, verify that the **Office Interior** viewpoint is active.
22. Select the new door in the scene view. The door highlights in the *Selection Tree*. Note that depending on your current *Selection Priority*, the **Corridors 2011** room might select. If so, use <Ctrl>+<H> to hide the room and reselect the door.

23. Notice that this new door is highlighted in the *Selection Tree*. Drag it from the *Selection Tree* and drop it on the **Wood Door-Single (80)** item in the *Quantification Workbook*. The new door is added as the new **C.10.20.01.2.81** item and the number of doors updates to 81.

    Note: *When updating and working with the Quantification Workbook, after objects have been added to a model, consider using the* ***Show Takeoff*** *and* ***Hide Takeoff*** *options to help identify the items that need to be added to the takeoff.*

Task 2: Export the Quantification Workbook.

1. In the *Quantification Workbook*, expand  and select **Export Catalog to XML**. This enables you to save the *Item Catalog* that was customized for use in another project.
2. In the *Export Catalog to XML* dialog box, browse to the *Navisworks BIM Practice Files\Quantification* folder, enter **Class Catalog.xml** as the name for the file, and save it.

    Note: *Consider setting up and saving to a network location so that multiple Navisworks users can use the new catalog.*

3. In the *Quantification Workbook*, expand  and select **Export Quantities to Excel**. This enables you to save all of the taken off quantities to an Excel spreadsheet.
4. In the *Export Quantities to Excel* dialog box, browse to the *Navisworks BIM Practice Files\Quantification* folder, enter **School Takeoff Report.xlsx** as the name for the file, and save it.
5. Click **Yes** to open the file once it has been created. Note that the file will open automatically only if you have Excel installed on your computer.

    Note: *If you receive a notification about missing pivot tables and are prompted to repair the file, select* ***Yes****. The file will be repaired automatically before it is opened.*

6. Review the takeoff quantities that have been added to the file. Close the file.
7. Save and close the file by clicking  in the Quick Access Toolbar.

Task 3: Restore the original School-Architectural file.

1. Open *Windows Explorer* and navigate to the *Navisworks BIM Practice Files\Project Files\Revit Files* folder.
2. Delete the Navisworks cache file of the architectural model, which is **School-Architectural.nwc**.
3. Rename School-Architectural.rvt to **School-Architectural_Revised.rvt**.

4. Rename School-Architectural_OLD.rvt to **School-Architectural.rvt**. Reverting back to the original architectural model is being done to complete the remaining practices in this learning content.

End of practice

Chapter Review Questions

1. Which of the following is NOT part of the *Quantification Workbook*?
   a. Navigation pane
   b. Summary tab
   c. Toolbar
   d. Takeoff pane

2. Contents in the *Resource Catalog* can be edited.
   a. True
   b. False

3. What is a GUID?
   a. Graphical User Interface Dock
   b. Globally Unique Identifier
   c. User guide/manual
   d. General Unit Imperial Distance

4. What is a virtual takeoff used for? (Select all that apply.)
   a. Calculating quantities in the Autodesk Cloud.
   b. Objects planned for the model but not yet placed.
   c. Objects part of a future phase of the model but not yet placed.
   d. Objects that have been deleted from the model.
   e. Objects located only in certain viewpoints.

5. Which of the following is NOT part of the *2D Takeoff* tools?
   a. Linear takeoff
   b. Area takeoff
   c. Volume takeoff
   d. Count takeoff

6. What formats can you export the quantification to? (Select all that apply.)

a. .HTML

b. .DBF

c. .DWFX

d. .XLSX

Command Summary

Button	Command	Location
	**Add Vertex**	• **Quantification Workbook:** *2D Takeoff* toolbar
	**Add Viewpoint**	• **Quantification Workbook**
	**Appearance of items**	• **Quantification Workbook**
	**Area**	• **Quantification Workbook:** *2D Takeoff* toolbar
	**Backout**	• **Quantification Workbook:** *2D Takeoff* toolbar
	**Bucket Fill**	• **Quantification Workbook:** *2D Takeoff* toolbar
	**Count**	• **Quantification Workbook:** *2D Takeoff* toolbar
	**Erase**	• **Quantification Workbook:** *2D Takeoff* toolbar
	**Find Items**	• **Ribbon:** *Home* tab
	**Formula Input**	• **Quantification Workbook**
	**Hide background and annotations**	• **Quantification Workbook:** *2D Takeoff* toolbar
	**Hide Takeoff**	• **Quantification Workbook**
	**Import/Export**	• **Quantification Workbook**
	**Import Sheets & Models**	• **Project Browser**
	**New Group**	• **Quantification Workbook>Item Catalog** • **Quantification Workbook>Resource Catalog**
	**New Item**	• **Quantification Workbook>Item Catalog**
	**New Resource**	• **Quantification Workbook>Resource Catalog**

Button	Command	Location
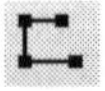	**Polyline**	• **Quantification Workbook:** *2D Takeoff* toolbar
	**Project Setup**	• **Quantification Workbook**
	**Quantification**	• **Ribbon:** *Home* tab>*Tools* panel • Ribbon: *View* tab>*Workspace* panel>*Windows* drop-down list
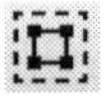	**Quick Box**	• **Quantification Workbook:** *2D Takeoff* toolbar
	**Quick Line**	• **Quantification Workbook:** *2D Takeoff* toolbar
	**Rectangle Area**	• **Quantification Workbook:** *2D Takeoff* toolbar
	**Rectangle Backout**	• **Quantification Workbook:** *2D Takeoff* toolbar
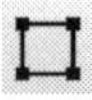	**Rectangle Polyline**	• **Quantification Workbook:** *2D Takeoff* toolbar
	**Show/Hide catalogs**	• **Quantification Workbook**
	**Show Takeoff**	• **Quantification Workbook**

Chapter 8

Animator

Communication is at the center of any efficient BIM workflow. Full communication ensures that all stakeholders fully understand how a project will look and function when it is complete. The Autodesk® Navisworks® Animator enables you to create movement in the model to show how objects interact with each other. Learn how to animate objects and create a simple animation to orbit a model. You will drive along one of the roads in the model and also create .AVI movies to share with others.

Learning Objectives

- Create an animation to tour a model.
- Drive along a Civil 3D road using the Civil Alignments tools.
- Modify the position, rotation, size, color, and transparency of objects to animate them.
- Create .AVI files to share videos of a project with others.

BIM Workflow: Communicate

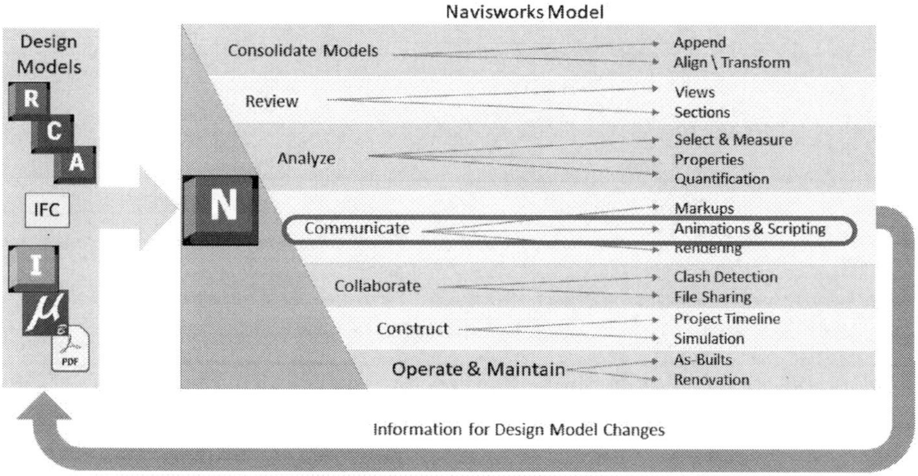

8.1 Creating Tours

You can create videos that simulate walking or flying through a model so that stakeholders can take a tour long before the structure is built.

Animator Window

Animator uses scenes along a timeline to create a slide show. The *Animator* window (shown in Figure 8–1) is broken into two key areas to reflect this: scenes display on the left in the *Tree* pane, while the scene's placement in the animation is shown in the *Timeline* pane on the right. The *Animator* toolbar sits above the *Tree* and *Timeline* panes.

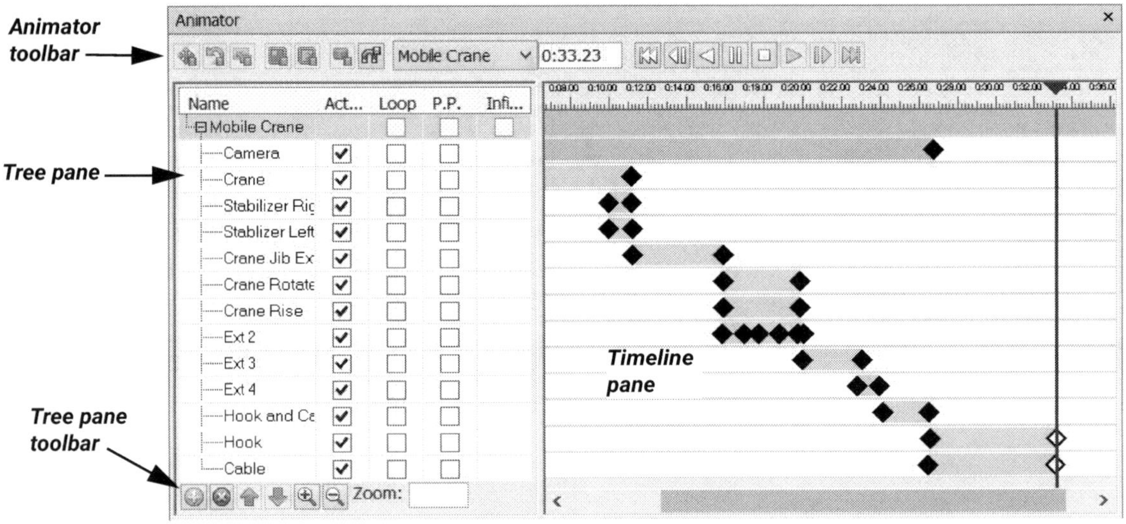

Figure 8–1

Tree Pane

You can add, view, and reorder scene components in the *Tree* pane. Scenes in the *Tree* pane can include:

- A camera
- Section planes for sectional views
- Animation sets of objects to be animated

Each scene can only contain one camera, but multiple scene views or viewpoints can be added to the camera.

- When using multiple viewpoints, the animation can jump from view to view or transition smoothly between views.

- When only one viewpoint is added to the animation, the scene continuously focuses on one spot as objects are animated.
- If no viewpoint is added to the camera, then the current view is used during the animation.

The *Tree* pane tools do the following:

- opens a menu that enables you to add a scene, animation set, section plane, folder, or scene folder, as shown on the left in Figure 8–2. You can also access these tools by right-clicking on a scene in the *Tree* pane, as shown on the right in Figure 8–2.

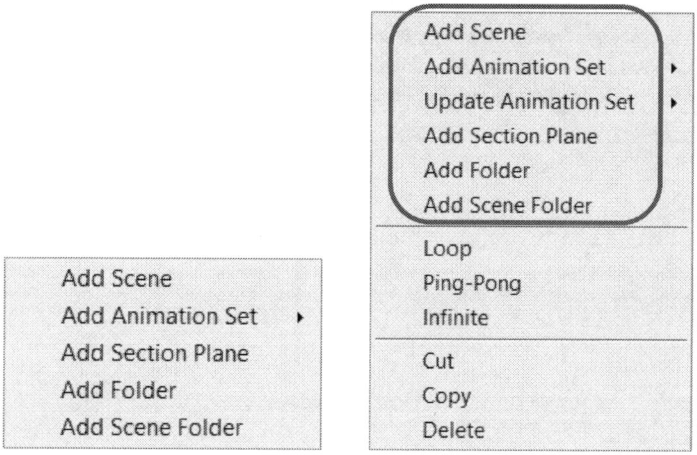

Figure 8–2

- deletes a scene or scene component.
- / changes the order of the scenes and scene components by moving them up or down in the *Tree* pane.
- / zooms in or out on the Timeline to make it easier to see the start, end, and duration of each item in the *Tree* pane.
- Zoom: 1/2 sets how many seconds display in the Timeline.

Timeline Pane

The *Timeline* pane is used to set when each keyframe is displayed in the animation and the length of the keyframe. A keyframe is a snapshot of a change to the model or the camera viewpoint. The animation bar indicates where on the Timeline the current keyframe falls. As the animation bar is moved, the scene view is updated.The start and end diamonds can be dragged to a new location on the Timeline to change when a keyframe displays in the scene view and the duration of the keyframe, as shown in Figure 8–3.

- In the *Animator* toolbar, click  (Capture Keyframe) to add the current viewpoint of the camera to the animation.

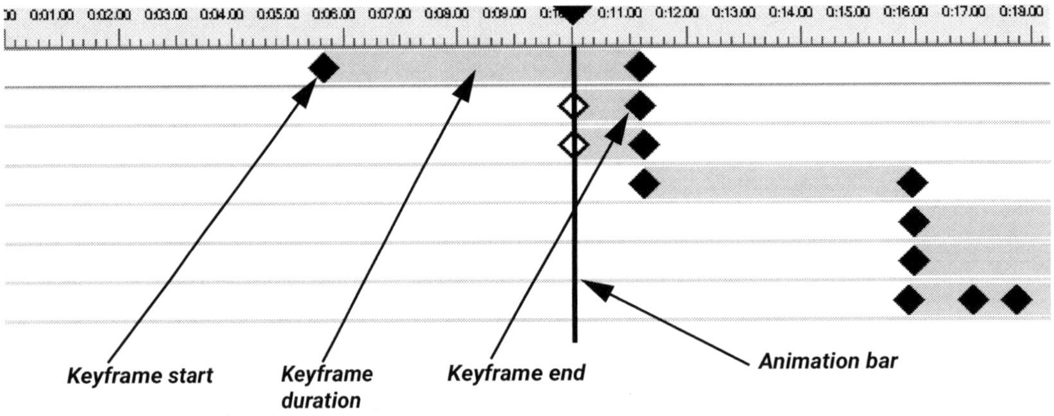

Figure 8–3

- Right-click on a keyframe to display additional tools, as shown in Figure 8–4.

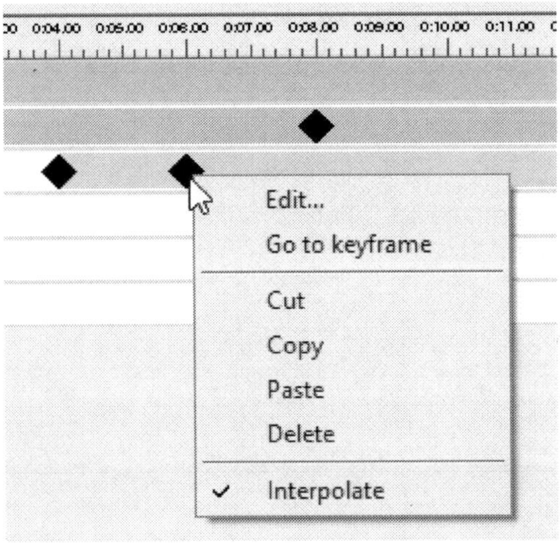

Figure 8–4

- **Edit:** Opens the *Edit Key Frame* dialog box (shown in Figure 8–5), which enables you to modify the keyframe focus, similar to modifying a viewpoint.

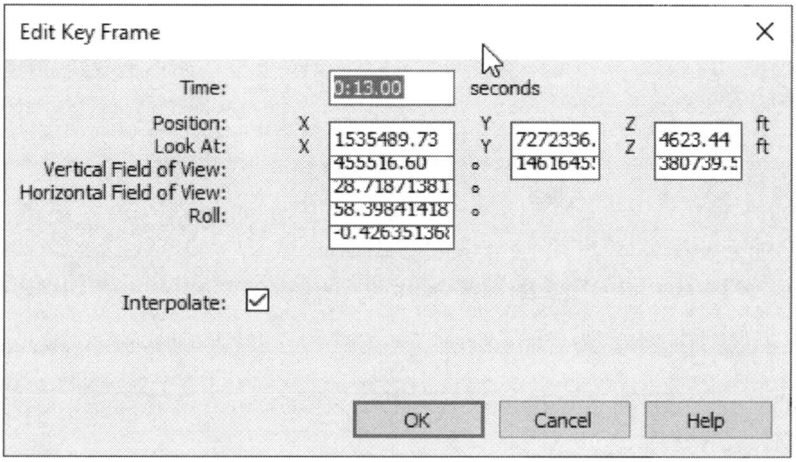

Figure 8–5

- **Cut:** Removes a keyframe from the Timeline and saves it in a clipboard for later use.
- **Copy:** Saves a keyframe to the clipboard for later use without changing the original keyframe.

Note: If Cut or Copy are selected, right-clicking anywhere on the Timeline provides a Paste option. **Paste** *enables you to place the last keyframe saved to the clipboard at the location where you right-click.*

- **Delete:** Removes the keyframe.
- **Go to keyframe:** Moves the animation bar to the selected keyframe, and changes the scene view to that keyframe's view.
- **Interpolate:** Creates a smooth transition between keyframes, as if panning or zooming in real-time.

How To: Create a Simple Animation to Display the Model

1. In the *Home* tab>*Tools* panel, click (Animator) to open the *Animator* window.
2. In the *Animator* window>*Tree* pane, click (Add Scene).
3. Enter a descriptive name for the scene.
4. In the scene view, set the current view as it is expected to display in the keyframe by reorienting or using saved viewpoints, as required.
5. Move the animation bar to the time that you want the scene to start.

6. Right-click on the scene name and select **Add Camera>Blank Camera**.
7. In the *Animator* toolbar, click (Capture keyframe). A black diamond displays in the Timeline to indicate the start of the keyframe.
8. Use the viewing tools (e.g., Pan, Orbit, Saved Viewpoints, etc.) to change the scene view to a new camera position.
9. Move the animation bar to where you want the scene to end.
10. In the *Animator* toolbar, click (Capture keyframe). This sets the end of the keyframe and its duration, as shown previously in Figure 8–3.
11. Repeat Steps 2 to 10 until all of the required scenes are added to the Timeline.

    Note: *Multiple keyframes can be added to the same camera.*

Play Animations

The *Animator* toolbar contains a variety of tools. The tools found on the right of the *Animator* toolbar helps you review the animations, as follows:

- Orbit (Scene Picker): Displays the active scene. Expanding this drop-down list provides a list of the available scenes.
- 0:36.25 (Time Position): Displays the current position of the black animation bar in the *Timeline* pane. You can enter a time to jump to that location in the Timeline.
- (Rewind): Moves the animation bar to the beginning of the animation and changes the scene view to match.
- (Step Back): Rewinds the animation one keyframe at a time.
- (Reverse Play): Plays the animation in reverse.
- (Pause): Pauses the animation.
- (Stop): Stops the animation, moves the animation bar back to the beginning of the Timeline, and changes the scene view to match.
- (Play): Starts the animation from the current position of the animation bar.
- (Step Forward): Moves forward in the animation, one keyframe at a time.
- (To End): Fast forwards to the end of the animation.

In addition to the tools in the *Animator* toolbar, there are four columns in the *Tree* pane that set the play options, as shown in Figure 8–6.

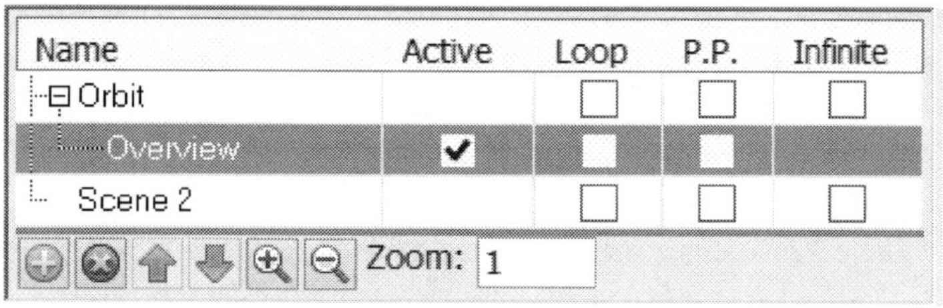

Figure 8–6

- **Active:** When checked, a scene component is active and is used in the animation. Clear the checkmark to make a scene component inactive.
- **Loop:** Causes the animation to automatically play again from the beginning once it reaches the end of the animation.
- **Ping-Pong (P.P.):** As the name implies, Ping-Pong causes the animation to play normally from beginning to end, and then plays it in reverse until it returns to the beginning again.
- **Infinite:** Makes the scene play indefinitely, or until you click (Stop).

Practice 8a
Create a Simple Animation

Practice Objective

- Create a tour of the model using Animator.

In this practice, you will create an animation to tour the model, as shown in Figure 8–7.

Figure 8–7

Task 1: Create an animation that orbits around the model.

1. Open **School-Orbit.nwf** from the *Navisworks BIM Practice Files\Animator* folder.
2. In the *Saved Viewpoints* window, select **Overview** in the *Animator* folder.
3. At the bottom of the graphics window, expand the *Animator* window and pin it.

   Note: *If the Animator window is not displayed, in the Home tab>Tools panel, click*  *(Animator) or in the View tab>Workspace panel, expand* ***Windows*** *and select Animator.*

4. In the *Animator* window>*Tree* pane, click  (Add scene) and select **Add Scene**. Note that **Scene 1** is added to the *Tree* pane.
5. Click on **Scene 1**, enter **Orbit** as the name, and press <Enter>. Ensure that the animation bar is at **0** on the Timeline. If it is not, drag the animation bar to 0.
6. Right-click on the scene name (Orbit) and select **Add Camera>Blank camera**.

7. Enter **Overview** as the name of the new camera and press <Enter>, as shown in Figure 8–8.

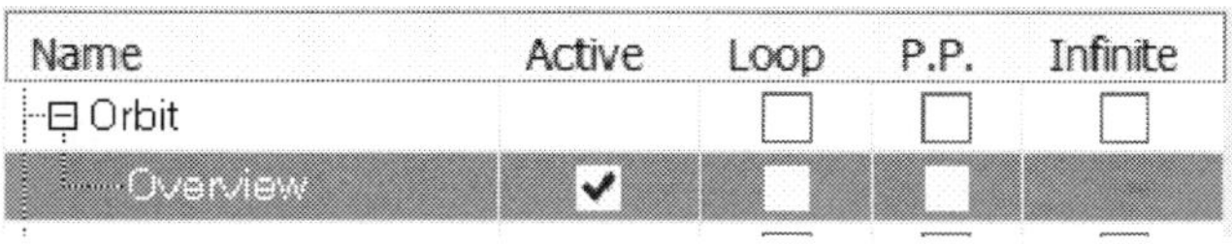

Figure 8–8

8. In the *Animator* toolbar, click (Capture keyframe), as shown in Figure 8–9. A diamond is added to the Timeline at 0 to indicate the start of the keyframe.
9. On the timeline, right-click on the new keyframe (diamond) and ensure that **Interpolate** is checked. If it is not, select it to toggle it on.
10. Move the animation bar to **4** seconds on the Timeline, or enter **4** in the *Time Position* field and press <Enter>. It displays as 0:04:00, as shown in the Figure 8–9.

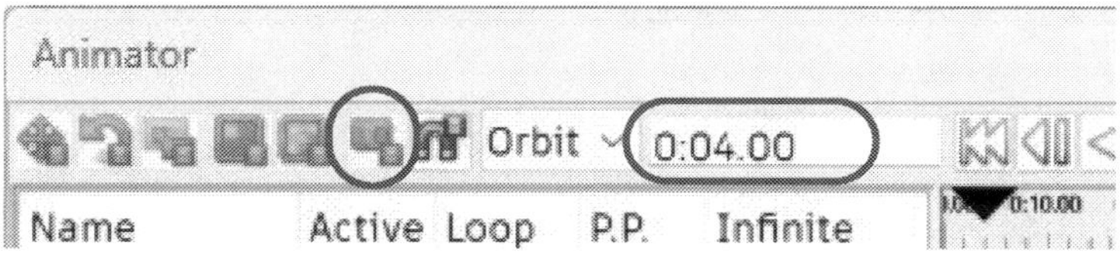

Figure 8–9

11. In the *Saved Viewpoints* window, select the **SE-Isometric** viewpoint in the *Animator* folder.
12. In the *Animator* toolbar, click (Capture keyframe).

    Note: *If you did accidentally move the viewpoint, you can restore the saved viewpoint.*

13. Repeat Steps 11 to 14 to create additional keyframes at the following times and viewpoints. All these viewpoints are in the **Animator** folder.
    - At **8** seconds, capture the **East Side** viewpoint.
    - At **12** seconds, capture the **NE-Isometric** viewpoint.
    - At **16** seconds, capture the **North Side** viewpoint.
    - At **20** seconds, capture the **NW-Isometric** viewpoint.
    - At **24** seconds, capture the **West Side** viewpoint.
    - At **28** seconds, capture the **SW-Isometric** viewpoint.
    - At **32** seconds, capture the **Overview** viewpoint.
14. In the *Animator* toolbar, click (Stop), and then click (Play) to play the animation from the beginning. Note how the animation moves through each of the viewpoints that you selected.

Task 2: Create an animation that walks into the model.

1. Continue working in the same animation that was created in the last task.
2. Move the animation bar to **36** seconds on the Timeline.
3. In the *Saved Viewpoints* window, select the **Front Entry** viewpoint in the *Animator* folder.
4. In the *Animator* toolbar, click  (Capture keyframe).
5. Repeat Steps 2 to 4 to create additional keyframes at the following times and viewpoints, as shown in Figure 8–10:
   - At **40** seconds, capture the **Turn1** viewpoint.
   - At **42** seconds, capture the **Turn2** viewpoint.

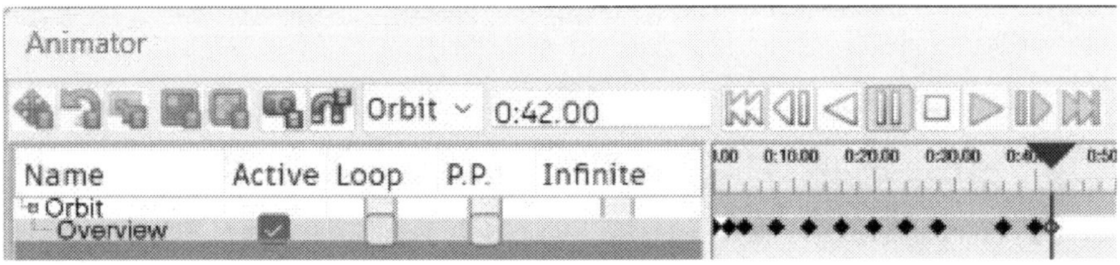

Figure 8–10

6. In the *Animator* toolbar, click  (Stop), and then click  (Play) to play the animation from the beginning.
7. Save the file.

End of practice

8.2 Civil Alignments

Roads created in Autodesk Civil 3D are known as corridors. Civil 3D corridors can also represent other features such as pathways, retention walls, breakwaters, berms, etc. The horizontal control lines of such corridors are known as alignments. In many cases, they represent the centerline of the road, but may also be medians, curblines, etc., depending on the design. They contain stations, which are points at regular distances along the alignment and at specific control points (such as beginning, midpoint, and end of curves, etc.).

Corridors can also be built from feature lines, which can be considered 3D polylines. However such corridors cannot be used for this Civil Alignments feature.

> ***Note:*** *Civil Alignments are part of Civil 3D drawings. In order to access them, you need to have either Civil 3D or the Civil 3D enabler installed. For more information on the Civil 3D enabler, see Appendix A - Coordination Best Practices.*

The Civil Alignments tools allow you to drive along a corridor from a driver's point of view. There are a variety of controls you can set to meet viewing requirements you may have.

When appending or merging a Civil 3D drawing or NWC file which contains corridors built with alignments, the civil alignment tools in Navisworks become available and are accessible on the *View* tab>*Civil Alignments* panel, as shown in Figure 8–11.

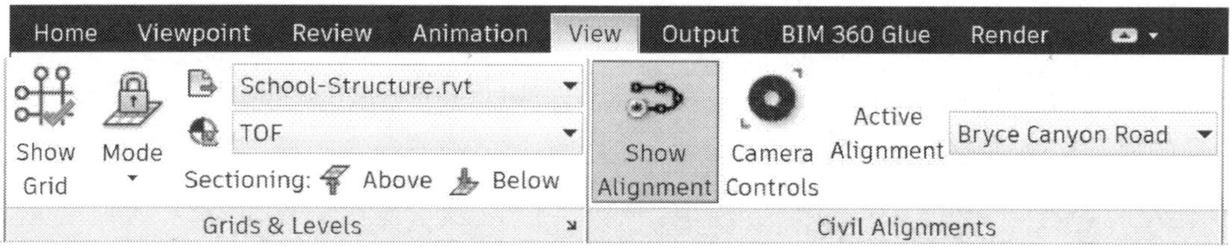

Figure 8–11

All eligible alignments (i.e., alignments that are used to define corridors) are listed in the *Active Alignment* drop-down list where you can select the alignment to focus on.

The **Show Alignments** button is a toggle that controls the visibility of the alignment. In the Top view, the difference is negligible; however, when driving along the road, it is quite noticeable as shown in Figure 8–12.

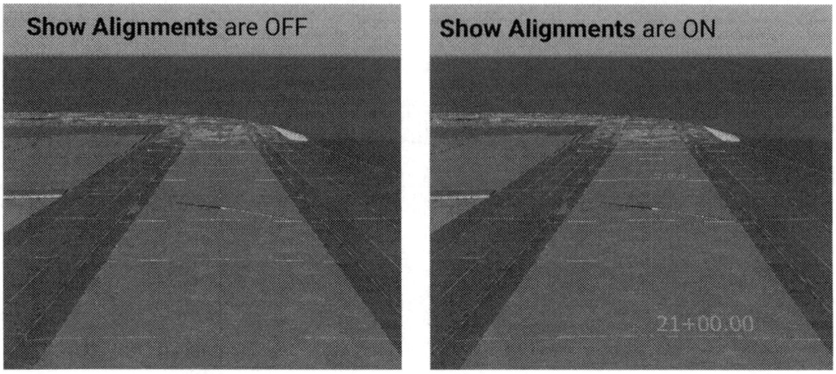

Figure 8–12

> **Hint: Alignment Colors**
>
> The color of the alignments, station labels, and station characters can be:
>
> 1. In the *Options Editor*, expand **Interface** and select **Civil Alignments**, as shown in Figure 8–13.
> 2. In the right panel, change the colors for the *Label color* (for the Stationing Labels) and the Alignment's *Line color*.
> 3. Choose what type of character you want the use as the abbreviation in the station values.

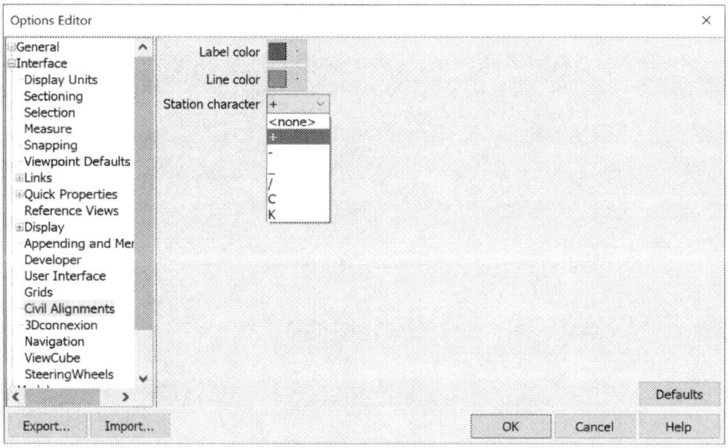

Figure 8–13

The **Camera Control** button toggles the display of the *Civil Alignments* window.

The *Civil Alignments* window

In the *Civil Alignments* window, you can "drive" along an alignment simply by pressing the  (Play / Pause) button. It also contains many options and settings to control the camera position and scene navigation relative to the civil alignment, as shown in Figure 8–14.

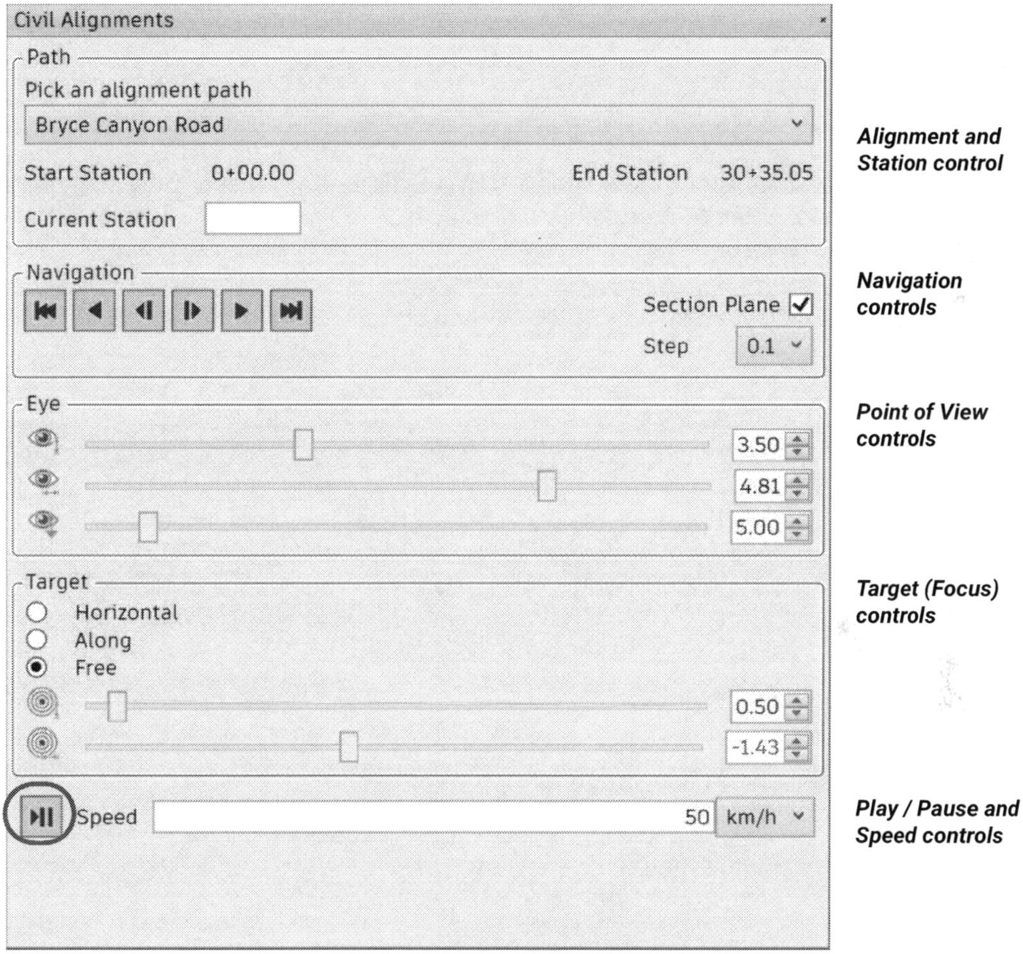

Figure 8–14

This window is modeless, meaning it remains open as you continue to work in Navisworks. It also can be docked on any edge of the Navisworks screen like other windows, or even be moved to a second monitor.

> **Note:** *The units are set in the Options Editor dialog box>Interface node>Display Units.*

Alignment and Station control (Figure 8–15)

Figure 8–15

- Make an alignment path current by selecting it from the drop-down menu. Only alignments that are active and connected to corridors are displayed.
- The *Start Station* and *End Station* are displayed for your reference.
- In the *Current Station* box, you can type in the desired current station, and press the <Tab> key to move to that station.

Navigation controls (Figure 8–16)

Figure 8–16

Use the following buttons to:

-  Go to the first station of the alignment.
-  Go to the previous major station of the alignment.
-  Go to the previous step of the alignment, as defined by the *Step* value.
-  Go to the next step of the alignment, as defined by the *Step* value.
-  Go to the next major station of the alignment.
-  Go to the end of the alignment.

Use the *Step* drop-down menu to select the size of the step between major stations. You can select a step size of **0.1, 0.2, 0.25** or **0.5.** For example, **0.1** will sets the step to one tenth of the distance between major stations.

The **Section Plane** check box enables the section plane. When enabled, the roadway is cut as you drive along it, however this is only noticeable when the Eye or Target controls are adjusted beyond the default settings, as shown in Figure 8–17.

Figure 8–17

Point of View / Eye controls (Figure 8–18)

Figure 8–18

Use the following buttons to adjust the point of view (eye position). You can either slide the slider button back and forth, use the up and down arrows or type in values. The camera adjusts interactively as the values change:

-  (Eye height) - The vertical distance between the camera and the alignment.
-  (Eye offset) - The horizontal distance between the camera and the alignment.
-  (Eye setback) - The horizontal distance between the camera behind the current station. When the Section Plane is selected (checked), this setting will help in showing the cut plane more clearly.

Target / Focus controls (Figure 8–19)

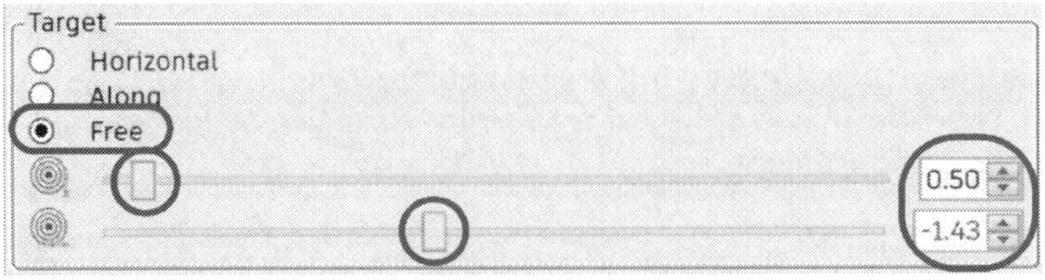

Figure 8–19

Use the following to adjust the focus or target of the camera as you "drive" along the road:

- **Horizontal** - The camera looks horizontally, even if the road slopes up or down.
- **Along** - The camera looks parallel to the road, thus tilting up or down as the road slopes.
- **Free** - Customize the focus while "driving" along the road. When this option is selected, the following buttons become available. As with the Point of View / Eye controls, you can either slide the slider button back and forth, use the up and down arrows or type in values. The camera adjusts interactively as the values change.
  - 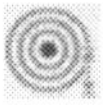 (Target height) - The vertical distance between the camera and the alignment. A value of **0** means the focus is on the horizon.
  - 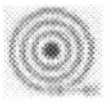 (Target offset) - The horizontal distance between the camera and the alignment. **Note:** A value of **0** keeps the focus on the centerline, a negative value turns it to the left, and a positive value to the right.

Play / Pause and Speed controls (Figure 8–20)

Figure 8–20

Use the following to adjust the speed of the "drive":

-  Play / Pause toggle - Press once to commence the drive, press again to pause.
- **Speed**: Set the simulated speed of the "drive". Type in the desired speed. From the drop-down menu, you can select units of the speed.

Type a value in the field and select units from the drop-down list to specify the speed.

> ***Note:*** *To record the drive for later playback, use the options on the Animation tab.*

Practice 8b
Take a drive along a Civil Alignment

Practice Objectives

- Drive along an active Civil 3D alignment.
- Change settings to fine-tune the drive.
- Set the focus on the school as you drive by.

In this practice, you will make a Civil 3D alignment current and then take a "test drive" along that road. Then you will make some changes to the way this drive is performed and examine the results, as shown in Figure 8–21.

> ***Note:*** *In order to access the Civil Alignments, you need to have either Civil 3D or the* ***2026.1 Civil 3D Object Enabler*** *installed. For more information on the Civil 3D enabler, see Appendix A - Coordination Best Practices.*

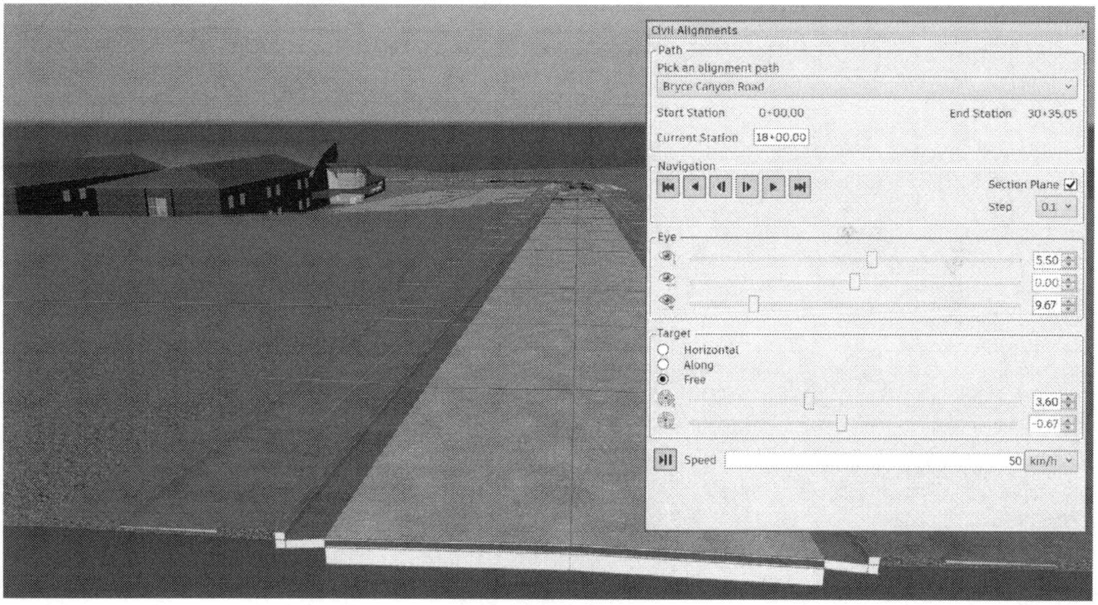

Figure 8–21

Task 1: Select an alignment and go for a "test drive".

1. Open **School-Alignments.nwf** from the *Navisworks BIM Practice Files\Animator* folder.
2. In the *View* tab>*Civil Alignments* panel, from the drop-down menu, select the **Bryce Canyon Road** alignment, as shown in Figure 8–22.

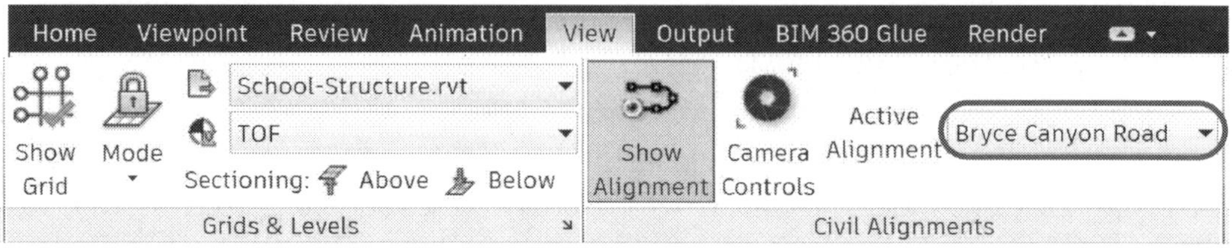

Figure 8–22

3. In the *View* tab>*Civil Alignments* panel, toggle on the **Camera Controls** button to open the *Civil Alignments* window.
4. In the *Civil Alignments* window, in the *Current Station* box, type **2550** for the desired current station, and press the <Tab> key to move to that station. As you press <Tab>, the *Current Station* box updates to **25+50.00** and the scene moves to that location, as shown in Figure 8–23.

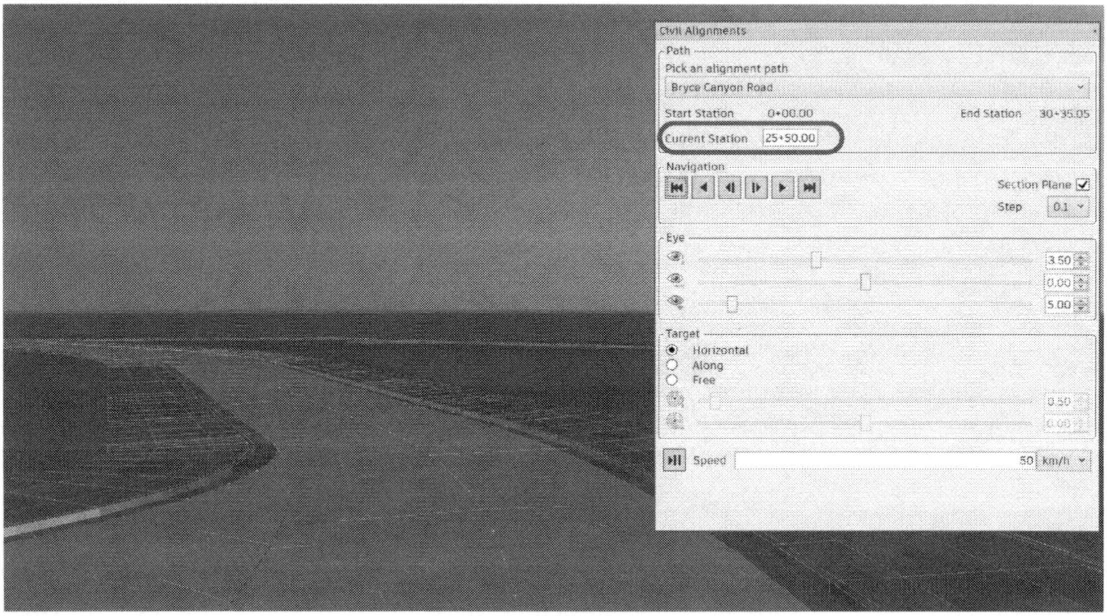

Figure 8–23

5. In the *View* tab>*Civil Alignments* panel, toggle the **Show Alignments** button a couple times to control the visibility of the alignment. Leave the alignment showing.

6. "Drive" along an alignment simply by pressing the (Play / Pause) button in the bottom left corner of the *Civil Alignments* window. You begin the drive at the station you had picked earlier and continue to the end of the alignment.

Task 2: Navigate along the Civil alignment.

1. In the *Civil Alignments* window, in the *Navigation* controls section, click on to go to the previous major station of the alignment, which is **30+00.00**. Click once more to move to the **29+00.00** station.
2. In the *Civil Alignments* window, in the *Navigation* controls section, ensure that the *Step* value is set to **0.1**, and that the *Section Plane* checkbox is toggled on, as shown in Figure 8–24.

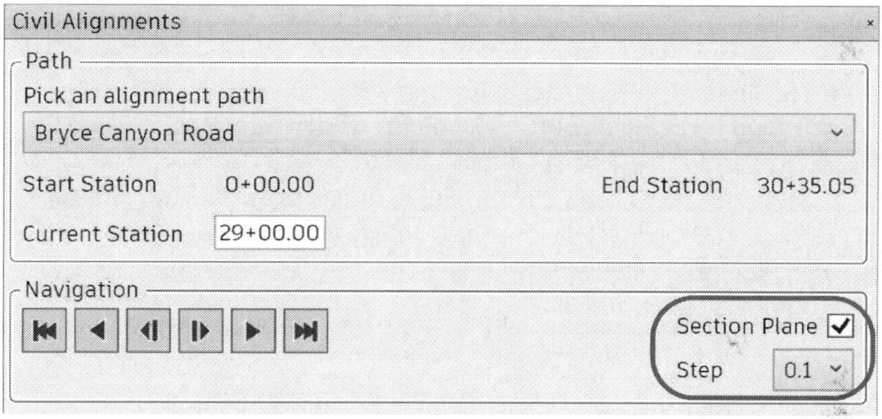

Figure 8–24

3. Now click on to go to the previous step of the alignment, which is **28+90.00**.
4. Use the *Step* drop -down menu to select the step size **0.5.**
5. Click on again to go to the previous step of the alignment, which will now be **28+50.00**, which is one half between the major stations.
6. Click on to go to the first station of the alignment, which is **0+00.00**.
7. In the *Current Station* box, type **1850** to go to station **18+50.00**.
8. In the *Civil Alignments* window, in the *Eye* controls section, slide the (Eye height) slider back and forth to raise or lower the vertical distance between the camera and the alignment. Use the up and down arrows for fine tuning.
9. Type in **15** to have the vertical distance at 15.00 feet.

10. Repeat the steps for (Eye offset), which controls the horizontal distance between the camera and the alignment. If you drive on the right side of the road, set the value to **3**, to be 3.00 feet off the center line.

11. Repeat the steps for (Eye setback). This sets the horizontal distance between the camera behind the current station. Set the value to **55**, so you are 55 feet behind your current station. The final values are shown in Figure 8–25.

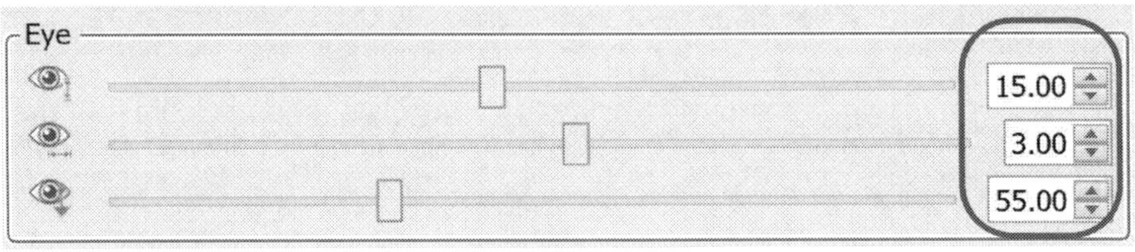

Figure 8–25

12. As you move behind the current alignment, you will notice the cut plane, since the *Section Plane* is toggled on (indicated by the checkmark). Toggle the *Section Plane* off and on and notice the difference of the roadway. Leave it toggled on.

13. In the *Civil Alignments* window, in the *Target* controls section, ensure that **Horizontal** is selected. This means that you will look horizontally as you drive, even if the road slopes up or down. This road has a minor slope.

14. Press the (Play / Pause) button in the bottom left corner of the *Civil Alignments* window to drive to the end of the alignment and notice that you are looking at the horizon.

15. In the *Current Station* box, type **1850** to go back to station **18+50.00**.

16. In the *Civil Alignments* window, in the *Target* controls section, select the **Along** option. This means that you will look parallel to the road, tilting downward, as the road has slopes.

17. Press the (Play / Pause) button in the bottom left corner of the *Civil Alignments* window to drive to the end of the alignment and notice that you are looking slightly downward with the downward slope.

18. In the *Current Station* box, type **1850** to go back to station **18+50.00**.

19. In the *Civil Alignments* window, in the *Target* controls section, select the **Free** option. This enables lower section of the section.

20. In the *Civil Alignments* window, in the *Target* controls section, slide the (Target height) slider back and forth to raise or lower the vertical distance between the camera and the alignment. **Note:** A value of **0** will keep the focus on the horizon. Use the use the up and down arrows for fine tuning.

21. Type in **10** to have the vertical distance at 10.00 feet.

22. Repeat the steps for (Target offset), which controls the horizontal distance between the camera and the alignment. **Note:** A value of **0** keeps the focus on the centerline, a negative value turns it to the left, and a positive value to the right. Set the value to **-8**, to be 8.00 feet to the left of the center line. This will focus on the school as you drive. The final values are shown in Figure 8–26.

Figure 8–26

23. In the *Civil Alignments* window, in the bottom section, in the drop-down menu, select **km/h** as the units and type **50**, so the speed of the drive will be 50 km/h, as shown in Figure 8–27.

Figure 8–27

24. Press (Play / Pause) toggle to drive and pause along the alignment.
25. In the *Current Station* box, type **1850** to go to station **18+50.00**.
26. In the *Civil Alignments* window, in the *Navigation* controls section, uncheck the *Section Plane* checkbox.
27. Press (Play / Pause) toggle and see the final result.
28. As you drive along the road, you can interactively change any of the above sections to change the drive.
29. Close the *Civil Alignments* window.
30. Save the file.

End of practice

8.3 Animating Objects

Touring a model is a great way to demonstrate to stakeholders the design intent and gain their buy-in. Being able to show how objects move and interact within the model helps stakeholders delve deeper into the project. Objects can be animated using a variety of tools found in the *Animator* toolbar.

- (Translate Animation Set): Provides a gizmo tool to modify the position of geometry objects.
- (Rotate Animation Set): Provides a gizmo tool to rotate geometry objects.
- (Scale Animation Set): Provides a gizmo tool to resize geometry objects.
- (Change Color of Animation Set): Displays the color palette in the Manual Entry bar, enabling you to modify the color of geometry objects.
- (Change Transparency of Animation Set): Displays the transparency slider in the Manual Entry bar, enabling you to modify the transparency of geometry objects.

  Note: *Capture Keyframe also adds viewpoints to the camera.*

- (Capture Keyframe): Adds the current objects' position to an animation set.
- (Toggle Snapping): Toggles snap on and off, enabling you to control whether you snap to other animation sets (translate, rotate, or scale).

How To: Animate Objects

1. In the *Sets* window, create a selection set or saved set that contains the objects that you want to move.
2. In the *Animator* window, create a scene and add any required cameras.
3. In the *Sets* window, select the selection set you created.

   Note: *The advantage of using a search set is that it automatically updates if the source file changes.*

4. In the *Animator* window>*Tree* pane, right-click on the desired scene and select either of the following options:
   - **Add Animation Set>From current selection**
   - **Add Animation Set>From current search/selection**
5. Enter a descriptive name for the animation set.

6. Move the animation bar to the location on the Timeline where you want the animation to start.
7. In the *Animator* toolbar, click (Capture Keyframe). Note that this captures the current location, rotation, or scale of the animation set.
8. Move the animation bar to the location on the Timeline where you want the animation to end.
9. In the *Animator* toolbar, click (Translate Animation Set), (Rotate Animation Set), or (Scale Animation Set).
10. Click and drag the center of the gizmo to move the origin point.
    - When (Rotate Animation Set) is selected, the pivot point for all of the selected objects is set.
    - When (Scale Animation Set) or (Translate Animation Set) is selected, you must hold <Ctrl> as you drag the gizmo to change the center of translation.
11. Use the appropriate gizmo shown in Figure 8–28 to translate (move), rotate, or scale the selection set, as required.
    - Red makes changes along the X-axis or in the X-plane.
    - Green makes changes along the Y-axis or in the Y-plane.
    - Blue makes changes along the Z-axis or in the Z-plane.

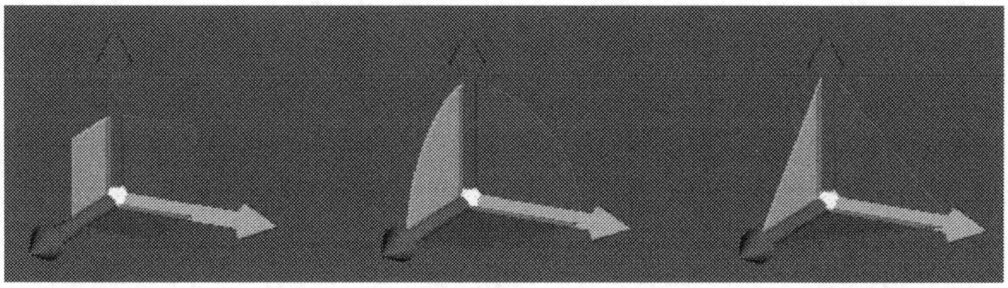

Translate ***Rotate*** ***Scale***

Figure 8–28

12. In the *Animator* toolbar, click (Capture Keyframe). This captures the new location of the animation set.

Practice 8c
Create an Animation I

Practice Objective

- Animate objects and note how they move in the model.

In this practice, you will animate the crane, as shown in Figure 8–29. Selection sets representing each of the specific components of the crane that will be moved and rotated have been created for you.

Figure 8–29

Task 1: Add views to the animation.

1. Open **School-Crane.nwf** from the *Navisworks BIM Practice Files\Animator* folder.
2. At the bottom of the graphics window, expand the *Animator* window and pin it.

   Note: *If the Animator window is not displayed, in the Home tab>Tools panel, click*

    *(Animator) or in the View tab>Workspace panel, expand* ***Windows*** *and select Animator.*

3. In the *Animator* window, verify that the **Active** option next to the **Overview** camera, is unchecked. This sets the animation as inactive.
4. In the *Saved Viewpoints* window, select the **Overview** viewpoint in the *Animator* folder.
5. In the *Animator* window>*Tree* pane, click  (Add scene) and select **Add Scene**.

6. Click on the scene name, enter **Mobile Crane** for the name, and press <Enter>.
7. Ensure that the animation bar is at **0** on the Timeline.
8. Right-click on **Mobile Crane** and select **Add Camera>Blank camera**. For the camera name, accept the default name of **Camera** and press <Enter>.
9. In the *Animator* toolbar, click (Capture keyframe). A diamond displays in the Timeline at 0 to indicate the start of the keyframe.
10. Right-click on the new keyframe and ensure that **Interpolate** is checked.

    Note: *Interpolate should be on by default. This is just a verification step.*

11. Move the animation bar to **4** seconds on the Timeline.
12. Pan and orbit the model so that the crane displays similar to the view shown in Figure 8–30. You can also use **Crane** in the *Saved Viewpoints* window in the *Animation* folder.

Figure 8–30

13. In the *Animator* toolbar, click (Capture keyframe).
14. In the *Animator* toolbar, click (Stop), and then click (Play) to play the animation from the beginning.

Task 2: Add a transition animation.

1. Open the *Sets* window and pin it open to make it easy to access.

    Note: *If the Sets window is not displayed, in the View tab>Workspace panel, expand* **Windows** *and select* **Sets**.

2. In the *Sets* window, select **Crane**. Note that the entire crane is selected in the model.
3. In the *Animator* window>*Tree* pane, right-click on the **Mobile Crane** scene and select **Add Animation Set>From current selection**.

4. Enter **Crane** as the name for the new animation and press <Enter>.
5. Verify that the animation bar is at **4** seconds on the Timeline.
6. In the *Animator* toolbar, click (Capture keyframe).
7. Move the animation bar to **8** seconds on the Timeline.
8. In the *Animator* toolbar, click (Translate animation set).
9. Use the Y-axis (green arrow) on the translate gizmo to move the crane forward, similar to what is shown in Figure 8–31.

Figure 8–31

10. In the *Animator* toolbar, click (Capture keyframe).
11. In the *Animator* toolbar, click (Stop), and then click (Play) to play the animation from the beginning.

Task 3: Add rotation animations.

1. In the *Sets* window, select **Raising Boom**.
2. In the *Animator* window>*Tree* pane, right-click on the **Mobile Crane** scene and select **Add Animation Set>From current selection**.
3. Enter **Raise Crane** as the name of the animation and press <Enter>.
4. Move the animation bar to **8** seconds on the Timeline, if not already set.
5. In the *Animator* toolbar, click (Capture keyframe).
6. Move the animation bar to **12** seconds on the Timeline.
7. In the *Animator* toolbar, click (Rotate animation set). The rotation gizmo is displayed.
8. In the *Animator* toolbar, click (Toggle snapping).

9. Click and drag the center of the rotate gizmo to the approximate center of the hinge pin shown in Figure 8–32. Orbit and zoom the scene as required to display the pin better. With snapping toggled on, you should be able to snap to the center of the circle.

   Note: *If you hold <Ctrl> when moving the gizmo, only the gizmo moves and not the selected objects.*

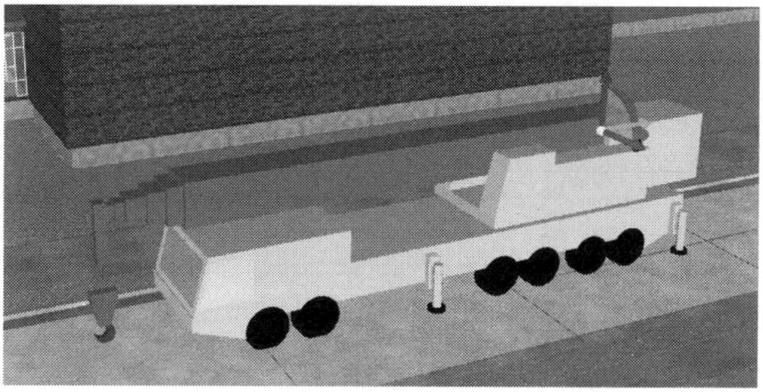

Figure 8–32

10. Use the YZ plane (red plane) of the gizmo to rotate the arm approximately **30°** about the X-axis, as shown in Figure 8–33. You can also enter the rotation value at the bottom of the *Animator* dialog box to assign an exact value.

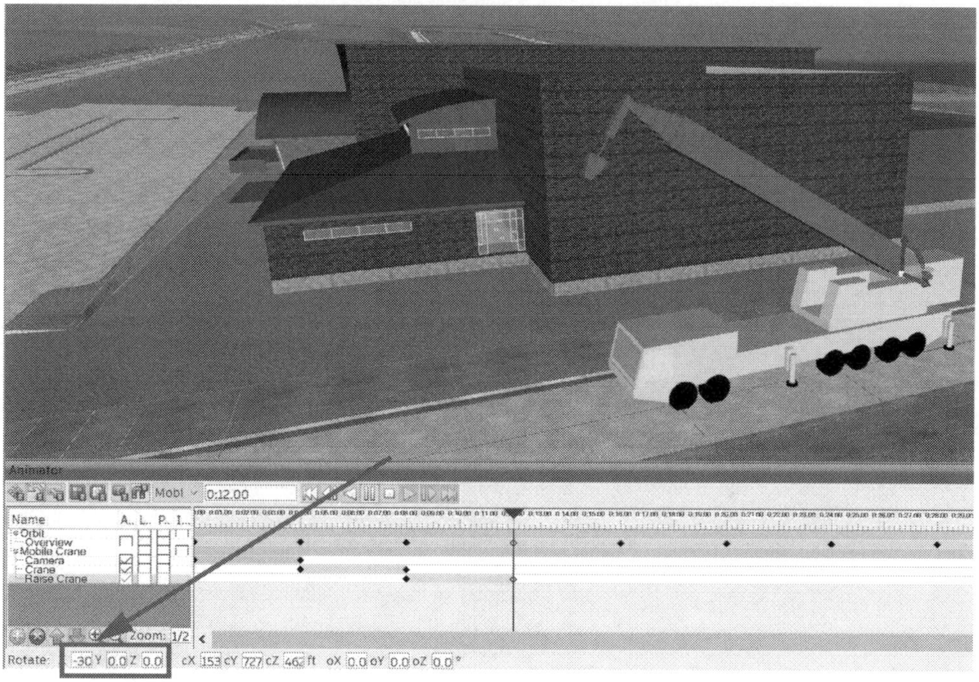

Figure 8–33

11. In the *Animator* toolbar, click (Capture keyframe). This captures the new rotation of the animation set.
12. Play the animation and note that the hook rotates with the boom, which is not realistic movement for the hook as it is hanging on a cable.
13. In the *Sets* window, select **Hook**.
14. In the *Animator* window>*Tree* pane, right-click on the **Mobile Crane** scene and select **Add Animation Set>From current selection**.
15. Enter **Gravity** as the animation name and press <Enter>.
16. Move the animation bar to **8** seconds on the Timeline.
17. In the *Animator* toolbar, click (Capture keyframe).
18. Move the animation bar to **12** seconds on the Timeline.
19. In the *Animator* toolbar, click (Rotate animation set).
20. Click and drag the center of the rotate gizmo to the top of the cable, as shown in Figure 8–34.

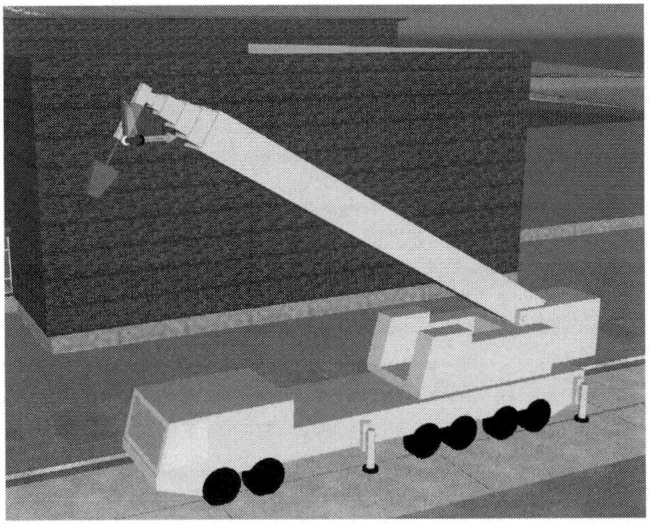

Figure 8–34

21. Use the YZ plane (red plane) of the gizmo to rotate the cable approximately **-30°** about the X-axis so that it is perpendicular to the ground as if gravity is pulling on it, as shown in Figure 8–35. You can also enter the rotation value of **0** at the bottom of the *Animator* dialog box to assign an exact value.

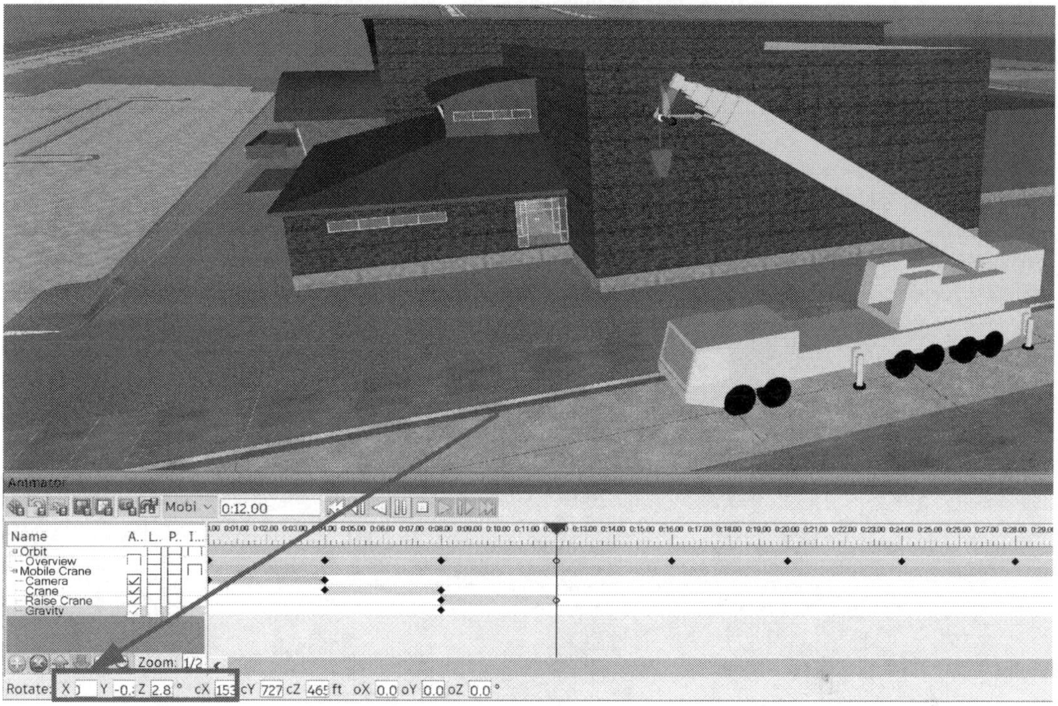

Figure 8–35

22. In the *Animator* toolbar, click (Capture keyframe).
23. In the *Sets* window, select **Rotating Boom**.
24. In the *Animator* window>*Tree* pane, right-click on the **Mobile Crane** scene and select **Add Animation Set>From current selection**.
25. Enter **Rotate** as the animation name and press <Enter>.
26. Move the animation bar to **12** seconds on the Timeline, if not already there.
27. In the *Animator* toolbar, click (Capture keyframe).
28. Move the animation bar to **16** seconds on the Timeline.
29. In the *Animator* toolbar, click (Rotate animation set).

30. Click and drag the center of the rotate gizmo to the center of the truck below the arm, as shown in Figure 8–36.

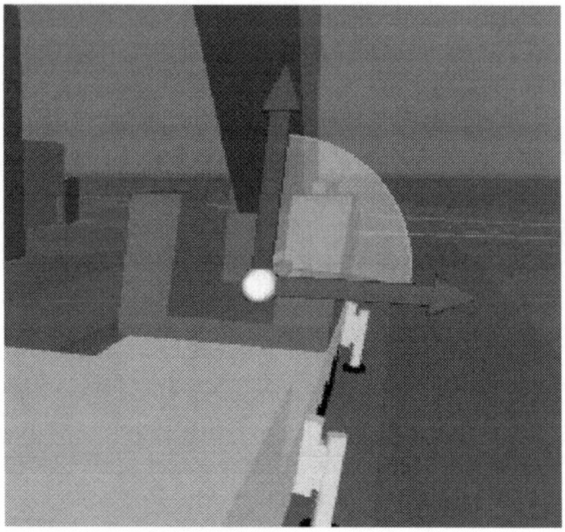

Figure 8–36

31. Use the XY plane (blue plane) of the gizmo to rotate the boom approximately **90°** about the Z-axis so that it is pointing at the building, as shown in Figure 8–37.

Figure 8–37

32. If need be, restore **Crane** in the *Saved Viewpoints* window in the *Animation* folder.
33. In the *Animator* toolbar, click (Capture keyframe).
34. In the *Animator* toolbar, click (Stop), and then click (Play) to play the animation from the beginning.
35. Save the file.

Task 4: Extend the arm.

1. In the *Sets* window, select **Crane Arm1**.
2. In the *Animator* window>*Tree* pane, right-click on the **Mobile Crane** scene and select **Add Animation Set>From current selection**.
3. Enter **Arm Extension** as the animation name and press <Enter>.
4. Move the animation bar to **16** seconds on the Timeline, if not already set.
5. In the *Animator* toolbar, click (Capture keyframe).
6. Move the animation bar to **20** seconds on the Timeline.
7. In the *Animator* toolbar, click (Translate animation set).
8. Use the X-axis (red arrow) and Z-axis (blue arrow) on the gizmo to extend the arm, similar to what is shown in Figure 8–38.

   Note: *It might be necessary to orbit the model after each move to ensure that the arm moves in the correct direction, and then restore* **Crane** *in the Saved Viewpoints window in the Animation folder.*

Figure 8–38

9. In the *Animator* toolbar, click (Capture Keyframe).
10. In the *Animator* toolbar, click (Stop), and then click (Play) to play the animation from the beginning.
11. Save the file.

Task 5: (Optional) Modify the animation.

1. Replay the animation and note that the hook collides with the building.
2. Drag the **Arm Extension** animation before the **Rotate** animation in the list, as shown in Figure 8–39.

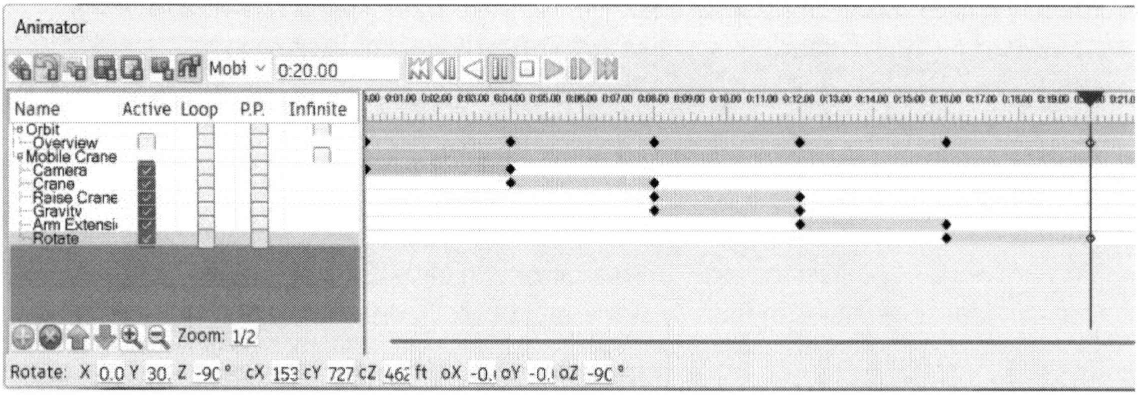

Figure 8–39

3. Play the animation and note that the keyframes are not in the correct locations. Drag them to the better timing. You will have to delete the keyframes at the end of the Arm Extension animation and recreate it in the proper direction.
4. Replay the animation and also note that as the crane moves along the road, the tires initially are off the surface. This is because the surface is not planar. To better approximate the movement, you can modify the keyframe at 8 seconds to translate and rotate the crane into a better final location.
5. Save the file.
6. To review a completed version of the model, open **School-Crane-Complete.nwf** from the *Navisworks BIM Practice Files\Animator* folder.

End of practice

Practice 8d
Create an Animation II

Practice Objective

- Create animations of objects to be used in interactive scripts.

In this practice, you will create two animations. The first will animate the action of the front and inside (as shown in Figure 8–40) doors opening as you walk through the entry. The final task has you practice the animation procedure a second time to create the door opening animations as two seperate animations that will be used in the Scripter learning content.

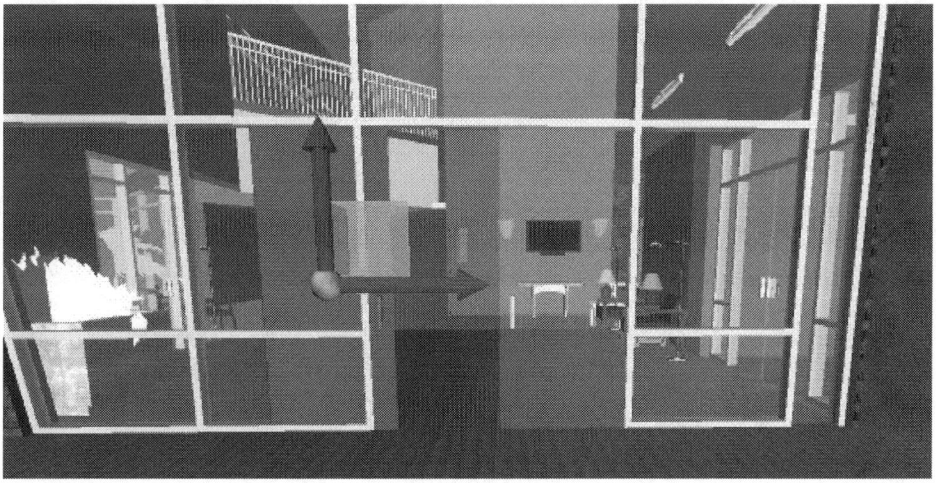

Figure 8–40

Task 1: Create an animation of the doors opening when walking through.

1. Open **School-Animation.nwf** from the *Navisworks BIM Practice Files\Animator* folder.
2. At the bottom of the graphics window, expand the *Animator* window and pin it.

   Note: *If the Animator window is not displayed, in the Home tab>Tools panel, click*

    *(Animator) or in the View tab>Workspace panel, expand* ***Windows*** *and select Animator.*

3. In the *Saved Viewpoints* window, select **Entry Doors**. This is a viewpoint that has been created for you.
4. Set the *Selection Resolution* to **First Object** (*Home* tab>expanded *Select & Search* panel>*Selection Resolution:***First Object**).

5. Hover your mouse over one of the front doors and wait until the tooltip displays. Note that the tooltip lists the *Item Type* as **Rooms**, as shown in Figure 8–41.

   Note: *Rooms are special organizational objects used in Autodesk Revit that have little to no value in Navisworks. Therefore, you can hide all the rooms.*

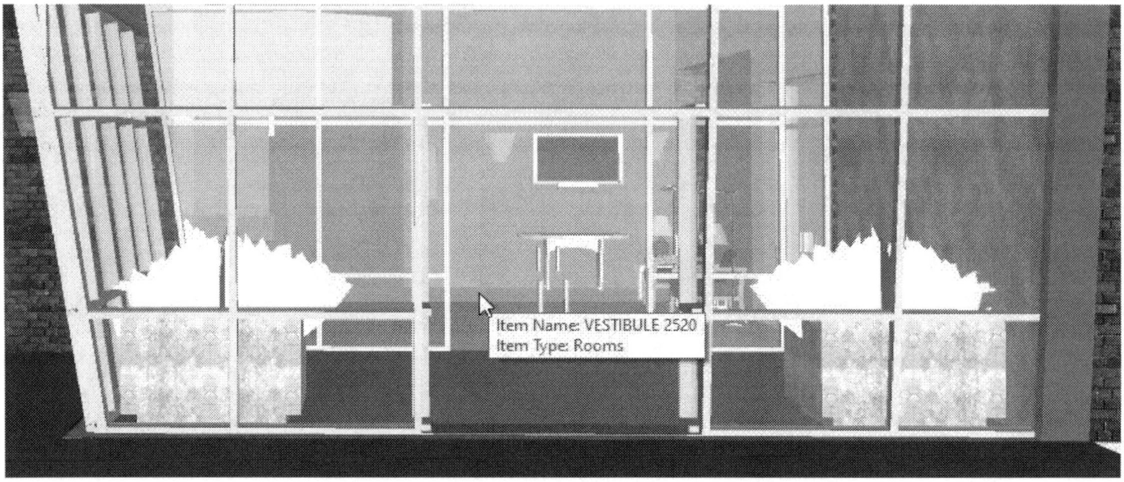

Figure 8–41

6. Select the item and note how the room is selected, not just the door.
7. Open the *Selection Tree* window. The *Rooms* node in which **VESTIBULE 2520** is located is automatically expanded.
8. Right-click on the **Rooms** node and select **Hide** to hide all of the rooms in the model. Now when you hover over the door, the tooltip confirms that the *Item Type* is **Curtain Wall Sgl Glass**, as shown in Figure 8–42.

Figure 8–42

9. In the *Animator* window>*Tree* pane, click  (Add scene) and select **Add Scene**.
10. Click on the scene name, enter **Entrance Doors** as the name for the new scene, and press <Enter>.

11. Compress the other two scenes in the model by selecting ⊟ adjacent to the **Orbit** and **Mobile Crane** scene names.
12. Select the **Entrance Doors** scene.
13. Ensure that the animation bar is at **0** on the Timeline. If it is not, drag the animation bar to 0.
14. Right-click on the **Entrance Doors** scene and select **Add Camera>Blank camera**.
15. Enter **Entering** as the name for the camera and press <Enter>.

    Note: *The outside entry doors of the school are pivoting doors that pivot inwards, while the inside doors slide.*

16. Select the **Entering** camera that was just created. Ensure that the view does not change as you are selecting the camera.

    Note: *Consider selecting the row in a column other than the Name column (as shown in Figure 8–43), so that the camera name field does not become editable.*

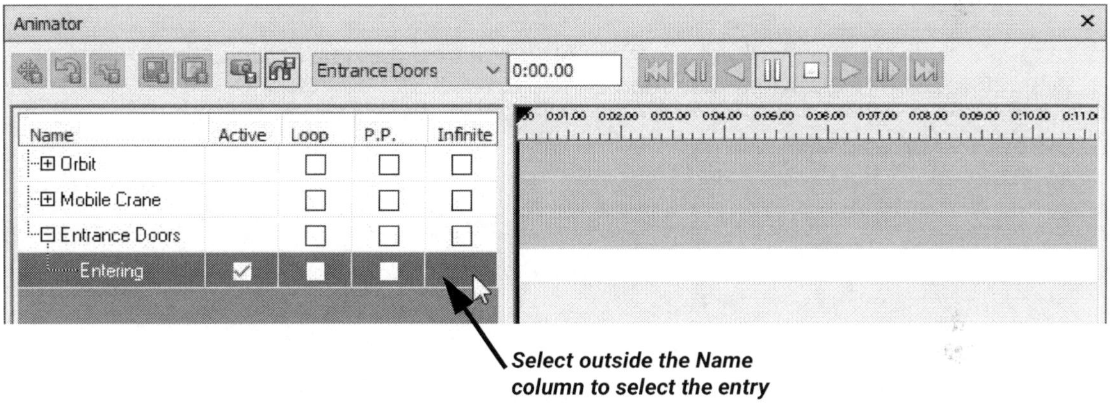

Figure 8–43

Note: *If you did accidentally move the viewpoint, you can restore the **Entry Doors** saved viewpoint before continuing.*

17. With the **Entering** camera row selected and the **Entry Doors** viewpoint displayed in the *Animator* toolbar, click (Capture keyframe). This captures a keyframe of the current view and places it at the beginning of the camera timeline.

18. In the scene view, select the left door, as shown in Figure 8–44.

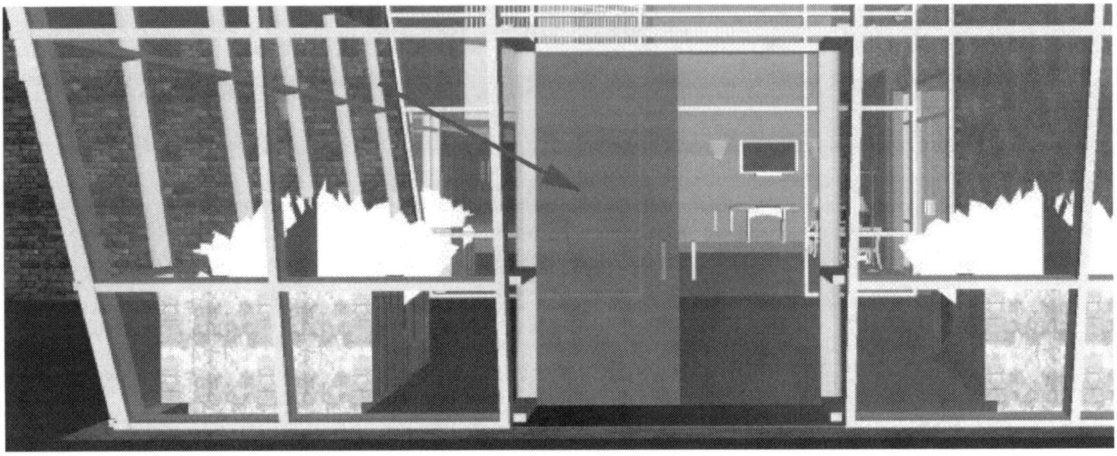

Figure 8–44

19. In the *Animator* window, right-click on the **Entrance Doors** scene name and click **Add Animation Set>From current selection**.

    Note: *You must right-click on the Entrance Doors scene name (not the Entering camera) to properly create the animation set.*

20. Enter **Hinge Outer Left** as its name and press <Enter>.
21. Repeat Steps 18 to 20 to add another animation set by selecting the right door and naming the animation set **Hinge Outer Right**.
22. Repeat the steps for the inner sliding vestibule doors, as follows:
    - In the *Saved Viewpoints* window, select **Inside Doors** to move to a better location to help you select the doors.
    - Name the two animation sets (one for each door) **Slide Inner Left** and **Slide Inner Right**, respectively.
23. Select each of the four door animation sets and note that when each is selected, the respective door is selected in the scene.

24. Before continuing, ensure that all of the animation sets are active, as shown in Figure 8–45. If not, select the checkboxes in the *Active* column.

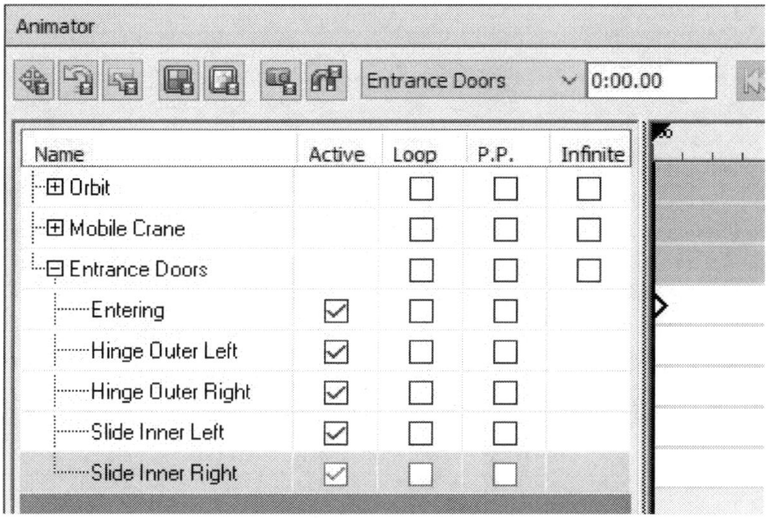

Figure 8–45

25. Save the file.

Task 2: Add cameras and keyframes.

1. An initial keyframe was created for the **Entering** camera using the **Entry Doors** saved viewpoint.
2. Select the **Entering** camera entry. In the *Timeline* pane, type **8** and press <Enter> or drag the animation bar to **8**.
3. In the *Navigation Bar*, use the  (Walk) navigation tool to walk towards the entrance doors and proceed until you are between the outer and inner doors.
4. In the *Animator* toolbar, click  (Capture Keyframe). This captures a keyframe of the current view and places it at the current camera timeline at the 8-second mark.
5. In the *Timeline* pane, drag the animation bar to **13** or enter the value in the *Time Position* field.
6. Using the  (Walk) navigation tool, walk into the center of the foyer, then click  (Capture Keyframe).
7. In the *Timeline* pane, go to **18**.
8. Using the  (Look Around) navigation tool, turn around to see the doors you have just walked through and capture this keyframe.

9. In the *Timeline* pane, drag the animation bar to **22**.

10. Using the (Walk) navigation tool, walk backwards from the entrance doors a few paces and then capture the keyframe. It should look like Figure 8–46.

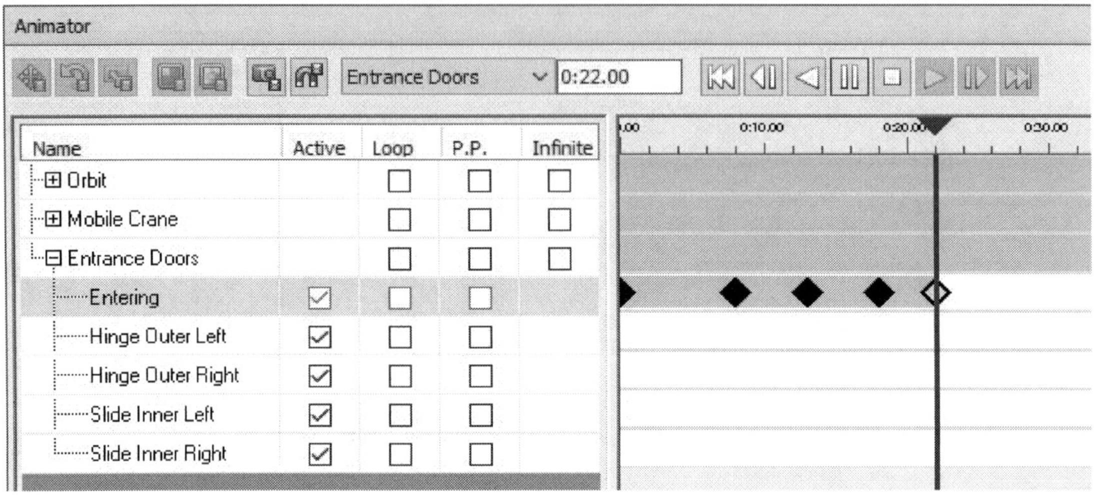

Figure 8–46

11. Click (Stop), then click (Play) in the *Animator* toolbar to view your newly created animation. The animation should walk through the doors, turn around to view the doors, then move backwards away from the doors.
12. Note how the doors were not animated. Only the camera has been animated.
13. Save the file.

Task 3: Open and close the hinged doors.

1. In the **Entrance Doors** scene, select the **Hinge Outer Left** animation set.
2. In the *Timeline* pane, drag the animation bar to **4** or enter the value in the *Time Position* field and press <Enter>.
3. In the *Animator* toolbar, click (Capture keyframe). This captures a keyframe of the current view and places it at the current position of the Timeline for the **Hinge Outer Left** set.
4. In the *Timeline* pane, drag the animation bar to **6** or press (Step Forward) twice or enter the value in the *Time Position* field.
5. Save this viewpoint and name it **6sec**, so you can return to this viewpoint later.

6. In the *Animator* toolbar, click (Rotate animation set). The rotation gizmo should be displayed near the center of selected door. Click and drag the circular dot at the center of the gizmo to the left frame of the door. This repositions the gizmo without moving the selected item. Place the center of the gizmo along the edge of the highlighted door, as shown in Figure 8–47.

Figure 8–47

7. Use the Orbit and Pan navigation tools to get a top view of the door or a similar view so that you can see the XY rotation plane. Hover over the blue XY rotation plane (blue plane), which will turn yellow. Swing the door inward by about 90°, as shown in Figure 8–48.

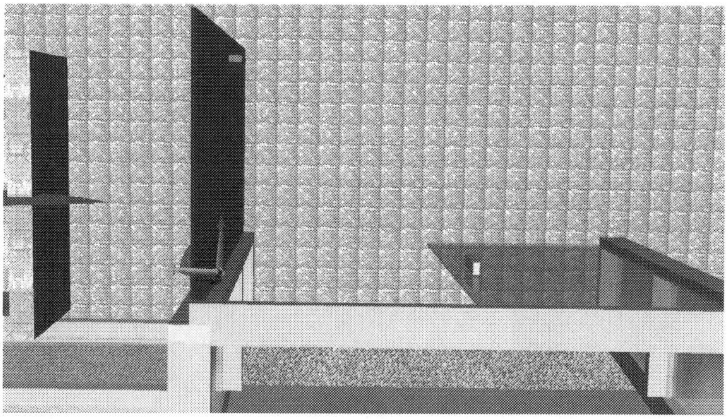

Figure 8–48

8. Restore the **6 sec** viewpoint.

9. In the *Animator* toolbar, click (Capture keyframe). This captures a keyframe of the current view and places it at the current position of the Timeline for the outer left door.

10. Right-click this new keyframe and select **Copy**, as shown in Figure 8–49.

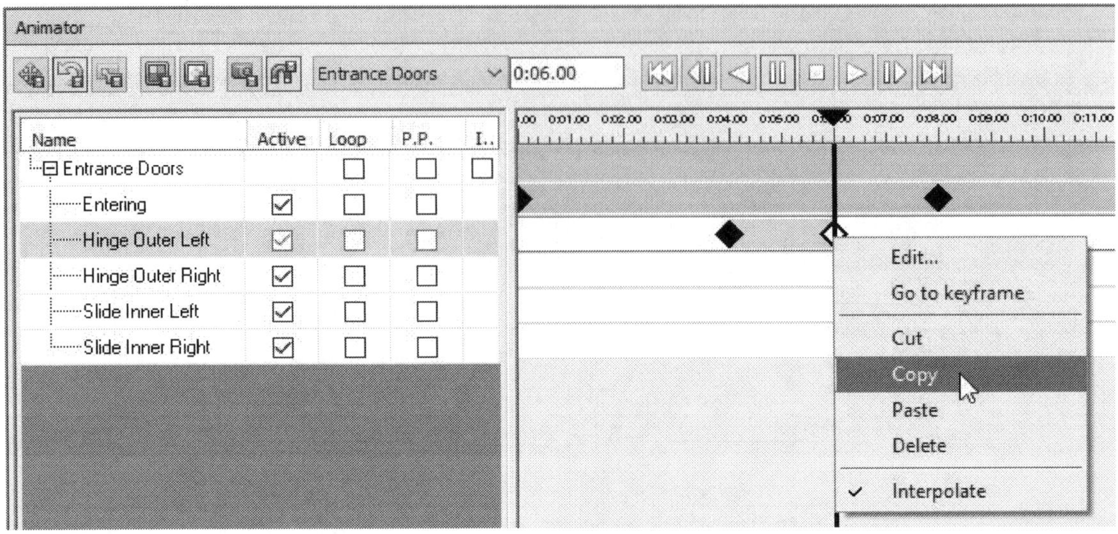

Figure 8–49

11. Drag the animation bar to **18** (or enter the value), then right-click and select **Paste**. This pastes a copy of the last keyframe at 18, which means the door remains open between 6 and 18.
12. Right-click the first keyframe at 4 and select **Copy**. Drag the animation bar to **21**, then right-click and select **Paste**, as shown in Figure 8–50. This pastes a copy of the first keyframe at 21 which means that door closes between 18 and 21.

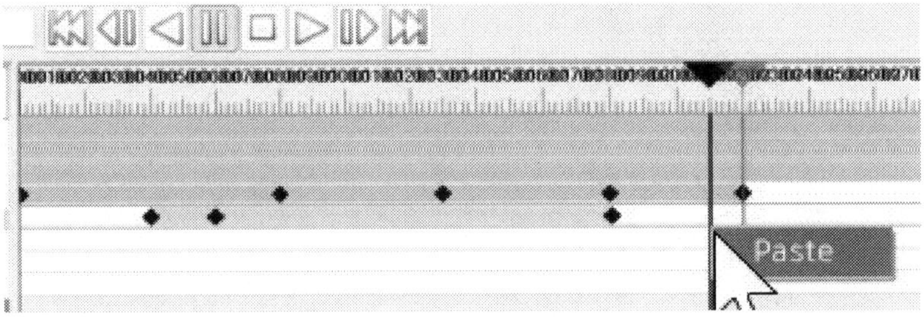

Figure 8–50

13. Click (Stop), then click (Play). As the entrance is approached, the left door should swing open, then the door should close as you move away from it at the end of the animation.
14. Repeat the steps to animate the right outer door.
    - Remember to restore the **6 sec** viewpoint prior to capturing the keyframe at 6 seconds.
15. Play the animation.

Task 4: Open and close the sliding doors.

1. In the **Entrance Doors** scene, select the **Slide Inner Left** animation set.
2. In the *Timeline* pane, drag the animation bar to **6** or enter the value in the *Time Position* field.
3. You may need to pan a bit to get the camera centered on the sliding doors.
4. In the *Animator* toolbar, click (Capture keyframe). This captures a keyframe of the current view and places it at the current position of the Timeline for the **Slide Inner Left** set.
5. While you are here, select the **Slide Inner Right** set and click (Capture keyframe).
6. Select the **Slide Inner Left** animation set again.
7. In the *Timeline* pane, drag the animation bar to **8** or enter the value in the *Time Position* field. You can also press (Step Forward) twice to get there.
8. Using the *Pan* tool, center the camera once again, if necessary.
9. Save this viewpoint and name it **8sec**, so you can return to this viewpoint later.
10. In the *Animator* toolbar, click (Translate animation set). The translation handles should be displayed on the sliding door, as shown in Figure 8–51. Select the red X-axis, which turns yellow, and slide the door all the way open.

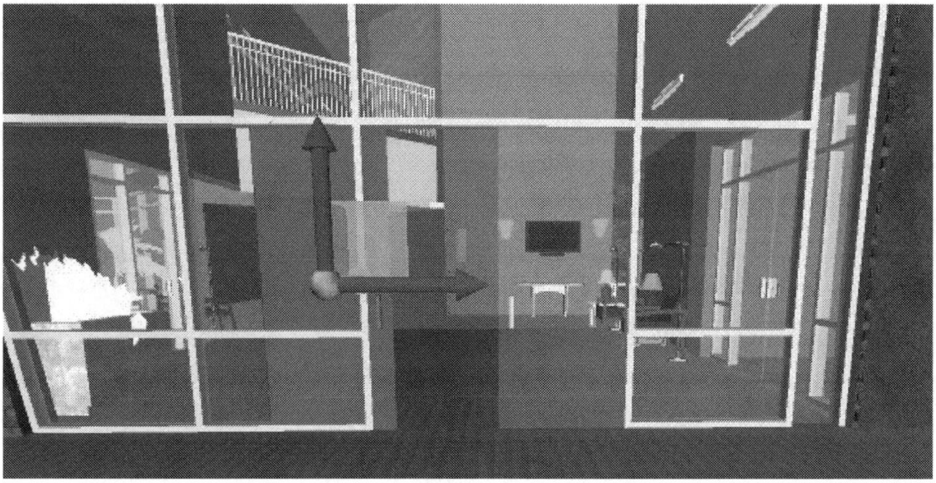

Figure 8–51

11. Restore the **8 sec** viewpoint if it has moved.
12. In the *Animator* toolbar, click (Capture keyframe). This captures a keyframe of the current view and places it at the current position of the Timeline for the **Slide Inner Left** set.

13. Right-click this new keyframe and select **Copy**.
14. Drag the animation bar to **18** (or enter the value), then right-click and select **Paste**. This pastes a copy of the last keyframe at 18, which means the sliding door remains open between 8 and 18.
15. Right-click the first keyframe at 6 and select **Copy**. Drag the animation bar to **21**, then right-click and select **Paste**. This pastes a copy of the first keyframe at 21.
16. Click  (Stop), then click  (Play). As the entrance is approached, the two front doors should swing open, then the left inner door should slide open, then as you move away from the door at the end of the animation, the left inner door and both front doors should close.
17. Repeat the steps to animate the right inner door.
    - Remember to restore the **8 sec** viewpoint prior to capturing the keyframe.
18. Play the animation to ensure the animation is as expected.
19. Save the file.

Task 5: (Optional) Create snippet animations for the Scripter.

In this task, you will complete steps similar to what were previously done for the doors; however, you will be grouping the doors independently so that they can be used separately with the Scripter functionality. Scripter will be discussed later.

1. Compress the current animations (Entrance Doors) in the *Animator* window.
2. In the *Animator* window>*Tree* pane, click  (Add Scene).
3. Click on the scene name, enter **Opening Outer Doors** as the name, and press <Enter>.
4. Ensure that the animation bar is at **0** on the Timeline. If it is not, drag the animation bar to **0**.
5. Select the **Entry Doors** saved viewpoint.
6. Select the left hinged door.
7. In the *Animator* window, right-click on the **Opening Outer Doors** scene and click **Add Animation Set>From current selection**.
8. Click the new animation set and rename it **Hinge Left**.

   Note: *A camera is not required since you are only recording the movement of the door. A camera would pre-determine the vantage point and this is not required for use in Scripter.*

9. In the *Animator* toolbar, click  (Capture keyframe) to save the left door in a closed position at the beginning of the animation.
10. Select the right hinged door and create a new animation set from this selection. Rename the animation **Hinge Right**.

11. In the *Animator* toolbar, click (Capture keyframe) to save the right door in a closed position at the beginning of the animation.
12. Select the **Hinge Left** animation set name.
13. In the *Timeline* pane, drag the animation bar to **3** or enter the value in the *Time Position* field and press <Enter>.
14. In the *Animator* toolbar, click (Rotate animation set).
15. As you did in the previous Entrance Door animation, move the rotation gizmo to the left edge of the door, hover over the blue XY plane, and rotate the door inward by about 90°. Keep in mind that you can reorient the scene as needed to position and rotate the gizmo.
16. In the *Animator* toolbar, click (Capture keyframe) to capture the open door.
17. Repeat the process for the **Hinge Right** animation set to rotate the right hinged door inward by about 90° and capture its keyframe at 3.
18. Return to the **Entry Doors** saved viewpoint.
19. Select the **Opening Outer Doors** scene.
20. Click (Stop), then click (Play).
21. Reorient the view and play the animation again. Because no camera was included in the animation, it only captures the positions of the doors.
22. Select the **Inside Doors** viewpoint.
23. Repeat the steps for the inner vestibule doors, as follows:
    - Name the scene **Opening Inner Doors**.
    - Name the two animation sets **Sliding Left** and **Sliding Right** accordingly.
    - Translate the two sliding doors open at 3 and capture keyframes for both.

24. Once complete, the *Animator* window should display as shown in Figure 8–52.

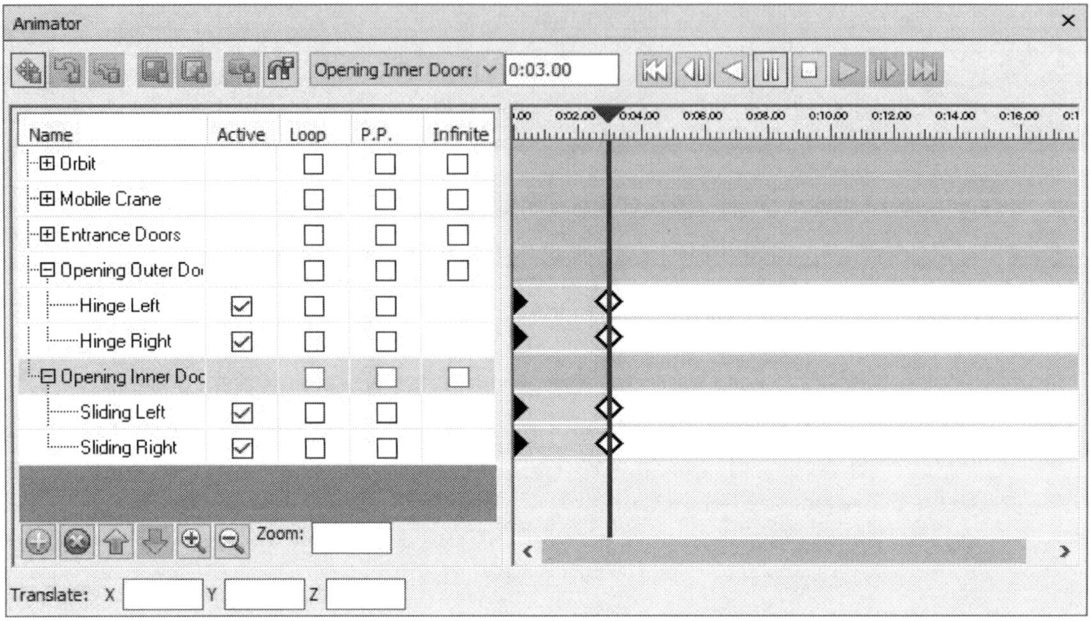

Figure 8–52

25. Return to the **Entry Doors** viewpoint and play each animation to test them.
26. To review a completed version of the model, open **School-Animation-Complete.nwf** from the *Navisworks BIM Practice Files\Animator* folder.
27. Save and close the file.

End of practice

Chapter Review Questions

1. In the *Animator* toolbar, what happens when you click  (Capture Keyframe)? (Select all that apply.)
   a. Captures a snapshot of the currently appended files.
   b. Captures a snapshot of the current viewpoint.
   c. Captures a snapshot of the current object positions.
   d. Captures key elements for later use.

2. What does the **Ping Pong (P.P.)** option do?
   a. Causes an animation to play in reverse when it reaches the end.
   b. Causes animations to randomly shuffle in the Timeline.
   c. Causes an animation to replay once when it reaches the end.
   d. Causes an animation to replay continuously when it reaches the end.

3. Using the Timeline, how do you change the length of time an animation plays?
   a. Select the animation set, right-click, and select **Set Duration**.
   b. Select the animation set and enter a duration in the *Time Position* field.
   c. Select the animation set and drag the animation bar in the Timeline to set the length.
   d. Drag the diamonds in the Timeline to lengthen or shorten the duration.

4. How many cameras can you have in a scene?
   a. 1
   b. 2
   c. 3
   d. Infinite

5. How can you move the point of translation when moving, rotating, or scaling an animation set?
    a. The point of translation cannot be changed.
    b. In the *Item Tools* tab>*Transform* panel, click **Move**.
    c. In the *Item Tools* tab>*Look At* panel, click **Focus on Item**.
    d. Hold <Ctrl> as you drag the center point of the gizmo.

Command Summary

Button	Command	Location
	**Add Scene**	• **Window:** *Animator*
	**Animator**	• **Ribbon:** *Home* tab>*Tools* panel
	**Capture Keyframe**	• **Window:** *Animator*
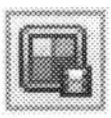	**Change Color of Animation Set**	• **Window:** *Animator*
	**Change Transparency of Animation Set**	• **Window:** *Animator*
	**Delete**	• **Window:** *Animator*
	**Move Down**	• **Window:** *Animator*
	**Move Up**	• **Window:** *Animator*
	**Pause**	• **Window:** *Animator*
	**Play**	• **Window:** *Animator*
	**Reverse Play**	• **Window:** *Animator*
	**Rewind**	• **Window:** *Animator*
	**Rotate Animation Set**	• **Window:** *Animator*
	**Scale Animation Set**	• **Window:** *Animator*
	**Scene Picker**	• **Window:** *Animator*

Button	Command	Location
	**Step Back**	• **Window:** *Animator*
	**Step Forward**	• **Window:** *Animator*
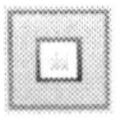	**Stop**	• **Window:** *Animator*
0:36.25	**Time Position**	• **Window:** *Animator*
	**To End**	• **Window:** *Animator*
	**Toggle Snapping**	• **Window:** *Animator*
	**Translate Animation Set**	• **Window:** *Animator*
	**Zoom In**	• **Window:** *Animator*
	**Zoom Out**	• **Window:** *Animator*

Chapter 9

Scripter

For communication to be effective, it needs to be interactive. The ability to record actions and validate different aspects of a model can be quite informative. To build such interactions with a model, scripts are required that allow for parts of the model to move on demand, messages to be exported to text files, the condition of properties to be recorded, events to happen upon collision, etc. Learn how to use the Autodesk® Navisworks® Scripter to create such scripts. You will create a simple script invoking animations developed in another chapter and will also examine how to create scripts based on certain keystrokes.

Learning Objectives

- Create a hotspot script and a keystroke script.
- Examine a message output file.

BIM Workflow: Communicate

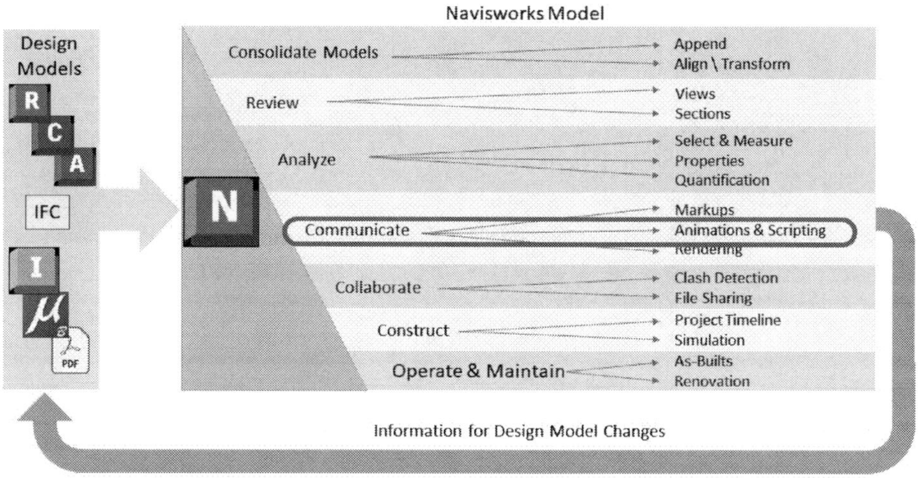

9.1 Scripter

Animation is good, but animation that is driven by interactivity with your model is better. The Navisworks Scripter is designed to add events to the animation based on triggers. By combining scripts with animations created in Animator, an animation can be triggered by an event created in Scripter. For example, doors open (animation) as you approach them (script) in your model. You could animate how a crane moves around a site or how a car is assembled or dismantled. You can also create interaction scripts, which link your animations to specific events.

Scripting

You need to create at least one animation scene to add interactivity to your model. Within this animation, certain events and actions must be created (scripted) that are carried out when those events are activated.

Each script can contain these two components:

- Events
- Actions

To open the *Scripter* window, in the *Home* tab>*Tools* panel or in the *Animation* tab>*Script* panel, click (Scripter). The *Scripter* window displays at the bottom of the Autodesk Navisworks window. The *Scripter* window consists of four panes, as shown in Figure 9–1.

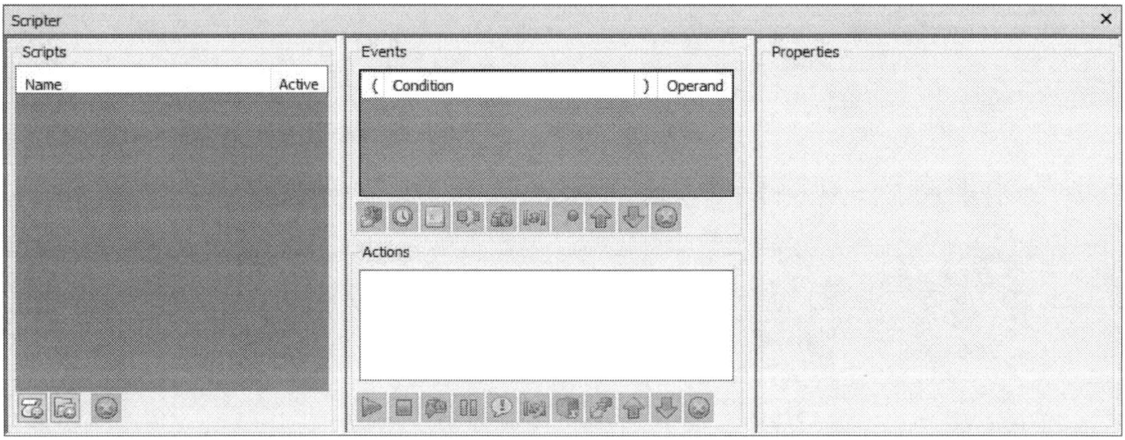

Figure 9–1

If the icons in the *Scripter* window are disabled (grayed out), it means scripts are enabled and thus not editable. To disable scripts, go to the *Animation* tab of the main ribbon and deselect (Enable Scripts), as shown in Figure 9–2.

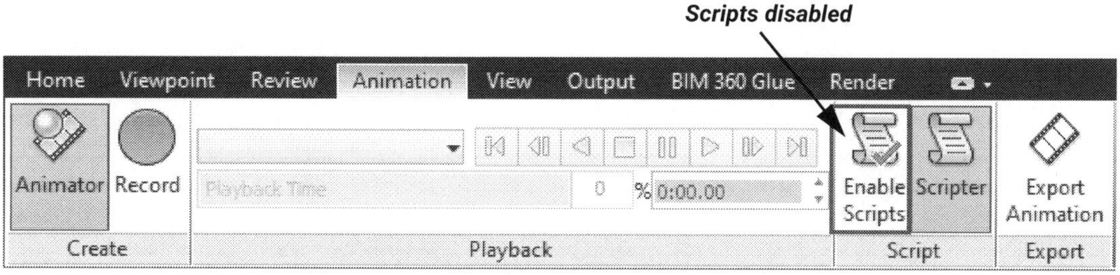

Figure 9–2

The *Scripter* window is divided into four panes, as follows:

- **Scripts:** The left pane of the *Scripter* window lists the available scripts and is where new scripts are added. If necessary, folders can be set up to house the various scripts. The *Scripts* pane also includes controls to add new scripts and folders or delete them.
- **Events:**The center top pane lists the events for the script. New event types can be added, edited, and reordered using buttons located at the bottom of the pane.
- **Actions:** The center lower pane lists the actions for the script. The *Action* pane also includes playback icons, action types, and reorder buttons located at the bottom to manage new and existing actions.
- **Properties:** The right pane displays the properties of the selected event or action. This pane displays the properties and options used to configure events and actions that were added in the central panes.

Creating and Managing Scripts

To add interactivity to your model, you first create a script. Events and actions are subsequently added to that script, and each event and action is configured for the desired interactivity. The scripts are then set up to work with the animations that have been created in Animator.

How To: Create Scripts

1. To add a new script, click (Add New Script) in the *Scripts* pane or right-click in the *Scripts* pane and select **Add New Script**.
2. Enter a new descriptive name for the script to help identify it and press <Enter>.

*Note: To delete a script, select it and click (Delete Item) or right-click the script and select **Delete Item**.*

How To: Organize Scripts

1. To add a new folder, click  (Add New Folder) in the *Scripts* pane or right-click in the *Scripts* pane and select **Add New Folder**.
2. Enter a new descriptive name for the folder and press <Enter>. The folder will be added to the *Scripts* pane, as shown in Figure 9–3.

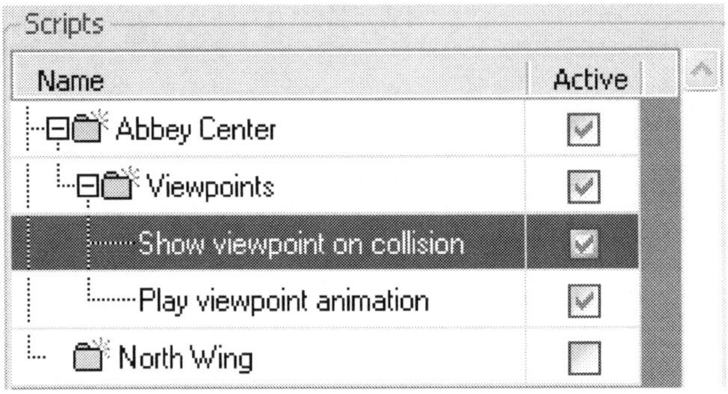

Figure 9–3

3. To move a script into a folder, drag the script using the left mouse button and drop it in the destination folder so that the black arrow head is displayed on the folder.

Practice 9a
Create a Script

Practice Objectives

- Add a script to open doors as one approaches.
- Organize scripts in folders.

In this practice, you will add a script to open doors as one approaches, as shown in Figure 9–4. The events and actions will be added later.

Figure 9–4

1. Open **School-Script.nwf** from the *Navisworks BIM Practice Files\Animator* folder.
2. Expand the *Scripter* window and pin it near the bottom of the graphics window.

   Note: *The Scripter window is displayed by clicking*  *(Scripter) in the Home tab>Tools panel, or in the View tab>Workspace panel, expand* ***Windows*** *and select* ***Scripter****.*

3. In the *Saved Viewpoints* window, select **Entry Doors**.
4. Check to ensure that the *Selection Resolution* is set to **First Object**.
5. In the *Scripter* window>*Scripts* pane, click  (Add New Script).
6. Click on the new script and name it **Open Exterior Doors**.

***Note:** If the icons are grayed out in the Scripter window, it means scripts are enabled and thus not editable. To disable scripts, go to the Animation tab of the main ribbon and deselect (Enable Scripts), as shown in Figure 9–5.*

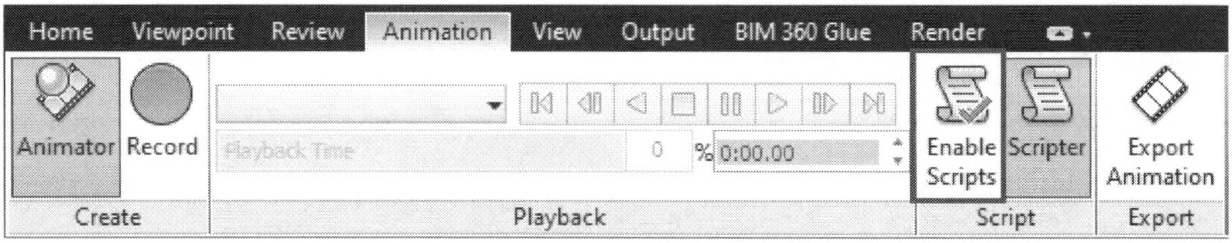

Figure 9–5

7. Repeat Steps 5 and 6 to add another new script and name it **Close Exterior Doors**.
8. In the *Scripter* window>*Scripts* pane, click (Add New Folder) and name it **Exterior Vestibule Doors**.
9. Click and hold the left mouse button on the **Open Exterior Doors** script and drag it to the *Exterior Vestibule Doors* folder so the arrow head is on the folder. Release the mouse to move the script into the folder.
10. Move the **Close Exterior Doors** script to the same folder.
11. Follow the same process to create two new scripts and name them **Open Interior Doors** and **Close Interior Doors**.
12. Create a new folder and name it **Interior Vestibule Doors**, then drag and drop the **Open Interior Doors** and **Close Interior Doors** scripts into the new folder.
13. The script structure should display as shown in Figure 9–6.

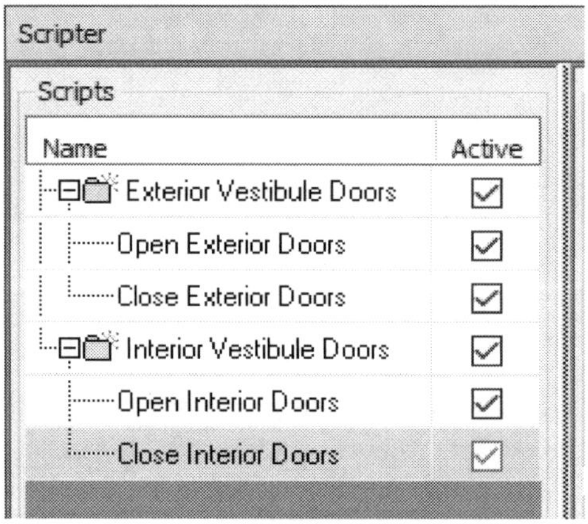

Figure 9–6

14. Save the file.

15. To review a completed version of the model, open **School-Script-Setup.nwf** from the *Navisworks BIM Practice Files\Animator* folder. This will be the file used in the next practice to ensure that the file was prepared properly.

End of practice

9.2 Creating and Managing Events

An event is created with certain actions, such as a mouse click, a pressed key, or a collision, which determine whether your script is activated or deactivated. Your script can have multiple events in it.

When you use several events in the same script, the event sequence becomes very important. You need to ensure the proper steps and logic make sense, the brackets are correctly closed, etc. Additionally, until the combination of all event conditions in the script is properly established, your script will not be able to run.

Event Types

There are seven event types available, which are displayed at the bottom of the *Events* pane, as shown in Figure 9–7. When an event is added, the *Properties* pane shows the properties for that event type. These properties may be configured at this time or can be deferred to a later time.

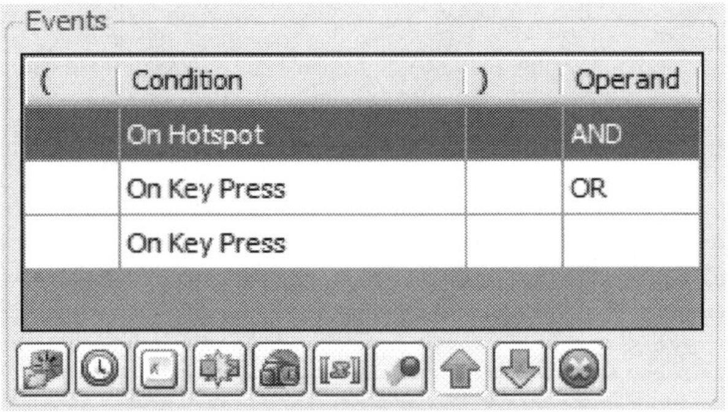

Figure 9–7

How To: Create an Event

1. In the *Scripts* pane, select the script you want to add an event to.
2. At the bottom of the *Events* pane, click an event type button (as described below) to define the event.
3. Review the properties in the *Properties* pane and change the property values, as required.

On Start Event

 (On Start Event) triggers a script when scripting is enabled. If scripting is enabled when a file is loaded, then any start events in the file are triggered, similarly to auto-executable commands or batch files. For example, On Start events can set initial conditions of your script, giving default values to variables or repositioning a camera to a proper vantage point. You do not need to configure any properties for this event type.

On Timer Event

(On Timer Event) triggers a script at predefined time intervals. You can specify the following properties for this event type:

- **Interval:** Enter the length of time in seconds between timer triggering.
- **Regularity:** Select the event frequency.
    - *Once After*: An event happens once only. Use this option when you want to have an event that starts after a certain length of time.
    - *Continuous*: An event is continuously repeated at specified time intervals. You can use this to simulate cyclic work on an assembly floor.

On Key Press Event

(On Key Press Event) triggers a script with a specific key on the keyboard. You can specify the following properties for this event type:

- **Key:** This is a read-only box showing the currently selected key.
- **Trigger On:** Select how the event is triggered.
    - *Key Up*: An event is triggered after you press and release the key.
    - *Key Down*: An event is triggered the moment you press the key.
    - *Key Pressed*: An event is triggered while the key is pressed. This option enables you to use a key press event together with Boolean operators such as AND, which would allow you to chain it with an On Timer event.

On Collision Event

(On Collision Event) triggers a script when your pointing device (such as a mouse) collides with a certain object. You can specify the following properties for this event type:

- **Selection to collide with:** Click the set and use the shortcut menu to define the collision objects.
    - *Clear*: Clears your currently selected collision objects.
    - *Set From Current Selection*: Sets the collision objects to your current object selection in the scene view.
    - *Set From Current Selection Set*: Sets the collision objects to your current search set or selection set.
- **Show:** This is a read-only box showing the number of geometry objects selected as collision objects.
- **Include the effects of gravity:** Select this option if you want to include gravity in collision detection. The event is triggered when you hit the floor.

On Hotspot Event

(On Hotspot Event) triggers a script when your pointing device (such as a mouse) is within a certain radius of a hotspot. You can specify the following properties for this event type:

- **Hotspot:** Select the hotspot type.
    - *Sphere*: A sphere from a given point in space.
    - *Sphere on selection*: A sphere around a given selection. This option does not require you to define the given point in space as the hotspot moves with the selected objects in the model.
- **Trigger When:** Select how the event is triggered.
    - *Entering*: An event is triggered when you cross into the sphere of the hotspot. This is useful for opening doors, for example.
    - *Leaving*: An event is triggered when you exit the sphere of the hotspot. This is useful for closing doors.
    - *In Range*: An event is triggered when you are inside the hotspot. This option enables you to use a hotspot event together with Boolean operators. For example, you can use AND to connect this event to an On Timer event.

The remaining options are valid depending on which hotspot option is selected.

- **Position:** Specify the position of the hotspot point in your model's units. If the hotspot type you select is *Sphere on selection*, this field is not available.
- **Pick:** Pick the position of the hotspot point. If the hotspot type you select is *Sphere on selection*, this button is not available. Click this button and then click a point for the hotspot in the main Navisworks window.
- **Set:** Select the hotspot objects. If the hotspot type you select is *Sphere*, this button is not available. Click **Set** and select an option.
    - *Clear*: Clears the current selection.
    - *Set From Current Selection*: Sets the hotspot to your current object selection in the main Navisworks window.
    - *Set From Current Selection Set*: Sets the hotspot to your current search set or selection set.
- **Show:** Displays the number of geometry objects linked to the hotspot. If the hotspot type you select is *Sphere*, this field is not available.This is a read-only field.
- **Radius:** Set the radius of the hotspot in your model's units.

On Variable Event

(On Variable Event) triggers a script when a variable meets a predefined criterion. You can specify the following properties for this event type:

- **Variable:** Specify the name of the variable to be evaluated.
- **Value:** Enter a value or a name of another variable to be tested against the value in your variable.
    - If you enter a number, the value is treated as a numeric value. If it has a decimal place, the floating-point formatting is preserved up to the user-defined decimal places.
    - If you enter an alphanumeric string between single or double quote marks, the value is treated as a string.
    - If you enter an alphanumeric string without single or double quote marks, the value is treated as the name of another variable. If this variable has never been used before, it is assigned a numerical value of 0.
    - If you enter the words **true** or **false** without any quotes, the value is treated as a Boolean (true = 1, false = 0).
- **Evaluation:** Enter an operator used for variable comparison. You can use the following operators with numbers and Boolean values, whereas when comparing strings, only the *Equal to* and *Not equal to* operators can be used.
    - *Equal to*
    - *Not Equal to*
    - *Greater than*
    - *Less than*
    - *Greater than or equal to*
    - *Less than or equal to*

On Animation Event

(On Animation Event) triggers a script when a certain animation starts or stops. You can specify the following properties for this event type:

- **Animation:** Select an animation that triggers the event.
- **Trigger On:** Select how the event is triggered.
    - *Starting*: An event is triggered when the animation starts.
    - *Ending*: An event is triggered when the animation ends. This is useful for chaining animations together.

9.3 Creating and Configuring Actions

An action is triggered by an event. Your script can have one or multiple actions in it. Actions are sequentially executed so it is important to get the order of the actions right. Scripter does not wait for the current action to be completed before moving on to the next action unless specifically scripted.

Action Types

There are eight action types available, which are displayed at the bottom of the *Actions* pane, as shown in Figure 9–8. When an action is added, the *Properties* pane shows the properties for that action type. These properties may be configured at this time or can be deferred to a later time.

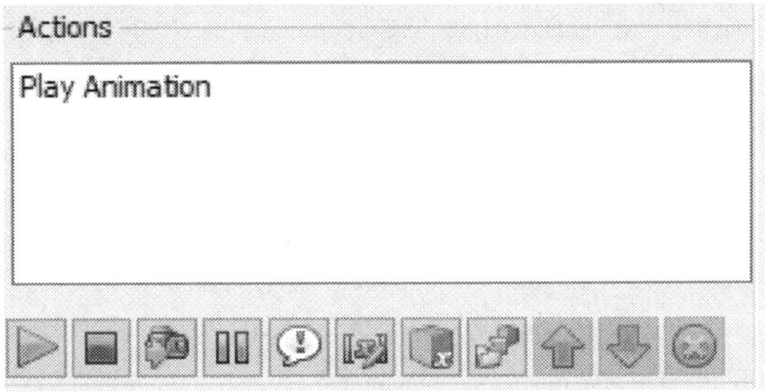

Figure 9–8

How To: Add an Action to an Event

1. In the *Scripts* pane, select the script to be modified.
2. In the *Events* pane, select the event requiring a specific action (or more).
3. At the bottom of the *Actions* pane, click an action type button to define the action. The action types are described below.
4. Review the properties in the *Properties* pane and change any of the property values, as required.

Play Animation Action

 (Play Animation Action) specifies which animation to play back when a script is triggered. You can specify the following properties for this action type:

- **Animation:** Select the animation to play. If you do not have any object animations in your Navisworks file, this field is unavailable.
- **Pause at End:** Select this checkbox if you want the animation to stop at the end. If not selected, the animation snaps back to the starting point when it ends.

- **Starting at:** Select where the playback starts.
  - *Start*: The animation plays forwards from the beginning.
  - *End*: The animation plays backwards from the end.
  - *Current Position*: The animation plays from its current position if the playback has already started; otherwise, the animation plays from the beginning.
  - *Specified Time*: The animation plays from the segment defined in the *Specific Start Time* field.
- **Ending at:** Select when the playback will end from the drop-down list.
  - *Start*: The playback ends at the beginning of the animation.
  - *End*: The playback ends at the end of the animation.
  - *Specified Time*: The playback ends at the segment defined in the *Specific End Time* field.
- **Specific Start Time:** Specify the start point of a playback segment.
- **Specific End Time:** Specify the end point of a playback segment.

Stop Animation Action

 (Stop Animation Action) specifies which animation is to stop when a script is triggered. The animation needs to be playing for it to be able to stop. You can specify the following properties for this action type:

- **Animation:** Select the animation to stop. If you do not have any object animation in your Navisworks file, this field is unavailable.
- **Reset To:** Select the position of the stopped animation:
  - *Default Position*: The animation returns to its starting point.
  - *Current Position*: The animation remains at its existing position.

Show Viewpoint Action

 (Show Viewpoint Action) specifies which viewpoint to use when a script is triggered. You can specify the following property for this action type:

- **Viewpoint:** Select the viewpoint to show. If you do not have any viewpoints in your Navisworks file, this field is unavailable.

Pause Script Action

Actions are executed one after another in a script, but Scripter does not wait for the current action to be completed before moving on to the next. With (Pause Action), you can interrupt the script for a specified amount of time before the next action is run. Alternatively, you can create several scripts to execute actions individually.

You can specify the following property for this action type:

- **Delay:** Enter the time period in seconds.

Send Message Action

(Send Message Action) outputs a text string to an external text file when a script is triggered. This can be useful in debugging when creating multiple interactive scripts. You can specify the following property for this action type:

- **Message:** Enter the text string to be sent to a text file.

The location of the text file can be configured in the *Options Editor*, under *Tools>Scripter*, as shown in Figure 9–9. When a script is triggered, the Send Message action sends the message to the location as configured.

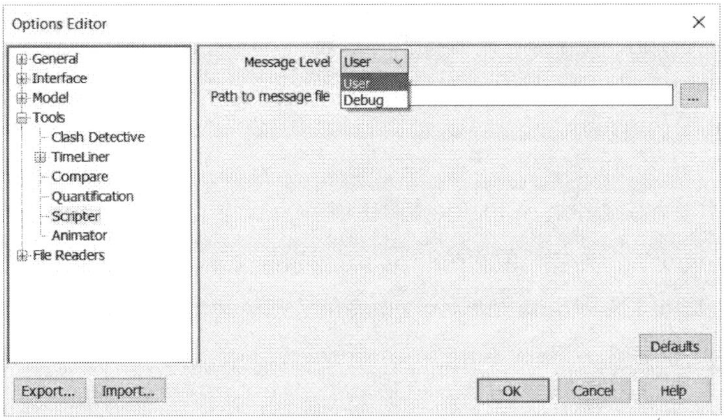

Figure 9–9

- For the *Path to message file*, enter a file location or click on the ellipses (...) to browse to a location.
- In the *Message Level* drop-down list, select the contents of the message file:
  - *User*: The message file only contains user messages (text strings generated by message actions).
  - *Debug*: The message file contains both user messages and debug messages (text strings generated internally by Scripter). Debugging enables you to see what is going on in more complex scripts.

Set Variable Action

(Set Variable Action) assigns, increases, or decreases a variable value when a script is triggered. You can specify the following properties for this action type:

- **Variable Name:** Specify the name for the variable.
- **Value:** Enter a value to assign.
  - If you enter a number, the value is treated as a numeric value. If it has a decimal place, the floating-point formatting is preserved up to the user-defined decimal places.
  - If you enter a string between single or double quote marks, the value is treated as a string.
  - If you enter the words **true** or **false** without any quotes, the value is treated as a Boolean (true = 1, false = 0).
- **Modifier:** Enter assignment operators for your variable. You can use any of the following operators with numbers and Boolean values. However, using strings is limited to the *Set equal to* operator only.
  - *Set equal to*
  - *Increment by*
  - *Decrement by*

Store Property Action

(Store Property Action) stores an object property in a variable when a script is triggered. This can be useful if you need to trigger events based on embedded object properties or data in an external database link. You can specify the following properties for this action type:

- **Selection to get property from:** Click **Set** and use the shortcut menu to define the objects, which are used to get the property.
  - *Clear*: Clears the current selection.
  - *Set From Current Selection*: Sets the objects to your current object selection in the main Navisworks window.
  - *Set From Current Selection Set*: Sets the objects to your current search set or selection set.

  Note: *If your selection contains a hierarchy of objects, the top-level object is used to get the property.*

- **Variable to set:** The name of the variable to receive the property.
- **Category:** The values in this drop-down list depend on the selected objects.
- **Property:** The values in this drop-down list depend on the chosen property category.

Practice 9b
Create and Configure Events

Practice Objective

- Create and configure events in a script.

In this practice, you will add to the script so that first the outer doors pivot open when one approaches and then the inner doors slide open. Finally, you will create a magical plant that grows and shrinks when pressing certain keys on the keyboard.

Task 1: Create and configure the events.

1. Open **School-Script-Setup.nwf** from the *Navisworks BIM Practice Files\Animator* folder.
2. Change to the **Entry Doors** viewpoint, if not already active.
3. In the *Scripter* window, in the *Scripts* pane, select the **Open Exterior Doors** script (in the *Exterior Vestibule Doors* folder).
4. In the *Events* pane, select (On Hotspot).
5. In the scene view (graphics window), use <Ctrl> and select both of the exterior doors.
6. In the *Properties* pane of the *Scripter* window, complete the following. The *Properties* pane should display as shown in Figure 9–10 once complete.
   - In the *Hotspot* drop-down list, select **Sphere on selection**.
   - In the *Trigger when* drop-down list, select **Entering**.
   - In the *Hotspot Type* area, click the *Set* button and select **Set From Current Selection** to attach the hotspot to both doors.
   - In the *Radius (ft)* field, enter **35.0**.

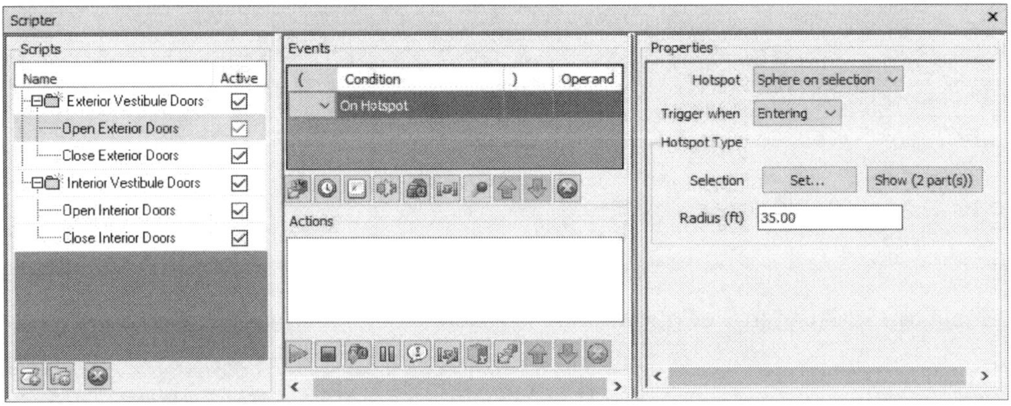

Figure 9–10

7. Leave the two doors selected.
8. Repeat Steps 3 to 6 to close the doors with the following exceptions, as shown in Figure 9–11.
    - Select the **Close Exterior Doors** script (in the *Exterior Vestibule Doors* folder).
    - In the *Properties* pane, in the *Trigger when* drop-down list, select **Leaving**.

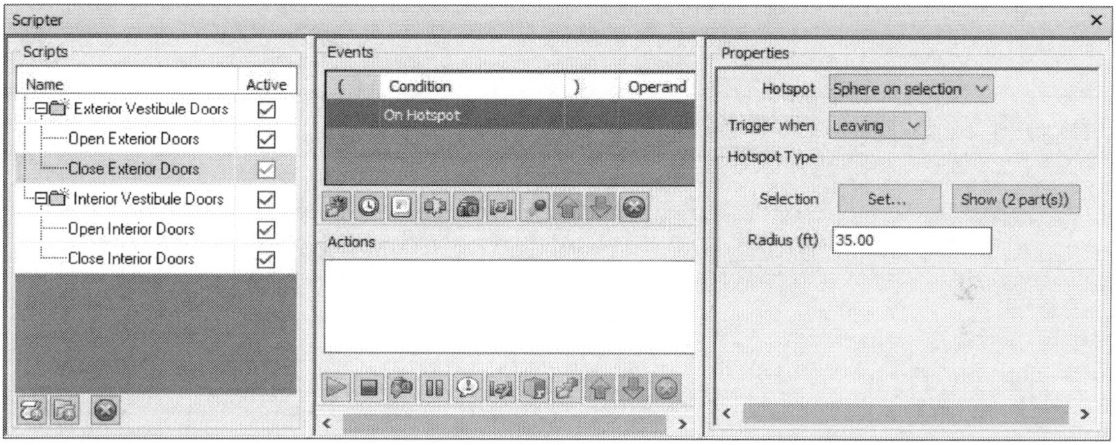

Figure 9–11

9. In the *Home* tab>*Select & Search* panel, click **Select None** to clear the selection of the two doors.
10. In the *Saved Viewpoints* window, select **Inside Doors** viewpoint.
11. Repeat Steps 3 to 7 for the two scripts contained within the *Interior Vestibule Doors* folder. Ensure that the inner two doors are selected for these scripts.
12. Save the file.

Task 2: Create and configure the actions required.

1. In the *Scripter* window, in the *Scripts* pane, select the **Open Exterior Doors** script (in the *Exterior Vestibule Doors* folder).
2. In the *Actions* pane, click (Play Animation) to add a play animation action.

3. In the *Properties* pane, click on the drop-down arrow in the *Animation* field and select the **Opening Outer Doors** animation, as shown in Figure 9–12.

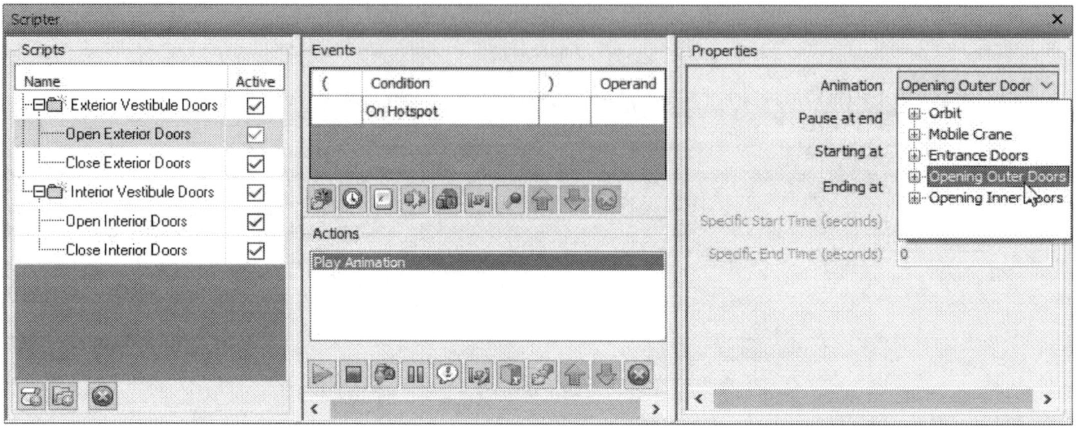

Figure 9–12

4. Ensure that the following settings are enabled in the *Properties* pane for the **Open Exterior Doors** script:
   - Enable the **Pause at end** checkbox.
   - In the *Starting at* drop-down list, select **Start**.
   - In the *Ending at* drop-down list, select **End**.
5. In the *Scripts* pane, select the **Close Exterior Doors** script.
6. In the *Events* pane, select the **On Hotspot** event.
7. In the *Actions* pane, click (Play Animation) to add a play animation action.
8. As you did previously, in the *Properties* pane, click on the drop-down arrow in the *Animation* field and select the **Opening Outer Doors** animation.
9. Ensure that the following settings are enabled in the *Properties* pane for the **Close Exterior Doors** script:
   - Enable the **Pause at end** checkbox.
   - In the *Starting at* drop-down list, select **End** (NOT Start).
   - In the *Ending At* drop-down list, select **Start** (NOT End).

   Note: *By reversing Start and End, the animation will play backwards (and close the doors).*
10. Repeat the process to apply actions to the two scripts within the *Interior Vestibule Doors* folder, using the **Opening Inner Doors** animation.
11. Save the file.

Task 3: Test out the interactive animations.

Now that you have added and configured actions to the hotspots in the scripts, you are ready to see the interactive animations. The created scripts need to be enabled to work with the navigation tools.

1. To enable scripts, in the *Animation* tab of the main ribbon, select  (Enable Scripts). Once enabled, the option turns blue, as shown in Figure 9–13.

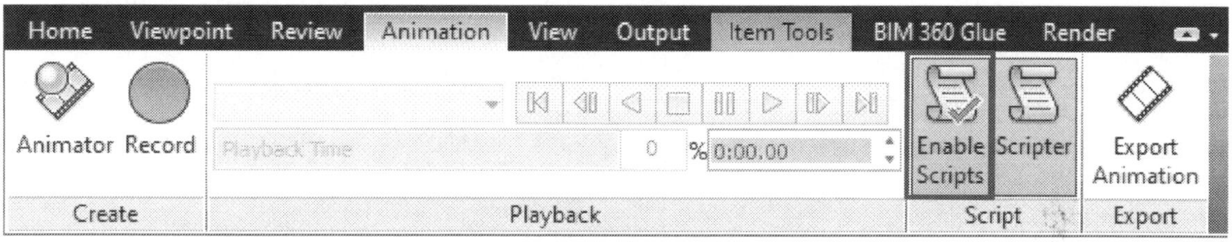

Figure 9–13

2. In the *Scripter* window, note how the *Events*, *Actions*, and *Properties* panes are now disabled. While scripts are enabled, you are unable to make any changes.
3. Select the **Entry Doors** saved viewpoint.
4. Use the **Walk** option in the navigation bar to move towards the doors in the scene view. When navigating towards the entrance doors, they should open and then close behind you as you proceed into the building. To review that the doors properly close as you walk into the building, use the **Look Around** option and then walk backwards away from the doors.
5. Save and close the file.
6. To review a completed version of the model, open **School-Script-Complete.nwf** from the *Navisworks BIM Practice Files\Animator* folder.

End of practice

Chapter Review Questions

1. Which of the following is NOT part of the *Scripter* window?
   a. Properties pane
   b. File pane
   c. Actions pane
   d. Events pane

2. Which of the following options are available for the **On Key Press** event? (Select all that apply.)
   a. Key Double Tap
   b. Key Pressed
   c. Key Held
   d. Key Up

3. Which of the following is NOT a **Scripter** event?
   a. On Collision
   b. On Timer
   c. On Hotspot
   d. On Saving

4. What is the issue when elements in the *Scripter* window are grayed out and cannot be edited?
   a. The script has not been saved.
   b. Scripts are enabled.
   c. The script is in read-only mode.
   d. There is an error in the script.

5. Can you specify the output file for exporting text strings?

a. Yes

b. No

c. It depends on the script.

d. You cannot export test strings.

Command Summary

Button	Command	Location
	**Add Folder**	• **Ribbon:** *Home* tab>*Tools* panel
	**Add Script**	• **Window:** *Scripter*
	**Delete Item**	• **Window:** *Scripter*
	**Enable/Disable Scripts**	• **Ribbon:** *Animation* tab>*Script* panel
	**Load Model**	• **Window:** *Scripter*
	**On Animation**	• **Window:** *Scripter*
	**On Collision**	• **Window:** *Scripter*
	**On Hotspot**	• **Window:** *Scripter*
	**On Key Press**	• **Window:** *Scripter*
	**On Start**	• **Window:** *Scripter*
	**On Timer**	• **Window:** *Scripter*
	**On Variable**	• **Window:** *Scripter*
	**Play Animation**	• **Window:** *Scripter*
	**Send Message**	• **Window:** *Scripter*
	**Set Variable**	• **Window:** *Scripter*

Button	Command	Location
	**Show/Hide Scripter Window**	• **Ribbon:** *Home* tab>*Tools* panel • **Ribbon:** *Animation* tab>*Script* panel
	**Show Viewpoint**	• **Window:** *Scripter*
	**Stop Animation**	• **Window:** *Scripter*
	**Store Property**	• **Window:** *Scripter*

Chapter 10

Project Scheduling

The next step in the BIM workflow involves constructing the project. By creating a 4D simulation, you can link a 3D model to a construction schedule, adding the fourth dimension of time. This approach enables users to more easily identify scheduling errors or address potential safety concerns.

You will learn to create and import a Gantt chart, then connect the model elements to this chart to create a construction simulation.

Learning Objectives

- Create a construction timeline.
- Import a construction timeline created in an external project management application.
- Run a time-based clash test.

BIM Workflow: Construct

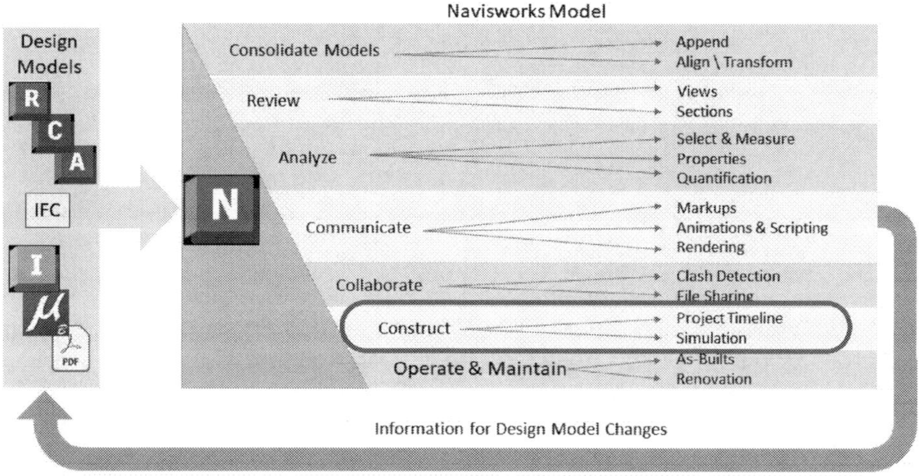

10.1 Introduction to TimeLiner

4D models visually communicate the relationships between model elements and the construction schedule. This can help stakeholders better understand any issues that might arise during the construction phase. The *TimeLiner* window (shown in Figure 10–1) is used to connect tasks in the Gantt chart with elements in the model to simulate construction.

You can create a Gantt chart in Autodesk® Navisworks® in two ways:

- Create a new chart from scratch.
- Import an existing chart from a project management software application.

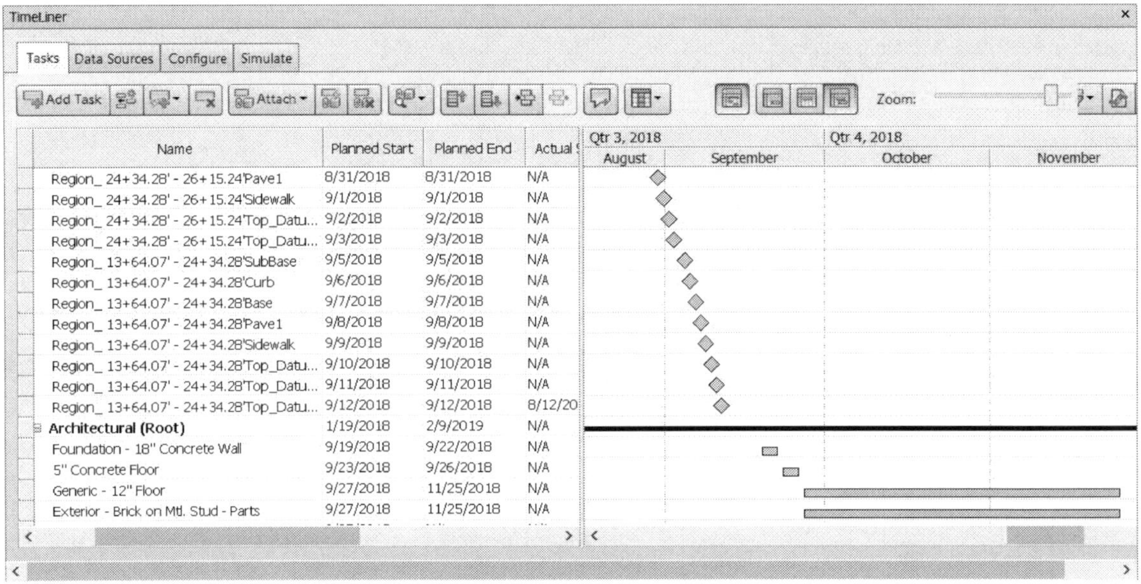

Figure 10–1

The *TimeLiner* window has four tabs, as shown above in Figure 10–1. Most of the work is completed in the *Tasks* tab.

Tasks Tab

The *Tasks* tab contains a list of all of the active tasks in the left pane and a Gantt chart in the right pane. Several columns are available in the task list pane that include information about each task. The columns can be reordered as required by dragging the column heading to a new location. The following information can be found in each column:

- **Active:** Displays a checkmark if the task is active and included in the simulation.
- **Name:** Displays the task name.

- **Status:** Displays two bars, as shown in Figure 10–2. The top bar represents the planned dates, while the bottom bar represents the actual dates. When the planned and actual dates match, the bars display in green. When they do not match, they display in red. If the date field is empty, the bar displays as clear.

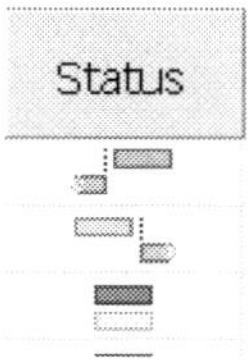

Figure 10–2

- **Planned Start/End Dates:** Displays the planned start and planned end dates of the task.
- **Actual Start/End Dates:** Displays the actual start and actual end dates of the task.
- **Task Type:** Displays the types of tasks that can be assigned, which determine the objects' appearance. The task types are set up in the *Configure* tab.
- **Attached:** Lists the objects attached to the task from the model.
- **Total Cost:** Displays a monetary ($) amount connected to the task.

Data Sources Tab

The *Data Sources* tab is used to connect to external project management software. There are multiple project management databases that can be connected, as shown in Figure 10–3. A database can be connected for each discipline or each model attached to the project, if required.

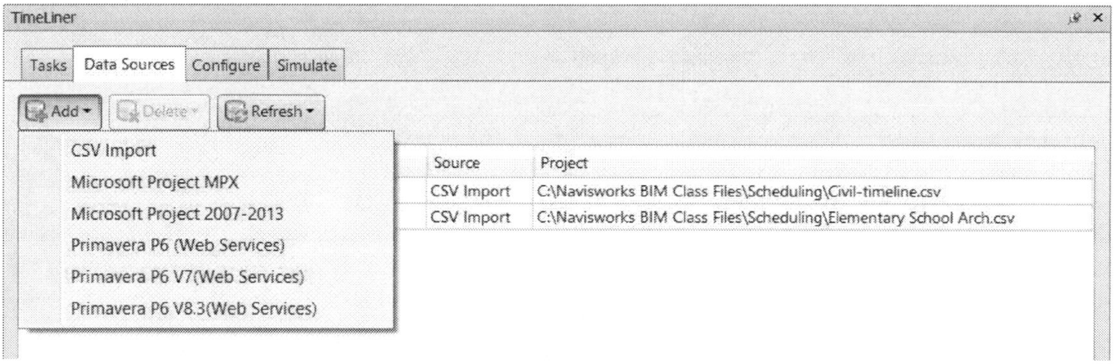

Figure 10–3

Configure Tab

The *Configure* tab enables you to set how you want objects to display at key times during a simulation. By default, there are three options, as shown in Figure 10–4:

- Construct
- Demolish
- Temporary (Constructed and demolished within the same key time)

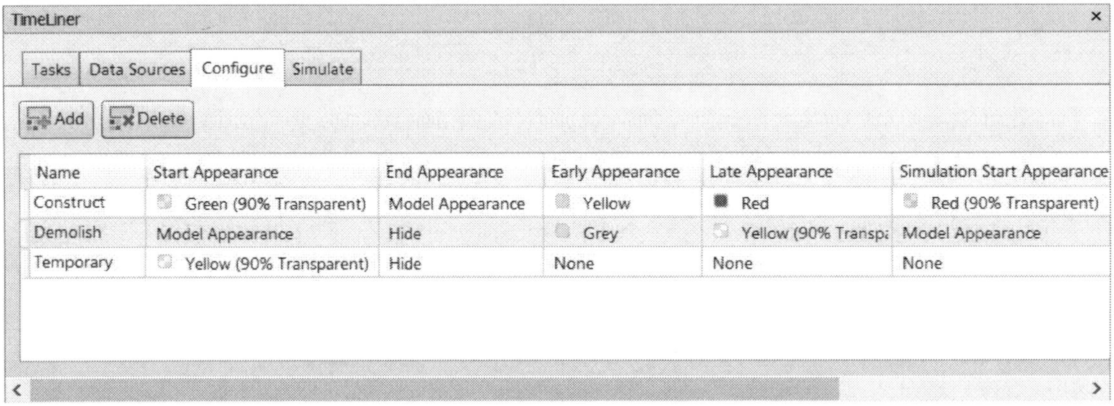

Name	Start Appearance	End Appearance	Early Appearance	Late Appearance	Simulation Start Appearance
Construct	Green (90% Transparent)	Model Appearance	Yellow	Red	Red (90% Transparent)
Demolish	Model Appearance	Hide	Grey	Yellow (90% Transp:	Model Appearance
Temporary	Yellow (90% Transparent)	Hide	None	None	None

Figure 10–4

Simulate Tab

The *Simulate* tab enables you to play, stop, and go to any point in the simulation. Similar to the *Tasks* tab, it contains two panes: the task list is on the left and the Gantt chart is on the right, as shown in Figure 10–5.

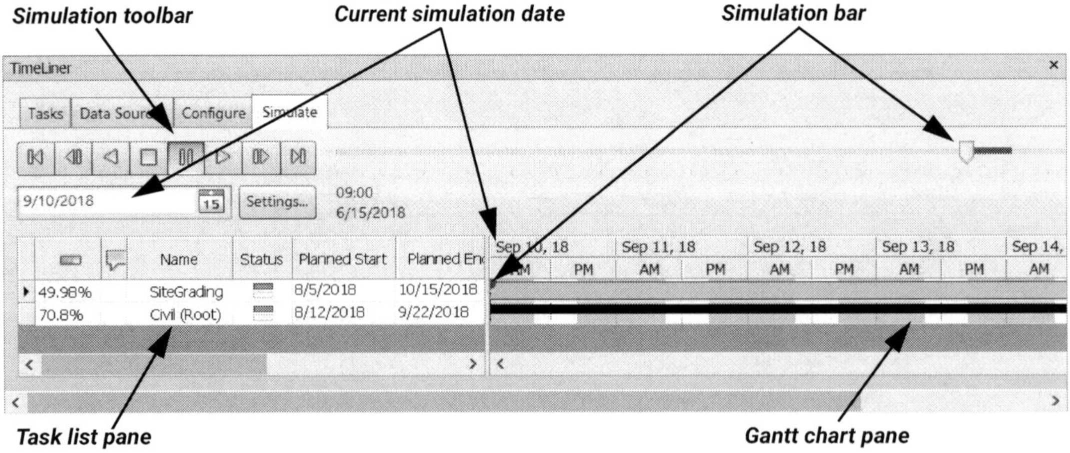

Figure 10–5

Task List Pane

The columns in the task list pane include information about each task. The columns can be reordered as required by dragging the column heading to a new location. The following information is found in each column:

-  **(Simulation Progress):** Displays a percentage for how much of a specific task is complete in the simulation.
-  **(Comments):** Lists the number of comments applied to a specific task.
- **Name:** Displays the task name.
- **Planned Start/End Dates:** Displays the planned start and planned end dates of the task.
- **Actual Start/End Dates:** Displays the actual start and actual end dates of the task.
- **Total Cost:** Displays a monetary ($) amount connected to the task.
- **Task Type:** Displays the task type that is assigned, which determines the objects' appearance.

Gantt Chart Pane

In the *Gantt chart* pane, columns list dates, while bars show each task's duration in the schedule. The beginning of the bar is located at the start date, and the end of the bar is located at the end date. Depending on the zoom level, the dates might display as months and days, months and weeks, or quarters and months, as shown in Figure 10–6.

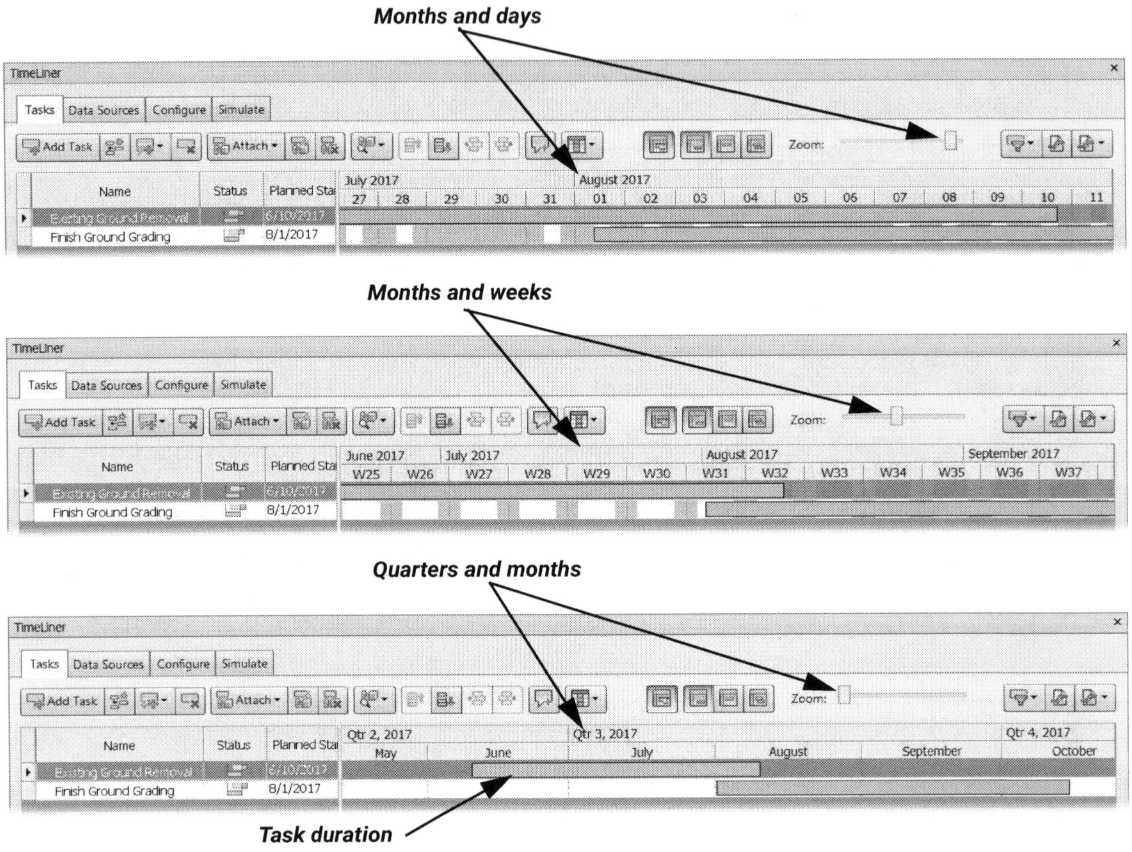

Figure 10–6

10.2 Manually Creating a Construction Simulation

Creating a construction simulation requires preparation. The models have to be created and then merged together. Next, the task list and Gantt chart must be created. Finally, the tasks must be connected to the task list.

General Steps

Use the following general steps to create a construction simulation:

1. Prepare the models.
2. Create saved sets and search sets.
3. Add tasks to the Gantt chart.
4. Configure how objects display during the simulation.
5. Link the simulation to any previously created animations.
6. Play the simulation.
7. Make any required changes.

1. Prepare the models.

In Autodesk® Revit® and Autodesk® Civil 3D®, multiple parts form one object in the model. For example, Figure 10–7 shows the parts that form a wall, while Figure 10–8 shows the parts that form a corridor model.

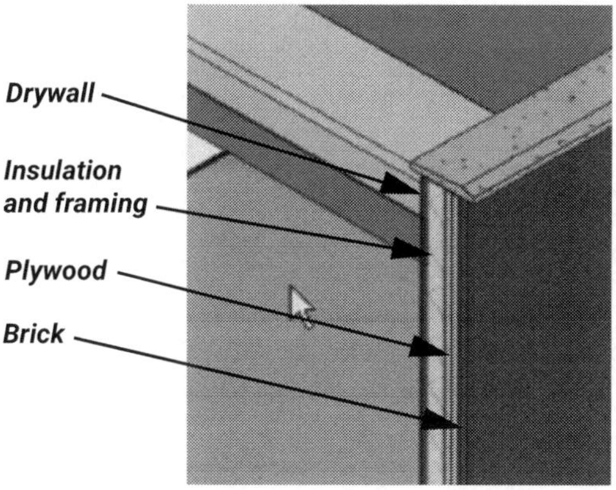

Figure 10–7

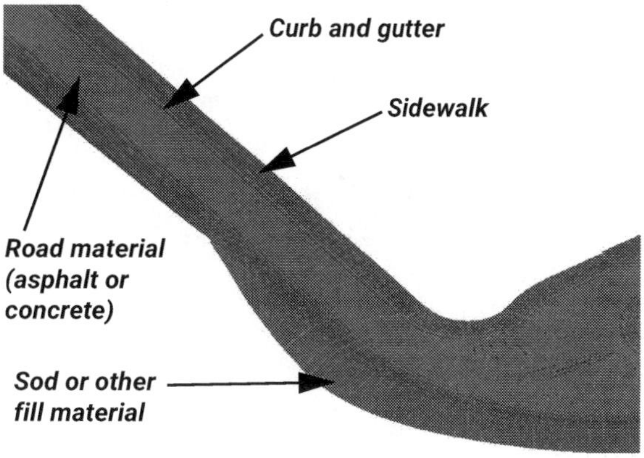

Figure 10–8

During construction, an entire road would not be built at once. First, grading would set the datum elevation, then the sub-base and base would be laid down. Next would come the sidewalks, curb, and gutter. Finally, the asphalt or concrete would be poured for the wearing course of the road.

When creating a construction animation using TimeLiner, you can create a simulation to match a real construction schedule. In order to do this, you must separate objects into parts in Civil 3D and Revit before importing the model into Navisworks.

> ***Note:*** *For more information on separating objects, see* ***Appendix C Preparing Models for TimeLiner****.*

2. Create saved sets and search sets.

Saved sets and search sets make connecting objects to the construction schedule much easier. You should use saved searches whenever possible to ensure that the sets are updated automatically whenever new or updated models are appended in Navisworks.

> ***Note:*** *For more information on creating saved sets and search sets, see* ***Chapter 4 Analyze Models****.*

3. Add tasks to the Gantt chart.

To manually create tasks in Navisworks, you must be on the *Tasks* tab of the *TimeLiner* window. Using this method, each task is created one line item at a time.

- Start and end dates must be manually input for each line item.
- You cannot set the end date in reference to the start date (i.e., you cannot set the number of days to complete).
- You cannot set the start of the next task to automatically follow the end of a previous task.

Hint: Date Standards

This guide uses the North American date standard of MM/DD/YYYY. If you are working in a region with a different date format, you will need to configure Navisworks to work with the MM/DD/YYYY date format for this course. In actual practice, you can configure Navisworks to work in your date format of choice.

To change the date format, go to the (Application Menu)>*Options Editor>Tools>TimeLiner* and change the *Date Format* to **7/26/2010**, which is the MM/DD/YYYY format, as shown in Figure 10–9.

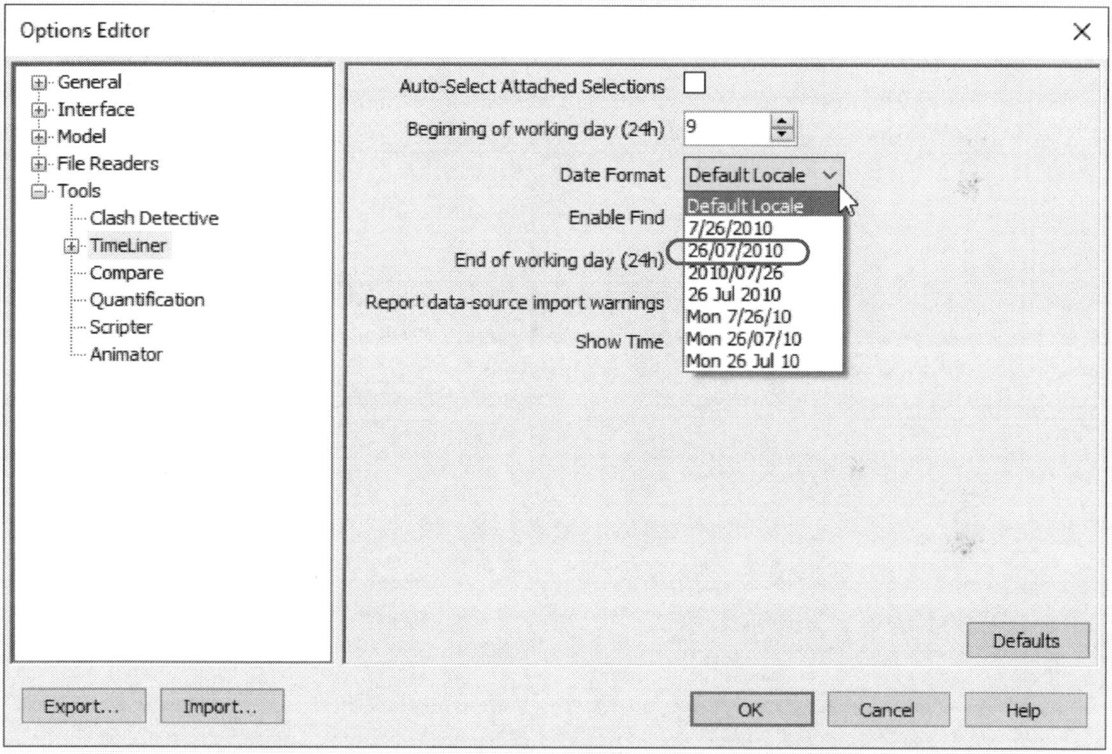

Figure 10–9

The **Default Locale** format is your system's format, controlled by your operating system and based on your location's standard.

How To: Manually Add Tasks to the Construction Simulation

1. In the *TimeLiner* window>*Tasks* tab, click (Add Task).

2. In the task's data fields, do the following:
    - *Name:* Enter a name.
    - *Planned Start Date:* Set the date (MM/DD/YYYY format).
    - *Planned End Date:* Set the date (MM/DD/YYYY format).
    - *Actual Start Date:* Set the date (MM/DD/YYYY format).
    - *Actual End Date:* Set the date (MM/DD/YYYY format).
    - *Task Type:* Expand the list and select a task type. Task types are defined in the *Configure* tab.
    - *Attached:* There are several options for attaching objects. Right-click on the field and select one of the options shown in Figure 10–10.

Note: *It is recommended to use search sets whenever possible to ensure that new items connect to the construction schedule.*

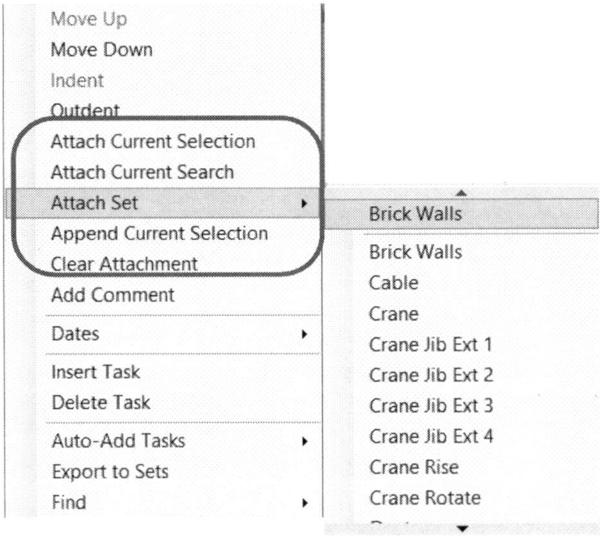

Figure 10–10

4. Configure how objects display during the simulation.

The *Configure* tab enables you to set how objects display at key times during the simulation.

- You can remove options by clicking 

(Delete), which deletes the selected row.
- You can create additional options by clicking 

(Add), which creates a new row. You can then use the down arrows in each column to select how you want objects to display.
- Additional appearance definitions can be created by clicking **Appearance Definitions**.

How To: Create a New Appearance Definition

1. In the *TimeLiner* window>*Configure* tab, click **Appearance Definitions**.
2. In the *Appearance Definitions* dialog box, click **Add**. A new row is added at the bottom of the list.
3. Select the new row and click on the **Name** field to change the name.
4. Double-click on the **Color** field to select a color from the color palette. Click **OK**.
5. Slide the **Transparency** slider to set the amount of transparency/opacity, as shown in Figure 10–11.

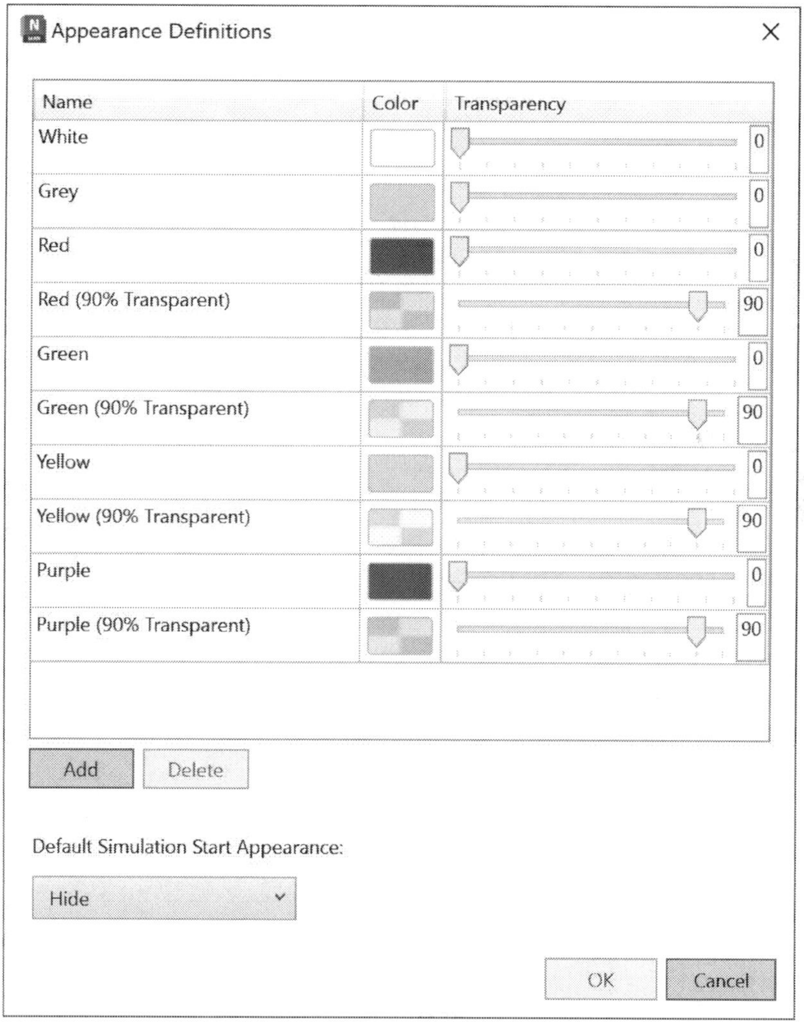

Figure 10–11

6. Expand the *Default Simulation Start Appearance* drop-down list and select the appearance you plan to use routinely at the start of the simulation.
7. Click **OK**.

5. Link the simulation to any previously created animations.

Simulations can be linked to any previously created animations to demonstrate how the project develops on the site as construction proceeds.

6. Play the simulation.

Tools at the top of the *Simulate* tab enable you to navigate the simulation. The tools are as follows:

- **(Rewind):** Moves the simulation bar to the beginning and changes the scene view to match.
- **(Step Back):** Rewinds the simulation a frame at a time.
- **(Reverse Play):** Plays the simulation in reverse.
- **(Pause):** Pauses the simulation, enabling you to resume play from the same spot by clicking (Play).
- **(Stop):** Stops the simulation, moves the simulation bar to the beginning, and changes the scene view to match.
- **(Play):** Starts the simulation from the current position of the simulation bar.
- **(Step Forward):** Moves forward a frame at a time.
- **(Forward):** Fast forwards the simulation to the end.

7. Make any required changes.

It is easier to make construction timeline adjustments before scheduling all of the sub-contractors due to complex project schedules. Being able to watch the construction virtually before breaking ground helps you to predict any issues that might occur during construction. Once an issue is discovered, you can go back to the *TimeLiner* window>*Tasks* tab to make any required adjustments to the construction timeline.

Scripter

By linking TimeLiner and scripted object animation together, you can trigger and schedule object movement based on start time and duration of project tasks. This can help you with workspace and process planning. For example, a TimeLiner sequence might indicate that when a particular site crane moves from its start to end point on a particular afternoon, a work group causes an obstruction along its route.

Practice 10a
Manually Create a Construction Simulation

Practice Objectives

- Review the model in preparation for use in TimeLiner.
- Create manual tasks in the *TimeLiner* window.
- Assign objects in the model to *TimeLiner* tasks.
- Play the TimeLiner simulation.

In this practice, you will manually add tasks to the *TimeLiner* window and attach them to objects in the model, as shown in Figure 10–12.

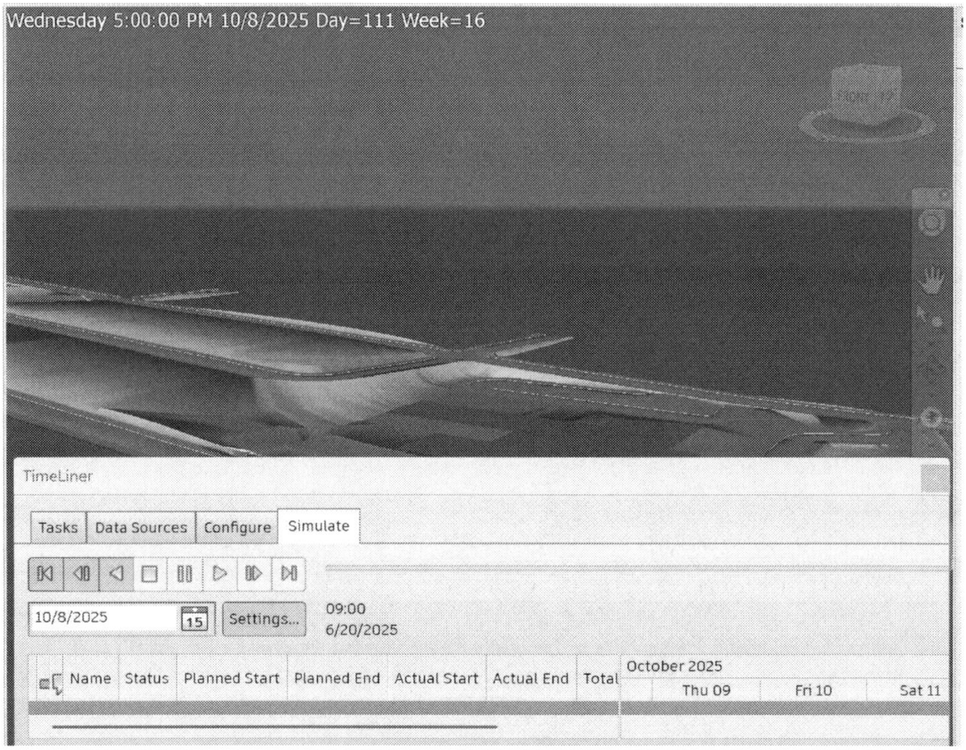

Figure 10–12

Task 1: Open and review the model.

For TimeLiner to work properly, the original files must be correctly organized and objects should be separated into objects. ***Appendix C Preparing Models for TimeLiner*** discusses how to set up the Revit file and the Civil 3D corridor models into separate objects for use in TimeLiner. In this practice, these models have already been processed in case you do not have access to Revit and Civil 3D.

1. Open **New-School-ManualTasks.nwf** from the *Navisworks BIM Practice Files\Scheduling* folder.
2. Review the *Selection Tree* and notice that there is an architectural and site layout appended to the file. Objects within these updated files have been separated for your use in the *TimeLiner* configuration.

Task 2: Create tasks manually.

In this task, you will add the existing ground to finish ground grading to the TimeLiner Gantt chart using the task pane.

1. Open the *TimeLiner* window and dock it near the bottom of the scene view (graphics window).

   Note: *The TimeLiner window is displayed by clicking (TimeLiner) in the Home tab>Tools panel, or in the View tab>Workspace panel, expand Windows and select TimeLiner.*

2. In the *TimeLiner* window>*Tasks* tab, click (Add Task).

3. In the task's data fields, enter the following, as shown in Figure 10–13:
   - *Name:* **Existing Ground Removal**
   - *Planned Start Date:* **6/20/2024**
   - *Planned End Date:* **7/10/2024**
   - *Task Type:* **Demolish**

   Hint: You can highlight the first cell and use the keyboard to type in the data, then use <Tab> to jump to the next cell and keep typing. For the *Task Type*, you can type the first letter and it will fill in, then press <Tab> or <Enter> to complete the selection or select the type from the drop-down list. You do not need to use the mouse for the data entry as using the keyboard can be more efficient.

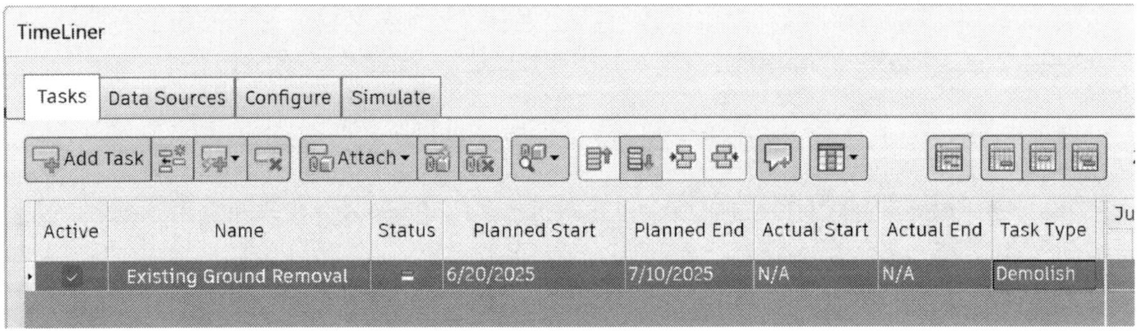

Figure 10–13

4. In the *TimeLiner* window>*Tasks* tab, click  (Add Task).

   Note: *If you pressed <Enter> after entering any data for your first task, a second task would have already been added and you will not have to manually create the second task using the **Add Task** option.*

5. In the task's data fields, enter the following:
   - *Name:* **Finish Ground Grading**
   - *Planned Start Date:* **7/1/2024**
   - *Planned End Date:* **8/10/2024**
   - *Task Type:* **Construct**

6. Save the file.

Task 3: Connect objects in the model to tasks.

In order to review the grading change from the existing ground to the finish ground, you must attach the objects to the tasks. In this task, you attach the existing ground to the first task and the proposed ground to the second task in TimeLiner.

1. In the *Selection Tree*, expand *Site Layout-Edited.dwg>C-TOPO-VIEW* and select **AIW_Existing_Ground**. This surface is currently hidden. Unhide the surface by pressing <Ctrl>+<H>. This surface represents the existing surface of the site prior to any construction.
2. Ensure that **AIW_Existing_Ground** is selected.
3. In the *TimeLiner* window, right-click on the **Existing Ground Removal** task and select **Attach Current Selection**, as shown in Figure 10–14.

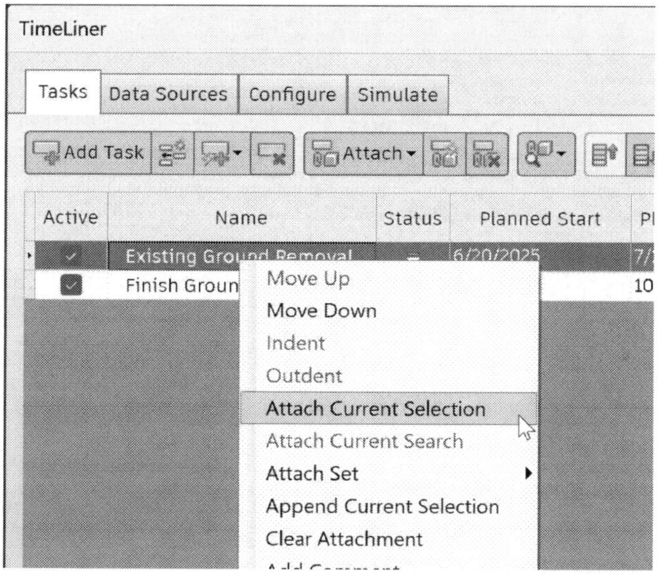

Figure 10–14

4. In the *Selection Tree*, expand *Site Layout-Edited.dwg>C-TOPO-VIEW* and select **Composite (All School Site FG Surfaces)**. Only this single item should be selected.
5. In the *TimeLiner* window, right-click on the **Finish Ground Grading** task and select **Attach Current Selection**.
6. Press <Esc> to deselect everything in the scene, or in the *Home* tab>*Select & Search* panel, expand the *Select All* drop-down list and select **Select None** (so that nothing is highlighted in blue).
7. In the *TimeLiner* window, select the *Configure* tab.

8. Set the following parameters for the appearance definitions, as shown in Figure 10–15. In each column, click near the right edge to display the drop-down list and then select the required setting.

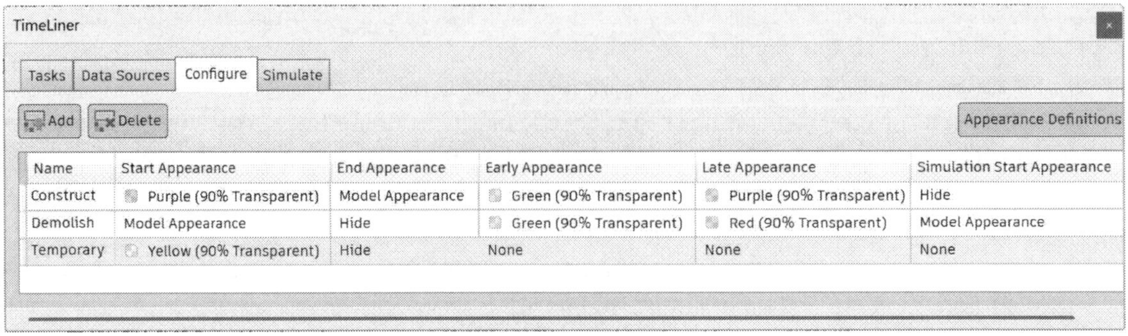

Figure 10–15

Construct:

- *Start Appearance:* **Purple (90% Transparent)**
- *End Appearance:* **Model Appearance**
- *Early Appearance:* **Green (90% Transparent)**
- *Late Appearance:* **Purple (90% Transparent)**
- *Simulation Start Appearance:* **Hide**

Demolish:

- *Start Appearance:* **Model Appearance**
- *End Appearance:* **Hide**
- *Early Appearance:* **Green (90% Transparent)**
- *Late Appearance:* **Red (90% Transparent)**
- *Simulation Start Appearance:* **Model Appearance**

Temporary:

- *Start Appearance:* **Yellow (90% Transparent)**
- *End Appearance:* **Hide**
- *Early Appearance:* **None**
- *Late Appearance:* **None**
- *Simulation Start Appearance:* **None**

9. In the *TimeLiner* window, open the *Simulate* tab. Note that the school disappears in the scene view. Only the existing site surface is displayed at the beginning of the timeline.

10. Click (Play) to run the simulation. Depending on your start date, it may take a while for anything to happen.
11. When done, return to the *Tasks* tab in the *TimeLiner* window (to restore the model to its finished state).
12. In the *Selection Tree*, expand *Site Layout-Edited.dwg>C-TOPO-VIEW* and select **AIW_Existing_Ground**. Press <Ctrl>+<H> to hide the surface.
13. Save the file.

End of practice

10.3 Importing an External Task List

Most architecture, engineering, and construction firms use project management software to manage their project schedules. These programs make it easier to set dates based on the start or completion dates of an earlier task.

You can use Navisworks TimeLiner to import project schedules from a variety of external data sources. Once imported, a task list can be created and automatically connected to model objects. The key to ensuring this information is correct is using saved sets and saved searches whose names match the task names in the project management database.

The following project management databases can be imported:

- .CSV files
- Microsoft Project MPX
- Microsoft Project 2007-2013
- Primavera P6 (Web Services)
- Primavera P6 V7 (Web Services)
- Primavera P6 V8.3 (Web Services)

TimeLiner Rules

TimeLiner rules assist in connecting tasks with items in the scene view. There are three rules available, as shown in Figure 10–16. In all cases, the name cases must match.

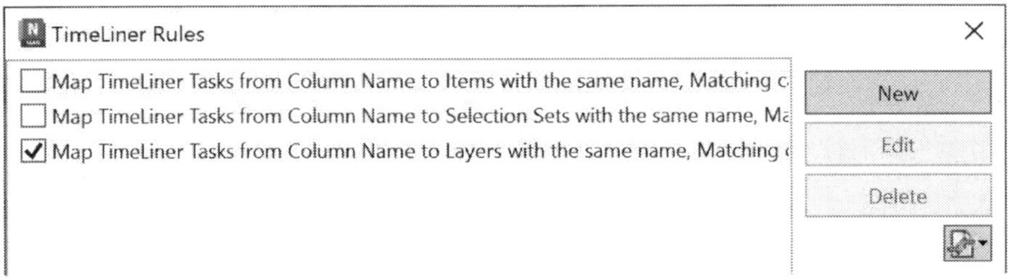

Figure 10–16

- Use the first rule when the item names in the *Selection Tree* match the task names in the project schedule.
- Use the second rule when the selection set names match the task names in the project schedule.
- Use the third rule when the layer names in the original file match the task names in the project schedule.

The first two rules are most often used with Autodesk Revit files, while the third rule is most often used to connect AutoCAD layers or Autodesk Civil 3D corridor shapes.

How To: Import a Task List

1. In the *TimeLiner>Data Sources* tab, expand  (Add) and select the source database.
2. In the *Open files* dialog box, navigate to the file and select it.
3. Click **Open**.
4. In the *Field Selector* dialog box, map the TimeLiner column names to the external database fields, as shown in Figure 10–17.

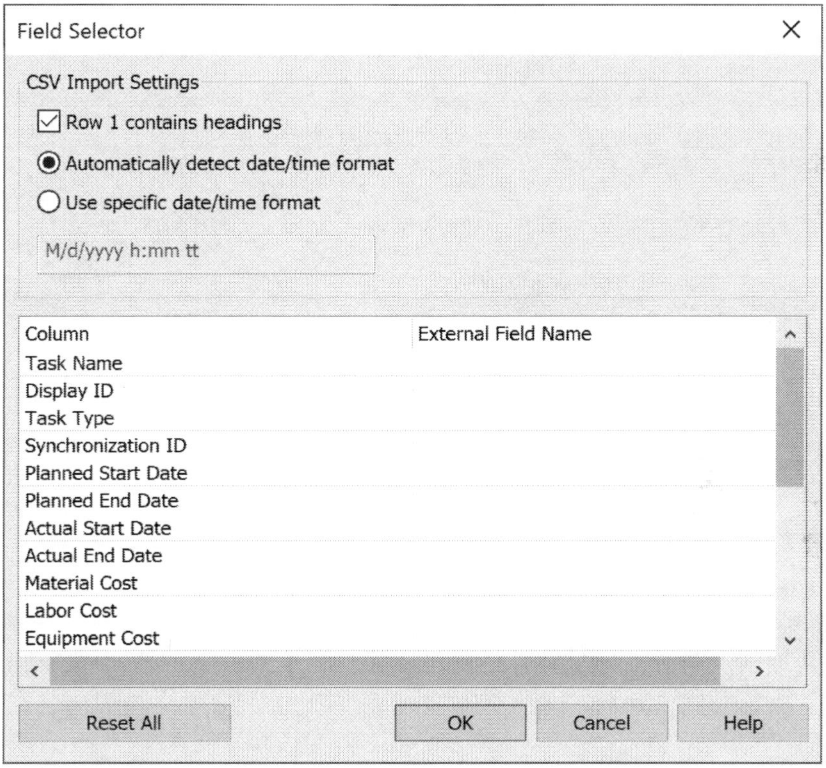

Figure 10–17

5. Click **OK**.
6. In the *TimeLiner>Data Sources* tab, right-click on the new data source and select **Rename**.
7. Enter an appropriate name. The name you use displays in the task pane.
8. In the *TimeLiner>Data Sources* tab, right-click on the new data source and select **Rebuild Task Hierarchy**.
9. If any fields are missing information, you might get an error message. Click **OK**.

10. In the *TimeLiner>Tasks* tab, click  (Auto-Attach Using Rules).
11. In the *TimeLiner Rules* dialog box, select the required rules and click **Apply Rules**, as shown in Figure 10–18.

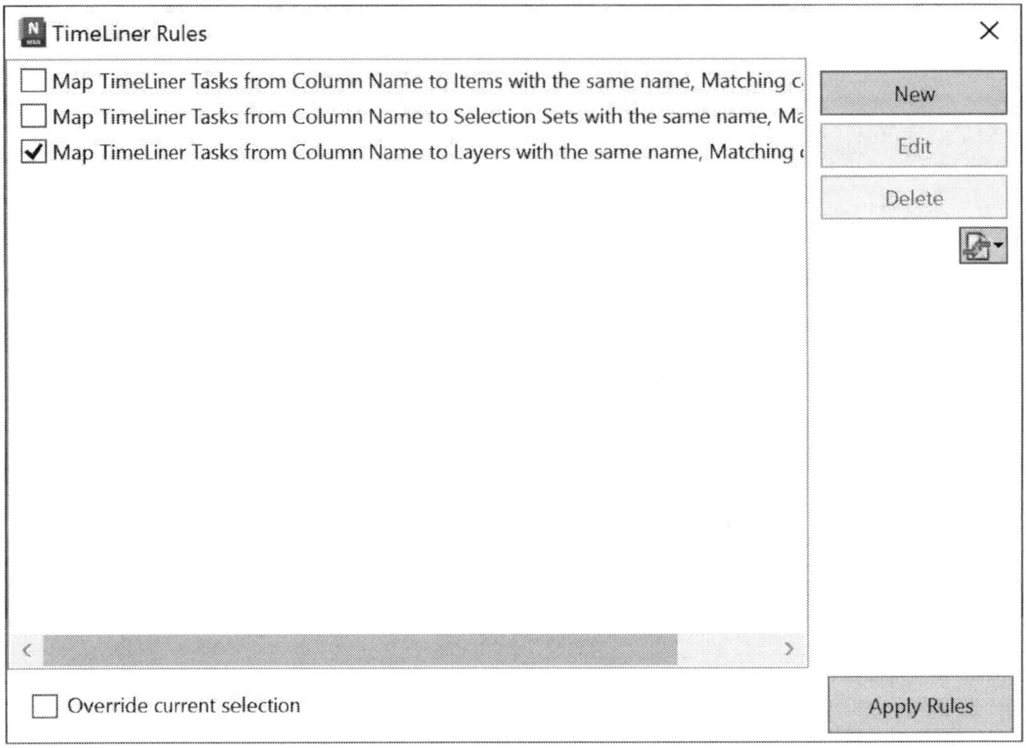

Figure 10–18

12. Ensure that all of the tasks have objects attached to them. If any are missing, manually attach the objects.
13. Play the simulation.

10.4 Combining TimeLiner and Animator

During a construction simulation, it can be helpful to view the model from multiple angles to understand how everything comes together. You can do this by setting up an animation first, and then connecting the animation to the project schedule.

Simulation Settings

The *Simulation Settings* dialog box enables you to connect an animation to the timeline and adjust a number of settings, as shown in Figure 10–19.

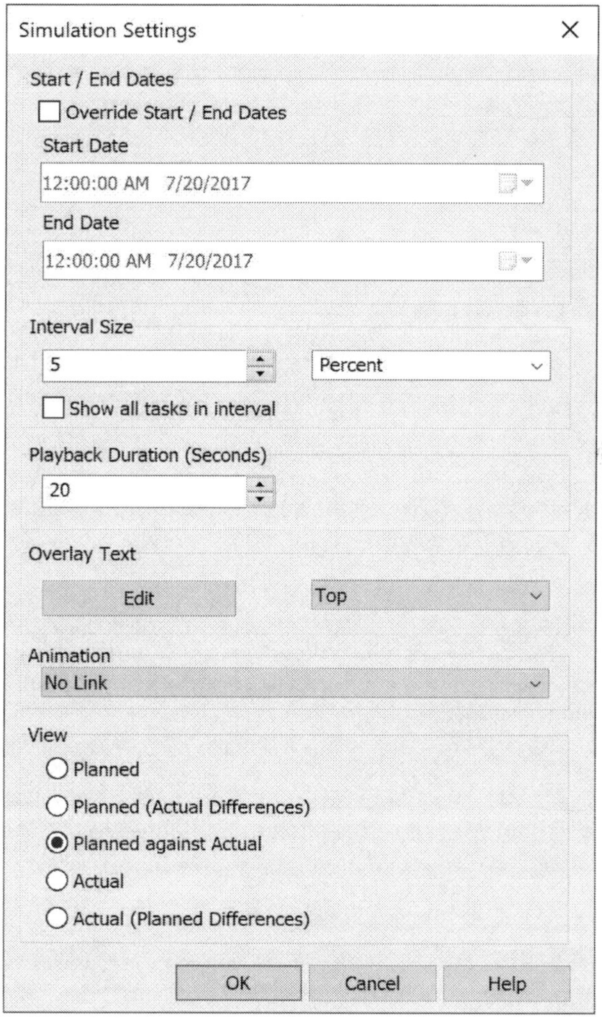

Figure 10–19

Start/End Dates

You can override the start and end dates for the animation, but this only changes what date the animation of the simulation starts. It does not automatically change the dates of the tasks according to the override start date. This means that if an override start date is selected that is the mid-point of the construction timeline, then half of the simulation shows as already being complete when you run the simulation.

Interval Size

The *Interval Size* determines how much of the Timeline plays at once. A numeric value, combined with one of the following, determine the interval:

- Percent
- Weeks
- Days
- Hours
- Minutes
- Seconds

Playback Duration (Seconds)

You can set the playback duration to control how long it takes to play the entire animation. The duration units are in seconds.

Overlay Text

Text can be added to the scene view to communicate information about the simulation. The text can be placed at the top or the bottom of the scene view.

Animation

The *Animation* drop-down list provides a list of previously created animations. By default, it is set to **No Link**. TimeLiner only uses the camera viewpoints from the animation to tour the model while the TimeLiner simulation plays.

View

The dates that are used to animate the simulation are selected in the *View* area. You have the following options to choose from:

- Planned
- Planned (Actual Differences)
- Planned against Actual
- Actual
- Actual (Planned Differences)

How To: Add an Animation to TimeLiner

1. Create an animation with the required camera viewpoints. **Note:** Object animations are ignored unless they are added to the task list.
2. In the *TimeLiner* window>*Simulate* tab, click **Settings**.
3. In the *Simulation Settings* dialog box, expand the *Animation* drop-down list and select the animation with the required viewpoints, as shown in Figure 10–20.

   Note: *Only animations that were previously created display in the list. You cannot create an animation at this point.*

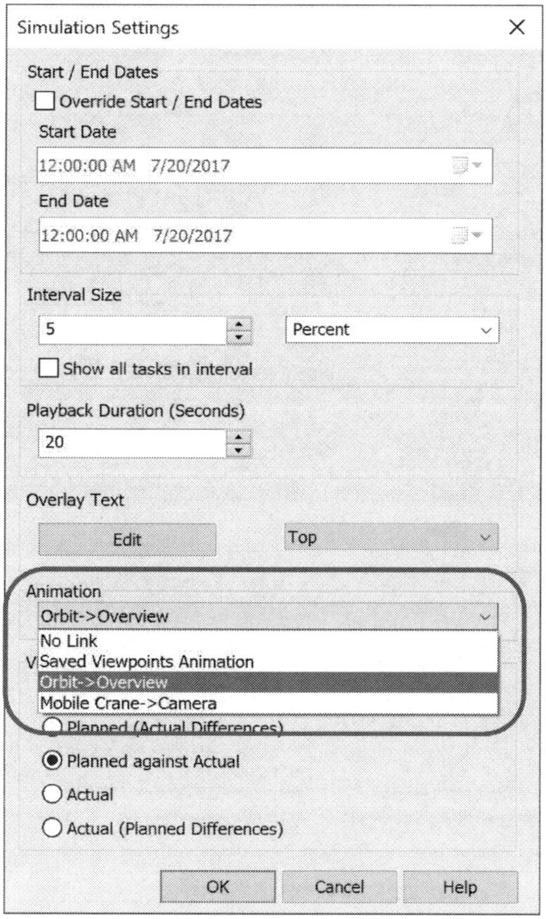

Figure 10–20

4. Click **OK**.
5. In the *Simulate* tab, click  (Play) to run the simulation.

Practice 10b
Import an External Project Schedule

Practice Objectives

- Import an external project management database to populate the TimeLiner task list.
- Connect objects to tasks automatically using rules.

In this practice, you will connect an external project management database to automatically populate TimeLiner tasks. Then, you will use rules to connect the tasks to the model automatically before running the simulation, as shown in Figure 10–21.

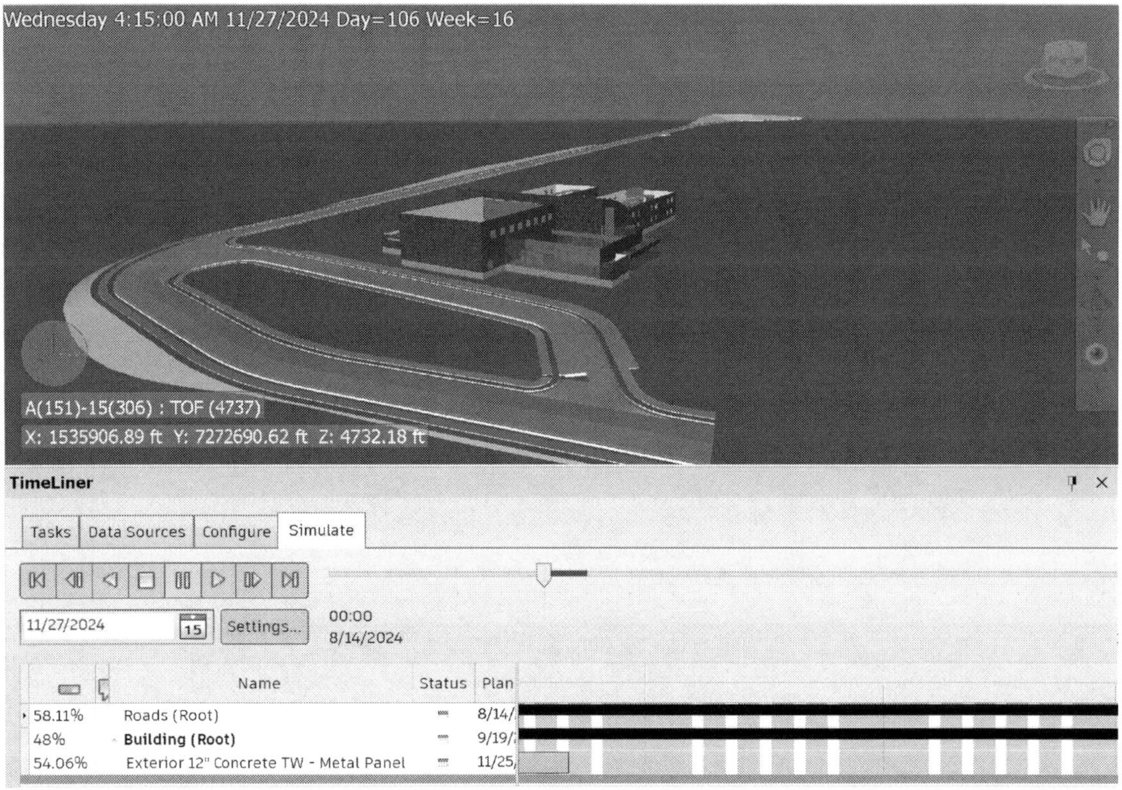

Figure 10–21

Task 1: Connect the corridor schedule.

In this task, you will connect a .CSV file to import the tasks for the road construction schedule.

1. Open **New-School-ImportTasks.nwf** from the *Navisworks BIM Practice Files\Scheduling* folder.
2. In the *TimeLiner* window>*Data Sources* tab, expand (Add) and select **CSV Import**.
3. In the *Open files* dialog box, navigate to the *Navisworks BIM Practice Files\Scheduling* folder and select **Civil-timeline.csv**. Click **Open**.
4. In the *Field Selector* dialog box, for each *TimeLiner Column,*use the drop-down list in the corresponding *External Field Name* to set the names, as shown in Figure 10–22. Note the options at the top of the dialog box.

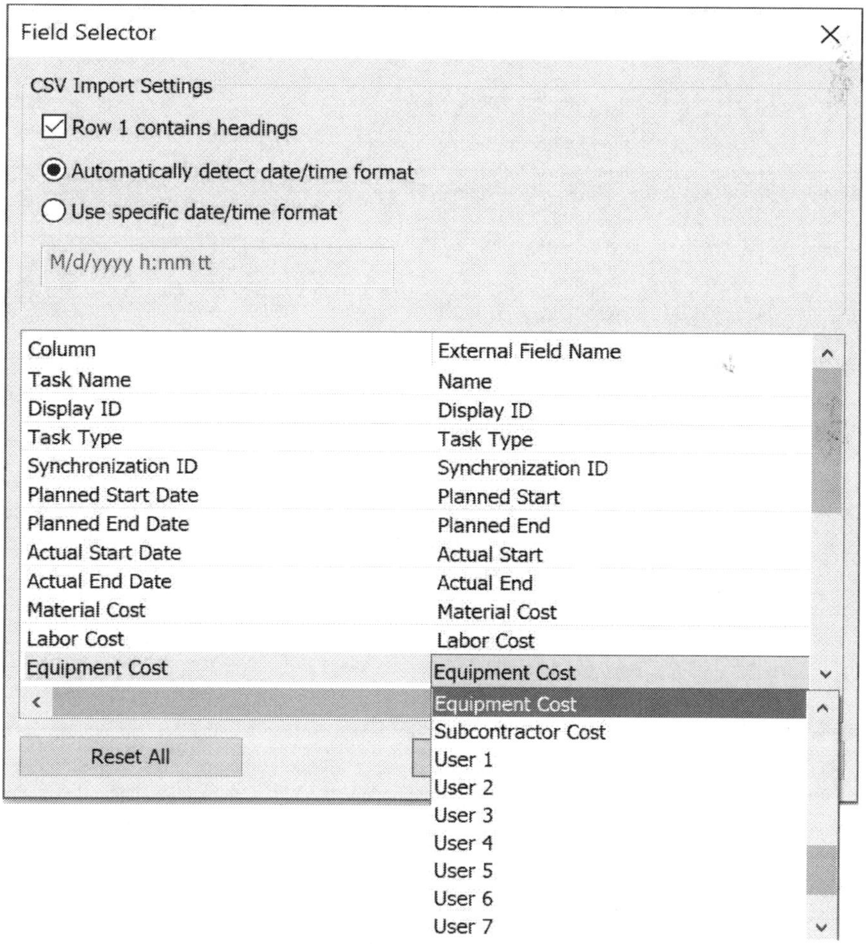

Figure 10–22

5. Click **OK**.

6. In the *TimeLiner* window>*Data Sources* tab, right-click on the **New Data Source** and select **Rename**, as shown in Figure 10–23.

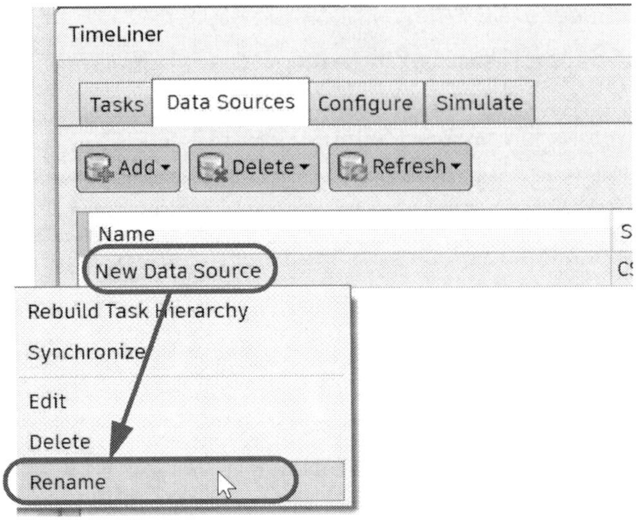

Figure 10–23

7. Enter **Roads** for the name and press <Enter>.
8. In the *TimeLiner* window>*Data Sources* tab, right-click on the newly renamed **Roads** data source and select **Rebuild Task Hierarchy**.
9. The *Problems in imported data* dialog box displays noting that some fields are missing information, as shown in Figure 10–24. For example, not all of the Actual Start and Actual End dates are entered in the spreadsheet. Click **OK**.

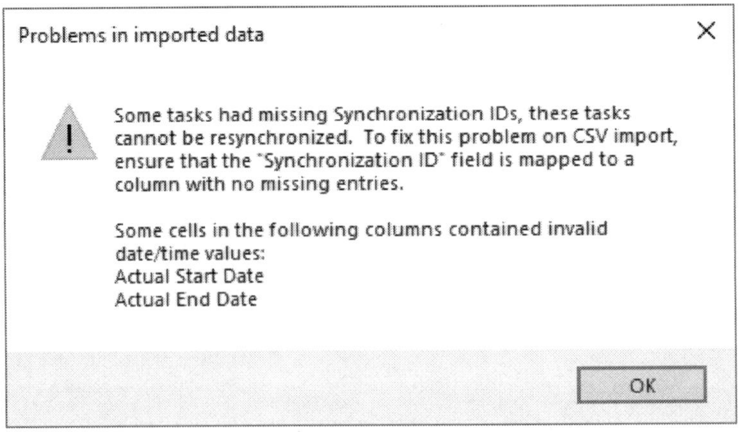

Figure 10–24

10. In the *TimeLiner* window>*Tasks* tab, click  (Auto-Attach Using Rules), as shown in Figure 10–25.

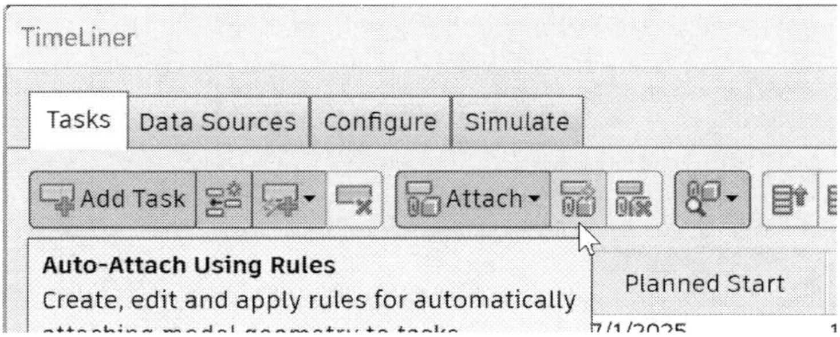

Figure 10–25

11. In the *TimeLiner Rules* dialog box, ensure that only the last rule, **Map TimeLiner Tasks from Column Name to Layers with the same name, Matching case**, is selected, as shown in Figure 10–26.

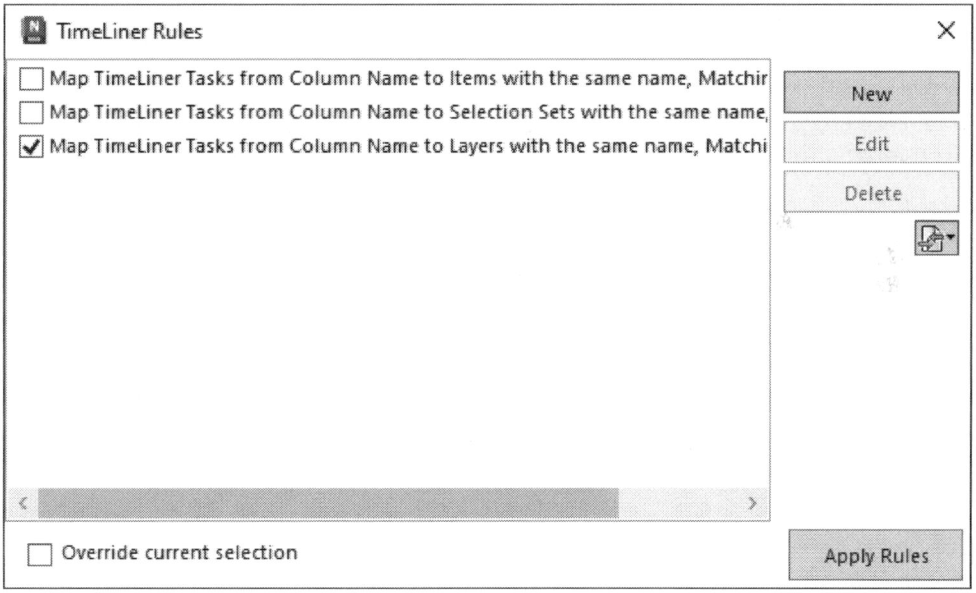

Figure 10–26

12. Click **Apply Rules**.
13. Close the *TimeLiner Rules* dialog box by clicking the **X** in the upper-right corner.

14. Use the scroll bar on the far right of the *TimeLiner* window to scroll down and ensure that all of the tasks have objects attached to them. Note that the root node (**Roads**) does not have objects assigned. In the *Attached* column, there should be an **Explicit Selection** text entry in blue, as shown in Figure 10–27. This means that the layer name in the Civil 3D drawing file matches the task name imported through the spreadsheet.

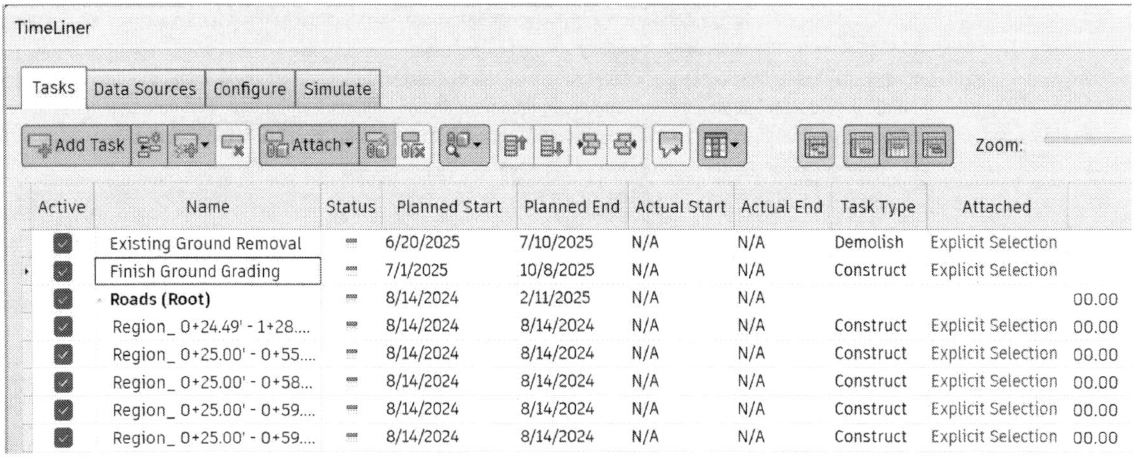

Figure 10–27

15. In the *Saved Viewpoints* window, select **Overview** to restore that saved viewpoint, if you have changed the view.

16. In the *TimeLiner* window, open the *Simulate* tab. Note that the school and site disappear. This is because the existing ground surface was previously hidden and it is the referenced geometry at the beginning of the simulation.

17. Click  (Play) to run the simulation. Note how the corridor is now added throughout the simulation. This is based on the surfaces and dates that were provided in the **Civil-timeline.csv** file.

18. When done, return to the *Tasks* tab in the *TimeLiner* window to restore the model to its finished state.

19. Save the file.

Task 2: Connect the building schedule.

In this task, you will import the project schedule for the building components. You will learn that not all of the object and set names match the task names in the imported .CSV file, and therefore will not all connect automatically. In these tasks, you can manually connect them.

1. In the *TimeLiner* window>*Data Sources* tab, expand (Add) and select **CSV Import**.
2. In the *Open files* dialog box, navigate to the *Navisworks BIM Practice Files\Scheduling* folder and select **School Arch-timeline.csv**. Click **Open**.
3. In the *Field Selector* dialog box, ensure that the TimeLiner column names are still mapped to the external database fields and click **OK**.
4. In the *TimeLiner* window>*Data Sources* tab, right-click on the new data source and select **Rename**.
5. Enter **Building** for the name and press <Enter>.
6. In the *TimeLiner* window>*Data Sources* tab, right-click on the **Building** data source and select **Rebuild Task Hierarchy**.
7. Note that some of the fields are missing information. Click **OK** in the *Problems in imported data* dialog box.
8. Before continuing in TimeLiner, open the Sets window. Noticethat additional selection sets,such as group wall, doors, windows, etc. on each floor, were created n this model. . These are required to make the connection between parts in the model and the Gantt chart.
9. In the *TimeLiner* window>*Tasks* tab, click (Auto-Attach Using Rules).
10. In the *TimeLiner Rules* dialog box, select the first two rules, as shown in Figure 10–28. Click **Apply Rules**.

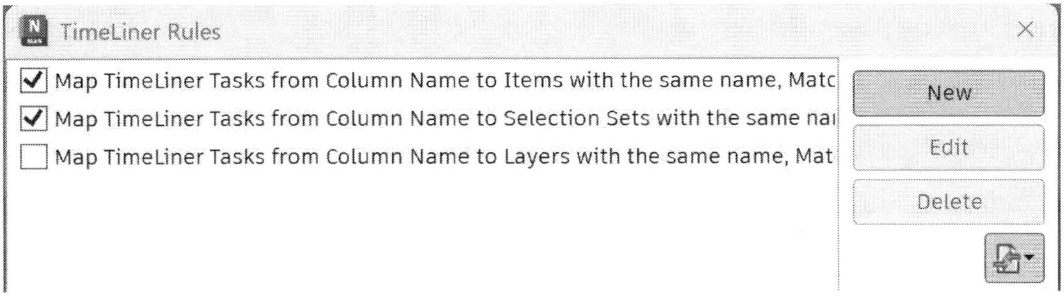

Figure 10–28

11. Close the *TimeLiner Rules* dialog box by clicking the **X** in the upper right corner.
12. Use the scroll bar on the far right of the *TimeLiner* window to scroll down until **Building (Root)** is displayed and review the tasks under it.

13. Note that not all of the tasks have objects attached to them (i.e., have an **Explicit Selection** or **Sets** text entry in blue), as shown in Figure 10–29.

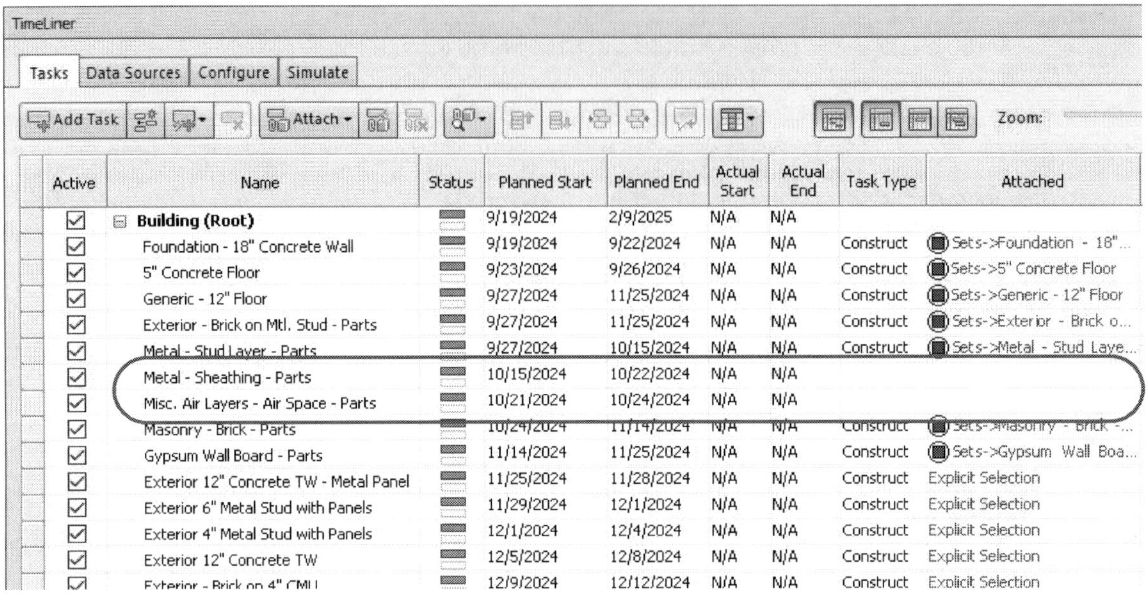

Figure 10–29

14. In the task pane, scroll down to *Metal - Sheathing - Parts*. In its row, right-click in its empty cell in the *Attached* column and select **Attach Set>Panels - Parts** to connect the paneling to this task. You will have to scroll down to find the **Panels - Parts** set, as shown in Figure 10–30.

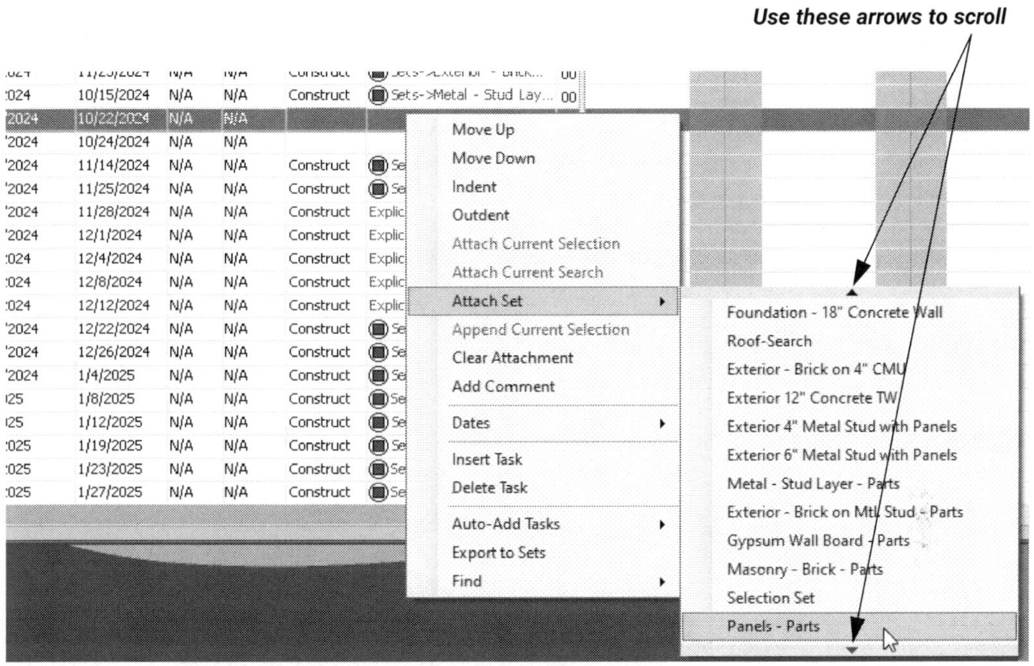

Figure 10–30

15. Set the *Task Type* to **Construct** for *Metal - Sheathing - Parts*.
16. You do not need to attach anything for the *Air Layers* because there is nothing to install for this layer. In the *TimeLiner* window, open the *Simulate* tab.
17. Click (Play) to run the simulation.

    Note: As the simulation is playing, you can navigate around the school to see the progress. You can also pause the play anytime.

18. When done, return to the *Tasks* tab in the *TimeLiner* window to restore the model to its finished state.
19. Save the file.

Task 3: Orbit the model as you play the simulation.

In this task, you connect an animation to the simulation to orbit the model as the simulation plays.

1. In the *TimeLiner* window>*Simulate* tab, click **Settings**.
2. In the *Simulation Settings* dialog box, expand the *Animation* drop-down list and select **Orbit>Overview**, as shown in Figure 10–31. This animation has been created for you.

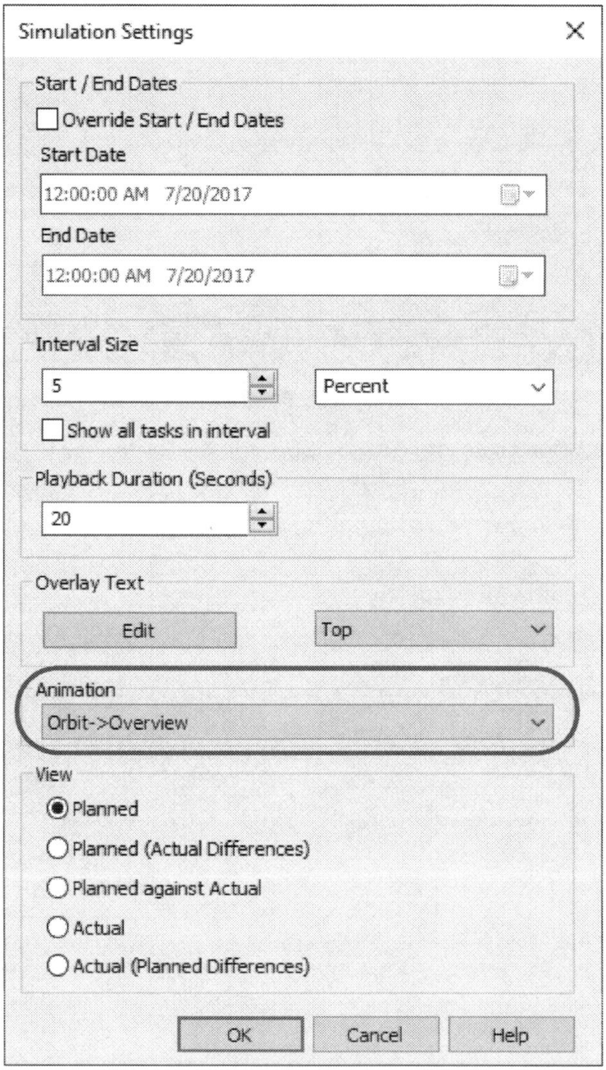

Figure 10–31

3. Click **OK**.

4. In the *Simulate* tab, click  (Play) to run the simulation.
5. This time the camera orbits during the simulation and ends inside the building.
6. When done, return to the *Tasks* tab in the *TimeLiner* window to restore the model to its finished state.
7. Save the file.
8. Close the *TimeLiner* window.

End of practice

10.5 Time-Based Clashes

A very costly and time-consuming situation may occur in construction when things fit together within the BIM model but do not fit together in the field. Construction simulations help you discover when a piece of equipment does not have the necessary room to maneuver on a job site. Combining TimeLiner, Animator, and Clash Detective, you can run a time-based clash test, as shown in Figure 10–32.

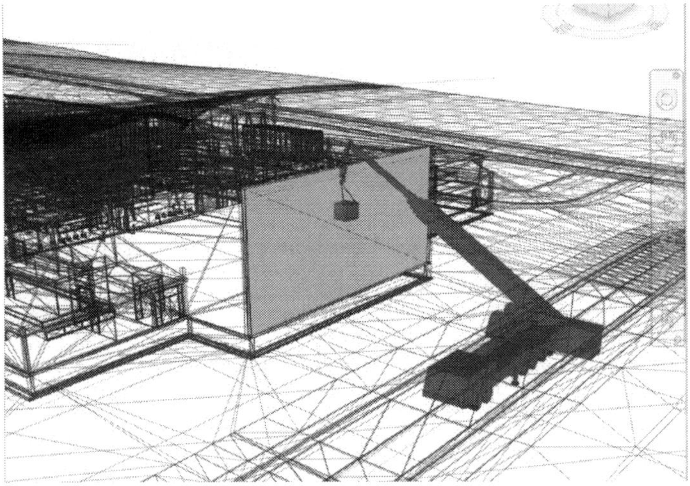

Figure 10–32

How To: Set Up a Time-Based Clash Test

1. In the *Clash Detective* window, click  (Add Test). Rename the test as required.
2. In the *Clash Detective* window, open the *Select* tab.
3. In the *Selection A* area, select the first item to compare.
4. In the *Selection B* area, select the second item to compare.
5. In the *Settings* area, expand the *Link* drop-down list and select either an animation or TimeLiner.
6. Click **Run Test**.

Hint: TimeLiner Could Interfere

If you have recently run a TimeLiner simulation, the model might still be displaying the ending scene view. This can interfere with the true results of a time-based clash test.

If you suspect that clashes should have occurred, but the result showed 0 clashes, go into the *TimeLiner* window, activate the *Tasks* tab, and then re-run the clash test.

Chapter Review Questions

1. What tab in the *TimeLiner* window would you use to manually create a Gantt chart?
    a. *Tasks* tab
    b. *Data Sources* tab
    c. *Configure* tab
    d. *Simulate* tab

2. What tab in the *TimeLiner* window would you use to set up how items display during the simulation?
    a. *Tasks* tab
    b. *Data Sources* tab
    c. *Configure* tab
    d. *Simulate* tab

3. Put the following general steps in the correct order for creating a construction simulation:
    a. Configure how objects display during the simulation.
    b. Prepare the models.
    c. Make any required changes.
    d. Create saved sets and search sets.
    e. Link the simulation to any previously created animations.
    f. Play the simulation.
    g. Add tasks to the Gantt chart.

4. Which rule would you most likely use to connect Autodesk Civil 3D corridor shapes to the task list?
    a. Map TimeLiner Tasks from Column Name to Items with the same name, Matching case
    b. Map TimeLiner Tasks from Column Name to Selection Sets with the same name, Matching case
    c. Map TimeLiner Tasks from Column Name to Layers with the same name, Matching case

5. Which window would you use to run a time-based clash detection?
   a. Selection Tree
   b. Animator
   c. TimeLiner
   d. Clash Detective

Command Summary

Button	Command	Location
	**Add Comment**	• **Window:** *TimeLiner>Tasks* tab
	**Add Configuration**	• **Window:** *TimeLiner>Configure* tab
	**Add Data Source**	• **Window:** *TimeLiner>Data Sources* tab
	**Add Task**	• **Window:** *TimeLiner>Tasks* tab
	**Attach**	• **Window:** *TimeLiner>Tasks* tab
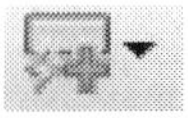	**Auto-Add Tasks**	• **Window:** *TimeLiner>Tasks* tab
	**Auto-Attach Using Rules**	• **Window:** *TimeLiner>Tasks* tab
	**Clear Attachment**	• **Window:** *TimeLiner>Tasks* tab
	**Columns**	• **Window:** *TimeLiner>Tasks* tab
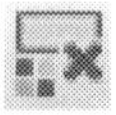	**Delete Configuration**	• **Window:** *TimeLiner>Configure* tab
	**Delete Data Source**	• **Window:** *TimeLiner>Data Sources* tab
	**Delete Task**	• **Window:** *TimeLiner>Tasks* tab
	**Export to Schedule**	• **Window:** *TimeLiner>Tasks* tab
	**Export to Sets**	• **Window:** *TimeLiner>Tasks* tab
	**Filter by Status**	• **Window:** *TimeLiner>Tasks* tab

Button	Command	Location
	**Find Items**	• **Window:** *TimeLiner>Tasks* tab
	**Forward**	• **Window:** *TimeLiner>Simulate* tab
	**Indent**	• **Window:** *TimeLiner>Tasks* tab
	**Insert Task**	• **Window:** *TimeLiner>Tasks* tab
	**Move Down**	• **Window:** *TimeLiner>Tasks* tab
	**Move Up**	• **Window:** *TimeLiner>Tasks* tab
	**Outdent**	• **Window:** *TimeLiner>Tasks* tab
	**Pause**	• **Window:** *TimeLiner>Simulate* tab
	**Play**	• **Window:** *TimeLiner>Simulate* tab
	**Play Backwards**	• **Window:** *TimeLiner>Simulate* tab
	**Refresh Data Source**	• **Window:** *TimeLiner>Data Sources* tab
	**Rewind**	• **Window:** *TimeLiner>Simulate* tab
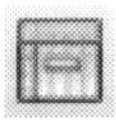	**Show Actual Dates**	• **Window:** *TimeLiner>Tasks* tab
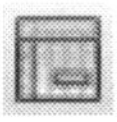	**Show Planned Dates**	• **Window:** *TimeLiner>Tasks* tab
	**Show Planned vs Actual Dates**	• **Window:** *TimeLiner>Tasks* tab
	**Show/Hide Gantt Chart**	• **Window:** *TimeLiner>Tasks* tab

Button	Command	Location
	**Step Back**	• **Window:** *TimeLiner>Simulate* tab
	**Step Forward**	• **Window:** *TimeLiner>Simulate* tab
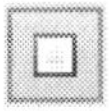	**Stop**	• **Window:** *TimeLiner>Simulate* tab
	**TimeLiner**	• **Ribbon:** *Home* tab>*Tools* panel

Chapter 11

Rendering

Autodesk® Rendering is an integral part of Autodesk® Navisworks®. It is a general-purpose rendering tool that enables you to customize a model to create physically correct renderings. Rendering uses the lighting, materials, and sun and sky settings in a model to shade the model's geometry.

Learning Objectives

- Open the Autodesk Rendering window and understand its interface.
- Select materials from the Autodesk Material Libraries and add them to the document library.
- Edit a material using the Material Editor and edit material mapping values for a material.
- Create and edit lights in an Autodesk Navisworks scene.
- Enable the use and display of the sun and sky lighting effects in the scene view.
- Understand the purpose of the fields in the *Environment* tab that deal with exposure.
- Render and save photorealistic images using the Autodesk Rendering tool.

BIM Workflow: Communicate

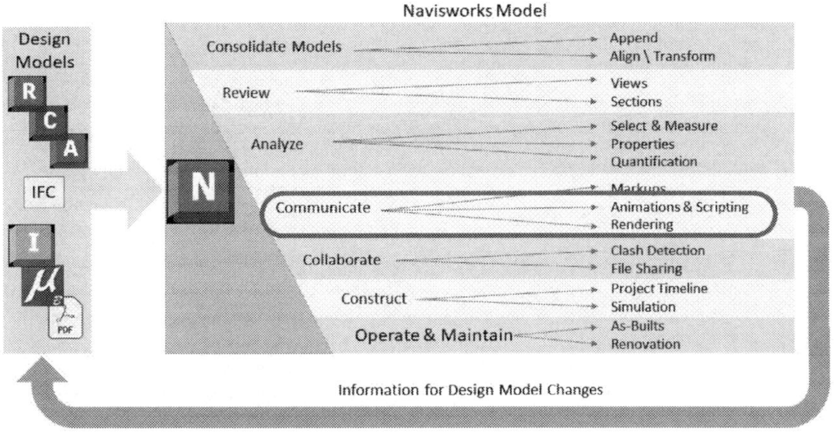

11.1 Autodesk Rendering Overview

Overview of the Autodesk Rendering Environment

The Autodesk Rendering window enables you to create, edit, and apply materials, lights, and environments to your Navisworks files. To open the Autodesk Rendering window, in the *Home* tab>*Tools* panel, click (Autodesk Rendering). Alternatively, in the *View* tab, expand the Windows options and click **Autodesk Rendering** in the drop-down list. You can also select the *Render* tab>*System* panel and click (Autodesk Rendering). The Autodesk Rendering window contains multiple commands and tabs. Each tab is broken into areas, as shown in Figure 11–1 for the *Materials* tab.

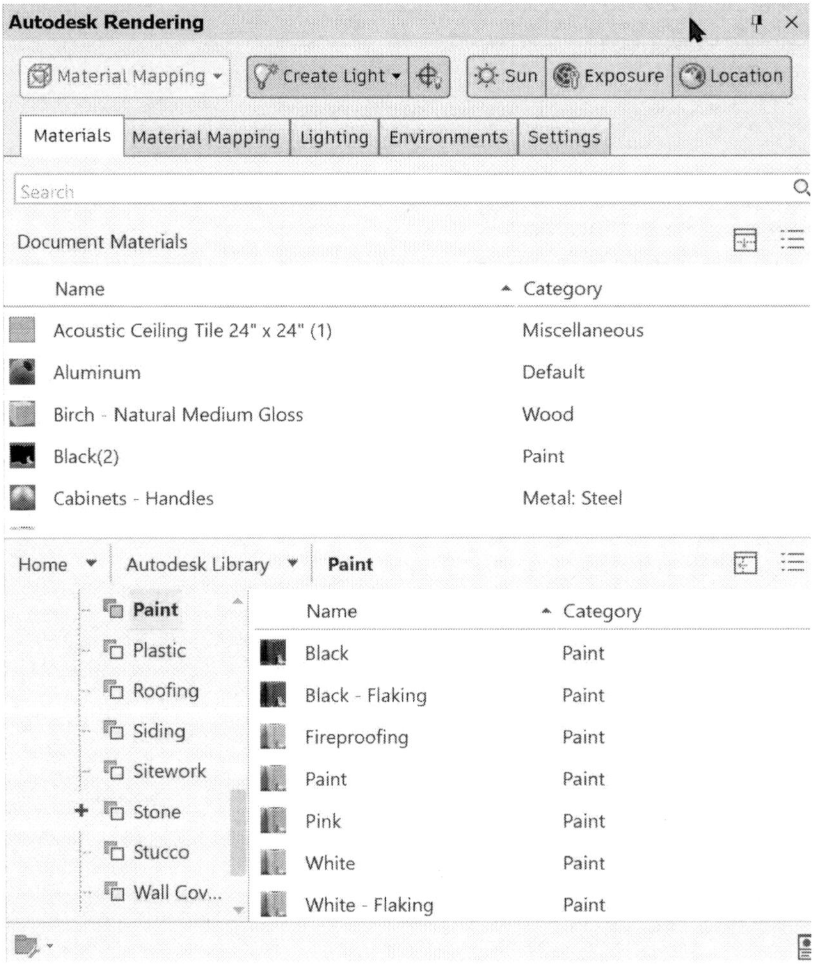

Figure 11–1

The buttons in the Rendering toolbar along the top of the Autodesk Rendering window enable you to define material mapping, create lights, toggle light glyphs, or enable/disable sun, exposure, and location settings. Selecting any of these options directly activates the appropriate tab for the button.

Overview of the Rendering Workflow

Using the Autodesk Rendering tools available in Navisworks enables you to create highly detailed and photorealistic images.

How To: Render a Navisworks Scene

1. Open the Autodesk Rendering window.
2. Set up the model geometry for the scene.
    - Apply materials and material mappings. You can apply materials to objects selected in the scene view.
    - Add artificial and natural lights. Photometric lights (artificial lighting) accurately define lights in a scene. Sun and Sky lighting simulates the effect of sunlight and sky illumination (natural lighting).
    - Define the exposure settings to control how real-world luminance values are converted into an image.
    - Orient the scene view with the required orientation and zoom level.
3. Select the rendering method (cloud or local).
4. Select the rendering quality.
5. Render the image.
6. Save (or download) the rendered image.

Hint: Navisworks Presenter Assigned Materials

In earlier versions of Navisworks, there was a rendering environment called Presenter. This tool has been removed from the software. Any materials that were assigned using the Presenter tool will have to be reassigned using the current Autodesk materials.

11.2 Materials

Materials are available in the Navisworks material libraries to enable you to assign real-world materials, such as plastic, wood, and glass, to objects in a model to give it a more realistic appearance.

Materials Tab

In the *Autodesk Rendering* window, select the *Materials* tab, as shown in Figure 11–2. The *Materials* tab provides access to the *Library* panel and the *Document Materials* panel.

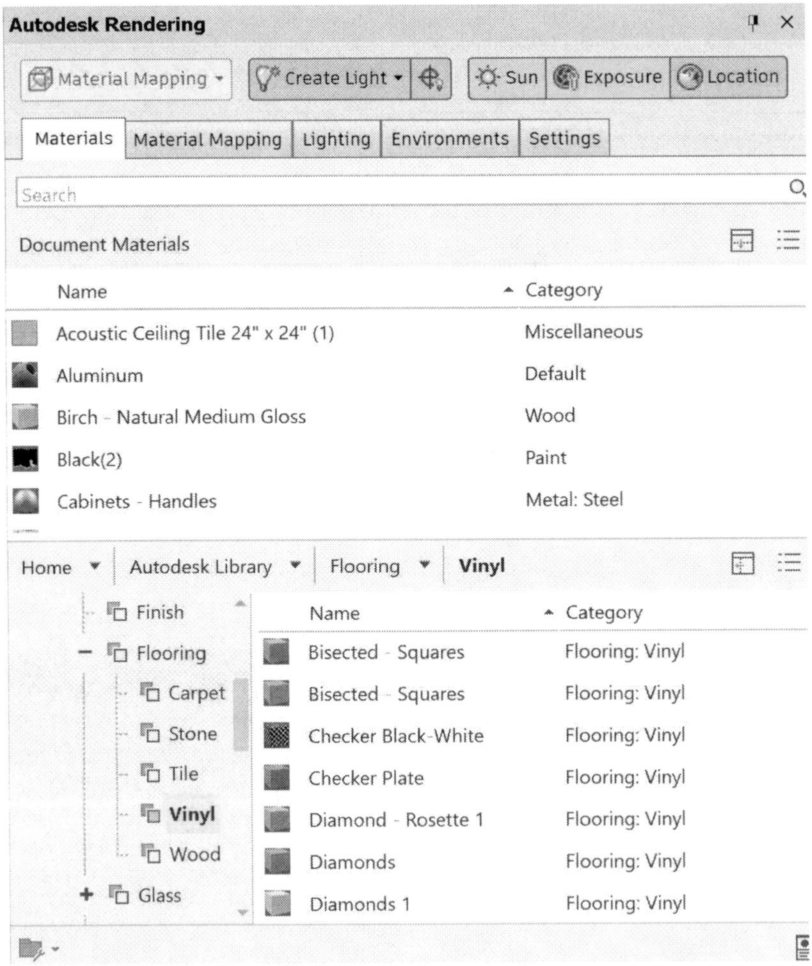

Figure 11–2

Library Panel

The *Library* panel is located in the lower half of the *Autodesk Rendering* dialog box, as shown in Figure 11–3. It provides access to the library of materials (standard and advanced) that are provided with Navisworks. Materials are selected in the library and then added to the current model for use.

To navigate the *Library* panel, expand the *Autodesk Library* folder in the left pane and then further expand any required nodes to find the required material categories. Select the category in the left pane to display its list of materials. Once a material has been located, select it in the pane on the right. When you hover your cursor over the material swatch, the buttons for applying or editing the material will display. The list of materials can be sorted by selecting the column headers in this panel.

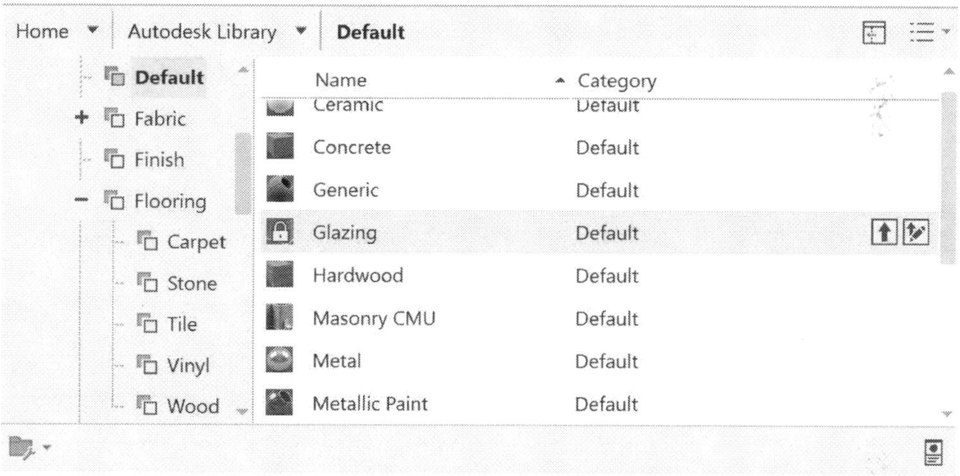

Figure 11–3

As you navigate through the nodes, the path is displayed at the top of the *Library* panel. You can use the drop-down arrows in the components of this path as another means of navigation, as shown in Figure 11–4.

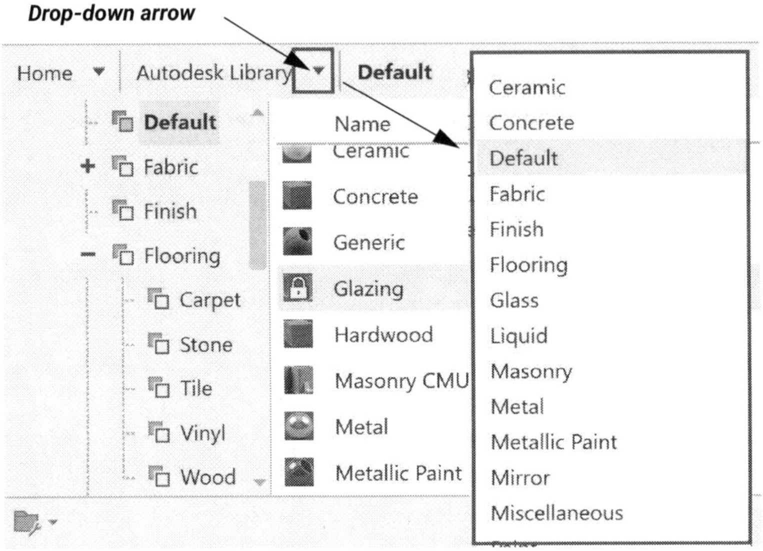

Figure 11–4

The following libraries are available in the *Library* panel:

- The *Autodesk Library*, which contains read-only materials provided by Autodesk.
- The *User Library*, which contains your own custom materials that you have modified and saved based on Autodesk materials or that you have created yourself.

The header for the *Library* panel lists the full path to the selected material category. Additionally, the header provides the  (Show/Hide Library Tree) and  (Display Options) icons to filter or control the display of the panel.  enables you to show and hide the Library tree.  enables you to customize the display type for materials. For example, you can control the library that is shown, the type of view (thumbnail, list, or text), how the list is sorted, and the thumbnail size.

Document Materials Panel

The *Document Materials* panel (shown in Figure 11–5) is located in the upper portion of the *Autodesk Rendering* dialog box and lists the materials that have been included for use in the document. These materials can consist of materials that have been applied or that have not yet been applied. Library materials must be added to the *Document Materials* panel if they are to be used in the model.

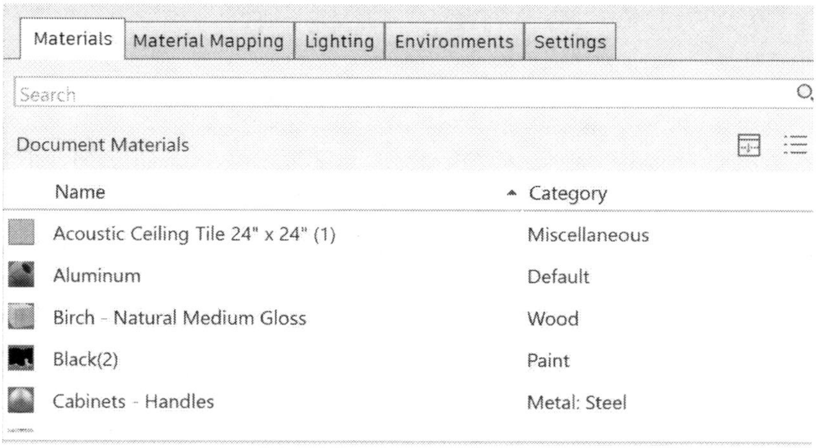

Figure 11–5

The header for the *Document Materials* panel also contains the and icons. These icons enable you to show or hide the *Document Materials* panel and customize the display type for the document materials, respectively.

Adding Materials to the Document

When a model is first created in Navisworks, it does not contain any materials unless they are brought in with the source CAD or BIM file. To assign materials to objects in the model, materials must be selected from a library and added to the document.

How To: Add Materials to the Document Materials Panel

1. Browse to the required material in the *Library* panel.
   - Consider using the **Search** field at the top of the *Materials* tab to locate specific materials in the library.
2. Select the material in the pane on the right and click to add the material to the current document. Alternatively, right-click the material and select **Add to>Document Materials**. A copy of this material is now available in the *Document Materials* panel for use in the current model.
   - If an object has been preselected in the scene, the material is also assigned to that object.
   - Click to add the material to the current document and immediately open the material in the *Material Editor*. If an object is selected, it also applies the material to that object.

Applying Materials to Model Objects

Once a model has been brought into Navisworks and materials have been added to the document, you can add materials to the objects in the model. You can apply materials to objects that have been selected in the scene view or in the *Selection Tree*. Materials are applied to an item, layer, etc., depending on the resolution setting of the Selection tool.

How To: Apply a Material to Items in the Scene

1. Select items in the scene using any of the following techniques:
    - Select individual items directly in the scene view or press and hold <Ctrl> to select multiple files.
    - Select individual items directly in the *Selection Tree* or press and hold <Ctrl> to select multiple items in the *Selection Tree*. To select a range of files, press and hold <Shift> while selecting two items to also select all of the items listed between them.
    - Select all of the items included in a selection or search set by selecting a name in the Sets window.

    Note: *Using search sets has the added benefit of materials being easily applied to items that are added to the model at a later stage.*

2. In the *Autodesk Rendering* window, use any of the following techniques:
    - In the *Document Materials* panel, right-click the required material and click **Apply to Selection**.
    - In the *Library* panel, navigate to and select the required material and click . Once selected, the material is copied to the *Document Materials* panel and assigned to an object if it is selected in the model.
    - Click and drag the required material directly onto an item from either the *Document Materials* panel or the *Library* panel. If you click and drag from the *Library* panel, the material is also added to the *Document Materials* panel.
3. Press <Esc> to clear item selection and view the item(s) with the applied materials.

Once a model has had a material assigned to it, that material can be overwritten with another material by selecting the object again and assigning a new material. Alternatively, you can remove the material that was previously assigned by selecting the object, right-clicking, and selecting **Reset Item>Reset Appearance**.

Rename and Manage Materials

Materials that are copied from the *Library* panel to the *Document Materials* panel have the same name as the one in the library by default. Once the material is copied to the document, you can maintain this name or rename it for easy reference, reuse, and management. Renaming materials is recommended if a library material is edited to help identify that it is different than the material in the library. Once materials have been customized in the *Document Materials* panel, they can be saved for reuse in other documents using the *Favorites* library.

How To: Rename a Material

1. Right-click the material in the *Document Materials* panel and select **Rename**.
2. Enter a descriptive name and press <Enter>.
3. It is useful to prefix the new material name with your company's initials for easy identification of a customized material.

How To: Manage Materials in the Favorites Library

1. Right-click the material in the *Document Materials* panel and select **Add to>Favorites**.
2. Navigate to the top of the *Library* tree and select the **Favorites** library node. The added document material displays in the pane on the right.
3. To further organize materials in the *Favorites* library, right-click the **Favorites** node and select **Create Category** to create a new category. Right-click the category, select **Rename**, and enter a new descriptive name for the category. Sub-categories can also be created. Materials can be dragged and dropped between categories, as required.
    - Once a category has been added to the *Favorites* library, you can add materials either to the top level or to a category when you use the **Add** option in the *Document Materials* panel.

Note: *Materials that are deleted from the Document Materials panel are also cleared from any object they have previously been assigned to.*

Material Editor

A material is defined by its properties. The available properties depend on the selected material type. Use the *Material Editor* to review and edit the properties of a material. Materials in the Autodesk materials library cannot be modified, but they can be used to create new materials.

To open the *Material Editor*, use one of the following techniques:

- Double-click a material in the *Document Materials* panel.
- Right-click a material in the *Document Materials* panel and select **Edit**.

- Select a material in the *Autodesk Library* and click [icon]. This option adds the material to the *Document Materials* panel and opens the *Material Editor* at the same time. If an object is selected, it also assigns the material to the model.

The *Material Editor* contains two tabs: the *Appearance* tab and the *Information* tab.

> ***Note:*** *Other Autodesk programs have more tabs when editing materials, such as Graphics, Physical Properties, and Thermal Properties.*

Appearance Tab

The *Appearance* tab is used to change how a material will display, as shown in Figure 11–6. The options available in this tab change depending on which material type is selected.

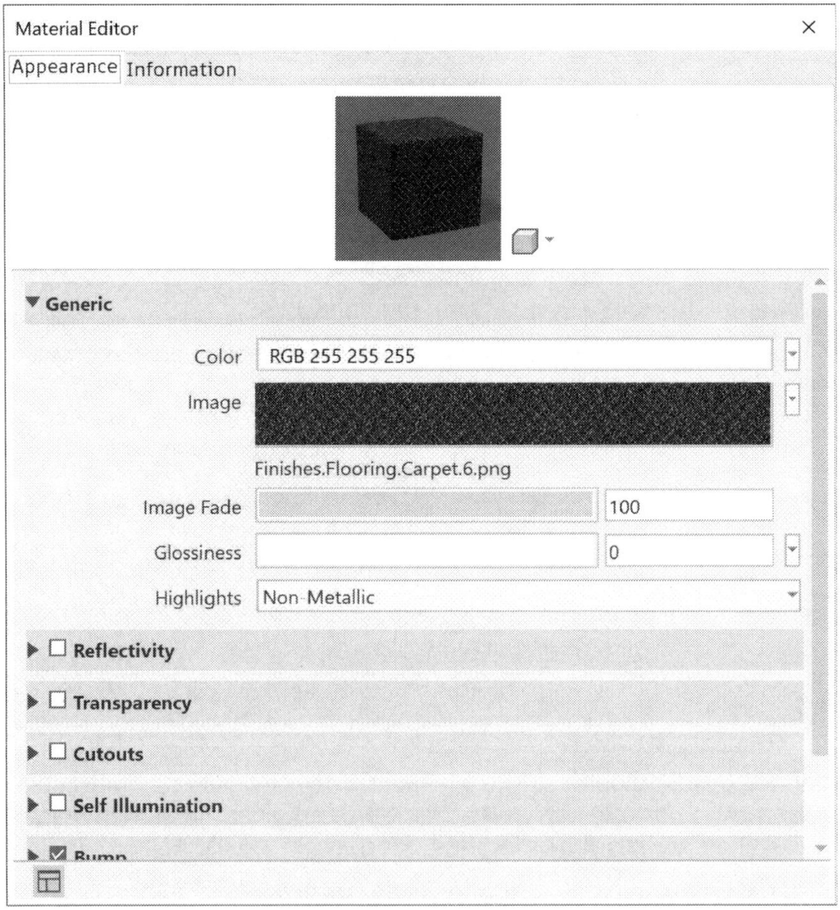

Figure 11–6

The following are consistent tools that are available for all material types when using the *Material Editor*:

- Click [icon] next to the lower right corner of the thumbnail image to access a list of display options for the thumbnail.
- The [icon] icon, at the bottom of the *Material Editor*, enables you to toggle the display of the Autodesk Rendering window on and off.

The following categories can be customized to define a material's properties:

> ***Note:*** *When creating or editing materials other than the Generic type, the list of available options for customizing the material might vary slightly.*

Generic: The *Generic* category is required for all materials.

- **Color:** Assigns the color of the material.
- **Image:** Assigns textures to a material's color. The texture would display on the assigned material color. Two types of textures can be used: image (1) and procedural-based (2), as shown in Figure 11–7.

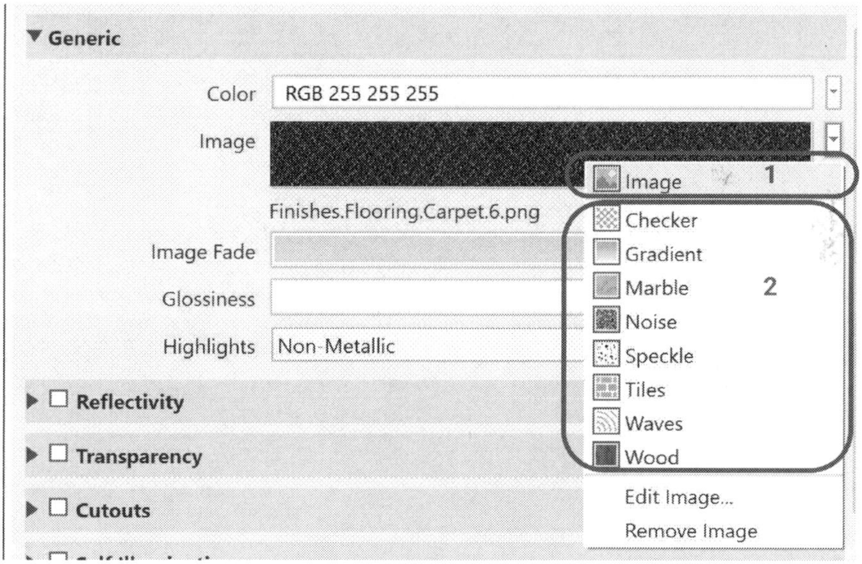

Figure 11–7

- Image textures (1) are assigned using the **Image** option and use an image representing a certain texture. For example, you can use an image representing wood, concrete, brass, or weave.

- Procedural-based textures (2) are selected from the predefined list and represent repetitive texture patterns, as shown in Figure 11–8.

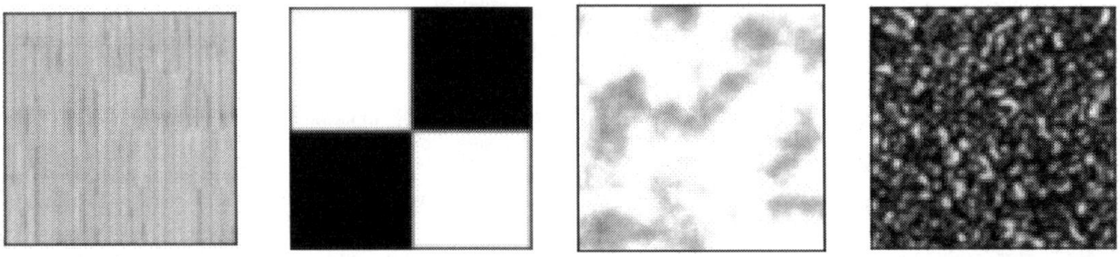

Marble ***Checker*** ***Speckle*** ***Noise***

Figure 11–8

Hint: Texture Editor

Navisworks has a *Texture Editor* that can be used to edit either image or procedural-based textures. To open the *Texture Editor*, double-click the image field when a texture has been assigned. Refer to ***Texture Editor*** in the Navisworks Help documentation for more information on using the *Texture Editor*.

- **Image Fade**
- **Glossiness**
- **Highlights**

The remaining categories can be selected to activate them and then expanded to assign values for them. These enable you to control reflectivity, transparency, cutouts, self-illumination, bump maps, and tint.

Information Tab

The *Information* tab (shown in Figure 11–9) contains general information on the material and its type.

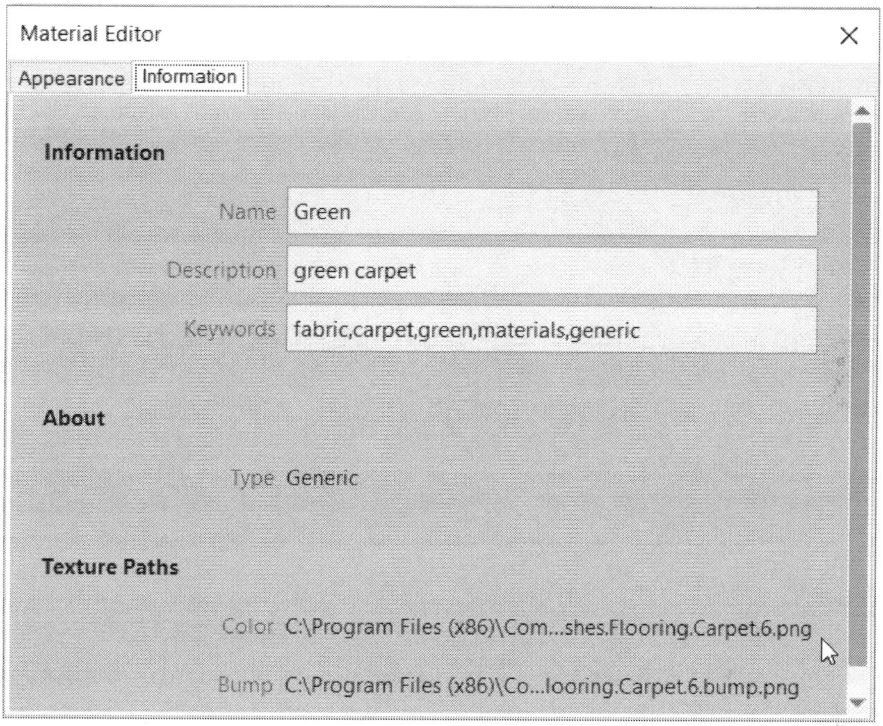

Figure 11–9

Creating Materials

You can also create your own custom materials for your project.

How To: Create a New Material

1. To create a new material, select an existing material from a library and add it to the *Document Materials* list using one of the following techniques:
    - Select the material in the pane on the right and click to add the material to the current document.
    - Select the material in the pane on the right and click to add it to the current document and immediately open it in the *Material Editor*.
    - Right-click the material and select **Add to>Document Materials**.

2. Double-click on the material in the *Document Materials* list to open the *Material Editor*. If you used the icon to add the material, the *Material Editor* will already be open.
3. Click the *Appearance* tab and modify the options in all of the required categories.
4. In the *Material Editor*, click the *Information* tab and enter a name, description, and any required keywords for the material.
5. Close the *Material Editor* to save the material to the *Document Materials* panel.

   Note: *Consider copying the material to a Favorites library for easy retrieval and reuse in other documents.*

Editing Materials

Materials can be edited once they have been added to the *Document Materials* panel. Editing materials enables you to adjust the properties of any *Autodesk Library* materials or any of the custom materials that have been created to improve or enhance their appearance.

How To: Edit an Applied Material

1. To open the *Material Editor*, do one of the following:
   - Double-click a material in the *Document Materials* panel.
   - Right-click a material in the *Document Materials* panel and select **Edit**.
2. Using the *Material Editor*, make the required changes to the options available in the *Appearance* and *Information* tabs.
3. Close the *Material Editor* to save the material to the *Document Materials* panel.
   - If the material has been assigned to the model, its appearance updates to reflect the changes.

11.3 Material Mapping

When mapping a material to an item, Navisworks initially determines the best mapping solution using one of the following options (shown in Figure 11–10). Each option will shrink-wrap the material texture to the geometry boundary as accurately as possible.

- **Planar mapping**
- **Box mapping**
- **Spherical mapping**
- **Cylindrical mapping**
- **Explicit mapping**

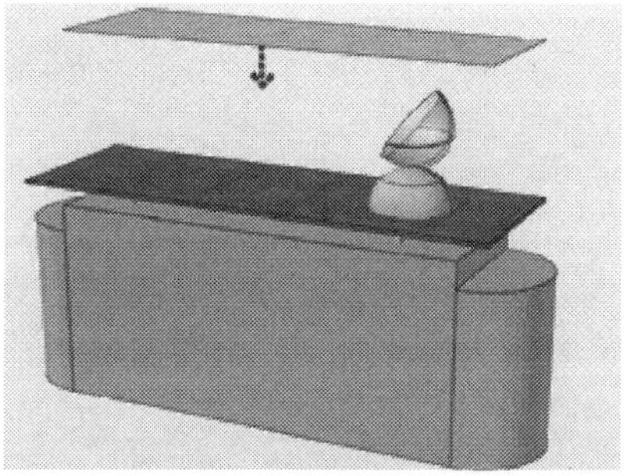

Planar mapping

Spherical mapping

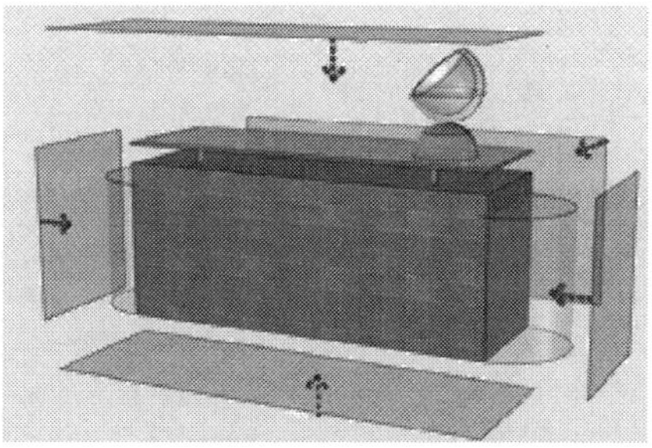

Box mapping

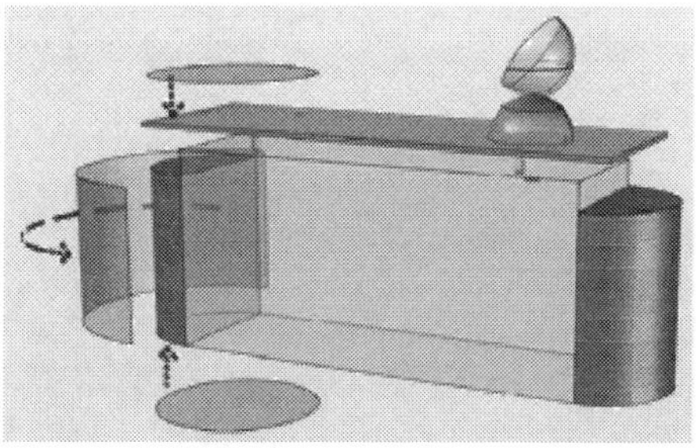

Cylindrical mapping

Figure 11–10

If the resulting mapping is not how you intended it, you can edit the texture space using the options in the *Material Mapping* tab.

Material Mapping Tab

The *Material Mapping* tab controls the texture spacing and proportions used when a textured material is assigned to an object. To change the type of texture spacing used, you select the object in the scene and then use the mapping type drop-down list. To edit the assigned texture space's settings, use the options in the *Material Mapping* tab, as shown in Figure 11–11.

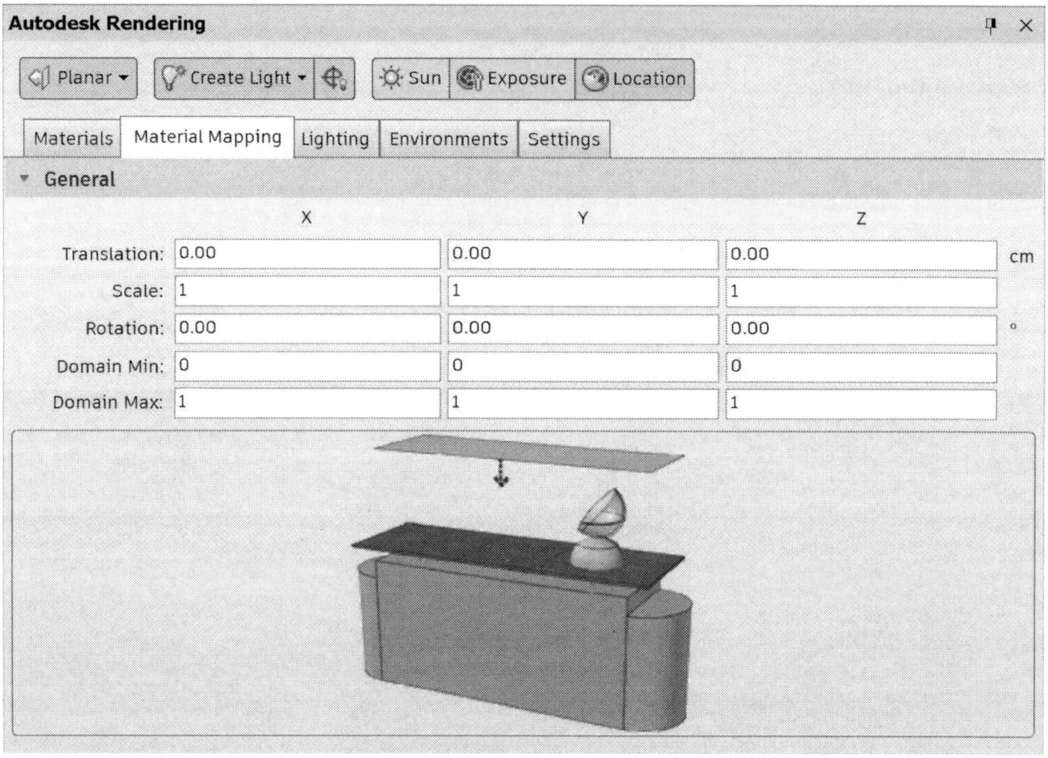

Figure 11–11

Material Mapping Drop-Down List

The *Material Mapping* drop-down list, shown in Figure 11–12, identifies the current texture space setting used on the object and can be used to assign a new type. Select the drop-down list to access and select another type.

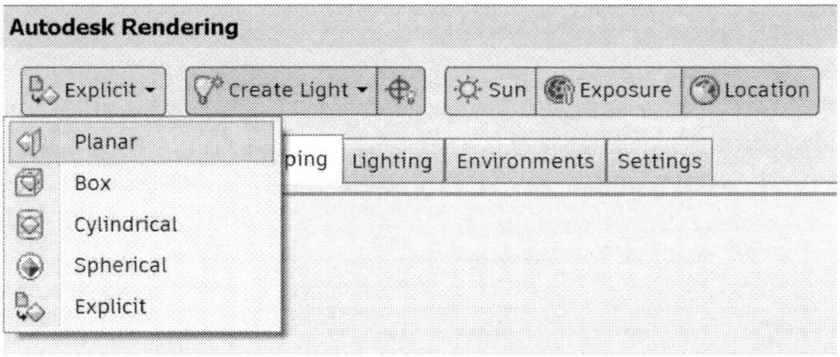

Figure 11–12

Material Mapping Settings

The *Material Mapping* tab provides fields that can be customized to refine the mapping settings, as shown in Figure 11–13. The fields are dependent on the active texture space setting.

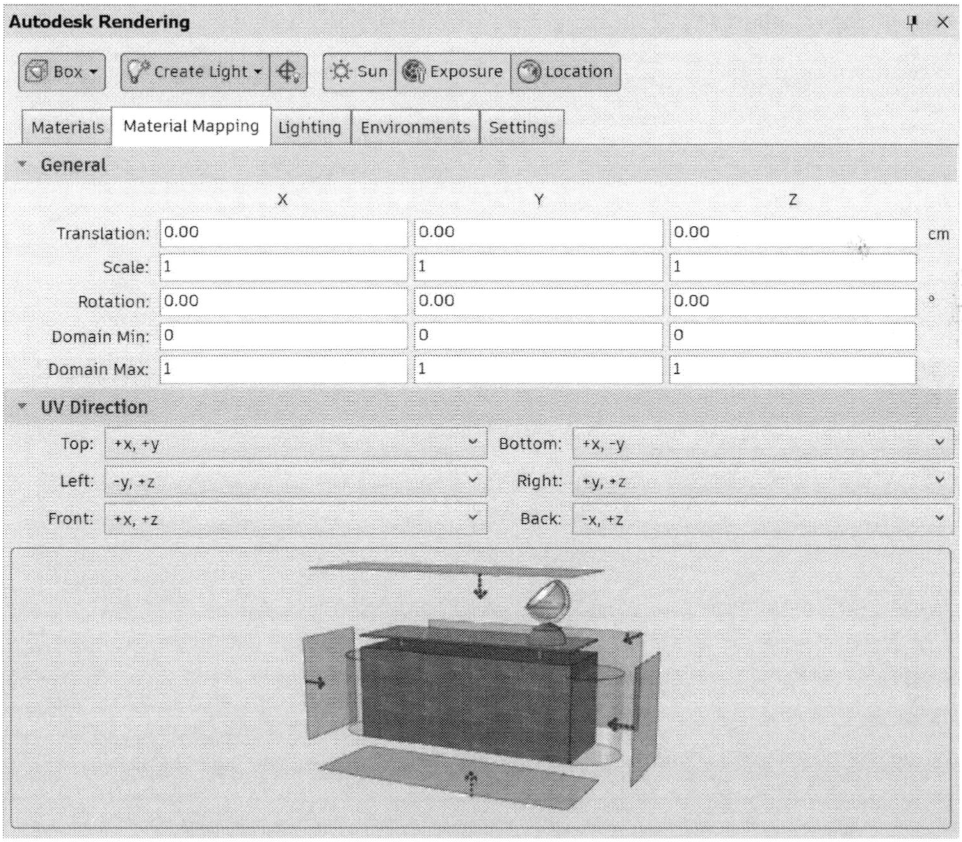

Figure 11–13

Adjusting Material Mapping

You can change the texture space setting in the *Rendering* toolbar by selecting a new option in the *Material Mapping* drop-down list. You can also adjust the fields that define the current mapping to adjust how a material map is placed, oriented, and scaled.

How To: Adjust the Material Mapping Settings

1. Select an object in the scene view or in the *Selection Tree* that you want to work with.
2. If no material has been previously added to the object, select the *Materials* tab, right-click on a material, and select **Assign to Selection**. Alternatively, you can click and drag the required material onto the object.
3. The current texture space setting is listed in the *Rendering* toolbar (e.g., Box, Cylindrical, Spherical, Planar, or Explicit). If this current setting is not appropriate, select a new type that is appropriate for the object.
4. Use the fields in the *Material Mapping* tab to adjust the mapping setting, as required. A preview of the result is shown in the scene view in real time.

Practice 11a
Add and Map Materials

Practice Objectives

- Navigate around the *Autodesk Rendering* window.
- Apply materials to objects.
- Apply material mapping to objects.

In this practice, you will study the *Autodesk Rendering* window, apply materials to objects, create a new material from an existing material, and map materials to better fit the object.

Task 1: Add materials.

1. Open **School-Lobby-Materials.nwf** from the *Navisworks BIM Practice Files\Rendering* folder.

2. In the *Home* tab>*Tools* panel, click  (Autodesk Rendering) to open the *Autodesk Rendering* window.

   Note: *The Autodesk Rendering window can also be displayed by selecting* ***Autodesk Rendering*** *in the View tab>Workspace panel>expanded Windows.*

3. In the *Saved Viewpoints* window, select **Lobby** to change the viewpoint to an internal view of the entrance lobby of the school.
4. In the *Viewpoint* tab>*Render Style* panel, expand **Lighting** and select **Scene Lights**. The **Scene Lights** option uses the lights defined in the source BIM model. The difference is noticeable as these light sources are imported from Autodesk Revit.
5. In the *Viewpoint* tab>*Render Style* panel, expand **Lighting** and select **Head Light**. This type uses a single directional light located at the camera (viewer) in addition to an ambient light. This mode is commonly used when working in Navisworks.

6. Select the other options in the *Lighting* drop-down list, as shown in Figure 11–14, and note the difference in lighting in the scene.

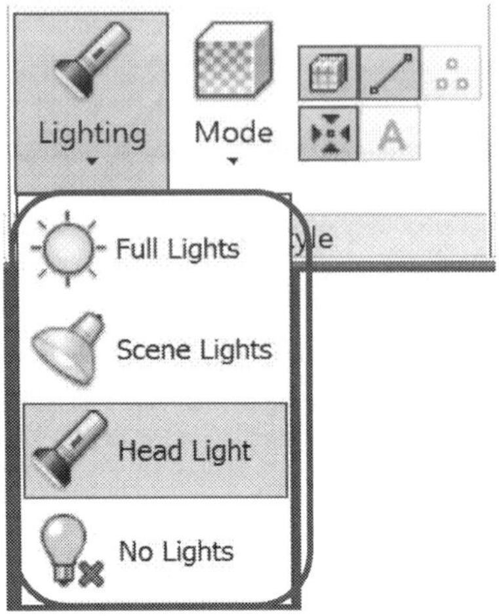

Figure 11–14

7. Change the *Lighting* style back to **Head Light**, if not already set.
8. In the *Render Style* panel, expand **Mode** and select all the options in the drop-down list to view the difference in lighting on the screen. Note that the icon in the panel changes to reflect the current mode, as shown in Figure 11–15. This is also true of the *Lighting* drop-down list.

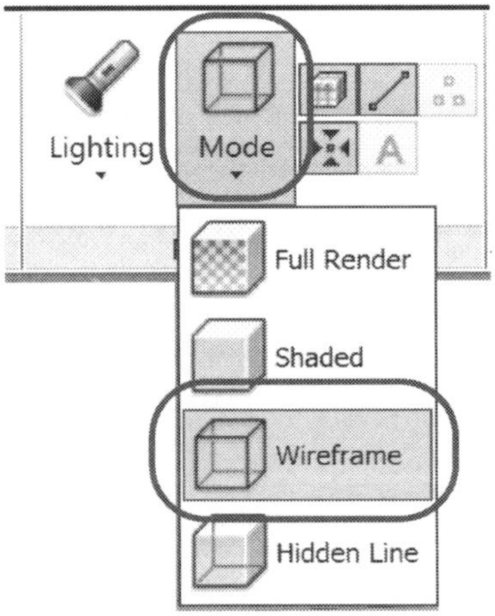

Figure 11–15

9. Change the *Render* mode back to **Full Render** to display a smooth rendering that includes all of the materials.
10. In the *Autodesk Rendering* window, select the *Materials* tab. The *Document Materials* panel is populated with the materials that have been brought in from the source Autodesk Revit model.
11. In the scene view, select a wall on the left side of the lobby and continue hovering your mouse over the wall until the tooltip displays. The tooltip lists the *Item Type* as **Rooms**, as shown in Figure 11–16. Also note that the selection is not just showing the wall selected; the entire room is highlighted.

Figure 11–16

12. *Rooms* are special organizational objects used in Autodesk Revit that have little value in Navisworks. Therefore, you can hide all the rooms to help avoid their selection. In the *Selection Tree*, go to the top of the branch of the selected object. Right-click on **Rooms**, and select **Hide**, as shown in Figure 11–17, to hide all of the rooms in the model. You could also press <Ctrl>+<H> to hide them.

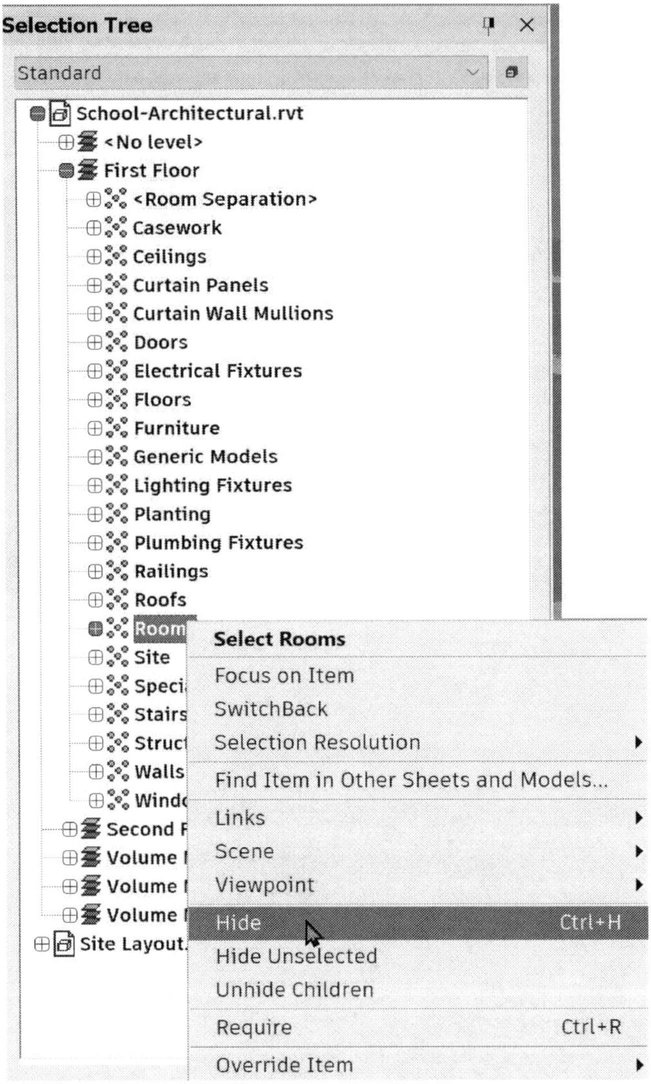

Figure 11–17

13. Set the *Selection Resolution* to **Geometry**.

14. In the scene view, select the two walls on the left side of the lobby so that only the two walls are selected, as shown in Figure 11–18. Hold <Ctrl> when selecting the second wall in order to select both walls.

Figure 11–18

15. In the Autodesk Rendering window, in the *Materials* tab, expand *Autodesk Library* and select the **Wall Paint** category. In the pane on the right, right-click the **Aquamarine** color and select **Assign to Selection**, as shown in Figure 11–19.

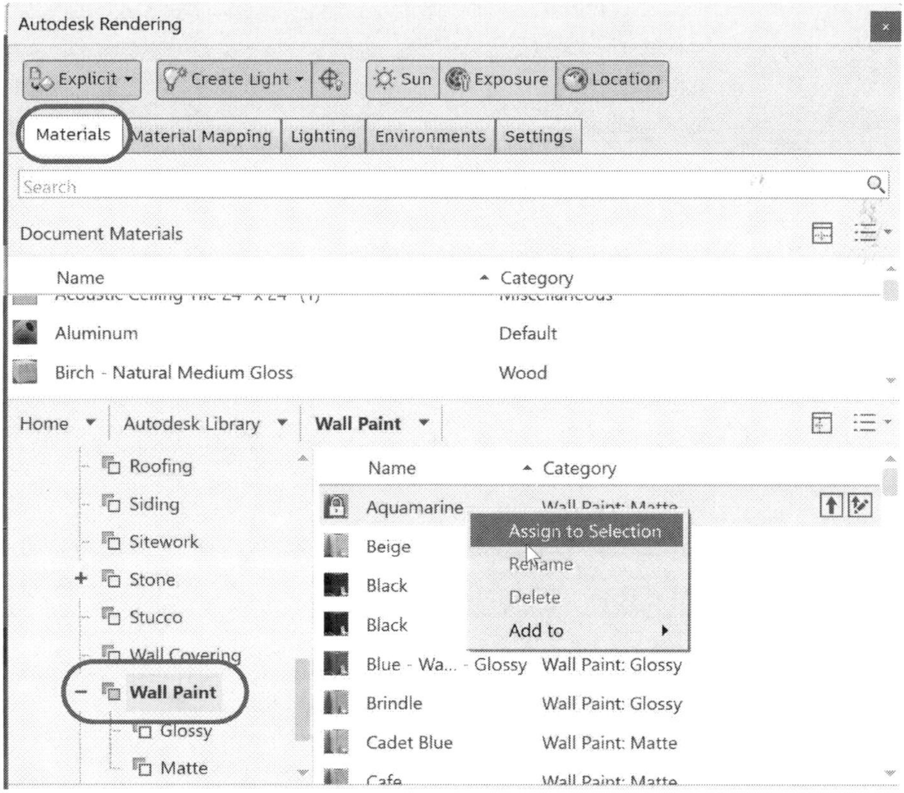

Figure 11–19

16. Clear the selection in the scene view by pressing <Esc> or clicking  (Select None) in the *Home* tab>*Select & Search* panel, and note that the **Aquamarine Wall Paint** material has been added to the wall. It has also been added to the *Document Materials* list, above the *Autodesk Library* list.

17. In the *Selection Tree*, expand **School-Architectural.rvt**>*First Floor*>*Generic Models*. Expand one of the **Table-Lamp** objects and select **Porcelain, Navy Blue**, as shown in Figure 11–20.

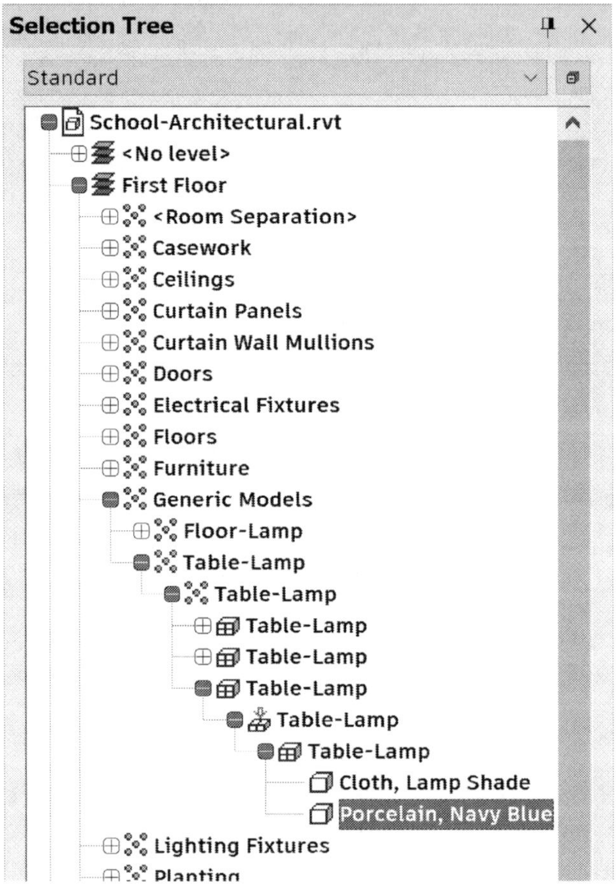

Figure 11–20

18. In the *Home* tab>*Select & Search* panel, expand **Select Same** and select **Same Name**. All three of the table lamp bases in the lobby are selected.

19. In the *Material Library*, expand the **Stone>Marble** category. In the right pane, right-click on the **Coarse Polished-White** material and select **Assign to Selection**.

20. In the scene view, select the hallway ceiling, which is at the top of the scene in the **Lobby** viewpoint.

21. In the *Material Library*, select the **Stucco** category. In the right pane, right-click on the **Exterior-Beige** material and select **Assign to Selection**.
22. Clear the selection.
23. In the *Autodesk Rendering* window, in the *Document Materials* panel, scroll to the **Metal - Aluminum (1)** material. Right-click on this material and select **Select Objects Applied To**. All of the curtain wall mullions and door handles are selected in the scene view.
24. Double-click the **Metal - Aluminum (1)** material in the list to open the *Material Editor*, as shown in Figure 11–21. Note that this material is **Satin Aluminum**, which is a matte material. Close the *Material Editor*.

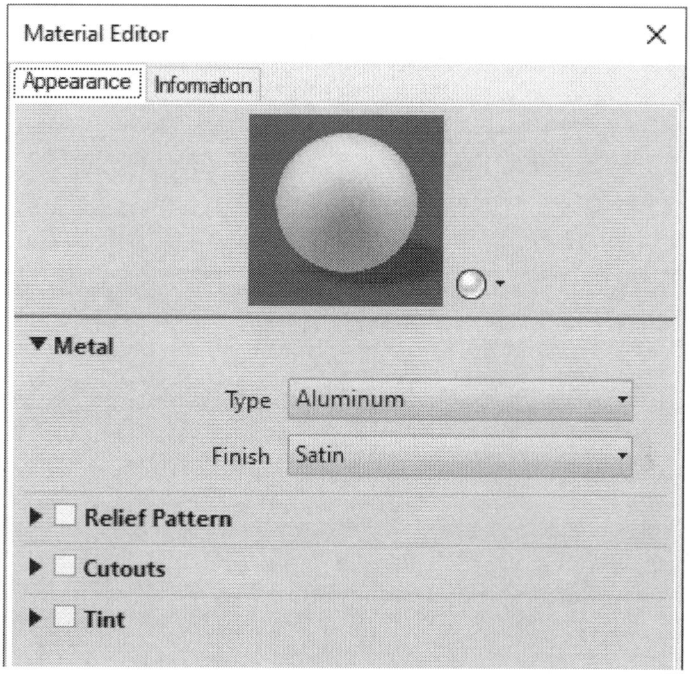

Figure 11–21

25. In the *Autodesk Rendering* window, in the *Autodesk Library*, select the **Metal** category. In the right pane, double-click the **Bronze-Satin Hammered** material to open the *Material Editor*, as shown in Figure 11–22. Note that this material is not a reflective material. Close the *Material Editor*.

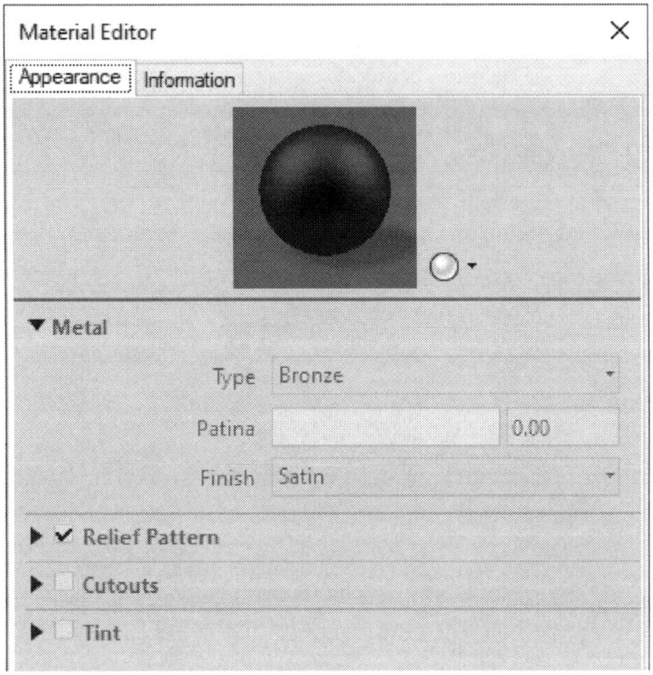

Figure 11–22

26. Ensure that all the mullions are still selected in the *Selection Tree*. In the *Material Library*, right-click the **Bronze-Satin Hammered** material and select **Assign to Selection**.

Task 2: Map materials.

1. In the scene view, select the gray floor of the lobby and hallways (not the shiny entrance tile). Verify in the *Selection Tree* that the **5" Concrete>Floor** object is selected.
2. In the *Autodesk Rendering* window, in the *Autodesk Library*, expand the *Flooring>Carpet* category. In the right pane, right-click the **Sisal - Lines** material and select **Assign to Selection**.
3. Clear the selection of the floor in the scene view. Note that the pattern is on the floor.
4. Select the floor (**5" Concrete>Floor** object) again.
5. In the *Autodesk Rendering* window, ensure that **Sisal - Lines** is selected in the *Document Materials* area. Select the *Material Mapping* tab.

6. In the *Material Mapping* drop-down list, select **Planar** to change the mapping type for the floor, as shown in Figure 11–23.

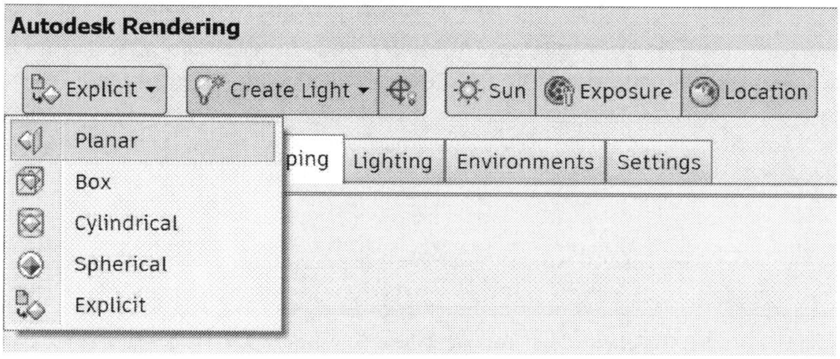

Figure 11–23

7. In the *Material Mapping* tab, in the *General* settings, change the *Rotation* to **90.00** for the X-direction, as shown in Figure 11–24. Press <Enter>.

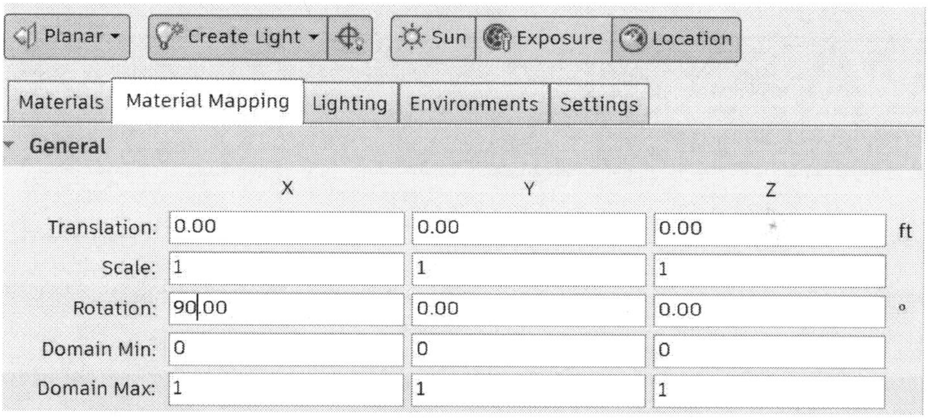

Figure 11–24

8. Clear the selection of the floor and note the rotated carpet pattern.
9. Save the file and leave it open. You can continue working on this file in the next practice.

End of practice

11.4 Lighting

Lighting is used in models to further customize a more realistic rendering then what materials alone can provide. Lighting also enhances the overall scene in which the model is presented. There are multiple types of lights that can be incorporated into a scene, including artificial lights and natural lights.

Artificial Lights

Scenes illuminated with point, spot, distant, or web lights are using artificially illuminated light sources. Artificial lights are subdivided into two types: photometric and standard.

Photometric lights provide lighting options as they would be in the real world. Point, spot, and web lights are photometric lights.

- **Point Light:** A point light illuminates everything around it.
- **Spot Light:** A spot light has a hotspot and falloff cone area that are defined by an angular value that radiates from the source.
  - The hotspot is the brightest area of the light beam.
  - The falloff defines the full cone of light.

  Note: *Using the light gizmos, you can adjust the sharpness or softness of the light by adjusting the hotspot and falloff angles.*

  - The difference between the hotspot and falloff angles determines the sharpness of the edge of the light beam. Angles that are near equal will produce a sharp edge while angles with a greater difference will produce a softer edge. These values can be adjusted directly using the light's gizmo.
- **Web Light:** A web light can use data provided by manufacturers of real-world lights to represent irregular light distributions, giving the light a more precise representation when rendered versus using spot or point lights.
  - You can set a light's distribution, intensity, color, and other characteristics, such as IES standard file format.

Standard lights are objects that mimic lights in a rendered image. The distant light type is a standard light. You can set its intensity and color values.

- **Distant Light:** A distant light shines uniform parallel light rays in a single direction. The light's intensity does not diminish and it is generally used to illuminate objects or uniformly illuminate a backdrop.

Use standard lights when you want to create and control a required effect in rendering and use photometric lights to enable the scene to render based on how the lights would look in the real world.

Natural Light

Natural light includes the **Sun** and **Sky** lighting system. Once enabled, the options for this are controlled in the *Environments* tab and the *Rendering* toolbar. Natural light does not use light glyphs because the sun lights up an entire scene.

Lighting Units

Both international (SI) and American lighting units are available.

Lighting Tab

The *Lighting* tab of the *Autodesk Rendering* window, shown in Figure 11–25, enables you to manage lights. The creation, use, and settings for those lights are managed using the following interface items:

- *Rendering* toolbar
- *Lights* panel
- *Properties* panel

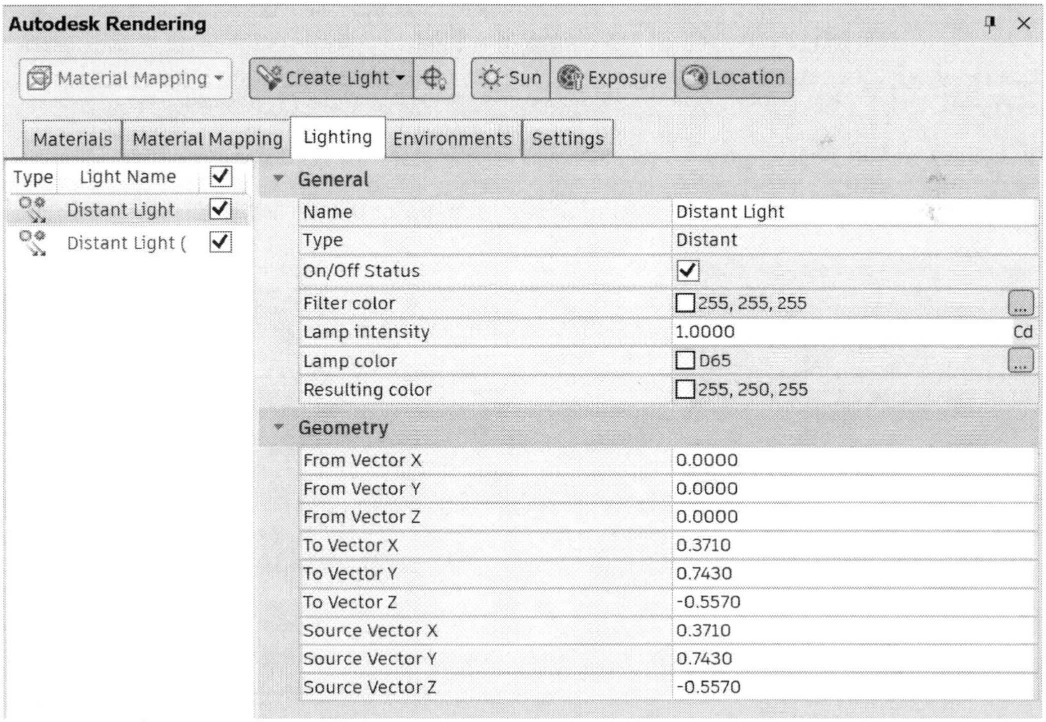

Figure 11–25

Rendering Toolbar

The *Create Light* drop-down list, located in the *Rendering* toolbar, enables you to create light sources in the scene view. The available light types are:

- **Point**
- **Spot**
- **Distant**
- **Web**

Once lights are placed in a model, they are represented by unique light glyphs indicating their location and type (point, spot, distant, or web). You can toggle the display of light glyphs on or off while you work by using (Light Glyphs) in the *Rendering* toolbar to control the display of the glyphs in the current viewpoint. **Note:** This does not toggle the light sources on or off.

Lights Panel

> ***Note:*** *The sun and sky light is not included in the Lights panel.*

The *Lights* panel is on the left side of the *Lights* tab. Use the **Status** checkbox to toggle the lights on and off, as needed. To display the light's properties, select it in the list. Selecting a light in the *Lights* panel also highlights it in the model (if the glyphs are displayed).

- An unlimited number of lights can be used in your model. To limit the lights used to a certain number of lights, click (Application Menu)**>Options>Interface>Display> Autodesk** and clear the **Use Unlimited Lights** option.

Properties Panel

The *Properties* panel displays the properties of the selected light. These can be modified as needed to update the lighting for the scene. The effects of changes are visible in the scene view in real time. The following general properties are available for artificial light types.

- **General Properties**
  - Name
  - Type
  - On/Off Status
  - Filter color
  - Lamp intensity
  - Lamp color
  - Resulting color
  - Hotspot and Falloff angle (spot light only)
  - IES filename and location (web light only)
- **Geometry:** Geometry properties enable you to enter specific values to control the light's location in the scene.

Creating Lights

The procedure for creating the four types of artificial lights is similar and involves the initial use of the *Create Light* drop-down list in the *Rendering* toolbar, as shown in Figure 11–26.

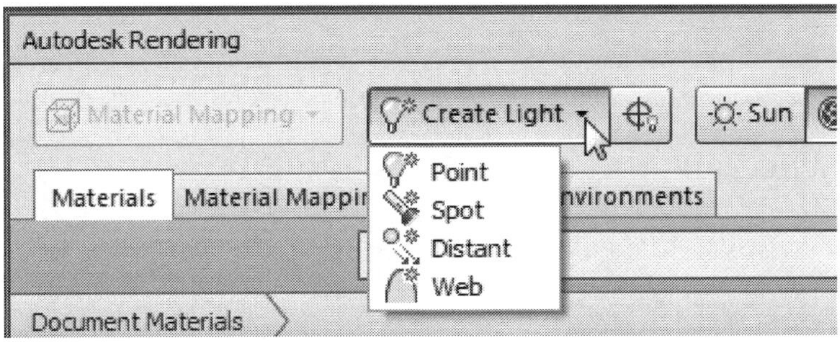

Figure 11–26

How To: Add a Point Light

1. In the *Autodesk Rendering* window>*Rendering* toolbar>*Create Light* drop-down list, click (Point).
2. Click in the scene view to locate the light. Adjust the light gizmo as needed to control the light's position in the model.
3. Use the *Properties* panel in the *Lighting* tab to adjust the light's properties, if required.

How To: Add a Spot Light

1. In the *Autodesk Rendering* window>*Rendering* toolbar>*Create Light* drop-down list, click (Spot).
2. Click in the scene view to locate the light.
3. Click to specify a target for the spot light. Adjust the light gizmo as needed to control the light's location and direction.
4. Use the **Properties** panel in the *Lighting* tab to adjust the light's properties, if required.

How To: Add a Distant Light

1. In the *Autodesk Rendering* window>*Rendering* toolbar>*Create Light* drop-down list, click (Distant).
2. Click in the scene view to locate the light.
3. Click to specify a direction. Adjust the light gizmo as needed to control the light's position and target.
4. Use the *Properties* panel in the *Lighting* tab to adjust the light's properties, if required.

How To: Add a Web Light with a Manufacturer's IES File

1. In the *Autodesk Rendering* window>*Rendering* toolbar>*Create Light* drop-down list, click (Web).
2. Click in the scene view to locate the light.
3. Click to specify a direction. Adjust the light gizmo as needed to control the light's position and target.
4. In the *Autodesk Rendering* window, in the *Lighting* tab, click in the *Web file* field. Browse to and open an IES file. The light properties update using the IES file data.
5. Use the *Properties* panel in the *Lighting* tab to adjust the light's properties, if required.

Autodesk Revit Lights

If the Autodesk Revit model contains lights, you can use them as light sources in Navisworks. In Revit, there are architectural and MEP lighting fixture families. The MEP lighting fixtures contain more BIM information for circuitry, switch networks, electrical panel identification, etc.

> ***Note:*** *Consult the Revit Help documentation about placing and managing light sources in Revit.*

Both Revit lighting types can be imported into Navisworks. First, you need to configure Navisworks to accept the Revit lights, which are disabled by default. Go to the Navisworks *Options Editor>File Readers>Revit* page and check **Convert lights**, as shown in Figure 11–27. By default, this setting is **OFF**.

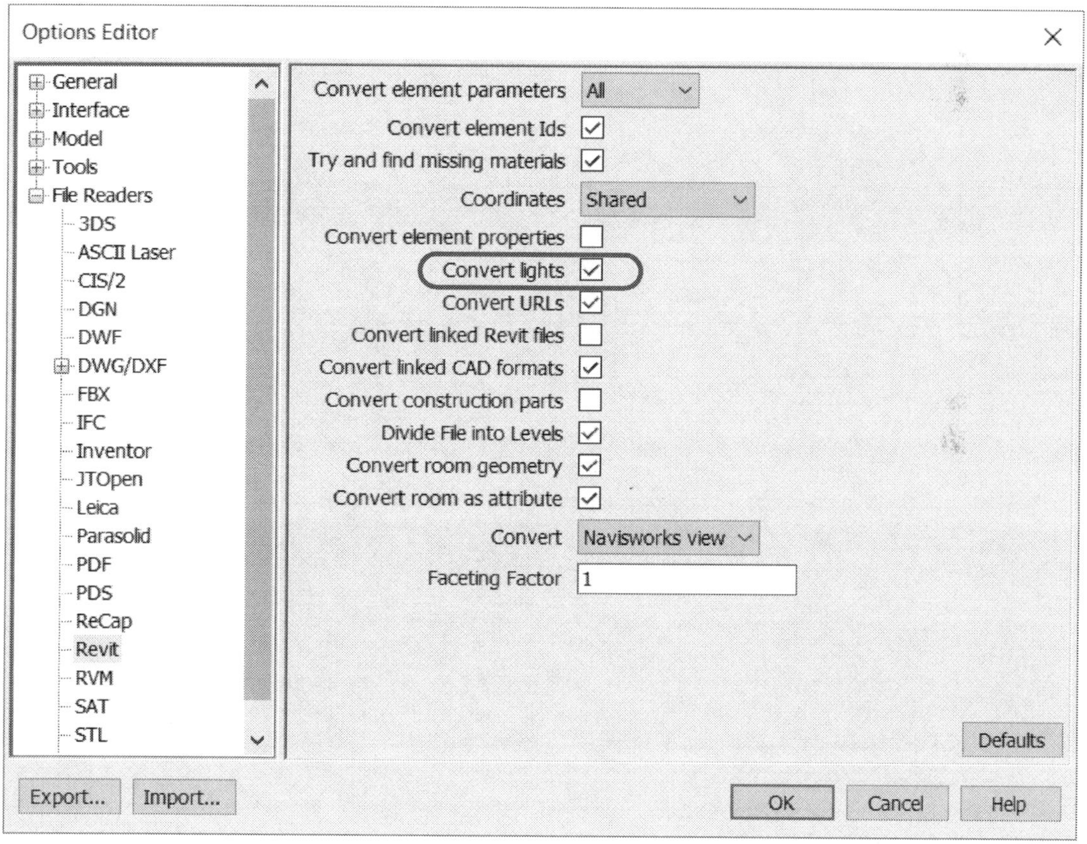

Figure 11–27

When the Revit file is appended, the lights and their properties will be extracted and defined as Navisworks light sources. They will automatically be assigned the proper lighting type (as defined in Revit), such as point light, spot light, or web light.

The *marks* (unique ID number in Revit) of the lighting fixture or the lighting groups established in Revit are **not** used in Navisworks. Instead, Navisworks assigns sequential numbers to the three light types. This makes it rather difficult to identify the individual light in the *Lights* panel, as shown in Figure 11–28.

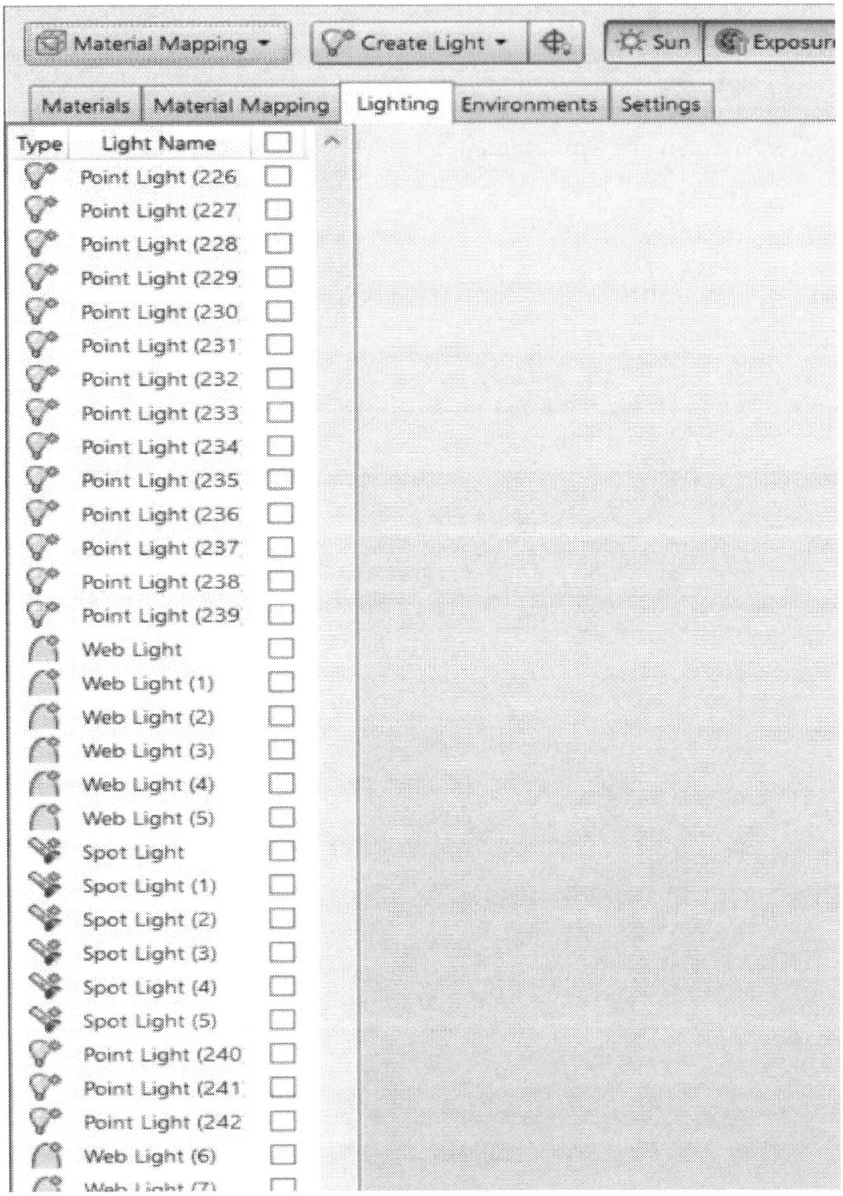

Figure 11–28

However, using Revit lights can save a lot of time, since no Navisworks lights need to be created. The output is very acceptable, as shown in Figure 11–29.

Figure 11–29

Note: *If a Revit file has been appended to the Navisworks model prior to the* ***Convert lights*** *checkbox being checked in the Navisworks Options Editor, you will need to delete the Revit file from the Navisworks model (through the Selection Tree) and add the Revit file again for the lights to be imported. Of course, you will need to check the* ***Convert lights*** *checkbox first.*

Editing Lights

Lights can be edited directly in the scene view or by using the *Properties* panel in the *Lighting* tab. When a light is selected in the model or in the *Lights* panel, a triad displays on the light's glyph, as shown in Figure 11–30. In the case of a spot light, hotspot and falloff cones also display. Additional property modification is done using the *General* properties in the *Lighting* tab. As you change the properties of a light, you will see the effect on the model.

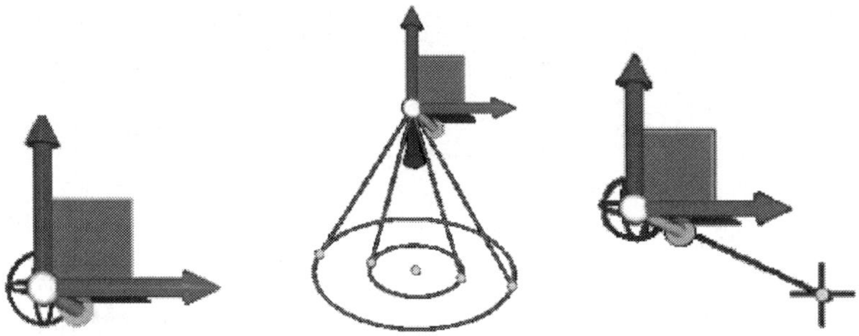

Point light ***Spot light*** ***Distant/web light***

Figure 11–30

- Select any of the direction arrows on the triad to translate the glyph (light) in that direction.
- Select the planar rectangle between arrows to move the glyph (light) in a plane.
- Select and drag the center of the triad to freely move the glyph (light) in the scene.
- Select the yellow dots that lie on the perimeter of the hotspot (inner) and falloff (outer) cones for a spot light and drag them to adjust their angle.
- Select the yellow dot that lies at the center of the cone for a spot light to relocate the target location. If the yellow dot is not visible, ensure that the **Targeted** option is enabled in the *Geometry properties* area.
- For distant and web lights, enter values in the *Geometry properties* area to change the location of the target.

You can also adjust a light's location and light's hotspot and falloff angle settings in the *Properties* view.

Filter Color

The filter color defines the color of the light that is being emitted. The default color is **white**. To modify this color, click ▢ and change the color using the *Color* dialog box that displays, as shown in Figure 11–31. Click **OK** to confirm and assign the new color for the light.

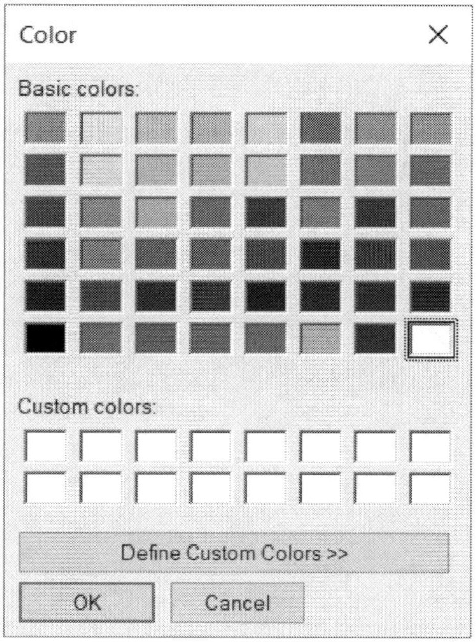

Figure 11–31

Lamp Settings

A lamp's intensity and color can be modified from its default values to customize the light's appearance.

- Clicking (...) adjacent to the *Lamp Intensity* field in the *General properties* area activates the Lamp Intensity dialog box.
- Lamp color can also be specified by clicking (...) adjacent to the *Lamp Color* field in the *General properties* area. Use the *Lamp Color* dialog box to modify the lamp color.

Deleting Lights

To delete an existing light in a Navisworks scene, right-click the light's name in the *Lights* panel and select **Delete**.

Controlling Lights in the Scene View

Lights in the scene view can be controlled in the *Autodesk Rendering* window or controlled globally.

Disabling Lights in the Autodesk Rendering Window

As an alternative to deleting lights from the scene, you can selectively disable lights that are not required. Disabling a light enables it to remain in the file, but temporarily removes it from use in the scene. To disable an existing light, in the *Lights* panel, clear the checkbox in the *Status* column, as shown for the Spot Light in Figure 11–32.

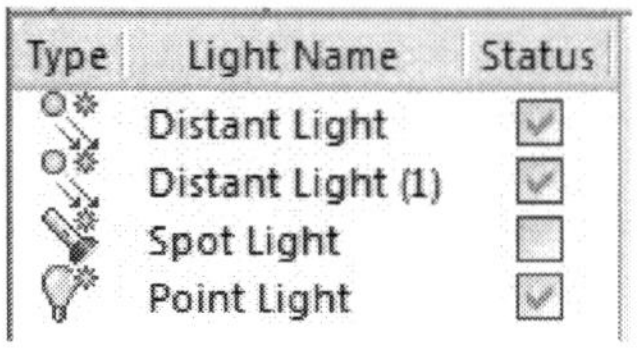

Figure 11–32

Controlling Lights for the Scene

The lights in the scene view can also be controlled using the **Lighting** options in the *Viewpoint* tab>*Render Style* panel, as shown in Figure 11–33. A scene consists of lights imported from the source CAD file and any lights that are created in the Autodesk Rendering environment.

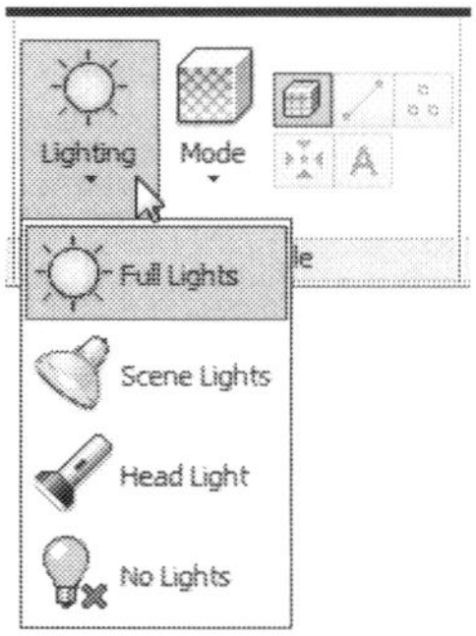

Figure 11–33

The following controls can be used to achieve the required lighting appearance.

Icon	Name	Description
	**Full Lights**	This mode takes into account the lights that are enabled in the *Lighting* tab of the *Autodesk Rendering* window (i.e., defined with Navisworks).
	**Scene Lights**	Uses the lights defined and imported from the source CAD model. If there are none available, two default opposing lights are used.
	**Head Lights**	Uses a single directional light located at the camera (viewer) in addition to an ambient light.
	**No Lights**	Disables the use of all lights, including any defined in the model.

Environments Tab

The *Environments* tab in the *Autodesk Rendering* window, shown in Figure 11–34, enables you to manage sunlight and sky illumination in a model. The settings are saved per file.

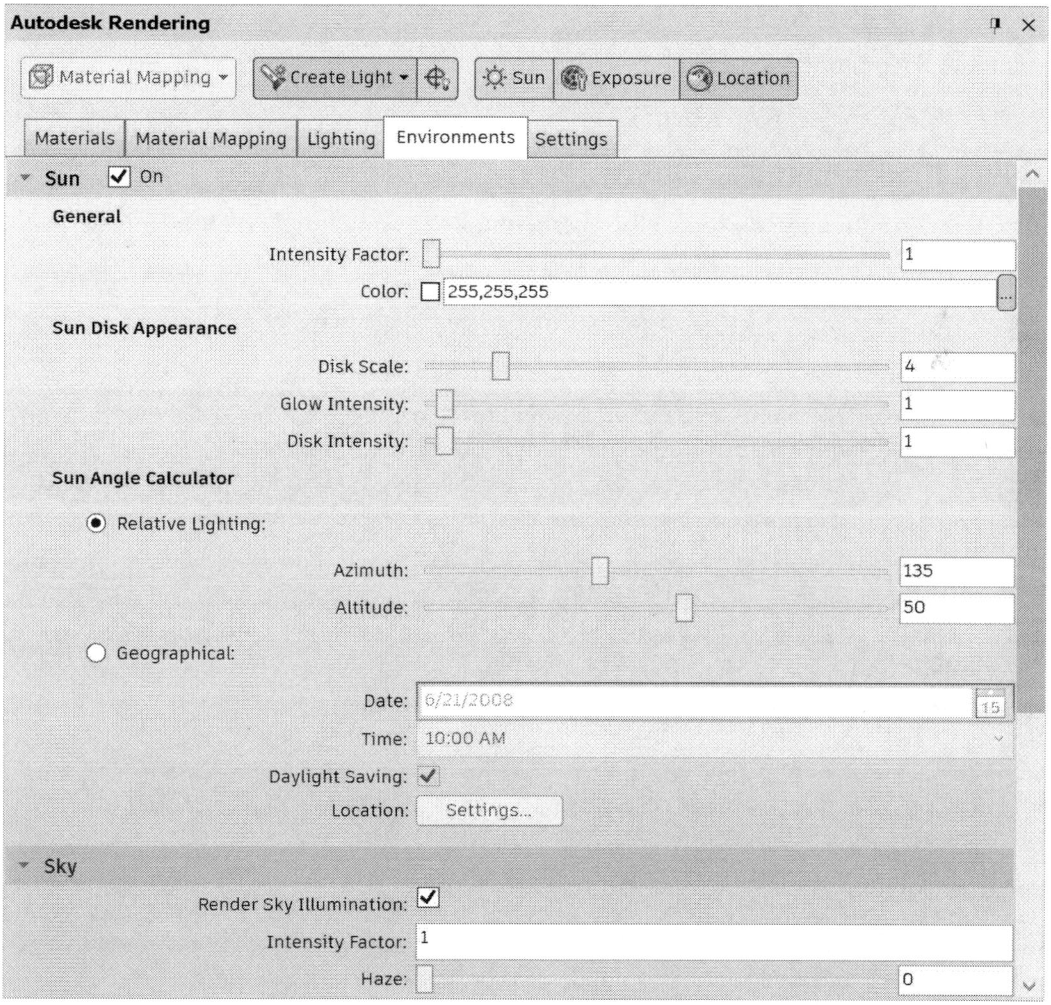

Figure 11–34

The options in the *Sun* and *Sky* panels enable you to modify the effect that these systems have in the scene.

Working with the Sun and Sky Environments

To add the sun and sky light to your model, use the following overall workflow:

1. Toggle on the sun light environment in the scene view.
2. Set the location of the sun.
3. Adjust the *Sun* properties, as required.
4. Adjust the *Sky* properties, as required.

Enabling the Sun Light System

Enabling the sun light environment in the scene requires you to toggle on the sun and then enable sky illumination.

How To: Enable the Sun Light System in the Scene View

1. In the *Autodesk Rendering* window>*Rendering* toolbar, click 

(Sun). Alternatively, you can select the **Sun** checkbox in the *Sun* panel in the *Environments* tab.
2. By default, the sun light effect is visible in the scene view. The sun's display in the scene view can be enabled/disabled as required.
3. The sun and sky effects are only visible in the scene view if the exposure is toggled on. By default, the exposure is enabled when the sun light is enabled, but it can also be disabled independently by clearing the **Exposure** option in the *Exposure* panel. If disabled, the background in the scene view displays as white.

Setting the Sun Location

Setting the sun location is done using the *Geographic Location* dialog box and the *Sun Angle Calculator* settings in the *Sun* panel. The position and angle of the sun can be defined using one of two methods:

- **Relative Lighting**
- **Geographical**

How To: Set the Geographic Position

1. In the *Autodesk Rendering* window, in the *Environments* tab, select **Geographical** in the *Sun Angle Calculator* area.
2. Click **Settings** in the *Geographical* area, or in the *Autodesk Rendering* window>*Rendering* toolbar, click **Location**.

3. In the *Latitude & Longitude* area, select a measurement type and enter the coordinates to locate the sun in the scene, as shown in Figure 11–35.

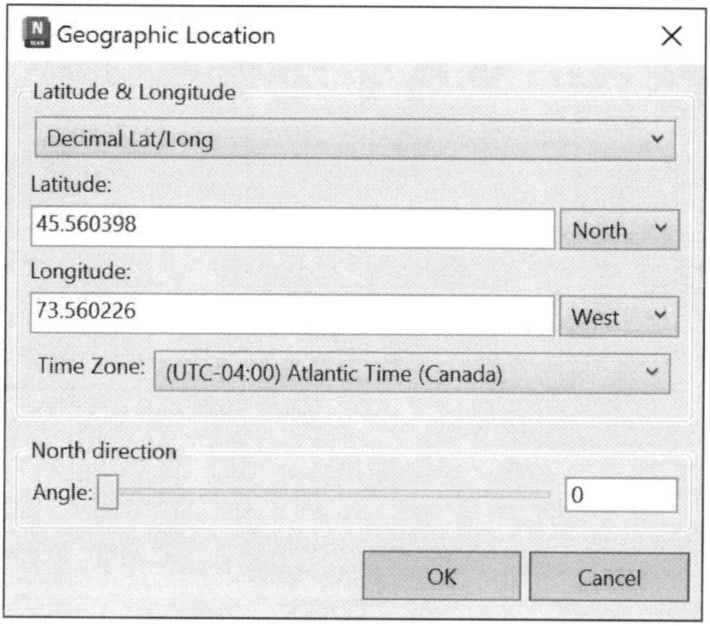

Figure 11–35

4. In the *Time Zone* drop-down list, set the time zone.
5. In the *North direction* area of the dialog box, move the **Angle** slider to define the angle of the position of the sun in the scene view.
   - **Note:** This setting does not have any effect on the model's coordinate system or the ViewCube compass direction.
6. Click **OK** to close the *Geographic Location* dialog box.
7. In the *Geographical* area, enter a *Date* and *Time* value for the sun, as shown in Figure 11–36.

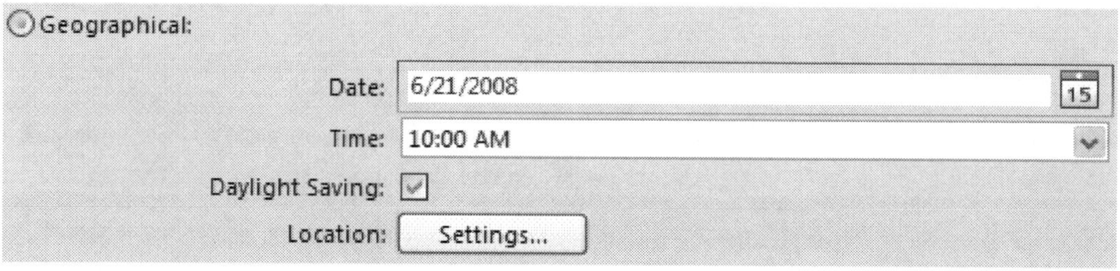

Figure 11–36

Adjusting the Sun Properties

You can further customize the default settings that are assigned for the sun using the *General* and *Sun Disk Appearance* options in the *Sun* panel, as shown in Figure 11–37.

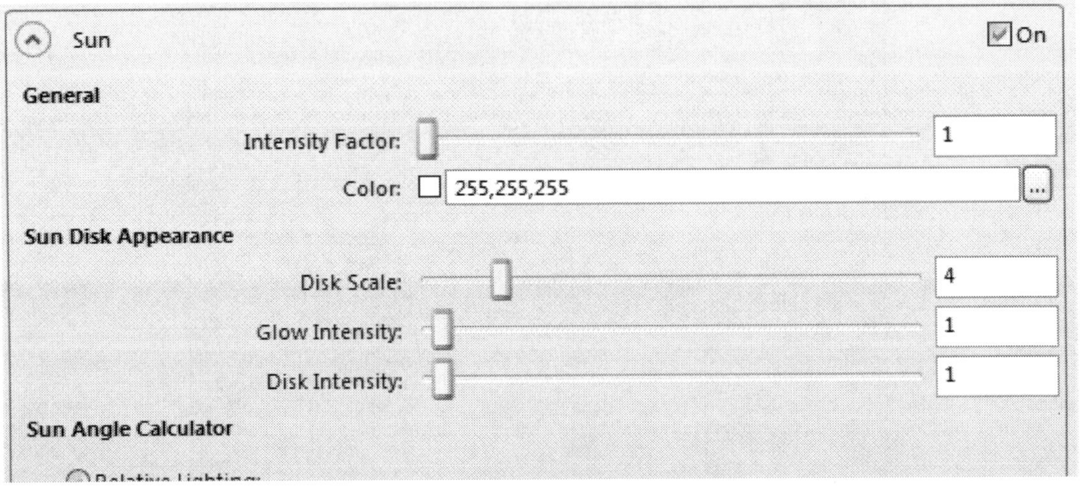

Figure 11–37

Adjusting the Sky Properties

The actual effect that all of the specified sun properties has on the scene can be further adjusted with the properties that are available in the *Sky* panel, as shown in Figure 11–38.

> ***Note:*** *The* ***Render Sky Illumination*** *option can be disabled, as required, to toggle off the sun light effect in the scene view.*

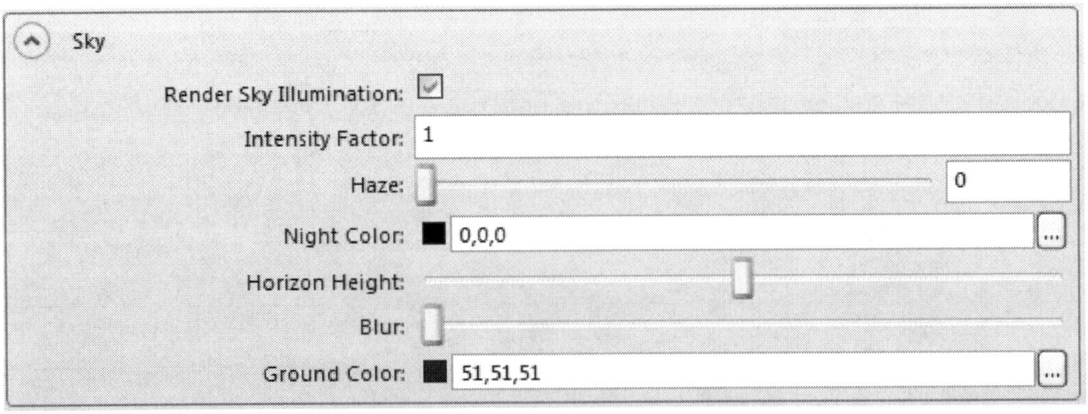

Figure 11–38

Practice 11b
Add Lights to a Model

Practice Objectives

- Place point lights and spot lights in the model.
- Adjust the lights.

In this practice, you will place lights strategically on walls and within light fixtures. Then, you will adjust the various settings of the lights and study the results. Finally, you will add some exterior lights.

There are light fixtures in the appended Revit file that have been imported. For this practice, the Lighting Render Style has been set to **Full Lights** and the exposure has been adjusted.

Task 1: Add point lights.

1. Continue to work on the file from the previous practice. If you did not complete that practice, open **School-Lobby-Lights.nwf** from the *Navisworks BIM Practice Files\Rendering* folder.

2. Click (Application Menu)>**Options**.

3. In the *Options Editor*, expand the **File Readers>Revit** page and make sure that the **Convert lights** checkbox is selected, as shown in Figure 11–39.

   Note: *If the* ***Convert lights*** *needed to be selected, you will need to refresh the models by clicking on* Refresh *(Refresh) in the Home tab>Project panel. This can take some time since it has to convert the lights from the Revit model.*

4. Click **OK** to close the *Options Editor* window.

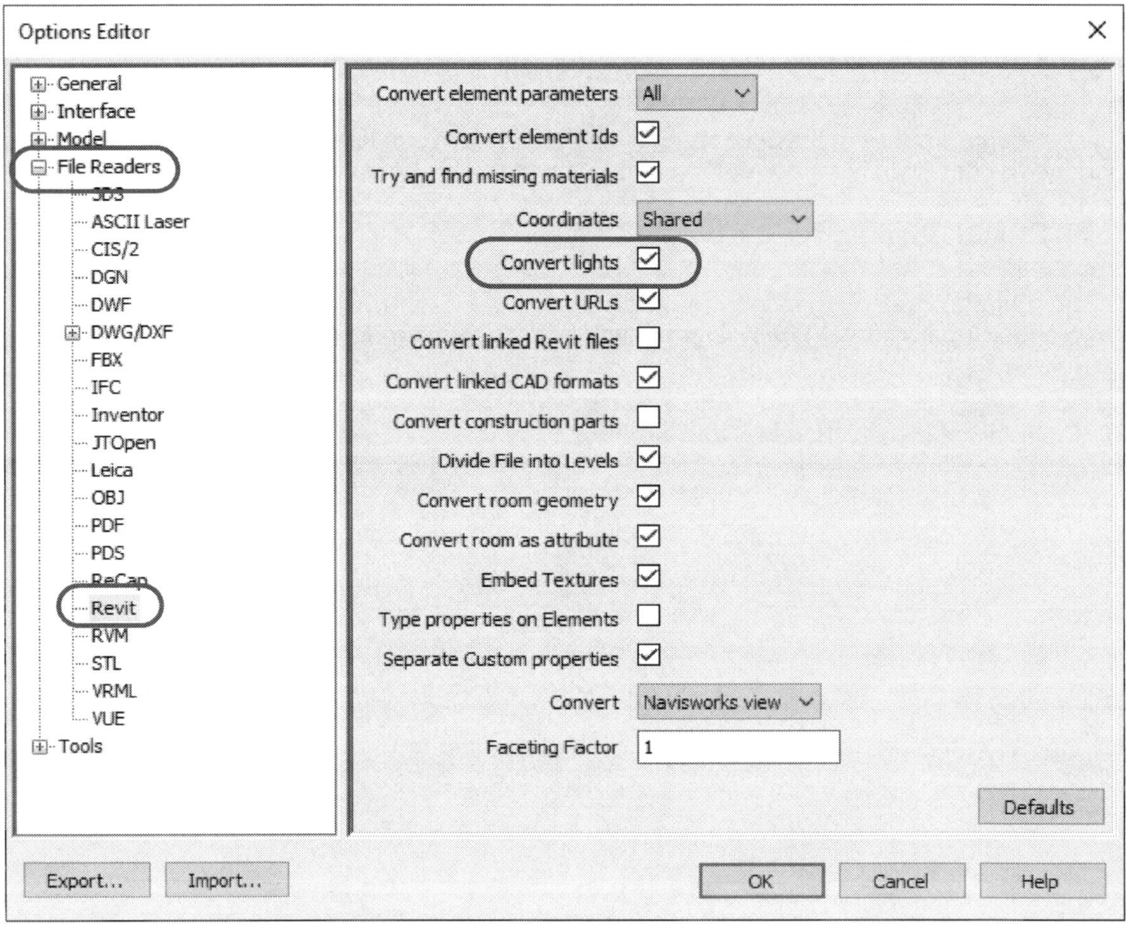

Figure 11–39

5. In the *Home* tab>*Tools* panel, click (Autodesk Rendering) to open the *Autodesk Rendering* window, if not already open.

6. In the *Saved Viewpoints* window, select **Lobby**, if necessary.

7. In the lobby and on the exterior are light sources from the Autodesk Revit model. The freestanding table lamps and floor lamps are not Autodesk Revit light sources, so these need to be supplied Navisworks light sources.

8. In the *Autodesk Rendering* window, select the *Lighting* tab. Note that there are multiple lights in the scene. These lights were brought in from the source Autodesk Revit model. For the interior scene we don't need the exterior lights. Disable all lights except for the first two web lights. To view the glyphs representing these lights, click (Light Glyphs), as shown in Figure 11–40.

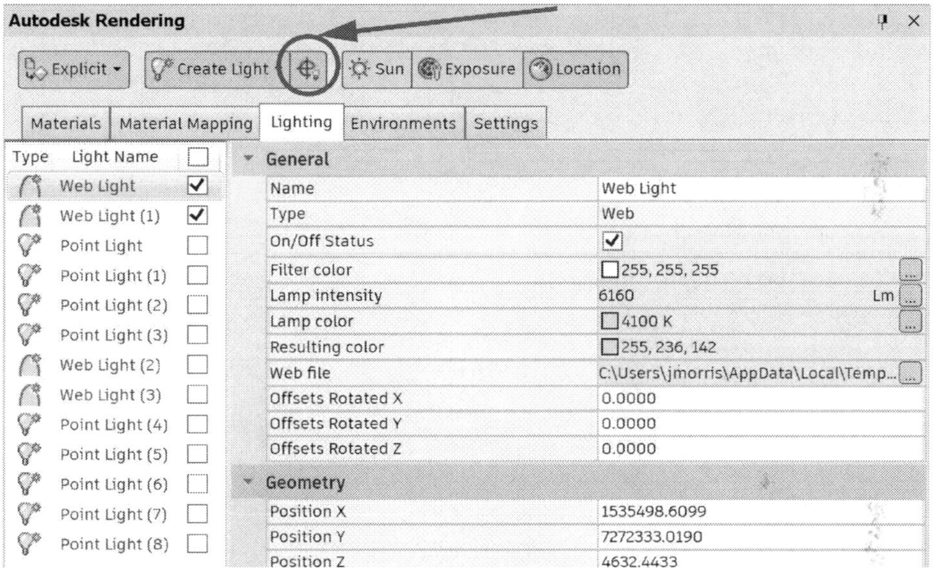

Figure 11–40

9. In the *Autodesk Rendering* window>*Rendering* toolbar>*Create Light* drop-down list, click (Point), as shown in Figure 11–41.

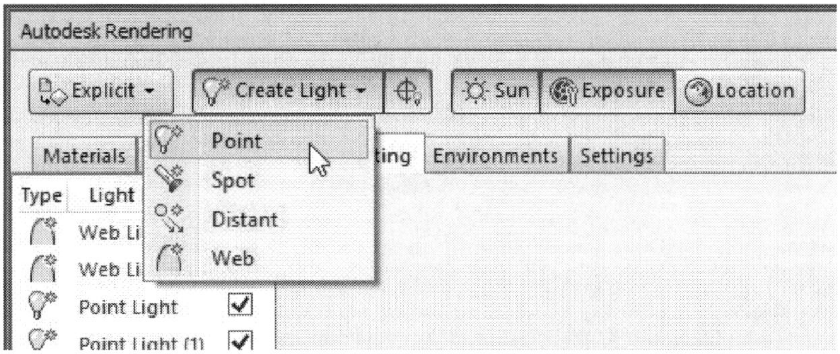

Figure 11–41

10. In the scene view, select the light shade of the table lamp to the right to place the point light, as shown in Figure 11–42.

Figure 11–42

Note: *When you create a new light source in Navisworks, the scene is fully rendered immediately. The glyphs of any other light sources are also revealed.*

11. For the *General* properties of the point light, enter the following, as shown in Figure 11–43:

- *Name*: **Table Lamp 1**
- *Lamp intensity - Intensity*: **60;** *Lamp intensity - Unit*: **Wattage (watt)** (click (*Ellipsis*) to the right of *Lamp intensity* edit box to open the *Lamp Intensity* dialog box. Select **Wattage (watt)** in the *Unit* drop-down list and then enter the *Intensity*. Click **OK**.)

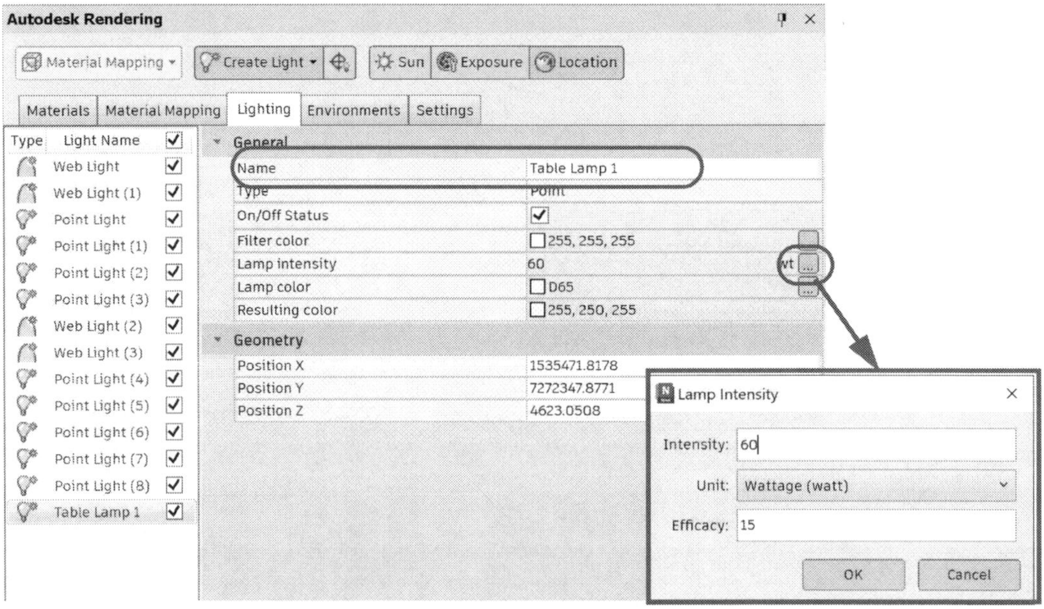

Figure 11–43

12. Select the red axis on the gizmo for the point light and drag the light toward the nearest chair, as shown in Figure 11–44. Note that the cursor displays as a hand when moving a light and the scene updates the lighting as the light moves.

Figure 11–44

13. Return the point light back to the lamp shade. Moving the light source was simply done to demonstrate the lighting effects when a light source is moved.
14. Create two more point lights for the other two table lamps along the far wall, rename them to **Table Lamp 2** and **Table Lamp 3** respectively, and change their intensity to **60 watts** as you did previously.

    Note: *You cannot select multiple light sources to edit in the General properties; they have to be edited one by one.*

15. Save the Navisworks file.

Task 2: Add spot lights.

1. In the *Create Light* drop-down list, click (Spot).
2. In the scene view, select the floor lamp nearest you (in the right side of the view) to place the spot light and select the black chair near it as the target, as shown in Figure 11–45.

Figure 11–45

3. For the *General* properties of the spot light, enter the following, as shown in Figure 11–46:
   - *Name*: **Floor Lamp 1**
   - *Filter color*: Salmon (click the ellipsis to select a color)

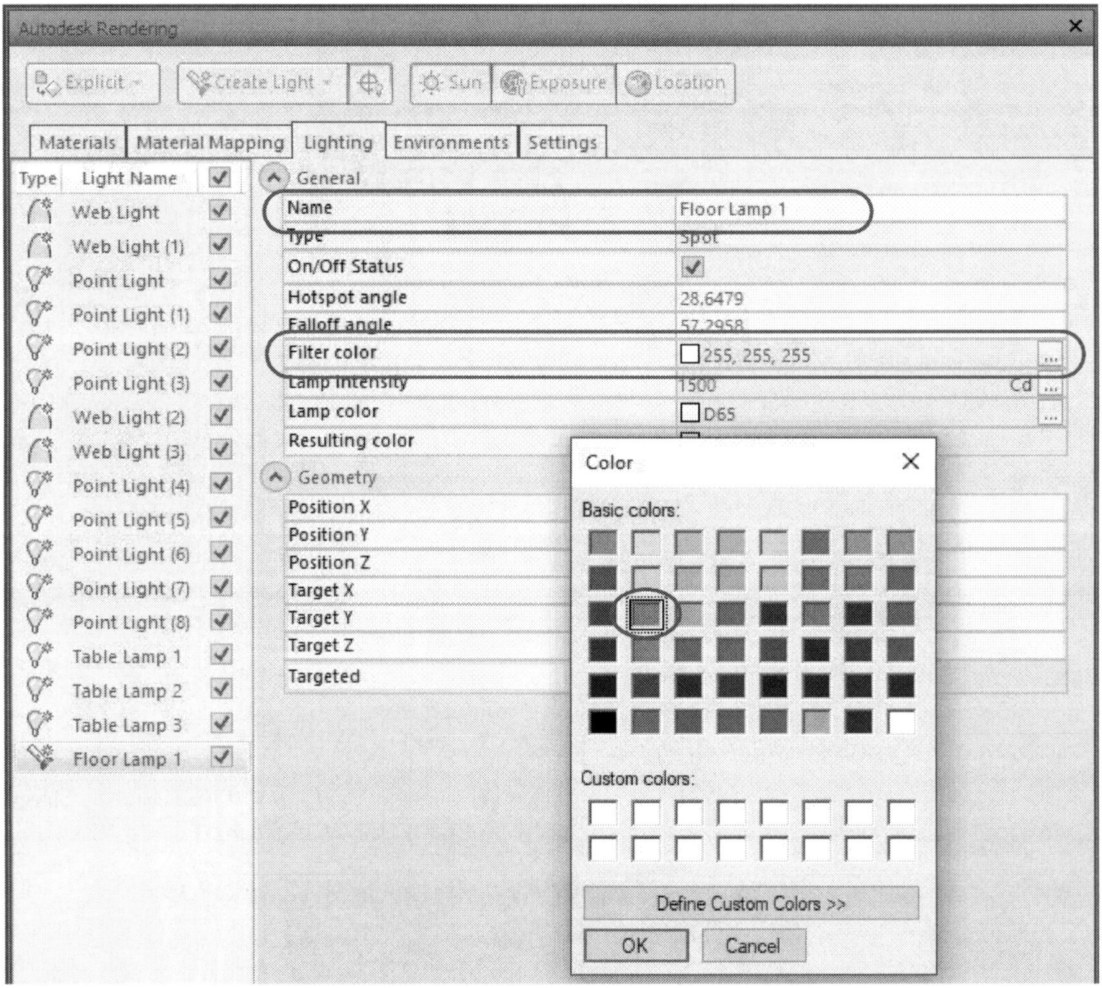

Figure 11–46

4. Select the black dot on the outside of the inner ring that is centered on the target and drag by selecting the arrow to make it smaller, as shown in Figure 11–47. This is the hotspot angle. Note how the *Hotspot angle* changes in the General properties for this light.

Figure 11–47

Note: *If you need to reselect the light, click on its name from the list in the Autodesk Rendering window.*

5. Select the black dot on the outside of the outer ring that is centered on the target and drag by selecting the arrow to make it smaller, as shown in Figure 11–48. This is the falloff angle. Note how the *Falloff angle* changes in the *General* properties for this light.

Figure 11–48

6. In the *General* properties for the spot light, adjust the *Hotspot angle* to **17** and the *Falloff angle* to **36**, as shown in Figure 11–49.

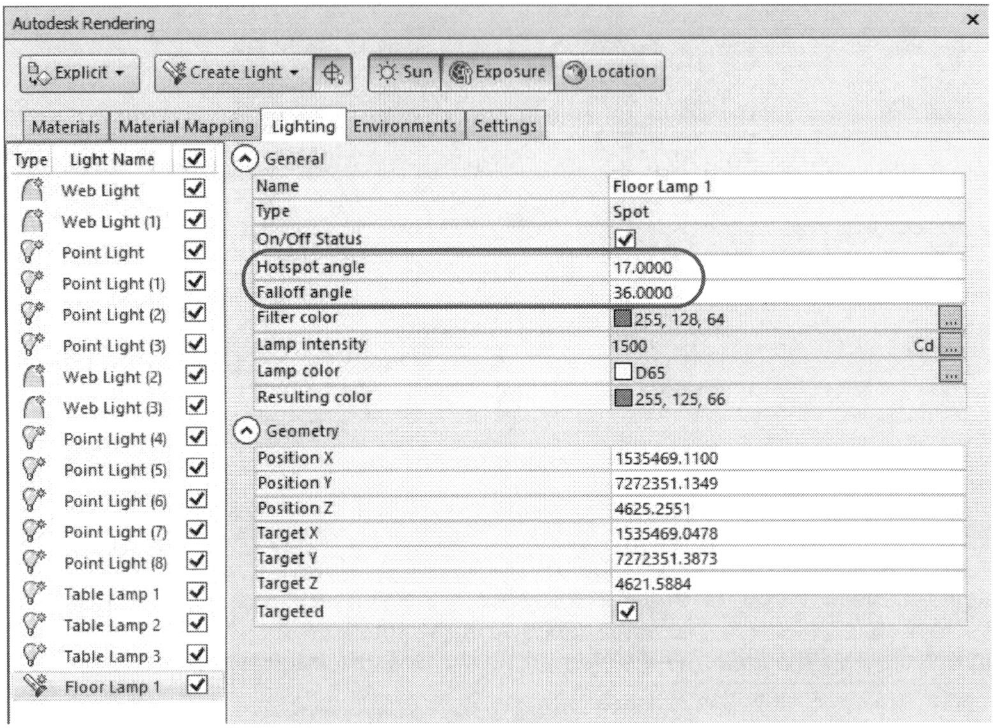

Figure 11–49

Note: *If the scene view goes black, you need to restore a viewpoint to resume.*

7. Create five more spot lights for the other floor lamps in the scene, aiming them onto the chairs nearest to them. You can zoom and pan within the scene for easier placement, if necessary.
8. In the *General* properties, adjust the *Hotspot angle* and *Falloff angle* and change the names of the spot lights. Keep the *Filter color* as the default.
9. You may have to reset the **Lighting** in the *Viewpoint* tab>*Render Style* panel to **Full Lights** to view the lights in the scene once complete.
10. Save the file.

End of practice

11.5 Exposure Control

Exposure settings enable you to control how the lights that have been defined in the scene are processed in a the final rendered image, providing real-world characteristics to the scene's lighting.

> ***Note:*** *The sun and sky effects are only visible when the exposure is toggled on; otherwise, the background in the scene view becomes white.*

Environments Tab

The use and settings for exposure control are managed using the *Exposure* panel in the *Environments* tab, as shown in Figure 11–50. As settings are specified, their effects are immediate in the scene view.

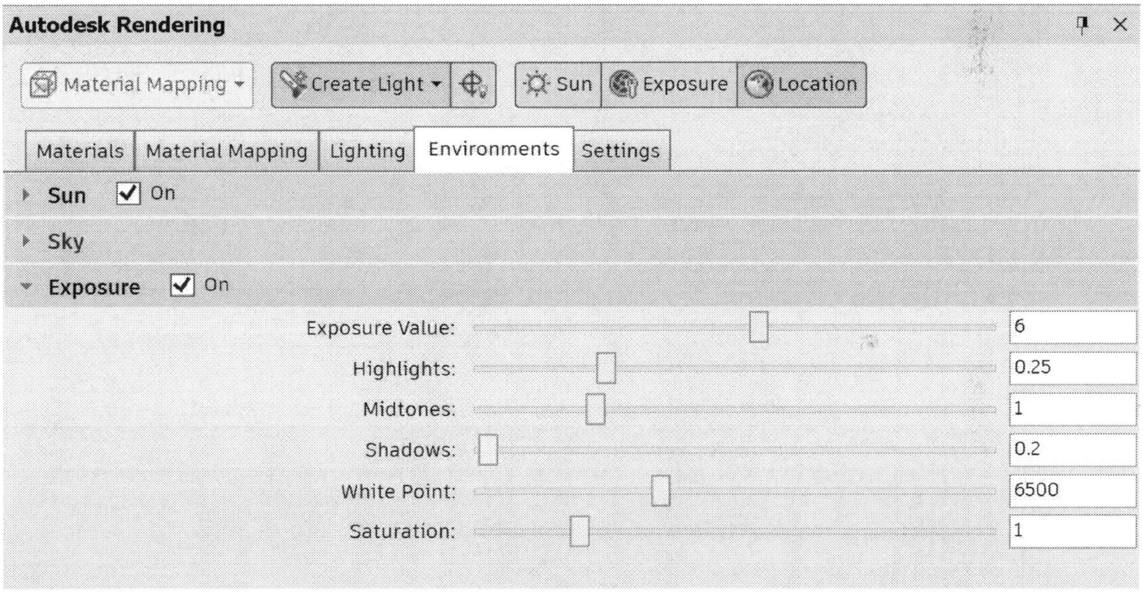

Figure 11–50

The options in the *Exposure* panel allow you to enable or disable the use of exposure and customize the effect that it has in the scene.

Enabling and Adjusting Exposure

Adjusting the exposure of the scene enables you to refine the results of the rendering to obtain a more real-world effect.

How To: Adjust the Exposure in a Scene

1. In the *Autodesk Rendering* window>*Rendering* toolbar, click **Exposure**.
    - Alternatively, in the *Environments* tab>*Exposure* panel, you can select **On**.
2. Refine the exposure controls using the sliders for the following options:
    - **Exposure Value:** Controls brightness (range is between **-6** (brighter) and **16** (darker)).
    - **Highlights:** Adjusts the light level for the brightest area of the image (range is between **0** (darker) and **1** (brighter)).
    - **Midtones:** Adjusts the light level for areas between the highlights and shadows (range is between **0.1** (darker) and **4** (brighter)).
    - **Shadows:** Adjust the light levels for the darkest areas (range is between **0.1** (lighter) and **4** (darker)).
    - **White Point:** Controls the color of the light source.
    - **Saturation:** Controls the intensity of the colors (range is between **0** (gray/black/white) and **5** (more intense colors)).

11.6 Photorealistic Rendering

Rendering creates highly detailed and photorealistic images in Navisworks, as shown in Figure 11–51. The renderings are created using all of the materials, lights, and environments that were applied to the scene view using the **Autodesk Rendering** window. Rendering can be run in Navisworks (Autodesk Rendering) or it can be done using Autodesk Rendering (Render in Cloud). Rendering involves complex calculations that can occupy your computer for an extended time, which may help you decide which render location is best.

Once the scene is rendered, small changes to the scene might be required to further refine it, which requires re-rendering the scene. Thus, creating photorealistic images can be quite time-consuming.

Figure 11–51

Rendering Not Working as Expected

As of the release of this learning guide (January 2026), the renderings for this task were not generating the expected result. This issue has been submitted to Autodesk.

Autodesk Rendering

When the **Autodesk Rendering** option is enabled in the *Render* tab, the viewpoint is rendered directly in Navisworks. During rendering, the output displays directly in the scene view, along with a progress indicator showing the completed rendering percentage.

Rendering in the Cloud

When the **Render in Cloud** option is enabled in the *Render* tab, Autodesk Rendering is used to create photorealistic images and panoramic renderings without using the resources on your system, enabling you to continue working in your local software. To render using Autodesk Rendering, Navisworks creates a version of the project containing just the information required to render and then transmits it to the rendering service. By accessing the online render gallery, you can access your renderings, re-render images as panoramas, or re-render with other settings. Additionally, you can preview and download the rendered image.

Once a rendering is complete, you can save it as an image.

Defining the Render Style

When rendering in Navisworks, you must define the render style that is to be used. There are six default styles available for use:

- **Low Quality**
- **Medium Quality**
- **High Quality**
- **Coffee Break Rendering**
- **Lunch Break Rendering**
- **Overnight Rendering**

The higher quality rendered images take more time to render. For the final photorealistic finish, you can select a high-quality rendering style to create the final image, but consider using a lower quality to initially test the rendering settings.

Custom Render Settings

The six render styles that are provided in Navisworks may not provide the exact rendering settings that you require. For these situations, you can customize the settings using the *Settings* tab in the *Autodesk Rendering* window, as shown in Figure 11–52.

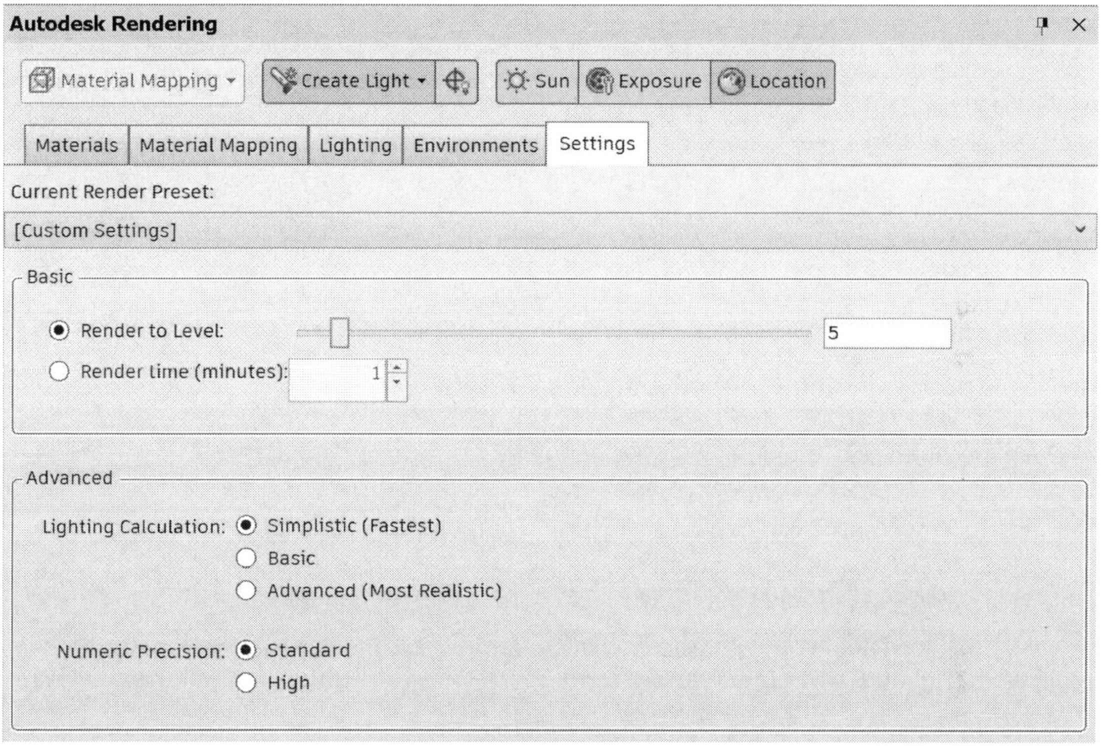

Figure 11–52

When rendering, the computer system slows down considerably and may appear to become unresponsive. Patience is required. During the rendering process, a status of the rendering is tracked in the lower left corner (below the HUD), as shown in Figure 11–53.

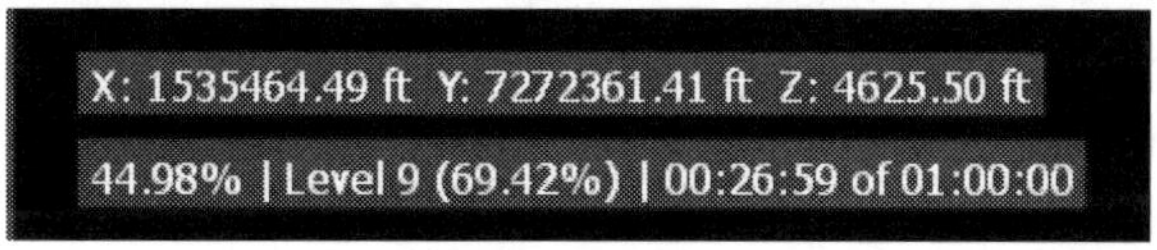

Figure 11–53

Rendering Workflows

The process for rendering directly in Navisworks or using the Autodesk Rendering cloud service are slightly different. To access either rendering method, use the *Render* tab in the Navisworks ribbon, as shown in Figure 11–54.

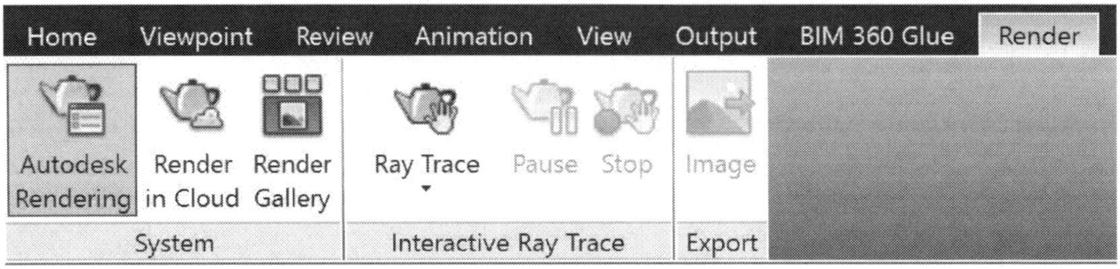

Figure 11–54

How To: Render a Scene in the Autodesk Software

1. Open the *Autodesk Rendering* window using one of the following options:
   - In the *Render* tab>*System* panel, click (Autodesk Rendering).
   - In the *Home* tab>*Tools* panel, click (Autodesk Rendering).
2. Set up the scene using the *Autodesk Rendering* window. This includes materials, material mapping, lighting, environments, and creating the viewpoint (orientation and zoom level).
   - **Note:** You can change the size of the rendered image by resizing the scene view before rendering.

3. Select the rendering quality. In the *Render* tab>*Render* panel, expand the **Ray Trace** option to provide the list of available render styles, as shown in Figure 11–55.

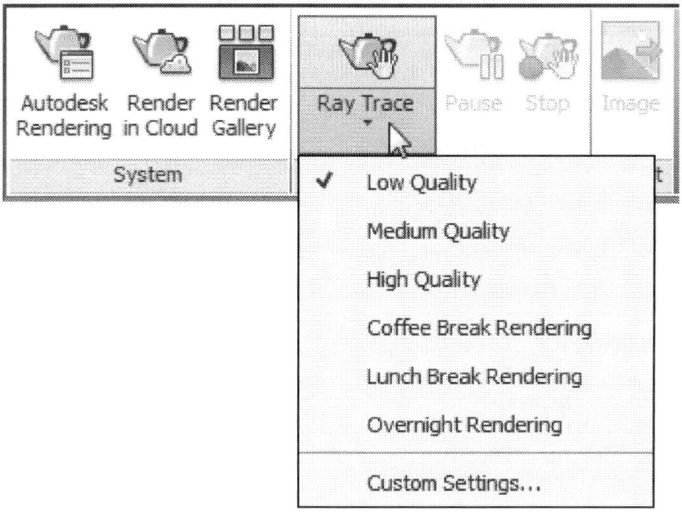

Figure 11–55

Note: Real-time navigation during rendering causes the process to restart from the beginning.

4. In the *Render* tab>*Render* panel, click  (Start) to start rendering. Click  (Pause) to temporarily pause the process.

5. Save the rendered image. When the scene is rendered, click  (Export) in the *Render* tab. In the *Save As* dialog box, select the required file format, browse to a storage location, and enter a name for the file. Click **Save**.

To stop a rendering and return to the scene, click  (Stop).

How To: Render a Scene Using Cloud Rendering

Rendering Not Working as Expected

As of the release of this learning guide (January 2026), the renderings for this task were not generating the expected result when rendering in the cloud. This issue has been submitted to Autodesk.

1. Set up the scene using the *Autodesk Rendering* window. In the *Render* tab>*Render* panel, click  (Render in Cloud) to access Autodesk Rendering.

2. In the *Render in Cloud* window, define the render settings and click **Start Rendering**, as shown in Figure 11–56. If you want the system to email you when the rendering is complete, select **Email me when complete**. The file is uploaded to the cloud where the rendering process is completed.

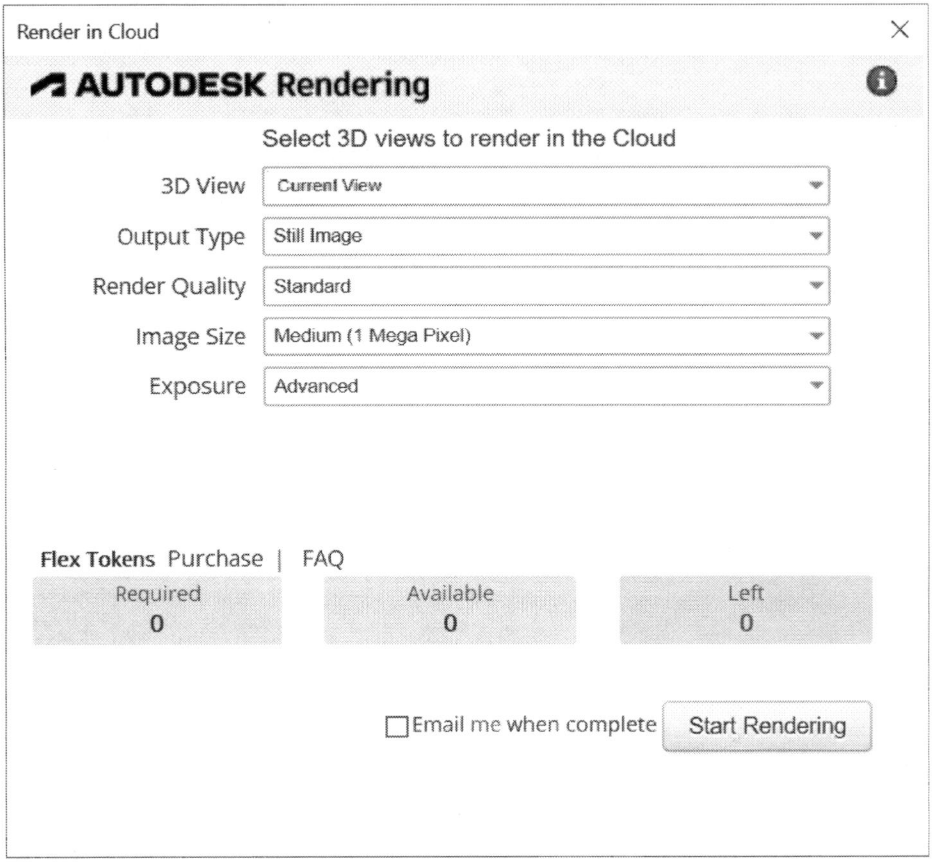

Figure 11–56

- Autodesk Rendering renders the Navisworks viewpoint in a project by making it the current view before starting the **Render in Cloud** command.
- Autodesk Rendering is a highly optimized engine. It is not the same as the rendering engine used in Navisworks.
- Autodesk Rendering automatically applies advanced exposure controls to simulate real-world lighting conditions.

3. Click  (Render Gallery) in the *Render* tab to review the file in Autodesk Rendering once it has been rendered.

   The following describes what can be done with the file.

   - Select **Re-render using new settings** to define new render settings and re-render the file.
   - Select a **Render As** setting.
   - Create panoramas of your scene.
   - Perform solar studies of designs in progress during the day.
   - Perform illuminance simulations of scenes.

- Show or hide the preview image.
- Download the image.
- Delete the image from Autodesk Rendering.
- Adjust the exposure settings using the **Adjust Exposure** option, as shown in Figure 11–57.

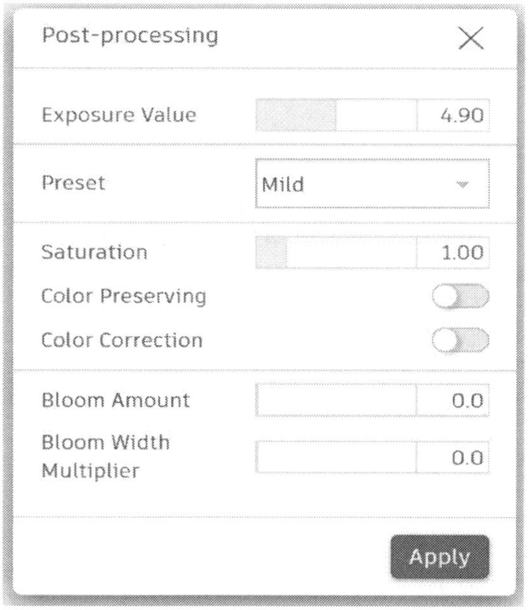

Figure 11–57

Ground Planes

Ground planes provide a visual base for the model. They can also hide the foundation geometry of a model.

You can append the ground planes that have been created in CAD software to the model files in Navisworks.

How To: Add a Ground Plane

1. In the *Home* tab>*Project* panel, click  (Append). Browse, select, and open the required ground plane file.
2. In the scene view, right-click the ground plane and select **Override Item>Override Transform**. The *Override Transform* dialog box displays, as shown in Figure 11–58.

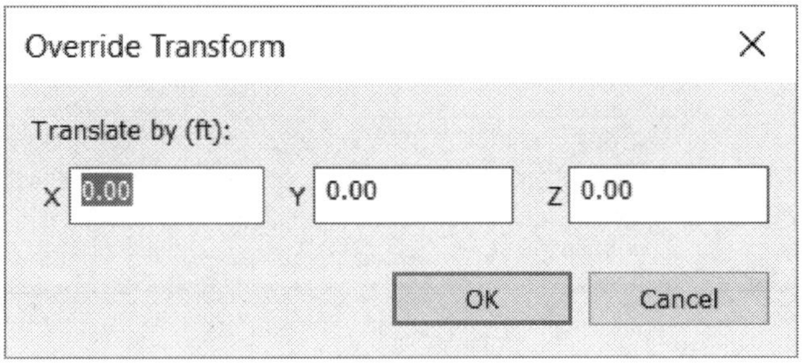

Figure 11–58

- You can move the ground plane by selecting it, right-clicking, and selecting **File Units and Transform**.

3. In the *Override Transform* dialog box, change the *X*, *Y*, and *Z* dimensions, as required.
4. Click **OK** to save the changes and close the dialog box.

Practice 11c
Render a Model

Practice Objectives

- Render an interior scene.
- Render an exterior scene.

Now that the materials are properly mapped and adjusted and the light sources placed and modified to suite the scene, it is time for action. In this practice, you will render an interior scene and an exterior scene and study the results. If you have access to an Autodesk Rendering account, you will also send the interior scene to the cloud for expedient rendering.

Task 1: Render the scene and make adjustments.

Hint: Rendering Not Working as Expected

As of the release of this learning guide (January 2026), the renderings for this task were not generating the expected result. We have to overexpose the scene in order to get satisfactory results.This issue has been submitted to Autodesk.

1. Continue to work on the file from the previous practice. If you did not complete that practice, open **School-Lobby-Render.nwf** from the *Navisworks BIM Practice Files\ Rendering* folder.
2. If necessary, restore the **Lobby** viewpoint.
3. In the *Viewpoint* tab>*Render Style* panel, expand **Lighting** and select **Full Lights**.
4. In the *Render Style* panel, expand **Mode** and select **Full Render** if not already set.

5. In the *Autodesk Rendering* window>*Rendering* toolbar, turn off (Sun) and turn on (Exposure), as shown in Figure 11–59. When toggled on, the buttons have a blue sheen.
6. In the *Environment* tab of the *Autodesk Rendering* window, you can use the sliders (or the left and right arrow keys of your keyboard) to set the exposure control as follows, as shown in Figure 11–59. These values are only approximate.
   - *Exposure Value:* **-0.5 (negative)**
   - *Highlights:* **0.15**
   - *Midtones:* **1.5**
   - *Shadows:* **0.3**
   - *White Point:* **7500 (+/-)**
   - *Saturation:* **1.5**

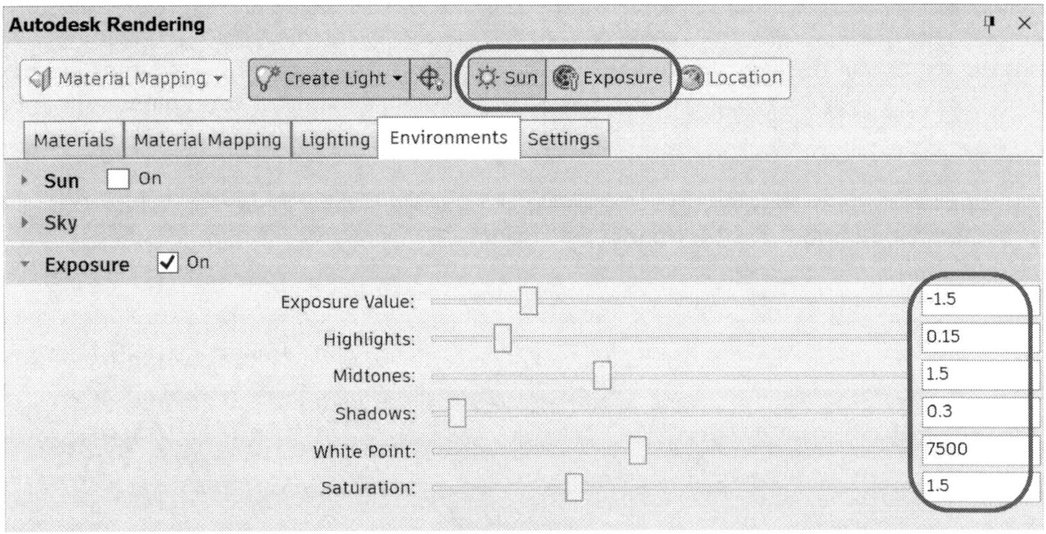

Figure 11–59

Note: *Even though the scene is overexposed, the resulting rendering is satisfactory. You can turn the Render Style (on the Viewpoint tab) to Scene Lights after the rendering is complete.*

7. Select the *Render* tab in the ribbon to access the rendering tools.

8. In the *Interactive Ray Trace* panel, expand the **Ray Trace** option and select **Medium Quality**, as shown in Figure 11–60. This sets the rendering quality as medium.

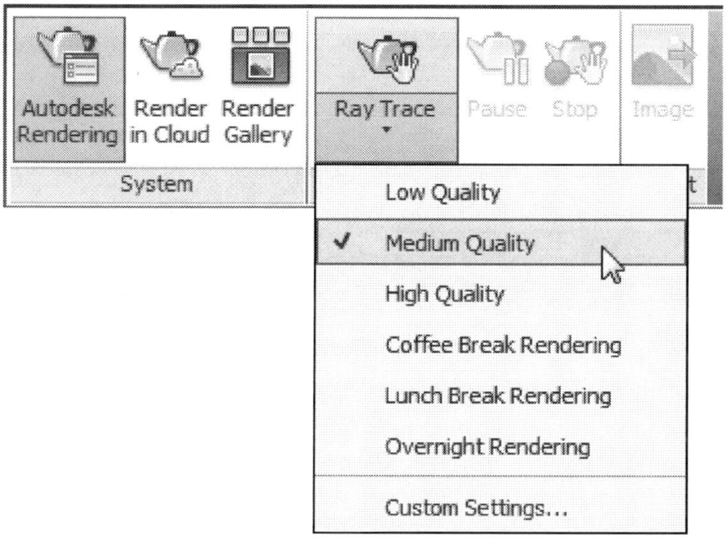

Figure 11–60

- The **Low Quality** style is the fastest to render and the **High Quality** style is the slowest to render. It is recommended that you begin rendering using a lower quality as you are developing appropriate material and lighting settings and then render at the higher quality once done. Consider using the other options for specific rendering settings based on time.

9. In the *Interactive Ray Trace* panel, click  to start rendering, as shown in Figure 11–61.

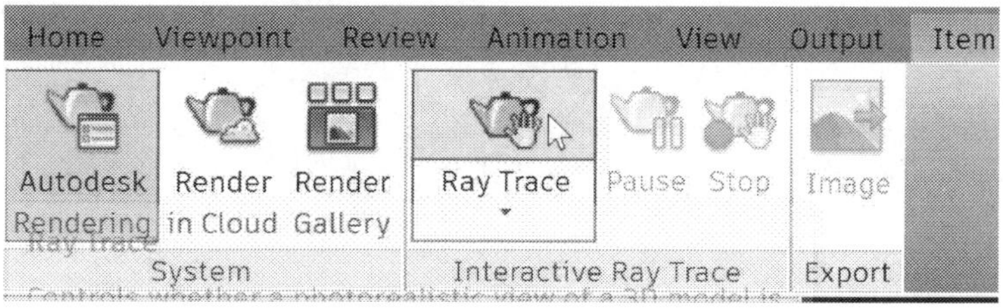

Figure 11–61

10. Notice that **Interactive Ray Trace is Running** in the upper left corner of the scene window indicating that the scene is being rendered. As the rendering is progressing, you will see the scene slowing becoming clearer with each successive pass.

    Note: *The rendering progress (Level and Time) is displayed near the bottom left corner of the scene window, as shown in Figure 11–62.*

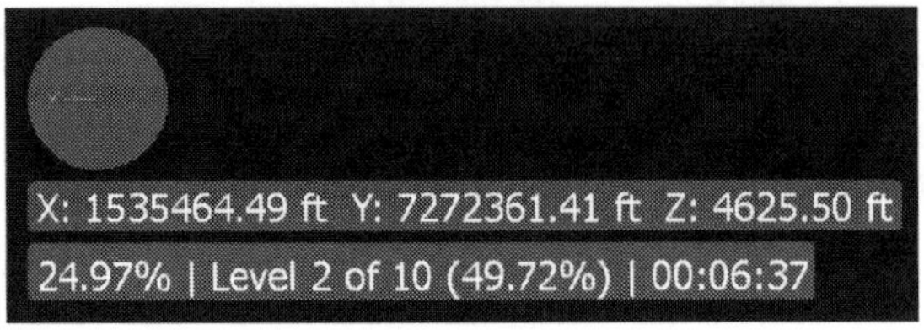

Figure 11–62

11. In the *Interactive Ray Trace* panel, click (Stop) to return to the realistic visual style. You can see the final rendering of this setting, navigate to the *Navisworks BIM Practice Files\Rendering\Images* folder and open **Lobby-Rendering-Local.jpg**. For reference, it took about 6 hours to complete the rendering. shown in Figure 11–63.

Figure 11–63

12. To preview the space for an evening setting without rendering, set the following:

    - *Exposure Value:* **9**
    - *Highlights:* **0.10**
    - *Midtones:* **1.3**
    - *Shadows:* **0.5**
    - *White Point:* **7500 (+/-***Saturation:* **1.5**

13. You can adjust these settings to see how the scene changes interactively, as shown in Figure 11–64.

Figure 11–64

14. Click (ellipses) adjacent to the *Lamp color* property. In the *Lamp Color* dialog box, select **Quartz Cool** in the *Standard colors* drop-down list, as shown in Figure 11–65. Click **OK**.

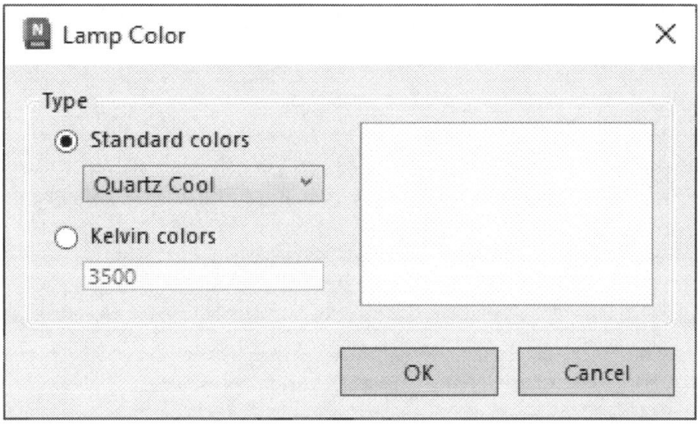

Figure 11–65

15. Repeat this for the other two table lamps.

16. In the *Lighting* tab in the *Autodesk Rendering* window, select **Floor Lamp 1** to access its properties.
17. Click (...) adjacent to the *Lamp color* property. In the *Lamp Color* dialog box, select **Quartz Cool** in the *Standard colors* drop-down list. Click **OK**.
18. Repeat this for the other floor lamps.
19. Figure 11–66 shows the results. Yours might vary slightly depending on the placement of your lights.

Figure 11–66

20. Save the file.
    - Rendering using Autodesk Rendering enables you to take advantage of its powerful rendering engine and tools. To review an image of the lobby rendered using the cloud and some of its settings, navigate to the *Navisworks BIM Practice Files\Rendering\Images* folder and open **Lobby_Cloud_Rendering.jpg**.

Rendering Not Working as Expected

As of the release of this learning guide (January 2026), the renderings for this task were not generating the expected result when rendering in the cloud. This issue has been submitted to Autodesk.

Task 2: Navigate to an exterior viewpoint and prepare the scene.

1. In the *Saved Viewpoints* window, select **Start** to change the viewpoint to an external view of the model. Zoom, orbit, and pan so you have a vantage point similar to the one shown in Figure 11–67.

Figure 11–67

2. Save the viewpoint as **Rendering-Exterior**.
3. In the *Autodesk Rendering* window>*Rendering* toolbar, click Location (Location). In the *Geographic Location* dialog box, set the *Time Zone* to **(UTC-05:00) Eastern Time (US & Canada)**, as shown in Figure 11–68. Click **OK**.

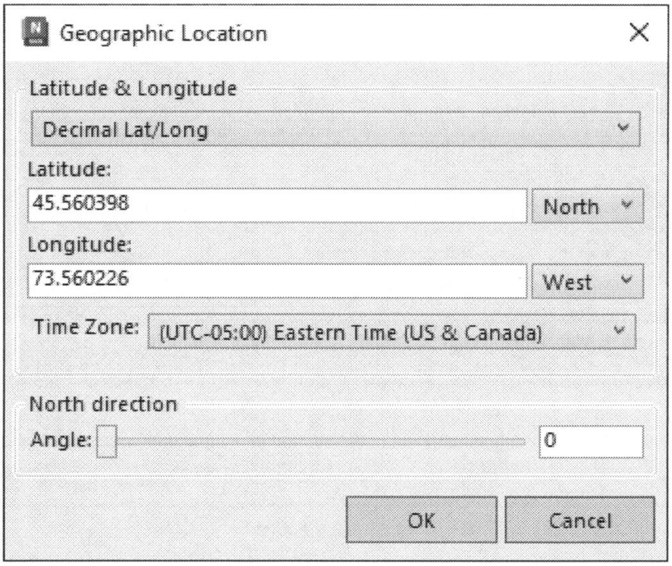

Figure 11–68

4. In the *Autodesk Rendering* window>*Rendering* toolbar, ensure that the  (Sun) option is enabled so that the sun is toggled on in the scene view.
5. In the *Autodesk Rendering* window, select the *Environments* tab. Make the following changes to the Sun properties, as shown in Figure 11–69:
   - Enter **4** as the *Intensity Factor*.
   - Select the **Geographical** option and enter the current date in the *Date* field.
   - Enter **11:45 PM** as the *Time*.

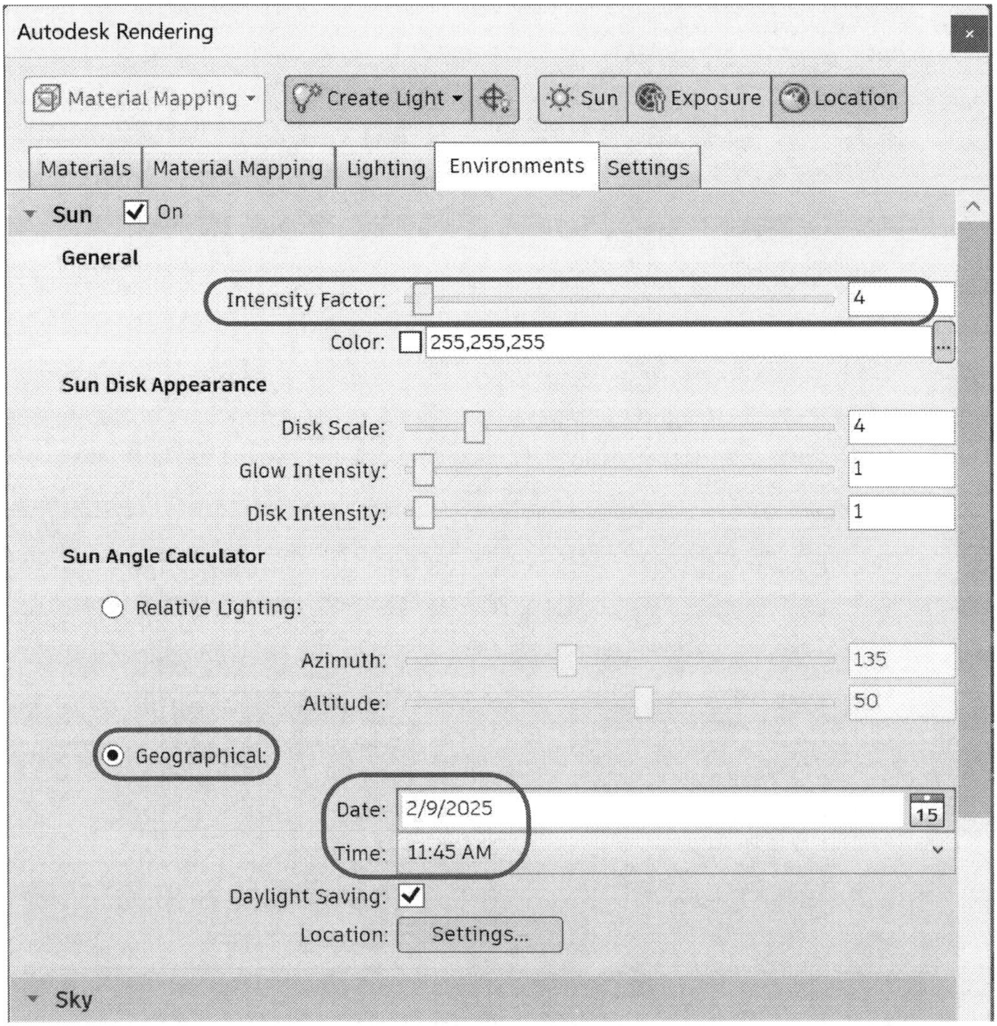

Figure 11–69

6. In the *Environments* tab, make the following changes to the *Sky* properties, as shown in Figure 11–70:
   - Enter **2** as the *Haze* factor.
   - Lower the *Horizon Height* using the slider.
   - Increase the *Blur* using the slider.
   - Change the *Ground Color* to a dark green by picking it from the color palette available from the (...) button.

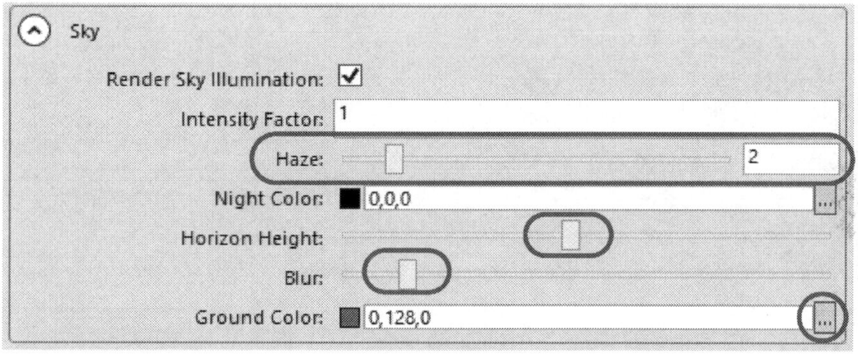

Figure 11–70

7. In the *Environments* tab, in the *Exposure* properties, set the following:
   - *Exposure Value:* **6**
   - *Highlights:* **0.4**
   - *Midtones:* **2**
   - *Shadows:* **1**
   - *White Point:* **3500 (+/-)**
   - *Saturation:* **2**
8. Save the file.

9. In the *Rendering* toolbar, toggle the Sun (Sun) and Exposure (Exposure) options off to simulate a night scene in the scene view shown in Figure 11–71.

Figure 11–71

> **Hint: Rendering Values are subjective**
>
> The variety of different settings and their values have been chosen for a satisfactory result. Experiment with different settings for your own individual preferences.

10. Change the *Exposure Value to* **9,** toggle the Sun (Sun) and Exposure (Exposure) options on and in the *Render* tab>*Interactive Ray Trace* panel, click (Start) to start rendering.

11. When the scene is rendered, click (Save) Interactive Ray Trace, select a file type, and save it to a local folder. You can see the final rendering of this setting, navigate to the *Navisworks BIM Practice Files\Rendering\Images* folder and open **Exterior_Rendering-Local.jpg**. For reference, it took about 7 hours to complete the rendering, as shown in Figure 11–72.

Figure 11–72

12. Save and close the Navisworks file.

End of practice

Chapter Review Questions

1. Which of the following are Navisworks lights? (Select all that apply.)
   a. Spot light
   b. Distant light
   c. Sun light
   d. Web light

2. You can select multiple lights and edit them in the Lighting panel.
   a. True
   b. False

3. Which render style mode includes the materials and textures of items, including lights, reflections, and shadows?
   a. Full Render
   b. Hidden Line
   c. Wireframe
   d. Shaded

4. Which of the following is NOT an option for mapping materials in Navisworks?
   a. Planar
   b. Box
   c. Surface
   d. Cylindrical

5. Which of the following is NOT an option for rendering styles in Navisworks?
   a. Coffee Break
   b. Full Day
   c. High Quality
   d. Overnight

Command Summary

Button	Command	Location
	**Append**	• **Ribbon:** *Home* tab>*Project* panel
	**Autodesk Rendering**	• **Ribbon:** *Home* tab>*Tools* panel • **Ribbon:** *View* tab>*Workspace* panel>*Windows* drop-down list • **Ribbon:** *Render* tab>*System* panel
	**Distant Light**	• **Autodesk Rendering window:** *Rendering* toolbar> *Create Light* drop-down list
	**File Options**	• **Ribbon:** *Home* tab>*Project* panel
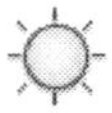	**Full Lights**	• **Ribbon:** *Viewpoint* tab>*Render Style* panel>*Lighting* drop-down list
	**Head Lights**	• **Ribbon:** *Viewpoint* tab>*Render Style* panel>*Lighting* drop-down list
	**Light Glyphs**	• **Autodesk Rendering window:** Rendering toolbar
	**No Lights**	• **Ribbon:** *Viewpoint* tab>*Render Style* panel>*Lighting* drop-down list
	**Pause**	• **Ribbon:** *Render* tab>*Render* panel
	**Point Light**	• **Autodesk Rendering window:** *Rendering* toolbar> *Create Light* drop-down list
 Ray Trace	**Ray Trace**	• **Ribbon:** *Render* tab>*Render* panel
	**Render Gallery**	• **Ribbon:** *Render* tab>*Render* panel
	**Render in Cloud**	• **Ribbon:** *Render* tab>*System* panel
	**Save**	• **Ribbon:** *Render* tab>*Render* panel
	**Scene Lights**	• **Ribbon:** *Viewpoint* tab>*Render Style* panel>*Lighting* drop-down list
	**Select None**	• **Ribbon:** *Home* tab>*Select & Search* panel

Button	Command	Location
	**Show Grid**	• **Ribbon:** *View* tab>*Grids& Levels* panel
	**Spot Light**	• **Autodesk Rendering window:** *Rendering* toolbar> *Create Light* drop-down list
	**Start**	• **Ribbon:** *Render* tab>*Render* panel
	**Stop**	• **Ribbon:** *Render* tab>*Render* panel
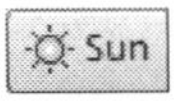	**Sun**	• **Autodesk Rendering window:** *Rendering* toolbar
	**Web Light**	• **Autodesk Rendering window:** *Rendering* toolbar> *Create Light* drop-down list

Appendix A

Coordination Best Practices

When you are working in multiple software packages, it is often necessary to prepare your models before providing them to the BIM coordinator for use in the Autodesk® Navisworks® software. This appendix introduces some of the best practices for Autodesk software users who plan to share their models in the Navisworks.

Learning Objectives

- Create views in Autodesk® Revit®.
- Add a real-world coordinate to an Autodesk Revit model.
- Install the Autodesk® Civil 3D® Object Enabler.
- Share an Autodesk® InfraWorks® model with Navisworks.

A.1 Creating a View in Autodesk Revit

When you append or open an Autodesk Revit model in Navisworks, the display matches what was toggled on in the Revit view when the model was saved. In order to ensure that unnecessary items (such as masses) do not display and that other necessary items (such as walls) display in Navisworks, you should create a view in Revit.

There are a couple of key things to keep in mind when creating the view, which are:

- You must start with a 3D view.
- The view must have "Navis" in its name for Navisworks to recognize it.

How To: Create a Revit View

1. In Autodesk Revit, set the view to a 3D view.
2. In the Project Browser, right-click on the view, expand **Duplicate View**, and select **Duplicate**, as shown in Figure A–1.

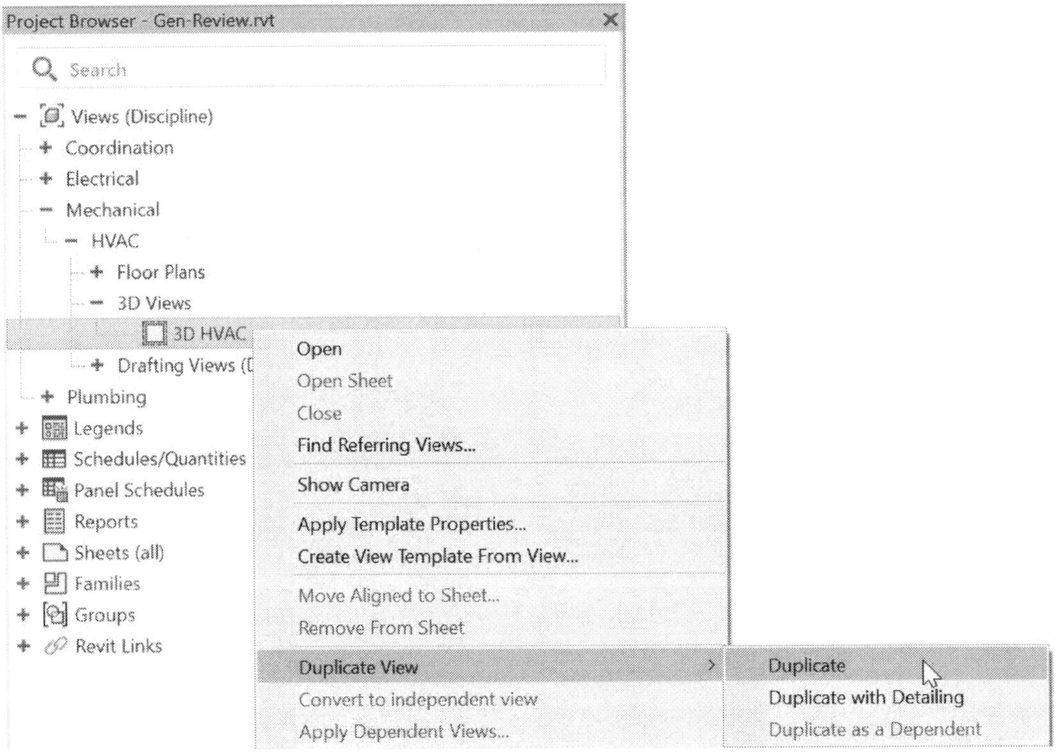

Figure A–1

3. In the Project Browser, right-click on the duplicated view and select **Rename**, as shown in Figure A–2.

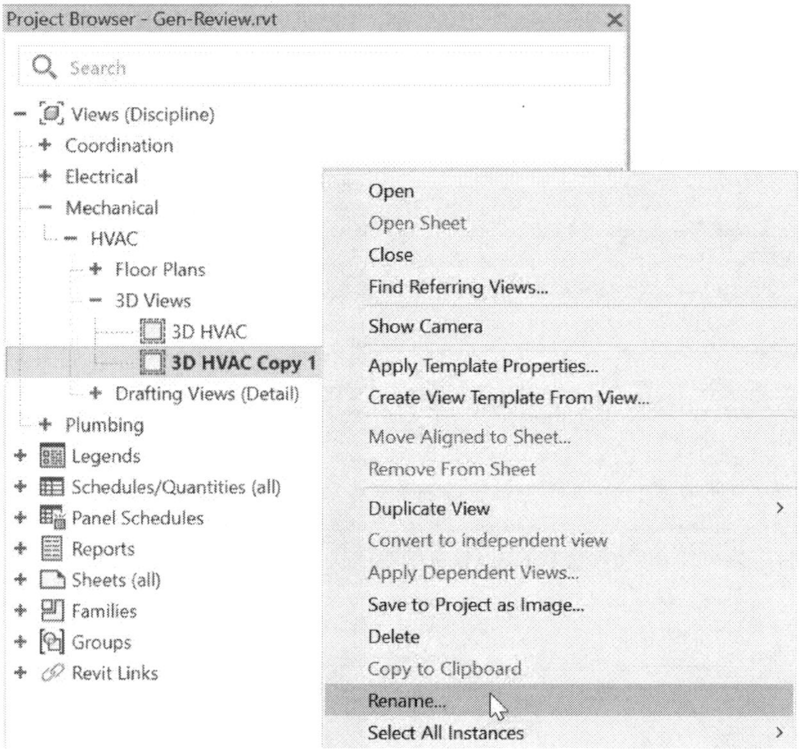

Figure A–2

4. In the *Rename View* dialog box, enter **Navis** for the name and click **OK**. This step is important to ensure that Navisworks recognizes the view.

5. In Properties, next to *Visibility/Graphics Overrides*, click **Edit**, as shown in Figure A–3. Alternatively, you can type **VV** to open the *Visibility/Graphic Overrides* dialog box.

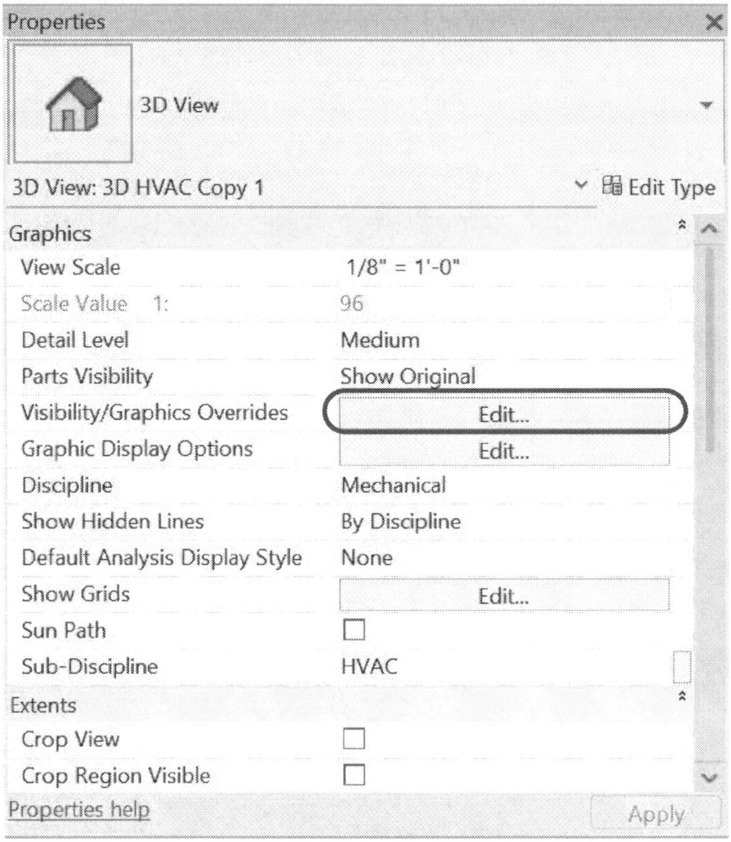

Figure A–3

6. In the *Visibility/Graphic Overrides* dialog box, in the *Model Categories* tab, clear the selection of any items that are not required and select all of the items that need to be displayed in Navisworks, as shown in Figure A–4.

   Note: *Toggle off items such as masses, areas, and lighting. Toggling off lights ensures that there is no duplication from the electrical model.*

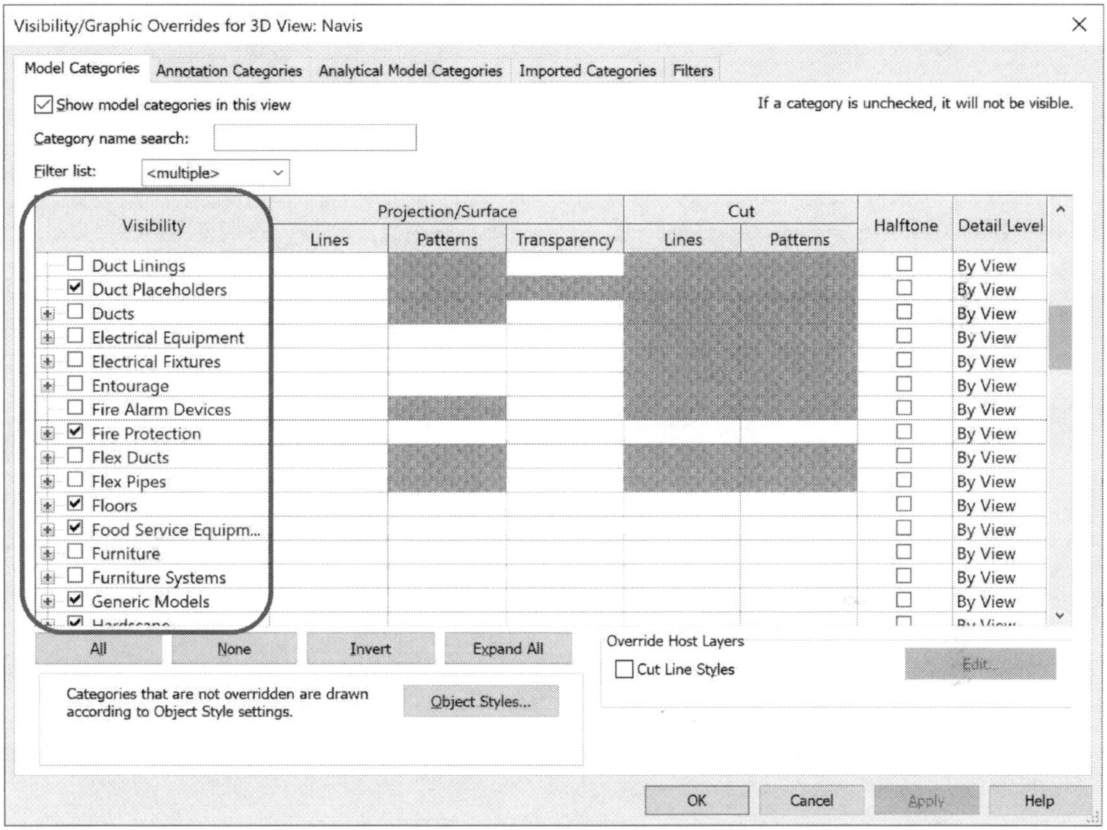

Figure A–4

7. Click **OK**.
8. Save the file and close Revit.

9. In Navisworks, in the *Options Editor*, expand **File Readers** and select **Revit**. Ensure that you set the options as shown in Figure A–5 before appending the Revit model so that the view is recognized.

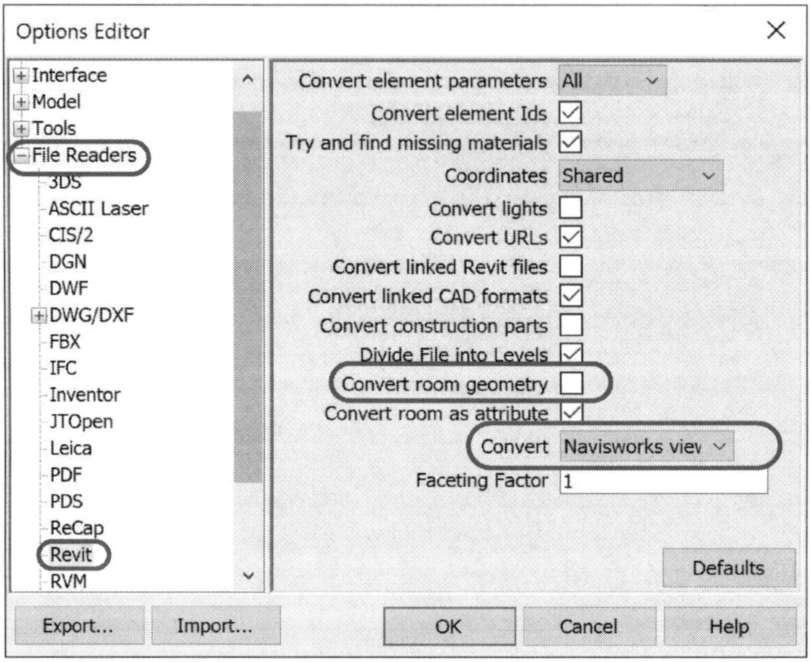

Figure A–5

A.2 Setting a Project Point in Autodesk Revit

Architectural models often have a base point of 0,0,0. However, when you import that model into Navisworks and combine it with other files that use real-world coordinates for their base point, the models do not line up. To fix this, you need to move and rotate the architectural model manually using the *Units and Transform* dialog box in Navisworks, as shown in Figure A–6.

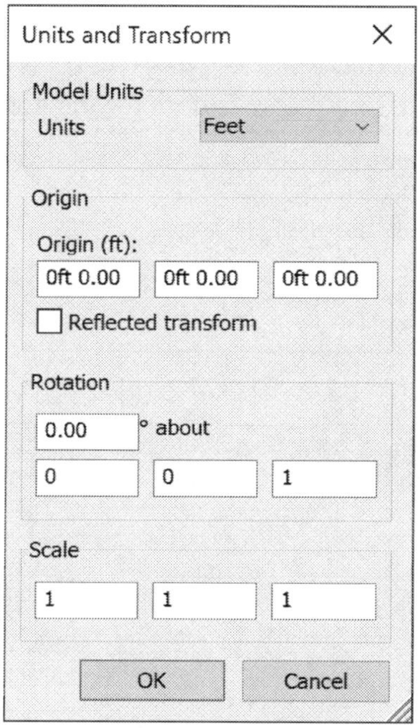

Figure A–6

The coordinates used for the transformation process is the centroid of the Revit model. Because of this, figuring out the correct coordinates to enter can be challenging. Additionally, if there are multiple Revit models, you will need to move and rotate each model individually.

In order to avoid this, Revit users can include a project point in their model. The project point can be a point of their choosing. This makes it much easier to coordinate a building's location with other team members that are using different software.

Before you can set a project point, you must:

- Communicate with the civil team members (engineers or surveyors) to know what coordinates to use.
- Use a 3D view in Revit to pick a point.

How To: Set a Revit Project Point

1. In Autodesk Revit, open the model that needs a project point.
2. Ensure that you are in a 3D view.
3. In the *Manage* tab>*Project Location* panel, expand the coordinates tool and click  (Specify Coordinates at Point).
4. In the Revit model, click the point on the building where you want the reference point to sit. Ensure that you use the snap option appropriate for the selected point, as shown in Figure A–7.

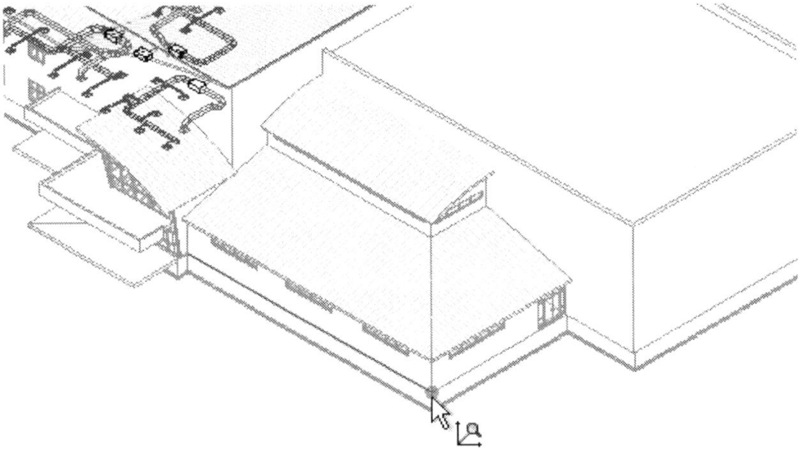

Figure A–7

5. In the *Specify Shared Coordinates* dialog box, enter the *North/South*, *East/West*, *Elevation*, and *Angle from Project North to True North* values, as shown in Figure A–8. Click **OK**.

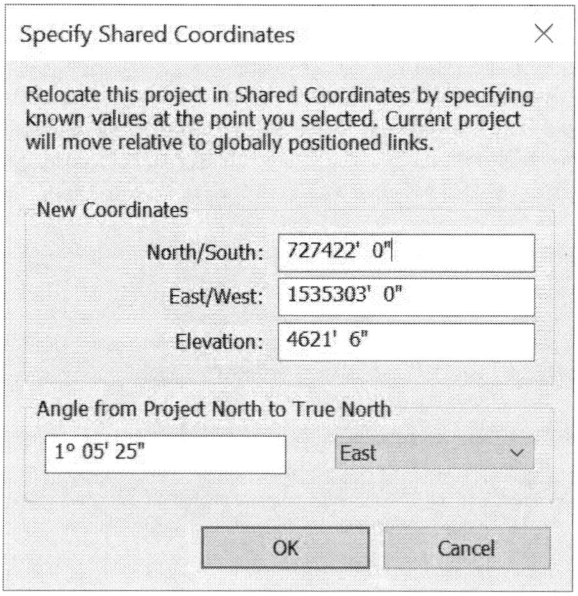

Figure A–8

Hint: The Autodesk Shared Reference Point Extension

There are two separate installations for this extension, one for Autodesk Civil 3D and one for Autodesk Revit.

It provides functionality to export a point with known coordinates and north direction from Civil 3D via an .XML file, which can be imported into Revit. This facilitates collaboration between Revit and Civil 3D. Navisworks will be able to read these shared coordinates as well.

The location of these extensions is shown in Figure A–9.

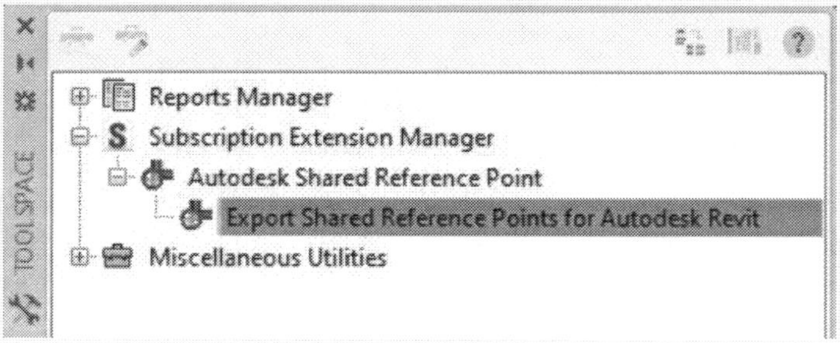

Civil 3D Toolspace

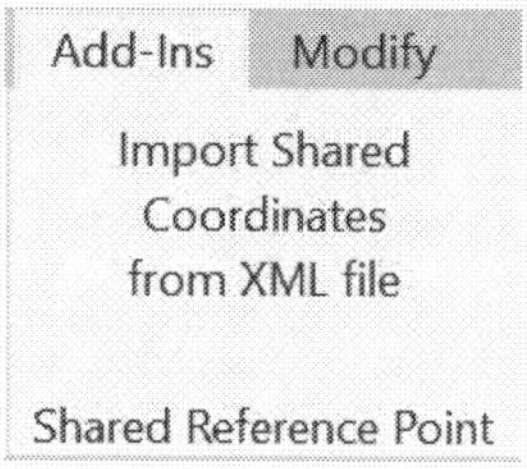

Revit Add-ins tab

Figure A–9

A.3 Autodesk Civil 3D Object Enabler

If you open or append an Autodesk Civil 3D drawing in Navisworks and boxes display where surfaces and roads should be (as shown in Figure A–10), then you need to install the Autodesk Civil 3D Object Enabler. The Object Enabler ensures that objects that are created in Civil 3D can be used outside of Civil 3D.

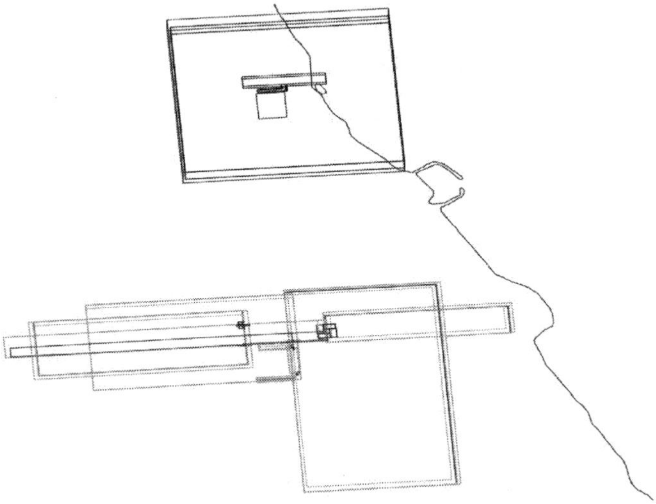

Figure A–10

To download the newest version of the Object Enabler, go to your Autodesk account page and select **All Products and Services**. Select **Navisworks Manage**, and on the *Updates* tab, click **Download** next to **Navisworks Manage 2026.2.1** (or a newest version), as shown in Figure A–11.

Once the update is installed, return to the same page. Open the *Plug-ins* tab and click **Download** next to the **Civil 3D Object Enabler 2026.1** to download and install the application.

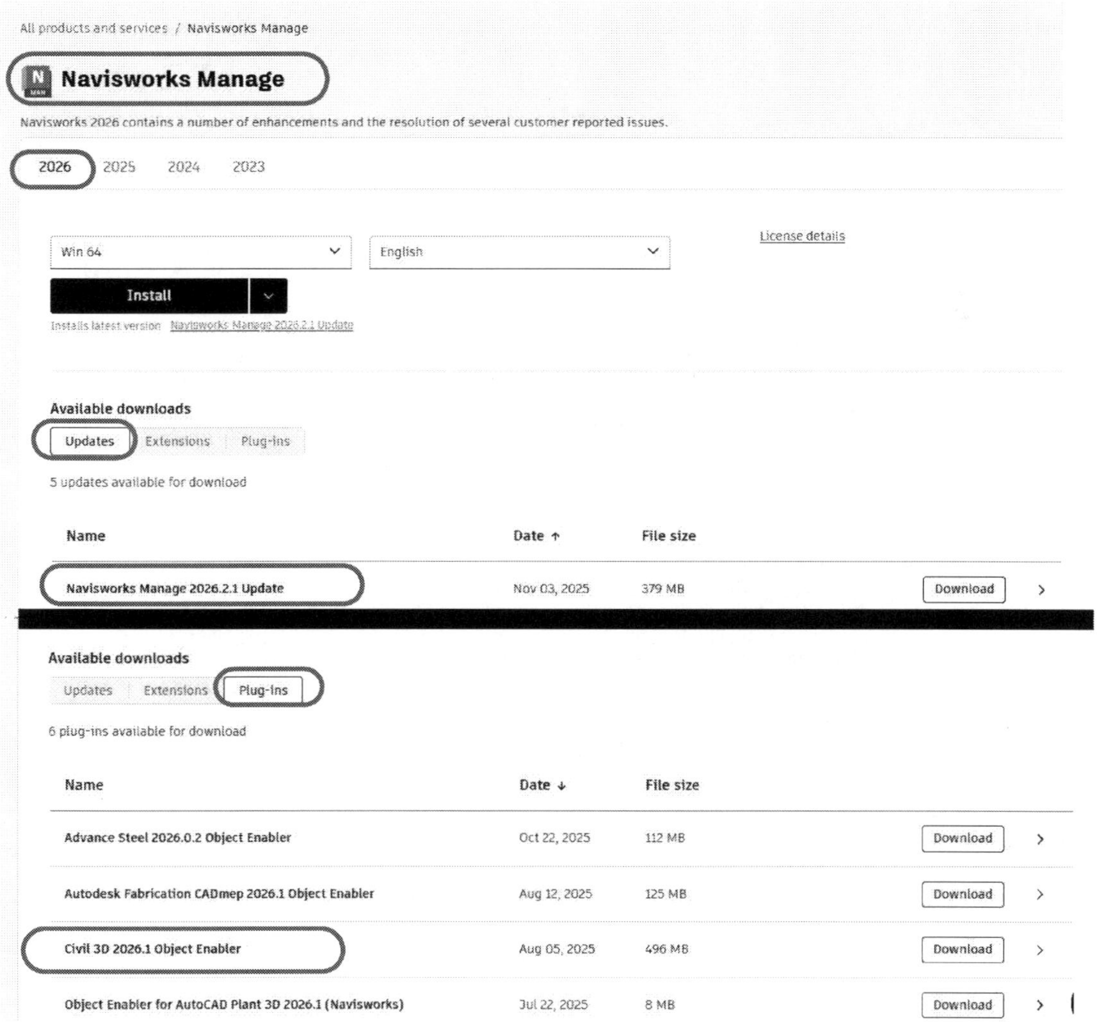

Figure A–11

Exporting Civil 3D drawings to AutoCAD format

In Civil 3D, you have the option of exporting a Civil 3D drawing to a regular AutoCAD drawing format. This will "dummy down" all Civil 3D objects to regular AutoCAD objects. With this option, no Civil 3D Object Enabler is required.

However, we do not recommend this method, for three reasons:

1. The visual fidelity of actual Civil 3D drawings is much richer. Surfaces, roadways, parking lots and other intelligent Civil 3D objects can be configured to be render-ready. These materials come through in Navisworks, as shown in Figure A–12.

Appended Civil 3D drawing with Civil 3D objects

Appended Exporting Civil 3D drawings with only AutoCAD objects

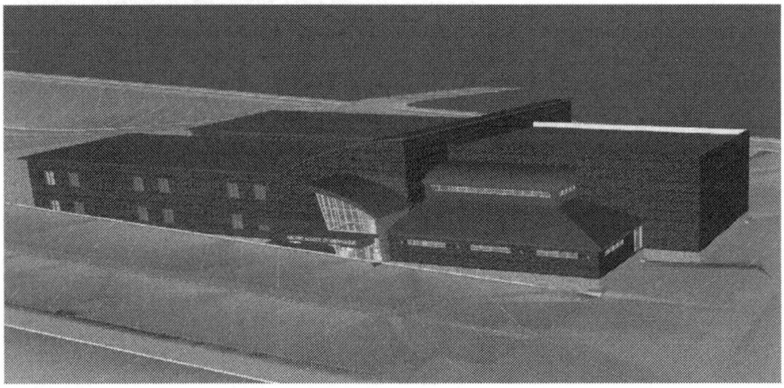

Figure A–12

2. Exported Civil 3D drawings are not dynamic. Each time the Civil 3D drawing goes through changes, it needs to be exported again. This can lead to gaps and errors.

3. The Civil 3D Alignment feature in Navisworks can only work with Civil 3D objects, not with an exported drawing. All the advantages of this feature, such as roadway construction, alignment stationing, "getting the feel for the road", etc. (as shown in Figure A–13) are negated when exporting a CIivl 3D drawing to regular AutoCAD objects.

Figure A–13

Hint: Civil 3D Corridors

In Civil 3D, corridors require alignments, profiles (or feature lines) and assemblies. These can either reside in the Civil 3D drawing with the corridor or be referenced into the corridor drawing through Data Shortcuts.

When appending a Civil 3D drawing that contains assemblies, the drawing becomes cumbersome with these additional design tools such as assemblies and profiles. This results in more layers and the extends of the drawing is wide, as shown in the upper part of Figure A–14.

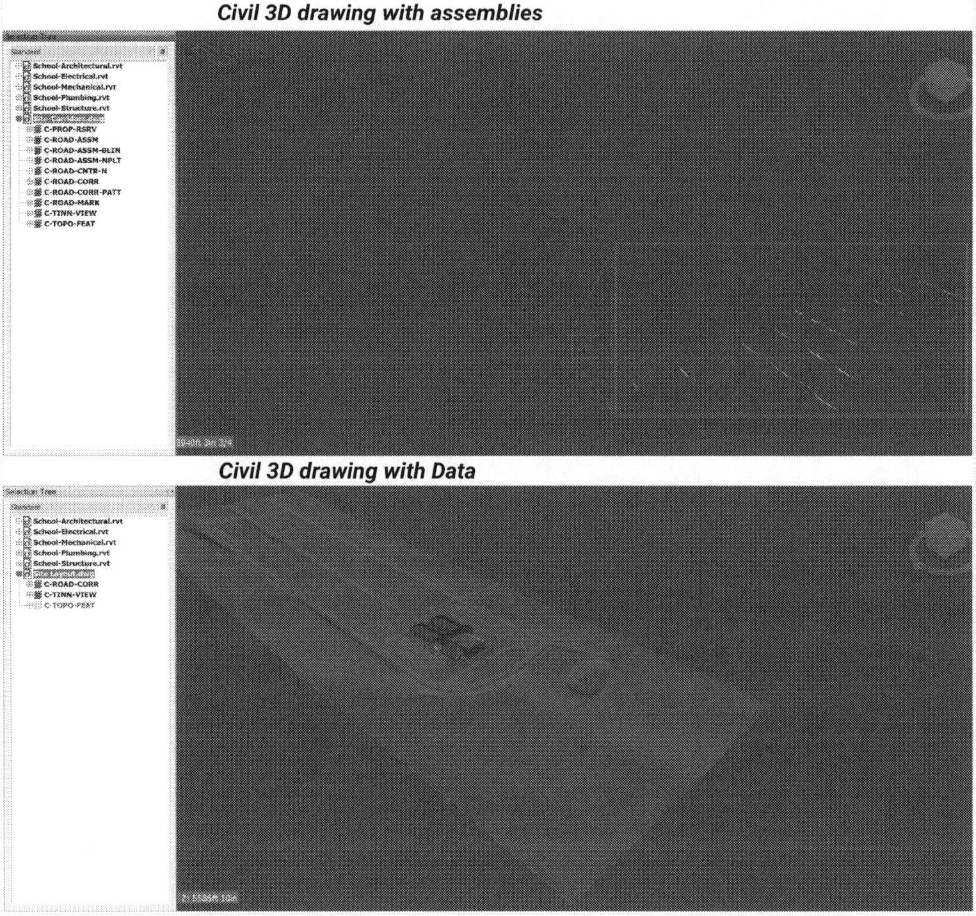

Figure A–14

When using Data Shortcuts, only the corridors are appended, leaving the design data behind, resulting in fewer more layers and the extends of the drawing is as expected, as shown in the lower part of Figure A–14.

> ***Note:*** *For more information on Data Shortcuts, refer to the Ascent Civil 3D Beyond the Basics for General Design learning guide.*

A.4 Creating an .FBX File in Autodesk InfraWorks

The best BIM workflows take full advantage of any software that adds value to the project. The photorealistic 3D models created in Autodesk InfraWorks provide a way to display designs in context with their surrounding areas. For infrastructure projects, the ideal workflow looks similar to the one outlined in Figure A–15. The software recommendations listed at the left of each phase provide the highest benefit to the project.

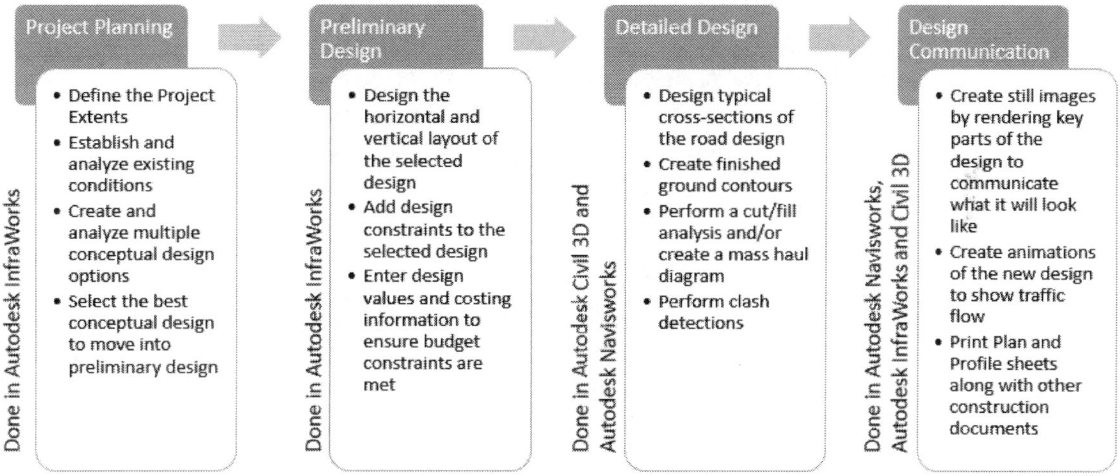

Figure A–15

If you follow this workflow, you can take advantage of using an early stage InfraWorks model inside Navisworks to uncover design problems and constructibility issues more effectively. In InfraWorks, you can export the model as a single file or multiple files. By using multiple files, you can select specific features in the model to export.

How To: Export an Autodesk InfraWorks Model to Navisworks

1. In InfraWorks, open the model you want to import into Navisworks.
2. In the *Present/Share* tab>*Share* panel, click  (Export 3D Model).

3. In the *Export to 3D Model File* dialog box, do the following, as shown in Figure A–16:
   - Define the area to export.
   - Set the *Target Coordinate System*.
   - Determine if you want one file or several files.
   - Click **Export**.

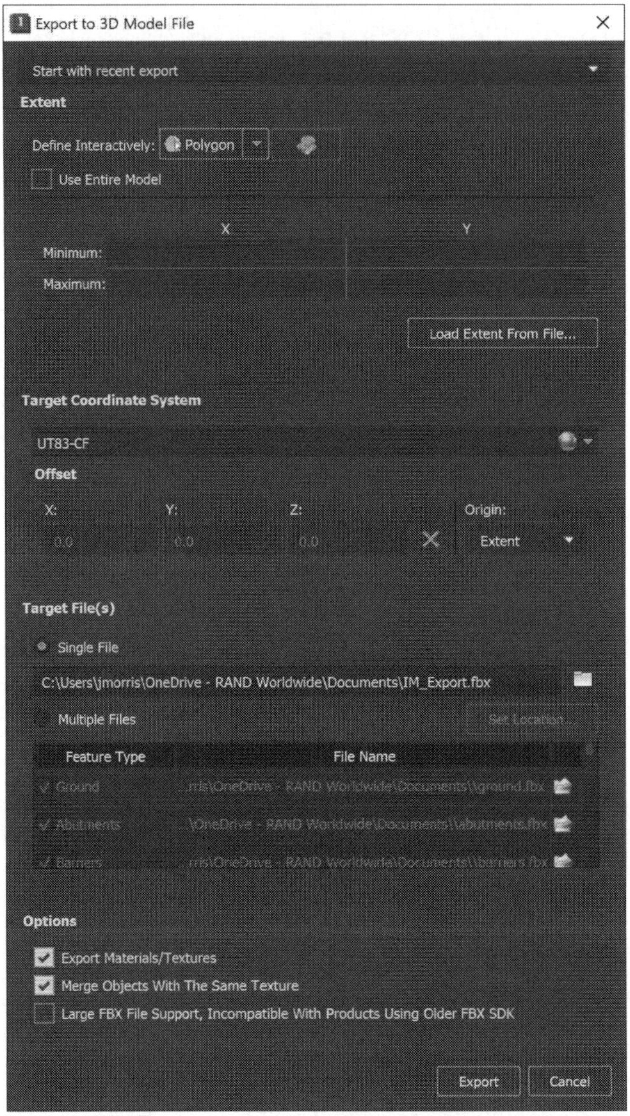

Figure A–16

4. In Navisworks, you can open the .FBX file or append it to an existing Navisworks model.

Appendix B

Preparing for Animator

There is a lot of work that goes into a project. In a classroom environment, you might not have time to create all of the viewpoints required for the class project. This appendix provides extra practice to help you test your skills. If you cannot complete the practice, it is recommended that you still review the referenced section to refresh your memory on how to complete the tasks.

Learning Objective

- Create a viewpoint.

Practice B1
Save Viewpoints

Practice Objective

- Save viewpoints for easy navigation and communication.

This practice provides extra practice on creating viewpoints on the model shown in Figure B–1. This model and the viewpoints are used in the Animator content. If you do not complete this practice, you will be provided a model to work with in the Animator content.

Figure B–1

Note: *Some viewpoints and sets that were created earlier in the guide have been removed for simplicity. Additionally, a model of a crane has been added.*

Task 1: Create a series of views around the building.

1. Open **School-Views.nwf** from the *Navisworks BIM Practice Files\Extra Practice* folder.
2. In the *Viewpoint* tab>*Camera* panel, ensure that the **Perspective** view type is selected and the FOV is set around 100, as shown in Figure B–2.

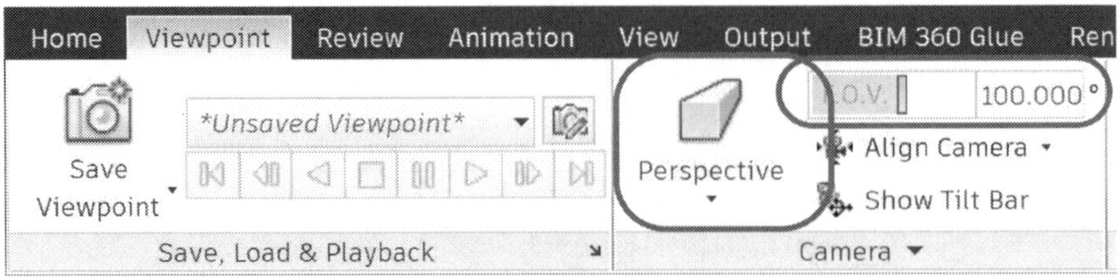

Figure B–2

3. Open the *Saved Viewpoints* window, if it is not already open and pin it for easy access.
4. Create a folder in the *Saved Viewpoints* window (using the right-click menu) and name it **Animator**.
5. Pan, zoom, and orbit the model until the scene view displays similar to that shown in Figure B–3.

Figure B–3

6. In the *Viewpoint* tab>*Save, Load & Playback* panel, click (Save Viewpoint).
7. In the *Saved Viewpoints* window, in the *Animator* folder, enter **Overview** for the name and press <Enter>.
8. Repeat Steps 5 to 7 to create the following saved viewpoints in the *Animator* folder, using the names and figure references provided. To ensure that the view is created in the *Animator* folder, select the folder in the *Saved Viewpoints* window prior to clicking the (Save Viewpoint) option.

- Save the view shown in Figure B–4 as **SE-Isometric**.

Figure B–4

- Save the view shown in Figure B–5 as **East Side**.

Figure B–5

- Save the view shown in Figure B–6 as **NE-Isometric**.

Figure B–6

- Save the view shown in Figure B–7 as **North Side**.

Figure B–7

- Save the view shown in Figure B–8 as **NW-Isometric**.

Figure B–8

- Save the view shown in Figure B–9 as **West Side**.

Figure B–9

- Save the view shown in Figure B–10 as **SW-Isometric**.

Figure B–10

Task 2: Create a series of views to walk into the building.

1. Pan and orbit the model until the scene view displays similar to that shown in Figure B–11. Save the viewpoint in the *Animator* folder as **Front Entry**.

Figure B–11

2. In the navigation bar, click (Walk).
3. Click and drag the mouse forward until the scene view displays similar to that shown in Figure B–12. Save the viewpoint in the *Animator* folder as **Turn1**.

Figure B–12

4. Pan and orbit the model until the scene view displays similar to that shown in Figure B–13. Save the viewpoint in the *Animator* folder as **Turn2**.

Figure B–13

5. Save and close the file.

End of practice

Appendix

C

Preparing Models for TimeLiner

When you are working in multiple software packages, it is often necessary to prepare your models before providing them to the BIM coordinator for use in the Navisworks® TimeLiner tool. This appendix introduces some points for consideration in your Autodesk® Revit® and Autodesk® Civil 3D® models.

Learning Objectives

- Prepare an Autodesk Civil 3D corridor model for use in TimeLiner.
- Prepare an Autodesk Revit model for use in TimeLiner.

C.1 Preparing a Corridor Model for TimeLiner

In order to use the Autodesk Navisworks TimeLiner to display a simulation of a road being constructed, you must turn the corridor model into solid parts. This conversion is done in the Autodesk Civil 3D software. By creating separate parts for each material (e.g, sub-base, base, sidewalk, etc.), you can animate the road being constructed one layer at a time, just like it would be during construction. It also enables you to break the road up into specific distances, since the contractor does not build the entire road at one time.

When converting a corridor to solids, it is important that the *Layer Name Template* match the item names in the Gantt chart, as shown in Figure C–1.

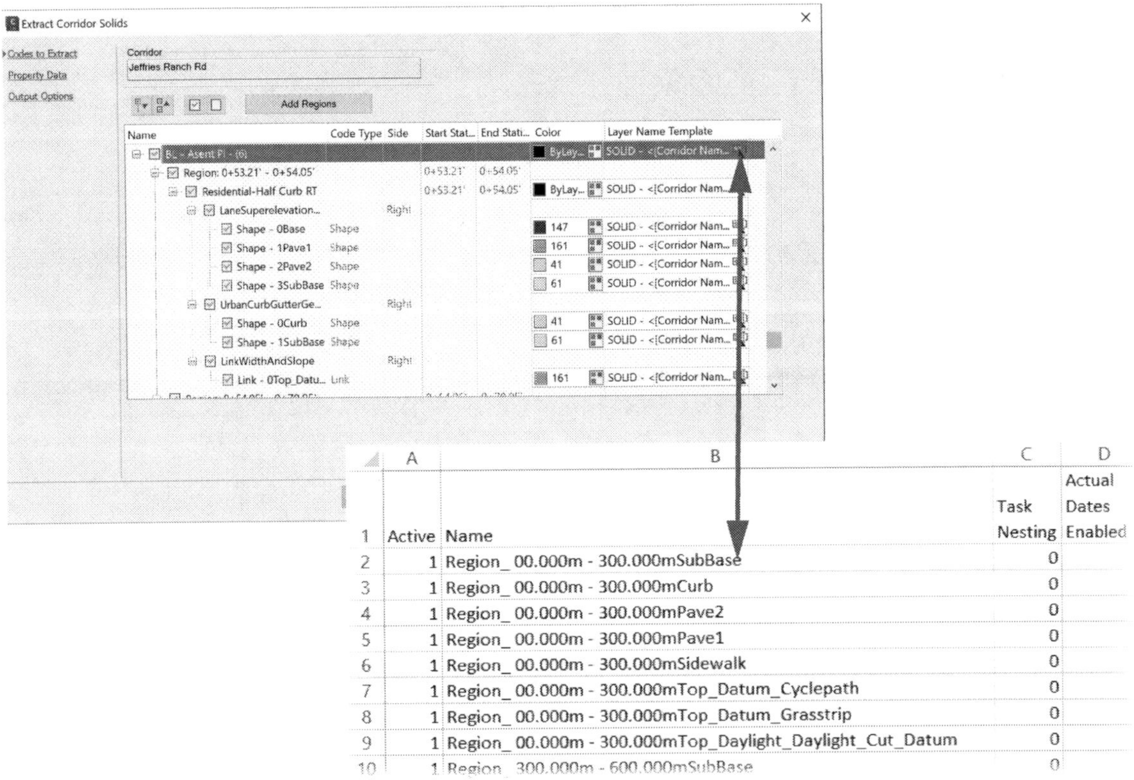

Figure C–1

How To: Extract Corridor Solids

1. In Civil 3D, select the corridor.
2. In the *Corridor* contextual tab>*Corridor Tools* panel, click (Extract Corridor Solids).
3. In the model, select only the regions for the area you want to extract. The options include:
   - **Station Range (S):** Select a region first, and then you are prompted to specify the start station. You can use the cursor to select it or you can enter a start station in the command line. After setting the start station, you are prompted to set the end station.
   - **Within Polygon (P):** Enables you to select a previously created polygon.
   - **All Regions (A):** Selects the entire corridor model.

   Note: *Type **S**, **P**, or **A** in the command line to select the associated option.*
4. In the *Extract Corridor Solids* dialog box, ensure that the *Layer Name Template* matches the item names in the Gantt chart. If you are using the Gantt chart (.CSV file) included in this guide, do the following to ensure the names match:

- In the *Layer Name Template* column, click (Modify Name Template) next to the **Baseline**, as shown in Figure C–2.

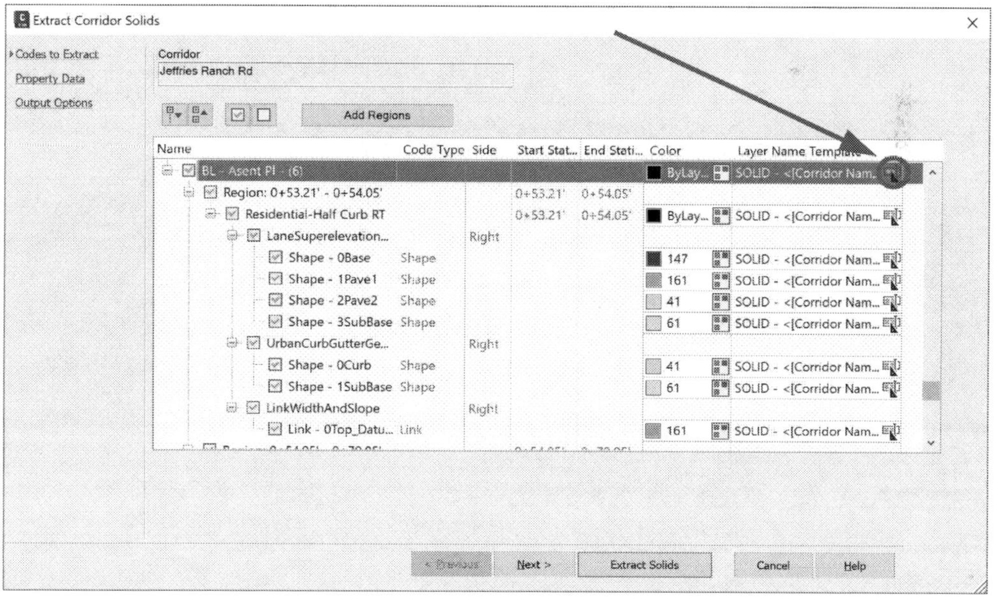

Figure C–2

- In the *Name Template* dialog box, do the following, as shown in Figure C–3:
    - In the *Name* field, highlight everything and press the <Delete> key to erase the existing name.
    - In the *Property fields* drop-down list, select **Construction Region Name**.
    - Click **Insert**.
    - In the *Property fields* drop-down list, select **Construction Codes**.
    - In the *Name* field, place the cursor at the end and click **Insert**.
    - Click **OK**.

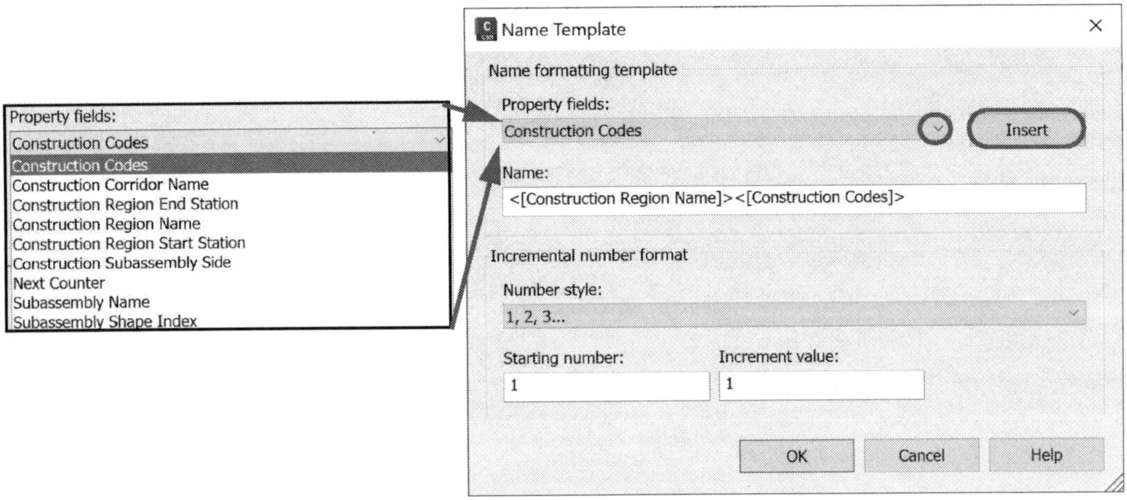

Figure C–3

Note: *Selecting the name template for the baseline ensures that all of the regions are updated to the new name template. You must do this for each baseline listed in the Extract Corridor Solids dialog box.*

5. In the *Extract Corridor Solids* dialog box, click **Next** twice.

6. In the *Extract Corridor Solids* dialog box>*Output Options* page (shown in Figure C–4), ensure that **AutoCAD 3D Solids (based on corridor sampling)** is selected, then select where you would like the solids stored:
   - **Insert into current drawing**
   - **Add to an existing drawing**
   - **Add to a new drawing**

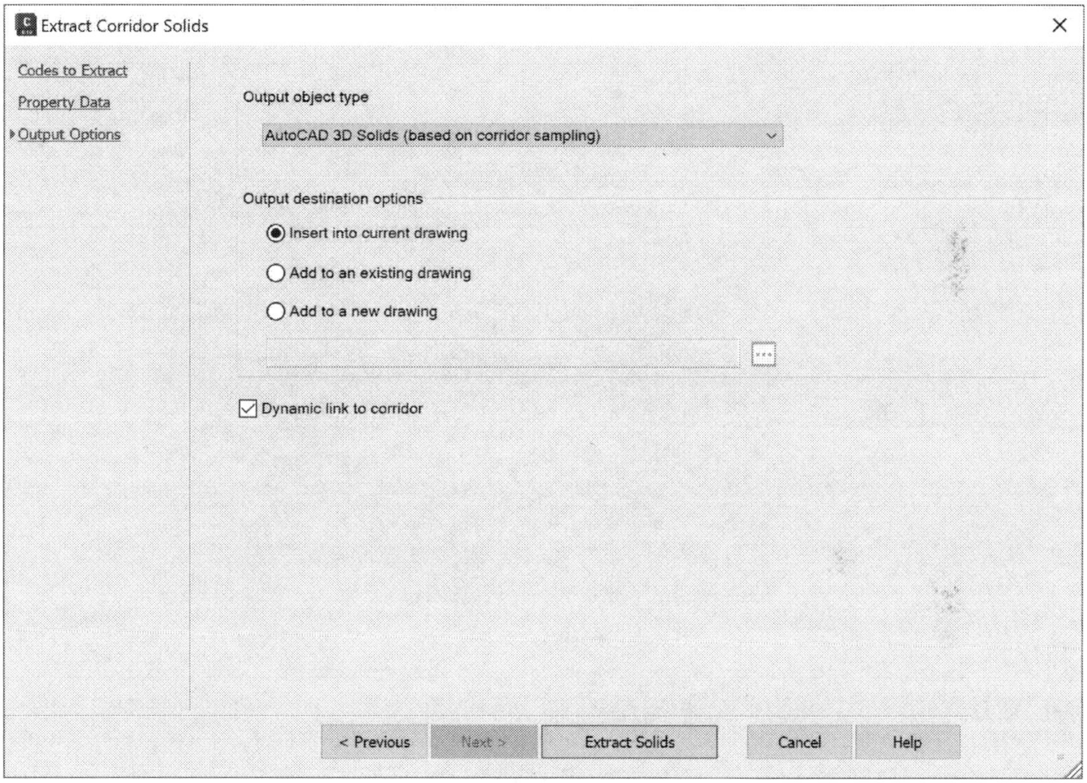

Figure C–4

7. Click **Extract Solids**.

C.2 Preparing a Revit Model for TimeLiner

In Autodesk Revit, multiple parts form a single object. For example, Figure C–5 shows the parts that form a wall. However, during construction, a wall is built in parts, rather than as a single piece. Framing might be the first thing to go up, then plywood on the outside, insulation, drywall on the inside, windows, and finally the brick on the outermost part of the wall. These Revit parts can be selected in Navisworks when the *Selection Resolution* is set to **Geometry**.

When creating a construction animation using TimeLiner, you want to simulate as closely as possible the construction schedule as laid out in the Gantt chart. In order to do this, you must separate all of the walls, ceilings, floors, etc. into parts in Revit before importing the model into Navisworks.

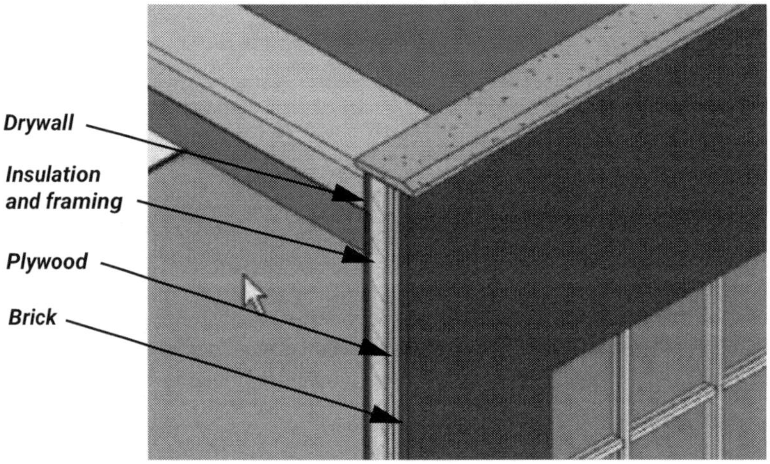

Figure C–5

How To: Separate Objects into Parts

1. In Revit, select the objects (all exterior walls, all interior walls, etc.) you want to separate into parts. It can be helpful to use selection sets for this.
2. In the *Modify (Object)* tab>*Create* panel, click (Create Parts).
3. Save the file.

Index

T

U

V

W

Made in United States
Orlando, FL
04 November 2026

90200363R00317